GARCIA

GARCIA
An American Life

BLAIR JACKSON

VIKING

VIKING
Published by the Penguin Group
Penguin Putnam Inc., 375 Hudson Street, New York, New York 10014, U.S.A.
Penguin Books Ltd, 27 Wrights Lane, London W8 5TZ, England
Penguin Books Australia Ltd, Ringwood, Victoria, Australia
Penguin Books Canada Ltd, 10 Alcorn Avenue, Toronto, Ontario, Canada M4V 3B2
Penguin Books (N.Z.) Ltd, 182–190 Wairau Road, Auckland 10, New Zealand

Penguin Books Ltd, Registered Offices: Harmondsworth, Middlesex, England

First published in 1999 by Viking Penguin, a member of Penguin Putnam Inc.

1 3 5 7 9 10 8 6 4 2

Grateful acknowledgment is made for permission to reprint excerpts from the following copyrighted works:
Farrar, Straus & Giroux, Inc.: *The Electric Kool-Aid Acid Test* by Tom Wolfe. Copyright © 1968 and copyright renewed © 1996 by Tom Wolfe. Reprinted by permission of Farrar, Straus & Giroux, Inc.
Ice Nine Publishing Company: Lyrics by Robert Hunter. "The Golden Road (To Unlimited Devotion)" © 1967 Ice Nine Publishing Company. "Dark Star" and "That's It for the Other One" © 1968 Ice Nine Publishing Company. "China Cat Sunflower," "Cosmic Charlie," "Doin' That Rag," "Mountains of the Moon," "Rosemary," and "What's Become of the Baby" © 1969 Ice Nine Publishing Company. "Attics of My Life," "Black Peter," "Box of Rain," "Candyman," "Casey Jones," "Cumberland Blues," "Dire Wolf," "New Speedway Boogie," "Ripple," "Truckin'," and "Uncle John's Band" © 1970 Ice Nine Publishing Company. "Bird Song," "Deal," "Loser," "Sugaree," "To Lay Me Down," "Wharf Rat," and "The Wheel" © 1971 Ice Nine Publishing Company. "Brown-Eyed Women" © 1972 Ice Nine Publishing Company. "Mississippi Half-Step Uptown Toodeloo" and "Stella Blue" © 1973 Ice Nine Publishing Company. "Scarlet Begonias" and "Ship of Fools" © 1974 Ice Nine Publishing Company. "Blues for Allah," "Comes a Time," "Crazy Fingers," "Franklin's Tower," "Help on the Way," and "Mission in the Rain" © 1975 Ice Nine Publishing Company. "Cats Under the Stars," "Lady with a Fan," "Palm Sunday," "Reuben and Cherise," and "Terrapin Station" © 1977 Ice Nine Publishing Company. "Fire on the Mountain" and "Stagger Lee" © 1978 Ice Nine Publishing Company. "Althea" © 1980 Ice Nine Publishing Company. "Midnight Getaway" and "Run for the Roses" © 1982 Ice Nine Publishing Company. "Black Muddy River" and "Touch of Grey" © 1987 Ice Nine Publishing Company. "Built to Last," "Foolish Heart," and "Standing on the Moon" © 1989 Ice Nine Publishing Company. "Days Between," "Lazy River Road," and "Liberty" © 1993 Ice Nine Publishing Company. "Down the Road" © 1996 Ice Nine Publishing Company. Excerpts from *Dead Heads* newsletter. By permission of Ice Nine Publishing Company.
Ram's Horn Music: "Knockin' on Heaven's Door" by Bob Dylan. Copyright © 1973, 1974 by Ram's Horn Music. All rights reserved. International copyright secured. Reprinted by permission of Ram's Horn Music.
Sony/ATV Music Publishing: "Sing Me Back Home" by Merle Haggard. Copyright © 1967 Sony/ATV Songs LLC. (renewed). All rights administered by Sony/ATV Music Publishing, Nashville, Tennessee.
Warner Bros. Publications U.S. Inc.: "Morning Dew" by Bonnie Dobson and Tim Rose. © 1967, 1968 (renewed) Warner-Tamerlane Publishing Corp. "Dear Mr. Fantasy" by Steve Winwood, Chris Wood, and Jim Capaldi. © 1968 (renewed) F. S. Music Ltd. and Island Music Ltd. All rights o/b/o F. S. Music Ltd. administered by Warner-Tamerlane Publishing Corp. All rights o/b/o Island Music Ltd. administered by Island Music Inc. "Like a Road Leading Home" by Don Nix and Dan Penn. © 1971 Irving Music, Inc., Deerwood Music and Dan Penn Music. All rights reserved. Used by permission of Warner Bros. Publications U.S. Inc., Miami, Florida.

LIBRARY OF CONGRESS CATALOGING IN PUBLICATION DATA
Jackson, Blair.
Garcia : an American life / Blair Jackson.
p.   cm.
Includes bibliographical references (p.   ) and index.
ISBN 0-670-88660-2
1. Garcia, Jerry, 1942–1995.   2. Rock musicians—United States—Biography.
3. Grateful Dead (Musical group).   I. Title.
ML419.G36J33   1999
782.42166'092—dc21   99-28775
[B]

This book is printed on acid-free paper.

∞

Printed in the United States of America
Set in Aldus • Designed by Francesca Belanger

*This book is dedicated with love
to my wonderful children.
Kyle and Hayley.*

*"Without love in the dream
it will never come true."*

CONTENTS

A Hopeful Candle Flickers

I was walking across the little parking lot outside the Grateful Dead's San Rafael, California, headquarters on a beautiful late-January morning in 1993 when Jerry Garcia came roaring into the lot in his giant dark gray BMW. The tires screeched and the car came to an abrupt halt at an odd angle, blocking three other cars. Garcia bounded out of the driver's seat with a big smile on his face, then ran around to the other side of the car to assist his passenger, an attractive woman who was also beaming. He took her by the hand and came over to me, saying, "You've *got* to meet Barbara Meier!"

Now, this was an unexpected development. I had interviewed Garcia many times over the years—that morning would be our ninth since 1981—and we'd chatted on a number of other occasions in more casual circumstances at the Dead office and at the band's recording studio, Club Front. In all that time, I'd never seem him quite so giddy, and he'd certainly never introduced me to a girlfriend before.

As the three of us walked up the back stairs and into the kitchen of the century-old house that served as the band's main office, Garcia protectively put his arm around Barbara and breathlessly told me the tale of how they had been lovers when they were teenagers, but her parents had forced her to break up with him. "I guess they knew I was trouble," he said with mock serious-ness, followed by a little laugh. Barbara and Jerry had reconnected recently and were now, obviously, quite in love.

In the kitchen and surrounding office rooms, Garcia introduced Barbara to every person he saw, repeating bits of the marvelous story of their reacquain-tance thirty years after their young love had been cruelly snuffed out. In no time the kitchen was crowded with people from the upstairs offices who'd come down to see what all the laughter and gaiety was about. Visits from Gar-cia, while not unusual, were rarely this boisterous, and his good mood was clearly infectious. Several others on hand, all of whom knew Garcia better than I did, also seemed stunned by the sight of him holding court in the kitchen, laughing and being so openly affectionate with Barbara.

These were heady times, particularly in contrast to the dark days the previous August, when Garcia collapsed from exhaustion and serious heart and lung problems just a few days after his fiftieth birthday. Coming almost exactly six years after a diabetic coma nearly killed him, the episode was another omen, another reminder of the preciousness of life.

As he had after his 1986 meltdown, Garcia took the warning seriously for a while. He became a strict vegetarian, adopted a strenuous workout regimen, lost sixty pounds, stopped using hard drugs and cut back his cigarette habit. His guitar playing and singing improved along with his health, and at the Dead's December 1992 concerts his fans couldn't help but be encouraged by his ebullient demeanor onstage.

So things were looking good that morning in January 1993. Once the commotion in the kitchen had died down a bit, Garcia and I adjourned to a nearby office for our interview, which was to be about Pigpen, his beloved bandmate, who had died two decades earlier, at age twenty-seven, of liver disease aggravated by years of drinking rotgut wine. Garcia had enthusiastically agreed to share his memories of Pigpen for an article I was writing, and when Jerry was excited about anything, he was an interviewer's dream—the stories poured out in rich detail and were punctuated by his frequent chuckles and guffaws. His eyes twinkled, and you could feel the intensity of the memories as the anecdotes flowed from him.

That morning, once we were alone, he still wanted to talk about Barbara, so we did for a while longer. Finally, though, it was Garcia who got the ball rolling, saying, "Okay, man, let's talk about Pigpen." He leaned forward in his chair as I explained my approach to the article, which I hoped would be an upbeat memoir of the fallen singer as told by his friends. "Here's my dilemma, Jerry," I said. "I want to write a positive story about Pigpen, but it seems as though no matter what I say in the main body of the article, it has to end in tragedy because that's how his life ended."

Without any hesitation Garcia replied, "Yeah, yeah—gotcha. I know exactly what you mean. But here's the thing about Pigpen: He was not a tragic figure. The fact that he died was a tragedy, but he wasn't tragic in the sense of being a doomed personality—brooding and suicidal, or any of that. He was more like a pixie; like an elf. And those of us who knew him and loved him got so much from him during the time he was with us, we can't be too sad about him not being around anymore. And of course he'll always be with us, just like anyone who's been important in your life and then moves on."

And so it is with Jerry Garcia's story. It must end in tragedy—a life cut short with devastating suddenness. But in the words of Bob Bralove, one of the Grateful Dead's technical wizards, "Jerry isn't a tragic figure because his accomplishments are so vast that it's hard to look at him as anything other than an incredibly positive force. He changed lives; he changed my life. His death may be a tragedy, but his death in no way overpowers his life. He died young, but he did so much in his time here."

Indeed, Garcia packed a lot of living into his fifty-three years. He was a perennial noncomformist and outsider, always fording unpredictable tributaries that branched off the American mainstream. Had he been born ten years earlier, he almost certainly would have become a beatnik; as it was he rode in the wake of the Beat wave and learned more than a few life lessons from reading Kerouac, Ginsberg and other rebels and malcontents. In his late-teen and early-adult years Jerry learned that he wasn't really cut out for school, the military, marriage, fatherhood or steady employment—all traditional avenues to the American dream. But he had a passion for playing music, and that love would eventually take him to the pinnacle of American celebrity. Along the way, he and his friends helped shape a part of America in their own image by obliterating traditional notions of freedom and liberty, and by questioning and ignoring the mores and social structures that had evolved through generations since colonial times. The hippie counterculture of the late '60s would have flowered without the Grateful Dead, but Garcia and the Dead came to symbolize the best and worst aspects of that libertine movement, from the communal spirit and healthy disrespect for the capitalist paradigm to the dangerous hedonism and unconscious self-absorption.

That Garcia became a true icon—and likely will remain so for decades, if not centuries, to come—is both surprising and ironic. Surprising because he had few of the traits we normally associate with entertainment stars. Ironic because he constantly tried to disavow his celebrity, insisting that he was just a guy who played guitar and wrote and sang songs. Which is why people loved him: There were flashier guitarists and better singers, but there was something about the way *he* played and sang that affected hundreds of thousands of people deeply enough that they wanted to hear him as often as they could. His fans offered him the ultimate gift: total artistic freedom. They supported every move he ever made and followed him down every twisting, turning road, every strange left turn, every cul-de-sac and lonely byway.

No modern popular musician ever worked so deeply in so many different styles as Garcia did. A true musical omnivore, he was equally enthralled playing old English ballads or completely formless improvised pieces. He thought nothing of playing Chuck Berry and Hoagy Carmichael songs in the same set, or of juxtaposing a Miles Davis tune with some ageless sea chantey. His guitar style was the sum of a million influences, yet it was distinctive enough that his playing was instantly recognizable, no matter what the genre. There was nothing he liked more than playing music in a band in front of dancing people. He didn't care if the group was acoustic or electric or if the audience was large or small—it was all about hearts and souls coming together through music; ecstatic communion and transformative epiphanies. "Magic is what we do," he once said of the Grateful Dead. "Music is how we do it."

He wrote melodies to another man's words and rarely spoke onstage, yet the people who came to see him play night after night felt they knew him intimately, as one knows a family member. A few put him on a pedestal and believed he was a god. But he had the frailties and the life of pain that are an unmistakable part of mortal territory.

He was well-read and street-smart; quick, funny and articulate when he wanted to be; hipster and prankster, skeptic and optimist, pragmatist and dreamer, philosopher and fool. A keen and voracious intellect, he was interested in almost everything, could speak knowledgeably about most things, yet he made his most profound statements with his fingers.

"I've prefaced interviews in the past by saying that I can't really do anything but lie, all talking is lying, and I'm lying now," he said in 1975. "You can go hear me play—that's me, that's what I have to say; that's the form my thoughts have taken, so I haven't put that much thought into really communicating verbally. It's all open to misinterpretation, just like the songs are."

And so is a life as portrayed in a book. The biographer chooses what to emphasize and what to ignore, chooses the voices that tell the tale, and interprets events that were lived by others. Objectivity is a fiction; writing is as subjective as listening to music. And writing a biography is by definition presumptuous.

I should state up front that I am not a dispassionate observer when it comes to Garcia and the Grateful Dead. I am a fan; a Deadhead. I first saw the band in the spring of 1970 when I was a junior in high school, and over the next twenty-five years I went to more than 350 Dead concerts, and dozens more by Garcia's various solo groups. I've been writing about the band since I saw my first show, though as often as not trying to explain the ineffable and mysterious qualities that make them so special ends up being an exercise in futility—like capturing lightning in a bottle. I suppose I persisted through the years because I felt that Garcia and the Dead were badly misunderstood and had never earned the sort of critical respect I always felt they deserved. Instead, they were routinely dismissed as lazy, aimless hippies playing for an army of burnouts and would-be flower children bent on recapturing the lost spirit of the '60s. But take away the colorful hippie following and the counterculture baggage that is so much a part of their history, and what's left is one of the most extraordinarily creative ensembles in twentieth-century music.

"The fact that they had so many periods of Olympian greatness is truly amazing," says David Gans, a musician and longtime chronicler of the Dead. "That's the stuff of jazz careers. Only a handful of the greats ever delivered as many peak seasons; certainly in the rock 'n' roll domain, there just hasn't been anybody who has sustained that level of inventiveness for so long."

And Jerry Garcia is surely one of modern music's most underrated figures. For my money, no popular guitarist ever took more chances, visited more uncharted realms or played more soulfully. But his genius as a musician and songwriter was always overshadowed in mainstream culture by the force of his personality. From his "Captain Trips" persona in the late '60s to the smiling, grandfatherly figure he became late in his life, his iconic self was much easier for many people to grasp than his nimble-fingered instrumental flights or his wrenching ballads where every note sounded like a deep human cry. It will be fascinating to see how future generations judge Garcia without the distraction of his wit and intelligence, not to mention the Deadhead carnival.

This book is neither hagiography nor exposé. I am much less interested in the sordid details of Garcia's personal life than I am in exploring and illuminating his splendid creative gifts. The Forces of Light win the battle in this book—not because I'm a starry-eyed revisionist, but because Garcia's musical legacy is larger than his life and will endure long after all of us have joined him in the sweet by-and-by.

—Blair Jackson
Oakland, California
December 1998

CHAPTER 1
Another Time's Forgotten Space

 a Coruña is a small, picturesque seaport on Spain's rugged northwest Atlantic coast. This isn't the sun-drenched Costa del Sol glamorized in postcards and guidebooks—that's hundreds of miles to the south on the Mediterranean. Geographically and climatically, the north coast has more in common with the rocky and rainy parts of western Ireland or Cornwall or Brittany than it does with most of the generally dry Iberian Peninsula. In ancient times the region was populated by small Celtic tribes who had migrated there from central and northern Europe. The Romans conquered the territory, which they called Galicia, in the second century B.C. The city now known as La Coruña was a small but important trading post for the Romans for several centuries. The collapse of the Roman Empire left the area vulnerable to invasion from outside forces, and over the course of several hundred years, hordes of Visigoths, Normans and Arabs swept through and controlled the area for long stretches.

By the beginning of the sixteenth century foreign invaders had been banished from the Iberian Peninsula and the various Christian kingdoms that had sprung up began to consolidate under more centralized rule. Galicia was always a bit isolated from the rest of the land, both politically and culturally (the inhabitants, known as Gallegos, spoke their own language, which has much in common with Portuguese), and even physically to a degree—Gallegos tend to be fairer-skinned than their neighbors to the south.

As a trading center, La Coruña has absorbed cultural influences—and sailors—from ports far and near, and it has also served as a point of emigration for thousands of Spaniards heading west to the Americas. The Gallegos themselves emigrated west in huge numbers, beginning with the first New World settlements at the end of the fifteenth century, for Galicia has historically been one of the poorest regions of Spain and the sea has always held the promise of a better life wherever mighty sailing ships could go. Even today there are more Gallegos and their descendants in Buenos Aires, Argentina, than there are in all of Galicia.

If you were to scour the streets and alleys of La Coruña, you might well encounter a Garcia who can trace the lineage of Jerry's family back many centuries. But in the United States, where two branches of the Garcias settled in the second decade of this century, we must rely on the memories of the lone surviving sibling from the original transatlantic voyage, Leonor Garcia Ross—still spry at ninety—and on family lore passed along to Jerry's brother and cousins.

Though Leonor considers La Coruña the family's ancestral home, the Garcias who emerge from the family's oral history in the mid-nineteenth century actually came from a nearby coastal fishing village called Sada, on an inlet called the Ría de Betanzos. Jerry's great-grandfather Manuel was a solidly middle-class entrepreneur who ran his own drayage business in the area, carting goods for merchants in a large wagon pulled by six workhorses. He had four children—two boys and two girls—and though tradition dictated that at least one of his sons would join the business and eventually take it over, the eldest son (Jerry's grandfather), also named Manuel, was not interested in his father's trade. "He was an adventuresome type who wanted to go to sea," says Jerry's cousin Daniel, "so he became a seaman and traveled all over, leaving for months at a time. In fact, he bought my grandmother a dry-goods store to keep her occupied, because he was away so much of the year." On his rare stays home, Manuel and his wife, Aquilena (who was from a comfortably middle-class La Coruña family), managed to start a family: Manuel (Daniel's father; it was traditional to name the eldest child after the father) was born in 1901; Jose (Jerry's father, named after his mother's father, Jose Lopez) was born in 1902; Leonor came along in 1908; and in 1912 Lena (short for Aquilena) completed the brood.

Eventually Manuel's wanderlust subsided, and by the time World War I swept across the continent he had decided that what he really wanted was to settle down with his growing family in America. Although he'd traveled extensively to ports in Europe and South America, "Like so many people around the turn of the century, he believed that America was the place to come for economic and other reasons," Daniel says. "He was in New York a few times, but he made trips to San Francisco and he liked it better there."

"He thought the climate in San Francisco would agree with my mother more," adds Leonor. "It was much more like La Coruña than New York, which was so terribly cold in winter. And also, because San Francisco was still being rebuilt after the [1906] earthquake and fire, there were more job opportunities there than in New York. My father's sister and her husband moved to New York first, and I know my father visited them there, but he didn't like it much."

And so, in early 1918, Manuel Garcia traveled alone to San Francisco, rented a furnished apartment on Filbert Street, half a block off tree-lined Washington Square in the bustling, mainly Italian North Beach section of the city, and quickly landed a job working for one of the railroads in the area. When he felt sufficiently settled, he arranged to have Aquilena and the four children—then ranging in age from six to seventeen—join him there. In the late fall of 1918, they sailed by steamship to Havana, then on to New York, where they were "processed" at Ellis Island before traveling by train to California. "We brought quite a few things with us on the boat," Leonor remembers, "but this cousin of ours, Antonio Dalmau, wanted to come with us, and he was slightly crippled—he'd had polio as a child—so when we got to Ellis Island they wouldn't allow him into the United States and they sent him back. It was sad. And he had a trunk of my mother's with all her prize possessions in it, as well as his own things, and it was sent back to Spain with him. We lost a lot of family mementos; we never saw any of it again."

The trip across America by train in the cold of December seemed long and hard, and Leonor says that when the travel-weary family arrived in Oakland and looked across San Francisco Bay to their new home, her mother exclaimed, "Oh my God, do I have to go to sea *again?*" Fortunately, the voyage took only about an hour, and according to Daniel Garcia's telling of the tale, Manuel "picked them up and had a hot meal waiting for them on the table at home."

"We lived in North Beach the first three years," Leonor says. "During that period, North Beach was like a Little Italy; almost everybody was Italian, though there were also a few Spaniards. In fact, my father got upset because he thought we were learning Italian instead of English. None of us spoke English when we got here, of course. In Spain, the second language you learned was French, which didn't do any good here. But my brothers went to both regular school and night school and they learned English much faster than I did."

"My grandfather was very much for education," Daniel says, "and my father took well to it and went into engineering. My uncle Joe [Jerry's father] didn't like school that much; he was much more interested in music. My grandfather had insisted that they both learn an instrument. My father studied piano and was quite good at it. And Uncle Joe studied clarinet [after initially learning piano basics]. They had a teacher there in North Beach who was a real Italian maestro and he drilled them on the scales and gave them good fundamentals of music. They continued to play for a while, but my dad kept on with school and my uncle hooked up with a group of musicians and ultimately left the area."

In 1922 the family left North Beach and moved across town to the outer Mission district, settling in a house on Precita Avenue, which in those days was nearly at the city's southern border; beyond was sparsely developed ranch land, although that would change in the late '20s and early '30s. Today the Mission is mainly populated by Mexican and Central American immigrants, but "it was totally different in the '20s," Daniel says. "The area was settled by Irishmen and some Spanish; there were no Mexicans at all. They came later. San Francisco was a very ethnically divided city in those days; no one mingled with anyone else much. It was even that way when I was a boy in the '40s."

It was always Manuel Garcia's intention that he and his family become fully integrated into American society. He applied for U.S. citizenship almost immediately after arriving in California. In the early 1920s he landed a job as a steam engineer for Pacific Gas & Electric and ended up working there for more than forty years. "My grandfather was a patriot from the word go," Daniel says. "Spain could sink into the ocean as far as he was concerned. He was a great believer in Roosevelt and the New Deal and [in the '30s and '40s] he used to keep a picture of Franklin Roosevelt on the wall; in those days a lot of Americans did that. Those were days of fierce patriotism. He loved America."

He came to speak English well (though with a heavy accent), but his wife "didn't want to learn English," says Jerry's older brother, Tiff Garcia. "My father, on the other hand, would not teach us Spanish. He was totally into America and wouldn't speak Spanish, even to his mom. I remember she'd be speaking to him in Spanish and he'd be saying back to her, 'No, you mean the *key,* the *car,* the *stove.*' " To solidify his own American credentials, Jose Garcia became Joe Garcia to both his family and friends; on city and county documents his name was listed as "Joseph" Garcia.

According to Leonor, her brother Joe became consumed by music in his late teens, "and he was very, very good in no time at all. All the kids in the neighborhood started taking lessons from him, and he decided, 'Hey, this is pretty good.' My father had future plans in mind for all of his kids and he had wanted Joe to be a machinist, but very early Joe said, 'No way I want to be that,' because once he started playing the saxophone that's all he wanted to do—just like Jerry and the guitar. Joe decided he wanted to be a musician, and after a while my father came to accept that." (Jerry once described himself as a "black sheep of a black sheep," but actually Joe Garcia's parents and siblings were supportive of Joe's music career.)

Leonor remembers Joe playing clarinet and saxophone in small groups at Sunday picnics in city parks and at dances in various ethnic halls around town. He also worked in local clubs, playing jazz mainly, but also the popular music of the day—standards, show tunes, vaudeville pieces—and during Prohibition, like many musicians, he took his share of jobs playing speakeasies. While still in his mid-twenties, Joe traveled across the country as part of an orchestra sponsored by the then-thriving Orpheum Theater chain. In fact, it's likely that he even played San Francisco's Orpheum Theater—site of numerous Grateful Dead and Jerry Garcia Band shows in the '70s and '80s. (Leonor says Joe definitely played a couple of blocks down Market Street at the Warfield Theater, another venue later used by both the Dead and the Garcia Band.)

"He was hip for his day, apparently," Jerry said in 1984. "I've looked at some of the arrangements that his band played. I remember poking around and looking at them and I thought they were pretty hip. I would have liked to have been able to experience his music because he was a musician who was interested in American music, also. He was a genre player, like I am; an idiom player."

As the Roaring Twenties gave way to the Great Depression, Joe Garcia settled for two or three years in Los Angeles, where he played in a small combo known as Lada's Lads, and also worked for an orchestra that played music for films; "talkies" were suddenly all the rage, and music for the movies became a growth industry for a while. Joe worked on several films for a studio run by screen great Mary Pickford, and, Daniel Garcia relates, "My dad was in the movies one day in San Francisco watching a film and the camera panned to the band, and my uncle Joe was in the front row. My dad jumped up and shouted, 'That's my brother! That's my brother!' He was so impressed that Joe was in a movie." Adds Leonor, "We were all so proud of Joe, and he was very excited because he got to meet Mary Pickford. That was a big thing back then!"

While working at a nightclub in L.A., Joe fell in love with a young blond dancer named Sunny (Leonor doesn't remember her real first name or her last name) and the two were married for a brief period. Daniel Garcia recalls his father, Manuel, referring to the woman as a "floozy"; Tiff says with a smile, "I like to think she was like Carmen Miranda, but she probably wasn't." Whatever the case, Joe wanted to start a family, Sunny wanted to remain a dancer, and they soon divorced. Joe headed back to San Francisco, where he lived for a period in the family house on Precita Avenue and worked hard to reestablish himself as a band leader in an increasingly depressed economy.

"It wasn't just the economy, though," Daniel says. "My father said that one of the things that killed the music business was 'canned music.' Records started to become very popular and people stopped going to live performances as much." Still, Joe Garcia's band was a fairly popular group around the city in the early '30s. "One of his main 'instruments' was actually the baton, since he was a band leader," Tiff Garcia says of his father. "He had a case for all his batons, plus he had all sorts of reed instruments—saxophones, clarinets. Even after he stopped playing professionally, he kept all his instruments around the house, and he'd play them pretty often."

Sometime in 1934 Joe met the woman of his dreams, a twenty-four-year-old nurse at San Francisco General Hospital named Ruth Marie Clifford. Ruth also had deep immigrant roots stretching back even further than the Garcias': Her grandfather Patrick Clifford was born in Ireland in the middle of the nineteenth century and emigrated to California, where he married another Irish expatriate named Ellen Callahan. Ruth's father, William Henry Clifford, was born in San Francisco in 1883. In his twenties he got involved in the laundry business and married nineteen-year-old Tillie May Olsen, whose ancestors had sailed to California from Sweden around the time of the Gold Rush. Shortly after they were married, Bill and Tillie bought a newly built home on the fringes of the Excelsior district. The house at 87 Harrington Street, where Jerry would spend much of his youth, was built in 1908. In June 1910 Jerry's mother, Ruth, was born at that address. She lived there until she married Joe Garcia.

By the time Joe and Ruth became serious about each other, Joe was already having some doubts about continuing on in the music business. "He wanted to have kids and have a stable family, and you couldn't do that as a musician," his nephew Daniel says. Joe and Ruth were married on April 29, 1935, and moved into a small, one-story four-year-old house at 121 Amazon Street, about a mile south of Harrington Street in the Crocker-Amazon district. Then (and now) the area was a bright, clean, ethnically diverse middle-class section of the city—in those days it was Spanish, Italian and Irish, with some German; today it is mainly Hispanic and Asian. All three of Joe's siblings lived nearby, and he always kept in close contact with them. Ruth quit her job at the hospital and became a housewife, as was typical in that day, but she always kept her nursing license up to date, and indeed, she would return to that profession twenty-five years after she married Joe. In April of 1937 Ruth became pregnant with her first child, news that was greeted with great excitement in the Garcia clan. (Before this, the four children had produced just one grandchild for Manuel and Aquilena—Manuel Jr.'s daughter Anita, who was born in 1932.) Unfortunately, also around this time an incident occurred that forced Joe Garcia to quit playing music professionally. In Jerry's recounting of the story in a 1971 interview, "I understand there was some hassle: He was blackballed by the union or something 'cause he was working two jobs or something like that—some musicians' union trip—so he wasn't able to to remain a professional musician." Tiff Garcia is shaky on the details as well, but Aunt Leonor says she remembers the particulars of her brother's exit from the music world very well:

"He'd been out of work for a little while, and then he was offered a good job: There was a big, new nightclub being opened in San Francisco out at the beach [perhaps the Nut Club], and they asked him if he and his orchestra would like to play, and of course that was a big break, so he said sure. They told him they wanted to put him on the radio to show people what a great orchestra he had, but they told him, 'We won't pay you the first time you play; we just want to see how it turns out.' Joe was very ignorant about this kind of stuff and they did play for the radio for free and then when the club opened they played there for free the first time, too. When the musicians' union found out he'd played for free they suspended him for six months and fined him something like $1,500, which was a lot of money in those days. Joe was shocked. He didn't know he had done anything wrong. So he said, 'To hell with this,' and he quit playing and he and a friend opened up a bar down at the waterfront, a seaman's bar with a hotel upstairs—a dollar-a-night kind of place. It did really great, and he stayed with that for quite a long time; he was in that business until he died. I think he liked it, too—not the same way he liked music, but he was happy there."

Joe and his partner opened their business in the summer of 1937. The bar/restaurant, called Garcia's, was at the corner of First and Harrison Streets in downtown San Francisco, on the site of what is today the beautiful and stately WPA art deco–style Sailors Union of the Pacific building. In the '30s and '40s that section of the city was a rough area whose (low)life centered on the nearby docks. In fact, Rincon Hill, where the bar was located, had been the site of bloody battles between striking maritime workers and local police just three years earlier. Run-down seamen's hotels and cheap restaurants dotted the area, and, sailors being sailors, there was plenty of nefarious activity to be found. The cheery, well-scrubbed boulevards and cedar-shaded parks of the Crocker-Amazon district must have seemed paradisiacal in comparison.

Joe had only been in the bar business for about six months when, on December 20, 1937, his first son, named Clifford Ramon (after Ruth's maiden name and Joe's middle name), was born at Children's Hospital in San Francisco. By all accounts, the Garcias had a very happy home life. Though the bar business was extremely time-consuming, Joe and Ruth managed to keep in close touch with their many relatives in the area, and large family dinners involving various Garcias and Cliffords were common. "The Cliffords were lovely people," Leonor remembers. "We all got along very nicely and they were very fond of my parents, so we'd get together quite often."

On August 1, 1942, Joe and Ruth's second son, Jerome John Garcia, was born at Children's Hospital. He was named after the great American composer Jerome Kern, whose bright, tuneful songs and music for the Broadway stage and Hollywood musicals made him a legend in his own lifetime. There's no question that Joe Garcia would have encountered Kern's sumptuous melodies during his own musical career; Kern's music was an integral part of American popular culture from the late '20s (when he wrote his best-known musical, *Showboat*, with lyricist Oscar Hammerstein II) until his death in 1945.

During the first few years of Jerry's life the family lived together in the small Amazon Street house. Clifford, who was forever branded with the nickname "Tiff" after his toddler brother's mispronunciation of his name, went to Epiphany School, in the shadow of the majestic Church of the Epiphany about six blocks up Amazon, while Jerry stayed home with his mother; or if she was helping out downtown at the bar, he might spend the day with his mother's parents over on Harrington Street or at one of his aunt's or uncle's houses. Tiff recalls going on a couple of family vacations when Jerry was still very young—to Las Vegas by train, and on a tour of some of California's missions by car.

The whole Garcia clan often got together on Sunday afternoons down in Burlingame, just south of San Francisco, where Manuel, the family patriarch, had moved during the late '30s. "He was a very bright guy," his grandson Daniel says. "He spoke broken English, but boy, he could talk about any political issue, and those were the kind of discussions that were held around the table when Jerry and I and all of us were little kids. I think it's part of the reason Jerry was an articulate guy. There were hot and heavy discussions, arguments even, between my grandfather and my dad and Uncle Joe. That was before dinner. Then after dinner there would inevitably be singing. Mostly it was songs from the flapper era—the '20s and '30s. We'd all be sitting around a big supper table, all the cousins and the aunts and everybody, and we'd sing for hours. It was a big deal. We'd sing American songs mainly—George M. Cohan, show tunes, popular tunes from the '20s, '30s, '40s."

Tiff and Jerry both took piano lessons when they were young—Jerry was four or five when he started—"but we both hated it," Tiff says. "Even though I was older, Jerry was better than me, but neither of us liked to practice, so we never got very good." Ironically, years later Jerry composed some of his most memorable songs on the piano, though he never did become more than a rudimentary player.

Although Joe Garcia's days as a professional musician were over, he still played music whenever he could. He entertained the seamen who frequented his bar with the mellifluous strains of his saxophone and clarinet, and he also played regularly at home and at family gatherings. Ruth played piano fairly well, but her taste ran toward Chopin rather than popular music. She listened mainly to classical music on the family phonograph. Joe liked swing music— Benny Goodman, Glenn Miller and others. "There was always music in the house," Tiff recalls, "either records or my dad playing. He had played clarinet mainly with his group, but I feel like I saw him playing saxophone more at home. There are pictures of me and Jerry with his saxes and clarinets."

Jerry once said he had only fleeting memories of his father, but the sound of the clarinet wafting through the Amazon Street house was ingrained in his memory: "The clarinet is a wonderful instrument. It has a nice, sonorous quality. I remember the sound of the clarinet more than the tunes. The clarinet had that lovely wood quality, especially in that relaxed middle register. And that sound is very present in my ear. Sounds linger in my ear; I can recall 'em. Some people can recall smells. I can recall specific sounds—I can hear a sound and all of a sudden it will transport me to places."

"I was in awe of Uncle Joe," cousin Daniel says, "He would take out the saxophone and play for us and we'd sit there completely mesmerized." Daniel remembers his uncle as "a very mild, kind, decent guy. I never heard him say a bad word about anybody. In a way Jerry reminded me of him. But Jerry's mom was that way, too—very nice and sweet and kindhearted."

Tiff says that both of his parents could be stern disciplinarians, too: "My dad once burned my hand to teach me a lesson because I accidentally set fire to the neighbor's house. Actually, I set fire to some papers under a garage, but the guy happened to be a cop. Big mistake."

The family was nominally Catholic. According to Tiff, "We went to church every Sunday, and later, when we moved down to the Peninsula, we went to church there. But my parents never came, my grandmother never came. They'd just push us out the door and say, 'Go!' Sometimes we'd go and sometimes we'd cut out and go get a milkshake." In later years, Jerry recalled being alternately spooked and transported by the impenetrably mysterious

Latin mass that echoed through all Catholic churches until 1962, when the Vatican II council authorized switching to the vernacular.

In 1945, when Jerry was three, the Cliffords and Garcias bought a small parcel of land and built a summer house in Lompico, an undeveloped, heavily wooded part of northern Santa Cruz County, about a two-and-a-half-hour drive south of San Francisco in those days. Ruth's handyman father, Bill Clifford (known as Pop), and Joe Garcia built the redwood cabin on West Drive over the course of a couple of summers. In the early years it had no electricity. "We used lanterns, and the kids all bunked together," Daniel says. It was hard to beat the location—just steps up the hill from Lompico Creek, which was dammed in the summer to create a swimming area, and Lompico Lodge, which was the main gathering place and watering hole for the summer revelers.

It was behind the Lompico cabin, in either the summer of 1946 or the spring of 1947, that one of the formative incidents of Jerry's early life occurred. As Tiff tells the story, "Jerry [who was four] and I were chopping kindling outside near the fire pit—they didn't call them barbecues back then. He would put a piece of wood down, take his hand away and I would chop. He'd put another one down, I'd chop it in half. These are long sticks, redwood branches. We got into a rhythm, him pushing the sticks with his finger and taking it away as I chopped, but in a split second we got confused and wham!—I hit his finger. It wasn't cut clean off but we couldn't get him to surgery fast enough and so they had to amputate it."

"My mother had my hand wrapped in a towel, and I remember it didn't hurt or anything," Jerry recalled, "it was just sort of a buzzing sensation. I don't associate any pain with it. For me, the traumatic part of it was after the doctor amputated it, I had this big cast and bandages on it. And they gradually got smaller and smaller, until I was down to, like, one little bandage. And I thought for sure my finger was under there. And that was the worst part, when the bandage came off. 'Oh my God, my finger's gone!' But after that it was okay, because as a kid, if you have a few little things that make you different, it's a good score. So I got a lot of mileage out of having a missing finger when I was a kid."

And so the middle finger on Jerry's right hand was amputated down to the second joint, thereby creating what would in his later years become another iconic symbol: the unmistakable Jerry Garcia handprint, seen on T-shirts, bumper stickers and car window decals. "It was a total accident, of course," Tiff Garcia says, "but deep down I felt I was responsible. I was the older kid and I was the one who actually did it. I don't think Jerry ever held it against me, though."

In the summers, Jerry, Tiff, their mother and various cousins and aunts would typically spend weeks on end in Lompico, while the working men in the family—Joe and Manuel Garcia, Pop Clifford and his son, Bill, who was a San

Francisco fireman—mainly came down on weekends. In the last week of August 1947, Tiff went down to Lompico to spend some time with his cousins, while five-year-old Jerry accompanied Ruth and Joe on what was to be a week-long fishing vacation up in the wilds of Humboldt County before Jerry started kindergarten. Joe loved outdoor leisure sports like fishing and golf; Tiff says their garage at home was filled with his father's sports equipment.

On Sunday, August 24, Joe, Ruth and Jerry began the long but scenic drive north to Arcata, about 275 miles up the coast from San Francisco. They probably spent the night somewhere off Highway 101; the next day they made it to Arcata, where they were planning to stay for the week, and then drove about 30 miles inland to an area near the tiny logging town of Willow Creek so Joe could fish for steelhead in the clear, sparkling waters of the Trinity River. That part of the Six Rivers National Forest is breathtakingly beautiful, with dense forests covering the foothills of rugged mountains that range from 3,000 to 5,000 feet near Willow Creek to 7,000 feet or more in the nearby Trinity Alps. The Trinity River is rocky and wild, its currents unpredictable.

At about 5:30 in the afternoon on the twenty-fifth, Joe Garcia was in his waders, fishing in the river, when he slipped on a rock and was swept into the raging waters. Although he was a good swimmer, he was no match for the fierce current, and within a matter of moments he was pulled underwater into a deep hole and pinned there. A couple of youngsters playing on some nearby rocks saw Joe go under and immediately went for help. Three vacationing fishermen rushed to the scene and managed to pull Garcia from the water, but only after he'd been underwater ten to fifteen minutes. By coincidence, shortly after the three men brought Joe's seemingly lifeless body onto land, a Humboldt county medical officer happened by, and for the next five and a half hours he attempted to resuscitate the victim, even using a pulmotor brought in by ambulance from Arcata. The struggle was futile, however, and at 11:15 that evening Joe Garcia was pronounced dead. He had turned forty-five ten days earlier.

(Though in a few interviews Jerry claimed to have witnessed his father's drowning—"I actually watched him go under; it was horrible"—Tiff, based on what his mother told him, questions that. The detailed newspaper account of the drowning the following day in the *Humboldt Times* makes no mention of either Ruth or Jerry being on the scene; indeed, Jerry is misidentified in the story as Joseph Garcia's "small daughter." This is not to minimize the impact of the death upon Jerry, however.)

The next day, Joe Garcia's body was shipped from the Chapel of the Redwoods in Arcata down to a mortuary in San Francisco. That same day, Tiff says, "My grandfather [Pop Clifford] had to drive down to Lompico from the city in his old Model A panel truck laundry wagon to tell us, because we didn't have a telephone. He never took that wagon out of town, so we knew something was wrong when he pulled up in that. It was crushing, to say the least. It was the first death in that generation."

"That was the biggest tragedy we'd ever had in our family," Leonor says. "We couldn't believe it. It took us all a long, long time to get over it." Adds Daniel Garcia, "My father and his brother were very, very close so this was just devastating."

Though Jerry was only five at the time, he said in 1984 that his father's death "emotionally crippled me for a long time. I couldn't even stand to hear about it until I was about ten or eleven. The effect it had on me was really crushing, maybe because it affected my mother a lot and I sensed that. And also, it was something I wasn't allowed to participate in, and I think now that that was a real problem. They tried to protect me from it. That was the reason I was sent to live with my grandparents after my father died."

Without warning—like some monstrously cruel twist of fate in a nineteenth-century English novel—everything changed for the Garcia family. Tiff briefly moved in with his uncle and aunt—Bill Clifford, the fireman, and his wife, also named Ruth—while Jerry stayed with his mother in the Amazon house. Tiff was taken out of Epiphany School and moved to a nearby public school, Guadaloupe. That's also where Jerry spent his first six months of kindergarten. Manuel Garcia (Joe's brother) and his family lived right near Guadaloupe, so Jerry and Tiff would usually go there after school, and then later someone would drive them back home.

"Then my mom sold the house on Amazon, so she could get into the bar business, buy out the other partner, and Jerry and I ended up moving in with my grandmother and grandfather [Pop and Tillie Clifford, known in the family as Nan or Nana]," Tiff relates. "We lived there at 87 Harrington Street, and my mom lived across the street in a cottage that my grandmother and grandfather also owned. So we lived close to my mom still, but we didn't see her much, except on weekends. She'd take us out for dinner, or make us dinner, or we'd go out somewhere, but my mom never drove—in fact, I got my driver's license before she did. She tried to drive after my father died, but she crashed up a couple of cars; she was a terrible driver. So for Jerry and me, our main role models for a long time were my grandparents, which was not bad.

"Before my father died we used to visit my grandmother every weekend and we spent a lot of time there, so it wasn't that new a thing to be there year-round. In fact, it was kind of nice because we got to go out after school and play, and my grandmother worked late and my grandfather would read the paper and drink his beer—he was the type who made his own liquor during Prohibition. He was very dapper, with a vest and a chain watch. My mom was a whole lot like him; she was very neat."

According to Leonor, most of the Garcia side of the family disapproved of Ruth's decision to stay in the bar business. "She had been a nurse making good money, so we thought that would be better for her," she says. "We thought the bar was kind of a rough place for a woman to be, but she wanted to stick with it, and she did for a few years. We didn't see as much of her or the children after Joe died. Mostly they were with their grandparents, the Cliffords."

Tiff says that shortly after he and Jerry moved into Harrington Street, Ruth bought them the first television on the block "and also this big freezer, with a complete food program. I guess she felt a little guilty that we had to stay with our grandparents. But she was only paying twenty-five dollars a month rent for the house across the street."

In Jerry's posthumously published book *Harrington Street,* a slender but beguiling collection of paintings, drawings and writing about his youth up until about age ten (he described the book as "auto-apocrypha, full of my anec-doubts"), he talks about how Bill and Tillie Clifford seemed like such a mismatched pair. She was vivacious, spunky, "a ball of fire; she was really hot." Pop was "so dull. He was such a quiet person. This was one of the Irish guys that *didn't* have the gift of gab."

Tillie *was* a bright, active, very independent woman. Bill had been a laundry worker most of his adult life—he was a laundry driver mainly—and he supported his wife, but it was Tillie who made a mark in that business. She helped organize the laundry workers' union in San Francisco, and she spent more than two decades as its secretary-treasurer. She traveled extensively in that position, attending and occasionally speaking at labor conventions. She was modern in another way, too, Tiff says: "She had a boyfriend for like twenty or thirty years that she would travel with when she took trips; he'd go along and he was a single guy and didn't have a family. My grandfather knew, but the guy never came to the house. It was a discreet situation."

Outwardly at least, Tiff and Jerry's years at their grandparents' house were fairly normal. They attended Monroe School on Excelsior Boulevard, the same school Ruth Garcia had gone to when she was a child living on Harrington Street. It was Jerry's third-grade teacher at Monroe, Miss Simon, who first "made me think it was okay to draw pictures," he said. "She'd say, 'Oh that's lovely,' and she'd have me draw pictures and do murals and all this stuff. She was very encouraging, and it was the first time I heard that the idea of being a creative person was a viable possibility in life. 'You mean you can spend all day drawing pictures? Wow! What a great piece of news!' She enlarged the world for me."

"Jerry and I used to like drawing together," Tiff says. "I was really into drawing structures, and Jerry was more into drawing characters. When we were growing up at my grandfather's house we used to draw on these laundry pads we had all over the house. We'd draw a little house, then get a razor blade and cut the window out of the house and go into the next page and cut another little slot for the door and so on and make these flip books.

"We also used to make instruments out of my grandfather's antique cigar cases, which he used to keep his tools in. We'd make little ukuleles that were actually playable. We didn't know chords or frets or anything. But we'd string them with fishing line. We went through periods where we'd make dozens of them. We were always fashioning our own little toys. My grandmother had a rumpus room under the house on Harrington Street and with my cousin [Daniel] we'd all sing and bounce around the room, and have parties."

It's not surprising to learn that thoroughly modern Tillie Clifford played the oh-so-'20s banjo-ukulele—"Four strings, short neck, strung like a banjo," Tiff says. "She didn't actually play it in our time. In fact when Jerry got into bluegrass, I gave it to him. He probably traded it somewhere along the line."

Jerry often said that one reason he eventually got into playing country music was that Tillie listened to broadcasts from the Grand Ole Opry on Saturday nights, but Tiff firmly says, "She wasn't into country music. Jerry is fantasizing all this. We knew about it because of her tours she would take and when she'd go to these conventions. She'd bring back memorabilia from these various places. She'd been to the Opry, but she didn't listen to it on the radio."

Of course in the early '50s everyone heard country-pop crooners like Tennessee Ernie Ford and Vaughn Monroe, and Roy Rogers and Dale Evans were going strong still. There was also a fellow in the Bay Area named Rusty Draper: "He had a kids' show on in the afternoon when TV first came out," Tiff says, "and in fact, one of the first 45s Jerry ever bought was a song [Draper recorded] called 'Gambler's Guitar.' It was sort of countryish and it had some riffs in it, little guitar solos, and I think that's part of what got him and myself interested in that kind of music."

Down at the bar, the jukebox was mainly filled with a mix of big band music and sentimental ballads—a reminder of Joe Garcia's days around the place. Sometime in the late '40s, the Sailors Union of the Pacific bought the corner lot where the bar and hotel were located so it could erect its moderne granite-faced meeting hall. "So they made a deal for my mom to have the property across the street, which at the time was an abandoned Curtis Candy Company factory, with a hotel on top called the Claremont Rooms. It had been a funky old seamen's hotel. Jerry and I used to go upstairs and clean out the rooms for my mom and we'd look at all the girlie magazines they'd leave."

"It was a daytime bar, a working guy's bar, so I grew up with all these guys who were sailors," Jerry said. "They went out and sailed to the Far East and the Persian Gulf and all that, and they would come and hang out in the bar all day long and talk to me when I was a kid. It was great fun for me."

In late '40s–early '50s San Francisco, kicks were easy to find for kids. The streets were relatively safe, so Tiff and Jerry roamed the city freely, taking advantage of the long leash their grandparents gave them. "You could take a bus or streetcar downtown, or ride your bike," Tiff says. "The trolleys had stopped going on Mission Street, but they were still on Market. They had trolley buses that we used to climb on the back of. We went all over the place: we'd go out to Sutro Baths [a defunct indoor swimming pool next to Ocean Beach in San Francisco], and Playland [an amusement park] was out there. You could go down there and spend all day. Sometimes we'd go to Fleishacker's—it was such a beautiful pool; it was like a *lake*. We'd go to the zoo [also out at the ocean], too."

Closer to home there were inexpensive movie theaters and plenty of small parks and playgrounds to keep the kids busy. Jerry spent much of his playtime in the late '40s and early '50s with his brother and older cousins Daniel, Diane (the daughter of Bill and Ruth Clifford) and Dave Ross (Leonor's son). Hanging with the big kids undoubtedly exposed Jerry to many things other kids his age hadn't experienced, but the influence wasn't always positive.

"I remember there was a police station over in the Ingleside district, next to Balboa Park, below City College, where they used to board horses; there was a big corral in the back," Tiff says. "This must have been '48, '49. Jerry, myself and my cousin Diane were in the back there and we noticed all these broken windows and a lot of rocks around, so we started breaking windows. We figured there were so many broken ones, what difference would it make? We were bored. And it was fun—until the cops came running out from all over the place and rounded us up. I don't remember them having weapons— Jerry liked to say they did, but I don't know—but they scared the shit out of us. So my parents had to pay for some of the damage and we were in *big* trouble at home. It was a big deal to me at the time. I was very impressionable. You know—first run in with the law, twelve years old."

Daniel Garcia remembers another run-in with the SFPD around the same time: "Right around the corner from Harrington Street, on Mission, there was a barbershop that had one of those turning barber poles out front. It had some kind of keyhole or something at the bottom and Jerry, Tiff and I put a cherry bomb in it. Obviously we didn't realize the power of it because it blew this thing off the wall. Glass came down; it was a mess. Of course the barber came out and he chased us down the street and then the cops came by and picked us up and put us in the backseat of the car. Then, while the cop was talking to Tiff, Jerry opened the door and jumped out and ran away, and I did, too. [In Tiff's version of the story Jerry even kicks the policeman before running away.] We went down to Tillie's house and Jerry was wheezing like crazy from his asthma; he even turned a little blue. It was scary. He couldn't run for more than half a block without wheezing. I remember that well because we used to run away from stuff that we did."

Jerry's asthma flare-ups were infrequent, but fairly debilitating when they occurred. The typical treatment in those days consisted of getting a shot of the bronchial muscle relaxant epinephrine and then staying in bed for a few days. "He liked to say he had a sickly childhood, but that's bullshit," Tiff says. "He had asthma once every couple of years, and it would last for maybe a week or two. And every time he got sick, he *got* something. I remember he got his first 45 record player and some records when he got sick."

But Sara Ruppenthal, Jerry's first wife, says that Jerry once "told me a story of being sick in bed with asthma. His mother came to visit and then left before he was ready for her to leave. There's this image of him looking out the window as she leaves, and having a massive asthma attack—making that connection between the abandonment and the illness."

Though by all accounts Ruth Garcia tried to be a good mother to her children, the fact is she was not around much during these formative years; the bar took up most of her time. Then, in 1949, Ruth married a carpenter-piledriver named Ben Brown, who'd been working on the Sailors Union construction project, and she saw the kids even less for a while. "It only lasted a year or two," Tiff says. "But they were friends for a long time after that. He was a drunk, but he was an okay guy."

In 1953 Ruth married her third husband, a merchant seaman named Wadislof "Wally" Matusiewicz, in a modest ceremony in Reno, Nevada, that was attended by both Jerry and Tiff. (In fact, the two kids got stuck in a hotel elevator during this trip and had to be rescued by the fire department.) Wally had grown up in Bayonne, New Jersey, the son of Polish immigrants (which didn't stop seamen from dubbing him "Russian Wally"). He was seven years younger than Ruth and had never been married before. When they got married, Ruth and Wally jointly decided that Ruth should take a greater role in the lives of her children, so Wally took over most of the day-to-day operations of the bar.

"Then Union Oil decided they wanted to put their office building where the bar was," Tiff says, "so the business moved across the street again, to another corner. There was a seamen's hotel there, too, and on the ground floor there was the 400 Club. The original 400 Club had been a bawdy seaman's bar, but my mom turned that into a typical '50s nightclubish-type place with the emphasis on the little restaurant. It had red Naugahyde stools and a solid mahogany circle bar. It was classy, a nice place considering the other one she had. So my mom had the daytime bar business there with a little restaurant. At the time, she had the biggest day business of any bar in the city. They were selling beer at six in the morning. You had to peel some of these guys out of the bar at night. They'd go up to a hotel room upstairs. People would rent these rooms for months at a time.

"When I was in the service [in the late '50s], my mom turned the top floor into this real flashy apartment—three bedrooms with a total view of downtown and the Bay Bridge. She had a doberman pinscher named Rusty and you could see him running around the roof as you drove over the bridge into the city."

With the 400 Club booming, the family made the same radical move as hundreds of thousands of other middle-class American families in the early '50s—they bought a ranch-style home in the suburbs; in this case in the town of Menlo Park, about thirty miles south of the city in San Mateo County.

"We moved to the Peninsula [as the area is known] in that furious rush to get kids out of the city—sort of a half-hearted attempt by my mom," Jerry recalled. "I was being a kid in San Francisco. I later became a hoodlum [there]. . . . The thrust of her thinking was to get out of the city, so we went to Menlo Park, a real nice place which was just bursting out of the ground at that point. Everything was new there."

The Matusiewiczes' nice, if nondescript, home was on a quiet cul-de-sac off Santa Monica Avenue, half a block east of Middlefield Road, one of the main arteries that cuts through the Peninsula. Across the street were the sprawling grounds of St. Patrick's Seminary, and close by was the Golden State Dairy. Santa Monica Avenue has no sidewalks, so the overall feeling of the neighborhood is sort of rural-suburban. Certainly it was a much different world than the Excelsior district of San Francisco, which was the point, of course.

"The house was right out of *Sunset* magazine," Tiff says. "We moved down there and none of us knew anybody. Still, we were pretty excited. We got all new clothes, new furniture. We had a new beige Cadillac. My mom really set this guy Wally up! He'd been a first mate in the merchant marine, but when he married my mom he became a bartender.

"But it was a culture shock, big time. There was nothing familiar. My mom was on this fetish about getting her family back together. She had a new husband, she had her kids back, she had a successful bar business. She wanted to be a housewife, really. My mom even started making some of our clothes, not because she had to, but because she wanted to. She did all this drudgery and loved it.

"My father's side of the family was really crushed when we moved down there. We still went up to visit my grandparents on weekends, and as soon as I got my driver's license I'd go up almost every weekend.

"Before my mom took me to the Peninsula, I was raised, if I can call it that, by my grandparents, who left me largely unsupervised," Jerry said. "I think that probably ruined me for everything—or made me what I am today. They were both people who worked and they were grandparently. They didn't have much stomach for discipline, so I was pretty much unsupervised and I was used to having things exactly like I wanted them. I was used to getting up and doing things, doing what I wanted, coming in when I wanted and going where I wanted and not asking anybody if they cared. I was much too much that person by the time my mom tried to get us down to the suburbs. It was really too late. But the change did me a lot of good for other reasons."

Jerry moved to Menlo Park when he was ten and was there through early adolescence, from part of sixth grade through eighth grade, which he had to repeat because of poor grades. "I was too smart for school," he said in 1984, a chuckle in his voice. "I knew it; I don't know why anyone else didn't know it. I went to school; I just didn't do any work. It's not that I had anything against school or even learning. The point was I was reading things and I had my own education, my own program going, and I was really, really bored with school. I already had things decided for myself. I had things I wanted to do, I had plans, and I had my own interests and my own rate of learning and I couldn't see slowing down or stopping and wasting my time for schoolwork."

Alienated though he was from the day-to-day of school life, "I had incredible luck with teachers," he said. "I had a couple of teachers that really opened up the world for me. I was a reader, luckily, because I was sickly as a kid. I spent so much time in bed because I was sick, so I read; that was my entertainment. That separated me a lot from everybody else. Then when I got down to the Peninsula, I had a couple of teachers that were very, very radical, absolutely far-out. I was lucky."

In interviews, Jerry often cited a teacher at Menlo-Oaks Middle School named Dwight Johnson for broadening his outlook on life and learning. "He's the guy who turned me into a freak," he said. "He was my seventh-grade teacher and he was a wild guy. He had an old MG TC, and he had a Vincent Black Shadow motorcycle, the fastest-accelerating motorcycle at the time. And he was *out there*. He opened lots and lots of doors for me. He's the guy that got me reading deeper than science fiction [Ray Bradbury was Jerry's favorite writer]. He taught me that ideas are fun."

It was through the influence of teachers like Dwight Johnson, too, that Jerry was admitted to what he called "a fast-learner program" in school, sponsored by Stanford University in nearby Palo Alto. "So I had the advantage of this elaborate accelerated program at school and a couple of far-out teachers who were willing to answer any questions and turn me on to where to go—'If you want to find more, this is what you read.' "

When he wasn't devouring George Orwell's *1984* (a favorite of his) or more complex tomes by European philosophers, Jerry was engaged in typical adolescent stuff. Through Wally he developed what would become a lifelong interest in comic books; in those days he collected the ghoulish, "ultra-horrible" EC comics—*Tales from the Crypt, Vault of Horror* and such—as well as *Mad Comics* (a forerunner of *Mad* magazine). Tiff was still a major influence in Jerry's life, although he was nearing the end of his days at Sequoia High in Redwood City, and before he graduated he joined the marine reserves.

"I had a driver's license so whenever we could we'd go up to the city and visit our friends," Tiff says. "I remember Jerry and I hot-wired a car that was in my stepfather's charge; a little MG roadster. We drove it up to the city from Menlo Park. My car [Tillie Clifford's green '42 Chevy coupe] wasn't working so we used this one. I didn't even know how I was going to do it—I undid a couple of bolts under the dash and I grabbed a bunch of tin foil and I zapped it up there, and it worked, although I singed my hands. We were mischievous in that way."

On those weekends in the city, Jerry spent much of his time palling around with his cousin Daniel, who recalls, "We spent a lot of time at the movies; that was something we both loved. We used to go down and see every movie that came out about a musician. I remember going down and seeing *The Glenn Miller Story* on a Sunday afternoon with Jerry. We always had no money, so we'd go through Tillie's pocketbooks to try to scrounge enough money to go down to the Golden Gate Theater, which was a movie theater in those days.

"I also remember going down to the Fox Theater on Market Street and Eleventh when they had the debut of *Rock Around the Clock* [in 1956] and that place was jumpin'! Jerry and I and two girls went to see it together. We came out of that movie with the burning desire to be rock 'n' roll musicians. I remember him telling me, 'We can do that; we can play like that.' I remember that very clearly."

Jerry was already falling in love with rock 'n' roll by the time that Bill Haley and the Comets movie came out. Again, Tiff was his main influence—Tiff began listening to local R&B radio stations in the early '50s, so by the time the first true rock 'n' roll records came out, the Garcia brothers were primed. "I remember going out with a friend to this record store on Mission near Geneva called the Record Changer, and buying this record, 'Crazy, Man, Crazy,' which was Bill Haley's first release out here—before 'Rock Around the Clock,' " Tiff says. "I bought it on 78 and Jerry bought it on 45. He got a pretty good 45 collection, because my mom, being in the bar business, used to get all these 45s from the jukebox. We had tons. Most of those weren't rock 'n' roll, but there was some good stuff in there."

Besides Tiff and Daniel, Jerry's other early rock 'n' roll buddy was a kid named Laird Grant, who lived a few blocks away from Jerry in Menlo Park. Like Jerry, Laird had moved to the suburbs from San Francisco—he'd lived in the outer Mission district, not far from Harrington Street. The two, who became lifelong friends, met when Jerry was in seventh grade at Menlo-Oaks.

"I met him because he hazed me," Laird says. "That's something that went around a lot back then, though it was usually a college thing; occasionally it trickled down. The bully kids—and I wouldn't say Jerry was a bully, but he hung out with some kids who were, and he was rougher than your normal, average kid—would haze other kids. So there they were, smearing me with lipstick and shaving cream, and there may have even been some perfume involved, and one of the guys was trying to pants me. They'd do that and then throw your pants up in a tree. Jerry was one of the guys and I thought, 'There's gotta be more to this guy than this.' After that we started hanging out together and we found out we actually had a lot in common. We hung out together because we realized that all the rest of the kids weren't the same as we were."

Tiff didn't feel like he was fitting in very well either in school or at home, so after he graduated from Sequoia High in 1956, "I was really anxious to get out of the house because I felt like there was some kind of tension there," he says. "My mom and Wally would argue—nothing too heavy, but I didn't like it. It hadn't felt right to me since we moved out of the city, so as soon as I was eighteen I was ready to get the hell out of the suburbs. I wanted to go back to the city. Instead I went into the marines. The Korean War was over by then, but you still had the drill instructors who were Korea veterans; a tough bunch, boy. *Mean*. But I thought if I was going to be in the service I was going to be in the tough one. I wasn't going to be in the army or navy."

Laird spent a fair amount of time at the Matusiewicz house (and later, at the bar) and he remembers Wally this way: "He was kind of like Popeye. He had a set of forearms on him—man, the last thing you wanted to do was piss this guy off because he'd reach out and grab you with a couple of canned-ham hands. He could get pissed off and rant and rave, but I never saw him raise a hand on anybody. He could go off—*BAM!*—like a firecracker, and then two minutes later he was cool."

"Wally was a no-nonsense, hard-nosed guy," adds Daniel Garcia. "He had a temper but he also had a great sense of humor. He used to get pissed off all the time because Jerry and Tiff wouldn't do enough work around the house."

And with Laird Grant in the picture, Jerry spent even less time at home than before. The Peninsula was their playground, and they darted around constantly—on bike, on foot and in buses, day and night. One of the duo's favorite late-night activities was to sneak out of their houses and break into the nearby Golden State Dairy. "People at the dairy would be packing up the trucks for morning with ice cream and chocolate milk and all that stuff," Laird says. "It was really easy to climb up these pine trees, throw a jacket over the cyclone fence and climb over into the place. We'd get chocolate milk and ice cream. The ice cream trucks were hard to get to, but we could always get chocolate milk."

In 1957 the family—minus Tiff, who was taking abuse from D.I.s down at Camp Pendleton in San Diego—moved back to San Francisco. They settled briefly in the Westlake district, on a steep hill overlooking the Pacific—"in the fog zone," as Tiff calls it—before moving back into Harrington Street, and then into the large apartment Ruth had created above the 400 Club. Jerry was enrolled at James Denman Middle School, a notoriously tough place then and now. "Denman was sort of like an intermediate penitentiary," says Daniel, only half-joking. "Then they'd parole you to Balboa [High] next door, which wasn't much better."

Jerry said that Denman and Balboa in the late '50s were "razor-toting schools. It was a matter of self-preservation. Either you were a hoodlum, or you were a puddle on the sidewalk. I was part of a big gang, a nonaffiliated gang. At that time in the 1950s, San Francisco was broken up into two loose groups, called the Barts and the Shoes. The Shoes were the white-shoe, Pat Boone–looking types, out on the Avenues among the upscale people. The working-class neighborhoods were where the Barts were—Black Bart greasers would be another expression for them. The city was divided bilaterally like that, and there would be incursions into other neighborhoods where you'd beat everybody up, or everybody would beat you up. It was a state of war, and I didn't last long in that. I spent a lot of time in Mission Emergency Hospital, holding my lip together, or my eye, because some guy had hit me with a board."

Jerry Garcia, in *fights?* "It might have happened," says Tiff, who was in the marines at the time. "It probably did a couple of times. Hey, it's colorful. And there was definitely trouble to be found. When he left the Peninsula and came back to San Francisco and went to Balboa, it was a big change for him. It was going from the suburbs to the city, no doubt about it. I mean, when we first moved down to Menlo Park, I had a reputation for being a bad guy just because I was from the city. Thirty miles back then seemed like it was halfway across the state; it was just a different world. If we had stayed in the city back then, we probably both would have wound up in jail."

Daniel Garcia's perspective is a little different: "Jerry liked to think of himself as a tough guy, but he was anything but. He had more of his mother in him than you'd think. He was a very benign guy, in fact. I can never remember being in a fight with him, and I was in plenty of fights. Tiff could knock your lights out at the drop of a hat. But Jerry wasn't a tough guy. He went to a tough school. Jerry was a clean-cut guy, if you want to know the truth. We were into music and we smoked cigarettes and that's about the wildest thing he did. I don't remember him drinking booze; that wasn't part of our lives at all. And I don't remember Jerry dating at all at that time. We were too shy to go to dances."

On August 1, 1957, Jerry turned fifteen, and that's when things really started to change for him. That birthday was the joyous occasion when his mother, finally recognizing the musician inside Jerry that was straining to be heard, broke down and got him what he'd always wanted: an accordion. Wait a minute! It's a story Jerry told with relish to any interviewer who asked him about it: "I went nuts—'Aggggh! No! No!'—I railed and I raved, and she finally turned it in, and I got a pawnshop electric guitar and an amplifier. I was beside myself with joy." In another interview he said, "I [had] developed this deep craving to play the electric guitar. I fell in love with rock 'n' roll; I wanted to make that sound so badly."

"The accordion came from one of the people who owed my mom money; that's how she got it," Tiff says. "There was an electric mandolin there, and a couple of other instruments my mom had taken on from other people. So it was like, 'Here, Jerry, want this?' It wasn't that big a deal. Jerry liked to sensationalize that story a bit, but that's okay; it's basically true."

"I went over to Jerry's one day and there he was fiddling with this guitar, an inexpensive, used guitar," Daniel remembers. "He was plucking it but didn't really know what to do with it. He knew how to hit a few notes, but he couldn't form a chord yet. He couldn't have had it more than three days. And I was so impressed that very day he and I went down to that hockshop on Third Street and I bought my first guitar for $25. He helped me pick it out—a lovely little acoustic guitar. So we started to learn it on our own and from a few books. We learned together and we played a lot together."

Jerry recalled that his stepfather taught him how to put the guitar in "a weird open tuning, and I learned to play a lot of stuff before somebody showed me how to tune it [normally] and some real chord positions and things like that." Jerry didn't take any lessons; didn't even know anyone who played electric guitar: "I mean, the electric guitar was, like, from *Mars*, you know. You didn't *see* 'em even," he said. "I was stuck because I just didn't know anybody that played guitar. . . . That was probably the greatest hindrance of all to learning the guitar. . . . I used to do things like look at the pictures of guitar players and look at their hands and try to make the chords they were doing: *anything, any little thing.*"

His idols were the hot electric guitar pickers of the day—Chuck Berry, who pretty much defined rock 'n' roll guitar in 1956–57, Gene Vincent and his guitarist Cliff Gallup, Eddie Cochran, Buddy Holly, Bo Diddley, and though he didn't know his name then, James Burton, who played on most of Ricky Nelson's records. Also, "At the time, the R&B stations were still playing stuff like Lightnin' Hopkins and Frankie Lee Sims, these funky blues guys," he said. "Jimmy McCracklin, the Chicago blues guys, the T-Bone Walker–influenced guys, that older style, pre–B. B. King stuff. Jimmy Reed actually had *hits* in those days."

Jerry had always loved to sing—it was a singing family, after all—and he and Tiff and Daniel used to try to sing doo-wop and R&B tunes they heard on records and the radio, just like thousands of other kids across America in the '50s. In fact, street-corner harmony became something of a national obsession among young people for a while. It didn't require any instrumental proficiency, and everyone, it seemed, knew the songs of the day.

"I remember teaching Jerry harmony to a commercial for S&W Foods," Daniel says with a laugh. "Their slogan, which was sung, was 'S&W Foods / S&W simply wonderful / S&W foo-oo-oods.' It had this big Broadway ending and the last two lines were harmonized. So that was one of the first songs I used to illustrate harmony. That and some of the songs the family used to sing, like 'Down by the Riverside' and 'In the Evening by the Moonlight,' an old Stephen Foster song. Jerry and I spent a lot of time harmonizing on that."

Two other seminal events in Garcia's life occurred shortly after he got his first guitar—he discovered pot and he went to art school.

"I was fifteen when I got turned on to marijuana," Jerry said in a 1972 interview. "Finally, there was marijuana: Wow! Marijuana. Me and a friend of mine went up into the hills with two joints . . . and just got so high and laughed and roared and went skipping down the streets doing funny things and just having a helluva time. It was great, it was just what I wanted . . . that wine thing was so awful, and this marijuana was so perfect." In the late '50s scoring pot was fairly difficult, but he and Laird Grant occasionally managed to buy skinny little joints for fifty cents apiece. More commonly they dabbled in pills of various kinds—uppers and tranquilizers of indeterminate origin and potency; the gamble was part of the adventure.

Jerry's mother might not have known about his occasional weekend pot and pills escapades, but she did know that Jerry was doing badly in school and was getting harder to discipline at home. He kept his own hours, ignored most of his schoolwork and sometimes disappeared for the weekend with friends without warning. Ruth's occasional attempts to crack down on his bad behavior were largely unsuccessful. He wasn't exactly hostile to her; it was more his style to figure out ways around her attempts to control him by being charming for a while and *then* going back to doing what he wanted.

And he wasn't completely rudderless. After all, he spent hours diligently trying to learn how to play guitar, and in the summer of 1958 he suddenly became serious about studying art, too. "I was thinking I was going to be an artist, 'cause when I was a child, that's where I showed the most talent," he said. "As I grew up, most of the encouragement I got was, 'Well, be in the arts. You're obviously gifted.'"

A teacher at Balboa spotted Jerry's interest in art, and that summer, "He and a friend of his named Mike Kennedy came over to the Art Institute [then called the California School of Fine Arts] as part of a program that the Institute had to provide summer instruction for high school students who had been referred from their own school because they had some real aptitude in that area," says Wally Hedrick, an artist who was teaching at the school then. "I remember these two guys walking in one morning and they became part of the class and immediately both of them began to paint up a storm. They were really quite good for their age. Of course at that time, to me, Jerry Garcia was just another student. During subsequent semesters he took more classes, not only with me, but other faculty members.

"At that time there were two major directions the school was going, stylistically," he continues. "One of them was abstract expressionism. But Jerry was more taken with the so-called California figurative style, which hadn't been named at that time, but several people on the faculty were sort of known for starting it. He studied with at least one of them—Elmer Bischoff. But even before he did that, I think the idea of the figurative style was more evident in his work. I was on neither side, so whatever happened was fine with me.

"Jerry never became a full-time student, but he did become a personal friend and we'd invite him over to our parties and various social activities."

The California School of Fine Arts was a vital bohemian hub in a city that was exploding with creativity of every kind in the 1950s. The wild, rapturous brushstrokes of the CFSA's abstract expressionists found their musical analog in the soaring bebop flights of sweaty saxophonists blowing hard and free in a dozen big and small nightclubs around town. In the bold, imaginative forms and striking colors that burst or oozed or coolly glided off the canvases of the school's great figurative painters, there was the same vivid sense of life and rhythm and release that flew like hot sparks off the pages of beat poets working on broken-down Royal typewriters and ink-smeared notebooks and napkins at North Beach hangouts like Vesuvio's, Caffe Trieste and the Place. Then there were the "Funk" artists at CFSA, whose constructions and contraptions and mixed-media *whatevers* had some of the bite, wit and absurdity of hipster word jockeys like Lord Buckley, Ken Nordine and the incomparable Neal Cassady.

Wally Hedrick, Jerry's mentor at CFSA, had been in the thick of the city's bohemian renaissance since he arrived at the school as a promising painter at the dawn of the '50s. As early as 1953 he experimented with a sort of proto–light show machine that projected splashes of color while he played music on a keyboard. The following year, he and Deborah Remington turned a former auto repair shop on Fillmore Street into a combination gallery/performance space called the Six Gallery. It was there on October 13, 1955, before an audience of about a hundred cognoscenti and illuminati, including Jack Kerouac, Neal Cassady, Michael McClure, Philip Whalen, Gary Snyder, Lawrence Ferlinghetti, Beat paterfamilias Kenneth Rexroth and scores of others, that Allen Ginsberg gave his first public reading of "Howl."

By the time Jerry arrived at CFSA in 1958 some of the early Beat energy had dissipated or moved elsewhere, but there was still very much a scene in North Beach. Laird Grant remembers, "We'd hang out in front of the Anxious Asp, the Green Street Saloon, the Co-Existence Bagel Shop, Coffee & Confusion, and we'd go to parties here and there—there was a lot of action around; this is still before they drove the beatniks out." Jerry, Laird and their friends also devoured the latest books by Beat writers—a dog-eared copy of Jack Kerouac's *On the Road* was eagerly passed around as if it were some secret mystic text.

In the winter of 1958 Jerry's mother had bought a vacation home for the family up on Austin Creek near the Russian River town of Cazadero, about sixty miles north of the city. Tiff Garcia, who visited the house only a few times while he was on leave from the marines, says the house was "rustic but modern. It had a nice big living room, a lot of windows; it was in a really pretty area."

Daniel Garcia recalls, "We used to go up to Cazadero and sit in the family room and smoke Bull Durham cigarettes and play our guitars for hours. Hours and hours until my fingers literally bled. We'd play Chuck Berry, Bill Haley, *everything.*"

The family still went down to Lompico for part of each summer, too, though for shorter periods, and Tiff remembers a time at the Lodge there in the late '50s when "Jerry and my cousin Danny and I played some Wilbur Harrison tunes up on the dance floor. They were playing guitars and I think I was beating on a cymbal and a box. It used to be the place for the kids to hang out, and for adults there was a bar, so they would go in there and get blasted. It was really quite a busy place; *crowded.*"

Daniel says that he and Tiff and Jerry practiced and played together on a number of different occasions: "I seem to remember we called ourselves the Garcia Brothers among the bunch of us. Jerry and I played lead guitar and we'd argue about who was going to play what. Jerry used to kid me—'Hell, I play better with four fingers than you guys do with five.' Tiff would play bass sometimes. Mostly we played by ear and copied records." Daniel also says that in Lompico he and Jerry would practice their guitars at a nearby dam "and a couple of times we'd even get a little group around us and people would actually clap when we were done, which surprised us.

"When we were first learning, we used to go up to Stowe Lake in Golden Gate Park and practice out there. We also practiced a lot at my mom and dad's house, because they'd put up with it."

Jerry's younger cousin Dennis Clifford recalls a big Garcia-Clifford Thanksgiving bash in '58 or '59 where Jerry entertained the families with his guitar playing. "I know he was self-taught," he says, "but he was really pretty good." Daniel Garcia also remembers a "family reunion at [Aunt] Lena's house in San Francisco where Jerry and I played. Boy, we knocked 'em dead! They hadn't heard us before and we played 'Donna' by Ritchie Valens."

During this period Daniel and Jerry also wrote a few simple songs together. "I still have a book where we wrote down the fingering and lyrics," he says. "They were typical love songs. One was called 'Fly Trap'—'words by J. Garcia and D. Garcia.' But mostly we played standard stuff—'Church Bells May Ring,' 'Whispering Bells,' Everly Brothers songs."

Sometime in the middle of 1959 Ruth decided that it would be in Jerry's best interest to get out of the city, so they moved up to the house in Cazadero full-time and that fall Jerry was enrolled at Analy High School in Sebastopol, a thirty-minute bus ride away. Jerry was *not* pleased about this turn of events, though he acknowledged once that "things were just getting too intense for me in San Francisco. Then I started cutting school up there at Analy, and I'd steal my mother's car and I'd go down to the Peninsula—I had a girlfriend down there [in Redwood City]."

When the fall semester ended at Analy in late January 1960, Jerry decided he'd had enough. He was unhappy in school, unhappy at home and had no notions of getting a job, either. After bumming around for two months, splitting his time between his girlfriend's house and various friends' pads in San Francisco, he made a decision that obviously came more out of desperation than rational analysis: he joined the army, enlisting at a recruiting office in Oakland on April 12. Since he was still only seventeen at the time, his mother had to sign the papers; now both of her sons were in the military. At least it was peacetime.

To say that Jerry Garcia wasn't exactly "army material" would be putting it mildly. He related more to the rebellious Brando in *The Wild One* than to John Wayne in *Sands of Iwo Jima,* and he wasn't about to leave Kerouac and Chuck Berry behind just because his hair was short and he wore a khaki uniform. By his own admission, he was lazy and "pathologically anti-authoritarian," but no doubt the military has made "men" out of tougher cases than his, and he was always such a genial and enthusiastic fellow that he probably convinced the recruiters, and maybe even himself, that this was the best move for him. Tiff says he tried to talk Jerry out of enlisting—after all, he knew both the military and his brother—but, as Jerry put it, "I wanted so badly to see the world; it was the only hope I had. The only reason I wanted to go into the army was to go someplace—Germany, Korea, Japan, *anyplace.*"

From mid-April to July of 1960, Jerry did his basic combat training at Fort Ord, a scenic if slightly desolate base near Monterey, on the Pacific Coast 125 miles south of San Francisco. He wasn't a total washout as an army man: at Fort Ord he earned decorations for carbine sharpshooting and for "Basic Missileman (Surface to Air Missile)" training. Clearly, though, he had things other than soldiering on his mind. There was his girlfriend, whom he visited in Redwood City whenever he could, and Laird Grant helped make sure that Jerry's time at Fort Ord wasn't *too* dull:

"I'd go on base and we'd go to the PX and get a bunch of beer and put it in my '47 Cadillac convertible and drive around and throw beer cans at the sentries," Laird says. "I had a whole bunch of crazy people that were dressed in weird costumes, people from Redwood City, like his girlfriend. I drove around with a leopardskin vest and cutoff patent leather shorts and a top hat with a dead mole on top of it."

In July and August of 1960 Jerry was in an advanced individual training program at Fort Ord learning how to be an auto maintenance helper. He had always been interested in cars, but Laird Grant says, "The army said, 'What do you want to do?' and he said, 'I want to do electronics,' but instead they gave him motor pool! He told me, 'If I'd asked for motor pool they would have given me electronics!' That's the way the army was in those days—if you were interested in something, they weren't interested in you being interested in it. They want to mold you their own way."

When Private Recruit (PV1) Garcia completed his service school training in late August, the army gave him his initial base assignment: not to some exotic foreign port of call, but to Fort Winfield Scott in San Francisco's Presidio, "a beautiful, lovely spot overlooking the Golden Gate Bridge and all that, and these neat old barracks, and almost nothing to do." Jerry said of that period, "Once you're out of basic training, being in the army is like having a bad job. I didn't take it seriously. They're very tough about showing up for the morning roll-call trip—reveille. And if you're not there, that's called AWOL. You pile up nine or ten of those and it doesn't look good on the record.

"In the army you get involved in these soap opera scenes," he continued. "I had this friend who I had met when I was in base training at Fort Ord. This guy had married the oldest sister of the girl I was going with [in Redwood City]. He was one of those incorrigible guys, one of those guys with a 'Live Fast, Die Young' tattoo; that kind of guy. A great guy but a total fuckup. So he was doing stuff like robbing banks and getting into tremendous big trouble, and the family was asking me to help out, because I was the way this guy had gotten into this little working-class family and [I] put him together with the sister he'd married. So [one time] I was hung up with this guy and he was threatening to commit suicide in a hotel room in Redwood City. So *of course* I was late the next morning to roll call. I thought it was more important to sit there and bullshit with the guy. It was stuff like that; things that I didn't have that much control over. I didn't do it on purpose, certainly, but the way it works is these things pile up."

The flip side to Garcia's relationship with this acquaintance who was, in Jerry's words, "trouble incarnate," is that he was a good fingerpicking guitarist and "I was totally fascinated by it." Garcia had brought his second electric guitar, a Sears Silvertone, into the army with him, but "I was just a three-chorder then" (a slight exaggeration; by all accounts he played competent rock 'n' roll guitar), and learning the rudiments of acoustic fingerpicking opened up a new world for him. "That's how I got into fingerpicking the acoustic guitar, country music, the banjo, folk music, the traditional stuff, all that," he said in 1971.

The episode in the Redwood City hotel may or may not have been the incident that actually led to Garcia's being convicted at a Summary Court-Martial on October 19, 1960. That military court found that "On or about October 15, 1960, [JG] broke restriction to battery area." It's unclear how long he was illegally off-base, but cousin Daniel Garcia recalls a time during this period when "U.S. marshals came to my house looking for him because he'd gone AWOL. You can't walk away from the army; they take a dim view of that. It scared the hell out of my mother, as you can imagine."

According to Jerry, not longer after the court-martial, "My company commander asked me in one day and said, 'Hey Garcia, would you like to get out of the army?' I said, 'Yeah, that would be nice.' " What might have gone on behind the scenes to expedite Jerry's departure from the service—did his commander simply want this insubordinate bad egg out of the army?—we may never know; that sort of information is sealed in his military records.

Thirty-five years later, Daniel Garcia is still incredulous that getting out of the military could have been that easy: "You can't just say, 'I don't want to be here, bye-bye.' Half the army would leave. It doesn't work that way. It's nearly impossible to get out of there unless you're a Section 8, and you have to prove that you're really a nutcase to get that." Actually, there is another criterion, which might have been used in Jerry's case: "Failure to Adapt," which includes the category "Not suited to the military lifestyle." Indeed.

"You've got to remember that this is the guy who could fall in the proverbial bucket of you-know-what and come out like a rose," Daniel says. "If he and his brother and I would get in trouble, Jerry would get out of it and Tiff and I would get in trouble; it never failed. We once stole some Silly Putty from a department store and his mother found this big stash of it in his room and I got in trouble because he told his mother I had given it to him. But you couldn't stay mad at him too long because he was such a likable guy. He was always getting out of scrapes like that, and the service was probably just another one for him."

And so, on December 14, 1960, Jerry's dubious military career came to an end, and he was out on his own for the first time—eighteen years old, with no plans, no family attachments (at last!), no commitments and no job prospects; finally *free*. Better take a page out of *On the Road* for this one:

"It was drizzling and mysterious at the beginning of our journey. I could see that it was all going to be one big saga of the mist. 'Whooee!' yelled Dean. 'Here we go!' And he hunched over the wheel and gunned her; he was back in his element, everybody could see that. We were all delighted, we all realized we were leaving confusion and nonsense behind and performing our one and noble function of the time, *move*. And we moved!"

CHAPTER 2

Recall the Days
That Still Are to Come

e'll probably never know precisely what was going through Jerry's head when he got out of the army, but one thing is certain—he made a conscious effort to disconnect from his family. Tiff had only sporadic contact with him over the next few years, his cousin Daniel didn't see him at all for a couple of years and he completely ignored his mother and grandmother. Pop Clifford had died in February of 1960, and later that year Ruth split up with Wally and moved back into Harrington Street to be with Tillie, whose health and mental faculties had become somewhat precarious. Ruth sold her liquor license at some point, and later the building that housed the 400 Club was torn down to make way for a new entrance onto the Bay Bridge. Ruth returned to her first career—working as a pediatric nurse at San Francisco General Hospital—and Wally went back to being a seaman full-time for the Pacific Far East Lines. He and Ruth remarried and divorced again but continued to live together on and off at Harrington Street. Early in the afternoon of February 12, 1962, Wally was driving Ruth to work when he suffered a massive heart attack. Ruth had to wrestle the car to the side of the road and then drive Wally to San Francisco General, where he was pronounced dead at 3:20 P.M. After a funeral a couple of days later (which Jerry did not attend), Wally's body was shipped to Jersey City for burial.

"I broke off all communication with my family when I went into the army," Jerry said, "and they didn't even know that I was out of the army. . . . I just didn't want to say anything to anybody. . . . I just wanted to be goofing off. I didn't want to get a job or go to college or do any of that stuff. So there was nobody after me to do it. I heard from people who had heard from [my family]. They knew I was okay."

Jerry said that he migrated back down to the Peninsula after his stint in the army because "that's where my friends were. I had a girlfriend in Redwood City when I was in the army and I met some people, this older couple, who lived in Redwood City—very nice people from Salt Lake City—and they moved down to Palo Alto and they offered me a place to stay when I was discharged. I thought, 'Oh gee, that would be great.' So I went to Palo Alto and I hung out there in the good graces of these nice people from Salt Lake City who put me up."

Located about forty miles south of San Francisco, Palo Alto is a genteel

suburban city of about 59,000 (it had about 52,000 in 1960) with a nearly perfect climate and block after block of American-dream houses and Edenic yards
brimming with an exceptionally large variety of trees, shrubs and flowers.
There are long, wide roads lined with white-blossomed magnolias, and great
grassy parks dotted with willows and rhododendron. It's probably best known
as the home of Stanford University, itself an incredible California dreamscape,
not to mention one of the best schools in the world. There's lots of old and
new money in Palo Alto; it's filled with professionals who have chosen to
bring up their children in more idyllic surroundings than the big city offers.

Of course there's more to Palo Alto than that neatly manicured portrait.
And that's hardly the world that Jerry dropped into when he dropped out of
the military.

Like most progressive university towns, Palo Alto has always been home
to a sizable bohemian element—artists, dancers, musicians and freethinking
literary types either connected to Stanford in some way or attracted by the
surrounding creative-intellectual milieu. There's always a lot happening on
and around campus, so it's hardly surprising that the area was a magnet for
bright, curious teenagers and young adults. And in those days it was easy to
live cheaply by renting rooms in any of dozens of old clapboard Victorians
near campus, or by moving away from the downtown area altogether: Menlo
Park to the north has more affordable housing, and in Palo Alto the farther
west you move from Stanford's towering eucalyptus groves, date palms
and golden-stoned buildings, the more you encounter ordinary middle-class
homes that were built in the late '40s and early '50s to accommodate an influx of baby boom families. And then, east across Highway 101 as you approach the shores of San Francisco Bay, there's East Palo Alto, mainly black
and poor, a thousand miles away from lily-white Stanford culturally, if not
geographically.

It's not clear how long Jerry stayed with the couple from Salt Lake City—
whether it was a matter of days or weeks—but sometime right after he arrived on the Peninsula, his bad-news army buddy showed up unannounced at
the house, parking his stolen car outside: "He's got a fella with him, both of
'em dressed in suits and packing irons, and they had just done a string of bank
robberies up and down the coast!" Jerry recalled. "I thought, 'Hmm, maybe
I'd like to not see so much of this guy and his crime scene any longer.' "

Jerry had no visible means of support when he arrived in Palo Alto, but
through his friend Laird Grant and his own natural openness and affability he
managed to plug into several different social scenes almost immediately. The
main one revolved around Kepler's Books, on El Camino Real, just a few
blocks from Stanford in neighboring Menlo Park. More than just a bookstore,
Kepler's was a serious hangout that attracted all sorts of interesting characters,
and indeed, it was at Kepler's that Jerry met a number of the people who
would be part of his remarkable odyssey over the next three-plus decades.

One person he encountered very quickly after moving to the Peninsula was a slight eighteen-year-old Englishman named Alan Trist, who had moved to Palo Alto in November 1960 when his father began a yearlong fellowship at Stanford's Center for Advanced Studies in Behavioral Sciences. To occupy his days and keep his mind sharp for the three years of study at Cambridge he still had in front of him, Alan was auditing courses at Stanford, until fate intervened:

"One of the other Fellows at the center had a daughter, Karen Kaplan, and they had a dinner party one night and she said, 'Well, if you want something to do here, you should see what's going on down at Kepler's,' " Trist says. "So the very next day I went down to Kepler's, where I met Jerry. He was sitting on a coffee table playing the guitar and we struck up an instant relationship. Jerry had this amazing way about him, and it happened the first time I sat across the table from him—he would just sit there and play and look at you and smile. His charisma was really attractive. After that I didn't want to audit any more courses at Stanford, because here was a bookstore where Roy Kepler allowed people to sit around all day and read the books and play music and talk. You could even take the books home overnight if you wanted."

Kepler's was more than just a boho hangout, for owner Roy Kepler was also one of the area's best-known peace activists, so the store attracted people from that world, too. Both Kepler and Ira Sandperl, who worked at Kepler's and also taught at the progressive Peninsula School nearby, had been instrumental in starting the Peninsula Peace Center in the late '50s over on Stanford Avenue in south Palo Alto. The Peace Center became an organizing hub for all sorts of pacifist political activity during that era, such as mobilizing against further nuclear proliferation and testing. "Ban the Bomb" was the slogan of the day, when the devastation of the Korean War was fresh in people's minds and the cold war was still heating up.

To help pay the rent on the ramshackle house that was headquarters of the Peace Center, Kepler and Sandperl used to rent out most of the rooms, at first mainly to needy Stanford students, but then to anyone who could afford the dirt-cheap monthly rent. Sandperl says that the staff at Kepler's also regularly helped its more indigent customers—which in short order came to include Jerry and most of his friends—to find places to live or crash for a day or two.

"The Palo Alto Peace Center was a great place for social trips," Jerry said. "The Peace Center was the place where the sons and daughters of the Stanford professors would hang out and discuss things. And we, the opportunist wolf pack—the beatnik hordes—would be there preying on their young minds and their refrigerators. And there would be all of these various people turning up in these scenes and it just got to be very good; really high."

One character he met at the Peace Center who became a lifelong friend was Willy Legate, a brilliant, red-haired, red-bearded College of the Redlands dropout and would-be communist—"I didn't know Marxist theory then and I don't know it now," he says, "but I enjoyed giving the impression that I might be some kind of commie." A deep-thinking and introverted historian, philosopher and theologian, Willy was also the first person in Garcia's Palo Alto crowd to take LSD: In February 1959, he ingested about 100 micrograms of illegally obtained Sandoz LSD with a couple of acquaintances in his dorm at Redlands. "We listened to a lot of Bach," he recalls. "I remember the dormitory's hallway seemed to be miles long, and the chapel jutted out like gingerbread against the cut-glass sky.

"These guys seemed to be saying that such hallucinogens were the answer, the end—a religious thing," Willy says. "I considered the experience a mental act, not a spiritual reality."

Another group Jerry ran with during these first days on the Peninsula lived in rented rooms in a rambling old house known as the Chateau, on Santa Cruz Avenue in Menlo Park, a couple of miles from Kepler's. "The Chateau was this large house that was probably built in the late '20s or early '30s on this little knoll there," says Laird Grant. "At the time it was owned by a guy named Frank Serratoni, who was an artist. He'd do these drawings and then put a watercolor wash on them; they sold at the City of Paris [an elegant San Francisco department store] and places like that."

"The Chateau was mainly the various people from the Kepler's crowd," adds David Nelson, who met Garcia in the summer of 1961. "And defining that is kind of elusive, because a lot of them were people who had been traveling and used Kepler's as a stopping point or meeting place. You'd be hitchhiking and coming from Big Sur or Monterey, where Emerson College was, and you'd be on your way to Oregon, where Reed College was, or to Berkeley, which had a scene, too. So there was all this commerce and traffic and different stopping places. Kepler's was one because it was a public place. The Chateau was another because it was so loose—it was always filled with people staying with other people, and partly because of that it became a really serious party place. They were big affairs, with pot for the people who were wise to it, usually smoked out back discreetly, and big jugs of wine inside. People would play music endlessly and Frank Serratoni just let it all happen."

Yet another meeting place was one of the local folk music spots, St. Michael's Alley on University Avenue in Palo Alto. It's there that the area's most celebrated singer and activist, Joan Baez, got her start while she was still a student at Palo Alto High School, and as Alan Trist puts it, "Kepler's was the main spot in the daytime and at night everyone would go over to St. Michael's Alley." Besides drawing some of the Kepler's crowd, St. Michael's also attracted a number of Stanford students and even local high school kids, since no alcohol was served there. Garcia and Phil Lesh met at St. Michael's during that year.

Garcia also struck up close relationships with a number of high school students who hung around the scene, including Charlotte Daigle, a senior at

Palo Alto High School whom he dated on and off for about a year after they met at Kepler's; Barbara Meier, a sophomore at Menlo-Atherton High in Menlo Park, who would become one of his first serious loves; Danya Veltfort, a bright, politically active Peninsula School alumnus and Willy Legate's girlfriend; and a sixteen-year-old Menlo-Atherton student named Paul Speegle Jr., whom Garcia and Laird Grant knew from their time at Menlo-Oaks.

Speegle was by all accounts a very interesting character. He was the son and namesake of the well-respected drama and music critic for the *San Francisco Call-Bulletin* newspaper, and he certainly had a taste for the theatrical himself. A painter of considerable renown, he regularly dressed in elegant, semi-Edwardian finery, and he was active in two local drama groups, the Teen Players at the Palo Alto Community Center, and the Comedia Theater. "Paul and Lowell Clukas were totally into Rimbaud and they were just flaunting it," says Barbara Meier. "Menlo-Atherton High School at the time was so '50s preppy—white bucks, crewcuts. They were definitely effete young men, but very, very bright. They were cultured. They were erudite. They had very refined taste and I think they were appalled, as I was, by our high school."

Garcia and Speegle spent a fair amount of time together in early 1961. Jerry greatly admired Paul's painting and his colorful personal eccentricities (this was no typical sixteen-year-old), and it was through him that Garcia became briefly involved with the Comedia Theater group. "I was just getting to be good friends with Paul," Garcia said of this period. "We didn't know each other that well yet, but it's like how you *know* you're going to be good friends with somebody. It's just getting hot. I could feel that coming. We were starting to cook. . . ."

At about 1:30 in the morning on February 20, 1961, a party at the Chateau was breaking up and Garcia, Speegle and Alan Trist all piled into a 1956 Studebaker Golden Hawk owned by one of the Chateau's residents, Lee Adams, to drive Paul back to his mother's house in the Los Altos Hills. Jerry, Paul and Alan had been playing charades—with Paul and Alan donning black cloaks at one point to mime what Trist calls "a game of death"—and they'd all had a lot to drink, including Adams, the driver. At about 1:50 A.M. the car was speeding south on Junipero Serra Boulevard near the U.S. Veterans Administration Hospital at about ninety miles per hour when Adams failed to negotiate a curve and lost control of the Stude, which slashed through a fence, rolled over several times and finally came to rest on its wheels—on top of Paul Speegle, who was pronounced dead at the scene. "It was just *wham!*" Garcia remembered. "We went flying, I guess. All I know is that I was sitting in the car and that there was this . . . disturbance . . . and the next thing I was in a field. I went through the windshield and landed far enough away from the car where I couldn't see it. It was night. It was very, very quiet, you know. It was like a complete break in continuity—from sitting in the car roaring down the road, to lying in a field wondering what had happened; nothing in between."

The force of the crash was so severe that Garcia was literally thrown out of his shoes, and Adams and Trist were tossed clear of the car as well. All three were taken to Stanford Hospital—Jerry with a shoulder injury, Alan a hurt back, and Lee Adams with a mild head wound and various cuts on one side of his body. The story of the calamity made the front page of the *Palo Alto Times:* Under a brooding photo of Paul Speegle Jr. was a headline that read SPEEGLE'S SON KILLED IN CRASH, and the accompanying story gave the vital stats on the car's other occupants, mentioning "Jerry Garcia, 18, 1339 Willow Road, Menlo Park, 'fair' condition with a shoulder injury."

In interviews Jerry often spoke of the crash as one of the early turning points in his life: "This was crushing. This was serious. For me—I was not really going anywhere special. I wasn't going to art school anymore, but I was playing the guitar an awful lot, sitting around and poking around the guitar. But I wasn't thinking about myself as a guitar player or musician. I was still thinking of myself as an artist. But that was really drifting away from me and I hadn't really admitted it to myself one way or another. . . . I was awfully happy to be alive, certainly. I was a changed person. It was cosmic. In fact, it affected our whole little community. . . ."

In another interview Garcia went even further, saying the crash was "where my life began. Before then I was always living at less than capacity. I was idling. That was the slingshot for the rest of my life."

Sara Ruppenthal, whom Jerry would meet and marry two years later, says that "He would talk about the accident a lot. I remember him driving me by the V.A. and saying, 'Here's where the accident was. I remember going through the barbed-wire fence.' He'd broken his collarbone and was in a lot of pain but managed to walk to the V.A. hospital, but they told him, 'Sorry, we don't have any emergency services; we can't help you.' That was such an awful part of his life. It was something that was still weighing heavily on his mind when we met."

Garcia didn't really make any radical changes in his life after the crash. He was still essentially a homeless drifter with no money, bouncing around to different friends' houses for as long as they would have him. Alan Trist's parents let Jerry stay off and on in the small Spanish-style house they were renting for the year and, as Trist puts it, "He always had a graciousness about him that you never felt imposed upon."

"In those days," adds David Nelson, "you could basically walk around with some stuff—maybe just a knapsack, or a little bag and a guitar—and you'd set it down somewhere and that'd be where you *were*. There were occasional nights one place and then you'd move on to another place, and you really didn't have to sweat it that much; you'd always wind up *someplace*."

Shortly after the accident, Garcia met Barbara Meier, a bright, vivacious fifteen-year-old student who was already an entrenched member of the Kepler's/Peace Center crowd. As she puts it, "My parents knew they could call up Kepler's pretty much any time to find out where I was, or [the Kepler's clerks] would cover for me and tell them I was fine." She describes her parents as "very cool, bright, extremely literate and politically liberal.

"Part of why I flowed into [the Palo Alto beatnik] scene so easily is that at the same time my parents were in Menlo Park, my aunt, who was a fashion executive at Joseph Magnin [department store] in San Francisco, had an apartment in North Beach so I would go and spend weekends up there. I think the turning point for me, when it really fell into place, was 1959, somewhere around my fourteenth birthday. I read *On the Road* and then I got what that scene in North Beach was all about."

Through her aunt, Barbara started to land modeling assignments, and her career was in full swing when she met Jerry—she often appeared in Macy's and Magnin's ads in the San Francisco newspapers, and nationally she appeared in *Life* magazine and in a Pepsodent toothpaste commercial. Jerry mocked her modeling but was more than willing to reap the benefits of the hundred dollars a day she made doing it. Barbara gave him money in dribs for nearly two years, and even bought him two guitars during that time.

In March 1961 Garcia was filling some of his evenings working the lights for the Comedia Theater's production of *Damn Yankees* when he met a very interesting, seriously intellectual, similarly bohemian nineteen-year-old who had been bumming around town looking for adventures and kindred spirits following a stint in the National Guard. This was Robert Hunter, who was, coincidentally, a former boyfriend of one of the girls Jerry was dating at the time, Diane Huntsburger. Hunter and Garcia hit it off immediately, discovering they had many interests in common, including Beat culture, mysticism, James Joyce, drawing, poetry, singing, playing guitar, girls and getting high. Just a couple of not-so-regular American teenagers on the prowl for good times.

Like Garcia, Bob Hunter had been bounced around by fate most of his life. "I'm from up and down the West Coast," he said. "I've lived in Portland, Seattle, San Francisco, Palo Alto, Los Angeles, Long Beach, all that, a couple of years in Connecticut, in my growing-up period." At age nine he went through at traumatic family breakup that led to his being placed in a series of boardinghouses for a couple of years: "Made a melancholy lad of me," he once wrote. "I was never in one place too long. I think Palo Alto about the longest of all— I spent between eighth and eleventh grade there. Up till then I think I went to a different school every year, which certainly helped develop my outsider feelings; always the new kid in school."

One way Hunter dealt with his loneliness was to dive headlong into both reading and writing: "I always had my nose in a book," he said. "I was getting away from it. . . . I thought that a lot of [the other kids] were just better than me. I didn't feel that I was particularly smart, and I felt they didn't like me for some reason. I think the reason they didn't like me was that I was too defensive and I would strike first. But I'd just forget it all and bury my nose in *Robin Hood* or something like that. I think my real life was books, in my growing up. So it was only natural that I started writing. I started my first novel when I was eleven."

Certainly there were plenty of books around the Hunter household. His stepfather, Norman Hunter, was a book salesman for Harcourt Brace and later a prominent book editor, whose high-profile authors included William Saroyan among others, "so we had a splendid library around the house." He said, "My father certainly didn't discourage [my writing] . . . although he told me there was no money to be made in the profession. I wasn't as discouraged from that as I was from my trumpet and violin, which after a hard day at work, he would tolerate but not encourage."

Besides his stabs at those instruments, Hunter took up the guitar, but it was trumpet that he played in a group called the Crescents during his senior year of high school in Stamford, Connecticut, forty-five minutes north of Manhattan on the venerable New York–New Haven Railroad line. It was an unusual quartet—drums, electric guitar, trumpet and bass clarinet. "We played Dixieland and I played trumpet and we played rock 'n' roll and I even wrote a song called 'Rock 'n' Roll Moon.' We used to play for dances on Saturday afternoons over at the Jewish Community Center and at the Veterans Hospital, where I had a good fantasy trip: 'Blue in the Night' with a blue spotlight on me. I got some of my Harry James fantasies out of my system."

After graduating from high school in Stamford, Hunter had a brief and ignominious stint at the University of Connecticut: "It was my first taste of real freedom. I arrived for freshman year a week early and spent all the money my father had given me for textbooks on pinball. Fortunately, I flunked out." Before that happened, however, he played in a folk music trio at UConn, and his second semester there he was president of the folk music club. After dropping out of school, Hunter traveled to California to pursue a girl he was in love with, but when he finally found her she was no longer interested in him. Heartbroken, he attempted to join the Coast Guard, but they weren't accepting enlistees, so he signed on with the National Guard, which required just six months of active duty, followed by five and a half years as a reserve.

So there he was, fresh out of Fort Sill, living on his meager mustering pay in a room in the Palo Alto Hotel, when he met Garcia. Within a month of their meeting the two of them were living side by side in their cars in a vacant lot in East Palo Alto—Jerry in an old Cadillac (with the words CALL PAM written in the dirt on the back window) and Hunter in a 1940 Chrysler straight-eight he'd picked up for fifty bucks a day or two after he'd arrived in town. "Hunter had these big tins of crushed pineapple that he'd gotten from the army,"

Garcia said, "and I had this glove compartment full of plastic spoons, and we had this little cooperative scene, eating this crushed pineapple day after day and sleeping in the cars and walking around.

"He played a little guitar; we started singin' and playin' together just for something to do. And then we played our first professional gig. We got five bucks apiece." Their innocuous little folk act was billed as Bob and Jerry, but they performed only two real gigs—at the Arroyo Lounge on May 5, 1961 (for a payday of five dollars, which Hunter says "we decided to frame as the first musical earnings for either of us, but spent on cigarettes instead"); and a concert at the Peninsula School's eighth-grade graduation ceremony in early June. That gig had been arranged by Danya Veltfort, whose younger sister was matriculating. Danya says Bob and Jerry took home fifty dollars for their troubles, good money for those days (and that crowd). The only known tape of Bob and Jerry was recorded by Barbara Meier's father in the living room of her house at her sixteenth birthday party. As Danya says, "It was a big deal to be able to make a tape in those days; not like today where everyone has recorders."

Alan Trist viewed his new friend Bob Hunter as "another fellow traveler. Like me he was really into reading; we'd spend hours having literate discussions, picking books off the shelves and getting into them. Jerry was carrying his guitar around and Hunter and I had our notebooks and we'd go places and Jerry would play and Hunter and I would write. Or we'd go to a cafe somewhere and we'd write and sometimes Jerry would sit there and draw. We'd talk and then move on to some other place.

"Hunter tells me now that Jerry and I were the ones who were raving around at the time, full of theatricality and spouting lines of poetry and being totally wild, and he was more circumspect. I think his recollection is probably correct, but what's interesting to me is that's not the person I later became. But Jerry was *always* outgoing and always had a very positive outlook on life. That's the thing that was most important to me during that period—a pure positiveness that we were all experiencing with each other, and affirming back and forth."

When one of them had a working car, they often would go up to San Francisco to wander around North Beach and soak up what was left of the Beat scene at places like City Lights Books and the Coffee Gallery. "It was still a vital scene, especially to those of us who were just coming of age," Trist says.

But their outlook on life was always much sunnier and more optimistic than that of the Beats they so admired. As Barbara Meier explains, "We weren't sitting around in our black turtlenecks, smoking Gauloises and talking about existentialism. We weren't doing that. We were raving. The music was happening; we were singing. We were partying. We were running around the beach or the mountains. The age difference [between the Palo Alto crowd and the original Beats] was crucial. I don't think we were saddled with that morose energy at all."

"It's funny, you know," Hunter remarked. "Back in those days there weren't a lot of people on the street, and I thought me and Garcia and Trist and the people who were hanging around there were really unique. I thought we were the new thing. It was quite arrogant: we felt that we were the legitimate rulers of the world."

At least they were rulers of the back room at Kepler's for a while. Garcia had traded his Sears electric guitar for an acoustic model shortly after arriving in Palo Alto, and late that spring Barbara bought him a better guitar, and shortly after that, a lovely sounding Stella twelve-string. Jerry spent hours in the back room at Kepler's practicing and playing the limited folk repertoire he had mastered, which consisted mainly of straight-ahead popular tunes by the Kingston Trio, Joan Baez, the Weavers, Pete Seeger and other leading lights of the burgeoning folk revival movement.

Of course folk music wasn't exactly new in the late '50s and early '60s, but its widespread popularity in America was, particularly in urban areas. This renaissance was driven largely by college students who had rejected rock 'n' roll as the anointed musical voice of their generation. By 1960 rock's initial flash had dimmed considerably, as the first generation of '50s rockers all but vanished from the scene (Chuck Berry went to jail; Jerry Lee Lewis was tainted by scandal; Buddy Holly and Eddie Cochran were dead; Elvis was in the army), replaced by bland teen idols whose white-bread take on rock 'n' roll was seriously lacking in soul and grit. And then there was the matter of rock's lyrical content, which was mainly limited to teenage love, lust and heartbreak. Folk music, on the other hand, drew from a wide variety of established traditions, including American blues, Southern mountain music, songs from the labor movement and the dust bowl diaspora, ballads from the British Isles, sea chanteys and tunes from around the world. In an America that was furiously promoting *The Donna Reed Show*, *Leave It to Beaver* and *Father Knows Best* as visions of the perfect postwar world, folk musicians—like the Beat writers all through the '50s—provided an alternative vision of the world to thousands of kids who believed that the gray-suited Madison Avenue man paradigm was just smoke and mirrors obfuscating a darker national reality that included McCarthyism, segregation, an aggressive, even jingoistic, foreign policy and an unhealthy compulsion to manufacture a perfect cookie-cutter culture.

"Having been born at the beginning of the '40s and coming of age during the '50s, there was an expectation of conformity," says Suzy Wood, who met Jerry in 1961. "My sense is that there was a huge feeling of unrest, starting with those of us who had that '50s kind of background: This is what we expect you to do—go into advertising, go into engineering, wear a suit, wear a skinny little tie, wear a dress with petticoats under it. You never fuck anybody except somebody you're married to. And in real life people weren't doing that. And so instead of saying, 'Here's the structure we're going to fit into,' we said, 'Let's trash the structure entirely. Let's just do anything we want.' And that was the appeal of people like Jerry, because he was doing exactly what he wanted. He certainly wasn't being in the army and wearing a suit."

Adds Eric Thompson, who became one of Jerry's musical partners later that year, "The people of our generation looked up and said, 'Wait a minute. We've got enough to eat. We're not at war. Everything seems to be fine. Why do I have to anesthetize myself? Why do I have to strive for this? Why can't I strive for something that actually interests me?' This was not something that previous generations had really done on any kind of wide scale. I think folk music's popularity was partly a response to the repression of real life that was happening. When all of a sudden you came across this wealth of emotional music, it seemed like it was coming from a different world than the one my parents talked about, and it seemed a lot more real to me and a lot of other people."

A musical turning point for Jerry came in the late spring of 1961. Marshall Leicester, who'd had a passing friendship with Garcia back at Menlo-Oaks Middle School, returned to the Peninsula from a year at Yale. One day, "I walked into Kepler's and Jerry was sitting there playing a twelve-string guitar and singing tunes like 'Everybody Loves Saturday Night,' which was one of those kind of Pete Seeger 'love-your-worldwide-neighbors' songs in which the verses are the words 'everybody loves Saturday night' in about fifteen languages—sort of the last gasp of the politically oriented folk music of the '30s and '40s. I think I asked to borrow his guitar and play some of my kind of music on it, and I think we were mutually impressed with each other. We remembered having met before and we hit it off."

Leicester taught Garcia the rudiments of the fingerpicking guitar style and also introduced Garcia to the main traditional white folksong forms of the South—old-time string band music and bluegrass. "He was playing more strum stuff, Kingston Trio–oriented songs," he notes. "He wasn't playing melodically oriented guitar at all. I think he'd gotten away from rock 'n' roll, too, so he wasn't using a flat pick, either. So I taught him how to play stuff like [Elizabeth Cotten's] 'Freight Train,' and he just took it and ran with it on his own—I never saw anybody learn how to do something as quickly as he picked up on that. So from there he went and made himself into someone with a sense of style."

The model for Garcia and many other aspiring old-timey music pickers in the early '60s was the New Lost City Ramblers, a trio of New York City boys who were faithfully devoted to uncovering, preserving and performing rural folk songs. One of the founding members of that group was Mike Seeger, Pete's younger brother, who had learned how to play fiddle, guitar, banjo and autoharp mainly from listening to old Library of Congress recordings made in the South as part of the library's Archive of Folk Song project. In the mid-'50s Seeger had traveled through the South himself with a tape recorder, capturing dozens of obscure folk and blues performers in their living rooms and back porches.

"In those days we all wanted to be Mike Seeger, so we were all trying to learn to play five or six instruments," says Marshall Leicester. "I played guitar, banjo, autoharp and a little mouth harp. I didn't become a fiddler, which is mostly what I am these days, until a couple of years later. Jerry was just playing the guitar at first, but then of course he took up the banjo and got really good at that, too." By 1963 Jerry was trying his hand at mandolin, dobro, fiddle and autoharp as well.

Another huge influence on nearly everyone playing folk music at this time was Harry Smith's multivolume *Anthology of American Folk Music*, which brought dozens of folk tunes that had been originally cut as 78s between the '20s and the '50s to a new audience. "Back in 1961 there was only one copy around our scene, belonging to Grace Marie Haddie," Robert Hunter said. "The six-disc boxed collection was too expensive for guitar-playing hobos like me and Garcia, even if we had a record player, or a place to to keep a record player. Grace Marie had a job and an apartment and a record player. We would visit her apartment constantly with hungry ears. When she was at work, we'd jimmy the lock to her apartment door or crawl through the window if the latch was open. Had to hear those records."

Early in the summer of 1961 a pair of folk music enthusiasts, Rodney Albin and George Howell, launched a small coffeehouse called the Boar's Head in a loft above a bookstore called the Carlos Bookstall in San Carlos (north of Menlo Park). "George was a renegade high school student and a wanna-be beatnik," said Peter Albin, Rodney's younger brother, later a founding member of Big Brother and the Holding Company. "My brother played banjo and fiddle and guitar; I played a little guitar, and a lot of our friends played various instruments. So we opened the Boar's Head and we had little get-togethers there on Fridays and Saturday nights."

Besides the Albin brothers and George Howell, one of the other key members of the Boar's Head scene was David Nelson, who in June of 1961 had graduated from Carlmont High School in San Carlos. Nelson was another bright, well-read kid with music in his soul. He began taking guitar lessons when he was in second grade and even studied steel guitar when he was in grade school.

It was through the Albin brothers that Nelson met Garcia: "I still remember that moment at Kepler's when Pete and I were peeking through some books, and we saw this hairy, swarthy guy with an open Levi's shirt and a real brooding look and an olive wreath in his hair, playing a Stella twelve-string. It was Garcia, and he had some notoriety even then. There was something scary about him; something awesome, some invisible quality. We talked to him and Rodney put a banjo in my hand and I thought, 'Oh no!' I had learned a little bit of banjo from a Pete Seeger book Rodney had given me, but here I was playing with Garcia the first minute that I met him!

"So we asked him to come play at the Boar's Head. That night at the Boar's Head it was Garcia, who played some songs on guitar, and then Bob Hunter came on wearing his army boots, as he always did in those days, and he sang a couple of songs. And there was also David X [David McQueen, a black man in his forties who was part of the Chateau scene] and Sherry Huddleston, who's the one who gave Pigpen his name [the next year]. It was very low-key. The Boar's Head always seemed more like a party than a real gig. It became another place for friends to get together and play and sing."

After Boar's Head gatherings, Suzy Wood, Carlmont High class of 1960, often hosted parties at her parents' large, lovely home on Debbie Lane, on a hill above the College of Notre Dame in nearby Belmont. "The way the house was set up, there was an extra lot behind the house, sort of secluded by fences and bushes, and we'd go hang out back there and pass hats and collect change and somebody would go off and buy gallons of wine," Wood says. "That was a place that summer where there was a lot of partying, for as long as anybody could stand to lie around drinking wine. I don't remember Jerry being into drinking particularly.

"My father was very intrigued by him," she continues. "Even though Jerry was a dropout, because of the kind of intelligence and charm and insight that he had, he always seemed more like a leader than a bad guy. My dad thought he was a wonderful person but he'd say, 'Why doesn't he *do* something with his life?' If there was any disapproval of Jerry back then, it was usually from the parental generation, but even so he was charming enough that they kind of threw up their hands—'Oh, the darling boy! What*ever* will become of him?' "

Marshall Leicester's parents were a little more negative in their assessment of Jerry's character. After the ever-homeless Garcia spent a couple of weeks crashing at the Leicester family pad, Marshall's parents made it clear to their son that it was time for this charming "freeloader," as they branded him, to move on.

Bob Hunter spent most of July 1961 in a National Guard summer training camp at Hunter-Liggett Military Base in San Luis Obispo, a few hours down the coast, but when he returned, he, Garcia and Willy Legate all lived for a time at the Peace Center. Willy, at least, had a political streak, but Hunter and Garcia had little interest in the center's activities, a fact that was not lost on Ira Sandperl and Roy Kepler, who tolerated them there and at Kepler's but never really warmed up to them personally.

At Jerry's urging, Barbara Meier attended the California School of Fine Arts that summer of 1961, and, like Jerry before her, became close to Wally Hedrick. Unlike Garcia, however, Barbara stuck with art through the years; indeed, she is still a painter. Garcia spent quite a bit of time in San Francisco that summer, too. "Jerry lived with John 'The Cool' [Winter] in this hotel on O'Farrell Street, which was just down from Magnin's," Barbara says. "So I'd walk those five blocks from Magnin's down to the hotel to see him. It's hard to say what they were doing. I think they had a little benzedrine and they were kind of racing around the city. I remember being with them and we'd rave around. We'd go to parties or drive over to KPFA [in Berkeley]. Little impromptu gigs and parties would turn up.

"They'd do crazy things like go down to Fisherman's Wharf and boost [steal] a big fifty-pound bag of carrots, for instance, and they'd live on that! He never had any money, but I was sort of supporting him. I remember that I made a point of never showing up to see Jerry without first stopping to pick up a pack of cigarettes, for instance, because he never had cigarettes. Once he had a car he could never afford gas, so I was always filling up his gas tank, too."

Eventually Garcia and Winter moved briefly into a nice attic apartment on Noriega Street, in the Sunset district of San Francisco, that was shared by Jerry's occasional girlfriend in this era, Phoebe Graubard, and Elaine Heise, the former girlfriend of Paul Speegle (as Elaine Pagels she went on to write *The Gnostic Gospels*). Phoebe had grown up in Palo Alto, where she was close friends with Danya Veltfort, but she moved up to the city to attend San Francisco State. She thought nothing of having Jerry, John and sometimes others crashing at her pad for days at a time. "It was part of that wave of Beat energy," Phoebe says. "If you read a Kerouac book, like *On the Road*, it was like that. They just kind of arrived, there was this frenetic *On the Road* kind of energy for a while, and some of those *On the Road* kind of experiences and these characters, and then one day they were gone."

Phoebe says that Jerry spent nearly all his time on Noriega Street playing guitar, trying to master old-timey fingerpicking styles, and even gigging occasionally as a solo act: "Jerry was playing in dives in North Beach, these remnants of the Beat Generation's places, but no one was going to them anymore. He would walk in at seven-thirty or eight and there might be nobody there, and sometimes nobody ever came and he'd play his set and go. But he had an amazing perseverence.

"Jerry used to take his guitar with him wherever he went, and one time we went down to Aquatic Park on the bus. We were sitting on the grass and he was playing the guitar and this old Basque man, who worked in a restaurant or something, had a pot full of food that he was going to feed to the birds, but he said he liked Jerry's guitar playing so he gave us the big pot of food instead. It was very sweet. And this was at a time when none of us had any money; we were very poor."

Alan Trist bid a fond farewell to his Palo Alto mates in September of that year and returned to England fundamentally changed. He had spent the year "experiencing life in the moment," he says. "We weren't thinking about the future. We were aware that we were experiencing something deep at that time. There was a lot of coherence to that little scene. It was this bunch of us going all around and hanging out just for the purpose of enjoying each other and sharing intellectual and artistic experience. We were all, in the broadest sense, involved in the arts—writing or drawing or both; playing music, listening to music. We were proto-artists; that was our sense of ourselves."

"Jerry, John, Alan, Phoebe and I stayed up all night rapping at Phoebe's before driving up to Twin Peaks at dawn, then driving Alan to the airport for his return to England," Robert Hunter recalled. "I consider that the end of our old scene. We all thought so. Alan was really the prime mover of our group cohesiveness. Without Alan's social focusing skills, the main group splintered, by main force of entropy, into several scenes rather than one."

Also departing at summer's end was Marshall Leicester, who returned to Yale. Leicester pops back into the scene during Christmas and summer vacations for the next couple of years, but his absence forced Garcia to look for new playing partners, as he dug deeper into the old-time string band repertoire and also began to explore bluegrass a little more.

Despite the generosity of Barbara Meier, who became Garcia's girlfriend that autumn, Garcia was perennially broke, but his friend David McQueen reveals that from time to time Jerry would do odd jobs to earn a little scratch:

"Aside from my regular job, I used to do yard work for extra spending money. I knew Jerry was broke and I enjoyed his playing at Kepler's, so we'd go on these yard jobs so he could earn some money for cigs. It was fun for both of us. Jerry used to call me a lousy blues singer, and I said he was equally lousy at yard work. Neither of us got offended; it was the truth.

"Jerry always had a guitar with him wherever he went," McQueen continues. "One day, after doing a yard job, we were on the way back to my house in East Palo Alto. It was summer, kids were out playing in the streets, and Jerry was playing guitar and we were singing as we walked. I looked behind us at one point and saw there was a whole group of little black kids following us and dancing, like in those great but politically incorrect Marx Brothers movies. I was impressed—those kids were for real! When we stopped, they were all over Jerry: 'Play some more! Play some more!' Jerry loved it.

"He was listening to a lot of Reverend Gary Davis at that time. But blues, gospel, jazz—he'd play it all. He used to jam with the drummers who came to play at Pogo's [Norm Fontaine's] house. I'm sure Jerry was influenced by some of the music he heard in East Palo Alto. Sometimes he'd go to the Anchor Bar—white owned, black run—which had music on weekends. There was a house band, but anyone with a union card could sit in, and name players would come by and jam after hours for drinks."

That fall Garcia moved to the Chateau. Actually, he moved into a broken-down car that had its windows whited out and was collecting dust behind the main house. He already knew all the Chateau's denizens, having partied there on numerous occasions since his arrival in the area, and no doubt he'd crashed there before, but this was the first time he'd actually lived there. By the middle of November, Bob Hunter was living there, too, having managed to snag a room in the main house when Carl Moore moved out. A while later Garcia moved inside to drummer Danny Barnett's old room.

It was in that autumn, too, that Jerry first encountered twenty-one-year-old Phil Lesh, who'd been kicking around the Peninsula on and off for a couple of years, and, like nearly everyone in the area with a rebellious streak and boho tendencies, eventually found his way to Kepler's and the Peace Center. Phil came from a very different world from Garcia's, and there was nothing in the early days of their relationship that would have suggested they would someday become musical soul mates.

Phil, who grew up in El Cerrito and Berkeley—the East Bay, as it is known—was initially interested in classical music almost exclusively. In third grade he began violin lessons and he stuck with it long enough to become second chair in a local youth orchestra after a few years. At fourteen he dropped violin and took up the trumpet, playing in the El Cerrito High School marching and concert bands. Midway through high school Phil's parents moved to neighboring Berkeley so Phil could go to Berkeley High, which had a much more serious music program.

Although he mainly played the classical repertoire, Phil also became a jazz aficionado during his high school days. At first he was attracted most to the music of Stan Kenton and the big, horn-heavy bands that were popular on the West Coast in the late '40s and early '50s. But at age seventeen, he met a bassist at a summer music camp who turned him on to John Coltrane (whom Phil dismissed initially: "I was incensed—How dare he play like that?"). It took him a while to warm up to the hot (or should we say cool?) jazz trumpeter of the day, too: Phil found Miles Davis's sound too airy and breathy at first—"not the kind of trumpet tone I'd been taught was the hip thing," he said.

After high school he moved to the Peninsula to attend the College of San Mateo, where he played in the school's jazz band for two years. During his second year there, Phil wrote a pair of original compositions for the jazz band, an experience that opened up a new world to him: "That was the first real flash that I had of having ideas and writing them down." Eventually he dropped the trumpet completely because he had decided that what he really wanted to do was become a composer—"with a capital C," as he put it.

Throughout his time at CSM he'd become increasingly interested in both the pioneers of electronic music such as Stockhausen and Berio, and modern composers like Schoenberg and Charles Ives, who was Phil's favorite. Operating under the mistaken belief that the University of California at Berkeley's music program was more plugged in to this progressive world, Phil enrolled there for the fall semester. It wasn't until he got to Berkeley that he discovered that the music department was geared to musicologists rather than composers. But on the day he was registering for classes in the department he met a fellow intellectual and modern-music freak named Tom Constanten, who became his roommate in Berkeley, and, several years down the line, the Grateful Dead's second keyboardist.

That fall of 1961, on November 18, the crowd at the Chateau got together to throw a giant party, dubbed the Groovy Conclave, which was attended by Lesh, Constanten, Bobby Peterson and about two hundred other people—intimates from the post-Beat and folk worlds, as well as friends of friends of friends. The party lasted nearly three days. Laird Grant, who didn't actually live at the Chateau but instead was settled in the wilds of the nearby Los Trancos Woods, even printed up "tickets" for the party. Garcia and others played music in the front room. Pot was smoked discreetly in the backyard, and the crowds went through gallons and gallons of jug wine and white port–and–lemon juice. It truly was a "groovy" scene; it was also the first time that nearly everyone from the bohemian/beatnik community on the Peninsula had gotten together in one place. These were pre-hippie days, but already some of the freak mindset was established in this crowd: they disdained the straight nine-to-five workaday world; they helped each other survive their sometimes desperate poverty; their scene was always more inclusive than exclusive, embracing misfits and outcasts as long as they were interesting; they enjoyed eclectic tastes in books and music; and they certainly seemed to share a hedonistic bent.

Alcohol was still the main drug then, but, as Bob Hunter said, "Those were seriously demented times. We were taking anything to get high: Asmador, Contac capsules—you could open them up and separate the little white caps out and take them; God, *anything*. There was hardly any weed around—maybe a matchbox or so every now and then. And it was nothing like what came along later; it was brown Mexican." As the early '60s wore on, the route from the Bay Area down to Los Angeles, and even all the way to Mexico, became increasingly well-traveled by couriers smuggling cellophane-wrapped bricks of Mexican pot back to an ever-expanding base of customers. There was also a fair amount of methedrine in the scene, which laid waste to more than a few promising souls back then, and on occasion strange things like the cough medication Romilar and various prescription drugs would turn up and be eagerly ingested. The truly desperate might even eat the cotton wadding from the insides of nasal inhalers, which were reputedly soaked in a mild upper.

Of his own preferences during this era, Garcia said, "We did a lot of playing around with these weird drugs, cough medicine kind of drugs. I didn't like to drink ever and drugs were always much more fun for me. I loved pot. Pot was just right up my alley. Anything that makes you laugh and so you love to eat—that's fun. To me there was no contest. That constituted our scene—we laughed a lot, really a lot. Still do. That was part of the orientation. We were basically looking for something, too. Seeking. And determined. And there was nothing pressing us to be any more structured than that, really."

As the months passed, Garcia devoted more and more of his time to practicing the guitar and his new love, the five-string banjo, a legacy of Marshall Leicester's influence. In fact, many days went by when Jerry literally played all day and well into the evening; this was a passion that bordered on the obsessive, no question about it. And the better he got, the more like-minded pickers he encountered.

One friend he made in the folk and bluegrass world around this time was a guitarist named Eric Thompson, a precocious and very well-connected fifteen-year-old who was a high school senior bound for UC Berkeley when he met Jerry. Though he lived on the Peninsula, Thompson had been floating around the more established Berkeley folk and bluegrass scene for about a year.

Berkeley had been the birthplace of the first Bay Area bluegrass band to come out of the folk boom in the late '50s, a group called the Redwood Canyon Ramblers, who amassed a small but dedicated following and influenced many other aspiring players. Berkeley had a few choice nightspots that catered to the string band music crowd, including the Peppermint Stick, the Jabberwock and the Cabale; an annual folk festival put on by guitarist Barry Olivier; a couple of music stores where pickers could hang out and swap licks—Jon and Deirdre Lundberg's Fretted Instruments and Campbell Coe's Campus Music Shop—and even a radio station, listener-sponsored KPFA, that regularly featured folk and bluegrass programming. Indeed, Barry Olivier had started the acoustic music program *The Midnight Special* in 1956—before the New Lost City Ramblers hit with their eclectic mélange, and well before Flatt and Scruggs came through town in 1961 and blew away every would-be picker from Marin to San Jose, leaving them slack-jawed and envious.

KPFA was also very supportive of avant-garde and modern classical music, which is one reason Phil Lesh did some volunteer engineering work for the station during his time in Berkeley. Among the programs he regularly engineered was *The Midnight Special*, and one night at a party at the Chateau Phil was listening to Garcia singing and playing the guitar when he had a flash that Jerry should play on that radio show. Phil recalled, "I said, 'Hey Jerry, if we could make a tape of you playing and singing, would you mind if I took it to Gert Chiarito [host of *The Midnight Special*] and played it for her?' He said, 'Shit no, man.' . . . He rode with me back to Berkeley to get the tape recorder—this is when we had all the time in the universe!—and he sang and played five or six songs."

Phil played the tape for Gert Chiarito, who was so impressed that she arranged to do an entire hour-long program with Garcia, which was called "The Long Black Veil," after the classic murder ballad that was part of Jerry's repertoire at the time. "After that he was almost a regular," Phil said. "Then he started to bring his buddies up from Palo Alto." The exposure on KPFA helped established Garcia as one of the premier pickers in the area.

"Bluegrass had kind of a shock value, like rock 'n' roll had shock value in a way," says Neil Rosenberg, a founding member of the Redwood Canyon Ramblers. "Electric instruments were considered *outré* by all of us. So if you wanted to do something that really set people's teeth on edge and kind of kicked butt, bluegrass was it. It was an exciting ensemble form and it appealed to the jazz sense—there was improvisation and trading of licks back and forth. There was a whole bunch of us young guys learning together and being very excited about it."

Actually, there was a fair amount of enmity between some hard-core bluegrass musicians and some old-timey string band players—"people looking down their noses at each other and being sort of cliquish," as David Nelson puts it—but Garcia and his crowd embraced both disciplines and basically played anything that caught their fancy. Jerry's first forays on the banjo had been influenced by the frailing style he heard on old-timey records, but as he investigated bluegrass more closely he naturally gravitated to the incredible picking of Earl Scruggs, who had popularized his rolling banjo technique first as part of Bill Monroe's seminal band in the mid-'40s, the Blue Grass Boys, and then with fellow Monroe alumnus Lester Flatt in the Foggy Mountain Boys. Actually, 1962 was a high-water year for Flatt and Scruggs and bluegrass in general. The duo's theme song for the hit television series *The Beverly Hillbillies* hit number 1 on both the country and pop music charts and spurred a brief bluegrass craze and some attendant grassploitation in the form of commercials using bluegrass music.

"It's hard to learn how to play bluegrass," says Marshall Leicester. "It's got a lot of rules and it's complicated music and that creates a kind of natural elitism around it. The banjo player has to learn to play Scruggs's three-finger style and that's a rather complicated and demanding way to play the instrument. It takes a lot of practice, it takes a lot of thinking. You have to get around the fingerboard in a way that an old-timey banjo player normally doesn't. And you have to learn to play fast and loud, which is also difficult."

Records and tapes were one way to learn about old-timey and bluegrass—Jerry said he spent hours listening to records slowed down to 16 rpm to learn solos off them—but he and his musical friends also took advantage of every opportunity they could to see touring acts from the East and South. Since Berkeley had always had an active folk scene—it was sort of "Cambridge West," though it didn't have a venue as established as the East Coast folk mecca's Club 47—the big folk and bluegrass acts would generally pass through on their infrequent tours. But the real action was down in Los Angeles at a club called the Ash Grove, which was run by a string band enthusiast and political activist named Ed Pearl. "He was one of the early guys to bring roots music to the West Coast," says Brooks Adams Otis, a musician and record collector in the Peninsula folk scene. "Not only bluegrass, but blues. He brought out the Stanley Brothers, Doc Watson, Bill Monroe. He brought out this succession of great people and you'd go to the club and then later Ed would have parties at his house with the musicians. A lot of people from the Bay Area went down to the Ash Grove."

Jerry and his friends made the pilgrimage south to L.A. many times, and in the process they befriended the members of what was unquestionably the best homegrown bluegrass band in L.A., the Country Boys, who changed their name to the Kentucky Colonels in 1962. The Colonels are probably best remembered as the group that launched the influential flat-picking guitar wizard Clarence White, but all four core members were hot pickers—Clarence's older brother Roland White, who played mandolin and guitar, banjo player Billy Ray Latham and bassist/banjoist Roger Bush. Though Garcia was friendly with the entire band, he later became closest to Clarence White, and many years later he said, "Clarence was important in my life both as a friend and a player. He brought a kind of swing—a rhythmic openness—to bluegrass and a unique syncopation. His feel has been incorporated by a lot of other players, but nobody has ever quite gotten the open quality of his rhythm. Clarence had wonderful control over the guitar. He's the first guy I heard who really knocked me out."

When Marshall Leicester returned from Yale in the spring of 1962, he and Garcia and a classically trained violinist turned fiddler named Dick Arnold, who had gotten the string band music bug from hanging around the Chateau, formed a group called the Sleepy Hollow Hog Stompers ("Jerry and I had a mutual taste for that kind of absurdity," Leicester says of the name). "Our repertoire was always about 80 to 90 percent from the first few New Lost City Ramblers records and reworked; and then a few other things from elsewhere, like the tapes that Adams Otis had and Chris Strachwitz's records. So we got a pipeline directly into the music and not just as mediated by a band like the Ramblers."

Garcia finally found a way to make some money on a semiregular basis when he started teaching guitar and banjo at Dana Morgan's Music Shop in downtown Palo Alto. This wasn't about to make him rich, but it allowed him to make enough to keep the wolf away from the door while still devoting most of his time and energy to practicing and playing music. And as Barbara Meier says, "That's *all* he did. That's it. He played music. He was totally dedicated. He would play all day long. If he was trying to learn something, he would practice it until he got it. And it wasn't something he ever had to force himself to do. For some reason, he was absolutely charmed, in the sense that it never occurred to him that he would have to earn a living. He was totally content.

"I did two paintings of him at that time, and in each one of those he's wearing the same shirt. Do you know why? Because it was just about the only shirt he owned. There was a short-sleeved white shirt that he wore when he went to Dana Morgan's to teach, and he had this other shirt. And he *did not care*. He did not care about anything, as long as he had that guitar, as long as he had cigarettes. There was always somewhere to stay, food always manifested somehow. He lived on less than nothing for a long, long time. And he allowed himself to have this incredible space, this time to devote to his craft. And he had no plan, either. This was just what he liked to do and this is what he was interested in. I don't think it ever occurred to him that he wouldn't be able to do whatever he wanted."

CHAPTER 3

There Were Days
Between

he Sleepy Hollow Hog Stompers played at the Boar's Head, which had moved to the San Carlos Jewish Community Center in the summer of 1962, and a few other places on the Peninsula, but they could never get too serious because they knew that come fall Marshall Leicester would be going back to Yale. Still, Suzy Wood, who would later marry Marshall, says, "I remember making vests for the Sleepy Hollow Hog Stompers—they looked so clean and straight playing this straight old-timey music. Even at the time I couldn't help thinking that the kind of morality, the kind of emotionality that the people who originated that music—these Appalachian, old-timey people—was very different from the people who were picking it up and saying, 'Oh, this is the kind of music we're going to learn how to play.' The real old-timey lifestyle could not have been nearly as much fun as the imitators of the old-timey music probably thought it was. The [original players] were mainly poor people, rural people—farmers and millworkers—whereas this crowd was filled with intellectuals and kids from the suburbs, although a lot of them were genuinely poor—I guess you could say by circumstance—too."

There's no point in getting too hung up on the names and membership of the various acoustic bands Jerry played in during the period between 1962 and 1964, because the personnel was always fluid, depending on who was around and available, and there were relatively few real gigs—mainly at Peninsula folk haunts and a few in North Beach at places like the Coffee Gallery and Coffee & Confusion. Among the short-lived aggregations were the Hart Valley Drifters (Garcia, Leicester, Ken Frankel and Worth Handley were one incarnation; there were others); the Badwater Valley Boys (Garcia, Frankel, Leicester and Hunter) and the Thunder Mountain Tub Thumpers (Garcia, Nelson, Hunter, Joe and Jim Edminston). Other players who turned up in groups with Garcia at this time include Brooks Otis, Norm van Maastricht, Eric Thompson, Ellen Cavanaugh and a golden-haired fiddler named Kathy Ledford.

At the same time that Garcia's friends were delving deeply into string band music, other players on the scene were intent on exploring country blues, which became popular in folk circles around the same time. Just as old-timey music had never really enjoyed much popularity outside of the rural

South before the late '50s, country blues had rarely been heard at all by whites before musicologists such as Mike Seeger, Alan Lomax, Sam Charters, Kenneth Goldstein, Frederic Ramsey Jr. and others scoured the South looking for surviving musicians from the first generation of "race record" artists, who'd recorded in the '20s and '30s. Many players were long gone, having died broke and in obscurity; others had given up music and taken jobs outside of music to survive. But there were great rediscoveries, too, and the same white, urban college audiences that propelled the folk and old-timey boom heartily embraced a legion of country blues greats, many of whom were able to make a good living playing music (most for the first time in their lives) on the folk club and festival circuit. This group, which also had a profound influence on many rock musicians who came up in the mid-'60s, included Skip James, Mississippi John Hurt, Mance Lipscomb, Sleepy John Estes, Reverend Gary Davis, Sonny Terry and Brownie McGhee, Mississippi Fred McDowell, Sam "Lightnin' " Hopkins, Eddie "Son" House, Gus Cannon and Scrapper Blackwell.

Ever the musical omnivore, Garcia tried his hand at some of the popular fingerpicking blues styles of the day, but not with the same dogged determination he brought to his old-timey and bluegrass playing. It helped that Barbara Meier's father had given him a stack of rare blues 78s, which Jerry dutifully studied in that obsessive way of his. But the best blues picker on the Peninsula in 1962 was probably twenty-year-old Jerry Kaukonen (whose real first name was Jorma), a Washington, D.C., native who had been playing blues guitar since the mid-'50s and had come west to attend Santa Clara University. He quickly became a regular at various local clubs like the Folk Theater in San Jose, the Top of the Tangent in Palo Alto and St. Michael's Alley, and Garcia was duly impressed. "Jerry said to me, 'You gotta hear this guy Jerry Kaukonen,' " says David Nelson. "Here was a guy playing Blind Boy Fuller and Reverend Gary Davis stuff the real way. We were totally blown away by him.

"One of the great aspects of the whole folk thing," Nelson continues, "was you could be in a room hearing somebody playing and then say, 'Here, let me try that.' And if you have a good memory like Garcia, you can retain that. He could hear a song once and remember all the words and the chords and put together a rough idea of the picking stuff."

By this time Jerry was already good friends with a blues-loving Peninsula kid named Ron McKernan, who had started hanging around Kepler's, the various folk clubs and the tough bars over in East Palo Alto when he was still in his mid-teens. Ron was the son of one of the Bay Area's original R&B/blues deejays, Phil McKernan, who was known by the colorful name "Cool Breeze" on KRE in the '50s. By the late '50s, though, the senior McKernan had quit the radio business to become an engineer at the Stanford Research Institute and he moved the family into a tract house in a working-class section of Palo Alto, near the East Palo Alto border. Ron became obsessed with the blues and R&B at a very young age, and he learned the rudiments of guitar and har-

LEFT: Jerry's mother, Ruth Clifford *(right)*, with her brother Bill in San Francisco, early 1920s. *(Courtesy of KrisAnne Clifford Crow)*

BELOW: Part of the Garcia clan in the late 1930s. *Left to right:* unknown, Manuel Garcia Jr. (Jerry's uncle), Leonor Garcia (Jerry's aunt), Manuel Garcia (Jerry's grandfather), Ruth Garcia (Jerry's mom), and (with head between the legs) Leonor's husband, Barney Ross. *(Courtesy of Daniel Garcia)*

Jerry and his dad, 1947.
(Courtesy of Daniel Garcia)

BELOW: The fateful day. Jerry and Joe on the banks of the Trinity River on the day Joe drowned, August 25, 1947. *(Courtesy of Daniel Garcia)*

LEFT: Cowboy Jerry, circa 1949. *(Courtesy of KrisAnne Clifford Crow)*

BELOW: The old swimmin' hole in Lompico, near Santa Cruz, early 1950s. *Left to right:* Tiff, Jerry and cousin Diane Clifford. *(Courtesy of KrisAnne Clifford Crow)*

LEFT: Outside the Church of the Epiphany in San Francisco's Crocker-Amazon district, 1954. *Left to right:* Jerry, Tiff, grandma Tillie Clifford (aka Nana); uncle Bill Clifford, Jerry's mother, Ruth (holding baby Julie Clifford); stepfather Wally Matusiewicz, aunt Ruth Clifford and cousin Diane Clifford. In the foreground are Jerry's young cousins Dennis and Michael Clifford. *(Courtesy of KrisAnne Clifford Crow)*

LEFT: Christmas 1957, the year Jerry got his first guitar and started smoking pot. *Rear, left to right:* Jerry, aunt Ruth Clifford, Diane Clifford and Tiff. *Front:* Nana, Julie Clifford, Pops, Michael and Dennis Clifford. *(Courtesy of KrisAnne Clifford Crow)*

ABOVE: With Robert Hunter,
Stanford University, 1962.
(Jer Melrose)

LEFT: Pickin' at the Hamilton
Street pad in Palo Alto, 1963.
(Rick Melrose)

With Barbara Meier at
Disneyland, 1962. *(Courtesy
of Barbara Meier)*

One of the first photos of the Warlocks, 1965. *Clockwise from back left:*
Bill Kreutzmann, Bob Weir, Phil Lesh, Jerry, Pigpen. *(Herb Greene)*

ABOVE: Haight-Ashbury Americana. Jerry at 710 Ashbury, 1967. *(Herb Greene)*

Snuggling with Mountain Girl in Golden Gate Park, 1967. Note the cool Pigpen T-shirt. *(Herb Greene)*

ABOVE: Billy, Pigpen and Jerry at the Newport Pop Festival in Costa Mesa, California, August 4, 1968. *(Jim Marshall)*

RIGHT: The Dead at the Family Dog on the Great Highway, February 4, 1970. *(Robert Altman)*

BELOW: Resplendent in tie-dye at the Capitol Theater in Port Chester, New York, June 24, 1970. *(Randy Berge)*

Early New Riders in the wilds of Marin. *Left to right:* David Nelson, Garcia, John "Marmaduke" Dawson, Mickey Hart, Dave Torbert. *(Herb Greene)*

LEFT: Playing pedal steel guitar at a New Riders recording session at Wally Heider's studio in San Francisco, December 1970. *(Robert Altman)*

BELOW: Cosmic cowboy, 1971. *(Herb Greene)*

monica on his own. Most of his friends in school were black, and in his teens he started frequenting the bars of East Palo Alto. He had always looked older than his age, and he fit into the black street culture surprisingly well. He even acquired a nickname in East P.A., long before he was dubbed Pigpen: Blue Ron. He started drinking cheap screw-top wines like Ripple, Thunderbird, Hondo and Night Train when he was twelve or thirteen, to fit in with his black friends and to emulate the blues musicians he admired so much.

"When I first met Pigpen," Garcia said, "he was hanging around Palo Alto and I was the only person around that played any blues on the guitar, so he hung out with me. And he picked it up, just by watching and listening to me, the basic Lightnin' Hopkins stuff. . . . All the black people [in East P.A.] loved Pigpen. They loved that he played the blues. And he was a genuine person— he wasn't like a white boy trying to be black. And he was pretty good, too. You know, Pigpen's best shot was sitting around a room with a bottle of wine and an acoustic guitar, playing Lightnin' Hopkins. He could improvise lyrics endlessly; that was his real forte.

"I spent a lot of time over at the Pigpen house, but it was mostly in Pigpen's room, which was like a ghetto! I sat in his room for countless hours listening to his old records. It was funky, man! Stuff thrown everywhere. Pigpen had this habit of wearing just a shirt and his underpants. You'd come into his house and he'd say, 'Come on in, man,' and he'd have a bottle of wine under the bed. His mom would check in about once every *five hours* to see if he was still alive. It was hilarious! We'd play records, I'd hack away at his guitar, show him stuff."

McKernan played some with both Jorma and Jerry, but mainly he worked alone, singing the blues at the Tangent, the Boar's Head and at parties. Garcia and others noted that Ron didn't seem to have the drive to be a real performer; mostly, he sang just because he loved it. Though not as overtly intellectual as a lot of people in the Kepler's/Chateau crowd (which he became part of), he had read his share of Beat writers and poets, and he could quote Lord Buckley routines verbatim, not to mention make up his own weirdly imaginative stories, which he delivered in his characteristic black slang patois. As Laird Grant, who became one of Ron's closest friends, said, "He wasn't white. He had no color."

In the fall of 1962 Garcia formed his first true bluegrass band, the Wildwood Boys, with Hunter, Nelson and Norm van Maastricht. "This was a major configuration of relatively long duration for those days," Hunter recalled. "We even had a professional promo picture."

It was in this group that Garcia honed his bluegrass banjo chops. He said that Earl Scruggs was "the number one, primo influence" on his bluegrass banjo work, but his playing was also informed by a number of other players, including Don Stover, who played with Bill Monroe in the '50s, and then with the Lilly Brothers; Allen Shelton, who played with Jim and Jesse McReynolds;

Ralph Stanley of the Stanley Brothers; and J. D. Crowe. "Those are my favorite banjo players," he said. "I think there's something about [three-finger] rolls—you know in those days, pre–[Bill] Keith banjo style, you either played rolls, or else there were guys who played single-string stuff like Don Reno [of Reno and Smiley] and Eddie Adcock [of the Country Gentlemen]. I preferred the kind of problem-solving thing of trying to figure out how to make melodies work out of rolls."

Speaking more generally about what attracted him to bluegrass banjo, he said it was "just the sound of the instrument, and then the fire, you know; the speed and all that. I was attracted by the intensity of it, really. And I was drawn to that incredible clarity—when something is going along real fast and every note is absolutely clear. That, to me, was really amazing—the Earl Scruggs instrumentals . . . the Mercury album that's got 'Foggy Mountain Breakdown' on it and 'Pike County Breakdown.' I just couldn't believe the sound of it. It was just *startling*."

But Garcia refused to commit himself to just one style of music. Though bluegrass became his overriding obsession for about two years, he still dabbled in folk, old-timey and blues whenever the opportunity arose and there were players around. For instance, at the College of San Mateo Folk Festival in November 1962, put on by Rodney and Peter Albin, Garcia played as a solo act, in a duet with David Nelson, and then with a full group—one tape in circulation has him playing as part of the Hart Valley Drifters with Hunter, Nelson and van Maastricht; Hunter's recollection is that the group was the Liberty Hill Aristocrats, with Hunter, Nelson and the Albin brothers. Whatever the particulars, over the course of a single day Garcia was onstage playing folk, old-timey and bluegrass.

David Parker was a twenty-year-old student at CSM and a friend of the Albin brothers at the time of the festival. "It was the first time I'd ever seen Garcia play," Parker recalls. "He was playing guitar and singing. It was funny, because he didn't go over too well. At that time he was sort of exploring the roots of American music and playing a lot of old-timey stuff. He played a lot of songs by the Carter Family, for instance. Most of the audience was fairly clean college kids into the Kingston Trio and the slicker kinds of sounds, and this sort of authentic old-timey stuff was a little strange to most of them. Also, most of the acts playing then would come on, do two or three songs and then go off, but Jerry got up there and he wanted to play a full set. So people first of all couldn't relate to the songs he was playing, and then they started feeling like he was staying on too long, and giving him a rough time. But he went along and finished his set, playing what he wanted to play. The reaction didn't seem to bother him too much. Then the next group that came on started by saying, 'This song we're going to do is *not* by the Carter Family,' and that got a big laugh."

"Jerry did bomb in his solo set," Hunter remembered. "The sound system sucked to the point of inaudibility, and he just kept playing one *ballade* after another to the baffled crowd of scornful noninitiates. Too cool for words!"

It seems as though nearly everyone in the boho/folkie scene was broke most of the time, and a running automobile was considered a luxury. At one point, an acquaintance of Jerry's named Bob Fees even chauffeured Garcia around on a semiregular basis in exchange for guitar lessons. As David Nelson put it, "It was the usual thing where people would be working temporarily. Employment was a thing you did sort of like houses—you'd work for two or three or four months someplace and then change to something else, and then you might not work at all for a while, and somebody else you knew would have a little money."

Or not. David Nelson says that one of the staples of his diet during this era was ketchup sandwiches (twenty years before Ronald Reagan's administration declared ketchup a vegetable!). "A box of Ritz crackers could be considered a meal. The refrigerator at the Chateau usually had like an old bottle of ketchup and something unidentifiable in a jar in it—like a science project, with three colors of mold on it."

Bob Hunter was one of the more motivated members of the gang. He took on a number of odd jobs to make ends meet, such as driving a truck for a photo developer and working as a busboy, and later as headwaiter, at St. Michael's Alley. He spent his free time reading, working on a novel, playing music when he could and dissecting James Joyce's famously impenetrable *Finnegans Wake*. "I can remember Jerry and Hunter would read some of it, and then they'd close the book and *continue;* just making it up," Barbara Meier says. "Jerry would laugh so hard. He loved that; he loved wordplay and he was very good at it."

It was in 1962 that Hunter happily earned some money as a guinea pig in the government's top-secret tests of psychedelic drugs at the Veterans Hospital in Menlo Park. He was given mescaline, psilocybin and finally LSD in a sterile, clinical setting that was somewhat hostile and forbidding; certainly a far cry from the tripping-gaily-in-the-redwoods model that would come into vogue when the lysergic genie came out of the (lab) bottle a couple of years later. Still, Hunter said, "I had no problems with acid. They gave it to me, and left me in a white room. I had no idea what was going to happen, although they had warned me about hallucinations, so I was prepared for that, psychologically."

Ever the writer, Hunter typed up his experiences while they were still fresh in his mind, and of course he raved about what he'd been through to his friends. David Nelson remembers sitting in a coffeehouse with Garcia after the experiments and pumping Hunter for information, never imagining for a moment that psychedelics would ever make it out of the white rooms.

Garcia and Barbara Meier broke up late that fall after Barbara's father learned that they had been sleeping together and insisted that she not see him again.

She "cut off from him completely," she says. "I left Menlo Park the minute I graduated from high school [in 1963] and I moved to San Francisco," where she drifted into a much different world after she became the girlfriend of jazz drummer Tony Williams, the powerful but exquisitely tasteful skinsman in Miles Davis's classic Quintet of the time. She reappears in Jerry's life much, much later.

One evening in the winter of 1963 Jerry was hanging out and playing music at Kepler's with Bob Hunter and David Nelson when he met nineteen-year-old Sara Ruppenthal, then in her sophomore year at Stanford. Their paths had undoubtedly crossed before, since Sara was good friends with Ira Sandperl and had done her share of hanging out at Kepler's. "Ira was my mentor," she says. "I loved that guy. When I went to Paly High there were a bunch of us intellectuals who were into folk music and the peace movement, working with the American Friends Service Committee."

Sara was also friends with Joan Baez, who was four years older: "She was an important person in my life in those days, and I idealized her powerfully. She and Ira were the only people I could talk to about my life, from the heart. I would go down with Ira to visit her at Big Sur Hot Springs, where she lived in a little cottage on the cliff—that place became Esalen.

"Joan and Jerry weren't really friends," she continues. "He resented the fact that she had records out and he thought he was a better musician. He felt competitive with her and didn't care for her nontraditional approach to music—the way she took from any source and personalized it." During the early days of Jerry and Sara's relationship, Baez approached Sara about accompanying her on what was to be her first European tour. "I'd traveled a lot and I knew how to get around in a foreign country," Sara says. "She wanted me to come with her and be her companion, but that's right when I was getting together with Jerry, so I made a choice between them."

Sara played music, too, though before she met Jerry she had been more interested in sociopolitical folk songs than the sort of rootsy, traditional fare being served up by Jerry and his buddies in the back room at Kepler's. Still, that first evening she was intrigued *and* amused: "Jerry, Hunter and Nelson were this funny trio; kind of like the Three Stooges. They were all so funny and I loved their music. They were very smart boys and always going so fast and hot and heavy with the witty repartee. It seemed like they were sort of all the same person. I remember I went home with Jerry to the Chateau because I had my roommate's car. That was a treat for him because none of them had cars. It was so interesting to me to see kids who were my age but already off on their own.

"Hunter took me off the next morning out into the garden and said, 'Here, try this, it's a funny cigarette,' and I didn't know what it was; I was very naive. I had kind of a nice time wandering around the garden with him, high.

"I don't know where Hunter lived in that house, but Jerry had this little room—you went around from the front door off the porch, around to the back of the house, which was on a hill, and into this basement storage room. It could have been a root cellar or a can cupboard kind of place. I think it had a dirt floor. He'd stuck a bed in there and there was a box with a candle on it, and that was it. There was no electricity. There were spiders. It was really funky. He didn't spend much time there. Shortly after I met them, Nelson talked his parents into letting him come to live at the Chateau. Since he had some money from his parents, he got the front bedroom, which had probably been the old sitting room."

For Jerry and Sara it was love and lust at first sight. Sara recalls, "He called me up a couple of days after we met—it was so sweet—saying 'I'm really fucked up. I need to be with you. I can't eat, I can't even play music, man! You've gotta come and be with me.' He was lovesick. He could be very sentimental."

And careless. Just a few weeks into their relationship, Sara learned that she was pregnant. She told Jerry the news one afternoon while they were window-shopping at Stanford Shopping Center. "It was probably a Sunday—everything was closed," Sara remembers. "I was pretty miserable and scared. I didn't know what to do. And he said, 'Well, I've always wanted to get married. Let's get hitched.' So then I took over and made the plans. I remember we went to Sears or Penney's and bought him a suit. I think he was indulging my fantasy of having a white wedding, doing it up the way I wanted to do it. Everybody in his crowd was pretty excited that we were going to have a 'shivaree.' "

It would be an understatement to say that Sara's parents did not greet the news of her daughter's impending nuptials with quite the enthusiasm she had hoped for. "My parents were horrified!" she says with a laugh. "He hadn't completed high school. He had no future whatsoever. When we came to them saying we wanted to get married—at first we didn't tell them I was pregnant—my dad said, 'Look, we'll send you around the world for the year. Think about it. Anything but that!' They tried to talk us out of it.

"I had already gotten myself kicked out of school for being with him overnight, because in those days the dorms had very strict rules. This was a serious offense, to break the social honor code. It was pretty terrible for my family. But I was itching to have some life."

Meanwhile, back at Kepler's and the Chateau, some of Jerry's friends were almost as surprised as the Ruppenthals that Jerry and Sara were getting married. "I was just the sort of kid who didn't want them to get married," says David Nelson. "I wanted to keep Jerry as part of the boys in the parking lot playing music. I was thinkin', 'It's not going to be the same. He's not going to be one of the boys.' He took me and Hunter to the coffeeshop and said he was thinking about getting married and he wanted our opinion. I'm saying, 'Oh no, don't do it!' and of course Hunter was very serious, saying, 'Well, you know, Jerry, it's a big undertaking, but if you can do it . . .' "

"When we decided to get married," says Sara, "I insisted we invite his mother and grandmother, so we came up to the city and went to Harrington Street—just surprised Tillie out of the blue. He hadn't been in contact with them for several years. Tillie and his mom were really glad to see him."

Sara's white-wedding fantasy was fulfilled on April 25, 1963, at the Palo Alto Unitarian Church. Tillie and Ruth made it down from San Francisco. Tiff Garcia was there, too. David Nelson was Garcia's best man, and many of Jerry's friends were in attendance, including Hunter, Laird Grant and others from the Chateau scene. The wedding even made the *Palo Alto Times:* SARA LEE RUPPENTHAL WEDS was the headline over a nice story about the event featuring a lovely formal head-and-shoulders portrait of the bride and groom—she with a lace mantilla draped over her head, he in a dark suit and a flower in his lapel—looking happily and dreamily off into space, their heads nearly touching. The caption under the photo read, "Stanford student is bride," and in smaller type below that, "Mr. and Mrs. Jerome John Garcia." Ah, young love!

The wedding reception was a big catered affair for about seventy-five people at Ricky's, a ranch-style hotel on El Camino Real that Sara says was "the fanciest hotel in Palo Alto in those days." Phil Lesh was among the revelers; it was he who summed up the reception in an oft-quoted remark: "It was priceless—all of her friends were at the booze; his friends were all at the food."

"I remember after the wedding reception," Sara says, "we went to my parents' house with his family members and mine for a little private family gathering. Then we went back to the hotel to spend the night. Suddenly it hit us that we'd gotten married and we had *no* idea what this meant. And we both started to freak out, big time. 'Oh my God! What have we done?' I had been seeing a psychiatrist—part of the deal of Stanford suspending me was if I went to a psychiatrist they'd let me back in—and he'd given me a sleeping pill because I was pretty anxious about all this wedding stuff. So Jerry and I opened up this one little capsule very carefully and we each took half of this foul-tasting powder so we could get some sleep."

The next morning, "We drove my parents' '59 Mercedes to Yosemite and we had a nice time there," Sara says. "It was an adventure. We stayed in Camp Curry in one of those platform tent-cabins. We hiked around Angel Falls and bought him a cowboy hat. We stopped in the Gold Country. It was a sweet time; really, in a way we were just beginning to get to know each other. I think that was the most time we'd ever spent together up to that point."

Shortly after they were married, Jerry and Sara moved to Mountain View, south of Palo Alto, "into a nasty little one-room shack behind a house for $75 a month," Sara says. "Jerry would go off with his guitar in one hand, his banjo in the other, in his white shirt and black pants and vest, and hitchhike in from Mountain View to Dana Morgan's—if he could get a ride, because he looked a little disreputable. He missed many of his lessons just because he couldn't get there. And I'd be home in this miserable low-ceilinged little space listening to old-timey music and memorizing it, learning it by heart." Sara's parents gave her $100 a month to encourage her to stay in school, and she also worked part-time for her father in the Stanford Business School, where he taught.

Sara says she and Jerry started singing together almost immediately after they met. She was an eager pupil, learning the intricacies of the old-timey style for the first time. "I was never much of an instrumentalist," she says, "but I always sang," and their voices—his low tenor, her alto—blended nicely. As a duo called Jerry and Sara, they made a few public appearances, singing such nuggets as the Delmore Brothers' "Deep Elem Blues" (which was later part of the Dead's repertoire), "Long Black Veil" and the Carter Family's "Foggy Mountain Top" at places like the Tangent and St. Michael's Alley. But as she got further along in her pregnancy, Sara stopped playing. "I was feeling discounted and unappreciated," she says. "We weren't figuring out ways to connect well at all during the pregnancy. Motherhood became my primary preoccupation and that wasn't interesting to him. Parenthood wasn't something he could participate in—he had such ambivalent feelings about his mother that when I became a mother . . . you know, the madonna-whore syndrome: you can't make love to your wife if you think of her as a mother. So he was running around and I didn't know about it. And I was so innocent, so naive. And I got so uptight. It was not a happy marriage. We stopped being friends basically after we married."

Which isn't to say there weren't good times along the way. Their mutual love of music allowed them to form a deep bond, and she was always very supportive of Jerry's musical aspirations. "He was very ambitious," Sara says. "He wanted to do something big. The Rooftop Singers came out with this old Gus Cannon song, 'Walk Right In,' and we thought, 'Oh, we can do better than that.' That was our plan. The phrase we used then was 'destined for greatness.' It felt very apt. Everybody recognized that he had some genius that he needed to do something with. It was obvious to me. That's why I signed on to help support him make something of himself. I thought if he had a good woman behind him he could go far," she adds with a chuckle.

"After we got married, we traded in his old banjo, my dear little rosewood Martin and another guitar, added to the money we'd received for wedding presents and from some wedding gifts we'd returned, and got him the fancy banjo of his dreams—a Weyman from the '30s with the name 'John' inlaid on the peg head. Everybody called the banjo 'John.' That banjo had a very distinctive tone; sharp and metallic. We invested in this instrument because it was to be the source of our livelihood, and Jer played that sucker night and day, and got to be very good. He was a very dedicated musician, an aspiring virtuoso. If he couldn't get in about four hours of practice a day, he'd be in a foul mood."

Near the end of May 1963 the first Monterey Folk Festival brought together some of the biggest names in folk and traditional country music, as well as numerous local groups, for a weekend of pickin' and singin' at the Monterey County Fairgrounds, site of the famous jazz festival (and four years later, the Monterey Pop Festival). The lineup was impressive: Peter, Paul and Mary, the Weavers and the Rooftop Singers were the darlings of the moment in the mainstream folk world; Bob Dylan had still put out only one record, but his reputation was growing by the month. (Sara says she and Jerry walked out of Dylan's performance at Monterey to protest his use of an amplified acoustic guitar.) Bill Monroe and Doc Watson, perhaps the most revered figures in bluegrass and old-timey, respectively, were on hand. So were three of the best young traditional bands—the New Lost City Ramblers, the Dillards and the Kentucky Colonels. The California bluegrass and string band communities turned out in force to see their heroes, and quite a few Bay Area players had the opportunity to play on smaller stages on the fairgrounds. The Wildwood Boys, with Garcia, Hunter, Nelson and Ken Frankel, won an amateur bluegrass open competition there. Garcia also entered (but didn't win) a banjo contest that was judged by Doug and Rodney Dillard and the Kentucky Colonels' banjo ace, Billy Ray Latham.

In the bluegrass community in 1963 the big buzz was about the young Amherst-educated banjo player in Bill Monroe's band named Bill Keith. The Monroe band played an extended run at the Ash Grove as well as other shows around California around the same time as the festival, so the serious bluegrass fans, like much of Garcia's Palo Alto crowd, got to check out Keith's colorful and intricate style on many occasions.

"Garcia reacted to Keith's playing immediately," writes Sandy Rothman, one of Garcia's bandmates in the Black Mountain Boys beginning in late 1963. "It changed his life, as it did for many banjo pickers worldwide, and from that point on I didn't hear Jerry work as hard on any other banjo technique. With great diligence he set to work mastering the entire fretboard, 'Keith-style.' . . . Keith's banjo approach allowed for dazzling displays of arpeggiated passages that swooped dramatically up the neck like musical parachute jumps.

"Jerry's playing in the early '60s might have been described as note-rich, maybe overstated at times, but it was always expressive and full of energy. Any way you looked at it, it was damn fancy banjo picking, consistently well executed. He was admired by progressives and staunch traditionalists alike."

Eric Thompson, who preceded Rothman as guitarist in the Black Mountain Boys, formed just weeks after the festival, says of Jerry's banjo playing, "He was pretty good, and inventive, but he didn't have the sort of perfection that is the norm in that kind of music. Usually, bluegrass music—especially in the banjo playing—tends to be very perfection-oriented because Earl Scruggs was so amazing; he never had a note out of place. It was a very, very high standard. His role in the music never falters. He never plays extraneous notes. You can't say that about Jerry, but on the other hand, he was very inventive, and that was great."

Frank Serratoni stopped renting out rooms in the Chateau in the fall of 1963, so part of the crowd that was living there got together with other friends and moved into a huge turn-of-the-century Victorian in downtown Palo Alto, where Garcia's recurrent paramour Phoebe Graubard had lived in a room. The two-story house at 436 Hamilton Street (long since demolished) housed David Nelson, Dave Parker, Willy Legate, Bob Hunter and Grace Marie Haddie. Actually, Hunter and Legate lived in a separate barnlike structure that had been divided into lofts, located behind the main house. Not surprisingly, the Hamilton Street house became a new locus of activity for all the residents' friends.

Garcia spent a lot of time over at Hamilton Street because it was where a lot of his friends were, and because, as Sara noted, he had a difficult time preparing himself psychologically for the birth of his child. This is, after all, a guy who thirty years later told Sara, "I don't have to grow up and I'm not going to." So Jerry spent a lot of time away from his pregnant bride, hanging with the boys instead.

At least he was around for the big day when it came. On December 8, 1963, Sara went into labor, and she and Jerry went to Stanford Hospital together. Dave Parker and a couple of other friends went to the hospital to offer Jerry support. "We hung out in the hallways waiting and waiting for however many hours it was, smoking cigarettes and talking," Parker says. "Then, finally, the baby was born and we got to see it through the window, and then we split and Jerry stayed with Sara for a while. He seemed really happy about being a new father and he and Sara seemed very much in love; it seemed like a good time for them."

Sara says, "The day Heather was born Jerry stayed with me while I was in labor, which was lovely and nice, and he was there waiting for the news from the delivery room. [Fathers were usually not allowed in the delivery room in this era.] Parker was in the waiting room keeping him company. I remember Jerry skipping down the hall saying, 'It's a broad! It's a broad!' He was so happy. He'd dreaded having a son. He just didn't think he'd be able to parent a boy, because he hadn't really had a father to raise him.

"The next morning I remember waking up and, before I opened my eyes, sensing that someone was sitting next to the bed, and feeling this deep sense of satisfaction that I'd given birth, the baby was healthy, it had been a good, easy birth—hard, but no problems. I felt such a sense of accomplishment and satisfaction. And here was my husband sitting next to me, keeping me company. Then I opened my eyes and it was *Hunter*. I was disappointed, crushed that it wasn't Jerry. But it was great that there was Hunter. Hunter was a really good friend to me, a constant reliable presence. When I was doing homework, housework, taking care of the baby, he'd come by and just hang out and talk about stuff that was important to me."

Hunter became baby Heather's godfather (and he is also godfather to Sara's son, Julian).

New Year's Eve 1963 is a date that holds special significance in Grateful Dead lore because it was on that night that Jerry Garcia and Bob Weir supposedly first talked about playing together in a band. As Weir said, "I was wandering the back streets of Palo Alto with a friend when we heard banjo music coming from the back of the music store. We walked to the door and came in and it was Garcia waiting for his pupils, unmindful that it was New Year's Eve and that they wouldn't show up. We sat down and started talking and had a great old rave. I had my guitar with me and we played a little and decided to form a jug band."

Garcia and Weir had met before this, but they weren't exactly friends. Bob was a misfit rich kid five years Garcia's junior, from nearby Atherton, which Bob once accurately described as "the Bel-Air of Northern California" (a reference to the exclusive L.A. suburb). He was born in San Francisco in 1947, and became the second adopted son of a very successful mechanical and electrical engineer who designed heating and cooling systems for big buildings, hotels and factories. Frederick Weir also designed the modern-looking Weir homestead at 89 Tuscaloosa Avenue in Atherton, which was ready for the family in 1950. Bob was a jock growing up, into baseball and track. He had problems in school because he was "dyslexic in the extreme, and nearly functionally illiterate. . . . But they had never heard of dyslexia when I was young so they figured I was lazy, which I was."

Even though he was essentially a nonreader, Weir says he managed to get good grades by developing a good memory and "an ability to bullshit teachers. I managed to stay awake for at least half my classes, and got A's. . . . My main hobby and pastime was girls. I went to seven—count 'em—seven schools, and I was kicked out of every one I attended." Actually, he dropped out of the last one—the exclusive Drew School in San Francisco—when he was sixteen.

Bob got his first guitar at fourteen as a gift for graduating from junior high school: "It was a pretty miserable guitar, but I learned to play it a little bit," he said. "The first song I learned to play on it was [the Beach Boys' version of] 'Sloop John B.' " Weir was also heavily influenced by Joan Baez, and as he got further into playing he discovered other players and styles. "I started hanging out in the folk scene in Palo Alto," he said. "Whatever was hot around there, including Jerry, was what caught my attention. There was a guy named Michael Cooney who showed me a lot of stuff. And Jerry, too."

"His musical leader was Jorma," Garcia said of Bob in a 1967 interview. "He used to go every time Jorma played, when he played in coffeehouses. Weir would go there with his tape recorder, tape the whole show and talk to Jorma extensively and watch him play the stuff, and study it all and go home and work it out. Jorma is where he learned a lot of his technique. . . . His whole approach to guitar playing was like Jorma's, essentially." At this point, Bob was viewed by most of the older pickers as "the kid," tolerated but not particularly respected.

Weir's New Year's Eve tale notwithstanding, it was actually quite a while before the jug band got going beyond a couple of very informal get-togethers. In early 1964, Garcia, Sandy Rothman and David Nelson were still going strong as the Black Mountain Boys, and Jerry and Sandy were hatching a plot whereby they'd travel back East, collect some bluegrass tapes and maybe get themselves hired by Bill Monroe. Their link was to be Neil Rosenberg, of Redwood Canyon Ramblers fame. Rosenberg had managed Bill Monroe's Indiana music park, the Brown County Jamboree (known far and wide as Bean Blossom) in the summer of 1963, had played banjo for Monroe on occasion and was living in nearby Bloomington.

In February 1964 Rothman wrote a letter to Rosenberg that read, in part, "Jerry Garcia and I, plus his wife and baby may (probably will) have a chance to drive out your way this summer some time after June to hear and tape music and relax. For me, the music and a chance to get unhung-up; for them the trip and bluegrass. If Jerry's wife does come along, they of course will have to stay in a hotel or the like, and I will probably have no problem finding a place to sleep."

"We were excited," Sara says. "To get the opportunity to play with Bill Monroe—that was the pinnacle. The idea was that Jerry was going to play with Bill Monroe, get hired to be in the band. The South was like a foreign country, potentially dangerous. He and Sandy were worried about getting rousted by the rednecks, and rightly so. There was such a strong suspicion of Northerners, and then of weird kids. . . . We thought at first that Heather and I would go along with them, but it didn't work out. I needed to stay in school to get the hundred dollars a month from my father; it was a little bribe.

"It felt like, 'This is something hard for us, but it'll be good for him and then if he gets work, when school is over in June I'll move there.' Another plan was I was going to go to school in ethnomusicology. I was the scholar. While he was playing music I could pursue my academic fortune."

At Stanford, Sara had become a communications major, with a particular interest in film and broadcasting, but, she says, "as with playing an instrument, I got hung up on not being technically proficient, but it was a lively time and I did make a few little films, some using guys like Dave Parker and David Nelson as my actors." Jerry also performed the soundtrack for a movie that one of the graduate students made about a camp for diabetic children. "That's a treasure probably nobody even knows about—Jerry playing pretty guitar or banjo music. I can't remember which."

Meanwhile, Bob Hunter, David Nelson and Willy Legate were among a large group on the scene who became interested in the Church of Scientology, which in the early '60s was just beginning to catch on in Los Angeles and the Bay Area. L. Ron Hubbard's popular book *Dianetics* had come out in 1950, and in the intervening decade-plus the tenets of Scientology had been codified and a church hierarchy established, in which students of the discipline worked their way up through different courses, or "processes," on their way to becoming "clear"—supposedly operating at full capacity without being dragged down by their own psychological baggage. Of course, that's just scratching the surface of what goes on in Scientology—there's a whole science fiction side involving human mental evolution to a sort of super-being, in control over thousands of years of past lives, and much more.

"I couldn't figure out what these guys saw in this," Dave Parker says of his friends. "Intellectual gamesmanship was certainly a key factor—it's something those guys in particular were really good at. They could do that kind of stuff all day long, and that's actually a lot of what went on in those houses— verbal fencing with ideas. So I guess it suited them that Scientology was something that was highly complicated and which presented you with this way to confront the world—and 'confront' was a word that Scientologists used to use a lot. I thought it was totally odd."

Willy, Hunter, Nelson and Grace Marie Haddie got into Scientology deeply enough that they moved from the Bay Area down to Los Angeles, in part because more advanced courses were taught at a center there. Whether he was just naturally skeptical or too busy working on his music, Jerry never showed much interest in Scientology: "Jerry would never even have considered distracting himself with someone else's scam in that way," Legate says today.

And he certainly wasn't about to give up smoking pot, which was strictly *verboten* in the Scientology world. Sara was anti-pot in those days, too, but for another reason: "I was kind of an uptight young mom," she says. "But the main reason is Jerry got more irresponsible when he was stoned and even less reliable. He wouldn't show up when he was supposed to or do what he said he was going to do, or the meager paycheck wouldn't come home when we needed it for rent. If I would show up at Dana Morgan's on the last day of the week, then I could make sure the check got into the bank. I put on a brave front but I wasn't having a very good time."

Shortly before his big trip east with Sandy Rothman, Jerry shaved off his goatee and cut his hair, in part, Sara says, because "he was afraid he'd get bothered by the rednecks with that beard. So I got to see what he really looked like—that was a shock," she adds with a laugh. Sara's photo album has a page of pictures of Jerry and Heather outside their little cottage taken on the morning Jerry left on the trip—"a sad day," Sara says wistfully.

That day, in early May of 1964, Jerry and Sandy hopped into Jerry's '61 Corvair (finally—*wheels!*), went to a Payless store in Palo Alto to buy a case of reel-to-reel tapes and drove down to Los Angeles, where they stayed for a couple of days with Bob Hunter. Hunter recalls that Billy Ray Latham, the hot banjo picker from the Kentucky Colonels, came over one night and jammed with Sandy and Jerry. A day or two later, the Corvair headed out to the San Fernando Valley and linked up with all four members of the Colonels, who were driving east in Roland White's station wagon to play at the Newport Folk Festival, Cambridge's Club 47 and various other spots. The Colonels were definitely on a roll at this time—in February they had recorded what remains one of their finest works, a sprightly album of bluegrass instrumentals called *Appalachian Swing!*

The two cars caravaned east, mainly traveling Route 66, with its truck stops and Burma Shave signs and innumerable small towns. The early part of their route took them through Flagstaff, Albuquerque, Kingman and Amarillo, "where we stopped and went to all the Western shops," Sandy says. "We mainly slept in the car and ate cheap Mexican food." They alternated cars a bit, too—Sandy remembers Clarence crammed into the small backseat of the Corvair, and Sandy rode in the Colonels' station wagon for stretches, too. Jerry mainly drove his Corvair.

They spent endless hours trying to tune in cool radio stations as they roared through town after town, and there was time for some pickin', too. Rothman says, "We'd pull up at some truck stop with each car going to a different pump, sometimes really far from each other, and we'd agree to play the same tune in each of our cars in hopes of freaking out the guys at the gas station. But nobody ever said a thing. We tried that endlessly and thought it was just so entertaining."

During their time in the Midwest, Jerry and Sandy spent nearly every waking hour on their bluegrass quest. In Indiana, Rosenberg introduced them to a tape collector (and musician) named Marvin Hedrick, who let them spend untold hours copying reels he'd made at Bean Blossom since the '50s. On May 24, Rosenberg says, Jerry even recorded a Bill Monroe show himself.

Jerry and Sandy tried to persuade Rosenberg to introduce them to Monroe, but as Rothman recalled, "Neil was steadfast in saying we should talk to him ourselves. I remember as if it was yesterday how we tried to approach Bill, exactly where we stood, and how we posed with our instrument cases upright in front of us, slightly leaning on them, maybe like one of those Stanley Brothers album cover shots. Jerry and I always reminisced about this: How in the world did we think he was going to get our message—mental telepathy? Neither one of us had the courage or the slightest idea, or plan of action, how to tell him we wanted to play with him or ask him for a job. We were petri-fied. We never said a word."

Jerry and Sandy spent about ten days with Rosenberg around Bean Blos-som, making tapes and playing music together. They journeyed as far east as Sunset Park, a country music jamboree in Pennsylvania, where they encoun-tered one of the hottest bluegrass mandolinists on the East Coast, a New Jerseyan named David Grisman. They also made a whirlwind trip south to Panama City, Florida, where Scott Hambly, onetime mandolinist for the Redwood Canyon Ramblers, was stationed in the air force.

Sometime in June, though, Jerry abruptly decided to head back to Califor-nia. Sara says, "Sandy tells me this sweet story about how they were going along and having this adventure when Jerry suddenly said, 'I've gotta go home. I've got to get back to Sara.' Jerry wrote wonderful letters to me while he was gone—funny, delightfully descriptive letters about their adventures. When we broke up I burned them, and I'm so sorry I did." Rothman elected to stay longer in the East, and later that year he actually did get to play with Bill Monroe, but he says the main mission of the trip with Garcia had been fulfilled by the time Jerry left: "We got our pot of gold; we got a whole case filled with tapes."

Back in the Bay Area that summer, Jerry, Eric Thompson and a New York mandolinist named Jody Stecher formed a trio they called the Asphalt Moun-tain Jungle Boys, and played a few gigs at places like the Tangent and Curt's Copy Cat in San Francisco before Stecher went back to City College of New York for the fall semester. It was during this summer, too, that Garcia hooked up with Bob Weir and Ron McKernan (now and forever dubbed Pigpen, after the unkempt character from Charles Schulz's *Peanuts* comic strip) to form Mother McCree's Uptown Jug Champions, or, as it's invariably referred to in Dead circles, "the jug band."

Talk about a blip on the cultural landscape: jug bands had a very brief run as a popular form of folk music in the mid-'60s. As with the old-timey revival, the craze started in the East. The major proponent of the style was Jim Kweskin and the Jug Band, which, like the late-'50s generation of string band players, went back to 78s by the original jug bands of the '20s and '30s for some of their material. In the years before the Depression, jug bands had sprung up like dandelions all over the South, though the most famous—like Cannon's Jug Stompers and the Memphis Jug Band—originated in Tennessee. While most of the popular jug bands from the music's first era were black, in the '60s revival the musicians were overwhelmingly white. Still, the instrumentation and the repertoire were similar. Jug bands invariably played a lot of humor-ous material—novelty tunes—and ribald blues-based numbers were also popular. Kweskin's group also did a few rock 'n' roll tunes jug band style, like Chuck Berry's "Memphis." Jug bands were usually loose and anarchic-sounding; they ended up having the perfect vibe for a place like the Tangent, filled with irreverent Stanford students.

"The jug band didn't have the egregious discipline that bluegrass required," notes Marshall Leicester. "And there was no way to make a living playing bluegrass. Jerry was married, he had a kid, he was looking for a way to find an accommodation with adult responsibilities—a problem he had for the next thirty years. But he was genuinely trying, working for Dana Morgan, and he was always trying to get together some kind of band that would keep him playing. And it was a real strain. Mother McCree's was fun for him and it allowed him to get in touch with musicians who had been on different paths. We'd known Ron McKernan for years, but aside from sort of playing Lightnin' Hopkins backup to Ron at parties and the Boar's Head and places like that, making him part of the same musical scene sort of hadn't arisen before."

For a change, Jerry didn't have to worry about whether this player or that was going back to school in September or after Christmas break: Mother McCree's was mainly folks who were part of the same dropout culture he was from. The personnel was always changing: Bob Matthews thinks as many as twenty different people played with the group at one time or another; that may be an exaggeration. "I think I only lasted six months," said Matthews. "I went from washboard to first kazoo, to second kazoo, to being out of the band. I think I was out of the band the night we were playing and Jerry leaned over to me in the *middle* of a tune and said, 'Why don't you take a break,' and I got off the stage."

Sara confirms, "In music, Jerry could take people on and be very direct and actually quite cruel to bandmembers if they met with his displeasure. People were scared of him. He was a hard taskmaster." Adds Dave Parker, "Jerry was definitely the leader. He pulled it together and made it the way it was. He went out and found the gigs. Jerry came up with most of the tunes, too, though Pig knew a lot of blues."

As for Bob Weir—well, he was spirited and kind of goofy and he played jug and Gary Davis–style fingerpicking guitar and sang decently, and already girls were crazy for his boyish good looks. "I was only sixteen at the time," he said, "and I was kind of in awe of these guys I was playing with, because I was not any kind of journeyman musician at that point; I really had almost no experience."

"That boy is a real space case," Sara says fondly. "He was kind of lost, a poor little rich kid. He was such an adorable kid. Jerry and I kind of adopted him. Actually, a lot of people seemed to idealize our little family. We were parental figures for a lot of young musicians."

The jug band rehearsed anyplace it could—at the Hamilton Street pad, Weir's parents' house or, as likely, in the garage of the cozy two-bedroom cottage Jerry and Sara rented after he returned from his eastern odyssey. Three fifty-one Bryant Court was a sunny little house with a small yard surrounded by a white picket fence, a great improvement over their previous residence.

Like the Kweskin band (and New York's Even Dozen Jug Band, featuring David Grisman), Mother McCree's took its repertoire from everywhere, it seemed: They lifted liberally from Jim Kweskin and company (colorful tunes like "Borneo," "Beedle Um Bum," "Washington at Valley Forge," "Overseas Stomp"); there was a dose of old-time string band tunes like "Cold Rain and Snow" and "Been All Around This World"; there were jug blues taken from Cannon's Jug Stompers ("Viola Lee Blues," "Big Railroad Blues") and the Memphis Jug Band ("Stealin'," "On the Road Again"); relatively modern folk blues, like Jesse Fuller's "Beat It On Down the Line" and "Monkey and the Engineer"; and Pigpen brought in his own repertoire of popular and obscure blues songs by Lightnin' Hopkins, Jimmy Reed, Howlin' Wolf and others.

Dave Parker estimates that Mother McCree's probably played twenty-five to thirty gigs over the course of seven or eight months. "There was no way we were anything even close to commercial," he says. "It was really just a good-time thing. It was a little eccentric even for what tastes were in folk music at the time. I don't think it was conceivable to any of us that it could be recorded and sold. But it sure was a lot of fun."

At the same time the jug band was going, Jerry and Pigpen were also playing occasionally in an electric blues/rock group called the Zodiacs, fronted by a guitarist named Troy Weidenheimer. "While Jerry was teaching folk guitar, Troy was teaching electric guitar; he was known around town," says Eric Thompson. "Troy had an R&B band that played Stanford frat parties and Jerry sometimes played bass in it and Pigpen was the singer. Troy could not only play exactly like Freddy King, he could move like Freddy King, too. During that period, Freddy had his blues song hits in the chitlin' circuit and his instrumental hits in the frat circuit, and he was playing both kinds of gigs. So that was part of the Troy niche, those instrumental hits Freddy King had— 'Hideaway,' 'San Hozay,' 'The Stumble.' The way white kids were relating to it it was like surf guitar in a way; instrumental music that you could dance to.

"When Jerry got interested in the electric guitar again, he devoured the Freddy King stuff, but he'd already been watching Troy do it, so he already knew a lot about it. The way Jerry was, every new wave of stuff that came along, he'd get really excited about it and just devour it. When he got excited about old-time music he learned lots of old-time songs and he did them with Sara and everything. When he got excited about bluegrass banjo he got all the tapes and dove into that. Same thing when he got back into rock 'n' roll. He'd get going on something and there'd by no way to stop him—he'd get other people excited along with him."

It's hard to believe that the same guy who'd driven across the country determined to become one of Bill Monroe's Blue Grass Boys all but gave up the banjo and bluegrass by year's end. Part of the problem, Jerry explained in 1981, was that "in the area I was in there were virtually no bluegrass musicians; very few, certainly nobody very good. I got to be quite a good banjo player, but I was really operating in a vacuum, and what I wanted was to have a great bluegrass band, but I only got occasional chances to put a bluegrass band together that was by my standards even acceptable. Although I had fun, none of them was serious or a very good attempt."

"I think he got disenchanted with bluegrass," Sara says. "It was clear he wasn't going to make it in that world. Socially, it was just too foreign. This was all these West Coast kids, some of them were Jewish, some of them had Hispanic surnames, and there was no way they were going to be part of the bluegrass establishment. It wasn't a good match socially."

But there was something else tugging at Garcia as 1964 turned to 1965. For one thing, like half of America under the age of twenty-five, Jerry had been seduced by the Beatles, especially their film *A Hard Day's Night*, which depicted life in a rock 'n' roll band as just about the most fun that could be had on planet Earth. The Beatles were deliciously irreverent and in-your-face anarchic; untamable gadabouts on an endless lark, always living in a completely different universe than the pitiably straight forces that were constantly trying to control, or at the very least, restrain them. Certainly the jug band had some of that off-the-wall spirit, but the Beatles were a whole different level of fun—that was obvious. And the screaming girls were *real*.

"[The Beatles] were real important to everybody," Garcia said. "They were a little model, especially the movies—the movies were a big turn-on. Just because it was a little model of good times. . . . It was like [they] were saying, 'You can be young, you can be far-out and you can still make it.' They were making people happy. That happy thing—that's the stuff that counts— was something we could all see right away."

"The Beatles were why we turned from a jug band into a rock 'n' roll band," said Bob Weir. "What we saw them doing was impossibly attractive. I couldn't think of anything else more worth doing."

But poking at Garcia's other shoulder, all gruff and grumbly but still the essence of a different kind of *cool*, was Mr. Pigpen McKernan: "He'd been pestering me for a while; he wanted me to start up an electric blues band," Jerry said. "That was his trip. Because in the jug band we used to do blues numbers like Jimmy Reed tunes and even played a couple of rock 'n' roll tunes, and it was just the next step. . . . Theoretically it's a blues band, but the minute we get electric instruments it's a rock 'n' roll band. Because, wow—playin' rock 'n' roll, it's *fun!*"

"It was always my impression that it was Jerry's decision to form the electric band," Dave Parker says. "That he was not that interested in playing the kinds of music he'd been doing before, and he'd *done* the jug band thing. That wasn't something you could really do for a long time, and the excitement of electric rock 'n' roll—what the Beatles and the Stones and Dylan were doing—was happening, and Jerry had this surge of energy to go and do that and make something happen.

"There was a feeling all around—and I think a lot of it came from Garcia— that anything was possible, so just pick out what you want to do and *do it*."

CHAPTER 4

I Can't Come Down,
I've Been Set Free

kay, Jerry's the lead guitarist; no question about that. Weir is certainly a good enough guitarist to take a stab at playing rhythm; after all, he's already beyond the sort of simple chords required in most rock and blues songs. Pigpen's been known to play some blues piano—get him an electric organ and you've got a double threat who can play keys and harmonica. Drums—that's a sticky one. Dave Parker says, "I had good enough rhythm to play something like the washboard, but I hadn't ever played drums, so when Jerry wanted to start an electric band, right at the first there was some thought maybe I could learn to play the drums—that's how funky it was! But Bill Kreutzmann was already a skilled drummer who'd played around a bit and taught, so he was a much better choice."

Ah yes, Bill the Drummer, as he was known for the *longest* time. Bill Kreutzmann was another Palo Alto product. His father was a small businessman and his mother was a choreographer who taught dance at Stanford. He started taking drum lessons when he was about twelve, and he got his first drum kit shortly after that. Though teachers and friends urged him to get involved with his high school band, "I wouldn't have anything to do with it," he said. "I went and heard the band one day and said, 'Are you kidding?!' It was just lame orchestra stuff, with nothing for the drummer to do." Instead he gravitated to rock 'n' roll, which he'd loved since he was a tyke listening to Elvis and Fats Domino. He was in a band called the Legends for a while, playing rock 'n' roll and R&B—"whatever was popular. It wasn't too soulful, though, and I think I was probably the most serious about music then; we were just teenagers."

While still in high school, Kreutzmann started hanging out at the Tangent, where he heard Mother McCree's on numerous occasions. "I went down there faithfully and listened to them all the time," he said. "I really got off on those guys; I really liked them a lot. My heart just said, 'This music is really cool.' " Bill also got a job at Dana Morgan's as a drum teacher, so he and Garcia were tight by the time the jug band was winding down and the dream of starting an electric band was coming to the fore.

For a bass player, the obvious, easy choice was Dana Morgan Jr., who already played electric bass, ran the music store his father had founded and also provided some of the equipment the band needed, as well as an after-hours rehearsal space. (The back room at Kepler's wasn't about to accommodate this noisy bunch.)

The fledgling band called themselves the Warlocks, an appropriately sinister name for such a motley-looking group. Pigpen was the closest thing the band had to a frontman, and he looked like some tough mutha who'd just roared up on a Harley. His acne-scarred face was nearly obscured by dark bangs and a mustache, and he dressed in black chinos, boots and either a jeans jacket or a leather vest. Garcia was letting his hair grow longer, and he too went for the Keith Richards/Bill Wyman look, with long bangs and hair down over his ears, though it wasn't quite to his shoulders yet. In fact, in look and feel there was definitely a parallel with the Rolling Stones, who were a strong early influence on the Warlocks, since they drew from many of the same musical sources—American blues, R&B and rock 'n' roll. Of course the Warlocks also dug every Beatles album that came out, but they couldn't really imitate the Fab Four. They didn't have the looks or the vocal chops, to put it mildly. More to the point, the Warlocks were more in tune with the rough-and-tumble vibe of the Stones or the Animals or even Van Morrison's band, Them.

And let's not forget that this group had metamorphosed from the jug band. A lot of the songs the Warlocks played came straight from the Mother McCree's repertoire, which meant that even in the group's nascent days it was stunningly eclectic and quite a bit different from most of the other electric groups on the scene. Yes, there were other bands around that played "Smokestack Lightning" and "Johnny B. Goode" and "It's All Over Now," but they weren't playing "Stealin' " and "Overseas Stomp" (also called "Lindy"), "I Know You Rider" and "Viola Lee Blues." And they didn't have the same reckless abandon that nearly everyone who heard the Warlocks could sense immediately. "We were always motivated by the possibility that we could have fun, *big fun*," Garcia said. "I was reacting, in a way, to my bluegrass background, which was maybe a little overserious. I was up for the idea of breaking out. You know: 'Give me that electric guitar—*fuckin' A!*' "

In retrospect, it's remarkable that the Warlocks were able to survive their first few months together, because what they offered musically wasn't what most kids going to clubs and dances were looking for in a rock 'n' roll band in early 1965. There was no Bay Area "scene" yet, and most of the local rock bands that enjoyed any kind of commercial success were so heavily influenced by the British Invasion bands in look and sound that no one took them too seriously. The San Francisco group the Beau Brummels and the Peninsula's own Vejtables rode the wave with enough panache to actually score regional hits on Autumn Records, the label run by the popular KYA disc jockeys Tom "Big Daddy" Donahue and Bobby Mitchell. But it was clear that most of these bands, in their imitation Brit threads or worse—hideous "theme" outfits (picture, if you dare, groups that looked like low-rent versions of Paul Revere and the Raiders)—were never going to get beyond the local CYO dance. There are still a few souls out there who speak with some fondness of groups like the Baytovens (a Beatles rip), William Penn and His Pals (with Gregg Rolie of Santana and Journey fame), the Syndicate of Sound and the Mojo Men, but by and large the bands were patently unoriginal, and none of them survived very long.

For one thing, there weren't many places to play. High school and YMCA dances were the big time for most groups. Some of the lucky ones got to play on the college fraternity circuit, but it was rare that bands played much outside their immediate area. In other words, Peninsula and South Bay (San Jose) groups usually worked that territory almost exclusively; same with San Francisco and East Bay bands. The *really* popular groups might get to play a couple of songs at one of KYA's multiact extravaganzas at the Cow Palace, on the same bill with national headliners like the Righteous Brothers, Sonny and Cher and Phil Spector's various aggregations (who themselves would play only a handful songs at the most). And then, of course, there were a million smaller "Battle of the Bands" shows all over the Bay Area, as Eric Burdon clones went up against George Harrison imitators and Gerry and the Pacemakers wanna-bes for *that night's* and *that club's* embarrassingly small cash prize (and the attendant bragging rights). Mike Shapiro, lead guitarist for William Penn and His Pals, said that "We used to battle-of-the-bands with [the Warlocks] at the Cinnamon Tree on Industrial Road in San Carlos. We actually lost to them and I thought they were the shits."

By conventional standards, the Warlocks likely *were* "the shits." There were probably fifty local bands who could play Kinks and Beatles covers more faithfully, who could nail the drum and bass parts off the first couple of Stones records *exactly*, who could hit the high notes of those tight British Invasion harmonies with ease. Fortunately for the Warlocks, right from the start they attracted a decent-sized following of like-minded dropouts, crazies and adventurous party animals who didn't care for note-for-note reproductions of 45s that were on the radio and weren't interested in lead singers wearing ruffled Edwardian shirts, but who wanted something a little rawer and more *real*. Many of the people who had supported the jug band also followed Garcia, Weir and Pigpen when they started playing electric music.

One of the group's original fans, Sue Swanson, remembers early Warlocks rehearsals at Dana Morgan's where the group would listen to records and try to learn songs. "My job was to change the 45s," she said. " 'Play that part again!' It was a crummy little phonograph that would sit on the counter. I'll never forget the sound of them practicing in there, and all the cymbals and everything in the whole room would be going. The *whole room* would be making all this noise."

It was mainly a big contingent of Peninsula friends and a few curious onlookers who made the scene at Magoo's Pizza Parlor on Santa Cruz Avenue in

Menlo Park, where the group played some of its first gigs in May of 1965. Pigpen and pizza: what a combination! It's hard to say whether Magoo's was a step up or a step down from local haunts like the Continental Roller Bowl in Santa Clara or Big Al's Gas House in Redwood City, but at least it was a place to play, and the fans turned out in force. "When we were in the Warlocks," Garcia said, "the first time we played in public [at Menlo College], we had a huge crowd of people from the local high school, and they went fuckin' *nuts!* The next time we played it was packed to the rafters. It was a pizza place. We said, 'Hey, can we play in here on Wednesday night? We won't bother anybody. Just let us set up in the corner.' It was *pandemonium,* immediately."

During this time, Jerry and Sara were living in the cottage on Bryant Court with baby Heather, now a year old, and trying to keep the marriage together despite Jerry's overriding obsession with his music and his apparent lack of interest in being a family man. "Before Heather's first birthday, sometime that fall, my mom said, 'Why don't you guys go away together?' " Sara says. "She was worried about us because clearly we weren't spending much time together. 'I'll take Heather,' she said. So we drove down to Disneyland and just *played.*"

There were a few changes in the inner circle of friends. David Nelson returned from his Scientology training in L.A. as the new guitarist of a fine, already established bluegrass band called the Pine Valley Boys, which included an L.A. fiddler named Richard Greene and two hot Bay Area pickers, banjoist Herb Pederson and mandolinist Butch Waller. Nelson says he had intended to return to L.A. for more Scientology courses, "but we got more and more gigs with the Pine Valley Boys. Then one day I was in Palo Alto seeing Dave Parker and we were talking and he brought out a joint. He said, 'You're going to tell me you're taking Scientology over *this?*' And I said, 'Uh, *no!*' " he laughs. Willy Legate and Robert Hunter stayed with Scientology a little longer before arriving at the same decision.

And then along came LSD. "One time Rick Shubb got some," relates David Nelson. Rick Shubb was from the Berkeley bluegrass world, a friend of the Redwood Canyon Ramblers and a talented banjo player himself. "It coincided with Rick needing a house, and Dave Parker and I needed a house, too. He found this place on Gilman Street [in downtown Palo Alto], right across from this piano store. We got the rent money together and Rick said, 'I've also got some LSD.' We thought, 'Great, we'll take it on the day we move in.'

"So we all go down there—me, Rick, Butch Waller, Dave Parker, Bonnie [Guckel, later Bonnie Parker, Dave's wife], Garcia, Sara and Eric Thompson. We were all taking it for the first time. We'd seen that book *The Psychedelic Experience,* which gives you information like, 'You might want to be by yourself for a while.' So we all started out alone and then we came together slowly. 'Hey, you look different.' 'Yeah, everything is in Technicolor.' And all of a sudden we were just this house full of insane kids giggling and saying, 'Hey, man, *look at this!'* 'Wow, man. . . ." We had a superball inside that we were playing with, and later we played basketball outside. That was a great day. I think we listened to Ravi Shankar. I thought that was appropriate.

Sara says, "I remember after the evening was over and Jerry and I went home, we freaked out badly; the two of us. It was another one of those 'Oh my God, what are we gonna do?' situations, just like when we got married and when Heather was a newborn. We drove over to Hunter's house, not realizing that we were capable of doing *something* if we could drive and find our way. But we were absolutely freaked out. We beat down the door, woke up Hunter and said, 'We're scared. We don't know what's happening. We don't know what to do.' We went to him because he had *The Tibetan Book of the Dead,* so clearly he could help us. So he kind of pontificated and after maybe consulting the book, he said, 'It's okay.' 'But you don't understand—' 'It's *okay!'* He just cut through the freak-out and we were so relieved. 'Of course it's okay! Thanks, man. Sorry we woke you up!' "

"The world was really innocent then," Garcia commented. "Or at least innocent of those experiences. So you could go around and be completely crazy, and the most people would suspect you of was being crazy. They didn't think it was *drrrrugs!* I was glad to be in on that. That was a remarkably lucky moment historically; that was fun."

Explaining psychedelics to someone who has never taken them is nearly impossible; it's as difficult as it is to use words to describe a piece of music so a person can "hear" it. Descriptions of acid trips, in particular, invariably just sound scary and weird, to the point where the uninitiated undoubtedly wonder why *anyone* would put themselves through such an unpredictable and potentially frightening experience. There are as many answers to that as there are people who have tried psychedelics—and at this point that would have to be millions of people worldwide. Some are seeking some sort of spiritual fulfillment or enlightenment, some are intent on exploring unseen corners of their own minds, and some are just thrill-seekers out for what they hope will be a good time.

Various natural psychedelics—peyote, psilocybin mushrooms, ayahuasca, morning glory seeds and others—have been used for more than ten thousand years by different peoples and tribes, mainly for religious purposes. "This particular chemical family has always been a key to a spiritual dimension or a parapsychological dimension," says Steve Silberman, a Grateful Dead scholar and veteran psychedelician. "You don't have to even speculate about *whether* there is a God out there; its obvious from accumulated cultural evidence that these chemicals are a key to the experience of the sacred."

The use of psychedelics in Western culture was rare until the mid–twentieth century, when knowledge of the revelatory properties of psylocibin mushrooms, peyote and LSD (which was synthesized by the Swiss chemist Albert Hoffman in the late '30s) began to spread among the ranks of researchers and intellectuals. The British writer Aldous Huxley wrote glowingly of his transformative experiences with psychedelics in the widely read books *The Doors of Perception* and *Between Heaven and Hell*. Henry Luce, founder of *Time* and *Life* magazines, took LSD a number of times, and in May 1957 he personally approved a seventeen-page *Life* story by the American ethnomycologist R. Gordon Wasson about his ecstatic experiences in Mexico with "magic mushrooms." That article, in part, inspired Timothy Leary, a young clinical psychologist and lecturer at Harvard, to make his own journey of psychedelic discovery to Mexico, and later to use psyilocibin as a psychiatric tool. Not surprisingly, psychedelics spread into the Beat world, too. Through Leary, Allen Ginsberg obtained a large quantity of psilocybin, which he distributed to various Greenwich Village poets, artists and jazz musicians.

Most of the people in Garcia's crowd had already read writings on psychedelics by Huxley, Leary and philosopher Alan Watts, so they were tuned into the spiritual possibilities of the experience. Perhaps what they didn't expect, however, was that psychedelics would provide hours and hours of funnyscary goofball *fun*.

Garcia said, "That first trip . . . we just wandered 'round and 'round the streets bumping into each other and having these incredible revelations and flashes. It was just dynamite; it was just everything I could hope for it to be for me.

"It was like another release, yet another opening. The first one was that hip teacher when I was in the third grade; and the next one was marijuana and the next one was music and the next one was—it was like a series of continually opening doors."

In May 1965 Phil Lesh reenters our story. He was living in the Haight-Ashbury section of San Francisco with Tom Constanten (T.C.), and working for the post office as a driver—shooting speed and driving aggressively through downtown rush-hour traffic, blasting a little transistor radio he smuggled onto his truck, digging Bob Dylan, the Beatles, the Stones, the Lovin' Spoonful and all the other hip groups that were suddenly transforming AM radio and a lot of the people who were tuned in to it. This was a relatively new world for Lesh, who, after his unhappy tenure in Berkeley's music program in 1962, had studied at Mills College in Oakland with the eminent modern composer Luciano Berio, then drifted to Las Vegas (T.C.'s hometown), where he took odd jobs and spent his days composing. From Las Vegas, Phil moved to Palo Alto, and then to San Francisco, where he began his wild ride as a driver for the post office. Phil's career as a postal worker came to an abrupt halt one afternoon after his superior complained that the haircut he'd forced Phil to get wasn't short enough. "I said, 'Fuck you,' and I quit," Phil said. "And the rest of that spring I spent letting my hair grow and taking acid and fuckin' off, having fun, and being supported by my girlfriend."

Then, "somebody came in with the word that Garcia's band was playing such-and-such a night at Magoo's Pizza Parlor," Phil said. A week earlier, in what he called "a stoned moment" at a party in Palo Alto, he'd told Garcia that he'd been thinking of taking up an electric instrument, possibly the bass. He and a few friends dropped acid and bopped down to Magoo's to check out the Warlocks, and "During the set break, Jerry took me off to a table and said, 'How'd you like to play bass in this band? Our bass player's not a musician and we have to tell him what notes to play.' I said, 'By God, I'll give it a try.' " Phil had been duly impressed by what he heard at Magoo's that night: "It was really happening. Pigpen ate my mind with the harp, singing the blues. They wouldn't let you dance but I did anyway."

Around the first week of June, Phil moved down to Palo Alto to devote himself full time to the Warlocks. At first he borrowed an instrument; then his girlfriend, Ruth, bought him his first electric bass—"a single-pickup Gibson with a neck like a telephone pole," he said—and he picked up pointers on the rudiments of the instrument from whoever was around: Garcia, a young folk picker named John Dawson (who would later form the New Riders of the Purple Sage), David Nelson, Eric Thompson. "I remember exactly when it was clear that Dana Jr. was not exactly with the program on bass," says Eric Thompson. "Jerry said, 'We're gonna get Phil.' Phil moved to the room across from me in this house and he'd never touched an electric bass before. I remember him picking up the bass for the first time and saying, 'Oh, how does this work?' and he started figuring out how to play scales on it immediately, very methodically."

One of the things that made Phil such an interesting player from the start is that he didn't have any preconceived notions about what the bass's role in rock music should be. This is not someone who had studied James Jamerson's solid, steady bass work on Motown singles, or Bill Wyman's thick grooves with the Stones. Nor had he spent time investigating the more inventive rock bass players of the era, like Paul McCartney, whose melodic approach made the instrument sing in ways it never had before, and the Who's redoubtable thunder machine, John Entwistle. What Phil *had* heard, and no doubt subconsciously absorbed, were some of the great acoustic bassists in jazz—Charles Mingus, Scott La Faro, Jimmy Garrison, Ron Carter and others—who succeeded in moving the bass beyond a mainly rhythmic supporting role into complex and sophisticated new realms that more fully exploited the instrument's broad range of sonorities. Even so, Phil said in 1990, "I don't study other bassists, and I don't think I've really drawn much from them. In my own style of playing, I've been influenced more by Bach than any bassists. Actually, you can go back even further—Palestrina, sixteenth-century modal counterpoint." That's all well and good, but at the beginning Lesh had to work his way through some of the basic blues-based progressions just like anyone else, if only to understand them well enough to be able to discard them with confidence on his way to finding something more interesting and challenging.

Garcia and Weir would have to have been considered novices on their instruments, too. Weir had never played electric guitar before, and Garcia hadn't played it since he moved to the Peninsula at the end of 1960, more than four years earlier. And in between his stints playing electric, Garcia had ventured far afield from the chugga-chugga simplicity of his Chuck Berry days into various acoustic country and blues fingerpicking styles, and then on to banjo, with an evolution from frailing to Scruggs-style, with a daring dash of Bill Keith thrown in there at the end. The Warlocks' eclectic mélange was a new world for Garcia, as was his axe, a red Guild Starfire. He said that in his early days with the Warlocks he listened extensively to Freddy King and B. B. King, and indeed, those influences can easily be heard in his playing from 1965 through the middle of 1967. But the country and bluegrass influences were also present in his electric work.

"I put my first real energy in music into the five-string banjo," Garcia said. "That was the first time I ever said, 'How do you do this?' It was like cracking a combination lock. I slowed the records down and painstakingly listened to every lick and worked them out. I did a complete breakdown—as close as I was able—to learn how to play bluegrass banjo. And having gone through that process with banjo, when I went to electric guitar I knew how to learn it. And my taste in music is kind of informed by the banjo in a way, too. I like to hear every note. I like that clarity and separation of notes. And that characterizes my guitar playing, too. So I came at it sort of backwards."

On the other hand, Garcia noted, "For me, just going and playing the electric guitar represented freedom from the tremendous control trip that you have to have to be a banjo player.

"I'd put so much energy and brainwork into controlling the banjo that, after psychedelics, what I wanted to do more than anything was not be in control nearly so much. And playing the electric guitar freed me! So for me, it was a combination of the times, a lucky moment, and it was much easier putting together a rock 'n' roll band or an electric band than having a bluegrass band."

Garcia didn't completely turn his back on bluegrass when he started playing electric music. He'd occasionally do some acoustic pickin' around Gilman Street with David Nelson and the other members of the Pine Valley Boys, and on a couple of occasions in 1965 he traveled down to the Ash Grove in Los Angeles to see his friends the Kentucky Colonels. During 1965 the Colonels added fiddler Scott Stoneman, the troubled black sheep of the famous Stoneman Family of country musicians (whose lineage stretched all the way back to the '20s), and this player made a lasting impression on Garcia:

"I get my improvisational approach from Scotty Stoneman, the fiddle player. [He's] the guy who first set me on fire—where I just stood there and don't remember breathing. He was just an incredible fiddler. He was a total alcoholic wreck by the time I heard him, in his early thirties, playing with the Kentucky Colonels. . . . They did a medium-tempo fiddle tune like 'Eighth of January' and it's going along, and pretty soon Scotty starts taking these longer and longer phrases—ten bars, fourteen bars, seventeen bars—and the guys in the band are just watching him! They're barely playing—going *ding, ding, ding*—while he's burning. The place was transfixed. They played this tune for like twenty minutes, which is unheard of in bluegrass. I'd never heard anything like it. I asked him later, 'How do you do that?' and he said, 'Man, I just play lonesome.' "

Garcia definitely saw the connection between what the Warlocks were playing and his former life as a bluegrass picker: "It's a string band fundamentally, even though it's electric. And the addition of drums made it more like bluegrass, which is a more intensely rhythmic kind of music. I viewed the Grateful Dead from the beginning, or the Warlocks, as a blues band in one sense, in other words the instrumentation is traditionally what a blues band has had. But it's also a kind of mutated bluegrass band on a certain level. Bluegrass is a nice metaphor for how music can work as a group. Bluegrass is a conversational music and I thought it would be nice to have an electric band that was conversational—where the instruments talked to each other. It's a way to organize music."

The coup that ousted Dana Morgan Jr. from the Warlocks and installed Phil Lesh as the new bassist signaled the end of the bandmembers' association with Dana Morgan Music, too, so the action shifted to another instrument store, Guitars Unlimited in Menlo Park. After the group was forced to return some of the equipment they'd borrowed from Dana Morgan's, Garcia's mother and Bill Kreutzmann's parents helped the group buy some new gear, and for a while Billy acted as their de facto manager, dealing with club bookers trying to get them gigs. Later, Phil's friend Hank Harrison did a brief stint as their manager. The Warlocks rehearsed wherever they could, including in the homes of various friends' parents. Garcia drove the band hard, insisting they practice nearly every day, even though gigs were scarce for a while.

All that changed in September when the Warlocks started playing regularly at the In Room, a lounge in a Belmont hotel that was trying to attract a younger crowd. Five nights a week, five sets a night for six weeks, the Warlocks held court at the In Room, getting weirder and louder, but also *better*, with each passing week. The crowds varied from night to night; not surprisingly the band drew best on weekends. Working in the same environment night after night gave them a chance to hone their chops and get to know each other's idiosyncrasies as players and performers. In essence, they learned to play their instruments together (though obviously the learning curve was higher for some than others), and that is one reason why the Warlocks, and later the Grateful Dead, played so well *together.* "When we first started work-ing," Garcia said, "we were really working hard. I never saw anybody. When we were working the bars, I lost contact with almost all my friends 'cause the Warlocks were playing every night, and on Sundays, afternoons *and* nights. We were booked solid."

In another interview Garcia said, "The only scene then was the Holly-wood hype scene, booking agents in flashy suits, gigs in booze clubs, six nights a week, five sets a night, doing all the R&B-rock standards. We did it all. Then we got a job at a Belmont club and developed a whole malicious thing, play-ing songs louder and weirder. . . . For those days it was loud, and for a bar it was ridiculous. People had to scream at each other to talk, and pretty soon we had driven out all the regular clientele. They'd run out clutching their ears. We isolated them, put them through a real number, yeah."

With the exception of Pigpen, who eschewed drugs in favor of his beloved screw-top wines, the Warlocks smoked pot whenever it was around—and by 1965 it was rolling up the coast in increasing quantities as more and more peo-ple discovered it. And they took LSD, which was still legal (though under-ground), with increasing regularity. At this point there was no regular, reliable source for the drug, but it was popping up simultaneously in San Francisco, Berkeley, the Peninsula and the South Bay, so obtaining it wasn't *that* diffi-cult. At the In Room, "we'd be sneaking out in the cars, smoking joints be-tween each set and so forth," Garcia recalled. "One of those days we took [acid]. We got high and goofed around in the mountains and ran around and did all kinds of stuff, and I remembered we had to work that night. We went to the gig and we were a little high, and it was all a little strange. It was so weird playing in a bar being high on acid. It was just too weird; it definitely wasn't appropriate."

Heads, in the drug sense of the word, were few and far between on the Peninsula in 1965—there weren't many beyond the Warlocks' scene and the crowd that had hung out around the Offstage club in San Jose. But not too far away, just up over Cahill Ridge, across Skyline Drive, down twisty Highway 84, and deep in a magical redwood-forested community midway between Palo Alto and the Pacific known as La Honda, something big was cookin'. The word came down through the jungle telegraph that there were strange doings at Ke-sey's place.

Ken Kesey was already a semilegendary figure by the time the Warlocks cruised over to La Honda for the first time in the fall of 1965. An Oregon na-tive who had attended the University of Oregon in Eugene and distinguished himself as a wrestler and drama student in the mid- and late '50s, Kesey and his wife, Faye, moved to Palo Alto in 1958 after the aspiring novelist won a Woodrow Wilson Fellowship and was admitted to the Stanford Writing Pro-gram, which was founded and spearheaded by novelist Wallace Stegner. Ken and Faye moved into a little cottage on Perry Lane, a bohemian enclave in

Menlo Park since the '20s, and fell in with a hard-partying intellectual crowd that included Ed McClanahan, Robert Stone, Larry McMurtry, Chloe Scott and Kesey's future Merry Pranksters partner Ken Babbs. Though a country boy at heart, Kesey became intoxicated by the Beat scene in San Francisco (and its ripples on the Peninsula)—so much so that he abandoned a novel he was writing about football and began a book called *Zoo*, which chronicled the adventures of a rodeo rider's son who moves to North Beach and becomes part of the Beat scene.

There were other intoxicants, too: Kesey was introduced to pot on Perry Lane, and like Robert Hunter a couple of years after him, he made the life-changing decision to volunteer for the government's tests of psychotomimetic drugs at the Veterans Hospital in Menlo Park. It's only in the past fifteen years that the truth about these experiments has been revealed—how the CIA wanted to study the effects of psychedelics on people, with a notion that perhaps drugs could be used against our enemies in some way: disorienting them, scaring them, perhaps making them tell us truths and secrets that conventional interrogation could not elicit. Kesey's and Hunter's descriptions of their test environments are fairly similar—the bright white rooms and dispassionate scientists who clearly had no handle on what was really going on *inside* their test subjects; whose periodic checks of Kesey's blood didn't tell them anything *real*; who never got an inkling of the completely indescribable profundity of the experiences they were routinely dispensing in pill and capsule form; who never once suspected that a guy like Kesey would be so moved by what he felt that he would take it upon himself to secrete away his own stash of these substances.

Peyote also made it to Perry Lane, direct from a place in Texas called Smith's Cactus Ranch. It was legal, too—it probably never occurred to government types that anyone other than Native Americans would have any use for the stuff. Kesey said that the first part of the book he was writing at night while he worked in the psychiatric ward at the Veterans Hospital, *One Flew Over the Cuckoo's Nest*, had emerged and crystallized while he was high on peyote. So it's not too surprising that the pivotal character in the book is an Indian, Chief Broom.

"It was a real tribal scene at Perry Lane," said novelist Robert Stone in Ken Babbs and Paul Perry's superb oral history of Kesey's world in the early and mid-'60s, *On the Bus*. "It was tribal in part because we were amusing ourselves with these experimental drugs. . . . We were young and thought we were just incredibly sophisticated and bohemian to be doing all this far-out stuff."

During the year that Alan Trist was in Palo Alto, "My parents had a Spanish house right there behind Perry Lane; in fact, the backyard of my house looked over into the backyard of Kesey's house, when he had his little cabin there. And Jerry often stayed over [with me]. We didn't know Kesey, but we were aware of him, because he already had a reputation as a writer and he had a little scene around him. So we were curious about that, and I remember being in my backyard and peering over the fence with Jerry and hearing a party going on there, so we went around—I can't remember if it was that night or another night—and we tried to gate-crash the party. So we did and we were unceremoniously thrown out. The person who connected our scene—what would be the Grateful Dead scene later on—to Kesey, was Page Browning, who was part of the Chateau scene."

Kesey finished *One Flew Over the Cuckoo's Nest* in the spring of 1961, and that summer he and Faye and their two kids moved back up to Oregon so Ken could do research for his next novel, *Sometimes a Great Notion*, a sprawling saga about a logging family. That autumn they returned to Perry Lane, and for the next year-plus Kesey worked diligently on his opus, while still finding lots of time for extracurricular partying, psychedelic and otherwise. The cottage on Perry Lane was razed by developers in June 1963 and was eventually replaced by more upscale housing. By the time the bulldozers arrived, though, Kesey had already found a cabin deep in the La Honda redwoods that was perfect for his needs. It offered the isolation he needed to complete his book, and it was a *great* party pad, if a bit off the beaten track from Menlo Park. Kesey hoped that the spirit of the old Perry Lane scene would somehow follow him over the mountain down to this magical, sylvan hideaway that looked like something out of Tolkien. But the vibe around Kesey was beginning to change—he had started to attract more friends who shared his interest in chemical exploration, and a sizable contingent of the Perry Lane crowd chose not to make the drive over the hill to La Honda once things started to get more psychedelic than literary.

Kesey was changing, too. By the time he completed *Sometimes a Great Notion* he had become somewhat disenchanted with the novel as an art form and was looking for new, less static media in which to express himself. Like everyone else in the hip culture of 1964, he was turned on by the Beatles and Dylan and innumerable filmmakers, artists, dancers and writers who seemed to be in the vanguard of some bold but undefinable new movement outside mainstream culture that was picking up steam with each passing month. Kesey talked about what he called the Neon Renaissance: "It's a need to find a new way to look at the world, an attempt to locate a better reality, now that the old reality is riddled with radioactive poison. I think a lot of people are working in a lot of different ways to locate this reality: Ornette Coleman in jazz, Ann Halprin in dance, the New Wave movies, Lenny Bruce in comedy, Wally Hedrick in art, Heller, Burroughs, Rechy, Günter Grass in writing and those thousands of others whose names would be meaningless, either because they haven't made *it* yet, or aren't working in a medium that has an *it* to make. But all these people are trying to find out what is happening, why and what can be done with it."

In the spring of 1964 Kesey decided to drive from California to New York with a few buddies to check out the New York World's Fair and attend a publication party for *Sometimes a Great Notion*. Originally, Kesey, his friend George Walker and a couple of others talked about throwing a mattress in the back of a panel truck and cruising across the heartland that way, but then the idea seemed to take on its own incredible momentum, and the result was the fabled psychedelic bus trip of song, story and a never-completed *cinema weirdité* film. Convinced that film was the new way he and his friends could make art that was more immediate, pliable, real and relevant, Kesey had invested a good chunk of his royalties from *Cuckoo's Nest* into buying film and audio recording equipment.

Ken Babbs, who had been part of the Stanford Writing Program, returned from a tour of duty as a chopper pilot in the quickly escalating Vietnam War and signed on with Kesey to go east for the great adventure. Babbs also helped find the mode of transport for the trip, a 1939 International Harvester school bus that Kesey bought for $1,500 and which he and his friends transformed into the perfect tourmobile for the dawn of the psychedelic age—complete with bunk beds, a kitchen, a cut-out rooftop perch, plenty of room for all the wires, speakers and odd equipment that were needed to make the movie, and a paint job (by everyone!) that mixed a million eye-popping colors, swirling patterns, mandalas, op-art geometrics and symbols of unknown origin and meaning, all slopped and glopped on with brushes, walked on with paint-covered feet, poured on in great rainbow streams and sometimes even meticulously labored over in the fashion of Michelangelo high on his scaffolding in the Sistine Chapel. And who was to say that pulsating green curlicue leaping from a field of crimson and midnight blue on the right front fender *wasn't* Adam's finger touching the hand of God? The destination sign on the front read FURTHUR, and on the back WEIRD LOAD.

By the time the bus pulled out of La Honda in mid-June for points south and east, the crew, dubbed the Merry Band of Pranksters (or Merry Pranksters for short), numbered fourteen and included a strange assortment of old and new friends, neighbors, relatives (Kesey's brother Chuck and Babbs's brother John) and, to share the driving duties with George Walker, none other than Neal Cassady, the fast-talking, larger-than-life hipster hero of Kerouac books—he was Dean Moriarty in *On the Road*, Cody Pomeray in *The Dharma Bums* and *Visions of Cody*—and Beat-era associate of Ginsberg and Burroughs. Everyone got a new name—Sir Speed Limit (Cassady), the Intrepid Traveler (Ken Babbs), Zonker (Steve Lambrecht), Gretchen Fetchin' (Paula Sundstun), etc. Almost nothing was planned: "In the bus trip we were working at being spontaneous," Ron Bevirt (aka Hassler) said in *On the Bus*. "And we were working at having fun. We were really having fun! And we were Pranksters." Added Ken Babbs: "We were astronauts of Inner Space, which is as big as outer space. As above, so below. We popped acid, flopped on the floor, hooked up tape recorders and rapped out whole novels. We got up on our feet and played musical instruments, acting out parts we made up on the spot. This wasn't a summer lark, but a legitimate literary endeavor of artistic merit, holding the promise of commercial success."

Mainly it was an acid-drenched coast-to-coast goofin' and freakin'—sort of a traveling dada circus; a rolling conceptual art piece that we now know was actually the signal flare for the great psychedelic bombardment of America that was to follow shortly in Furthur's Day-Glo wake. You have to give the Pranksters credit for chutzpah: their route to the World's Fair took them through the heart of the South at a time when racial tensions were at their absolute highest—civil rights workers were being murdered, their bodies dumped by the roadside, that horrible summer. It was mile after mile of cultural weirdness and potentially bad vibes, yet here was the bizarre-looking contraption just *swarming* with laughing, barely coherent young men and women, spilling out of the magic bus with cameras and musical instruments and God knows what else. They were greeted mainly by delighted, if puzzled, faces—"Gee, never had one of *those* come through here before"—and curious police patrol cars making damn sure the thing kept movin' right on through town.

Not surprisingly, the bus caused quite a sensation when it finally arrived in Manhattan. Even though New York is a city that takes weirdness in stride, no one had ever seen anything quite like this blur of bright colors clattering noisily through the midtown streets like some hyperkinetic vehicle from a '30s cartoon. The World's Fair, out in the Flushing Meadows section of Queens, was already good and strange, so the Pranksters weren't quite as conspicuous in that setting. Hell, they could have put the bus in there next to GM's Futurama or Buckminster Fuller's mammoth geodesic-domed U.S. Pavilion—which had spaceships outside and Warhol paintings inside—and attracted a line of sight-seers in no time.

The bus arrived back in La Honda near the end of August 1964 after a relatively quick and calm (by Pranksters standards) journey across the northern Midwest, the Canadian Rockies and down the Northwest coast. Cassady and Hassler had returned to California separately in advance of the bus, so the Pranksters' exploits were already infamous on the Peninsula by the time the bus rumbled, sputtered and gasped its way onto Kesey's property.

Before we get back to Garcia's story, we need to meet one more significant new character—Carolyn Adams, Jerry's future girlfriend and wife, who became an integral part of the Pranksters' scene almost immediately after the bus trip. "It was shortly after that that I ran into Neal Cassady and Bradley Hodgman at St. Michael's," she says. "They had just come back from the Prankster bus trip. They came up to my table and said, 'Do you want to go for a ride and smoke a joint?' and I said, 'Yeah!' I guess I was sort of the 'babe.'

"I knew who Neal was, of course. Plus he had all his clippings in his wallet! I was an attractive eighteen-year-old and he was a celebrity and I thought he was a weird old guy. Bradley had a Beatle haircut and had been a tennis star at Stanford who also liked speed, and I guess he ran into Neal on the speed circuit. I thought Bradley was really quite cute. Anyway, I decided these guys looked interesting and I went for a ride with them and the ride ended up at Kesey's and I was like, 'Oh my goodness, *look* at these people!' The bus was there in the trees. It was incredible. This beautiful place and the bus was just shimmering in the gloom. And here were all these weird people. I felt *instantly* at home with them. They'd just gotten back from New York and they were still very high on it, partly with exhaustion I think."

Carolyn had only been in Palo Alto about a year when Cassady swept her into the Pranksters' orbit. She had grown up in Poughkeepsie, New York, in the Hudson River valley, the daughter of an entymologist/botanist and a grade school teacher. She had two brothers, five and seven years older, who went to Swarthmore and Haverford out of high school. "They were golden, they could do no wrong; on the crew team, great grades," she says. "I came along and I did really well for a while, and then when I was about twelve or thirteen it all fell apart for me and I got into the heavy rebelling. I got suspended, which was rough for my parents because my mom was on the school board. I couldn't stand all that stiffness and regulation. There was just too much of it. I became a sort of class clown, as well, and pulled lots of stunts and was thrown out of high school a few weeks short of graduation."

She managed to collect her diploma by mail, and in the summer of 1963 Carolyn and the younger of her brothers drove to Palo Alto. "He was in the psychology program [at Stanford] with rooms full of monkeys; I thought it was the nastiest possible scene," she says. "So I got a job at Stanford. I immediately got hired by the organic chemistry department, making over $400 a month, which was really good back then. But all these organic chemistry guys were leching on me when I was on the graveyard shift, so it wasn't as cool as it sounds."

Unbeknownst to Carolyn when she took the chem job at Stanford, some of the scientists she worked with were involved in complex drug research: "They were working on psychedelic drugs and they never told me. What I did know is that when they would send this stuff down for analysis they would look at me really funny and tell me to be really, really careful with the samples. There was a lot of unspoken stuff going on that I had no clue about. I had no idea about consciousness-expanding drugs.

"Then this *Life* magazine article came out and it had Timothy Leary and Richard Alpert talking about seeing God, and I thought, 'Wow! I want to see God, too,' and I vowed that if any psychedelics came my way I'd try it."

So she did. "I tried one of the drugs, which turned out to be this leafy African drug called ibogaine. It changes your head and initiates you into the channel of the ancestors. I ended up passing out at my workstation, and when my boss came in at seven-thirty the next day, there I was."

A few weeks later Carolyn was fired, and shortly after that Cassady showed up. Her boyfriend in Palo Alto had already turned her on to pot, "but I took acid for the first time twenty-four hours after meeting the Pranksters. They were having their debriefing—they'd gotten back from New York and everyone had gone back to their houses to see how everything was, do the laundry and all that. It was a couple of weeks after the bus trip. And of course the debriefing was an excuse for a party, and I got high with them. I thought it was the greatest stuff in the world. My first dose was a really light dose—just enough to see the redwood needles start rearranging themselves in all sorts of intricate Celtic patterns."

Cassady gave Carolyn her Prankster name, Mountain Girl (to this day, most of her friends call her "M.G."), but it was with Kesey that she bonded immediately. "We had an instant rapport because I had read Sartre and Albee; I was a reader," she says. "In my family we read Shakespeare to each other; we had a literary tradition." Their relationship became physical soon after they met. "I was an interloper to Faye," Carolyn says. "It was very difficult for her and I was pretty unsympathetic, as young people will be. But I just adored her kids and I thought she had a marvelous family."

Over the next several months the scene at La Honda continued to grow "and more and more people started glomming onto it and showing up," Carolyn says. "Ken developed the idea of having these Saturday night parties, and that's what eventually led to the Acid Tests. It became just a huge social scene." The Pranksters had set up loudspeakers and colored spotlights in some of the trees on Kesey's property, and the house itself became a chaotic multimedia center, with music usually blasting at all hours, and M.G. and others working in fits and starts trying to edit the bus footage and audiotapes into a manageable feature film. There were forty-five hours of film to wade through, much of it poorly shot and as incoherent as one might imagine a film of people on LSD and/or amphetamines shot by cameramen high on those same substances would be.

It was only a matter of time before the Warlocks hooked up with Kesey and the Pranksters. In the fall of 1965 the Warlocks were experiencing a bit of an identity crisis. Not that they weren't getting along and playing music that *everyone* agreed was evolving to be more interesting, more far-out, every day. It's just that Phil, or someone, thought they saw a 45 in a record store one day by another group called the Warlocks—beaten to the punch!—though to this day no one has ever confirmed that the record or the other band even existed. Maybe it was a sign; at the very least it was an auspicious opportunity to come up with a moniker that had more weight, in the cosmic sense. "The Warlocks" was a little too Roger Corman B-movie—it was easy to imagine it as the title of a bad mid-'60s gore film. But it wasn't easy coming up with a new name. The group bandied about a thousand possible names—serious, funny, surrealistic tags that didn't quite resonate for one reason or another. When they drove up to San Francisco on November 3 to record their first demo tape at Golden State Studios, they went under an interim name, the Emergency Crew; not bad, but not really *them* either.

That tape, often bootlegged through the years, is the only surviving musical artifact of the band's pre–Grateful Dead period, and it barely hints at the group's power as a live act (a problem that would dog the Dead for the rest of their album-making days). In 1964 and '65, Golden State Studios was the place where up-and-coming bands recorded demos and albums for Autumn Records, the label owned by Tom Donahue and Bobby Mitchell. The studio was geared to cranking out tapes quickly and cheaply, and Sylvester Stewart, later famous as Sly Stone, was a house producer, known then for being somewhat autocratic and more than a little crazed. John Haeny generally engineered the sessions.

The Emergency Crew cut six songs that afternoon, four originals and two cover tunes. Garcia sang lead on only one song, "Can't Come Down," a Dylan-inspired number (shades of "It's Alright Ma") in which Jerry sings/raps verses such as the following: "They say I've begun to lose my grip / My hold on reality is startin' to slip / They tell me to get off this trip / They say that it's like a sinking ship / Life's sweet wine's too warm to sip / And if I drink I'll surely flip / So I just say as I take a dip: I can't come down / It's plain to see / I can't come down / I've been set free / Who you are and what you do don't make no difference to me." It ain't Dylan, or Robert Hunter for that matter, but at least it's an attempt to put into words some of the feelings and attitudes of the early psychedelic age. And the music isn't bad, either: Pigpen blows harp with zest and power all through the tune, Billy drives the track with his sure, steady beat and Garcia gets in a nice speedy guitar run as the song fades at the three-minute mark.

"Mindbender" (also known as "Confusion's Prince") is dominated by a guitar riff that sounds as if it were lifted off Johnny Rivers's "Secret Agent Man," and the group's vocal weaknesses are clearly brought to the fore—Phil and Bob's tandem lead vocal is anemic and slightly off-pitch, and the harmonies are ragged, to put it charitably. Instrumentally, Pigpen's piercing Vox Continental organ predominates, though Garcia also gets in a fine solo. The next track, "The Only Time Is Now," with Phil's vocal again highest in the mix, has an unmistakable Byrds quality to it, complete with heavy vibrato on Garcia's guitar and stacked harmonies that the Emergency Crew couldn't pull off if their lives depended on it.

The remaining three songs each showed a different side of the group (which, of course, is usually the point of a demo tape). "I Know You Rider" was from the folk and blues world; it was an electrified holdover from the days of Mother McCree's Uptown Jug Champions. "Early Morning Rain," written by Gordon Lightfoot, was arranged by the group as a mild slice of folk-rock, which was all the rage then. But the song where the band really cut loose was "Caution," a locomotive blues jam that Bob Weir said had been inspired by Them's "Mystic Eyes." The interweaving of Phil's relentless, propulsive bass line, Weir's slashing rhythm guitar attack and Garcia's wiry lead offers a glimpse of what was ahead; alas, it fades abruptly at just over three minutes. Live, it was one of the songs that the band stretched out on a bit.

It was sometime in November 1965, while the band and a few friends were sitting around Phil's apartment on High Street in Palo Alto, smoking DMT and thumbing through a gargantuan Funk and Wagnalls dictionary, that the group's name was *revealed* (cue biblical trumpets!). As Jerry said in his oft-quoted 1969 description of the episode, "There was 'grateful dead,' those words juxtaposed. It was one of those moments, y'know, like everything else on the page went blank, diffuse, just sort of *oozed* away, and there was *grateful dead*. Big black letters edged all around in gold, man, blasting out at me, such a stunning combination. So I said, 'How about Grateful Dead?' and that was it." Later, he noted, "Nobody in the band liked it. I didn't like it, either, but it got around that that was one of the candidates for our new name and everyone else said, 'Yeah, that's great.' It turned out to be tremendously lucky. It's just repellent enough to filter curious onlookers and just quirky enough that parents don't like it," he added with a laugh.

Perhaps the most common misconception about the name is that it derives from *The Egyptian Book of the Dead*. In fact it comes from a folktale that is found in many cultures dating back hundreds of years. As that Funk and Wagnalls dictionary defined the term, it is "a motif of a cycle of folk tales which begin with the hero's coming upon a group of people ill-treating or refusing to bury the corpse of a man who died without paying his debts. He gives his last penny, either to pay the man's debts or to give him a decent burial. Within a few hours he meets with a traveling companion who aids him in some impossible task, gets him a fortune, saves his life, etc. The story ends with the companion disclosing himself as the man whose corpse the other had befriended."

Garcia stumbled upon the name during a period when the band wasn't playing many gigs, but they still rehearsed regularly to keep their chops up and try to develop new material. Garcia admitted that the grind of playing five sets a night, six days a week eventually became stultifying: "We just did it and did it and *did it*. And we got good doing it. It was a great way to get good. And we were young enough to love it. And we made enough so we could quit our day jobs. That happened immediately; that was the first thing that happened with us. But we were already burning out on the professional level that was available to us about the time the Acid Test came to our attention."

CHAPTER 5
Can YOU Pass the Acid Test?

o one seems to know exactly when Garcia and the others first connected with Kesey and the Pranksters. Garcia and a couple of other members of the group were definitely at the party that is usually considered the first Acid Test, held in late November at Babbs's spread near Santa Cruz. Neal Cassady and Allen Ginsberg were there, as were all the Pranksters who were around, and even a few curious thrill-seekers who responded to a little sign Hassler had put up in the Santa Cruz bookstore he ran: CAN YOU PASS THE ACID TEST? The evening was fun and profound enough that by the end of the night, as Prankster Lee Quarnstrom put it, "It was like a Mickey Rooney movie where we suddenly said, 'Hey, I know—we can put on a show!' "

"Before there were Acid Tests," Garcia said, "there were parties, and we got invited to one of these parties and we went down and plugged all our stuff in and played for about *a minute.* Then we all freaked out. But we made a good impression on everybody in that minute, so we were invited to the next one. So we just started playing at these things and they were great fun. . . . We were ready for something completely free-form. It kind of went along with where we were going, which is we were experimenting with psychedelics, as much as we were playing music."

The next Acid Test took place in the wee hours of December 4, 1965, after the Rolling Stones had played a show at the San Francisco Civic Auditorium, with the Dead and Kesey's gang in attendance. The Pranksters had unsuccessfully tried to rent a hall in San Jose for a party, so in the end Kesey called a bohemian acquaintance in that city known as Big Nig and talked him into hosting the postshow gala. As the Stones concert ended, the Pranksters swung into action, handing out "Can YOU Pass the Acid Test?" handbills to the masses filing out of the auditorium, then hopping onto the bus and hustling down to San Jose. Tom Wolfe's description of the evening in his funny, hip and hallucinatory 1968 book *The Electric Kool-Aid Acid Test* gives some of the wild flavor of these early acid parties:

"They come piling into Big Nig's, and suddenly acid and the worldcraze were everywhere, the electric organ vibrating through every belly in the place, kids dancing not *rock* dances, not the frug and the—what?—*swim,* mother, but dancing *ecstasy,* leaping, dervishing, throwing their hands over their heads like Daddy Grace's own stroked-out inner courtiers—yes!—Roy Seburn's lights washing past every head, Cassady rapping, Paul Foster handing people weird little things out of his Eccentric Bag, old whistles, tin crickets, burnt keys, spectral plastic handles. Everybody's eyes turn on like lightbulbs, fuses blow, blackness—wowwww!—the things that shake and vibrate and funnel freak out in this blackness—and then somebody slaps new fuses in and the old hulk of a house shutters back, the wiring writhing and fragmenting like molting snakes, the organs vibro-massage the belly again, fuses blow, minds scream, heads explode, neighbors call the cops, 200, 300, 400 people from out there drawn into The Movie, into the edge of the pudding at least, a mass closer and higher than any mass in history, it seems most surely . . ."

On December 10 the Grateful Dead played its first show under the new name in San Francisco at the Fillmore Auditorium, a black-run nightspot that had hosted countless great R&B shows through the years. The occasion was a benefit for the radical performance group the San Francisco Mime Troupe, who had been seriously harassed by San Francisco police for performing their politically charged musical plays without the requisite permits from the disapproving city government. The Mime Troupe's business manager was Bill Graham, a brash New Yorker who once had acting aspirations of his own but who now brought the full force of his excitable personality to keeping the Mime Troupe solvent, defending them against the hostile powers that be and getting them lots of publicity however he could. Though not particularly a rock 'n' roll fan (he preferred Latin music and jazz), Graham was savvy enough to see the potential for making money to defray the Mime Troupe's mounting legal costs by putting on benefit concerts for the group using local bands as his drawing card. The first Mime Troupe benefit, on November 6, featured the Jefferson Airplane (who sometimes rehearsed in the Mime Troupe's loft), eclectic guitar virtuoso Sandy Bull and New York gutter-rockers the Fugs. At the December 10 Mime Troupe benefit, the Dead (whom Graham billed as "The Grateful Dead [Formerly The Warlocks]" because he was so uncomfortable with the name) shared the bill with some of the best young rock bands in the city, including the Jefferson Airplane, the Great Society and the Mystery Trend, as well as local jazz saxophonist John Handy.

While the Warlocks had been playing bars and getting deeper into acid on the Peninsula, an even bigger psychedelic scene was developing in San Francisco. A group called the Charlatans, conceived and led by an artistic San Francisco State student named George Hunter, spent much of the summer of 1965 in the arid hills of Virginia City, Nevada, near Reno, taking acid, strutting around town with their friends in Victorian finery they'd picked up in San Francisco thrift stores, taking target practice in the surrounding hills and playing their rough-hewn rock 'n' roll music in a Western bar called the Red Dog Saloon, which was built in a gambling hall that dated back to the 1860s. Word quickly got around San Francisco that there were high times to be had at the Red Dog, and for a while there was a small but steady stream of visitors from the city making the pilgrimage to Virginia City. Kesey and the Merry Pranksters even stopped by the Red Dog near summer's end, but their timing was off: one of the Charlatans had been busted back in the Bay Area, the police had traced his connection to what was going on in Virginia City and the scene was forced to disperse.

That fall, some of the folks who'd been part of the Red Dog summer and who were living together in a commune called the Dog House (in honor of various mutts who'd lived there) on Pine Street in San Francisco decided to seize upon the energy of the Virginia City romp and put on a dance with the Charlatans at Longshoremen's Hall in San Francisco, a big, funky space near Fisherman's Wharf that was often used for more conventional teen and young-adult dances. The first "Family Dog" dance concert, October 16, 1965, was billed as "A Tribute to Dr. Strange," after the Marvel Comics hero. Also playing that night were the Jefferson Airplane, who had begun to create a stir through their appearances at a San Francisco club called the Matrix, and the Great Society, with Grace and Darby Slick. The Warlocks had a connection to the Airplane before they ever shared a bill with them: guitarists Jorma Kaukonen and Paul Kantner had both been folkies in the South Bay during Garcia's bluegrass days.

The Family Dog's second dance, "A Tribute to Sparkle Plenty," was held the following weekend, with an even bigger turnout, mostly because word of mouth on the first event had been so positive. This time the headliner was the Lovin' Spoonful, the popular New York folk-rock group then riding high with their smash hit "Do You Believe in Magic," fresh from a sold-out week at the San Francisco music and comedy club the hungry i.

"The first time that music and LSD interacted in a way that really came to life for us as a band," Garcia said, "was one day when we got extremely high on some of that early dynamite LSD and we went that night to the Lovin' Spoonful. . . . That day, the Grateful Dead guys—our scene—went out, took acid and came up to Marin County and hung out somewhere around Fairfax or Lagunitas or one of those places up in the woods, and just went crazy. We ended up going into that rock 'n' roll dance and it was just really fine to see that whole scene—where there was nobody there but heads and this strange rock 'n' roll music playing in this weird building. It was just what we wanted to see. . . . We began to see that vision of a truly fantastic thing. It became clear to us that working in bars was not going to be right for us to be able to expand into this new idea." It was that evening, too, that Phil Lesh uttered his famous remark to Ellen Harmon of the Family Dog: "Lady, what this little seance needs is *us.*"

The Family Dog dances were mainly that: *dances,* though they also featured primitive light shows—strobe lights were the perfect accompaniment for LSD because, like that drug, they seemed to fracture both light and time. And people increasingly used the dances as an excuse to dress up in odd thrift-store clothes—capes and long coats and feathered boas and strange hats direct from grandma and grandpa's musty attic trunk. The Acid Test, on the other hand, made no pretense of being a concert of any kind. Yes, the Grateful Dead was part of the package, but as Garcia put it, "We had no significance. We weren't famous. Nobody came to the Acid Test to see us, particularly. We got to play or not play, depending on how we felt. We could play anything we could think of, which meant we didn't have any constraints on our performance. We didn't have to be good, or recognizable even. We had an opportunity to visit highly experimental places under the influence of highly experimental chemicals before a highly experimental audience. It was ideal. And that was something we got to do long enough to get used to it.

"Everybody there was entertaining. Everything there was entertaining; every event that happened. And you didn't need expertise. The musician's chauvinism—'I can do something you can't do'—all that stuff went up in smoke, which I think was very good for everybody; everybody learned a lot from that process. I think everybody who ever went to an Acid Test came out a different person and loved it."

Everyone who attended paid a buck to get in—musicians and Pranksters included—and there were no rules; whatever happened is what happened.

The night after the Dead's Fillmore debut, the third Acid Test was held at a club in Palo Alto called the Big Beat. This was the first Acid Test where the Dead got to play on a real stage, but as usual they were just part of a larger, more amorphous event. The Pranksters always commanded as much attention as the Dead at these affairs, with their piles of sound equipment, Roy Seburn's light show and the unholy triumvirate of Kesey, Babbs and Cassady always moving in three equally weird but compelling directions at once, doing strange things with microphones—laying down a rap or playing ghastly tune-less harmonica or chanting nonsense or narrating the insane scene in the room, sometimes even while the Dead were playing. There were times when the Dead were too high to play; other times they'd hit monstrous fat grooves that had everyone in the place dancing deliriously. "Our trip with the Acid Test was to be able to play long and loud . . . as long and as loud as we wanted and nobody would stop us," Garcia said.

The following week the Acid Test moved out of the South Bay/Peninsula area for the first time. Originally it was scheduled for a public lodge at Stinson Beach, on the coast twenty-five perilous but scenic miles north of San Francisco on Highway 1, but that fell through at the last minute and instead it took place in the log lodge at Muir Beach, a few miles closer to San Francisco. Perhaps because it was nearer to the city and the San Francisco freaks had already gotten a glimpse of the Dead at the Mime Troupe benefit, the Muir Beach Acid Test drew a lot of new faces. (It probably would have attracted even more if untold numbers hadn't shown up at Stinson Beach instead; which brings to mind the most famous Prankster axiom: "Never trust a Prankster.")

Owsley Stanley, who was already legendary in underground circles for making high-quality LSD, was at Muir Beach that night seeing the Grateful Dead for the first time. He had met Kesey about a month earlier in La Honda, after friends had tipped him off about the acid parties in the redwoods, and before too long he became a primary supplier to that scene, though he continued to live in Berkeley.

Owsley, known to most then and now as "Bear," was an interesting fellow. He was a few years older than the guys in the band—he and Kesey were the same age—and like Kesey, he had grown up in a very straight world. He was the grandson and namesake of a U.S. senator from Kentucky (Augustus Owsley Stanley) and the son of a Washington, D.C., lawyer (A. O. S. Jr.). His misfit tendencies showed up fairly early—in junior high he was expelled from Charlotte Hall, a military prep school in southern Maryland, "for smuggling a lot of booze into the school and getting the whole campus intoxicated," he says. Later he went to public high school in Arlington, Virginia, "where I ate at the same table in the school cafeteria where Shirley MacLaine held court; she was a year ahead of me."

Although he ultimately dropped out of high school after the eleventh grade, he managed to get into the University of Virginia's School of Engineering, where he studied for just a year before quitting. In 1956 Owsley joined the air force and, on the basis of experience he'd gained working as a rocket test mechanic for Rocketdyne, was assigned to the Rocket Engine Test Facility at Edwards Air Force Base, east of Los Angeles. There, "I wound up teaching myself electronics, which I knew nothing about. I was reassigned to the salvage yard, and took apart every piece of gear that came in—and there was some pretty high-tech stuff at Edwards." He also took and passed the tests for the ham radio and First-Class Radiotelephone Operator's licenses.

When he landed a job at the Jet Propulsion Laboratory in Pasadena, Owsley was released from his military obligations. Later, he worked at various Southern California radio and TV stations, including a stint as chief engineer at an AM station in San Diego. Eventually, though, he went back to college, this time to UC Berkeley. He lasted only two semesters there, but he liked the city of Berkeley, which was filled with people who were, like him, intellectually voracious, stimulating to be around and definitely weirder than your average citizen. Then, as now, he was given to expounding at length, lucidly and enthusiastically, on a startlingly broad assortment of pet theories, which he held with absolute conviction, no matter how far away from the mainstream thinking on a given subject they were. In early 1964, Owsley "got turned on to the Beatles' first album and LSD in the same week," he recalls. "It was amazing. It all seemed to fit together. We had *Meet the Beatles* within a few days of it coming out. One of my friends who was a folkie brought it in and said, 'Man, you gotta listen to this!' And I was off and running on it. I loved it."

But not quite as much as he loved LSD. Acid had a deep and profound effect on Owsley—so much so that with the help of his girlfriend, Melissa Cargill, a Berkeley chemistry grad student, he set up his own lab in the bathroom of his house to make the stuff, and in short order became renowned for the superior quality of his potion. Which is what led him to Kesey in the fall of 1965 and brought him that night to the lodge at Muir Beach.

There was a lot of weird energy in the air that night at Muir Beach. Owsley, for one, was overwhelmed by the totality of the experience—by what he saw as an almost maniacal edge to the Pranksters' mind-warping assault, and by the sheer power of the Grateful Dead: "I'd never heard anything like it," he says. "It was a little bit scary. Garcia was sort of frightening with that cosmic electric intensity he had back then. I remember at some point that night thinking, 'This band is going to be bigger than the Beatles.' That was my thought as I listened to this incredible cosmic shit they were playing. Of course I was out of my gourd that night. . . . But that was my thought, and I think on some level they proved me correct."

Mountain Girl, who was a few months pregnant with Kesey's child, remembers, "That was a strange night. The poor band couldn't get anything going. I know Pigpen got dosed and he was very unhappy about it. The lighting was bad in there and the band would go up and play for about five minutes and then they'd sit down; that was all they could do. 'C'mon guys! Why aren't you playing?' 'I dunno. Why do we have to play?' It was pretty funny. So then the Pranksters would play and that was perfectly dreadful. It sounded like a bad version of Sun Ra—screechy, but still kind of fun and upbeat; dissonant, goof-off kind of music. There were lots of silly costumes and colored smoke and bubbles and whatever I could come up with. I did a lot of light show stuff—I ran various slide projectors and film loops, mainly Prankster footage—the bus going down the road, and so on."

In Tom Wolfe's account of the evening, the night ended with Owsley screaming denunciations at Kesey for the dark power he had seen unleashed on the world during his peculiar night at Muir Beach. Owsley jumped into his car and started to roar off into the night, but crashed into a tree almost immediately and tumbled out of the car still raving and railing at Kesey and the Pranksters. As Garcia said later, "[Owsley's] mind was completely shot—he thought they'd come and taken it from him. . . . He didn't get along too well with our wilder version [than the Berkeley psychedelic scene Owsley was from] because the big, straight psychedelic scene always called our scene too high-energy—'You can freak out in there, you know.' That was what they always used to say."

Garcia explained the allure of the Acid Tests from his perspective in a 1969 *Rolling Stone* story on the band:

"What the Kesey thing was depended on who you were when you were there. It was open, a tapestry, a mandala—it was whatever you made it. Okay, so you take LSD, and suddenly you're aware of another plane, or several other planes. And the quest is to extend that limit, to go as far as you can go. In the Acid Tests, that meant to do away with old forms, with old ideas, try something *new*. Nobody was doing *something*, y'know. It was everybody doing bits and pieces of something, the result of which was something else.

"When it was moving right, you could dig that there was something that it was getting toward, something like ordered chaos. The Test would start off and then there would be chaos. Everybody would be high and flashing and going through insane changes during which everything would be *demolished*, man, and spilled and broken and affected, and after that another thing would happen, maybe soothing out the chaos, then another; it'd go all night 'til morning. . . .

"When we were playing, we were playing. When we weren't, we'd be doing other stuff. There were no sets; sometimes we'd get up and play for two hours, three hours. Sometimes we'd play for ten minutes and then freak out and split. We'd just do it however it would happen. It wasn't a *gig*—it was the Acid Test, where anything was okay."

Commented Bob Weir: "When we played the Acid Tests, we set up before the whole thing began—wisely so. Then we'd take acid and wait until we could kind of deal with the physical. Back then, God knows who decided what the doses were gonna be, so there were times when it was a couple of hours before we'd make a stab at trying to play. And oftentimes we'd pluck around a little and then abandon ship pretty quick. It was hard to relate when we were heavily into hallucination.

"We began turning up loud pretty quickly. From the start, it was faster, looser, louder and hairier. We were going for a ride. We were gonna see what this baby'll do. It helped that we were playing in an uncritical situation. What didn't help was that the fact that we were *completely* disoriented, so we had to fend for ourselves and improvise. When we would come around in a song to what should be a familiar chorus, it seemed completely unfamiliar. The jams made us rely on each other a lot. 'How are you doin', man?' 'I don't know! How are you doin'?' 'Well, I got *this*,' and you'd play a little line. 'Okay, I think I can relate to that.' So we had to hang together. We got better and better at it as time went on, so we could take a pretty massive dose and hang in there for a while."

Garcia often said that one of the biggest turn-ons of the Acid Tests for him was getting to know an ever-growing assortment of odd, interesting people who shared his own insatiable taste for adventure, the unexpected and the truly *weird*. It was under the aegis of the Acid Tests that Garcia encountered Kesey, Babbs, Bill Graham, Owsley, Wavy Gravy, Stewart Brand and many of the people who would become the movers and shakers of the blossoming San Francisco music scene. But the figure who impressed Garcia the most during this period was Neal Cassady, the *fastestmanalive!*, legendary for his verbal and physical dexterity and his death-defying feats of reckless driving. His exploits were dutifully chronicled by writers from Kerouac to Wolfe, and seemingly everyone who encountered him was affected by him.

"It's hard to even know what to say about Cassady," Garcia said in 1994. "He had an incredible mind. You might not see him for months and he would pick up exactly where he left off the last time he saw you; like in the middle of a sentence! You'd go, 'What? What the . . .' and then you'd realize, 'Oh yeah, this is that story he was telling me last time.' It was so mind-boggling you couldn't believe that he was doing it.

"If you'd go for a drive with him it was like the ultimate fear experience," Garcia continued. "You knew you were going to die; there was no question about it. He loved big Detroit irons—big cars. Driving in San Francisco he would go down those hills like at fifty or sixty miles an hour and do blind corners, disregarding anything—stop signs, signals, all the time talking to you and maybe fumbling around with a little teeny roach, trying to put it in a matchbook, and also tuning the radio maybe, and also talking to whoever else was in the car. And seeming to never put his eyes on the road. You'd be just *dying*. It would effectively take you past that cold fear of death thing. It was so incredible. . . .

"He was the first person I met who he himself was the art. He was an artist and he was the art also. He was doing it consciously, as well. He worked with the world. . . . He was that guy in the real world. He scared a lot of people. A lot of people thought he was crazy. A lot of people were afraid of him. Most people I know didn't understand him at all. But he was like a musician in a way. He liked musicians; he always liked to hang out with musicians. That's why he sort of picked up on us."

"The only thing I can really say is everybody who ever knew Cassady was tremendously influenced and affected by him," Kesey said. "People from all sorts of stations in life, from Stewart Brand to Garcia to Kerouac to Ginsberg to Burroughs to strange little teenage girls who had never read a book—were all very affected by him, and that in itself should say to people, 'Pay attention to this guy. There's more going on than you get in the first glimpse.' It takes a bit of study."

"One of the essential points of the Acid Tests is that you were safe in your idiosyncrasies and safe to be who you really were," M.G. says. "That idea is at the heart of Ken's nature, and it's also the heart of Jerry's nature. Jerry adored idiosyncrasies, and Ken as well. They would genuinely be charmed by weird people. Jerry would take people in who he thought had some special charm or something fascinating about them. It was an openness to weirdness.

"We also had this commitment to a group decision-making process and that worked fine as long as Ken or Jerry—in either one of the groups—hadn't already made a decision about things, in which case we were going to do what they wanted to do. That's the hilarious thing about it. We had this system which was truly democratic a lot of the time, but occasionally veered into being a dictatorship. I think Bill Graham shared that same oddness, of letting people do what they want to do and run stuff until suddenly it contradicted what he wanted."

The Grateful Dead's first performance of 1966 was an Acid Test at Beaver Hall in Portland—Kesey country—and then a few days later the Acid Test finally hit San Francisco's Fillmore Auditorium. Hundreds of heads turned out and had their minds blown by what they experienced. The Dead played an incredible set that night and the place was jumpin' in a way it never had before. "All I know," comedian–social satirist Paul Krassner said into a microphone at the Fillmore that night, "is that if I were a cop and I came in here, I wouldn't know where to begin."

Indeed. The "authorities" were not happy about these public carnivals of what was, by mainstream societal standards, deviant behavior on a mass scale taking place under their noses. Since LSD was still legal, they couldn't just shut the Acid Test down, but there's no doubt that they were taking notice of what was going on at these events. As early as the Big Beat Acid Test, newspapers began running stories about "drug orgies," and police and government officials started talking about making the drug illegal and cracking down on the anarchic scene.

"The Acid Test started expanding at an incredible rate," Garcia said. "It started from about enough people to fill a room this size, to enough to fill the Longshoremen's Hall in San Francisco. And it had virtually no advertising or anything. You sort of had to be a detective to even find out where they were gonna be. But even so they got to be immensely popular. More and more people came to them, more and more people got high. After about three or four months, it seemed like the Acid Tests were going to take over the world in about a year."

One person whose life was changed by seeing the Grateful Dead at the Fillmore Acid Test was Rock Scully, who as part of the Family Dog organization was actually putting on a competing dance concert featuring the Charlatans and the Jefferson Airplane at California Hall half a mile away the same night. In an early example of freak solidarity, Scully and the Pranksters worked out an arrangement where tickets were good for both events, and even set up a shuttle bus between the two venues. At one point Scully left his own show to check out what was happening at the Fillmore, and he was so mesmerized by what he saw and heard that he never returned to California Hall. Shortly afterward he became the Grateful Dead's first manager.

Just as UC Berkeley was the center of cultural upheaval in the East Bay in the mid-'60s, and Stanford the bohemian nexus on the Peninsula, San Francisco State, located on an often foggy stretch of land at the southwest end of the city, produced many of the "pioneers" of Haight-Ashbury, Rock Scully among them. Rock hailed from Carmel, an idyllic coastal village 125 miles south of San Francisco, but much of his youth had been spent in European boarding schools. After attending college in Switzerland he went to S.F. State for graduate school and fell in with a crowd of students that included members of the Charlatans, Rodney and Peter Albin, and a New York kid named Danny Rifkin, all of whom, like Scully, lived in the Haight-Ashbury district of San Francisco, near the eastern edge of Golden Gate Park. Rifkin was living in and managing a stately old Victorian at 710 Ashbury when the two became friends, and after a while Scully moved into the building. Through Luria Castell, a former 710 resident who'd moved into the Dog House, Scully became involved with the Family Dog, and he in turn persuaded Danny Rifkin to help put on the dance concert with the Charlatans that December night at California Hall. Scully first heard the Dead at the Big Beat Acid Test, where he claims he and Pigpen were the only people in the room not on acid, but it wasn't until he blasted into the Fillmore Acid Test, high as a kite, that he understood why so many people were latching onto this band.

That January the Dead also began playing regular gigs at the Matrix club in San Francisco, giving those who found the whole Acid Test scene a bit too strange, frantic and unpredictable (as well as those who simply dug the band and wanted to see more) a chance to groove on the Dead's music without the confusing distractions that pretty much defined the Acid Tests. The Jefferson Airplane had been the first group to play the club when it opened in August 1965, and by year's end they were signed to RCA Records. Though in early 1966 no one was beating down the door trying to get the Grateful Dead into a recording studio, the Matrix gigs certainly elevated their status around town and helped establish them as a "San Francisco" band, whereas before they had been considered a Peninsula group.

It was Stewart Brand, not Ken Kesey, who was the driving force behind a three-day multimedia extravaganza known as the Trips Festival at Longshoremen's Hall on January 21, 22 and 23, 1966. Brand's concept, or at least what he told the local media, was an event that would be like an acid trip, but *without the acid* (wink wink). What an extravaganza: Friday was to feature Brand's multimedia America Needs Indians Sensorium and something called the Open Theater, which consisted of everything from the Congress of Wonders comedy troupe to a recitation of an Aimee Semple McPherson sermon, to a group called the Jazz Mice. Saturday evening was turned over to Kesey and the Pranksters, with music by the Dead and Big Brother and the Holding

Company. Sunday's lineup brought together elements of Friday's and Saturday's events, along with such new stimuli as Henry Jacobs's Air Dome Projections and the Stroboscopic Trampoline. A flier for the Trips Festival offered this explanation to the curious: "the general tone of things has moved from the self-concious happening to a more JUBILANT occasion where the audience PARTICIPATES because it's more fun to do so than not. maybe this is the ROCK REVOLUTION. audience dancing is an assumed part of all the shows, & the audience is invited to wear ECSTATIC DRESS & bring their own GADGETS (a.c. outlets will be provided)."

Basically the festival was designed to be a three-day freak convention, a big party to usher in the dawn of the acid age. The gullible press completely bought into Brand's rap and gave the event lots of free publicity.

Meanwhile, Ken Kesey had a problem. Way back in April 1965 the police had raided his house in La Honda and busted him for possession of pot. He was released on bail, and it wasn't until just four days before the Trips Festival that the case finally worked its way through the crowded court docket. Kesey found himself on the receiving end of a stern lecture from San Mateo County court judge Louis Demateis. The judge said that the crime Kesey had committed could have landed him in the state prison, but since he was a first-time offender, Demateis instead sentenced Kesey to six months in the county jail, three years probation and a $1,500 fine. As part of the probation, the judge also ordered Kesey to sever all ties with the Merry Pranksters and the Acid Test. Kesey paid a $5,500 bond and announced his plan to appeal the sentence.

But that wasn't the worst of it. Kesey's situation was complicated further when the night after the sentencing he and Mountain Girl were busted on the roof of Stewart Brand's Telegraph Hill apartment. The pair had been lying around on the roof late at night, smoking pot, watching the stars above them, the lights of North Beach below them, and playfully tossing gravel from the rooftop. This was not a good idea: some of the gravel apparently hit the window of an apartment beneath them and a woman called the cops. Kesey and M.G. watched as police cars arrived in the street below them and officers entered the building they were on top of, but they failed to make the connection. The next thing they knew there were two cops on the roof with them. Kesey tried to throw away a baggie containing a small amount of pot, and the officers, with guns drawn, took the pair into custody. Mountain Girl bravely tried to take the rap, but nobody was buying her claim. No, Kesey had not only been busted a second time, but he was also caught consorting with a Prankster! This could land him in jail for an extended period—maybe even the three years the San Mateo judge had originally said was a probation period.

The Trips Festival was a huge success. Longshoremen's Hall was jammed all three nights, with more than 10,000 people attending overall. The event grossed $12,500, which was good money for its day, a fact that was not lost on the man Stewart Brand had hired to help run the event—Bill Graham. Contrary to Brand's pre-event assertions to the press, nearly everyone who attended the Trips Festival was high on *something;* acid was everywhere. It was, in fact, undoubtedly the largest concentration of psychedelicized people in one place that the world had ever seen. Kesey turned up Saturday night wearing a silver space suit and a bubble space helmet, and managed not to be too conspicuous, which gives an idea of how wild many people's outfits were.

The handbill ads for the Saturday night event promised "ken kesey, members of the s.f. tape music center, big brother & the holding company rock 'n' roll, the don buchla sound-light console, overhead projection . . . 'the acid test,' the merry pranksters and their psychedelic symphony, neal cassady vs. ann murphy vaudeville, the grateful dead rock 'n' roll, allen ginsberg, roy's audioptics, movies, ron boise & his electric thunder sculpture, the bus, hell's angels, many noted outlaws, and the unexpectable." In the middle of the hall the Pranksters constructed a giant tower—their command control center—which they filled from top to bottom with stacks and stacks of sound, lighting and movie equipment. What a pile of stuff: It was as if the little ol' Acid Test of yore had been zapped by some ray and mutated, like the Amazing Colossal Man!

"The Trips Festival was a continuation of what was happening at other events, but in a much bigger dose," says Steve Brown, who was managing a local band called the Friendly Stranger at the time. "Our thing was we did a liquid light show, strobe lights, a fog machine and projected cartoons. We had all that environmental thing going already. What this added to it was a more chaotic, unpredictable type of edge: tying everybody together with string, turning off the lights and throwing thousands of marshmallows down on everybody. Weird stuff that was sort of like performance art and got everyone participating. You'd be going along doing whatever you were doing and all of a sudden you'd find yourself in the middle of some other completely weird scene that somebody else was doing, so you did that until it ended or until something more interesting came along. And if a band happened to be playing and was good, that was an added bonus. The place was packed. There were people inside and outside, and people who didn't know if they were inside or outside. There were all these people just kind of bumping around Fisherman's Wharf scaring the tourists; it was great! What it really was, was a public drug event. Everyone was completely aghast that this many young people would *want* to do this. They couldn't believe it!"

For Garcia the Trips Festival was "thousands of people, man, all helplessly stoned, all finding themselves in a roomful of other thousands of people, none of whom any of them were afraid of. It was magic, far-out beautiful magic."

Facing a bail hearing on February 2, which would almost certainly result in his being jailed because of the rooftop bust, Kesey decided to go on the lam, but not before he hatched one more prank. He arranged to have an old panel truck driven up to the rainy northwestern corner of California, outside of

Eureka, and parked on a cliff overlooking the ocean. On the front seat he left a "suicide" note that concluded: "I Ken Kesey being of (ahem) sound mind and body do hereby leave the whole scene to Faye, corporation, cash, the works. And Babbs to run it. (And it occurs to me that nobody is going to buy this prank and now it occurs to me that I like that even better.)"

Of course the police *didn't* buy it; not for a second. But by leaving the truck so far north, Kesey led people to believe that he'd returned to his native Northwest, whereas in fact he'd hopped into a rented red Mustang convertible with Hassler, driven down to Los Angeles, then hooked up with Ron Boise and headed across the Mexican border in a truck. As the anointed successor, Babbs tried to keep the momentum of the Acid Tests going, and in fact there was more craziness to come in the weeks after Kesey's departure, but most agreed that the Acid Tests were never quite the same. This brings to mind Prankster axiom number two: "Nothing lasts."

All during this period, the band was still living in and around Palo Alto. Jerry, Sara and Heather had moved from the cottage on Bryant Court into a huge Victorian house a block or so from the Gilman Street pad, on the corner of Forest and Waverly Streets, along with Dave Parker, Robert Hunter, Rick Shubb and David Nelson. There were palm and avocado trees in the large yard, and most of the rooms were big and sunny. Inside, there was sometimes a palpable tension between Jerry and Sara, who were still drifting apart despite their shared love of tripping and of Heather. Jerry had been unfaithful to Sara on numerous occasions with a few different women, but what finally broke up the marriage was Sara's falling in love with Roy Seburn, one of the Pranksters:

"He and I started hanging out and then he came and stayed at our place on Waverly Street. The Acid Tests were going and I was just miserable with Jerry, absolutely miserable. One evening Roy was camping on the couch in the living room and I went down to be with him. And Jerry came down and found us hanging out together—we hadn't done anything together yet—but I had strong feelings about Roy and I hadn't had any strong feelings about Jerry, except disappointment, for quite some time. And Jerry basically said, 'I can't tolerate you being with somebody else,' so I said, 'Okay, that's *it*. We're done.' I threw away my wedding ring and burned the letters he'd written me and gave a lot of my stuff to Cassady's girlfriend and took off with Roy."

Garcia noted that one of the effects of his experimentation with psychedelics during this period was that "It freed me, because I suddenly realized that my little attempt at having a straight life and doing that was really a fiction and just wasn't going to work out. Luckily I wasn't far enough into it for it to be shattering or anything. It was like a realization that just made me feel immensely relieved. I just felt good and it was the same with my wife; at that point it sort of freed us to be able to go ahead and live our lives rather than having to live out an unfortunate social circumstance." Of course his "attempt at a having a straight life" was *never* very earnest, and it's doubtful that Sara, who continued to care for Heather, enjoyed the same relief that the now unburdened Garcia did.

In early February the Dead and the Pranksters headed down to Los Angeles. For the Pranksters this was a chance to bring the Acid Test to new crowds on their way down to Mexico to reconnect with Kesey. In the Dead's case, going to L.A. offered an opportunity to spend some solid time working on new material to expand a repertoire that new manager Rock Scully said was getting stale.

Owsley had also reconnected with the Dead in the weeks since his rough time at the Muir Beach Acid Test. While still somewhat distrustful of the whole Prankster ethos—"I thought they were probably messing with something that was probably very dangerous. It was not so good," he said—seeing the Dead again at the Fillmore Acid Test confirmed his earlier notion that *they* were onto something special. "I met Phil," he said. "I walked over to him and said, 'I'd like to work for you guys.' Because I had decided this was the most amazing thing I'd ever run into. And he says, 'We don't have a manager . . .' I said, 'I don't think I want to be the manager.' He said, 'Well, we don't have a sound man,' and I said, 'Well, I don't know anything about that, either, but I guess I could learn. Sounds like more fun.' That's how that happened."

Owsley knew Los Angeles well from his years in the air force, the electronics industry and radio/TV, and he'd actually made LSD there as recently as the spring of 1965. He had roots and connections there, and a little bit of money from his drug operation to help support the band, yet he says he was opposed to the Dead's moving there in that late winter of 1966: "The Acid Test went to L.A. and the Grateful Dead felt obligated. I argued long and strongly that it wasn't really a very good idea to do it because I didn't see any point in it. It was going to be expensive, none of us had a place down there to stay and there were no assurances there was any income; I had limited amounts of money. When I first met those guys they couldn't make enough to live on. If they went out and worked a show, there were five of them and they were lucky to get $125 a night. So there was no money in it; it was more like a hobby.

"But, like I said, they felt like they had to do it, that they were part of the Acid Tests, so they went ahead and did it. I missed the first one because I couldn't disconnect whatever I was doing [in Northern California], but I showed up the next week. We went down there and then somebody who was connected with the Pranksters had met some person who was in real estate and they located this house in Watts. I thought, 'Who the fuck wants to go there?' It turned out it was right next door to a whorehouse, and the whorehouse patrons would throw pot seeds out the window, so there were little pot plants growing all around—that's all we needed, since we were bringing the cops there almost every day because of the noise."

The big pink stucco house on the edge of Watts had no furniture in it at all, and, according to Rosie McGee (née Florence Nathan), who was Phil's girlfriend, "That whole scene down there was totally controlled by Owsley. He rented the place, paid for everything. They had very little income during that period. They'd do a few gigs here and there for a couple of hundred bucks, and there was a house full of people to feed. But because Owsley was in charge of it and paying for it and was the massive control freak that he was, he controlled every single thing, down to what we ate. I'll never forget that when you'd open the refrigerator there were big slabs of beef in there. The shelves weren't even in there—just these big hunks of meat. So of course behind his back people were sneaking candy bars in. There were no greens or anything— he called it 'rabbit food.'

"It was kind of an odd period because the band wasn't working very much," she continues. "They were home a lot and practicing in the house." And how did they sound? "They were very rough but they were working hard at it; at the same time they were all having a lot of fun. I'm not sure they really had a direction at that point, except to stretch—musically, with drugs or whatever. It all went off in so many directions at once. They weren't very focused. But that's to be expected, because they were pretty loaded much of the time."

For the record, Owsley acknowledges that he kept the band on the all-meat diet (which he preferred because he believed that humans are essentially carnivorous and that vegetables poisoned the body) and he admits, "I tend to be a control freak. I've had that epithet thrown at me a bunch. I like to see things done right." Still, he was no Svengali telling the Dead what to do or what to play. Phil Lesh once noted, "He was our patron, in the ultimate sense of the word. . . . He never once thought about the money. We were able to be the Grateful Dead, and if they hired us, great. But we could at least eat."

While the Dead contingent was staying in Watts, the Pranksters were spread out in several different locations around L.A., setting up Acid Tests at various odd places, including a Unitarian church in Northridge, Cathay Sound Studios, and the most notorious Test of them all, the Watts Acid Test, held in an old warehouse on Lincoln's Birthday in 1966.

"We got a couple of 30-gallon garbage pails and mixed Kool-Aid," Lee Quarnstrom said in On the Bus. "Owsley had a couple of glass ampules with pure LSD in them and he poured it into the Kool-Aid. We did some quick mathematics and figured that one Dixie Cup of Kool-Aid equalled 50 micrograms of acid. The standard dose, if you wanted to get high, was 300 mics. So we told everyone that six cups would equal a standard trip. After a couple of cups, when I was as high as I'd ever been, somebody recomputed and realized each cup held 300 micrograms. I remember hearing that and realizing I had just gulped down 2,000 micrograms. The rest of the evening was as weird as you might expect."

The other L.A. Acid Tests were considerably more benign, and there's no question that the Pranksters made quite an impression on the Angelenos who turned out. "It was a very different scene than San Francisco," says Rosie McGee. "The San Francisco scene and the Pranksters and all of that was always a really funky, real, hairy kind of thing. It was the true *edge* and it was gritty. We brought that down to L.A. and there was this overlay of the glitzy people trying to be hip coming to this event and not knowing what to make of it. There were always people at the L.A. Acid Tests who were not on acid and who were very Hollywood, so they were standing around like poseurs, looking at all this stuff while we were down on the ground, holding on for dear life, and getting down to it. Then, those of them who did get high . . . well, glitz and acid don't mix too well, so when these people started shedding their skin, so to speak, a lot of them got pretty freaked out. It was definitely a collision of cultures there."

Jerry and Sara were tripping at the same events, but were psychically far apart for most the L.A. Acid Tests. While Jerry and the band were shattering the peace of their Watts neighborhood (Rosie McGee says the band's response to noise complaints was "to open the window and put the speakers going toward the neighbors"), Sara and Heather were across town with Roy and the other Pranksters. "I loved being part of that scene," she says. "There was a can-do attitude about the Pranksters that was just thrilling in those days. There was great idealism. We were going to take the Acid Test across the country and save the country by opening people's minds."

Sara even took baby Heather to the Acid Tests with her: "I would always find a place for a little nest that would be safe and quiet for Heather, like the projection room in a theater or someplace like that, and set her up with her toys and crayons and snacks and a snug little bed." One time at an Acid Test in L.A., "Jerry wanted to see Heather," Sara says, "and I remember taking him up to this place where I had nested her, and him just kind of adoring her while she was asleep. He asked me to come back to him, and I said no."

After about six weeks in L.A. the Dead and the Pranksters finally parted ways, with the bus heading south to Mexico and the Dead returning to Northern California. "The Acid Test had sort of run its course and it was time to do something else and take it apart," Babbs says. "For one thing, we had a huge crew that was traveling with us, and we didn't have any money. The choice was either to take it on the road and head east and try to keep limping along, or to stop it. But it wasn't like people were after us to do it in their town or anything. Not that many people knew about it, really."

With the Pranksters suddenly out of their lives and the Acid Tests over (at least for the time being), it was time for the Grateful Dead to become more self-reliant and carry its own version of the Acid Test spirit into the clubs and ballrooms of San Francisco. It wasn't, Garcia noted, quite the same:

"In order to keep on playing, we had to go with whatever form was there.

Because for one thing, the form that we liked [the Acid Test] always scared everybody. It scared the people that owned the building that we'd rent, so they'd never rent twice to us. It scared the people who came, a lot of times. It scared the cops. It scared everybody. Because it represented total and utter anarchy. Indoor anarchy. That's something people haven't learned to get off with. But our experience with those things is that's where you get the highest. . . .

"The Acid Test was the prototype for our whole basic trip. But nothing has ever come up to the level of the way the Acid Test was. It's just never been equalled, really, or the basic hit of it never developed out."

But what it evolved into over the next three decades was no less remarkable.

CHAPTER 6

In the Book
of Love's Own Dream

he Grateful Dead stayed in Los Angeles for only about six weeks, but things were moving so fast in San Francisco in the winter of 1966 that the dynamics of the city's music world had changed fairly dramatically by the time the band returned to the Bay Area. While the Dead and the Pranksters were scuffling around L.A. digging up odd places to play, the scene in San Francisco was simultaneously solidifying and opening up in exciting new directions, as both Bill Graham and the loose-knit group known as the Family Dog began putting on dance concerts more frequently, showcasing both the city's own up-and-coming bands and out-of-town groups.

Because of what they became and their longevity, the Dead's role in the early days of the San Francisco rock 'n' roll renaissance has probably been somewhat overemphasized through the years. While the Acid Tests were unquestionably influential, the Haight-Ashbury scene might still have flowered as it did if Kesey had never left La Honda and the Warlocks had broken up after their third gig at Magoo's. The fact is, hundreds of sources of intense energy, bold musical statements, creative thinking and wild flights of imagination were germinating in the city. Drugs were certainly a major catalyst, but they proliferated independent of the Dead/Pranksters. And the dozens of bands that sprang up in the garages, basements and living rooms of drafty old Haight-Ashbury Victorians and nondescript apartments and row houses around town drew their inspiration, as the Dead did, from all over—the Beatles, the Byrds, Dylan, the Stones, the Lovin' Spoonful, Chicago blues cats, the Yardbirds, Ravi Shankar, Nashville country pickers, Miles and Coltrane, Mongo Santamaria and a thousand other musicians, famous and obscure, whom the city's young players listened to on records and the radio and in clubs of every variety.

And of course there was a lot more to the scene than just the music, though the bands and dances became the primary galvanizing force. Over a period of just a few months, the Haight became the center of a loose movement of adventurous and eclectic visual artists—poster designers, light show makers, painters, filmmakers and lithographers, some of whom became nearly as celebrated as the musicians. All of the artists shared a playful spirit of adventure and a willingness (or compulsion) to experiment. They drew from art nouveau, Hindu and Buddhist art, contemporary op and pop painters, Native American crafts, nineteenth-century woodcuts—everything was fair game, and each of the artists developed a distinctive style, much as each of the bands on the scene developed a unique musical signature.

Not surprisingly, the name "Grateful Dead" lent itself to interesting iconic possibilities, "because we had such an evocative name," Garcia said in 1987. "You can throw anything at it. 'Grateful Dead' is so huge and wide open that anything works. That's one of the reasons the artists loved it. . . . Because the artists came to the shows, they'd get all excited and come over and say, 'Look, here's the latest Grateful Dead poster. What do you think?' They liked to blow our minds, too. It got to be feedback on so many different levels with everyone trying to blow each other's minds. And it works! When everyone's putting all their energy into it full-time, pretty soon everyone's mind is blown."

With Danny Rifkin joining Rock Scully in actively working with the Dead—though there was little money in it at this point—there was talk about the Dead moving into 710 Ashbury, the rooming house that Danny managed and where Rock had a room, and various members crashed there for a week or so after they arrived back in town following the L.A. sojourn. But instead of immediately plunging into the world of the Haight, the Dead decided to take a scenic detour and headed into the country, where Rosie McGee and Owsley's girlfriend, Melissa Cargill, succeeded in renting a giant house for the group in the wilds of Novato, in northern Marin County, on a plot of land known as Rancho Olompali.

"It was a kind of Spanish-style, pseudo-adobe structure with at least two stories, and a whole bunch of rooms," Rosie McGee says of the house, which had been used as a home for retarded children before the Dead took it over. "The grounds were famous—there was the pool and several buildings; a building off in the back that some people stayed in."

"The Dead used to have some pretty good parties out in their place in the country, in Olompali," said Charlatans founder George Hunter. "Two or three hundred people would come, and of course, most of them probably took LSD. This was around the time that a lot of new ground was being broken, socially, and it seemed like a third to a half of the people at these parties would be naked, hanging around the pool. It was a great place. It was a sort of ranch estate that had a nice big house that looked kind of like Tara in *Gone With the Wind*. . . . In between the house and the pool the Dead would set up their equipment and play from time to time. Usually there'd be members of other bands there, too, like the Airplane and Quicksilver, and there'd be little jams with people who wanted to play. I remember the Dead would be playing and Neal Cassady would be doing this strange little dance—it was almost like break dancing; very fluid. . . . Those parties—I'm not sure how many of them there were—were always on a nice afternoon. Everybody would play all day in the sunshine—just doing *everything*—and then when the sun would start to go down and it got cold, people would pack it in. By the time it was dark most people were gone, but there were always enough people who were either around to begin with or who wanted to stay, that the party would continue inside. In fact, with the number of people hanging out there all the time, it was pretty much a party all the time anyway. I don't know if it was twenty-four hours a day, but every time I was there it was going."

"Novato was completely comfortable, wide open, high as you wanted to get, run around naked if you wanted to, fall in the pool, completely open scenes," Garcia said in 1971. "Everything was just super-groovy. It was a model of how things could really be good. . . . It was good times—unself-conscious and totally free."

If this all sounds like some sort of freak utopia, that's probably not too far off the mark. The spring and summer of 1966 were in some ways the apex of the whole San Francisco scene—the true "Summer of Love" a year before the media latched on to that tag; a time when the Bay Area's freak community was joyously coalescing, discovering its breadth and diversity, and people were turning each other on in a thousand different ways: with music, art, books, dope, endless conversations. . . .

Everyone knew that it was only a matter of time before LSD was made illegal—in California, legislators had already been whipped into an anti-drug frenzy by a rising tide of hysterical press associated with the Acid Tests—so in a sense this period was the last window of opportunity for people to trip without the paranoia associated with the knowledge that possessing acid could lead to jail time. And for the Dead, trying to eke out a living on the still growing local band circuit, and playing an increasing number of conventional dance concerts—as opposed to Acid Tests—meant that they could no longer get as high as they wanted and then either play or not play. People started coming to dance to the Dead because they were the Dead, and as Owsley puts it, "In the early days, we were almost always well lubricated [for shows]; till after the Acid Test period, when they started getting working gigs. Then there was a greater reluctance to get too screwed up because there was a certain level of professionalism that was required."

But out in the bucolic wilds of Olompali it was another matter altogether. Garcia and the others gobbled acid regularly in that beautiful, unpressured setting, psychically far removed from the sensory whirlwind that the Pranksters had created at the Acid Tests, and physically from the bustling, citified swirl of the Haight-Ashbury. Garcia said that some of his most profound LSD trips occurred during this magical period, which, though far from the end of his psychedelic days (he tripped occasionally for the rest of his life), marked the end of his serious exploratory phase.

"Psychedelics were probably the single most significant experience in my life," Garcia said. "Otherwise I think I would be going along believing that this visible reality is all that there is. Psychedelics didn't give me any answers. What I have is a lot of questions. One thing I'm certain of—the mind is an incredible thing and there are levels of organizations of consciousness that are way beyond what people are fooling with in day-to-day reality."

And how did psychedelics affect his music?

"I can't answer that. There was a me before psychedelics, and a me after psychedelics; that's the best I can say. I can't say that it affected the music specifically; it affected the whole me. The problem of playing music is essentially of muscular development and that is something you have to put in the hours to achieve no matter what. There isn't something that strikes you and suddenly you can play music.

"I think that psychedelics was part of music for me insofar as I was a person who was looking for something and psychedelics and music are both part of what I was looking for. They fit together, although one didn't cause the other."

Although mid-1966 probably represents the apex of the Dead's experimentation with psychedelics, the music the group played during this period wasn't nearly as twisted, weird and obviously chemically inspired as what they would unleash a year later, when, though their own psychedelic intake was down, they'd been playing together longer and the cumulative effect of their psychedelic consumption had become manifest in their original music. In 1966 the Dead were still essentially a cover band, and in terms of their song choices, what they played wasn't tremendously different from what was being churned out by other bands around town, except that the Dead always retained some of the jug band's feel and repertoire. (In fact, the band's first single release, in June 1966—a pressing of just 150 copies on a local independent label, Scorpio Records—featured electrified versions of two songs they'd played with the jug band: "Don't Ease Me In" and "Stealin'.") Everybody, it seemed, was playing blues-based rock 'n' roll of one kind or another. Some bands took their blues approach from British bands like the Stones, the Yardbirds, the Animals and Them; others looked directly at the Chicago blues artists the Brits had copied, such as Muddy Waters, Howlin' Wolf, Junior Wells and others.

Garcia noted, "As a band, the Grateful Dead has never thought of itself as being a psychedelic band. We've always thought of ourselves as a rock 'n' roll band. What we were playing back then [the mid-'60s] was basically a harder, rhythm and blues–oriented rock 'n' roll; especially Pigpen's stuff. We were going for a sort of Chess Records school of R&B—Howlin' Wolf and Muddy Waters. Those are the records we stole a lot of our tunes from. We didn't have that Midwestern authority—we weren't like the Butterfield band, but we were a funky blues band."

The Paul Butterfield Blues Band played fairly often in San Francisco in 1966 and 1967, and their influence on many of the Haight-Ashbury groups was considerable—it's fair to say that they set a standard for musicianship that other bands aspired to (and few could match). This Chicago group was the real deal: Butterfield blew harp as well as James Cotton, the rhythm section of bassist Jerome Arnold, drummer Sam Lay and pianist Mark Naftalin was as good as any in Chicago, and the group boasted *two* excellent guitarists: Elvin Bishop and Mike Bloomfield, who'd come up playing in Chicago's highly competitive blues circuit, where imitating Otis Rush and Buddy Guy and Hubert Sumlin wasn't enough: "It had to be the real thing; it had to be right," Bloomfield said.

John Kahn, who played with Garcia beginning in 1970 and also played extensively with Bloomfield, said, "Jerry told me that when he was first playing in San Francisco, Bloomfield was the one guitarist who really impressed him, because of the way he could endlessly come up with different ways of playing around a melody. I think Jerry would say he was influenced by Bloomfield a little, though Jerry had stronger country influences that shaped his tone. But they both had their own special kind of tone and they both played American roots music and were completely influenced by all different strains of American music." In a 1968 interview, Bloomfield said of Garcia's playing, "He sounds amazingly like he's trying to sound like me, but I don't think he is. I think he came that way himself."

In terms of their *approach* to playing, the Dead were as influenced by jazz musicians as they were by the classic electric blues bands. Phil Lesh had a lot to do with educating the other bandmembers, including Garcia, about jazz, though the Chateau had been a jazz hotbed, so Garcia had already heard plenty of jazz independent of Phil. Danya Veltfort remembers Garcia sitting around Phoebe Graubard's apartment in the summer of 1961 listening to Miles Davis's *Sketches of Spain* and Coltrane's *Soul Trane* over and over, though he was playing old-timey guitar at the time. Garcia also attended the Monterey Jazz Festival that autumn and saw Coltrane there. Miles and Coltrane were still the dominant figures in jazz five years later, and both were still evolving in fascinating directions when the Warlocks were starting off. By the early '60s, too, Ornette Coleman was making noise—literally and figuratively—in Los Angeles, pushing the limits of what was considered jazz with his daringly dissonant free improvisations that shocked and outraged the jazz establishment.

"We felt at that time, when we were listening to Coltrane, that we were hardly fit to grovel at his feet," Bob Weir said. "But still, we were trying to get there; our aims were pretty much the same."

One would be hard pressed to point to elements in the Dead's music in mid- to late 1966 that specifically echoed Miles or Coltrane or Ornette, but the group was definitely inspired by the questing spirit of their jazz contemporaries: the great jazz groups' willingness to abandon form and structure in search of wondrous new avenues of self-expression; the fluid and intricate dynamics of their highly intuitive ensemble playing; and their refusal to make commercial compromises with their work. The musical influences were more readily apparent in 1968 and 1969 and later, as the Dead became more proficient and took their jams farther "out," in the jazz sense.

Garcia noted, "I've been influenced a lot by Coltrane, but I never copped his licks or sat down, listened to records and tried to play his stuff. I've been impressed with that thing of flow, and of making statements that to my ears sound like paragraphs—he'll play along stylistically with a certain kind of tone, in a certain kind of syntax, for X amount of time. Then he'll, like, change the subject, then play along with this other personality coming out, which really impresses me. It's like other personalities stepping out, or else his personality is changing, or his attitude's changing. But it changes in a holistic way, where the tone of his axe and everything changes.

"Perceptually, an idea that's been very important to me in playing has been the whole 'odyssey' idea—journeys, voyages and adventures along the way."

In the early and mid-'60s Coltrane was a master of the introspective musical odyssey, a shamanic conjurer whose playing breathed fire one moment, floated in the ether the next, but always seemed to bubble up from some deep spiritual wellspring. During the Beat era, jazz was considered a transportational medium: it opened up your head and took you places. And from the beginning, that's also what the Dead's music was designed to do. The band's early music might not have had the compositional depth or improvisational sophistication of Miles's or Coltrane's groups (to say the least), but the conversational relationship between the instruments in the Dead—the way they engaged each other and seemed to always be simultaneously providing both melody and rhythm without explicitly defining either—clearly owed much to the jazz world.

"We're trying to think away from the standard routine of *these* members comp, *this* member leads," Garcia explained to Ralph Gleason in 1967. "We're trying to think of ensemble stuff. Not like Dixieland ensemble stuff; something else which we don't yet know anything about. The way Bill [Kreutzmann] plays is he plays a little with everybody. So if I'm playing a line, he knows enough about my playing and thinking that he can usually anticipate the way I'll think a line. And he's a great rhythmic reinforcement for any line that I can play, no matter how it relates to the rest of the time going on. He also plays beautifully with Phil, the bass player. . . . And Phil's way of approaching the bass is utterly different than any other bass players, 'cause he doesn't listen to any bass players. He listens to his mind!

"The problems we're having with all this [are] because all of us still think so musically straight, really, that it's difficult to get used to not hearing the heavy two and four [beat]. It's difficult to think rhythmically without having it there all the time, but we're starting to develop that sense better.

"There's not that feeling of the big rhythm going [in our music] because we do a lot of tricks within a bar and the tricks we do are like eliminating the beat entirely and just all of us *not* playing it. Like we're starting to use the space, rather than the time or whatever.

"We still feel that our function is as a dance band. . . . We like to play with dancers. We like to see [them] and nothing improves your time like having somebody dance. It pulls the whole thing together, and it's also a nice little feedback thing."

It helped that in 1966 and '67 particularly, the people who came to dance to the Dead were often close friends of the band, or, at the very least, kindred spirits with a shared sense of adventure and purpose. If there's one thing that nearly everyone who went through that time in the San Francisco underground agrees on, it's that the ballrooms were magical places where people could freak freely with friends and strangers alike and groove to an incredible range of bands, all of whom seemed to be getting better every week.

"The real magic time was '66, because the Fillmore and the Avalon were both going and the scene was still pretty much all local," Steve Brown remembers. "Everybody knew what we had going musically and were enjoying the drugs that were around and still legal, and we were identifying ourselves by clothing and appearance and having events that were our own things. It was a very sweet period that felt like it would keep going like that and be cool and be a new thing—a whole new culture that we'd grow up into and that would remain our own thing. We didn't look to promote it and nobody really felt like it was a crusade of any sort. We were just enjoying it ourselves."

"Going to the Fillmore and the Avalon and all those places was probably the most fun I ever had in my life," Rosie McGee says. "Considering that I personally probably knew a couple of hundred people at the Fillmore on a given night, the shows seemed more like parties than concerts, and there was always a wonderful sense of community, and great music obviously. Every part of it was wonderful; there was nothing bad about it. I loved to dance. We all did. And we never wanted the nights to end. It was one week after another, after another, after another. You look at the posters and the playbills from that period and you see who was playing. You'd go one week and hear Otis Redding. Another week somebody else great would be around. And then of course we all went and saw all the local groups, too. It was amazing that we were able to do anything else in between. But some of us had to earn a living."

Dick Latvala, who became the keeper of the Dead's tape vault in the late '80s (and who is the namesake of the "Dick's Picks" series of historic Dead CDs), says, "I went to shows every night. In '66 I didn't do anything *but* go to shows. . . . Because I thought, 'This is what I'm supposed to do—take acid and go see this music.' And it wasn't just the Grateful Dead, of course. It was the Jefferson Airplane and Big Brother and Quicksilver, too. Okay, Moby Grape was pretty good—sometimes. But basically, there were these four groups that were just devastatingly unique. It was music that was unique, exploratory, something you'd literally never heard before—that *no one* had ever heard before, including the people playing it a lot of times.

"And it was fuckin' awesome to be in a room of people who were tripped out. The fact that you could be really high on acid and be in a room with a whole bunch of other people was amazing! It was a real intimate experience, and everything I was looking for."

"The best thing about it," Garcia commented in 1992, "was that the audience all danced. Being there was being part of the experience; you didn't feel that performer-audience [dichotomy]. . . . We were part of that world. We were not performers. We were playing for our family, in a sense. It kind of had that feel, that kind of informality. The times when someone came in and gave a show it seemed freakish. It was like, 'Well, what's *he* doing up there?' "

"We'd all go to each other's gigs and we were all very supportive of each other," says David Freiberg, who was a founding member of Quicksilver Messenger Service. "You'd look down from the stage at the Fillmore or the Avalon and it wasn't at all unusual to see Garcia and Weir down there, smiling up at you, along with some of your other friends, and then a bunch of people you didn't know, but who seemed like they *could* be your friends.

"There was no real demarcation between the people who were in bands and the people in the audience, at least as far as I was concerned," Freiberg adds. "We weren't viewed as any big deal particularly. You'd walk around the Haight and people would smile at you and they definitely respected you, but we were their peers. At the same time, there *was* a little hierarchy. Owsley liked to say, 'It's the bands, man,' and that gave you a certain carte blanche. You never had to pay for acid or pot generally; it would just find its way to you. But after everything went to hell after the Summer of Love, it got more compartmentalized."

In 1966 it was Pigpen, not Garcia, who was viewed as the leader of the band by most people; certainly he had the most commanding stage presence. Though never a great singer technically, Pigpen had a way of putting a song across to an audience that made him sound believable. When he really threw himself into Jimmy Reed's "Big Boss Man," or Otis Redding's "Pain in My Heart" (which seriously tested Pigpen's vocal chops), or got into a groove on the venerable "Good Morning Little Schoolgirl," his singing seemed so effortless and unpretentious that he made you forget that he was just a white kid from the Peninsula singing songs by his idols. He wasn't really trying to sound *like* anybody; he was just being Pig—down and dirty when a song required some menace or a lascivious edge; funny and self-mocking in his raps during the group's endless versions of Wilson Pickett's "Midnight Hour"; and whipping the crowd into a frenzy with his heartfelt testifyin' on the uptempo R&B numbers. He was scary-looking, but he always had a twinkle in his eye that made him somehow not too threatening. You *rooted* for Pigpen (or the character he played onstage), and hoped that the pain he sang about in his blues would, by the show's end, be replaced by the joyous exhilaration that always came through on showstoppers like "Midnight Hour" or, beginning in 1967, "Turn On Your Love Light."

"Pigpen was the only guy in the band who had any talent when we were starting out," Garcia said. "He was genuinely talented. He had no discipline, but he had reams of talent. . . . He was the guy who really sold the band, not me or Weir. Back then, Weir was almost completely spaced; he was just barely there. And I was aggressively crazy. I could talk to anybody until hell froze over, but I wasn't really what made the band work. Pigpen is what made the band work."

Still, Sue Swanson noted, "It was always Jerry's band. But Pigpen was the only one who was really a showman. He'd get out there and work the audience and the band would be behind him. . . . But by no means were they a backup band for him or did he ever really lead them."

Indeed, it was always a struggle to get Pigpen to rehearse, and Garcia said that performing "meant nothing to [Pigpen]; it wasn't what he liked. We had to browbeat him into being a performer." But Pigpen liked to get a crowd going and he liked to the rock 'n' roll lifestyle—not having a regular job, sleeping late, getting high (alcohol was always his vice, not drugs), girls waiting by the back door at gigs, and so on.

Over the course of a few months in mid-1966, most of the original tenants of 710 Ashbury moved out and were replaced, one by one, by members of the Dead or their friends. By year's end Garcia, Pigpen and Weir lived there (Lesh and Kreutzmann lived up the hill a couple of blocks away on Belvedere Street), as did Rock Scully and his girlfriend Tangerine, Danny Rifkin, the two-man Dead equipment crew—Laird Grant and Bob Matthews—and Jim and Annie Courson, who had been brought in by Rock and Danny to run the house. The household was run communally, with everyone pooling their finances, and the young women in the scene, including Sue Swanson and Pigpen's girlfriend, Veronica Barnard, taking care of most of the domestic responsibilities.

"The men were doing the things that brought in the money," comments Rosie McGee, who lived with Phil but spent a lot of time hanging out at 710. "They were the creative ones and the breadwinners, although some of the women also earned money. But the gist of it was the women provided the comfort, which included keeping the home together, doing the laundry, getting the food together, cleaning. It was very male-dominated. Over time, if individual women had their shit together and manifested something, they definitely were respected. But as a group, the rest of the women were regarded as 'the chicks.' Later on it became 'the old ladies.' That was like the worst thing you could say: 'Oh yeah, well, the old ladies are here today,' " she adds with a laugh.

It didn't take long for 710 to become one of the most vital spots in the Haight, a constantly buzzing nerve center where musicians, artists, dope dealers and innumerable friends of the folks living there hung out at all hours of the day and night. The sixty-six-year-old Victorian didn't offer the same kind of wide-open spaces that the spring and summer living experiments in Marin County had, and of course the group couldn't actually play amplified music at 710 (the Dead rented a rehearsal space in a heliport in Sausalito, on the other side of the Golden Gate Bridge). But the trade-off was that the Dead were now at the hub of the evolving Haight culture, and they could both witness and be a part of everything that was going down. And by the fall of 1966 the scene was growing rapidly, while still being manageable for the most part.

"Our place got to be a center of energy and people were in there organizing stuff," Garcia said. "The Diggers [a communal group in the Haight dedicated to providing free food and clothing for anyone in need] would hang out there. The people that were trying to start various spiritual movements would be in and out; our friends trying to get various benefits on for various trips would be in and out. There would be a lot of motion, a lot of energy exchanged, and it was all real high in those days because at the time the Haight-Ashbury was a community. . . . It was just a very small neighborhood affair [and] we were all working for each other's benefit."

In the Haight, the principal movers and shakers included Ron and Jay Thelin, who ran the Psychedelic Shop; Emmett Grogan, who spearheaded the Diggers; Michael Bowen, a painter and a self-described Psychedelic Ranger; and Allen Cohen, who started an underground paper called the *Oracle*, which evolved into a stunningly beautiful source of art and writing about the community and psychedelic culture. There were "scenes" of various sizes surrounding each of these people, as well as all the major bands in the Haight, but there was a remarkable unanimity of purpose among all the different groups—stay high, have fun, be kind to your "brothers and sisters"—and everyone came together at the dances and free concerts in the park.

At the end of September, Kesey and the Merry Pranksters ended their Mexican adventure and drove Furthur back to the Bay Area. "It was just a very strange time," Mountain Girl says. "George [Walker] had gotten hepatitis, and Page [Browning] was sick, too, so Cassady drove a lot of it. And people were pretty depressed—it was depressing coming back to America. We didn't know what we were going to do. I had Sunshine with me, and I didn't have a plan or even an idea of what I was going to do next."

Mountain Girl had given birth to Sunshine Kesey in Mexico in early May, right on the heels of her "marriage" to George Walker there: "That was Ken's plot," she says. "He talked to his Mexican attorney who told him I would not be able to get a birth certificate for the baby unless I could show a marriage certificate, so a couple of weeks before I had the baby, in the middle of April, we got married at the registry office. They were laughing and laughing because I was *so* pregnant."

A lot had happened in San Francisco during the six months M.G. was with the Pranksters in Mexico. The Haight scene, which was just sprouting buds when she left in winter, was in full bloom that fall; the streets were teaming with freaks and glowing with new colors; *more* colors. "There was lots of energy and there was more interest in the Grateful Dead," M.G. says. "Suddenly *they* were the stars and we weren't. And we were kind of miffed, actually. But also it had gone from being interactive, like at the Acid Tests—the whole room is doing something together—to entertainer-audience. We were shocked—we didn't know how to fit into that; we couldn't fit into that. That helped our scene break up; plus, later, Ken had to go to court a lot."

Even though Kesey was still on the lam, he moved fairly openly, but carefully, in San Francisco that October—a bust waiting to happen. On October 3 he showed up late at night at a strangely subdued Acid Test called the Whatever It Is Festival put on by Stewart Brand at San Francisco State. The Dead dutifully supplied some of the music for the concert portion of the evening, and a few members of the group hung around to hear Kesey's ramblings in the wee hours of the morning.

And Kesey was there among the revelers for a while at the Love Pageant Rally, held in the Panhandle of Golden Gate Park on October 6 to celebrate the burgeoning Haight culture and to protest the new state law—which went into effect that day—making the possession and manufacture of LSD illegal. The Citizens for a Love Pageant Rally (led by Michael Bowen and *Oracle* editor Allen Cohen) had petitioned the Recreation and Parks Department for a permit for the gathering by saying, "Our party will be a celebration of community awareness and joy in communion with an international fellowship of those interested in the exploration of consciousness." But the invitations the rally organizers later sent to Mayor John Shelley and other city officials addressed the drug issue: "Opposition to an unjust law creates futility for citizens who are its victims and increases the hostility between the governed and the governors. In the case of LSD prohibition, the state has entered directly into the sacrosanct, personal psyches of its citizens." The Grateful Dead performed on a makeshift stage near the corner of Masonic and Oak Streets for several hundred dancing people—many of them tripping—and Kesey roamed through the crowd without attracting much notice.

Kesey stuck around San Francisco long enough to help plan one last big public event, the Acid Test Graduation, scheduled for Halloween night, appropriately enough. And he even managed to talk Bill Graham, who had been distrustful of Kesey and the Pranksters, into producing the event at Winterland, the 5,000-seat home of the Ice Follies, just a block up Geary Boulevard from the Fillmore Auditorium. The Grateful Dead were scheduled to play another gig at California Hall that night, but Kesey being Kesey, and the magnitude of the Graduation being readily apparent to every freak in the scene, the Pranksters prevailed and the Dead were released from their obligation. Now, defining what that event was supposed to be was the tricky part. It wasn't exactly designed to be an Acid Test—in fact, Kesey talked publicly about taking the whole scene "beyond" LSD, though he claimed not to know exactly what that meant. "Leary's supposed to be coming out and he's supposed to know pieces of it. And Jerry Garcia with his music knows pieces of it," Kesey said cryptically.

Kesey did an interview with the *San Francisco Chronicle* and even appeared on camera with a reporter from the local ABC-TV affiliate, KGO, hyping the event, but he refused to be goaded into actually renouncing LSD. And he was defiant about his outlaw status, saying, "I intend to stay in the country as a fugitive, and as salt in [FBI director] J. Edgar Hoover's wounds."

A few days later the law finally caught up with Kesey, and he was arrested by a station wagon full of off-duty FBI agents just south of San Francisco off the Bayshore Freeway. It seemed certain that Kesey would stay locked up this time; after all, he was now facing three felony charges: the two pot busts and one for unlawful flight when he skipped town and went to Mexico. Incredibly, though, his lawyers convinced the judge that Kesey should be allowed to remain free on bail because he was planning this event—the Graduation—where he would tell the assembled acidheads that LSD was not the answer. In *The Electric Kool-Aid Acid Test*, which contains vivid, Day-Glo-colored descriptions of all of these incidents, Tom Wolfe paraphrased Kesey's lawyer, Paul Robertson: "Mr. Kesey has a very public-spirited plan. . . . He has returned voluntarily from exile in his safe harbor, to risk certain arrest and imprisonment, in order to call a mass meeting of all LSD takers, past, present and potential, for the purpose of telling them to move beyond the pestilent habit of taking LSD."

Out on bail again, Kesey continued planning the Graduation. But the repentant image he presented to the media and the judge didn't prevent freaks from believing a very different scenario was planned for the Halloween celebration. A few days before the event, Bill Graham heard through the grapevine that Kesey and Owsley were planning to dose everyone who came to Winterland for the Acid Test Graduation. After calling Chet Helms and talking to others who knew Kesey better than he, Graham decided the rumors were probably true and backed out of the show the day before Halloween, forcing the Pranksters to scramble for a new place to stage their event.

The Grateful Dead dropped out of the Graduation ceremony, too, leaving a bizarre new multimedia group called the Anonymous Artists of America (or "Triple-A") to provide the entertainment for the assembled tripsters. Interestingly enough, the Anonymous Artists included none other than Sara Ruppenthal, who was living up on Skyline Boulevard in a commune known as Rancho Diablo with daughter Heather and various members of the troupe. "The reputation of the Dead is that they never sold themselves out," Sara comments. "Michael Moore had made the poster for the Acid Test Graduation announcing that the bands would be the Grateful Dead and the Triple-A. But the Dead backed out at the last moment because they were potentially getting a record contract and they were advised not to be associated with drugs, and since the Acid Test Graduation was potentially disreputable, it might harm their chances of getting signed. This was Triple-A's first gig and we were left to be the musical entertainment for this event. Half the people in our band had never played music before!"

The Dead played at the Dance of Death Ball at California Hall on Halloween, as originally planned. And the Acid Test Graduation took place in a dark, funky warehouse on Sixth Street, near downtown San Francisco, where some of the Pranksters had been staying since their return. In the end it was mainly friends and fellow travelers, not the hoped-for multitude they would've turned on with at Winterland. Not thousands but dozens of the right people, *their* people—"The Few and the Faithful" as Wolfe called them—pouring into the place, which the Pranksters had magically transformed with paint and props and a giant orange parachute billowing from the ceiling.

People tripped and danced and screamed and carried on as if it might be the last time this group would get the chance to be this high, this uninhibited, this free together. There were heavy moments, weird moments, scary moments, deep, dark, soul-searching moments, too. And sadness. And more dancing. And introspection. And eventually, inexorably, the dawn. With morning, too, a sense of finality. This *was* the last Acid Test. The Pranksters dispersed shortly after. Kesey took Furthur back home to Oregon, a few of the inner circle following close behind. Others scattered to points east and south, and a handful, including Mountain Girl, melted into the San Francisco scene.

CHAPTER 7
Come Join the Party
Every Day

y the fall of 1966, various L.A. and New York record business types had been sniffing around the Haight for a while, hoping to cash in on the rapidly developing scene, which some truly believed might be the American answer to the British Invasion. The Jefferson Airplane's first album, *Jefferson Airplane Takes Off*, hadn't quite lived up to RCA Records' commercial expectations, but in between that record and the sessions for their second album, which took place in Los Angeles in November 1966, the Airplane had brought in Great Society lead singer Grace Slick to replace the departing Signe Anderson, and the chemistry between Slick and singers-writers Marty Balin and Paul Kantner instantly took the group to a new level, both live and in the studio. It's a sign of how much respect the Airplane had for Garcia that they asked him to join them down in L.A. when the group was cutting tracks for their second album, *Surrealistic Pillow*, with producer Rick Jarrard and engineer David Hassinger. Garcia played acoustic guitar on four tracks—"My Best Friend," "Today," "Plastic Fantastic Lover" and "Coming Back to Me"—and served as an intermediary of sorts between the group, Hassinger and Jarrard. In addition, Garcia had a strong hand in rewriting the arrangement for "Somebody to Love" (written by Darby Slick for the Great Society), which became the Airplane's first hit single.

"The Airplane thought it would be helpful to have somebody there who could communicate to their producer who *they* could communicate to," Garcia said. "And since they all knew me and I understood their music and understood what they were doing pretty much at the time, it would be far-out. I went down there and hung out and was a sort of go-between."

Though he's not credited specifically for his contributions, which included the album's title, Garcia *is* listed on the record—as "Musical and Spiritual Adviser." Of course it was meant mainly tongue-in-cheek, but that credit was the first exposure most people outside of California had to the name "Jerry Garcia." *Surrealistic Pillow*, released in February 1967, was an immensely popular album, particularly in counterculture circles (it was the obvious product of *heads*), so Garcia's association with it boosted the mystique that was already starting to surround him.

Not surprisingly, as one of the top bands in the Haight, the Grateful Dead attracted considerable interest from record companies. Joe Smith, who was then an A&R man for Burbank-based Warner Bros. Records, came up to San Francisco and, at the urging of Tom Donahue, went to see the band at the Avalon Ballroom. Smith was already becoming known for his good musical intuition, but he'd never encountered anything quite like the Grateful Dead—Warners was a straight, mainstream label with a roster boasting names like Dean Martin, Petula Clark and Frank Sinatra. Smith showed up at the Avalon wearing a suit, and, as he said in Gene Sculatti and Davin Seay's *San Francisco Nights,* "There we were, walking up the steps of this startling place and there were these kids lying around painting each other's bodies and all of these lights and smells everywhere. Somebody wanted to dance with my wife. I told her, 'Don't come with me to meet the band. You must understand.' The Grateful Dead. Even the name was intimidating. What did it mean? No one knew."

The band had reservations about signing a deal with an L.A. record label—"They lived in terror of being ripped off," Smith said—but a few weeks after their first encounter, the Dead decided to accept the Warner Bros. offer of $3,500 (to be matched with a bonus if the record sold more than 15,000 copies, which it did, easily). Smith flew to San Francisco and met Scully and Rifkin at Tom Donahue's Telegraph Hill apartment to get the contract signed. Donahue remembered, "Joe walks out on the porch and Rock and Danny say to me, 'Listen, man, we gotta take acid with this cat. Then he'll really understand what it is we're doing.' "

"They told me I couldn't really understand their music until I dropped some acid," Smith said. "I informed them that under no circumstances would I do that." He didn't. And the band signed on the dotted line anyway.

There's no question that Scully and Rifkin were a new breed of manager; after all, they had virtually no experience, and they were completely distrustful of the straight show-business world. Actually, being a "manager" for the Grateful Dead was almost a contradiction in terms. But every band had to find that person or combination of people who had a "business head," and in the beginning it was that unlikely pair.

"The managers don't do things the old cigar-chewing-manager way," Garcia noted in early 1967. "When our managers go someplace, they go just the way they are around the house. They have long hair, wear outlandish clothes and beads, and they talk like people on Haight Street do, because that's the way they are. That's the way we all are, and we're not sacrificing any of ourselves to do business. When we go into the business part of things—when we talk to lawyers, the vice presidents of Warner Bros.—we talk to them the way we talk to our friends. We're being out front. We're trying to change the whole atmosphere of music, the business part as well as just the way it is, just by dealing with it on a more humanistic level, because it's a valuable commodity—it's an art."

Between October 1 and December 31, 1966, the Dead played the Fillmore Auditorium sixteen times, the Avalon five times, the Matrix four times, and they landed a few other gigs at odd places like the North Face Ski Shop in Berkeley, Las Lomas High School in Walnut Creek and the Old Cheese Factory in San Francisco. They became headliners that fall, second only to the Airplane as a popular draw (though the Dead *begged* Bill Graham to let the group open for the great R&B singer Otis Redding at the Fillmore in mid-December). Additionally, the band played occasionally for free in the Panhandle: in those days it was easy to load their equipment into Laird Grant's truck, drive a couple of blocks and play for a while using a generator for power. Between money the band earned through gigs and cash that passed through 710 from low-level pot and LSD sales, the Dead were able to live comfortably, though not lavishly, and support a few of their friends in the process. In that way, the Dead scene was a microcosm of the larger Haight economy, which was driven mainly by rock 'n' roll and dope dealing, but also supported craftspeople and hippie business entrepreneurs as the area thrived.

Asked in the spring of 1967 what would happen if the Dead somehow became successful (how unlikely *that* seemed then), twenty-four-year-old Jerry replied, "Then we'll see if there's a better way to become successful and wealthy! A way that's more rewarding to us. A way to spend our money so that it brings about more enjoyment for more people. More food certainly. A lot of what we make now is just money to live on for us and our friends and anybody else who doesn't have anything. I don't need anything. I don't really want anything. I've got instruments, I know I can eat, so there's nothing to worry about."

That fall of 1966 Garcia and Mountain Girl began spending more time together, at 710 and out in the world, and at some point what had long been just a close friendship developed into mutual affection. "Actually, I thought Jerry was really special from when I first met him [in 1964] because he played the banjo so well and I loved the banjo," she says. "I was knocked out by him. I was a little disappointed by Mother McCree's because Jerry wasn't really the leader; everybody took a turn. Then, in the Warlocks, it seemed like Weir and especially Pigpen were more out front and Jerry was in the background; he didn't push his way out there. But I wasn't that interested in amplified music at that time. I liked folk music and classical music and I loved the banjo, too. By the time we'd gone through the Acid Tests, though, I loved the Grateful Dead, and as time went on, Jerry got better and better and the same kind of special thing that I saw in his banjo playing was obvious in his [electric] guitar playing and he just had a really nice stage personality; really 'up' and smiling a lot. Always very positive."

Still, Jerry nearly got back together with Sara that December. As she recalls, "When Heather turned three [on December 8, 1966] I invited Jerry to my parents' home for a celebratory dinner. It felt good having our little family together, and we talked about giving it a try again. He invited me to come visit him at [710] Ashbury and see if it would work for Heather and me to move in there with him. I did go, but I didn't feel comfortable there, and I couldn't imagine a place for Heather and me in that life. There was a lot going on, no privacy, too chaotic for me. It didn't exactly feel 'family-friendly' to me."

Nineteen sixty-six ended gloriously with Bill Graham's first New Year's Eve concert at the Fillmore, an acid-soaked revel that found the Airplane, the Dead and Quicksilver trading sets until dawn. There was incredible optimism in the Haight as 1966 turned to 1967: the bands were getting better and more popular; the steady influx of freaks from other parts of the country brought new energy into the scene but still seemed manageable; and increasingly the neighborhood felt like an oasis far away from straight society—a vision of what many felt was a better world in every aspect.

"The utopian sentiments of these hippies was not to be put down lightly," Warren Hinckle wrote in perhaps the finest contemporary article about the rise of Haight-Ashbury, in *Ramparts* magazine in mid-1967. "Hippies have a clear vision of the ideal community—a psychedelic community, to be sure— where everyone is turned on and beautiful and loving and happy and floating free. But it is a vision that, despite the Alice in Wonderland phraseology usually breathlessly employed to describe it, necessarily embodies a radical political philosophy: communal life, drastic restriction of private property, rejection of violence, creativity before consumption, freedom before authority, de-emphasis of government and traditional forms of leadership."

From the outset, the Dead refused to get involved with overtly political activities, though not surprisingly they were often asked to appear at various marches and rallies. There's no question that as individuals, Garcia and the other members vehemently opposed the Vietnam War and supported the goals of the civil rights movement, to mention two of the hot-button issues of the day, but many freaks believed that protesting and trying to reform what they viewed as a corrupt, morally bankrupt political system was, in effect, buying into that system. Basically, the apolitical freaks in Haight-Ashbury wanted to create a world where people could get high (or not; most weren't doctrinaire about it), live and work together, support each other and police themselves, without conforming to what they viewed as tired and judgmental societal "norms."

"The politics of hip was that we were setting up a new world, as it were, that was going to run parallel to the old world but have as little to do with it as possible," said Country Joe and the Fish guitarist Barry Melton (who's now a lawyer) in the film *Berkeley in the Sixties*. "We just weren't going to deal with straight people. And to us, the politicos—a lot of the leaders of the antiwar movement—were straight people, because they were still concerned with government. They were going to go march on Washington. We didn't even want to know that Washington was there! We thought that eventually the whole world was just going to stop this nonsense and start loving each other as soon as they all got turned on. It's amazing that these movements [that] coexisted at the same time were in stark contrast in certain respects, but as the 1960s progressed, drew closer together and began taking on aspects of the other."

"What we're thinking about is a peaceful planet," Garcia told a reporter in an infamous 1967 CBS documentary called *The Hippie Temptation*. "We're not thinking about anything else. We're not thinking about any kind of power; we're not thinking about any of those kind of struggles. We're not thinking about revolution or war or any of that. That's not what we want. Nobody wants to get hurt. Nobody wants to hurt anybody. We would all like to be able to live an uncluttered life; a simple life, a good life. And think about moving the whole human race ahead a step, or a few steps."

And in another 1967 interview, Garcia said, "We're trying to make music in such a way that it doesn't have a message for anybody. We don't have anything to tell anybody. We don't want to change anybody. We want people to have the chance to feel a little better. That's the absolute most we want to do with our music. The music that we make is an act of love, an act of joy. We really like it a lot. If it says something, it says it on its own terms at the moment we're playing it, and it doesn't have anything to do with— We're not telling people to go get stoned, or drop out. We're just playing and they can take that any way they want."

On the cool but sunny Saturday afternoon of January 14, 1967, the freaks of Haight-Ashbury and North Beach and Berkeley and Marin and *everywhere* got together on a gorgeous patch of green in the heart of Golden Gate Park known as the Polo Fields. This was the Human Be-In, "A Gathering of the Tribes," and it drew more than 20,000 people in an unprecedented show of numbers by the emerging counterculture. The Be-In was really an extension of the energy that had gone into the Love Pageant Rally back in October, with Michael Bowen and Allen Cohen again leading the way. This time around though, there was an effort to broaden the scope of the event and to include Beat poets and writers, more bands, and even some of Berkeley's radical left firebrands. Allen Ginsberg, Lawrence Ferlinghetti, Lenore Kandel, Gary Snyder and Michael McClure read poetry and led chants and prayers. Millbrook vet Richard Alpert and activist Jerry Rubin spoke. Timothy Leary, a yellow flower tucked behind each ear, urged the assembled to "Turn on, tune in, drop out. . . . Turn on to the scene; tune in to what's happening; and drop out—of high school, college, grad school, junior executive, senior executive—and follow me, the hard way." (Rock Scully joked years later that the Grateful Dead's ethos in that era was "Plug in, freak out, fall apart.")

But "The few speakers were hardly intelligible over the microphone, the gathering being more interested in the great light show of nature and themselves," wrote the *Chronicle*'s Ralph Gleason in a poignant and amazingly sympathetic article in Monday's paper. "The rock bands—the Quicksilver, the Grateful Dead, the Airplane—came over well and the Dead's set was remark-

ably exciting, causing people to rise up wherever they were and begin dancing. Dizzy Gillespie, playing while a young girl danced over on one side, asked
who the Dead were and commented on how they were swinging."

The Hell's Angels cared for lost children (!) and helped provide security.
People threw Frisbees, watched their dogs run free, danced, sang, tripped in the
surrounding pine and eucalyptus groves, pounded on drums, played flutes,
strummed guitars, clinked cymbals and clonked cowbells. Incense and pot
smoke rose into air already colored by balloons, kites, flags and streamers. Acid
was everywhere, but there were no bad trips. "As the sun set, and the bands
played and the people glowed," Gleason wrote, "Buddha's voice [actually, it
was Ginsberg] came over the sound system, asking everyone to stand up and
turn towards the sun and watch the sunset. Later, he asked everyone to help
clean up the debris and they did.

"And so it ended; the first of the great gatherings. No fights. No drunks.
No troubles. Two policemen on horseback and 20,000 people. The perfect sun-
shine, the beautiful birds in the air, a parachutist descending as the Grateful
Dead ended a song. . . .

"Saturday's gathering was an affirmation, not a protest. A statement of
life, not death, and a promise of good, not evil. . . . This is truly something new
and not the least of it is that it is an asking for a new dimension to peace, not
just an end to shooting, for the reality of love and a great Nest for all humans."

All in all it was probably the the Haight scene's finest hour.

"I'd never seen so many people in my life," Garcia said a few weeks after
the event. "It was really fantastic. I almost didn't believe it. It was a totally
underground movement. It was all the people into dope of any sort, and like
20,000 people came out in the park and everyone had a good time. There was
no violence. No hassling."

However, many years later Garcia recalled one aspect of the Be-In that
was not sunshine and roses for him: "There was a whole contingent of people
from over in Berkeley, guys like Jerry Rubin. . . . And I remember standing
out in the crowd and I heard people like Allen Ginsberg got up—he 'ommed'
and played little finger cymbals and that felt very good out in the crowd. I had
taken some LSD; I was feeling really good. A lot of people were there and were
real happy. Then all of a sudden this voice came over the loudspeaker—it
turned out to be Jerry Rubin—and he was exorting the crowd. And all of a
sudden the kind of images that went into my mind were Hitler, you know,
every angry voice I'd ever heard popped into my head. So I felt, well, of all the
things I would like to avoid people having to feel, *that's* one of the things I'd
like to avoid. I'd like to avoid transmitting that message to people—that angry voice."

That said, the Grateful Dead opened their short set that afternoon with
one of the most powerful songs ever written about the perils of nuclear
war, "Morning Dew," by the Canadian folksinger Bonnie Dobson. The song's

setting is the world after a nuclear holocaust, and it takes the form of a conversation between the last man and last woman left alive:

> *I thought I heard a baby cry this morning*
> *Thought I heard a baby cry today*
> *You didn't hear no baby cry this morning*
> *You didn't hear no baby cry today*

Far from being some blatant political screed, however, "Morning Dew" is more evocative and elliptical, a mood piece that's really its own world. It instantly became one of the Dead's most popular tunes, and it remained so until Garcia's death. And in some ways the song exemplifies the kind of ballads Garcia and Robert Hunter would later write—melodically beautiful, even exultant, but lyrically bittersweet and mournful.

Less than a week after the Human Be-In, the Dead, their managers and a few friends, including Rosie McGee and Mountain Girl (who had just moved into 710 with Jerry), drove down to Los Angeles to record the Dead's first album for Warner Bros. Records. Dave Hassinger, who'd engineered classic Rolling Stones hits like "Satisfaction," "It's All Over Now," "Lady Jane" and "Paint It, Black," as well as records by the Lovin' Spoonful, the Yardbirds, Elvis Presley and the Airplane, was brought in to produce the sessions, which took place over four days at RCA's Studio A in Hollywood—the same studio where Garcia had helped the Airplane make *Surrealistic Pillow*.

"We went in and did the album very, very fast—less than a week," Hassinger recalled. "At that time I didn't know them, and looking back I wish we could have had more time and done some things a little differently. But it was my understanding that these were songs that they'd really played a lot and they wanted to essentially get them down the way they played them live. I'd made two or three trips up to the Bay Area and seen them at the Fillmore, and I thought they were dynamite. What I was after on the album was to capture as much of the energy as I could."

A month after the sessions, but before the record had been released, Garcia characterized the album as "honest. It sounds just like us. It even has mistakes on it. But it also has a certain amount of excitement on it. It sounds like we felt good when we were making it. It sounds like one of our good sets."

But by the early '70s Garcia's evaluation of the group's maiden effort had shifted a bit: "At that time we had no real record consciousness," Garcia said. "We were completely naive about it. . . . So we went down there and, what was it we had? Dexamyl? Some sort of diet-watcher's speed, and pot and stuff like that. So in three nights we played some hyperactive music. That's what's embarrassing about that record now: the tempo was way too fast."

In terms of the song selection, the record reflected "simply what we were doing onstage," Garcia said. "But in reality, the way we played was not really too much the way that record was. Usually we played tunes that lasted a long time because we like to play a lot. And when you're playing for people who are dancing and getting high—you can dance easy to a half-hour tune and you can even wonder why it ended so soon. So for us the whole thing was weird 'cause we went down there and turned out songs real fast—less than three minutes, which is real short." (In fact, five of the nine songs on the record were under two and a half minutes; very unusual for the Grateful Dead.)

Rushed tempos aside, the album nicely captures some of the breadth of the Dead's uptempo ballroom repertoire, with a solid mixture of blues- and folk-derived tunes, including "Morning Dew" (shortened slightly for the record); radical rearrangements of the '20s jug band blues "New Minglewood Blues," "Sitting on Top of the World" and "Viola Lee Blues"; the Blue Ridge Mountains chestnut "Cold Rain and Snow"; Bay Area folk/blues singer Jesse Fuller's early '60s number "Beat It On Down the Line"; and the late-'40s blues standard "Good Morning Little Schoolgirl" (which was Pigpen's lone lead vocal on the album). Additionally, the album featured two frenetic rock 'n' roll originals: "The Golden Road (To Unlimited Devotion)," written by the group under the fanciful pseudonym McGannahan Skjellyfetti (derived from a novel by pacifist author-artist Kenneth Patchen); and "Cream Puff War," with words and music by Garcia.

"The Golden Road" is a fine bit of aural fluff dominated by fast, ringing electric guitars and an overdubbed acoustic picked by Garcia, a swirling Pigpen organ line and Garcia's bright lead vocal, which almost sounds like he's smiling as sings:

> See that girl barefootin' along
> Whistlin' and singin' she's a-carryin' on
> Got laughin' in her eyes, dancin' in her feet
> She's a neon light diamond
> She can live on the street.

Then the band joins in on the chorus:

> Hey, hey, come right away
> Come join the party every day.

" 'The Golden Road' was our effort at nailing down some of that [early Haight] feeling, I guess," Garcia said. "That was sort of our group writing experience before Hunter was with us. We kept it simple. But what could you say [about the scene]? 'We took a bunch of acid and had a lot of fun'?"

Garcia's "Cream Puff War" is much darker both musically and lyrically. It sketches a portrait of a relationship gone bad (presumably not his) in a manner that's somewhat reminiscent of bitter Dylan tunes like "Positively 4th Street" and "Like a Rolling Stone," though not nearly as cleverly. Jerry once said he became a lyric writer "only by default. I felt my lyric writing was woefully inadequate." And about "Cream Puff War" specifically, he said in the mid-'80s, "That's one of those tunes that's so old its totally embarrassing. I'd just as soon everybody forgot about it." He tried to: a few months after the first record came out, Garcia dropped both "Cream Puff War" and "The Golden Road," and he never played either again (much to the chagrin of Deadheads).

Of the album's nine songs, only two gave the band a chance to stretch out much, "Good Morning Little Schoolgirl" and "Viola Lee Blues." In concert, "Schoolgirl" was always exciting because it contained a solo passage where the band quickened the tempo for a while before falling back to the song's midtempo shuffle. On the album, the song faded during the uptempo section; still, it was an effective showcase for the band's considerable blues chops. "Viola Lee Blues" had a similar construction, but rather than suddenly changing speeds, it contained a long middle jam that built slowly and deliberately, almost like a raga, with bandmembers expertly constructing an ascending line that over the course of a few minutes rose to a feverish crescendo of clanging guitars, screaming organ and sheer cacaphonous noise.

Live, the group sometimes kept the jam in "Viola Lee Blues" at the climax for upwards of half a minute—an extraordinarily long time for something that loud and furious—before the tension was released by dropping back to the tune's original gait. Though powerful by any standard, the album version of "Viola Lee Blues" is still tamer than what the band usually unleashed in the ballrooms, where writhing and jerking dancers frequently added to the mounting din with their own ecstatic screams and shouts as the music and earsplitting feedback and human wails joined to create a deafening tidal wave of sound that always seemed to lift the dance hall off the ground. In late 1966 and early 1967, "Viola Lee Blues" was the song that best showed the raging beast inside of the Grateful Dead, the chaotic and unpredictable edge that had been somewhat subsumed since the Acid Tests. Not surprisingly, it was the trippers' favorite song.

"We've always liked the long form," Garcia said. "For us, taking an idea and just *annihilating* it worked great in that context, because the dancers loved it. There they were, high on whatever, and they had the energy to dance for hours. So you could take [a song] and [do whatever you wanted to it] and you weren't violating the dancers' space and you weren't failing to entertain them. And they also had the option of stopping whenever they wanted to and going someplace else, and so the whole thing had a sense of free-flow about it. I've thought about this: There's no situation that I've been able to come up with that would have allowed the Grateful Dead to do what we used to do; the kind of range we wanted to cover. You couldn't have done it in a conventional bar, you couldn't have done it at a conventional concert."

If the album offered few hints about the direction the Dead's original material would take over the next year, it at least served as a strong showcase for the Dead's instrumental prowess. Hassinger and engineer Dick Bogert did an excellent job of capturing the intricacies of Phil Lesh's dynamic and tuneful bass work and Bill Kreutzmann's fluid, high-energy drumming, with its subtle cymbal splashes and rapid-fire cymbal-snare combinations that clearly owed more to Elvin Jones than Charlie Watts. But it is Garcia's guitar that is most prominent in the mix on most tunes, and even on this first major outing the breadth of his playing is readily apparent, as he moves easily from blues to heavily accented country picking, sometimes even within the same solo.

Since the Dead never decided to be a blues band or a country band or a straight-ahead rock 'n' roll band, or *any* particular style of group, Garcia had the freedom to take his inspiration from anything that caught his fancy, whether it was techniques he'd enjoyed as a banjo player, or B. B. King, or George Harrison, or sarod master Ali Akbar Khan, or Bakersfield country guitarists like Don Rich (from Buck Owens's Buckaroos) and Roy Nichols (from Merle Haggard's Strangers), or even the "hot" jazz of the great Belgian gypsy guitarist Django Reinhardt and his violinist partner, Stephane Grappelli. Garcia and the other members of the band reveled in their eclecticism and their personal eccentricities as players, with the result that they each developed a unique instrumental voice in their ceaseless exploration of different kinds of music.

The first Dead album, called simply *The Grateful Dead*, was released in mid-March of 1967, and it was an immediate smash hit—in Northern California, if almost nowhere else. Warner Bros. dutifully released a single of "The Golden Road" backed by "Cream Puff War," but there's little evidence that the record got much airplay on many AM radio stations outside the Bay Area, and the proliferation of progressive, "free-form" format FM radio stations was still a few months away in major cities—KMPX, the pioneering San Francisco FM rock station founded by Tom Donahue, started broadcasting in June.

Still, the album was a big deal in San Francisco, and it symbolized the rising fortunes of the cream of the local bands. Garcia appeared on the front and back covers of the album smiling benignly and dressed in an indigo paisley velour shirt, his long black hair crowned by an American flag top hat. In the credits he was listed as Jerry "Captain Trips" Garcia, a Prankster moniker concocted by Kesey in late 1965, which became an embarassing albatross around Garcia's neck almost immediately: "That's bullshit," he said of the tag in the early '70s. Garcia had no interest in being known as the "captain" of anything, let alone people's trips.

"Jerry was kind of like the patriarch, although that's not quite the right word," Rosie McGee says. "I remember very early on going to his house and it was like he was holding court, even back then. I got the impression that, well, I couldn't imagine him going to hang out at somebody else's house. People came to his house instead; certainly that was true in the Haight. People gathered around him naturally, and I think it was because of his intelligence and his imagination. Even back then he had charisma. But he was also always very self-deprecating: 'I'm just a guy who plays guitar.' "

A charmingly innocent description of Garcia, delivered in classic fanzine style, appeared in a spring 1967 edition of the *Olompali Sunday Times*, a humble but spirited free mimeographed newsletter put out by the Dead's fan club, The Golden Road to Unlimited Devotion, headed by Sue Swanson and Connie Bonner: "Jer—talented, talented . . . has a lot to say . . . digs girls . . . very open . . . loves orange juice . . . tells the best stories . . . warm . . . hates dishonesty (they all do) . . . owns a pedal steel guitar . . . Leo." (In the same article we learn that Pigpen has a bright red bathrobe, Weir's nickname is "Mr. Bob Weir Trouble," Bill "sleeps a lot . . . eats a lot . . . digs jazz drummers . . . has a shiny new Mustang . . ." and Phil "has a quick mind . . . doesn't bleach his hair.")

In late March the Dead played six shows at a short-lived San Francisco nightclub called the Rock Garden. The series is notable for two completely unrelated reasons: it marked the first time Garcia's mother had gone to see her son play since his folk days; and sharing the bill with the Dead for those shows was the jazzy Charles Lloyd Quartet, who unquestionably influenced the Dead's musical direction.

It was Jerry's brother, Tiff, who cajoled their mother to go see the Grateful Dead. "I'd say, 'Mom, you gotta hear this. Will you listen?' " Tiff remembers. "But she was very stubborn and only liked to listen to certain things. She liked easy-listening music. She saw Jerry a couple of times when he was with Sara down in Palo Alto, but she didn't want to know about the rock 'n' roll. And then of course there was the whole drug thing and 'Captain Trips' and all that. She was a nurse so she knew a bit about drugs. It didn't surprise her. She wasn't shocked or anything. She might not have liked it, but she was always proud of him. Then I took her to this place called the Rock Garden, in the outer Mission. The Dead were between gigs and I helped them get work there because I had helped this guy rebuild the club. So my mom went and saw them and she liked them. In fact she went a couple of times. But because of the experience my father went through, the music business wasn't the best thing you could do for a career in her eyes. She was from the era when a lot of people viewed all musicians as criminals and lowlifes who couldn't fit into society."

As for the attitude of the other members of the Garcia clan, Jerry's aunt Leonor says, "It was terrible during that time because they were calling him 'Captain Trips' and we were hiding that from my parents—we didn't want them to know that he was into drugs and all that. That sort of thing really shocked my mother. For a long time Jerry completely ignored everyone in the family. He didn't want any part of the family. I think it was because he was into drugs and he knew we didn't approve. I was even ashamed to admit he was my nephew."

The New York–based Charles Lloyd Quartet was a significant force in the San Francisco scene because they managed to make free-ranging improvisational jazz that was accessible to rock fans. Lloyd's band, which, besides the talented reedsman, included pianist Keith Jarrett, drummer Jack DeJohnette and bassist Cecil McBee, was one of the first jazz groups to be invited to play the Fillmore, and Lloyd jammed with the Dead at the Human Be-In, adding breathy flute to a long workout on "Good Morning Little Schoolgirl." It was Garcia's idea to book Lloyd's group at the Rock Garden, and he was such a fan of the group that when he and Phil Lesh appeared on Tom Donahue's KMPX radio program as guest deejays in April 1967, one of the songs he chose to play was Lloyd's trippy "Dream Weaver," a potent dose of acidy jazz from late 1966 that presaged some of the free-floating but intense places the Dead's music would go in the last part of 1967 and early 1968. "Dream Weaver" is a sort of proto–"Dark Star," complete with passages of spellbinding dissonance and gently cascading melody streams.

"I think we probably influenced them a bit to start opening up their improvisations," Lloyd says of the Dead. "When we were at the Rock Garden, we traded sets and they'd all be hanging around in the wings when we played, really listening. Jazz has always been a music of freedom and inspiration and wonder and consolation, and the Dead definitely got something from that."

By the spring of 1967 Mountain Girl was well settled in 710 and she and Jerry were unquestionably a couple. "It was a happy house, it really was," she says. "We had a great time. Tangerine was the only girlfriend living there at first. Veronica [Pigpen's girlfriend] would come by a lot. She was very sharp-tongued and hilariously funny. The fan club had an office downstairs. It was a lot of mouths to feed. I collected the money from everybody—fifteen dollars a week, except I don't think Pigpen ever paid, and I was mad at him for that. Then I'd go down to the Chinese grocery store down the street and buy pork chops and brown rice. I was not a good cook. I knew how to make Prankster stew—anything over brown rice, usually just brown rice and veggies. We went through lots of frozen orange juice, too."

There was a constant stream of visitors to 710 day and night, as each bandmember had his own intimates and acquaintances, "and then all the other people associated with the scene had people they brought around—Owsley and Hank Harrison had their own circles," M.G. notes. "Rock was the ultimate conduit for all sorts of weird people, like millionaires and people with foreign connections." Visitors from the Palo Alto days frequently stopped by, and Neal Cassady had his own little space in the attic, where he'd stay for a few days every month or so in the course of his travels.

"As far as I could tell [Cassady] never slept," wrote John Barlow, a childhood friend of Weir's (and his songwriting partner beginning in the early '70s) who first encountered the Beat hero at 710. "He tossed back hearts of Mexican Dexedrine by the shot-sized bottle, grinned, cackled and jammed on into the night. Despite such behavior, he seemed, at forty-one, a paragon of robust health. With a face out of a recruiting poster (leaving aside a certain glint in the eyes) and a torso, usually raw, by Michelangelo, he didn't even seem quite mortal.

"Neal and Bobby were perfectly contrapuntal. As Cassady rattled incessantly, Bobby had fallen mostly mute, stilled perhaps by macrobiotics, perhaps a less than passing grade in the Acid Tests, or, more likely, some combination of every strange thing that had caused him to start thinking much faster than anyone could talk."

"Weir had a whole cabinet in the kitchen for his weird macrobiotic things that he was eating," M.G. remembers. "I'd run into the macrobiotic thing before and I just sneered at him; I thought it was absurd. You get skinny and pale on this diet; it has zero nutritional content. He was not an untroubled person. He definitely brought emotional baggage with him from school experiences, his whole scene with his parents, and the feeling that he wasn't as big a dude as the rest of the guys: they pushed him around quite a bit. But he always took it with pretty good grace. He was always extremely gracious.

"Phil was hilariously funny in those days. With a little bit of LSD and a long night, Phil could keep you laughing until the point where you thought your face was going to fall off. He had a terrible, wicked, needly sense of humor. He was lots and lots of fun, and though he didn't live at 710 when I was there, he and Rosie were around most of the time it seemed.

"Jerry was sort of the indestructable, fast-moving guy. He talked a blue streak—talk, talk, talk, talk—always spinning ideas and concepts, philosophies and possibilities. If he had a genius, it was for recognizing possibilities, and he had this limitless enthusiasm. He'd get all enthusiastic about ephemeral stuff and get everyone all charged up in an instant. And he was a great supporter of people's ideas. There was a lot of sitting around bullshitting, shooting the breeze, getting enthusiastic about things and then dropping them just as fast—sending out so-and-so to research something; discussions about buying a boat and taking the show onto the waters; or buying a bus of our own and doing something with that. There were a million ideas about what we were going to do and it was really exciting to be around that, but what actually transpired was they rehearsed a lot and they played a lot and they stayed home a lot—the touring thing didn't really come on until later. The band's work ethic at that time was really strong. They rehearsed all the time and that's how they got so good."

On the last day of May the band flew to New York for its first shows away from the West Coast, with Warner Bros. footing the bill for the trip. The Airplane and Country Joe and the Fish had already played New York by this point, so the ground had been broken, so to speak. Amazingly, though, none of the Dead had been to New York before this trip; Garcia's bluegrass quest had taken him only as far east as Pennsylvania. As Laird Grant, who helped haul and set up the Dead's equipment, noted, "For California boys like us it was strange to be in New York. It looked like all the old gangster movies I'd ever seen. The place looked just as grimy as it did on black-and-white TV." Of course the Dead weren't lodging on Park Avenue, either. Rather, they stayed at the Chelsea Hotel, the notorious bastion of junkies, poets, artists, musicians and bohemian drifters of every stripe. "It was very strange, charmingly seedy," Mountain Girl remembers. "I'd never slept overnight in a big city. I couldn't believe it. Here we were, these acid-soaked, highly sensitive woods-bunnies from California, and I could hear every toilet flush and every siren passing."

Appropriately enough, on the Dead's first full day in New York the group played a free concert in Tompkins Square Park, in the East Village, immediately endearing themselves to the area's sizable freak population. All through the second half of 1966 and the first half of '67 there had been caravans of people traveling back and forth between New York and San Francisco, so actually there was already a contingent of folks in New York who'd seen the Dead in San Francisco and knew what the Haight scene was all about by the time the Dead arrived in the East. Mostly, though, Tompkins Square Park was filled with people who either didn't know the Dead at all or had perhaps heard something about them through the underground grapevine. And then there were the simply curious: "During the concert I was looking off to the side, and, sitting down under a tree drinking pink lemonade, with his Cadillac nearby, and his white chauffeur and his white butler, was Charles Mingus," Laird Grant says. "Phil went over and talked to him after the show. It was cool."

Though there were no bands in New York that were truly comparable to the Dead, Rosie McGee says, "Everything we were doing in San Francisco, they'd been doing in New York for a while longer. It was very different, of course, but they'd been having events in people's lofts and dances and really weird happenings, and the music scene had gone on through the folk years into rock 'n' roll like it did in California. But it was much more entrenched and serious and gritty in its own way. We were the Wild West people to them. If you compared us to the L.A. crowd, we were the gritty ones. But then we moved into New York and we were kind of the lightweights, or that's how it felt to me, anyway. We were treated that way, I thought. But maybe not so much musician to musician."

During their brief New York stay the Dead played a few nights on the cramped stage of the Cafe Au Go-Go, downstairs from where Frank Zappa's Mothers of Invention were playing at the same time; at the trendy, chrome-walled Cheetah Club; in the gym at the State University of New York at Stony

Brook (Long Island); and at another free concert, this one in Central Park. And though all the gigs went well, there was nothing about the two-week jaunt that indicated what a phenomenon the Dead would become in New York in the years to come.

"We were very insular on the road," Mountain Girl says. "We were considered very exotic almost everywhere we went. I would wear wild shit on the street. In New York, my diaper bag was made out of American flag bunting and I had some guy who attacked me and tried to rip it off my arm. I had it chock-full of baby diapers and baby bottles and here's this guy screaming some gibberish about desecrating the flag. 'You people should all be put in jail!' 'Really, for what, asshole?' That's the way it was on the street—we experienced a lot of naked hatred just for being different. I loved being different. For me it was the final expression of things I'd been feeling since high school—all that repression and pressure to conform."

Things were much more comfortable for the Dead at home, though the scene they returned to in the middle of June 1967 was starting to get a bit weird. The Summer of Love was in full swing, thousands of young people from all over the world were descending on the Haight each week and the hippie utopia was clearly beginning to fray around the edges.

CHAPTER 8

Poised for Flight,
Wings Spread Bright

ver since January's Human Be-In, which was the first Haight-Ashbury event to get extensive national media coverage, teenagers and young adults had been arriving in San Francisco in increasing numbers. They took buses from Des Moines and planes from Boston. They hitchhiked west with just a few clothes tossed into a backpack, or stuffed all their worldly possessions into old cars and Volkswagen microbuses. Some came from comfortable suburbs with a wad of cash supplied by Mom and Dad (who had no idea why it was so important, all of a sudden, to go to San Francisco). Others came from poor rural areas with just a few hard-earned dollars and wide-eyed expectations for the hippie promised land. Runaway rebels, dropouts and misfits were joined on the interstates and on buses by curious college students eager to check out the commotion in California. There was even a fluffy but infectious bit of folk-rock all over the radio that May and June that added to the buzz: "San Francisco (Be Sure to Wear Flowers in Your Hair)," written by the leader of L.A.'s Mamas and the Papas, John Phillips, and sung by another Angeleno, Scott McKenzie, promised "summertime will be a love-in there."

Time and *Newsweek*, *Look* and *Life* and all the major television networks covered the rise of the San Francisco counterculture with varying degrees of befuddlement. This was, after all, something genuinely new in this country, a cultural and generational rebellion of unparalleled scope and seriousness. Though it was easy for mainstream Americans to chuckle at the colorful external trappings of the revolution—the long hair, wild clothes and jargon-filled lexicon, not to mention *that noise these kids call music*—the majority of Americans truly believed that what they saw happening in the Haight, and maybe on a much smaller scale in their own cities and towns, was truly a threat to the traditional American Way of Life.

And it was. Hippies rejected many of the assumptions that are the foundation of Western materialistic society. They believed that working hard in an unfulfilling job to acquire enough money to live in a culture that values conformity over creativity and individuality was not a well-spent life. They believed that the competitive capitalist paradigm was outmoded and noxious, destined to be replaced by cooperative community. Further, they believed that the widespread expansion of consciousness through drugs or other means—

meditation, yoga, music, art of any kind—was the only way the Earth was going to survive what appeared to be a certain apocalypse, caused either by war or by the destruction of the planet's natural resources. There had never been such a public flaunting of out-and-out lawlessness and morally seditious behavior in this country before. And that scared the hell out of people.

"When the big media flash came out," Garcia said, "when *Time* magazine guys came out and interviewed everybody and took photographs and made it news, the feedback from that killed the whole scene. It was ridiculous. We could no longer support the tiny trickle that was really supporting everybody. The whole theory of hip economics is essentially that you have a small amount of money and move it around very fast and it would work out. But when you have thousands and thousands of people, it's just too unwieldy. And all the attempts at free food and all that—certain people had to work too hard to justify it.

"At the early stages we were operating purely without anybody looking on, without anybody looking through the big window. We were going along really well. And then the crowds came in. All the people who were looking for something. . . . [There were] too many people to take care of and not enough people willing to do something. There were a lot of people looking for the free ride. That's the death of any scene, when you have more drag energy than you have forward-going energy."

On the surface at least, the Haight-Ashbury scene must have seemed extremely appealing to independent-minded kids. Free music in the park! Cheap rent in communes or no rent at all in crash pads! Free food for those in need! Dope for the taking! A community run *by* freaks *for* freaks! According to Garcia, the Haight was originally made up of "all those kids that read Kerouac in high school—the ones who were a little weird. Then it became a magnet for every kid who was dissatisfied: a kind of central dream, or someplace to run to. It was a place for seekers, and San Francisco always had that tradition." And because rents were so cheap—an old house with a dozen rooms that could accommodate twenty or thirty people living in close quarters might cost only three or four hundred dollars a month—and there was a well-established cooperative economy, where barter was nearly as common as cash on the street, a subsistence hippie lifestyle was fairly easy to maintain. At least for a while.

Even with the Haight's population explosion beginning to strain the resources of the neighborhood (not to mention the patience of the area's sizable non-freak contingent of mainly working-class folks), the feeling on the street was still overwhelmingly positive as the summer solstice approached. Just a few blocks from 710 Ashbury, the Straight Theater was getting ready to open its doors. The long-abandoned theater, built in 1910, had been acquired by a group of local hippies in April 1966 with an eye toward making it a neighborhood rock 'n' roll hall and an arts center offering a broad array of cultural programs for adults and children. But it took more than a year and about $100,000 to completely renovate the decaying structure and fight through mountains of bureaucratic hassles and red tape, and some neighborhood merchants were still waging a bitter war against the theater when the Grateful Dead played at the "christening" party on June 15, 1967. The Dead also played the official opening of the Straight near the end of July, a gig notable for the appearance of Neal Cassady rapping onstage into a microphone as Pigpen and the Dead charged through a version of "Turn On Your Love Light," the Bobby "Blue" Bland rave-up that was a brand-new addition to their repertoire.

But the biggest event in the counterculture that June wasn't the Straight Theater christening or the giant solstice celebration at the Polo Fields a week later. In fact it wasn't even in San Francisco. Two and a half hours down the coast from Haight-Ashbury, the Monterey International Pop Festival drew thousands of people to the Monterey County Fairgrounds for three days and nights of music featuring some of the most popular rock 'n' roll bands from England and America, as well as various lighter pop groups and singers, and from India the great sitar master Ravi Shankar.

Though the event was organized by L.A. record business types, including promoter Lou Adler and "Papa" John Phillips, because the event was taking place in what was, figuratively at least, San Francisco's backyard, every effort was made to include the top Bay Area bands in the festival lineup. At first most of the local groups were wary of getting involved—it had the look of some slick L.A. scheme to cash in on the growing reputation of the San Francisco underground. Who knows—maybe the release of Scott McKenzie's "San Francisco" had even been designed to grease the wheels for the festival. In the end, though, entreaties by everyone from Paul Simon to Beatles associate Derek Taylor, and the obvious strength of the bands who had signed on for the festival, finally persuaded the Dead and some other San Francisco groups to participate. However, even after agreeing to play, the Dead remained suspicious of the motives of the organizers, did everything they could to stay away from Adler and Phillips, and flatly refused to sign a waiver, presented to them right before they went onstage, that would have allowed their performance to be filmed for a movie being shot by the noted documentarian D. A. Pennebaker.

Despite the troubles between the Dead camp and the festival organizers, the band was given a prestigious Sunday slot for their set at Monterey. Unfortunately, the way things worked out, that slot was between two of the most powerful and electrifying acts of the entire three days: the Who and Jimi Hendrix. Much to the consternation of Dead roadie Laird Grant, the Who left the stage in a shambles after ritually destroying much of their equipment during their grand finale, "My Generation." And Hendrix's performance was so eagerly anticipated by the throng that much of the crowd seemed distracted and uninvolved during the Dead's brief time onstage.

Nevertheless, the festival was hardly a washout for the Dead and their retinue. After all, the music was spectacular. The lineup included the sensational soul singer Otis Redding, the Byrds, African trumpeter Hugh Masakela, Eric

Burdon and the Animals, Simon and Garfunkel, Canned Heat and the Blues Project. The event turned into another gathering of the tribes, as freaks from up and down the West Coast and points east descended on Monterey to dig the music and each other. Owsley acid was everywhere, and the vibes were good all three days and nights. The Dead managed to organize a free campground on the football field of nearby Monterey Peninsula College, and even set up a stage there, powered by generators, where various musicians who were playing at the festival—Eric Burdon, Jimi Hendrix, lots of San Francisco band people—came and jammed late at night after the fairgrounds were closed. (Contrary to the impression given in Rock Scully's *Living with the Dead*, Garcia and Hendrix never played together there, or anywhere else for that matter.)

"Monterey was an incredible event," says Dick Latvala. "How could it not be? Jimi Hendrix was coming! We'd all heard about how great the Who were live. And of course Otis Redding already had a big following in San Francisco. Everybody looked completely stoned on acid. People were so high it was common to think that the Beatles were going to come out of the sky in flames! To have so many amazing personal experiences in the context of all these other people having amazing *group* experiences, gave everyone a huge sense of respect for each other. When you were there, it felt like everyone was in sync, and that was amazing."

About three weeks after Monterey Robert Hunter arrived in San Francisco, fresh from two and a half months of adventures in New Mexico and Colorado. His Scientology experiences behind him, Hunter had drifted in and out of the Dead's orbit during the latter part of 1966 and the first part of 1967, but he'd gotten heavily involved in what he called the "caustic" Bay Area methedrine scene, even contracting a case of hepatitis B. So he went to Santa Fe at the end of April 1967, in part to get away from that world. He spent his time in the Southwest doing psychedelically inspired pencil drawings—"but they were not the sort of things that rich Texans were going to buy," he said—and working on song lyrics, a relatively new pursuit for him.

"I first started waking up to the possibilities of rock lyrics being serious with *Blonde on Blonde* [Dylan's ambitious 1966 double album]," Hunter said. "It opened up everything; it said it was okay to be as serious as you wanted in rock. I had been writing unpublishable poetry. Joyce was my primary influence; it was really heavy Joycean stuff. I guess it made Joyce look more conservative, though—he didn't have acid."

Hunter mailed some of his lyrics to Garcia in San Francisco, and within a few weeks, unbeknownst to Hunter, Pigpen and Phil had worked out the music for one called "Alligator," with Pigpen even adding a verse or two of his own. As set lists from 1967 are rare, it's impossible to determine exactly when the song was first performed onstage. In the book *Deadbase*, which is regarded as the more-or-less official source of information about what the Dead performed when, the first listing for "Alligator" is the Dead's opening night at

New York's Cafe Au Go-Go in early June 1967, but chances are it was introduced sometime the previous month. Two other songs from the first batch of lyrics Hunter mailed from New Mexico, "China Cat Sunflower" and "Saint Stephen," were set to music later. In early June Garcia wrote a letter to Hunter—"incredible to think that Jerry would sit down and write a letter," he said—telling him that the band had set the lyrics for "Alligator" to music and urging Hunter to come back to San Francisco to work more with the group.

At the beginning of September the Dead, with Hunter in tow, drove north to the quaint Russian River community of Rio Nido to spend time at a friend's ranch honing some of the group's original songs in preparation for recording sessions in Los Angeles for their second album, set for mid-September. The newly written "Alligator" was developed further, and Phil Lesh and his poet friend Bobby Petersen had written a piece, sung by Weir, with the unlikely title "New Potato Caboose."

It was in Rio Nido, too, that the Dead's most famous improvisational vehicle, "Dark Star," was born. "I was in my cabin," Hunter recalled. "They were rehearsing in the hall [about 100 feet away] and you could hear from there. I heard the music and just started writing 'Dark Star' lying on my bed. I wrote the first half of it and I went in and I think I handed what I'd written to Jerry. He said, 'Oh, this will fit just fine,' and he started singing it. That's true collaboration. I mean, I actually heard the Grateful Dead playing and those are the words it seemed to be saying. I'm going to take a big stretch here and say the music seemed to be saying that and I transcribed it."

> *Dark star crashes*
> *Pouring its light into ashes*
> *Reason tatters*
> *The forces tear loose from the axis*
> *Searchlight casting*
> *For faults in the clouds of delusion*
>
> *Shall we go, you and I while we can?*
> *Through the transitive nightfall of diamonds*

"That did it for the time being," Hunter continued. "Then, a couple of days or weeks later—days, weeks, what were those in those days?—Jerry said he'd like as much material again. So I went out and sat in the Panhandle of Golden Gate Park. I was sitting there writing some more lyrics and a hippie came up and offered me a joint. I took a hit on that and he said, 'What are you writing?' I said, 'This is a song called "Dark Star." Remember that, it's gonna be important.' He said, 'Far out.' Off he went and I finished writing it. I suppose it *is* important within the context of the Grateful Dead, and the most we can ask for is importance within a context."

Though the song had begun from a groove Hunter had heard the band playing, Garcia noted that "the reason the music is the way it is, is because those lyrics did suggest that to me. That's what happened. They are saying, 'This universe is truly far out.' That's about it. You could take whatever you will from that suggestion. For me, that suggestion always means, 'Great, let's look around. Let's see how weird it really gets.' " From the outset, "Dark Star" was designed to be a tune with a constantly shifting interior between the two verses, though in its nascent stages it didn't have nearly the complexity it did a year later.

The Dead went down to Los Angeles in the second week of September to begin work on the group's sophomore album for Warner Bros., with Dave Hassinger once again producing. Though much has been made through the years about the Dead's apparent dislike of Hassinger, that was not based on their experience making the first record. In fact, part of the band's dissatisfaction with that album was that Hassinger didn't have more engineering input on the record, since that's what he was best known for. However, working at RCA Studios, Hassinger was forced to use RCA engineers, rather than relying on his own engineering chops. "That's a lot of what the band wanted from me," Hassinger recalled. "I was new to production, and the Grateful Dead really didn't need a producer to tell them what to play or how to play it. They needed someone to help them get the record to sound the way they wanted it to sound, and that's what I would have liked to have done."

This time around, the Dead were determined not to be rushed through the recording process as they had been on the first album. This was an era when albums rarely took more than a week or two to record and mix, though by the summer of 1967 there were starting to be records that took longer and showed more obvious studio craftsmanship—the Beatles' *Revolver* and *Sgt. Pepper's Lonely Hearts Club Band*, and the Beach Boys' *Pet Sounds* being the great shining examples that so many musicians, producers and engineers have cited through the years as having inspired them. Those albums had an incalculable impact on the recording industry because they showed that there could be more to making a record than simply documenting a performance; an album could be *art*, and, used creatively, the recording studio itself could be a tool to create that art. That meant thinking in new ways about how to work in the studio and make the most of the technology that was available. And if the Beatles could make such powerful, sophisticated and sonically detailed records using four-track recorders, imagine what the Dead could do with an eight-track, which became the de facto standard in top studios around the time the Dead started work on their second album. The Dead may not have aspired to make an album like *Sgt. Pepper's*, but from the outset they decided that rather than just playing live in the studio, they would layer the record, first putting down basic tracks—drums, bass, guitars, keyboards—then adding other parts to it to make the album more texturally interesting and involving.

During the two weeks or so the Dead were down at RCA Studios, they worked a little on the basic tracks for a number of different songs, but "we accomplished absolutely nothing," Garcia said. But they did play their biggest Southern California concert to date at the Hollywood Bowl ("Bill Graham Presents the San Francisco Scene in L.A."), taking the middle slot on a bill that had the Jefferson Airplane headlining and Big Brother and the Holding Company opening. Then, after a pair of shows at the Family Dog's Denver ballroom and a free concert in downtown Denver, the band headed back to San Francisco for two nights at the Straight Theater, which, after having been denied a dance permit because of city and neighborhood opposition, managed to operate as the Straight Theater School of Dance. There was, in fact, a bit of dance instruction at the Straight: Peter Weiss, a onetime dancer with Anna Halprin's troupe, said to the crowd, all of whom had to fill out dance class registration cards to attend, "What I would like everyone to do is close your eyes and relax and note how you breathe and how your heart is pumping. . . ." This rigorous instruction out of the way, the Dead broke into their raucous version of Martha and the Vandellas' Motown hit "Dancing in the Streets."

At the first of those two Straight shows the Dead took on a sixth member, a drummer named Mickey Hart. His addition to the lineup would have a profound effect on the direction the band's music was to take.

Brooklyn-born Michael Hart was the son of two drummers. His father, Lenny, was a national and world champion rudimental drummer, and Mickey's mother, Leah, took up drumming to get close to Lenny; together they won a mixed doubles drumming competition at the New York World's Fair in 1939. Shortly after Mickey was born in 1941 his parents split up and he and his mother moved in with her parents; Mickey didn't really meet his father again until he was about twenty. Though not a musician himself, Mickey's grandfather, Sam Tessel, was a huge fan of military drum-and-bugle corps, which were highly popular during World War II and in the years right after.

Growing up, young Mickey loved going to drum corps competitions, and though the absent Lenny Hart was scarcely mentioned in the Tessel household, Mickey "was acutely aware that I was the son of a great drummer," he wrote in his autobiography *Drumming at the Edge of Magic*. "That was my father's legacy to me; that and his drum pad and a pair of beautiful snakewood sticks he'd won in a competition." Mickey got his first drum when he was ten or eleven, but it wasn't until the Tessels had moved to Lawrence, Long Island, and Mickey was a freshman in high school, that he started to play seriously. Over the course of his four years in high school, he worked his way up from pulling (rather than playing) a giant bass drum on wheels in the high school marching band to first chair percussionist in the all-state band. Mickey practiced incessantly, on drumming fundamentals as well as just bashing along to records featuring big band jazz drummers like Gene Krupa and Buddy Rich, or to Elvis Presley and other rock 'n' rollers. But sometime during his senior year, Mickey abruptly quit school and joined the air force, "burning to test myself in the world of grown-up drummers. I wanted to become an adult as fast as possible, and the quickest way to accomplish that when I was young was the military."

Mickey got to play plenty of music in the air force. Stationed in Spain, he traveled the country playing military music by day and big band jazz at night. By 1965 he'd left the air force and returned to Long Island, hoping to make it as a drummer in New York. He got fired from the first and only drumming job he landed through the New York musicians' union—filling in for a drummer in a staid fox-trot band. Then, without warning, Mickey received a letter from his father asking if he wanted to work with his old man in a music store he was opening in San Carlos, California. Without hesitation, Mickey moved west and convinced his father that the guitar store the senior Hart had envisioned should—of course!—be a drum store. For the next two years Mickey spent his time working in the store and practicing his rudimental drumming.

Then, one night in late August 1967, Mickey went to see Count Basie's band at the Fillmore Auditorium. Mickey was friends with Basie's drummer, Sonny Payne; they hung out together whenever the Basie band was on the West Coast. At the Fillmore, a friend of Mickey's introduced him to Bill Kreutzmann, who was in the audience that night, and the two hit it off immediately. After the show, Hart and Kreutzmann hung around outside the Fillmore, talking and drumming on parked cars for a while. Then Billy suggested they go to the Matrix club to hear some friends of his, Big Brother and the Holding Company. Even though Mickey had been in the Bay Area since the early days of the San Francisco rock 'n' roll scene, he'd never heard any of the bands before, and that night at the Matrix the combination of James Gurley's deafening, feedback-laden guitar solos and Janis Joplin's raw, primal singing "cracked open my comfortable little notions about music," Mickey wrote. "In my excited and defenseless state I let myself be ravaged. . . . I felt like I'd fallen through a time warp into another universe. I was grinning so hard my jaws were starting to ache.

"Kreutzmann and I became drum brothers after that first night at the Matrix. We started hanging out, drumming together, cruising around Haight-Ashbury in Billy's Mustang." A couple of times Billy invited Mickey to Grateful Dead practices, "but I could never find the right warehouse where they were rehearsing," Hart wrote. And so, as fate would have it, the first time Mickey ever saw the Grateful Dead play was also the first night he played with them—September 29, 1967, at the Straight Theater. Mickey watched the first set and was blown away by the band's energy and power. Then, between sets, Kreutzmann suggested they round up another drum set so Mickey could sit in with the band during the second set. They drove to a friend's house, grabbed a kit, zipped back to the Straight, set up the drums as fast they could and "launched right into the first song of the next set, a tune they'd been fooling around with called 'Alligator/Caution.' Everything had been so frantic that it was only then, as the song gathered speed, that I was able to focus on the fact that I didn't have a clue as to what I was supposed to play. . . . One of the things Billy had stressed about his band was that the unexpected was welcome, indeed was actively sought—so I threw away my caution and dove in."

Hart's *baptismo del fuego* had been a triumph: "Suddenly, with two drums pounding away in the back," he wrote, "they had glimpsed the possibility of a groove so monstrous it would eat the audience. There seemed no question that it was an adventure we would all explore together." And from that night, Mickey Hart was in the band.

The intense civic resistance to the Straight Theater that fall was emblematic of the city's changing attitude toward its hippie enclave in Haight-Ashbury. All summer, as the crowds in the Haight got bigger, so did the police presence in the neighborhood. From the freaks' perspective, there seemed to be more police harassment. Drug busts became more common and in some cases more violent.

But the drugs in the area were changing, too. Amphetamines had been a problem in the Haight for a while, but in the summer of 1967 the problem escalated, as more and more dealers moved into the area and found easy prey among the thousands of out-of-towners looking for kicks. Heroin, too, made new inroads in the Haight, and with increased heroin use came more petty crime, as desperate young addicts turned to robbery to scrape up enough money for their next fix. Psychedelics had been the inspirational soma in the early days of the counterculture, but now a dark side began to manifest itself in the Haight, as poorly manufactured drugs were taken by kids who had no prior experience with psychedelics, no guidance from caring friends, no clue about what constituted a safe dose and no idea how to deal with the intense changes the drugs put them through. And it wasn't just bad acid that was going around. There were all sorts of odd substances being concocted in makeshift labs in the area, a veritable alphabet of bizarre and often dangerous synthetics—STP, MMDA, PCP—that would flood the streets for a few days or even weeks at a time, leaving dozens of people in hospital emergency rooms or, if they were lucky, in the capable and caring hands of workers from the increasingly important Haight-Ashbury Free Medical Clinic.

Not surprisingly, from the earliest days until Garcia's death in 1995, the Grateful Dead scene was a magnet for people on the dark periphery of the psychedelic drug world—lowlife dealers, kids who were barely functioning drug burnouts and out-and-out wackos attracted to the lunatic fringe of the hippie world. Anyone was welcome, it seemed, and few judgments were made. What this meant for the band, however, was that a certain amount of vigilance was required to keep the crazies away from the inner circle, and to recognize which folks trying to glom onto their scene were nice people with good ideas, and which ones were scam artists looking for money or power or both.

"Back in the Haight," Garcia said in 1981, "there were some Charlie Manson characters running around, really weird people who believed they were Christ risen or whatever, and who meant in the worst possible way to take the power. Some of them saw that the Grateful Dead raised energy and they wanted to control it. But we knew the only kind of energy management that counted was the liberating kind—the kind that frees people, not constrains them. So we were always determined to avoid those fascistic crowd-control implications in rock. It's always been a matter of personal honor not to manipulate the crowd."

"It got so we could recognize those kind of people in a heartbeat," Mountain Girl says. "The minute you looked at somebody you could tell by their vibe, by what was coming out of the tops of their heads kind of, whether they were going to be really dangerous to you or really dangerous to themselves or completely off the wall so you didn't know what they might do. I hardly ever felt personally threatened. The negative energy pretty much stayed away from me. But it would attach to Weir, and Jerry attracted it, too. If anybody tried to chase down Kesey at the Acid Test, it was usually because they were an English major who had freaked out and been in the nuthouse and then read *Cuckoo's Nest*. But for Jerry it was other types of nuts. He seemed to attract compulsive people; strange people that either wanted to be part of his life or part of the Grateful Dead—they would write themselves into the drama and it would just become this maddening compulsion for them and they'd follow us around. That stuff was going on pretty early, actually. Then there were these other types who would have some doom-filled message that they had to communicate to us. Or it would be something inter-hippie: 'So-and-so is an evil person,' and you had to be warned about stuff. Or there were a lot of warnings about incipient busts. There were a lot of false alarms."

There was also the real thing. At 3:30 in the afternoon on October 2, 1967, eight narcotics agents from the San Francisco police, accompanied by reporters and television crews they'd tipped off, pulled up to 710 Ashbury, knocked on the door and demanded to be let in, even though they didn't have a search warrant. When their entry was denied, police kicked in the door and searched the house from top to bottom, eventually finding about a pound of pot and hashish. They confiscated the files, money and address books of both the Dead and the Haight-Ashbury Legal Organization, which had an office in 710, and proceeded to arrest everyone in the house on marijuana possession charges, including Bob Weir and Pigpen, Bob Matthews, Pig's girlfriend Veronica, Sue Swanson, Rosalyn Stevenson, Christine Bennett and Antoinette Kaufman. Danny Rifkin and Rock Scully arrived once police were already in the house and were promptly busted, too, as was another late arrival, Rosie McGee.

After six hours in jail the suspects were released on bail. The next morning, the *San Francisco Chronicle*'s front page carried the news under a banner headline: ROCK BAND BUSTED. Below a very sinister-looking photo of Pigpen—ironically, the one person arrested who was not a dope smoker—was a subhead that read COPS RAID PAD OF GRATEFUL DEAD, and a long story detailing the arrests in "the Dead's way-out 13-room pad." That morning, too, the eleven bustees were arraigned in court, and then the entire Grateful Dead and their managers held a press conference in the living room of 710 to decry the bust, draconian drug laws and the police crackdown in the Haight.

In the end, the bust was more an annoying distraction than a serious threat to the band's future. No one believed for a minute that anyone would serve time, and no one did. In May 1968 the eleven defendants were fined $100 to $200 each. But the bust did have a somewhat sobering effect on the Dead, or at the very least taught them that they were being watched by disapproving forces from the straight world.

"The bust was kind of like the last straw for us," Mountain Girl says. "We were feeling too exposed. And Haight Street just wasn't any fun anymore. There were tour buses driving in front of our house, cops all over the streets. The Chinese grocery closed up so we were going to have to drive to shop. Everything started changing and becoming very trendy, so we started looking for a new place to go, but it was hard to find a place because the city had such a low vacancy rate in those days." Eventually Garcia and Mountain Girl found an apartment in the outer Sunset district—near the ocean but often fogbound—and lived there for five months or so. "It wasn't too great," M.G. says, "but at that point we were tired of sharing a house, so it was kind of nice to be off by ourselves." Jerry and M.G. didn't need a car to get around when they lived in the Haight, but once they moved to the western edge of the city they bought a used Plymouth station wagon with a rear window that didn't roll up, and they continued to bop down to 710, which remained the Dead's headquarters for a few more months after the bust.

If things were unsettled, even chaotic, on the home front, musically the Dead were entering a new phase in the fall of 1967, as Mickey Hart became integrated into the lineup and the group began to play more open-ended original compositions in addition to the blues, R&B and jug tunes that had been their stock-in-trade the first two years. The band spent untold hours rehearsing at the old, run-down Potrero Theater, clear across town, developing their new songs, investigating different kinds of beats and grooves, experimenting with dynamics and learning how to move seamlessly from one tune or musical feeling to another. The Dead had always been considered a jamming band, but during this period there was a quantum leap in the complexity of their musical constructions, the ferociousness and abandon with which they charged into uncharted realms, and the originality of their collective vision.

Although the group had occasionally linked two songs in the same key together to form one longer piece—on blues numbers like "Good Morning Little Schoolgirl" and "You Don't Love Me," for example—the songs the band wrote in 1967 and '68 were specifically designed to open up and give the band the flexibility to move in whatever direction their inventions took them. The first great jamming vehicle along those lines was the combination of "Alligator" and "Caution," which rolled from the chunky, syncopated rhythm of the former tune to the locomotive drive of the latter via a long and always unpredictable jam that served as connective tissue between the two. In the fall of 1967 the band also introduced another multilayered original that incorporated several different tempo changes and textural shifts—"That's It for the Other One."

The song opens with a lovely midtempo passage called "Cryptical Envelopment," written and sung by Garcia, and once described by him as "an extension of my own personal symbology for the 'Man of Constant Sorrow'—the old folk song—which I always thought of as being a sort of Christ parable. Something fuzzy like that; fuzzy Christianity."

> The other day they waited
> The sky was dark and faded
> Solemnly they stated
> He has to die, you know he has to die

Just as the Dead's version of "Morning Dew" derives much of its power from the stark contrast between the beauty of the melody and the bleakness of the words, the folky lilt and shimmer of "Cryptical Envelopment" is deceptive, masking a darker lyric thrust.

Garcia's part of the song ends abruptly, and then Hart and Kreutzmann come rat-tat-tatting in together, their drum lines rolling inexorably toward each other until they meet at a single point where they're joined by Garcia, Lesh, Weir and Pigpen in a fireball blast, which then gives way to the relentless, galloping gait of "The Other One." "That was sort of a serious, hole-in-the-wall psychedelic explosion," Garcia said of the song, which was based around a revolving pattern in 12/8 time conceived by Weir and Kreutzmann:

> Spanish lady come to me
> She lays on me this rose
> It rainbow spirals round and round
> It trembles and explodes
> It left a smoking crater of my mind
> I like to blow away
> But the heat came 'round and busted me
> For smiling on a cloudy day
> Comin', comin', comin' around, comin' around
> Comin' around in a circle

"The Other One" is less a tune than it is a rhythmic shell capable of housing an infinite number of variations within its constantly rotating figure. Lesh and Garcia might chase each other for several bars—stalker and prey—then become intertwined, the bass and lead notes tumbling over each other chaotically, or miraculously fusing together in an intricate upward dance, while Weir's rhythm guitar cuts deep slashes in the air around them and between them, and the drummers keep pushing the jam forward at a breakneck pace.

Eventually the "Other One" jam would make a final quick turn, like a speeding roadster trying to execute a hard left, the "tiger paws" rhythm (as Weir once called it) would break apart, and the band would fall back into the gentle strains of the last verse of "Cryptical Envelopment":

> And when the day had ended
> With rainbow colors blended
> His mind remained unbended
> He had to die, you know he had to die

That passage then flowed naturally into a series of jams that allowed Garcia to lead the others through a web of different but related melody-based variations rooted in "Cryptical" 's moderate, loping 4/4. If "The Other One" jam always seemed to be hurtling out of control and headed toward certain calamity, the jams after "Cryptical Envelopment" were more like watching the ocean at sunset, with waves undulating in the twilight, breaking on the sandy shoal and then receding, changing ever so slightly one to the next. That the Dead could create such a complex, colorful and intensely detailed sonic universe within the fifteen to twenty minutes "That's It for the Other One" usually lasted in those days was a remarkable achievement, unparalleled in the rock world at that point. And when the Dead then attached that song to "New Potato Caboose," which offered a whole other set of kaleidoscopic musical pictures, and linked that to "Alligator/Caution," the band could play for an hour or more without stopping between songs, taking the crowd through an amazing series of moods in the process. This had never been done before in rock. Even in jazz, where Coltrane, Ornette Coleman, Charles Lloyd and others had been playing twenty- and thirty-minute compositions for some time, there were rarely attempts at fusing pieces together the way the Dead did, much less figuring out on the spot, through inspired improvisation, ways to create transitions between songs that hadn't previously been joined; no easy feat. The Dead succeeded at this because they dedicated themselves completely and selflessly to developing their sound as *a group*, and then put in the hours to thoroughly explore every interesting musical possibility that presented itself.

"You can't play the way the Grateful Dead plays without working at it," Garcia said. "It's not something that just happened to us. It didn't happen overnight, either. There was a long, slow process that brought that into being."

"The essence of this kind of playing is really to be open to the context you're in," says David Gans, author of several books on the band and a guitarist who has played Dead music himself for more than twenty-five years. "When it's really working something happens and you are a delighted witness to its creation, just like everybody in the audience; you're just the person who has his hands on the guitar neck and can take something and go someplace with it. So if you're cruising along in a groove coming out of a song, and you're looking at a place, like where the signature part of a song starts to drop away and then you go somewhere else, what you're doing is listening to what the other musicians are doing, and that creates a space into which new music, ideally, will fall. So it's what you're doing, but it's also what the other guys are doing, and it's trusting each other and supporting each other. It's not about individual virtuosity as much as it is about how well you keep your periphery open to influence. It's what makes brilliant new structures emerge out of the void.

"I've always thought that part of what made the Dead so great was their willingness to cooperate," Gans continues. "Although everyone adored Jerry's solos, the thing that made him such a magical player was how well he blended in and cooperated with the others. Every band needs a reliable source of inspiration, and the glory of Jerry was that for many years he was almost never at a loss for a musical thought, but also never really obsessed with dominating everything. So if an idea needed to come up, he'd be there with one, but it was also an idea that was freely shared. Then somebody else could answer it, and that was the thing—laying out an idea and then listening to what it educed from the other guys. And it was that way with all of them. The job of playing Grateful Dead music is to open yourself up to divine inspiration, to put yourself at the disposal of the collective muse, and that means being a good listener."

For the musicians, listening to and making sense of the tremendous amount of musical information pouring out of the amplifiers and blasting from the drums in the heat of an intense jam required acute concentration, to say the least. Often it was unclear who, if anyone, was perched on the leading edge of the jam, and who was listening to whom at any particular moment. So the way jams progressed depended on each member of the band fitting his part into a fluid musical stream and at the same time trying both to direct that stream and to anticipate where it could or would go next. That meant that sometimes jams would unfold with a mellifluous all-for-one, one-for-all directivity, and sometimes it would be more like a clash of the titans. This is a band that always reveled in its differences and in fact turned them to its advantage.

The Dead went back to Los Angeles to resume work on their second album, which became *Anthem of the Sun*, in the middle of November 1967, this time at American Studios in North Hollywood rather than at RCA. Unfortunately, the change in scenery didn't have much effect on the band. They continued to have problems recording the basic tracks for their new songs tight enough to satisfy either themselves or Dave Hassinger, who was feeling increasingly frustrated by the band's seeming inability to realize their ambitious compositions in the studio. Basic tracks on "Cryptical Envelopment" and "New Potato

Caboose" were completed, but rather than continue on in L.A., Hassinger and the group decided to travel to New York to work in a pair of highly regarded eight-track studios there, Century Sound and Olmstead Studios.

"One of the things that we built into our contract which was unheard of at the time was unlimited studio time," Garcia said. "We knew we'd have to pay for it, but we wanted as much as we wanted. Our strategy was: 'We want to play in the studio. We want to learn how the studio works. We don't want somebody else doing it. It's our music, we want to do it.' So what we did essentially was we bought ourselves an education, and the way we achieved it was to spend lots and lots of time in the studio fooling around with stuff— 'Let's see what happens when you [turn this knob]: "Skrawwwwwkkk!" Oops, that's not going to work. Let's try this over here: "Eeee-eeee-eee!" Nope!' It was a trial-and-error kind of thing."

And it drove poor Dave Hassinger crazy, to the point where in the middle of the Century Sound sessions he quit the project and flew back to Los Angeles. "I gave up in New York," he said. "We'd been working a long time on that second album, and they had put down some new tracks in New York and no one could sing them. Nobody could sing the thing, and at that point they were experimenting too much in my opinion. They didn't know what the hell they were looking for. I think if you experiment you should have at least some sense of what you're ultimately going after, but they were going from one end of the spectrum to the other."

After Hassinger left, "We found ourselves with enough music on tape for maybe a third of an album, so we had to figure out what to do," Phil Lesh said. "But we did have a lot of live performances [recorded]," and it dawned on the band members that they could actually combine live and studio recordings into a sonic sculpture that would sound like, in Phil's original conception, "a thousand-petal lotus flowering from nothing." Amazingly enough, Warner Bros. decided to let the Dead finish the record themselves and even allowed them to record in a studio close to home—Coast Recorders, a well-equipped facility in San Francisco. To help them on the technical end the band enlisted Dan Healy, who had replaced Owsley as the Dead's principal live sound engineer after Bear was busted in the fall of 1967. Healy had been part of the Bay Area studio world before he became involved in the San Francisco rock scene, so he was the perfect choice to help the Dead on their maiden voyage of self-production. Armed with exceptional-sounding four-track live recordings made by Bob Matthews and Betty Cantor in Los Angeles in November 1967 and on a tour of the Northwest in late January 1968, Healy, Garcia and Lesh hunkered down at Coast for the complicated task of constructing the album.

"We weren't making a record in the normal sense," Garcia said, "we were making a collage. We were trying to do something completely different, which didn't even have to do with a concept. It had to do with an approach that's more like electronic music or concrete music, where you are actually assembling bits and pieces toward an enhanced nonrealistic representation. That is really the sense of what we were doing."

Indeed, *Anthem of the Sun* is a carefully constructed montage of live and studio performances that flow in and out of each other and are stacked to very strange effect. Each side is a continuous piece of music with no breaks. Side one opens with "That's It for the Other One," followed by a transitional section put together by Phil's old friend from the electronic music world, Tom Constanten, using some of John Cage's "prepared piano" techniques—in which gyroscopes and other objects were placed inside the piano to create unusual sounds for a bizarre, even scary, sonic tapestry. As T.C. said, "I was given the interesting task of whipping [the music] up into a greater frenzy, ultimately causing it to explode, and out of the rubble of the explosion and the smoke and the ashes and everything would come the delicious sounds of 'New Potato Caboose.' " That song is followed by Weir's unusual "Born Cross-Eyed."

Side two is a mind-bending meld of "Alligator" and "Caution" that, in addition to opening with a chorus of kazoos (shades of the jug band!), at points features multiple performances of similar but still different passages from different shows, all playing at once, as well as studio tracks that speed up and slow down unnaturally. Solos fade in and out, walls of feedback are erected then torn apart, three or four Pigpen vocals are woven together in parts. "There are places of extreme awkwardness," Healy admitted later, "but it wasn't hurting for imagination." Garcia said, "We mixed it for the hallucinations," and thirty years down the line, *Anthem of the Sun* is still a very, very weird album. No question about it, *Anthem of the Sun* was one for the heads, from the dizzying mix of sounds on the album to the seriously psychedelic cover painting—by Phil and T.C.'s friend Bill Walker—depicting the bandmembers as six heads of an incredibly intricate fire-breathing monster-deity out of Tibetan/Haight-Ashbury mythology.

The album as a whole works as a sort of metaphorical acid trip, with passages of clarity followed by passages of tremendous confusion, frightening and funny moments juxtaposed, fabulous detail emerging from dense sonic squalls and cryptic lyrics that somehow managed to mirror the album's variegated musical textures. It's an often dark, even troubling work that couldn't have been farther removed from the happy bounce of "The Golden Road (To Unlimited Devotion)." This was music made by people who had obviously spent lots of time perched precariously on the psychedelic *edge*, witnessing heavens and hells worthy of Hieronymus Bosch, and were reporting back on what they'd experienced. Anyone who bought *Anthem* expecting to hear San Francisco "flower power" in full bloom got quite a shock. But then the Dead were never that kind of band, despite how they might have seemed on a sunny Sunday in the Panhandle playing to blissed-out dancers under the tall eucalyptus trees. This was, after all, *the* acid band, born out of the chaos of Muir Beach and Watts and the Trips Festival, and always looking for new pathways to the deep beyond.

Driving away Dave Hassinger earned the Grateful Dead what they sought—the autonomy to make records their own way. And it effectively frightened off Warner Bros. executives from further meddling in the band's affairs. "The record company had a funny relationship with us," Mickey Hart said. "They were scared of us. They wouldn't visit us because it was too dangerous. They couldn't eat anything or drink anything around us because they were afraid everything had LSD in it, so they never really showed up."

At the same time, the group was establishing their independence in other ways, too. Their tour of the Pacific Northwest with Quicksilver Messenger Service in late January and early February of 1968 was booked without the aid of conventional promoters. And, closer to home, the Dead decided to circumvent Bill Graham and Chet Helms and play exclusively at the 2,000-capacity Carousel Ballroom on Van Ness Avenue in downtown San Francisco, which had been taken over by friends of theirs. The Carousel had been a popular venue for big band dances in the '40s and '50s as the El Patio Ballroom, and was all but unused by the winter of 1968, though it was still owned by a very successful Dublin-based ballroom operator named Bill Fuller. Ron Rakow, a onetime Wall Street whiz kid who'd moved to San Francisco in the mid-'60s and befriended Rock Scully, Danny Rifkin and, in time, the band, negotiated a deal with Fuller that allowed the freaks to lease the hall for no money down, but a guaranteed rent of $15,000 a month plus a percentage of the gross receipts. The Dead, along with Quicksilver, first played the Carousel on January 17, 1968, a Ben Franklin's birthday bash that was a rousing success. But the official grand opening came on Valentine's Day, with the Dead and Country Joe and the Fish sharing the bill for a concert broadcast on KMPX—quite a coup for both the Dead and the Carousel.

Phil Lesh once listed that show as his favorite Dead concert ever; certainly it was one of the best of that era, and one that shows the transition the Dead made around this time from a group that played mainly short cover tunes to one whose sets were dominated by original songs connected by long jams. It was one of those nights when it seemed as though nearly everyone in the place was dosed, which always put an interesting spin on things.

The Dead's first set opened innocently enough, with a typically serpentine version of "Good Morning Little Schoolgirl." But that would be just about the last glimpse of terra firma until the final "Midnight Hour" at the end of the evening, about three hours later. Everything in between was unrecorded material that showed the Dead at their spacey best. During the first set the band introduced the vast listening audience to a formidable sequence of three new songs written with Robert Hunter.

Just a few months after its unveiling in the fall of 1967, "Dark Star" was already beginning to stretch in all sorts of interesting directions, slowing down and elongating a little more with each playing.

Garcia had plucked the whimsical "China Cat Sunflower" from the first batch of lyrics Hunter had sent from New Mexico, and devised a bouncy, bopping musical setting loaded with clever contrapuntal melodic lines and neatly interlocking rhythms that were every bit as playful as the words, which owed a debt to Dame Edith Sitwell, Lewis Carroll and psychedelics:

> Look for a while at the China Cat Sunflower
> Proud-walking jingle in the midnight sun
> Copper-dome bodhi drip a silver kimono
> Like a crazy-quilt star gown
> Through a dream night wind

Musically, the song was a new form for the Dead, a harbinger of other interesting rhythmic numbers Garcia would create over the next five years. Each player laid down a different but complementary rhythm with his part, and then Garcia's light, skipping vocal pulled the pieces together into a "song." "China Cat" was an instant success with the Dead's fans, and it was the only late-'60s Garcia song that he performed for the rest of his career.

The third new song that night was "The Eleven," a furious, constantly mutating jam in 11/4 time (hence the title) that had been conceived by Phil and the drummers during marathon rehearsals at the Potrero Theater before the Northwest tour. Like "China Cat," it was quite obtuse lyrically (in fact, a section of the words was originally a verse that followed the three stanzas that became "China Cat"), but it was always less a song than a long monstrous groove that gave the musicians on opportunity to see how much music they could pack into a fast eleven-beat pattern—spraying bursts of notes, chords and beats in long and short phrases that somehow, incredibly, always ended up meeting at the one-beat of each measure as the song rolled through space like some planet threatening to spin out of its orbit.

"[Playing in unusual time signatures] really started when Mickey met [the Indian table master] Alla Rakha [in the fall of 1967]," Garcia noted. "What Indian music seems to have—the combination of tremendous freedom and tremendous discipline—really impressed Mickey, so he started right away studying with Alla Rakha. That influence got the rest of us starting to fool with ideas that were certain lengths."

At the Valentine's Day show, the jam after "The Eleven" eventually calmed down enough to segue into "Turn On Your Love Light," which became Pigpen's signature tune in the late '60s. The Dead never really got the credit they deserved for being innovative rhythm and blues players—on songs like "Love Light," "Dancing in the Streets" and, later, "Hard to Handle," the band was capable of jamming long and hard on different riffs and progressions that sounded like psychedelicized mutations of ideas swiped from James Brown's Fabulous Flames or Archie Bell and the Drells or any of the other funky kings of the day. Sometimes they would hit on one fat soul groove after another, with Pigpen endlessly improvising above the band, masterfully playing with words and phrases, bringing the energy in the room up and down at his whim.

And other times Pig would do his thing but the band would be on a completely different plane for much of the song, still out in space from the previous song, and perhaps unwilling to come back down to earth. But no matter which direction the "Love Light" jam took, eventually the song reached a climax that had Pigpen and Weir screaming call-and-response like preachers in a Baptist tent service, as the band played the song's finger-snappin'-catchy six-note riff louder and more intensely with each pass. "Love Light" never failed to get a crowd up on its feet and dancing, and Pigpen was never above cajoling the few people who weren't grooving with him to get loose and get *down*. "He always had more nerve than I could believe," Garcia once said with an admiring chuckle. "He'd get the audience on his side and he'd pick somebody out—like a heckler—and get on them. He'd crack us up, too. Sometimes he'd just kill me!"

The band dedicated their second set at the Carousel that Valentine's Day to the memory of Neal Cassady, whose body had finally given out while he was walking along the railroad tracks near the small Mexican town of San Miguel de Allende on the evening of February 2. A seriously psychedelic version of "That's It for the Other One" included a new verse by Weir that referred to "Cowboy Neal at the wheel of the bus to never-ever land," a fitting tribute their fallen comrade/hero. The rest of the set was composed of the other tunes that would make up *Anthem of the Sun*, played in order and played extremely well; in fact, parts of this show actually made it onto the album. It was the Dead at a magical peak, fully in command every step of the way, equally comfortable ripping through a fluttering Spanish-sounding jam or letting all their musical structures crumble and dissolve into dissonant sheets of white noise, feedback and, ultimately, silence, which is how they ended the set. On tapes of the show, there's barely audible clapping from about ten people in the crowd, but you sense that it's because the rest of the audience was probably too incapacitated by what they'd been through to know whether it was the end of the set, or the end of the world for that matter.

"It was right around that time that the Dead's music started to take on this huge, monstrous dimension and the unique qualities that really separated them from all the other bands," observes Dick Latvala. "Within a year we got 'Dark Star,' 'That's It for the Other One,' 'Alligator,' 'Caution,' 'Love Light,' 'China Cat.' They were steppin' out! Back in '66 it was mostly Pigpen singing, and that was great for what it was, and they had three songs they'd really jam on—'Viola Lee Blues,' 'Dancin' in the Streets' and 'Midnight Hour'—and that's the stuff you'd wait for. But when these other songs started coming in, that's when the big change occurred. Mickey came into the band at the beginning of that wave.

"It was like the music itself was escalating. Everything became a vehicle to go 'out' with, and the jamming was so focused but still totally on the edge of being out of control, I remember thinking, 'This music is way, *way* unusual.' Somewhere near the end of '67, the music started getting too far out for me to even dance; I had to just sit down and be as still as I could so it could come through me. I remember being scared sometimes. I mean, there were times when Phil was making the bass notes so big that I thought I was going to explode, and maybe I should leave. But then I'd think, 'Well, if I'm going to explode, let's do it here!' It was dense shit. Even today, you can't listen to that stuff all day—it's too much."

"People weren't afraid to let go and get really high at Dead shows because it felt like a 'safe' place to [trip]," Mountain Girl says. "You knew that you'd probably be taken some pretty interesting places during a show, but that you'd always come out on the other end in one piece. Experience, expectation and fine-tuning—the Dead were really good at being there for that. The music evolved to enhance that and people got into it. The music would not have developed the way it did if it wasn't for people's willingness to go on a big trip with it, and the band's willingness to help them along. That was pretty deliberate, and it made for a wonderful, musical, intuitive kind of mix. They definitely created the set and the setting, and then they played to that, both with the music and the lyric content, and the lights and the noise and the glorious and horrible sounds; *all* that stuff."

Though nobly intentioned, the Carousel Ballroom experiment was probably doomed from the start. "We were terrible business people!" said Jon McIntire, a friend of the Dead's who helped manage the Carousel. "We made mistakes from the outset. We opened up with the Dead and [Country Joe]. The place was crammed to the gills. The next weekend we didn't have anyone—the place went dark—and then we opened up the following weekend. Well, if you're trying to establish a place as a draw, that's death. But we simply didn't know that.

"To me, what the Carousel was about was freedom, true freedom," McIntire continued. " 'You can do anything here and it's okay, as long as you don't hurt anyone.' That's the kind of anarchy that shows that people at their basis are good; they don't need constraints to make them good. So that's what we were experimenting with there. I think that's what all of us in the Haight were experimenting with. The Carousel was the epitome of anarchy at its finest. A lot of people found it scary, but I think a lot of people in San Francisco found it to be exactly what was going on, and very important to them, and exciting, warm and wonderful."

Unfortunately, "warm and wonderful" doesn't necessarily pay the bills, and when the Dead and the Airplane were on the road (separately) that spring—the Dead played various clubs, ballrooms and armories in cities such as Miami, Philadelphia, New York, St. Louis (where the Dead opened for Iron Butterfly) and Los Angeles—the Carousel crew was forced to compete with Bill Graham and Chet Helms to book headlining acts. Graham, in particular, proved to be a formidable foe who was not above demanding that groups of national stature who played for him in San Francisco play *only* for him or he wouldn't book them into his new venue on New York's Lower East Side, the old Village Theater, which Graham renamed the Fillmore East. Graham was also looking for a new, larger dancehall for his shows in San Francisco in the wake of riots in the Fillmore neighborhood that spring after the assassination of Martin Luther King. So when it became clear that the Carousel was failing financially, Graham hopped on a plane and flew to Dublin to meet with the ballroom's owner, Bill Fuller, and he persuaded Fuller to let him take over the struggling operation. By mid-July Graham had opened his new San Francisco flagship, at first called Fillmore-Carousel, then the Fillmore West. During the time they'd controlled the Carousel, the Dead didn't play for Graham in San Francisco, but they did play at the Fillmore East, and after Graham took over the Carousel the group swallowed its pride and gigged there often. It *was* a great room, and by the end of 1968 the Dead were filling it easily, so it made good business sense to play there.

By mid-'68 most of the bandmembers had moved out of Haight-Ashbury and relocated in different parts of Marin County. In early March the Dead had bid a fond farewell to the old neighborhood with an impromptu free concert in front of the Straight Theater, drawing thousands of people into Haight Street for what turned out to be their final appearance in the neighborhood. Panhandle shows were part of the distant past by this time, the Straight was struggling, and by the summer of 1968 the vibe in the neighborhood had deteriorated so much that it had become a dangerous and forbidding place for many people— particularly those who had been around the Haight two years earlier.

"After a while, the police and the city just got sick of what was happening in Haight-Ashbury, and they cracked down," says Steve Brown. "They were edgy because the black community was rioting and there was a lot of right-wing reaction to the anti-war, liberal, hippie, drug-taking, commie, pinko element. These guys wanted to smack a few heads. They were *not* interested in keeping cool. They wanted to scare them and drive them out. And by the late '60s, especially with the change of the drug scene in the Haight-Ashbury, it was hard to blame them, because it had gotten pretty ugly there. In '67 the police sort of turned the other cheek and let the hippies and the flower children do their thing. There was enough media support that they would have looked like real ogres to have gone hot and heavy on the kids. But by '68 they'd had enough of it. 'Let's run 'em out!'"

The Dead had seen the storm clouds gathering ominously over the Haight for so long that by the time they left they had already moved past any feelings of disillusionment. As Rosie McGee put it, "They were never really a part of the flower power thing, so it wasn't too crushing for them when the Haight turned the way it did. We knew it couldn't last forever."

It was really like *a moment*," Garcia said in 1994. "There was a breath there for a moment that was like an open door—'Oo-oo, *look!*'—and then BAM! It slammed shut again immediately. . . . There was a moment there where there was a very clear, wonderful vision, but you see, it had to do with everyone acting in good faith. It had to do with everybody behaving right. There was a lot to it. It wasn't a simple thing.

"So the thing of this door opening—it was one of those things that we were all inducing it as well as perceiving it. I think probably everybody saw what they wanted to see or what they needed to see. They'd all been brought there somehow for that moment. And you can't even say what it was or when it was or what it boiled down to or anything like that. But for me it's been enough energy to keep me going this long and I don't see any end, at least for me, in terms of my work. . . . It doesn't matter to me whether it has any historical value or whether it's measurable in some objective way. I don't care. For me, the subjective reality is what counts—what I experienced, what happened to me. I know a lot of people who shared something like it, their own version of it, and who are still moving with that energy; that energy is propelling us. That energy has also gained enough momentum over the years [that] it's partly responsible for all the things that have happened historically since then, in some way. It's part of it. It's part of the gain in consciousness that the last half of this century has represented. And that includes all the technology that goes with it—the braincraft that subsequently sprang up. And it's still rolling, it's still happening."

CHAPTER 9

Where Is the Child Who Played with the Sunshine?

he band's exodus to Marin County began in the spring of 1968, when Jerry and Mountain Girl moved into a little house behind the Silver Peso bar in downtown Larkspur. Shortly after that, Weir and Mickey found a place in Novato; Phil and Rosie settled in Fairfax; and Billy moved out to rural West Marin, off Lucas Valley Road. Pigpen stayed in San Francisco a while longer than the others, living with Veronica in a converted church that was owned by the Dead's sometime lawyer Brian Rohan. Eventually they left, too, moving into Weir's digs, while Mickey moved onto a ranch in a rustic, undeveloped part of Novato. Actually, the ranch had been under hippie control for some time already—it was being leased from the city by Rock Scully and Jonathan Reister, a fourth-generation Kentucky horseman who had been one of the managers of the Carousel Ballroom and a pioneer of the West Coast acid scene before that. Dubbed the "Pondareister" (or, after Mickey moved in, "Hart's Delight"), the ranch became a bucolic hangout for the entire Dead scene, a place where people could ride horses and live out their fantasies of being pioneers of the new Wild West. Mickey eventually took over the lease for the ranch and built a recording studio—the first bandmember to do so—in the barn on the property.

After several years of everyone living on top of each other in the Haight and doing everything together, the move to Marin must have felt like getting a friendly invitation to slow down a tad, take it a little easier.

"It was never the same again after we left San Francisco," Rosie says. "That was definitely a transition. Before that, we were all living together and being together and we did that for a couple of years. It changed after that. Then it became different nuclear units—couples and families were starting. Then the gigs became the focal point, or the rehearsal place. But that was okay. By then we all needed a little more space."

Anthem of the Sun came out in July 1968 and proved to be a challenging disc for Warner Bros. to market, even in an era when free-form FM radio stations were popping up all over the country. Nothing on the record was remotely "commercial" in the traditional sense—short and punchy—and since each side tracked continuously, it was difficult for deejays to, say, drop the needle onto "New Potato Caboose" and play only that. Rather than touring to promote the record, the Dead stayed in California the entire summer and actually began working on their third album in early September. It was as if the *process* of making *Anthem of the Sun* had been the important thing for the Dead—learning how to make a record themselves—and the end result was secondary.

By that summer, the songwriting partnership of Garcia and Hunter was picking up steam. Joining "China Cat" and "Dark Star" in their canon that June was a big, rubbery rock song called "Saint Stephen," with music by Garcia and Lesh, tandem lead vocals by Garcia and Weir, and a catchy central riff that sounded almost like a spry Elizabethan dance played on rock instruments. Hunter said he wrote the lyrics over the course of a couple of inspired evenings with a light, lilting feel in mind, "and then [the band] put this up-against-the-wall-motherfucker arrangement on it. We came up with a hybrid that hit between the eyes!"

Lyrically, the song is quite obtuse—we never really learn who Stephen is or why "wherever he goes the people all complain," for instance. But in a way "Saint Stephen" is *the* prototypical Hunter composition, blending vivid psychedelic imagery ("Ladyfinger dipped in moonlight / Writing 'What for?' across the morning sky") with a scattershot of lines and couplets that might have been drawn from the yellowing pages of some now forgotten culture's Book of Wisdom, or its epic tales. In the jumbled swirl of images—"sunlight splatters dawn with answers"—and aphorisms—"Talk about your plenty, talk about your ills / One man gathers what another man spills"—there's an oddly reassuring tone to the piece as a whole, as if the poet is reaching out to share something with us, and what *that* is will become clear . . . when it becomes clear, if you'll pardon the Zen. Hunter made a point of never explaining what his lyrics "mean" or his intention with a given song, "because if it is that concrete, if I can really explain it, I might as well write books of philosophy," he said. "The poet is touching and questioning; it's open to interpretation." And as with all poetry, the way Hunter's lyrics resonate with someone depends on that person's sensitivity, openness, the particulars of his or her own life and a thousand other undefinable factors that sometimes magically allow insight to bloom where before there was opacity or confusion.

"Saint Stephen" was the first song the band tackled when they went into Pacific Recording in San Mateo in early September to begin work on their album. Armed with their extensive studio experience making *Anthem of the Sun*, the Dead were determined to take their time and make a record that was a true studio creation rather than something that reflected the way the group played live. Bob Matthews was elevated to chief engineer for the project, which, like *Anthem*, ended up sprawling over many months in between Dead tours. In fact, a few months into the project, Matthews was able to get a hold of the first sixteen-track tape recorder made by the Ampex Corporation (based on the Peninsula), and the original eight-track tapes that had been made on a few songs were transferred to sixteen-track and then added to. Now, in the case of the Grateful Dead, doubling the number of available tracks wasn't necessarily a good thing, because they took the increased tape capacity as a challenge to experiment even more in the studio, which meant everything took longer than expected. It didn't help, either, that the band was dabbling in all sorts of mind-altering drugs in the studio just to see how they affected their work. Besides the standard pot and LSD, Garcia said they sometimes sipped beverages laced with the powerful hallucinogen STP in the studio—"which made it a little weird; in fact, very weird," he said—and brought in tanks of nitrous oxide (laughing gas), a drug noted for the way it colors aural perception.

One track the band worked on that fall, Hunter and Garcia's "What's Become of the Baby," was recorded and mixed in part on nitrous oxide, and the finished song actually has some of the character of a nitrous experience, with its slow, surreal, electronically treated Garcia vocal floating eerily above a ghostly wash of feedback, reverb-laden gongs and other completely indistinguishable instruments. It's a truly odd number—essentially just voice and electronics—and light-years from Garcia's original conception of the song as "baroque. . . . The original setting I'd worked out was really like one of those song forms from the New York Pro Musica." Later, though, "I had a desire to make it much weirder than that and I didn't know how to do it. . . . I had something specific in mind, but simply couldn't execute it because I didn't have the tools. It's too bad, because it's an incredible lyric and I feel I threw the song away somewhat."

It's true that Garcia's sonic experiments did ultimately obfuscate some of Hunter's best late-'60s lyrics, which were filled with exotic psychedelic pictures and a strong metaphorical undercurrent that could easily be interpreted as being about lost innocence and the vanished promise of the acid culture's golden days:

> Scheherezade gathering stories to tell
> From primal gold fantasy petals that fall
> But where is the child
> Who played with the sunshine
> And chased the cloud sheep
> To the regions of rhyme?

There were strange goings-on outside the recording studio, too. In September and October 1968, three years into their history, the Grateful Dead faced a crisis that nearly derailed the group. Garcia and Lesh determined that Weir and Pigpen weren't pulling their weight musically in the band, weren't in tune with the more complex compositions the band was writing and, according to Rock Scully, "Jerry kind of put it on me to fire them. It was a totally musical decision. Bobby wasn't progressing—he was still playing the electric guitar like an acoustic guitar, and Jerry was trying to get him to loosen up and be a rhythm guitar player. Bobby was still a student, but not listening." Bobby had nearly been fired in the fall of 1967, and as Jonathan Reister, their road manager beginning in mid-1968, says, "Bobby was our little juvenile delinquent. Most of the band fights were about his guitar playing."

As for Pigpen, Scully said, "I don't think that Pig, without being high on LSD, could quite understand the direction the music was taking. And their music did change a lot in that period. Jerry spent a lot of time trying to describe and explain where he thought the music was going, and so did Phil. Phil was a *very* high dude in those days. Now he's considered a genius, but in those days he was just this weird ex–postal worker who'd just taken up the bass but had some really neat ideas musically. He was willing to push that envelope.

"But if the firing had to happen, it happened at a good time, because we were just sort of doodling in the studio. We weren't making any money. We didn't have any gigs booked, so there was really no loss, except emotionally. I was against it, but Jerry put it on me as the manager to do it. Phil was behind it and so was Kreutzmann. But to fire nearly half your unit . . ."

Scully said that Pigpen took the firing hard, but in Garcia's rosier memory, "we never actually let him go; we just didn't want him playing keyboard, because he just didn't know what to do on the kind of material we were writing. It seemed like we were heading some [musical] place in a big way and Pigpen just wasn't open to it."

No one seems to remember exactly how long Weir and Pigpen were out of the band. Weir suggested it was "a couple of months," but using *Deadbase*'s show list as a guide, it appears there was never a period of more than two weeks between Dead shows at any time during September or October 1968, so it couldn't have been too long. "It didn't take," Garcia noted with a laugh. "We fired them, all right, but they just kept coming back."

Nevertheless, during October the Dead minus Weir and Pigpen played a loose series of jam nights at the Matrix club as Mickey and the Hartbeats, and invited a variety of musicians down to play with them, including Elvin Bishop, Paul Butterfield, Jack Casady and Spencer Dryden. Though a few of the jams that came out of these evenings were centered on some of the Dead's most open-ended material, like "Dark Star" and "The Eleven," mostly the musicians stuck to blues tunes and various progressions that gave everyone plenty of room to blow.

The Weir problem evidently took care of itself over time—he rededicated himself to his instrument to the satisfaction of his detractors. To get around the problem of Pigpen's limited skills as a musician, the Dead hired Tom Constanten to play keyboards beginning in November 1968. "Pigpen was relegated to the congas at that point," said Jon McIntire, who was brought on board to help road manager Jonathan Reister in the summer of '68, "and it was really humiliating and he was really hurt, but he couldn't show it, couldn't talk about it. He never came up to me and said, 'I can't stand what they're do-ing to me,' or anything like that. I bet he didn't say it to anyone; I don't even know if he said it to himself—maybe when he went for the bottle the first time after it happened he said it to himself."

Constanten was even more a stranger to the rock world before he joined the Grateful Dead than his friend Phil Lesh had been. You'll recall that Phil and T.C. took music classes together at UC Berkeley (although T.C. originally en-rolled there to study astrophysics) and that they studied with Luciano Berio at Mills College in Oakland, and then T.C. continued working under Berio's tute-lage in Europe. Later, on Berio's recommendation, T.C. hooked up with another well-known avant-garde composer, Karlheinz Stockhausen, in Darmstadt, Ger-many, and in Brussels he studied with Henri Pousseur. Upon returning to the U.S. in the mid-'60s, T.C. enlisted in the air force as a way to avoid being drafted into the army. Though he regarded his stint in the military "like a bull-shit job with a silly suit," at least it gave him time to compose—indeed, T.C. was very prolific during his time in the military, and a few of his orchestral works were performed by the Las Vegas Symphony Orchestra.

On his furloughs T.C. would often go to the Bay Area, where Phil was playing first with a crazy electric blues group called the Warlocks, and then with the Grateful Dead. Not surprisingly, hanging out in the Dead scene brought T.C. in contact with the psychedelic underground, and he was per-sonally responsible for bringing quite a bit of LSD to his hometown of Las Ve-gas. He was still a short-haired serviceman when he worked with the Dead on *Anthem of the Sun* in the fall of 1967 and winter of '68.

Constanten was discharged from the air force on November 22, 1968, af-ter serving three and a half years, and he immediately took the group up on its earlier invitation to join the band on the road. He flew to Ohio the next day and played his first gig with them on November 23 at Ohio University in Athens. Although he hadn't had a chance to rehearse with the band, "I'd heard the albums, I knew the changes and knew I could land on my feet in impro-visatory situations." Immediately the Dead's jams took on a new richness with the addition of T.C.'s organ work, though he felt his playing was tentative at first.

T.C. said that he felt hampered by having to play the same cheesy-sounding Vox Continental organ that Pigpen usually took on the road: "I didn't like the sound it put out at all. There was something about the Continental in that par-ticular band that grated. The Dead's guitars were these strands of gold and fila-ments of light, but the Vox was like a hunk of chrome. I had terribly mixed emotions about everything I was playing because the sound didn't please me. After a bit of moving, shaking and agitating, I convinced them to let me play a Hammond B-3, which I was able to enjoy a bit more."

(Garcia changed his axe at some point in 1968, too, retiring his Guild

Starfire and picking up the warmer-sounding Gibson SG Les Paul model. In '69 he switched back and forth between that guitar and a regular Gibson Les Paul.)

In January 1969 the group returned to Pacific Recording to cut tracks for "China Cat Sunflower" and two new Hunter-Garcia songs, "Mountains of the Moon" and "Dupree's Diamond Blues," both of which Garcia decided to put in settings dominated by acoustic guitars. That's about all those two songs have in common, however—they couldn't be farther apart lyrically and in terms of the mood each creates.

With its flowery T.C. harpsichord line, "Mountains of the Moon" sounds like a throwback to an earlier age; it's practically a minuet. And Hunter's lyrics paint a picture of a mythical world far removed from our own:

> *Twenty degrees of solitude*
> *Twenty degrees in all*
> *All the dancing kings and wives*
> *Assembled in the hall*
> *Lost is a long and lonely time*
> *Fairy Sybil flying*
> *All along the all along the*
> *Mountains of the moon*

"That song turned out nicely," Garcia said. "I don't know what made me think I could do a song like that, but something at the time made me think I could do it."

Hunter once said that "Dupree's Diamond Blues" was the only song he ever wrote drunk, but that's not to suggest that lyrically it's sloppy or anything less than clever. "Dupree's" was the first of a handful of songs that Hunter and Garcia wrote together where they essentially plucked stories out of the folk/blues tradition and reworked the themes in their own way. In this case, there were already a number of songs, dating back to the '20s, that told the (true) story of Frank DuPre, who in December 1921 robbed an Atlanta jewelry store to get a diamond ring for his girlfriend and killed a policeman while escaping the scene. The dapper DuPre was hanged in September 1922, and he instantly became the subject of various songs in both white and black folk music circles. "Hunter and I always had this thing where we liked to muddy the folk tradition by adding our own songs to the tradition," Garcia said. "It's the thing of taking a well-founded tradition and putting in something that's totally looped. So that's Hunter's version of that [song]. Originally, it's one of those cautionary tales; one of those 'Don't take your gun to town'–type tunes. So Hunter elaborated on that in a playful way."

At concerts during the winter and spring of 1969, the band sometimes paired "Dupree's" and "Mountain of the Moon" at the beginning of their second set, with Garcia and Weir playing acoustic guitars onstage for the first time in the Dead's history. Then, more often than not, those songs gave way to "Dark Star," as the set would leave the warm, homey acoustic plane for more remote galactic destinations. The band loved to set up those kinds of juxtapositions—acoustic into electric music, country tunes coming out of space jams or an out-of-control, high-energy romp like "The Eleven" abruptly followed by a slow blues tune like "Death Don't Have No Mercy," which Garcia sang and played with such unbridled passion in the late '60s.

A third acoustic tune Hunter and Garcia wrote around this time was a wispy ballad called "Rosemary," which, according to T.C., Garcia brought into the studio as a completed four-track tape. It's just a Garcia vocal (altered by running the signal through a Leslie organ cabinet to give it a weird, treated quality) and two fingerpicked acoustic guitars, double-tracked by Garcia; there's no bass, drums or keyboards. The band never performed the song in concert, and there's no evidence the other members of the group ever played it at all. Lyrically, "Rosemary" feels almost fragmentary, as if it's just a part of some larger song.

The band worked up a couple of new electric Hunter-Garcia songs in the studio in the winter of '69, too. "Doin' That Rag" was a curious, quirky, lighthearted little number with a hint of a jug band feel in places. With its succession of quick tempo changes between verse and chorus and even within each chorus, it was a fairly difficult tune for the band to perform live. That's one reason Garcia only played the song for a few months in '69; he also once said he had a tough time getting into the lyrics, which do lean toward the cryptic and inaccessible:

> Sitting in Mangrove Valley chasing light beams
> Everything wanders from maybe to Z
> Baby, baby, pretty young on Tuesday
> Old like a rum-drinking demon at tea

"Cosmic Charlie" was a more successful song all the way around, a loping midtempo number with unison lead vocals by Garcia and Weir and a screaming Garcia slide guitar line that weaves through the entire song and is so on the money that it prompts the question: Why didn't Garcia play slide guitar *more* during his career? He also plays a fingerpicking acoustic guitar line that gives the blues-based tune a dash of Mississippi John Hurt or Reverend Gary Davis feeling. Hunter's words seem to be, at least in part, a gentle, mocking put-down of undirected, "cosmic" hippie types:

> Cosmic Charlie, how do you do?
> Truckin' in style along the avenue
> Dumdeedumdee doodley doo
> Go on home, your mama's calling you . . .

Say you'll come back when you can
Whenever your airplane happens to land
Maybe I'll be back here, too
It all depends on what's with you

Garcia admitted that in many of the songs he and Hunter wrote in 1968, "we were both being more or less obscure, and there are lots of levels on the verbal plane in terms of the lyrics being very far-out; too far-out, really, for most people." He also complained that some of the music he composed during that period was unnecessarily complicated and difficult to sing. Of "Cosmic Charlie," for instance, he noted, "It doesn't have any room to breathe" and "trying to sing that song and play it at the same time is almost impossible." "Cosmic Charlie" was not performed very often (the final version was in 1976), but it was always a fan favorite—during the '80s and '90s a group calling itself the Cosmic Charlie Campaign wrote letters and circulated petitions in a futile effort to get the band to play the song again.

In the winter of 1968–69 the Dead started to venture more regularly outside of California. In November and December of 1968 they hit three cities in Ohio, Chicago, Detroit, Philadelphia and Louisville on one swing, and Houston and Miami on another before closing the year as headliners for "The Fillmore Scene at Winterland" New Year's Eve bash that also included Quicksilver and two of the best "second-generation" San Francisco rock bands, Santana and It's a Beautiful Day. Then, after working more on their third album during the first three weeks of 1969, the band hit the road again, playing Chicago, Minneapolis, Omaha, St. Louis, Pittsburgh, New York City (opening for Janis Joplin at the Fillmore East) and Philadelphia—a grueling two-week trek across frozen tundra to snowbound cities that earned little money at most stops. Looking back from a time when rock tours gross millions of dollars and top bands routinely stay in luxury hotels, it's sometimes difficult to picture an era when there really wasn't a touring "industry" in rock, and bands had to continually scramble to find airplane flights, hotels to stay in and places to play.

"I got kicked off seven national airlines for holding up flights so that two hundred people missed their connections; things like that," says Jonathan Reister. "We were sometimes checking in two hundred or three hundred pieces of equipment as extra baggage. I'd have thirteen, fourteen, fifteen tickets [for the band, managers and crew] and I'd check in the equipment as extra baggage for each of us. It took forever, and sometimes it also made the plane heavier than it should have been."

Typically, the entire band and crew would travel from place to place using Rock Scully's American Express card as their collateral, whether Scully was there or not. "That was the only credit card we had and we owed $10,000 on it all the time—that was our limit," Reister says. "I was sending money back from the road all the time just to keep the card open for another day or another week. Everything was a hustle—not that we were burning people, just that we never had quite the right cards or documentation, and of course we looked outrageous. I finally told the band, 'Look, don't come anywhere near me when I'm getting the car; don't come to the rental desk with me.' Which, of course, Weir *loved* to do, and then he'd act weird. Jerry really stood out a lot in those days, too, because he used to wear this brightly colored serape and he had a big natural, and people had never seen anything like that in Nebraska. It was like walking with an apparition. I always had short hair and a cowboy hat, but everyone would stare at Jerry."

"Occasionally you'd arrive at these cheap hotels and they wouldn't know you were a bunch of longhairs until you got there, and they'd refuse to let you in," Jon McIntire remembered. "That happened to us several times. First you'd try to be diplomatic and try to convince them to let you stay there. Usually I was successful at that. But sometimes I couldn't do that and we'd have to scramble to find another place."

"We'd walk into a Holiday Inn or someplace and they'd say, 'Oh no you don't, *not here!*'" Garcia recalled with a laugh. "We got that kind of reaction the first couple of years we were out. People weren't used to seeing freaks back then. That was still a big novelty. That was fun for us 'cause it was the last chance you had to shock people, just by the way you looked, just by the way you were. You didn't have to think about it or work at it at all. You could just walk down the street and people would go, 'Oh my God!' That was fun. We got in on the last of that probably."

Of course the restaurateurs' and moteliers' fears were occasionally well-founded. As Weir put it in 1995, "We left some smoking craters of some Holiday Inns, I'll say that. There were a lot of places that wouldn't have us back."

And while the Dead were unknown in many cities in the late '60s, their reputation as free-spirited drug users preceded them in some areas. When the group arrived in Miami in the spring of 1969, for example, "the chief of police actually came onto our plane, asked who the road manager was and then told me, 'We're going to follow you everywhere you go,'" Reister says. "St. Louis was another bad town. The police showed up in force at the airport and introduced themselves. 'We're here. We're gonna watch you sons of bitches. We want you out of town as soon as possible.' They made it very clear they did not want us there. They thought we were going to get their daughters high and fuck 'em—and they were right," he adds with a chuckle.

Mostly, though, life on the road for the Dead in the late '60s was what it has always been for traveling musicians: tedious, uneventful; marking time between the gigs, which is where the band would really come alive and enjoy themselves. "Jerry was my roommate on the road, and he wasn't much into the late-night party scene in those days in hotels on the road," Reister says, "at least outside of the big cities on the East Coast. There was always more happening in New York or Boston, of course. But one of my favorite memories of Jerry is being in a motel somewhere, with him sitting on the edge of my bed watching *Captain Kangaroo* with no sound, playing scales on his guitar while I was on the phone to the next city or whatever. He was a marvelous guy; a great storyteller. Well-spoken, well-read, a lot of fun to travel with."

As 1969 rolled along, both Warner Bros. and the band became increasingly concerned about the group's precarious financial state. Though the group toured more in '69 than in any previous year, they barely broke even on the road, and the album was costing an astronomical amount for that era—close to $100,000. Then, from out of nowhere, came Lenny Hart—Mickey's dad—who had become a Christian fundamentalist preacher, full of fire-and-brimstone sermons and, strangely enough, a rap that convinced the Dead he could manage the group's business affairs and sail the good ship Grateful Dead into calmer waters. "Lenny was a preacher and he preached the gospel of the band," Hunter said. "He was dynamic and intelligent, and if he was a Jesus freak, then he could probably be trusted, so that was okay with the band.

"It was a signal moment: he asked us what we wanted. And we said it— we wanted to do this for the rest of our lives. It wasn't supposed to be possible in rock; it was a teenage phenomenon. You lasted five years and it was over."

"What we wanted to do was play music, and we didn't want to have to be businessmen," Garcia said. "We didn't even want to decide; we just wanted to play. . . . It never occurred to us that there were options. It never even occurred to us that you could plan. We were truly coming from an unstructured space."

Reister and Hunter were among a small group who say they never trusted Lenny Hart, and even warned the group against hiring him, but it would be several months before the wisdom of their position became apparent to everyone else.

"The band was always wishy-washy about these kind of things," Reister says. "One of Garcia's bad character defects is that he'd just go with the flow. Nobody wanted to hassle in those days, so they sometimes took the easy way out, which wasn't always the smartest way."

The Dead's third album, *Aoxomoxoa* (a title concocted by cover artist Rick Griffin in consultation with Robert Hunter; the Dead's original title for the record was *Earthquake Country*), appeared in record stores in late June 1969, after eight months of on-and-off recording and mixing sessions. Although the album contained nicely nuanced versions of Dead concert favorites like "Saint Stephen," "China Cat Sunflower" and "Cosmic Charlie," the record's overall feel was quite different from a Dead show during this era. There was no jamming to speak of; three of the songs were driven by acoustic guitars; there was the peculiar and not particularly successful vocal experiment "What's Become of the Baby"; and Weir and Pigpen had no lead vocals on the album—indeed,

Pigpen does not appear on the record at all. The album was not a commercial success—though "Saint Stephen" did get some FM airplay—and the single release of "Dupree's Diamond Blues," backed with "Cosmic Charlie," was an utter failure.

"I like that record personally, just for its weirdness really," Garcia said a couple of years after the album came out. "The tapes were well-recorded, and the music is well-played and everything on it is really *right*. It's just that it was our first adventure with sixteen-track and we tended to put too much on everything. We tended to use up every track, and then when we were mixing, we were all of us trying to mix. It came out mixed by committee. A lot of the music was just lost in the mix, a lot of what was really there."

It's telling that in late 1971 Garcia and Lesh went back into the studio and completely remixed the record, stripping away entire parts—like the otherworldly female backup vocals on "Mountains of the Moon" and the cute barbershop quartet–style vocal ending of "Doin' That Rag"—and generally making a leaner, better-sounding album. (The CD version of the album is the remix, so in essence the original *Aoxomoxoa* is "lost.")

The middle of 1969 found the group playing some of its most adventurous and challenging music, with long, beautifully developed versions of "Dark Star," "That's It for the Other One," "The Eleven" and "Love Light" being commonplace, and songs like "Saint Stephen" and "China Cat" becoming more powerful and assured almost with each playing. By then, most of the material from *Anthem of the Sun* had either receded to the background or, in the case of both "New Potato Caboose" and "Born Cross-Eyed," been dropped altogether, never to be played again by the Dead. The band's approach—born of endless rehearsal during the *Anthem* era—of connecting tunes together continued to be a vital part of their operating ethos all the way up until Garcia's death, but it's fair to say that by mid-1969 there was very little collective composition going on. The band still rehearsed occasionally (though less and less as they toured more), but their sessions were no longer characterized by the sort of obsessive pursuit of the unknown that had characterized late '67 and '68, when they were discovering the raw power of the sextet and, in essence, beginning to forge their mature group sound. By the spring of '69 it was also clear that Hunter and Garcia were becoming serious *song*writers, and that Garcia was as interested in directing his energy toward becoming a craftsman in that area as he had been in honing his instrumental voice in earlier years. This was the beginning of the golden era of the Hunter-Garcia partnership and a gradual simplification of the Dead's sound, as the duo moved away from the strange, often impenetrable imagery of their most psychedelic pieces into a somewhat simpler folk and country vein.

For Hunter, the epiphany that led him to pursue a new direction in his writing was hearing *Music from Big Pink*, the debut album by the Band. The onetime backup group for Bob Dylan had fashioned an extraordinary record that tapped into many of the same Southern roots the Dead originally drew upon, and in guitarist Robbie Robertson the Band had a songwriter capable of spinning the group's influences into something that was utterly new while still sounding familiar. And the Band's eponymous second album (aka "the Brown Album" after the dominant color on the cover), released in 1969, was even more successful at depicting characters who inhabited some mythic dimension from America's past yet seemed to speak clearly to a late-twentieth-century audience.

"I was very much impressed with the area Roberston was working in," Hunter said. "I took it and moved it west, which is the area I'm familiar with, and thought, 'Okay, how about *modern ethnic?*' Regional, but not the South, because everyone was going back to the South for inspiration at that time."

Hunter found that Garcia's own tastes were moving in the same direction as his—that Jerry was more interested in writing songs like "Dupree's Diamond Blues" (which would have fit nicely on either of the Band's first two records) than "What's Become of the Baby." And it helped that beginning in late '68 or early '69 the two actually lived together: Garcia and Mountain Girl gave up their Larkspur cottage and, with Hunter and his girlfriend, Christie, moved into a wonderful house at the end of Larkspur's redwood-studded Madrone Canyon, just a few blocks from Janis Joplin's Baltimore Canyon house, as fate would have it. The house at 271 Madrone sat on an acre of land, had a creek running behind it, tall trees surrounding it and morning light that came through the branches in great golden shafts.

"I'd be sitting upstairs banging on my typewriter, picking up my guitar, singin' something, then going back to the typewriter," Hunter recalled. "Jerry would be downstairs practicing guitar, working things out. You could hear fine through the floors there, and by the time I'd come down with a sheet and slap it down in front of him, Jerry already knew how they should go! He probably had to suffer through my incorrect way of doing them," he added with a chuckle.

"Hunter was up twenty-four hours a day, chain-smoking, and he'd come down in the morning and he'd have a stack of songs," Mountain Girl says. " 'Wow, Hunter, these are fantastic.' 'Do you really think so?' And he'd challenge Jerry to sit down right then and write a tune for it; or he might have already worked out some chord changes for it and Jerry would say, 'Oh no, man, that's not the way it should be; it should be like *this.*' But to see Hunter walk out of his room in the morning with a stack of freshly minted tunes was pretty exciting. It was just incredible how fast those tunes fell together once they got on them. It was a tremendous time for everybody."

The first three songs Hunter and Garcia produced in the Madrone house in the spring of 1969 were indicative of the direction their work was heading in this era:

"Dire Wolf," which Hunter wrote one night after staying up late with

M.G. watching the Sherlock Holmes film *The Hound of the Baskervilles*, told a tale of the struggle between man and nature, in which a settler in the snowy "timbers of Fennario," after having a supper of "a bottle of red whiskey," tempts fate by inviting a wolf into his isolated cabin and then playing a game of cards with the beast, presumably to determine the poor man's ultimate fate—sort of a backwoods version of the chess game in Ingmar Bergman's *The Seventh Seal*. In this case, the theme is much darker than the presentation. Garcia's musical setting for Hunter's story is light and folky—as if it might have come from the campfire sing-along mentioned in the last verse—even though the opening verse makes it clear that the narrator probably perishes ("I said my prayers and went to bed, that's the last they saw of me"). The chorus is a plaintive "Don't murder me / I beg of, you don't murder me / Please don't murder me," which Garcia always seemed to sing with a sort of amused "poor sucker" tone in his voice.

In its first versions in the spring of 1969, "Casey Jones" was much more country-flavored than the song that ended up on *Workingman's Dead* a year later, more like something that could have been lifted out of the repertoire of Buck Owens. Of course Buck Owens wasn't about to sing a song with lyrics like these:

> *Driving that train, high on cocaine*
> *Casey Jones you better watch your speed*
> *Trouble ahead, trouble behind*
> *And you know that notion just crossed my mind*

Like "Dupree's Diamond News," the Hunter-Garcia "Casey Jones" put a new spin on an old story, and actually blended two different song streams from the oral tradition. As Garcia explained, "There's a whole tradition of co-caine songs—'Cocaine's for horses, not for men / Doctors say it'll kill you, but they don't say when'; they have lyrics like that. Then there's a whole group of 'Casey Jones' songs, so we thought it would be fun to combine these two tra-ditional ideas and put them into one song." It was more than coincidence that the song was written at a time when cocaine first started to turn up in the Dead's scene with some regularity, though at first the white powder was re-garded more as simply a pleasant pick-me-up to be enjoyed when it was around, rather than as an essential tool for surviving the rigors of the road, as it was viewed later. And while the straight media were scandalized by the song's supposed glorification of cocaine—Hunter acknowledged he put cocaine in a "lightly romanticized context"—the lyrics reveal that it is a cautionary fable, not an endorsement of the drug. After all, Hunter's Casey Jones character, like the real early-twentieth-century figure all the tradition's songs are based upon—John Luther Jones of Cayce, Kentucky—dies in a train wreck.

"I always thought it's a pretty good musical picture of what cocaine is like—a little bit evil, and hard-edged," Garcia said. "And also that sing-songy thing, because that's what it *is*, a sing-songy thing, a little melody that gets in your head."

The third Hunter-Garcia song introduced that spring was the most hardcore country of them all, the exquisite, melancholy ballad "High Time." Musically, the song could have come from any one of the top Nashville or Bakersfield writers of the day, but lyrically it was much more complex than it appeared on the surface, with its deft intermingling of past, present and future, anticipation and regret, clarity and confusion. Garcia once complained that he wasn't a good enough singer to do the song justice; nevertheless, it became one of the group's most successful live songs in mid-'69, a plaintive little Patsy Cline saloon break in the midst of the band's nightly journeys through distant nebula and intricate psychedelic dreamscapes. The Dead in the second half of 1969 were really three bands in one—the jamming band that stretched in every conceivable musical direction in search of new sounds, new musical shapes and uncharted emotional terrain; the funky R&B machine that took over when Pigpen strutted the stage during the group's extended workouts on "Love Light" and "Hard to Handle"; and the country band that sparkled on the short, punchy new Hunter-Garcia originals and Weir-sung tunes like John Phillips's "Me and My Uncle" (actually a Dead staple since '66), the traditional song "Slewfoot," the Springfields' "Silver Threads and Golden Needles" and Merle Haggard's "Mama Tried."

The Dead's turn toward country coincided with (but was not necessarily influenced by) a movement in that direction in rock music as a whole. Near the end of 1968 the Rolling Stones released *Beggar's Banquet*, which contained a big dollop of country blues. The Byrds had ambled down a country road during Gram Parsons's brief tenure with the band; he and Chris Hillman then split off from the Byrds to form the countrified Flying Burrito Brothers. Bob Dylan emerged from the symbolist forest he'd created on *John Wesley Harding* and simplified his sound to cut *Nashville Skyline*. Poco had risen out of the ashes of the *original* country-rock band, Buffalo Springfield, and immediately developed a strong hippie following. In mid-1969 another Springfield alumnus, Stephen Stills, got together with another ex-Byrd, David Crosby, and former Hollies singer Graham Nash to form the mainly acoustic trio Crosby, Stills and Nash. They recorded an album that fairly glistened with bright harmonies and warm, acoustic textures, and had a deep impact on many bands, the Dead included. In fact, Crosby and Stills spent a lot of time around the Dead scene during 1969, mainly at Mickey Hart's ranch, and the band often credited those two with influencing them to spend more time working on their harmony singing, which had never been the band's strong suit, to put it kindly.

"They had listened to us a lot," Crosby said, "and they liked what happened when three-part harmony went over a good track. It's very generous of them to credit us with it, but we never sat down with them in a room and said, 'Okay, now, you sing this, you sing this.' That never happened. Those guys are brilliant. They knew exactly what they were doing, and they evolved their own version of it. They just credited us to be nice."

Of course Garcia had strong country inflections in both his singing and playing dating back to his folk and bluegrass days, but in March of 1969 he took it a step further when he bought a Zane-Beck (ZB) pedal steel guitar in Denver during the band's spring tour. Garcia had owned a Fender pedal steel back in 1966, but at that point he found it too complicated to set up and too difficult to find time to learn how to play, so he sold his instrument to Banana (Lowell Levenger) of the Youngbloods. When the Dead returned to California after the tour, Garcia took the pedal steel to the band's rehearsal hall in Novato and began teaching himself the rudiments of the instrument. Interestingly, in the mid-'60s and early '70s there were a number of city-bred banjo pickers who took up pedal steel, including Eric Weissberg, Winnie Winston, Tony Trischka, Mayne Smith and, perhaps most notably, Bill Keith, who had been one of Garcia's major banjo influences.

"When I heard that Jerry had bought a pedal steel," John Dawson recalls, "I boldly invited myself over to his house to hear what it sounded like. I brought my guitar along and I played him a couple of my songs and he literally sat there and dove into the pedal steel guitar, like jumping into a swimming pool without even checking the water. We had a nice evening and that was really the beginning of the whole New Riders thing."

Dawson had been on the periphery of Garcia's world since the Palo Alto days. He had been part of the early acid scene on the Peninsula and was a witness to the birth of the Grateful Dead, but he was never very interested in playing rock 'n' roll himself, and instead spent hours listening to Merle Haggard and Buck Owens, "getting off on how they used electric guitars to make this real sparse but beautiful sound," Dawson says. "Their harmonies were crisp and clean and the songs made good sense. If you were a guitar player and you wanted to play country, you had to listen to Don Rich [Owens's guitarist]. Everybody did, including Jerry, of course. We'd all listen to that Carnegie Hall record that Buck Owens did and try to figure out how [Rich] made those sounds."

Dawson had seen Garcia on and off through the Dead's first few years, but it wasn't until Garcia bought the pedal steel that their musical worlds finally intersected. "At that time, I had a gig at this coffeehouse/hofbrau in Menlo Park called the Underground, playing Wednesday evenings, and I invited Jerry to come down and join me," Dawson says. "It was just the two of us—me on guitar and Jerry on pedal steel. I would play my own songs and I was also doing covers—Dylan stuff like 'I Shall Be Released,' and Merle Haggard's 'Mama Tried' and Del Reeves's 'Diesel on My Tail.' At that point Garcia was already becoming *Garcia*. He was already a bit of a celebrity. So once the word got out that it was me and Garcia there—and it was more Garcia than me, of course, because no one knew who *I* was; but it was my thing that Garcia was doing his thing to—we got some pretty big crowds that summer. The teen crowd would come out of the nearby pizza parlor and they'd fill up the place. It got to be a nice little scene.

"At first, Jerry didn't have the slightest idea what the real steel players were up to. What he played was just his idea of what they were doing and what sounded good to him. He basically just put on the finger picks, turned the thing on and just started playing. He was checking it out: 'Let's see, this goes here. If I do this, *this* happens. What if I do *this*?' He didn't read any books; he just sat down and played it. Pick the thing, step on a pedal, move the slide.

"After a while we decided to make a little band out of this," Dawson continues. "David Nelson was available. He was living in Big Brother's warehouse up in San Francisco—he was going to be a member of Big Brother; this is after Janis left, of course. She went on and formed her own band somewhere along the line. But Nelson had always loved country music, so he was up for being in a band. Then we needed a bass player, and [Bob] Matthews tried it and Hunter was interested, but I can't actually remember ever playing with him. So finally we said, 'Hey Phil, won't you play with us? It's really simple shit—not like the stuff you play in the Dead.' And Mickey was into it, so he joined. But he was always a little weird to play with because he likes off-rhythms. Billy plays the straight shit and Mickey plays the weird stuff against that. Anyway, we got together and we rehearsed at Mickey's barn." The band was dubbed the New Riders of the Purple Sage, after the famous Western novel by Zane Grey (with a nod to a Western swing band called the Riders of the Purple Sage).

By the beginning of June, Garcia occasionally played the pedal steel on-stage at Dead shows, too, on songs like "Dire Wolf" and "Slewfoot." Then, beginning in late August 1969, the Dead played their first few concerts with the New Riders as the opening act. "It was great," Dawson says. "With simply two additions to the Grateful Dead's tour you had a whole five-piece band." It wasn't until the middle of 1970, however, that the Grateful Dead–New Riders partnership really blossomed on the road.

The Grateful Dead played 145 gigs in 1969, and in no other year did they play such a broad variety of venues. Close to home they usually played the Carousel/Fillmore West, Winterland (where the Dead were still second-billed to the Airplane) and the Family Dog at the Great Highway (after Chet Helms had to close down the Avalon Ballroom). But they also played one-nighters at local colleges and high schools and, at year's end, a few shows at the "New Old Fillmore"—a short-lived revival for the original Fillmore Auditorium. Out of town, shows happened at large and small colleges, medium-sized theaters, ballrooms here and there (though those were fast disappearing by mid-1969) and, of course, rock festivals.

Ever since Monterey in June 1967 there had been attempts all over the country to put on multi-act festivals, some of them successful, many of them not. The Dead had played a few of them—the Northern California Folk-Rock Festival in San Jose in May 1968; the Newport (California) Pop Festival in August '68; the Sky River Festival in Sultan, Washington, in September '68; the Big Rock Pow-Wow in West Hollywood, Florida, in May 1969—and by the summer of '69 they had a well-established reputation as a good-time, good-vibes live band that always succeeded in getting a crowd up on its feet. (It didn't matter that no one bought their records. The rap on the Dead was *always* "You gotta see 'em play live!"). So it's not surprising that the promoters of a three-day festival taking place on a farm near the upstate New York town of Bethel in the middle of August 1969 would book the Dead, along with two dozen other acts. This, of course, was Woodstock.

It was never easy persuading the Dead to play these kinds of gigs. They were just as happy booking smaller but potentially groovier shows like the Celestial Synapse Celebration at the Fillmore West, where everyone took acid and danced till dawn, or the Expanded Spiritual Music Concert—a psychedelic Easter celebration the Dead were supposed to headline at Miami's Dinner Key Auditorium but were eventually banned from because Jim Morrison had allegedly exposed himself there. The venue's director, George McLean, viewed the Dead as "the same type of people and the same type of music as the Doors; it's this underground pop," he said at the time. Initially, the Dead were apprehensive about appearing at Woodstock, "but [festival promoter Michael] Lang's people really went a long way to assuage us," Rock Scully said. "They went after the Pranksters to be kind of overseers of security, and Wavy Gravy to help feed people and look after bum trips and all that kind of stuff, so eventually they met most of our demands and we believed it might run fairly smoothly."

In the end, Bill Graham helped talk the Dead into playing the festival, and for his trouble Graham managed to land a then-unknown band he was managing—Santana—on the bill as well. The Dead were promised a hefty (for them) $15,000 for their hour-long set. "There were certainly other bands on the bill that were selling more records than us and could demand more money," Scully said, "but they really wanted us to be there and thought we *should* be there—even then back East we were sort of a mythological, sociological movement rather than a musical one."

The Dead were put on the schedule for Saturday afternoon—after Canned Heat, Creedence Clearwater Revival, Santana, Janis Joplin and Mountain, and before Sly and the Family Stone, the Who and the Jefferson Airplane; heavy company. The promoters put the band up in a Holiday Inn in the nearby town of Liberty, along with the Who, most of the Jefferson Airplane, Richie Havens and a few other acts, but there wasn't much time for partying there—by Thursday evening, the day before the festival opened, it was obvious that the event was going to be much bigger than anyone had imagined, and with every road approaching the area completely clogged with traffic, the band opted to take helicopters to the concert site a day early.

What they found when they arrived was staggering—people as far as the eye could see, and not just in front of the stage, but *everywhere*. By Friday night there were close to 250,000 people, and another 100,000 or more hiked miles from cars and buses they abandoned on country back roads and even the New York State Thruway the following day. With tens of thousands of people arriving by the hour, the promoters were forced to tear down the fences and let everyone in for free.

Garcia wandered casually around the festival site on Saturday, high on the Czechoslovakian acid that was making the rounds backstage. He spent some time at the Pranksters' encampment, where there was a small "free stage" with an open mike for anybody who had a song to sing. The old Prankster bus, Furthur, was parked in a semicircle with other hippie buses next to the stage—this would be its last big road trip before it was literally put out to pasture on Kesey's Oregon farm. Kesey himself didn't go to Woodstock; he stayed home and played farmer instead. Mountain Girl was a no-show, too—she was five months pregnant (by Jerry) and wasn't up for being in a crowded festival in hot and humid New York in August.

Hot, humid and *rainy*. There were fierce downpours on and off during much of Saturday, turning Max Yasgur's farm into a giant mud bowl. There wasn't enough food and fresh water to go around, and the limited number of portable toilets wouldn't have been enough for a crowd half the size of the one that actually turned up.

No doubt everybody who went to Woodstock has a different survival story to tell, of hardships that rivaled the Twelve Labors of Hercules. Yes, there were bad trips and injuries and thousands of people who didn't like it one bit and left early, dog-tired and disgusted. Everything we've ever heard about the festival is probably mostly true, even the stuff made up by the thousands of people who didn't go but *said* they did. The myth—the epic story of biblical proportions!—is all-encompassing enough to absorb every tall and small tale thrown at it, because the essential truth of the festival is not in dispute: the vibes really *were* good for the most part, people *did* help each other out and the music by and large *was* outstanding, occasionally even transcendent.

So that's some of the myth. But the Grateful Dead wouldn't be the Grateful Dead if their experience of Woodstock didn't deviate from that myth. They must have said it in countless interviews: "We sucked at Woodstock." Through the years the band members have delightedly told the particulars of their Woodstock debacle with a mixture of mock horror and actual glee, as if failing miserably—while high on acid, no less—at the most famous concert of all time was a badge of honor (remember, "Never trust a Prankster!"), or, more likely, part of a great cosmic joke that they were the butt of. All of a sudden the Dead found themselves onstage, several hours late because their equipment was so heavy that it broke one of the rotating pallets it was placed on and had to be taken down and set up again after it was fixed. They'd hoped to go on in the fading light of afternoon to help the trippers make that sometimes difficult transition from day into evening, but instead it was pitch-dark when they hit the stage, and a howling wind was blowing down the hillside, actually threatening to move the huge stage backwards in the mud.

"We were just plumb atrocious," Garcia said. "Jeez, we were awful! We were on a metal stage and it was raining to boot and I was high and I saw blue balls of electricity bouncing across the stage and leaping onto my guitar when I touched the strings." To make matters worse, random CB radio signals kept erupting out of the PA while the band played, and "people behind the amplifiers kept yelling, 'The stage is collapsing! The stage is collapsing!' " Garcia said.

"The thing about Woodstock," he noted many years later, "was that you could feel the presence of invisible time travelers from the future who had come back to see it. You could sense the significance of the event as it was happening. There was a kind of swollen historicity—a truly pregnant moment. You definitely knew that this was a milestone; it was in the air. As a human being I had a wonderful time hanging out with friends in the music business and sharing great little jams. But our performance onstage was musically a total disaster that is best left forgotten."

The Dead didn't have much time to lick their wounds and contemplate the magnitude of their failure at Woodstock, and that's probably a good thing. Four nights later they played at the Aqua Theater in Seattle, with the New Riders on the bill for the first time, and everyone was all smiles. The crowd dug the Riders' country-rock and loved seeing Garcia sitting behind the pedal steel, a big grin peeking through his bushy black beard for nearly the whole set. And there was a string of other smaller festivals that summer where the Dead played considerably better than they had at Woodstock. The Bullfrog 2 Festival in St. Helens, Oregon, and the Vancouver Pop Festival both took place within a week of the Dead's Woodstock appearance; the New Orleans Pop Festival was two weeks later.

Originally there had been plans to put on a three-day Wild West Festival the week after Woodstock at San Francisco's Kezar Stadium, right next to Haight-Ashbury, but the event collapsed in the face of civic opposition and the ceaseless harangues of various radical politicos who believed the fest was going to be overpriced (at $3 a ticket!), insensitive to the needs and desires of the non-hippie community and a poor excuse to bring dozens of police—"pigs" in the parlance of the Left—into the neighborhood.

That fall, however, a plot was quietly hatched to put on a giant free concert in early December at the Polo Fields in Golden Gate Park. Now ordinarily this might seem like off timing for an outdoor show in San Francisco, since December is smack-dab in the middle of Northern California's rainy season. But there was an ulterior reason for scheduling the show then: in late

November the Rolling Stones would be wrapping up their first U.S. tour in three years, and they thought it would be fun to play for free in the city where both the hippie movement and the concept of free rock 'n' roll in parks had been born. And, oh yes, the Stones were going to film the entire tour, and they liked the idea of using footage from the free show as a triumphant climax for their movie—a one-day mini-Woodstock that would put the Stones at the pinnacle of the rock heap as the '60s drew to a close. Take *that*, John, Paul, George and Ringo!

"Originally the idea was nobody would say anything," Garcia said, "and we'd sneak the Rolling Stones into the park or something like that, [they'd] play for half an hour or forty minutes and then beat it; it would be low-level. But they were making the documentary at the time and they saw it as kind of a photo op." So when asked about rumors of the guerrilla concert at a press conference in New York at the end of their tour, just two weeks before the event, Mick Jagger spilled the beans and confirmed that the Stones were hoping to play a free concert in Golden Gate Park on December 6.

"That was *it*," Rock Scully said. "Within half an hour of that announcement, I got a call from the Park [Department] saying we couldn't do it. Consequently we had to find a place really quickly to do it because everybody knew that they had just made an announcement in New York City that they were going to play for free in San Francisco and everybody was heading there." For the next two weeks the organizers frantically searched for a site that could accommodate an expected influx of 200,000 people.

Finally, just twenty-four hours before showtime, Dick Carter, who operated Altamont Speedway, forty-five minutes east of San Francisco in a hilly, windy, sparsely populated part of the East Bay, offered his facility. No one involved with the concert knew anything about Carter or Altamont, but there was no time for a thorough analysis of the situation. On the surface, at least, it must've seemed as though the day had been saved—the Speedway area appeared to be large enough to accommodate the expected deluge, and the site was accessible by a multilane interstate highway.

As soon as the venue was announced, the invasion began from every direction. As workers raced against the clock to build the stage, and equipment trucks filled with band equipment descended on the speedway, thousands of people arrived in the dark and staked out positions in front of the stage and on the surrounding hillsides. Luckily there was no rain, but it was bitterly cold that night, so people built bonfires to stay warm. By daybreak on December 6 there were already more than 250,000 people at the site and traffic was backed up for miles on every approach road. In all, about 350,000 showed up—or tried to. In the grand tradition of Woodstock, thousands of cars were abandoned along the highways and people hiked miles along the roads and over the grassy hills in the reddish glow of the first morning light. And why not? It was sure to be a helluva show—besides the Stones, scheduled acts included the

Dead, the Airplane, Santana, Crosby, Stills, Nash and Young, and the Flying Burrito Brothers.

By the time the concert got going in midmorning, however, it was clear that there had been a major miscalculation. The Stones had hired members of the Hell's Angels to provide security around the stage (in exchange for gallons of free beer), and apparently the Angels' idea of crowd control was to use violence and intimidation to keep people in line. Most of the senior members of the motorcycle club were elsewhere that weekend, so the security jobs fell mainly to relative neophytes. Memories of how peaceful the Angels had been when they guarded the generators and cared for lost children at the Human Be-In were quickly replaced by the nightmarish spectacle of tough young bikers high on alcohol, acid, amphetamines and barbiturates wailing on people with pool cues just a few feet from the stage. And the violence took an ugly, surreal turn when Jefferson Airplane lead singer Marty Balin was knocked unconscious *during* the band's performance when he tried to stop an Angel from beating someone right in front of the stage.

Shortly after that episode most of the Dead arrived at the site by helicopter. In *Gimme Shelter*, the film about the Stones' tour and Altamont made by the Maysle brothers, Santana drummer Michael Shrieve approaches Garcia and Lesh at the makeshift heliport and informs them of the bad scene going down inside the speedway. "Hell's Angels are beating on *musicians?*" Lesh asks incredulously. "It doesn't seem right, man."

"It was like hell; it was like a nice afternoon in hell," Garcia said years later, a fatalistic chuckle in his voice. "The light and everything was just so weird. The light was this kind of baleful red dusk, kind of particulate air, like [if there were] piles of smoking tires; the smell of sulfur. Jeez, it was horrible; it was so hellish."

The Dead were scheduled to go on right before the Stones, but at the last moment they backed out of the concert altogether. "We felt that it would not have done any good for us to play, and it would have only prolonged the agony," Lesh said. "Unfortunately, the Rolling Stones apparently were waiting for sundown [to go on] so they could make a film, and that's why it went on and on. So it turns out it probably would've been better for us to play, just to fill up that time. But when music was happening, the crowd would surge toward the stage, security would beat them back. So we didn't want to contribute to that."

The violence escalated during the Stones' set, with the Angels beating dozens of people in the crowd for the slightest transgression, and culminated in the stabbing death of a gun-wielding man just a few yards from the stage, as Mick Jagger sang "Under My Thumb." (The killing is captured in the Maysles' film.) The show limped to its conclusion, and though many who didn't see any violence enjoyed the concert, thousands came away from the event dazed and disillusioned.

"It was completely unexpected," Garcia said two years after Altamont. "And that was the hard part; that was the hard lesson there—that you can have good people and good energy and work on a project and really want it to happen right and still have it [go] all weird. It's the thing of knowing less than you should have; youthful folly.

"It was another big scene. Woodstock was the big beautiful scene and Altamont was the big ugly scene. I don't really know what conclusion to draw from it, except that big scenes can go either way. You can tie in a lot of stuff about the Rolling Stones and black magic and all the rest of that shit—karma and whatever. But anytime you have a big scene, you have that potential there; the potential for it to get *ugly*."

CHAPTER 10
Listen to the River
Sing Sweet Songs

iscussion about Altamont dominated the Bay Area rock world for weeks after the debacle, and more than a few people suggested that the Dead were partly culpable for the violence that occurred because of the group's longstanding relationship with the Hell's Angels. In the Stones camp there was a concerted effort to shift the blame to Rock Scully for supposedly arranging the Angels' security-for-beer deal, a charge Scully always denied. At the very least Scully approved of the idea, which most likely originated with Emmett Grogan, formerly of the Diggers cooperative and one of the first to approach the Stones about playing a free show in San Francisco. The Stones' tour manager, Sam Cutler, who worked closely with Mick Jagger in making logistical decisions, had also enthusiastically endorsed the plan. Whatever the facts—and they continue to be debated in '60s memoirs to this day—the events at Altamont unleashed a torrent of finger-pointing, hand-wringing, pontificating and deep, dark self-analysis in the counterculture press, a conversation that lasted for years. Altamont was variously described as the death of the '60s, the death of idealism, the death of rock 'n' roll, the death of hippiedom—an Old Testament–style cataclysm where evil momentarily triumphs, arousing the wrath of God.

The Dead didn't say much publicly in the days following Altamont—what was there to say, really?—but on December 20, 1969, two weeks after the concert, near the end of their second set at the recently reopened Fillmore Auditorium, the group unveiled a new song "about" Altamont. After roaring through what was really the Dead's grand trilogy for 1969—"Dark Star"> "Saint Stephen">"The Eleven"—the band fell into the ominous, rumbling introduction to Hunter and Garcia's "New Speedway Boogie," which Hunter had been partly inspired to write after reading *San Francisco Chronicle* columnist Ralph Gleason's stinging condemnations of the Dead and the other organizers of Altamont.

> *Please don't dominate the rap, Jack*
> *If you got nothing new to say*
> *If you please, go back up the track*
> *This train got to run today*

Spent a little time on the mountain
Spent a little time on the hill
Heard some say: "Better run away"
Others say: "You better stand still"

Now I don't know, but I been told,
It's hard to run with the weight of gold
On the other hand, I've heard it said
It's just as hard with the weight of lead

Ed McClanahan, essayist and former denizen of both the Perry Lane and Acid Test scenes, nicely described the heart of this strong and unflinching song in a 1971 article in *The Realist*:

"Hunter is not of the Altamont-as-*Götter-dämmerung* persuasion, and he does not agree that the quest after salvation—the voyage that began in the Haight-Ashbury and carried us all the way to Woodstock—has dead-ended at last in the molten yellow hills of California just 20 miles east of where it started, impaled on the point of a Hell's Angels rusty blade, skewered there like those suicidal Siamese frogs that travel great distances only to fling themselves upon the spikes of some rare thornbush. Rather, the poet suggests, the journey has only just begun, and the way is long and arduous and fraught with peril; Altamont is but one dark moment in the community's *total* experience, the first installment of the dues we must pay for our deliverance. On the Big Trip, the poet warns, the pilgrims will encounter suffering as well as joy, and those with no heart for the undertaking would do well to stand aside, because "this train's got to run today."

Two years after Altamont, Garcia said of "New Speedway Boogie," "I think that song's an overreaction myself. I think that it's a little bit dire. Really, the thing that I've been seeing since Altamont is that periodically you have darkness and periodically you have light, like the way the universe is in the yin/yang symbol. There's darkness and light and it's the interplay that represents the game that we're allowed to play on this planet."

Neither Garcia nor other members of the Dead ever came down hard on the Angels for their role at Altamont. To the contrary, Garcia said in an interview about a year after the festival that the Angels "behaved properly" at Altamont. "I mean, they did just what they would do, so they were not out of character. Also, I don't think that it was strictly a trip on the Angels, 'cause the Angels in California are surrounded by prospects—people who want to be Angels—and their way of showing that they could be Angels is to come on bad. And they're the ones who are mostly responsible. Most Hell's Angels I know are into partying."

Though Altamont was unquestionably a blow to the Dead—a surprise kick to the solar plexus—the fact is the band barely missed a beat after the fes-

tival, and their gigs in the rest of December and moving into 1970 were uniformly strong and spirited. They were definitely on a roll, inspired no doubt
by the slew of new songs they'd introduced since mid-'69. In the late fall of
1969 the group unveiled four more Hunter songs that would make it onto
their next album.

"Cumberland Blues," with music by Garcia and Lesh, was a tuneful,
harmony-filled portrait of a coal miner:

> *Lotta poor man make a five-dollar bill*
> *Keep him happy all the time*
> *Some other fellow makin' nothing at all*
> *And you can hear him cryin'—*
>
> *"Can I go, buddy*
> *Can I go down*
> *Take your shift down at the mine?"*
>
> *Got to get down to the Cumberland Mine*
> *That's where I mainly spend my time*
> *Make good money, five dollars a day*
> *Made any more might move away . . .*

"On 'Cumberland Blues,' " Garcia explained, "one part is modeled on the
Bakersfield country and western bands—electric country and western bands
like Buck Owens's old Buckaroos and the Strangers [Merle Haggard's group].
The first part of the tune is that style. And the last part is like bluegrass. That's
what I wanted to do: a marriage of those styles."

The song "Black Peter" started life as a "jumpy little tune," according to
Hunter, but "Garcia really turned that one inside out and made a monster of
it." Garcia slowed the song down to a mournful ballad tempo and played it like
a country blues with some Western overtones. Lyrically, it paints a somber
picture of a man on his deathbed, surrounded by sympathetic cronies:

> *Just then the wind*
> *Came squalling through the door*
> *But who can the weather command?*
> *Just want to have*
> *A little peace to die*
> *And a friend or two I love at hand*

It was at the Fillmore West two nights before Altamont that the Dead first
played what became one of their best-known songs, "Uncle John's Band," also
penned by Hunter and Garcia. A month earlier the group had been toying
with some of the progressions that would eventually become part of the song:

"At that time," Garcia said, "I was listening to records of the Bulgarian Women's Choir and also this Greek-Macedonian music—these penny whistlers—and on one of those records there was this little turn of melody that was so lovely that I thought, 'Gee, if I could get this into a song it would be so great.' So I stole it! Actually, I took a little piece of the melody, so I can't say I plagiarized the whole thing. Of course it became so transmogrified when Phil and Bob added their harmony parts to it that it really was no longer the part of the song that was special for me. That was the melodic kicker originally, though."

Hunter wrote the words for "Uncle John's Band" using a tape of the band playing what was essentially the finished tune. "I played it over and over and tried writing to it," he recalled. "I kept hearing the words 'God damn, Uncle John's mad,' and it took a while for that to turn into 'Come hear Uncle John's Band,' and that's one of those little things where the sparkles start coming out of your eyes."

In its earliest incarnation, "Uncle John's Band" had a slightly Latin flavor to it, though with its neatly arranged three-part harmonies and bright, buoyant chord progressions it was clearly a part of the American folk tradition. In 1969 there was a well-known precedent for combining those two types of feelings in a song—Stephen Stills's "Suite: Judy Blue Eyes" from the first Crosby, Stills and Nash record, which was all over the radio that summer and fall. Unlike Stills's opus, however, "Uncle John's Band" was no simple love song. Rather, Hunter fashioned a song that was effectively an invitation to his generation to learn from the past and move forward together into the future:

> Well, the first days are the hardest days,
> Don't you worry anymore
> 'Cause when life looks like Easy Street
> There is danger at your door
> Think this through with me
> Let me know your mind
> Whoa-oh, what I want to know,
> Is are you kind?
>
> It's a buck dancer's choice, my friend
> Better take my advice
> You know all the rules by now
> And the fire from the ice
> Will you come with me?
> Won't you come with me?
> Whoa-oh, what I want to know,
> Will you come with me?

In 1967 Hunter had invited us to go into "the transitive nightfall of diamonds" in "Dark Star." In 1968 he had chided "Cosmic Charlie" to "go on home, your mama's calling you." But "Uncle John's Band" was like a friendly outstretched hand that reached into the psychic darkness that was enveloping the culture and pulled the tattered survivors onto safer ground. After all, if the Dead had come through the violence, disorder and disillusionment of the late '60s with their family intact, with smiling faces and their voices soaring together in song, there was hope for the rest of us, too. Still, Hunter/the Dead were looking for guidance as much as everyone else:

> *I live in a silver mine*
> *And I call it Beggar's Tomb*
> *I got me a violin*
> *And I beg you call the tune*
> *Anybody's choice*
> *I can hear your voice*
> *Whoa-oh, what I want to know,*
> *How does the song go?*

The fourth new tune introduced that fall was "Easy Wind," written by Hunter alone and sung by Pigpen. It was the finest song ever written specifically for Pigpen's rough-and-tumble onstage persona—it casts him as a hardworking laborer whose mistreatin' woman "hides my bottle in the other room." Though Hunter said he originally wrote the song to be like a Robert Johnson blues, once the Dead got hold of it, it became a slinky slice of funk-flavored R&B, full of interesting counter-rhythms and slightly off-kilter guitar parts.

By the end of 1969 Tom Constanten and the Dead had decided to part ways. T.C. had been a valuable addition to the group during a time when their music was at its most complex, but he was not fundamentally a rock 'n' roll player, and he also didn't have roots in the sort of folk and country music that was increasingly part of the Dead's new direction. It didn't help, too, that T.C. had become a Scientologist, which "made me a nonparticipant in the chemical sacraments of the time, and that offended Owsley greatly," he said. "I tried not to proselytize, but I'm sure there's a certain amount you can't resist, and *that* I regret. It probably must have rubbed some people the wrong way."

From his standpoint, T.C. felt he was never really able to step out musically in the Dead, and in his spare time he became involved in a music/theater project called *Tarot* that gave him more creative space. "I wanted to be a bigger fish in a smaller pond, and *Tarot* was more edifying," T.C. said.

Constanten's last official show with the group was the final concert of a five-night series in Honolulu near the end of January 1970. But he traveled to New Orleans with the band right after those shows and appeared onstage with the Dead as a "guest" when they played a new ballroom called the Warehouse, with Fleetwood Mac and the Flock. On January 31, after the first of three scheduled concerts there, police raided the Dead's French Quarter hotel and busted the entire band—except for T.C. and Pigpen—on narcotics possession charges. Also busted were Owsley—whom the local papers crowed was "the king of acid"—members of the Dead's road crew and various "family" members who were along for the trip; nineteen people in all.

"After the show," Garcia recalled, "I went to somebody's house and hung around there for a long time and rapped, and finally went back to the hotel, and when I got there, [the police] were already pretty much cleaning out everybody's room. Everybody was gone, nobody was there, and I just happened to be walking down the hall with my guitar. I saw a couple of guys in the room and they said, 'Hey you, come here!' and they shook me down."

This was much more serious than the San Francisco bust in the fall of 1967. Louisiana had very tough drug laws—kids caught with pot were drawing sentences of five years and more—and the police claimed they had found large quantities of pot, LSD, barbiturates and amphetamines among the band's and crew's possessions. Lenny Hart managed to bail everyone out by posting $37,500, on a nonrefundable premium of $3,750, the Dead's earnings for the concert.

"The cops made it extra heavy for us," Lenny Hart told *Rolling Stone* at the time. "They detained the band, handcuffed them all together and lined them up in front of the building for press photos. The cops were enjoying it, just getting their own things on. They ended up having to spend eight hours in jail; even though the bail was ready right away, they hassled them that long. I don't think that's the way police are supposed to handle it."

This was Garcia's first bust, and the news couldn't have come at a worse time for Mountain Girl, who was back in California: "I called the hotel that day to tell Jerry that I was going into labor and going to the hospital, and the lady at the desk at the hotel said, 'I'm really sorry, but those guys are in jail; you'll have to call the police station.' So I was worried sick about that, and then I didn't see him until he got home, which was right after Annabelle was born."

Garcia was philosophical about the bust, noting, "I just consider it sort of an occupational hazard. I mean, it's like if you're working on a skyscraper—if you're paranoid about falling, you shouldn't be working. And that's like if you're playing rock 'n' roll music and you're paranoid about being busted, you shouldn't be in rock 'n' roll music. It's one of those things that happens; there's nothing you can do. There's no profit in worrying about it."

Shortly after the bust, the Dead went into Pacific High Recording—the studio where finishing work on *Aoxomoxoa* had taken place in the spring of 1969—and cut their fourth studio album, entitled *Workingman's Dead*, in just ten days. What caused the band to make such an about-face in their working methods? Partly it was the nature of the material—the simpler song structures evidently didn't require as much fussing as Hunter and Garcia's psychedelically inspired songs. But a lot of it was economic considerations.

After *Aoxomoxoa* the Dead were in debt to Warner Bros. for close to $200,000. The next record they delivered was the live double-LP set *Live Dead*, released in November 1969 and featuring spectacular performances that showed the early-'69 Dead at their spaciest and absolute best. That record was both inexpensive to make and successful enough that it wiped out about half of what they owed the label, but when the band went in to make *Workingman's Dead*, "we didn't want to incur an enormous debt like we had been," Garcia said. "So I was thinking, when we go into the studio next time, let's try a real close-to-the-bone approach, like the way they record country and western records—a few instruments, relatively simple and easy-to-perform songs. It was quite conscious, an effort to say, 'Let's not spend a year. Let's do it all in three weeks and get it the hell out of the way. And that way, if the record does at all well, we will be able to pay off some of what we owe to the record company.' So that worked very well. And it was a chance to expose a side of us that we hadn't exposed very much."

"We were into a much more relaxed thing about that time," he said in another interview. "And we were also out of our pretentious thing. We weren't feeling so much like an experimental music group, but were feeling more like a good old band."

That's when they were playing music. Offstage, there were big problems. There was the New Orleans bust hanging over their heads—jail was not inconceivable—and while they were recording *Workingman's Dead* they discovered that Lenny Hart had been stealing from them.

Road manager Jonathan Reister says he was the first to raise the red flag about Lenny, but that his warnings had been ignored and, in fact, others had sided with Mickey's father, ultimately leading to Reister's departure from the Dead scene. Still, the band recognized that the financial end of the operation was in such disarray that they needed some help from the outside. Well, sort of "outside": Dave Parker and his wife, Bonnie, friends of the the band from the Palo Alto days, had hooked up with Garcia again in December 1969, and even stayed with Jerry and Mountain Girl in Larkspur for a couple of weeks. Bonnie had accounting experience and David was a bright guy, so when suspicions arose about Lenny, Garcia hired them to work for the Dead. Around the same time, the Dead hired the Stones' road manager, Sam Cutler, to replace Jonathan Reister, and he, too, was involved in the investigation of Lenny Hart's financial shenanigans.

The Parkers' first order of business was to establish the Dead's true financial status, which was difficult because Lenny Hart would not cooperate with them. "Coming in, there was a feeling of suspicion that something was not quite right, but people didn't know for sure," Parker says. "I was starting from a set of books that Lenny Hart had kept in pencil, so it was very convenient to erase and change things. We had to struggle and scuffle just to get the books from him in order to start doing the job. He was reluctant to give them up. The bank account was practically empty and here was this dubious set of books. So finally I went to a lawyer and an accountant. Some suspicious entries were found and it actually resulted in an embezzlement charge [later]."

When it became clear that Lenny had doctored the books and taken an estimated $70,000 to $100,000 from the band, they confronted him with the information and Hart promised to pay back the money. Instead, after putting down $10,000, he disappeared, but not before stealing more of the group's money. "When he ran off on us," Rock Scully said, "he'd just gone to L.A. with Garcia to negotiate for music in *Zabriskie Point* [Michelangelo Antonioni's muddled "youth" film]. Well, he just took the check and split. We found out he had eleven accounts spread out through California."

The theft put the Dead in an even more precarious financial position. Dave Parker remembers that "there was no money to buy plane tickets for the next gig, so we had to borrow that from the booking agent so they could even get out to start earning some money. It was quite a blow coming just after the bust and having it be not just a manager, but Mickey's father."

We'll probably never know the true extent of the psychic damage Lenny's grand larceny had on his son, but it's probably not a coincidence that at the end of 1970 Mickey dropped out of the group for the next five years. "Mickey was dismayed," Garcia said. "He'd never expected anything like that, of course. He knew his father had been into shady trips before, but he thought he was reformed, just like we all did. He was really shocked, and he was right with us about our decision to get rid of Lenny."

In retrospect, it's remarkable the Dead could keep their minds on playing music during this weird time, but as Mickey himself pointed out, the band's business problems were a distraction "only when we came off the road. Not when we were out there, certainly, because we were *flyin'*. When the music's going, all is well. When the music stops and you come home, that's when art meets reality."

In December 1969 the band had experimented at a few shows by opening their concerts with a short set played on acoustic instruments, and in the winter and spring of 1970 this concept was expanded. This proved to be a format that was suitable not just for some of the band's new acoustic guitar–based songs, like "Dire Wolf," "Uncle John's Band" and "Black Peter," but also for a wide range of cover tunes, from traditional pieces like "Little Sadie," "Deep Elem Blues" and "I Know You Rider" (which the Dead also played electric, connected to "China Cat Sunflower") to numbers like the Everly Brothers' "Wake Up Little Susie" and Jesse Fuller's "The Monkey and the Engineer." The sets were loose enough that sometimes only Garcia and Weir would play on a tune. Other times they'd be joined by Lesh on bass, or Pigpen might sing a song like Lightnin' Hopkins's "Katie Mae" solo, with just his own guitar accompaniment. It was almost like sitting around a living room with the musicians—they'd joke around between songs, banter with the audience, play whatever struck their fancy.

Garcia introduced two new songs in the acoustic sets during this period. "Candyman" was another Hunter-Garcia variation on a familiar song theme— there were sexually suggestive "Candyman" songs in the blues tradition dating back to the nineteenth century, and Mississippi John Hurt had a popular fingerpicking song by that name in the late '20s, which he revived when he was rediscovered in the early '60s. The music for Garcia's "Candyman" sounded as if it had been pulled off a piano roll from some dusty, smoke-filled Western saloon, and Hunter's words matched that mood perfectly:

> *Come all you pretty women*
> *With your hair hanging down*
> *Open up your windows 'cause*
> *The Candyman's in town.*
> *Come on, boys, and gamble*
> *Roll those laughing bones*
> *Seven come eleven, boys*
> *I'll take your money home*

The other song was one that Hunter had actually started writing with John Dawson and intended for the New Riders of the Purple Sage. "Friend of the Devil" was a brisk little bluegrass-flavored tune about a desperado on the lam ("trailed by twenty hounds") who borrows twenty dollars from the devil, only to have the devil take it back later, leaving our hero (?) still running from the law, crying his lonely nights away as he dreams of both his "sweet Anne Marie" and the prospect of a life behind bars. As Dawson recalls, "Hunter came over to our house with the germ of the idea that became 'Friend of the Devil.' He had that great opening guitar part, but that's as far as he'd gotten. I came up with the melody for the hook: 'Set out runnin' but I take my time / Friend of the Devil is a friend of mine / If I get home before daylight / I just might get some sleep tonight.' We thought we had a complete song. But he took it back home to Garcia's house, where he was also living, and played it for Jerry and said, 'Well, what do you think?' Jerry said, 'It's nice, but it needs a bridge,' so Hunter got busy and scribbled out some more words and Jerry wrote the bridge. Garcia ended up liking the song so much that he immediately put it in their set. That was fine with me, because he sang it well and the song I'd helped write had grown up and found a nice home."

That spring, the Dead and the New Riders went on their first East Coast tour together, and it was a tremendous success from every standpoint. First of all, because the Dead were traveling with their own opening act, they were able to play concerts with no other group on the bill, so they could play longer sets and not have to worry about clearing another group's equipment from the stage before they went on.

"That first tour was fabulous," Dawson says. "We had a built-in friendly crowd waiting for us—'Wow, what's this new thing that Garcia's up to?' When Alanna [Dawson's wife of many years] was first getting into it, she asked somebody, 'So who are the New Riders?' And the guy told her, 'Oh, they're the guys who come on before the Dead and make everybody feel good.' I'll take that. That's great. That kind of sums it up. We were there to get people goin' and feelin' good, and then the Grateful Dead could go ahead and do their weirdness and all that."

There was definitely something warm and reassuring about the New Riders in the early days. Part of it really was just the sight of Garcia sitting at the pedal steel, picking out melodies that were sweet as molasses, and Phil thundering beneath the songs, playing simpler but still distinctive bass lines. But David Nelson was also a master of twangy Bakersfield-style electric guitar, and Dawson—or Marmaduke, as he was called—was a genial and engaging frontman in his cowboy hat and boots, kind of a Marin hippie on the range. And Dawson's early songs were catchy and compelling, from his bouncy ode to dope smuggling, "Henry," to mooning love ballads like "All I Ever Wanted" and "Portland Woman," to his grand saga of treachery and disaster, "Dirty Business," which featured Garcia playing wonderfully distorted pedal steel. The Riders also played some neat cover tunes, like "Truck Driving Man" and their usual set-closer, a countrified but still rocking version of the Stones' "Honky Tonk Women." The band particularly struck a chord on the East Coast, which was fast becoming the Dead's most lucrative market.

"I guess we represented something to East Coast people that was missing from their lives," Dawson suggests. "Maybe some of it was our disregard for the harsh realities of day-to-day life, which are always right in your face in the East, especially in New York City. Here we were coming in with a devil-may-care attitude and all those guys [in the audience] were having to work for a living, having to do the day-to-day grind and worry about what's happening on the FDR [Drive] or what's happening on the West Side [Highway]. We were high and obviously having a great time and doing what we liked and playing this stuff that everybody had sort of heard before, but it didn't sound like that crap that was on the radio. It was familiar but still different and new."

From the second half of 1969 all the way through 1970, Garcia lent his unique pedal steel touch to a number of different albums that were recorded in the Bay Area. His steel appeared on a song called "The Farm" on the Jefferson Airplane's superb record *Volunteers*. He played on a few tracks by a group called Lamb, one song on It's a Beautiful Day's *Marrying Maiden* album and one on the Kansas City–based duo Brewer and Shipley's *Tarkio*. (Contrary to popular myth at the time, Garcia did not play on their hit "One Toke Over the Line.") And in early 1970 he laid down what is probably, to this day, his most-heard solo—the steel break in "Teach Your Children," on Crosby, Stills, Nash and Young's mega-selling *Déjà Vu* album.

Around the same time that CSNY were finishing up their album, the Airplane's Paul Kantner was busy at Heider's working on what would become his first solo album, *Blows Against the Empire*, and he enlisted Garcia to play steel and some electric guitar on several songs.

"Jerry was doing a lot of pedal steel for people around that time, experimenting, and so we let him be on it; he was overjoyed," Kantner says. "So he went in and just experimented with sounds, seeing what kind of sounds he could get out of it, running it through various pedals and echoes and delays. We gave him a free hand, which made him happy. Before that he'd pretty much just been doing country licks on the steel, and this gave him the opportunity to get a little weirder, which he always appreciated."

Blows Against the Empire was one of the most interesting records to come out of San Francisco in that era, more a work of modern folk music than a rock 'n' roll album, and the first of several Bay Area projects that used members of several of the top local groups as a "cast" of players, rather than featuring a fixed band. From the Airplane, there was Kantner, Slick, Jack Casady (playing perhaps the most sonically intense bass lines of his career) and drummer Joey Covington. From the Dead, Garcia, Bill Kreutzmann and Mickey Hart appeared on various tracks. Graham Nash and David Crosby sang backup vocals, and Crosby also helped write a couple of tunes. Quicksilver's David Freiberg began his long musical association with Kantner and Slick at these sessions; he later played in the Jefferson Starship with them. It was a vibrant and uplifting record that unabashedly celebrated hippie idealism through an elaborate science fiction fantasy story.

"It's about us—me and Jerry Garcia and David Crosby—stealing a starship; hijacking a spaceship, going where whoever comes along wants to go," Kantner said in 1970. "It'd be the rock 'n' roll groups—us, the Dead, Crosby, Stills, Nash and Young, Quicksilver—being part of the plan to take all the millions that they earn from rock 'n' roll, buying an island in the Pacific or somewhere and setting Owsley up with a lot of bread and a lot of equipment. . . . If you gave him $50 billion and an island and a machine shop, he'd have the starship together in less than a year." In Kantner's vividly told tale, hippies escape from Earth to live idyllically in the outer reaches of the galaxy, where they tend hydroponic gardens, enjoy free music, take acid and make love, merging blissfully with the universe.

Derided by some as stoned hippie ravings run amok, *Blows Against the Empire* was nonetheless embraced by freaks from coast to coast, and it was certainly more compelling than the Airplane's rather disjointed next album, *Bark*, made without Marty Balin.

Garcia's playing on the record is both imaginative and impeccably tasteful throughout, from the aching cry of his steel on "Have You Seen the Stars Tonite?" which beautifully evokes the feeling of a starcruiser drifting through limitless space, to the round but wiry tones of his electric guitar work dancing spryly all through "Starship." Garcia also received a co-writing credit (with Kantner, Mickey Hart and Phil Sawyer) on a noisy instrumental interlude called "XM," which simulates the sound of a rocket blasting off using feedback, white noise, distorted gongs and multiple Garcia pedal steel tracks drenched in crackling fuzz and distortion.

As if playing gigs with the Dead and the New Riders and working in the studio with virtually anyone who asked wasn't enough, Garcia also managed to find the time to bop down regularly to the Matrix club to jam with a local keyboardist named Howard Wales and drummer Bill Vitt.

Wales was a Wisconsin native who had played and toured mainly with R&B performers like Ronnie Hawkins, Little Anthony and the Imperials, the Four Tops, the Coasters, Freddy King and James Brown. He'd jammed with rockers like Harvey Mandel and Jimi Hendrix, and when he moved to the Bay Area in 1968 he formed a moderately popular band called A.B. Skhy. Along the way Wales absorbed quite a bit of jazz, too, and he was one of the first rock/R&B keyboardists to try blending the different styles into something new. Certainly, jazz-fusion, as it became known, was in the air in 1970—that was the year of Miles Davis's seminal *Bitches Brew* band, who opened for the Dead at the Fillmore in April and were so hot the Dead felt positively humbled.

Vitt was another seasoned pro with a background that included a three-year stretch as a session drummer in the highly competitive Los Angeles studio scene in the mid-'60s, and a stint playing with Michael Bloomfield after the guitarist's group the Electric Flag broke up.

"Originally it was Howard and me playing at the Matrix on Fillmore, just the two of us, very informally," Vitt says. "The we added a couple of pieces and Jerry was one of the guys. It was a neat little club. It was all listening; nobody danced. Howard had known Jerry before, so he started coming down and jamming with us, and it got to be a regular thing for a while."

"The Matrix was always like a king-sized jam session," Wales adds. "We had all sorts of people coming in and out—Elvin Bishop, Harvey Mandel and Jerry, of course; anybody who was around there came down to play. Mostly it was just jamming and free-form spontaneity. And there were some incredible nights there. Later it solidified and we played more of my own material, but in the beginning it was real loose."

Sometimes Wales, Garcia and Vitt played as a trio, other times a bassist would sit in; the first bassist Vitt brought down to work with the group was a symphony player named Richard Favis. When he dropped out, he was replaced by another Bloomfield band alumnus named John Kahn, who would become one of Jerry's closest musical partners over the next twenty-five years.

The lanky, laconic Kahn had been raised in Beverly Hills, the son of a respected Hollywood talent agent who died when John was five. Kahn's mother stayed in the business and became a successful agent herself, so John was brought up around the movies. "I remember spending a lot of time around the 20th Century-Fox lot as a kid," Kahn said. "It was pretty boring, actually. But one thing that came out of it was Marilyn Monroe baby-sat for me a couple of times. That was cool."

He studied piano and music theory while he was still in grade school, and in high school he added rock 'n' roll guitar to his arsenal. "But then I got heavily into listening to jazz and all of a sudden all I wanted to do was be a jazz string bass player and listen to jazz records all the time," he said. "I loved Scotty La Faro and the Bill Evans Trio, and I also listened to a lot of Ornette Coleman and Coltrane. So I took up the string bass and studied classical music quite a bit."

After high school, Kahn attended the University of Southern California for a semester, then transferred to the San Francisco Conservatory of Music in late 1966. Gradually Kahn became somewhat disenchanted with jazz, and he started drifting into the rock 'n' roll world that was exploding all around him. In 1967 a roommate offered him a job as bassist in a rock cover band, so Kahn traded in his electric guitar for an electric bass, and he emulated the great R&B and blues players of the day—James Jamerson, Hamp Simmons (of Bobby "Blue" Bland's band), Duck Dunn and Chuck Rainey, to name a few. "Another guy who influenced me was Paul McCartney," he said. Over the next couple of years Kahn played in several different groups, including two that he led, Memory Pain and the Tits and Ass Rhythm and Blues Band. He met and jammed with Steve Miller and Michael Bloomfield during this period, and, suddenly brimming with confidence, he went to Chicago to try to land a job with Paul Butterfield's band. When that fell through Kahn returned to San Francisco and started playing with Bloomfield and doing session work in studios around town. It was Bill Vitt who invited Kahn down to the Matrix for one of Wales's Monday night jam sessions.

"So I went down there and it was a lot of fun," Kahn said. "I met Garcia and we became friends right away. Of course I'd heard the Dead quite a bit, but I can't say I was really a fan or anything. I'd been around them some. I lived in the Haight and was at their house a couple of times. But I didn't know their music very well and I didn't know much about how Garcia played. I didn't know what kind of music he and Wales would be playing down at the Matrix when I went down. And I still don't know! It was kind of a weird jazz with these other influences—it was mainly Howard's music, all instrumental.

"We played Monday nights there for a while, and for the longest time, hardly anybody would show up," Kahn continued. "We'd get ten people and split ten dollars four ways at the end of the night. We played there for something like six months but people just didn't seem interested, or maybe they didn't even know about it. After a while people did start to come. It got to be . . . 'crowded' might be stretching things a bit—and this place was the size of a living room. Maybe even 'full' isn't accurate. Let's say 'not empty.' "

For Garcia, the attraction was being able to play in a more relaxed context than the Grateful Dead offered, and a chance to branch out in directions he'd never pursued before. Wales was a serious player, and Garcia had to work hard to follow him. "[Kahn] and I would plug in and play with Howard and spend all night muttering to each other, 'What key are we in?' " Garcia said. "Howard was so incredible, and we were just hanging on for dear life. For some reason Howard enjoyed playing with us, but we were just keeping up. Howard was so *outside*. For both of us that was a wonderful experience. . . . Playing with Howard did more for my ears than anybody I ever played with because he was so extended and so different. His approach was all extensions and very keyboardistic; not guitaristic."

Sometime in April 1970, a few songs from *Workingman's Dead* filtered out to FM radio stations in advance of the album's release, and the response was both immediate and enthusiastic—the Dead had a bona fide hit on their hands. "Uncle John's Band" and "Casey Jones" were the tracks that made the initial splash—they were many people's introduction to the music of the Grateful Dead. By 1970, most young people who liked rock 'n' roll were at least aware of the Grateful Dead—they were more famous than they were popular—though they hadn't sold many records or appeared on any of the big television programs that showcased rock bands, such as *The Ed Sullivan Show* or the much hipper *Smothers Brothers Comedy Hour*. (In mid-1969 the Dead had gotten their only major national TV exposure when they played "Saint Stephen" and "Mountains of the Moon" on Hugh Hefner's *Playboy After Dark*, amid buxom women in miniskirts and young men who looked as if they'd learned about hip fashion from watching *The Mod Squad*. In grand Prankster tradition, someone from the Dead crew dosed many of the drinks on the faux bachelor pad set with LSD, leading to some strange times for the "party" guests after the taping was done.) The Dead were known far and wide as the band that just *might* play all night when they came to your town or college campus; the band that had been at Monterey and Woodstock (and Altamont); the band that was the living embodiment of that undefinable yet still compelling San Francisco spirit of the late '60s—high times, free concerts, a sense of family. And now they had a record filled with these catchy, instantly accessible songs that anyone could sing along with without having to wade through lengthy guitar solos and feedback.

The album contained only eight songs—"Uncle John's Band," "High Time," "Dire Wolf," "New Speedway Boogie," "Cumberland Blues," "Black Peter," "Easy Wind" and "Casey Jones." But each song was its own world, with a distinct tone and texture, and the cumulative effect of the tunes was powerful indeed. Hunter had drawn flesh-and-blood characters who possessed feelings and frailties anyone could relate to. The great paradox of *Workingman's Dead* is that lyrically it's a very dark record—filled with death, despair and hopelessness—yet the music is uplifting, even joyful. (In this way it shared a common characteristic of many bluegrass recordings.) It's an album full of images of man's insignificance in the face of nature's power and mysteries, while at the same time it celebrates the dignity and humanity of the poor beleaguered souls who populate Hunter's universe. There's something vaguely familiar about the music, but it never quite falls into any definable style.

"The album was a tremendous joy," Garcia commented. "Being able to do that was extremely positive in the midst of all this adverse stuff that was happening [with Lenny Hart]. It definitely was an upper. We were getting far into our own thing, without really a gallery to play to, or an audience to interact with. It's just us, bouncing off each other. It was the first record that we made together as a group, all of us. Everybody contributed beautifully and it came off really nicely. That was also our first really together effort at having our songs be groovy and everything; the whole thing."

Though the record was unquestionably a group effort, Garcia was clearly the dominant figure on the album—he co-wrote seven of the eight songs, sang lead on five and shared the lead with Weir and Lesh on two others. Coming on the heels of *Aoxomoxoa*, where Garcia was the main singer and songwriter, and *Live Dead*, which showed off his instrumental prowess (as well as the other players', but the lead guitarist usually gets more of the glory), *Workingman's Dead* affirmed the popular perception of Garcia as the de facto leader of the group. He was the personable storyteller onstage, rarely speaking, but singing Hunter's tales in a plaintive tenor that seemed to owe more to bluegrass great Ralph Stanley than to any pop singers; and offstage, Garcia was the thoughtful, funny and usually articulate spokesperson for the band, doing most of the press interviews, which became more numerous after the surprising success of *Workingman's Dead*. In a sense, Garcia's stage persona was a figment of Robert Hunter's imagination. But it could also be argued that the reason Garcia could sing Hunter's lyrics so convincingly and surround those words with music that matched the sentiments of the songs so beautifully was that he and Hunter fundamentally agreed about so many things that Hunter could truly function as Garcia's poetic alter ego. Hunter voluntarily subsumed some of his own ego to give a voice to Garcia:

"I have to smile when someone, with the best of intentions, tells me I'm as much a part of the band as any of the musicians," Hunter mused a year after Garcia's death. "Ever hear of lost-wax casting? The wax mold is melted away leaving only the casting. That is, I found through long experience, the proper stance for a writer of words in a musical situation. If you think of the writer when the singer is singing, something is wrong with the words."

Warner Bros. Records was understandably excited by the overwhelmingly positive response to *Workingman's Dead* when the album was released in May, and they tried to boost the record's fortunes by releasing a single version of "Uncle John's Band" to AM radio stations. There were a couple of problems with that choice, however. At four minutes and thirty seconds, the song was too long for most AM stations. And, even worse, there was a troublesome word in the third verse: "*Goddamn,* well I declare / Have you seen the like?" Warner Bros. engineers awkwardly deleted the offending phrase and also eliminated one chorus and truncated another in an effort to make the single more radio-friendly.

"I gave them instructions on how to properly edit it," an exasperated Garcia said in late 1970, "and they garbled it so completely and we didn't get a chance to hear it until way late, and it was—oh fuck, what an atrocity!" In the same interview, Garcia admitted his ambivalence about striving for a hit: "It would be nice to have a single, but a hit single usually means twelve-year-old audiences."

"Uncle John's Band" stayed on the *Billboard* Hot 100 chart for seven weeks in the summer of 1970, making it to as high as number 69, which sounds fairly impressive but probably is more a reflection of Warner Bros. promo men doggedly "working" the record than actual sales. The unclipped album version received much more airplay than the single, and the feared influx of twelve-year-olds never materialized.

The Dead also ran into trouble on the radio with "Casey Jones," because of the song's repeated references to cocaine. Actually, cocaine was barely a factor in the underground at the time—it was rarely seen outside of rock 'n' roll backstages, and even there it wasn't nearly as common as it would become in the mid- and late '70s. But drug references of any kind in songs—even cautionary ones like this one was meant to be—were considered to be endorsements of drug abuse by the virulently anti-hippie Nixon White House, and many radio stations chose not to play "Casey Jones," fearing retaliation by reactionary minions from the FCC. This wasn't exactly news: There were countless songs in the late '60s that drew fire from government and church leaders for allegedly promoting drugs, including such mainstream favorites as the Byrds' "Eight Miles High," the Beatles' "With a Little Help from My Friends" and Donovan's scandalous "Mellow Yellow" ("E-lec-trical banana, is gonna be a sudden craze"). As is usually the case with these sorts of controversies, the notoriety associated with the attempts to censor "Casey Jones" probably ended up helping the Dead rather than hurting them. After all, being a thorn in the side of Nixon was a badge of honor in the counterculture, and anything that shook up the straight, pro–Vietnam War "establishment" was regarded as a noble act of counterinsurgency.

Not that the Dead ever endorsed any particular political agenda or had any real interest in confronting the status quo. The group's "political statement," such as it was, was an extension of the Beat imperative to live an honest and soulful life free of the unreasonable dictates of disapproving moralists—"Here's who we are. This is how we're going to live our lives. Join us, or leave us alone." The Dead's staunch apoliticism actually put them in a weird position in the counterculture. Although the band had impeccable "underground" credentials because of their lifestyle, they refused to support the radical Left's ideology and confrontational protest methods, and so were dismissed by some for being spaced-out hedonists. True enough from one point of view, yet from another the Dead's whole enterprise could be seen as even more radical.

"On the West Coast it's already so crazy you can't believe it, with court-room bombings and all that going on," Garcia said in 1970. "But, see, every-body's had a chance to look at it, step away from it, and that isn't it—fighting and hassling and bloodletting and killings and all that shit; that ain't it. What-ever life's about, that's not it.

"I think everybody should take one step backwards and two steps side-ways, and let the whole thing collapse. Nobody vote, nobody work—let it collapse. You don't have to break things and fuck things up and kill people and make all those people uptight."

In another interview, from early 1971, Garcia noted, "Everything is going to pieces on the one hand, and everything is coming together on the other hand. I think that the revolution is over, and what's left is mop-up action. It's a matter of the news getting out to everybody else. I think that the important changes have already happened—changes in consciousness."

Music, he believed, was also an agent in the changes happening in the cul-ture. "It could be that music is one of those things left that isn't completely devoid of meaning. Talk—like politics—has been made meaningless by the endless repetition of lies. There is no longer any substance in it. You listen to a politician making a speech, and it's like hearing nothing. Whereas music is unmistakably music. The thing about music is that nobody listens to it unless it's real. . . . Music goes back before language does. And music is like the key to a whole spiritual existence which this society doesn't even talk about. We know it's there. The Grateful Dead plays at the religious services of the new age. Everybody gets high, and that's what it's about really. Getting high is a lot more real than listening to a politician. You can think that geting high ac-tually did happen—that you danced and got sweaty, and carried on. It really did happen. I know when it happens. I know when it happens every time."

Despite their dislike of any sort of organized political activity, the Dead occasionally turned up unannounced at events that had political overtones. On May 6, 1970, they played a free concert in Kresge Plaza at MIT to show their support for a nationwide campus strike protesting the killing by National Guard troops of four protesters at Kent State University in Ohio. The group also ex-pressed some admiration for the Oakland-based Black Panther Party, whom Gar-cia described in the fall of 1970 as "righteous. They have a rhetoric trip going on, but what they're doing is actual, practical things. They've got a free breakfast trip, and they're starting a free shoes thing—they're starting shoe factories and stuff like that. . . . We don't have any affiliations with any specific organizations, but if there's a righteous [benefit to play], no matter who's doing it, we'll do it. If it avoids bureaucracy and bullshit and goes right to something, we'll do it. That's the sort of thing we're interested in." (Garcia's support for the Panthers cooled significantly as the radical group's posturing became increasingly militant.)

Ever since the Dead's planned European tour in the spring of 1968 had fallen apart, the group had been looking for ways to go overseas, and for a while it looked as though they might be able to ride the success of *Workingman's Dead* across the Atlantic. As the New Riders' David Nelson said, "Originally, Sam Cutler was telling us that he was setting up this big tour of Europe. It was going to be the Dead, the New Riders, the Jefferson Airplane, any good San Francisco bands he could get, and we were all going to go over on a big ocean liner; it would be a big party boat. There were all these meetings, like a big one at Jerry's house in Larkspur where we all talked about getting passport photos taken and all. There were all sorts of changes, though, and it ended up being all these bands going across Canada on a train. We were disappointed we didn't get to go to Europe then, but the train was just fabulous. It couldn't have been any better."

The "Festival Express" train trip in late June and early July 1970 was definitely a career high point for the Dead, though it lasted less than a week. In its own way it was as special as their trip to Europe two years later, or even their trek to the Great Pyramid in the fall of 1978. The concept was simple: put a bunch of bands on a train and roll across Canada, playing twelve-hour festivals in a few key cities. On this rollicking journey the Dead were in splendid company; among the performers joining them were the New Riders, Janis Joplin's Full-Tilt Boogie Band, the Band, Mountain, Delaney and Bonnie and Friends, Chicago bluesman Buddy Guy, folksingers Tom Rush and Eric Anderson, and Ian and Sylvia's country-folk band, Great Speckled Bird. The twelve-coach train had a tiny sleeping compartment for each person on board, a dining car, a lounge and two club cars that were filled with amplifiers and musical instruments for impromtu jam sessions. In the original vision of the Festival Express there were to be five stops on a trip that was supposed to end in Vancouver, but due to financial and logistical problems the Express ended in Calgary, on the east side of the snowcapped Canadian Rockies, and the musicians went their separate ways from there.

The week started out on a down note. In Toronto, a coalition of students and street people calling themselves the May 4th Movement (or M4M), after the date of the Kent State killings, threatened to disrupt the festival, which they called the Rip-off Express. In a letter to the Canadian organizers of the train trip, the M4M's leaders wrote, "We demand that the Transcontinental (Rip-off) Express be free for everyone and all tickets be refunded; there be free food, dope and music for all the people there, with no cops. Failing these totally reasonable and just demands, we demand that 20 percent of the gate receipts be returned to the community. . . ."

The first show, at the Canadian National Exhibition Hall in Toronto, was marred by a violent assault by nearly 2,500 people trying to break into the concert, resulting in numerous injuries and arrests. According to David Dalton and Jonathan Cott's detailed account of the trip in *Rolling Stone*, "Jerry Garcia had helped cool things down by setting up a free festival at nearby Coronation Park, where the Dead, Purple Sage, Ian and Sylvia, James and the Good Brothers, and the People's Revolutionary Concert Band played to 4,000 kids the first day and 500 the second day." The first day's performance at the CNE was also marred by a stream of people climbing onto the stage and trying to make political announcements. At one point, Dalton and Cott wrote, "a kid came onstage and pointed to each member of the Dead and shouted, 'You're all phonies—you and you and you . . .' "

The M4M's campaign against the festival, and the attendant fear of violence, kept the crowds lower than expected in Toronto, and probably affected attendance at the other stops as well. But once the train left Toronto Coach Yard heading west, the party began in earnest. Because the Canadian border customs inspections were so rigorous, the musicians were afraid to bring dope into the country, so this trip was fueled by alcohol, lots of it.

"The train ride across Canada was just like one crazy party," John Dawson said. "I remember the times on the train a lot more than I remember the shows. It was just crazy. I remember that the only time I ever saw Garcia smashed on tequila was on that trip. It was a rare occasion indeed. We all got completely smashed on Cuervo Gold, and then he and Janis Joplin and me and Rick Danko and a couple of other people broke out our guitars and sang 'No More Cane on the Brazos' [a venerable Texas blues/worksong] until three or four in the morning as this train sped across Canada. Danko kept making up verse after verse. He just couldn't be stopped. Garcia and I were falling all over the place laughing."

The music cars were going twenty-four hours a day for nearly the entire trip, with everyone playing with everyone else—dozens of combinations of pickers and singers and tambourine shakers tackling any song that came up. It was musician heaven, with no one to please but themselves.

"The train trip wasn't a dream, it was a stone boss reality," Pigpen said right after the journey. "I'm still on that train. I just turn on the switch, and the fan's on and the train's still moving." A few months after it was over, Garcia was still beaming about the experience, too: "It was great. That was the best time I've had in rock 'n' roll. It was our train—it was the musicians' train. There were no straight people. There wasn't any showbiz bullshit. There weren't any fans. . . . It was like a musicians' convention with no public allowed."

The flood of inspired new tunes coming from Hunter and Garcia continued unabated during the spring and summer of 1970. In May the Dead introduced a beautifully ethereal ballad called "Attics of My Life," featuring heavenly three-part harmonies that were stacked in an almost choral arrangement, soaring over a spare instrumental bed. With its lovely, arching melismatic turns, "Attics of My Life" is perhaps the most successfully realized vocal piece Hunter and Garcia ever wrote together, a love song—to a woman? a man? Hunter's muse?—with deep spiritual overtones. The musical context is almost hymnlike, but the lyrics have the graceful simplicity of a Japanese ink drawing:

> In the attics of my life
> Full of cloudy dreams unreal
> Full of tastes no tongue can know
> And lights no eye can see
>> When there was no ear to hear
>> You sang to me
>
> I have spent my life
> Seeking all that's still unsung
> Bent my ear to hear the tune
> And closed my eyes to see
>> When there were no strings to play
>> You played to me

Many of the songs Hunter and Garcia wrote together during this period are plainspoken but eloquent; economical in construction yet emotionally expansive. Hunter's subject was the interior human landscape, but his imagery was drawn almost entirely from nature—his simple, elegant word paintings are filled with birds, clouds, rivers and trees. There's a quietude to some of these songs, as if they were suspended in a specific time, yet they are also eternal. "Brokedown Palace," which the Dead introduced in mid-August 1970, is so timeless and nonspecific that it could easily be mistaken for a nineteenth-century tune by Stephen Foster or a Hoagy Carmichael song three-quarters of a century later. The pace is languorous, like a muddy stream. The mood is one of weary resignation and sadness, but also, ultimately, acceptance:

> River gonna take me
> Sing me sweet and sleepy
> Sing me sweet and sleepy
> All the way back home
>
> It's a far-gone lullaby
> Sung many years ago
> Mama, mama many worlds I've come
> Since I first left home
>
> Going home, going home
> By the waterside I will rest my bones
> Listen to the river sing sweet songs
> To rock my soul

Not necessarily the sentiments one might expect from a twenty-eight-year-old rock 'n' roller. But as Garcia once noted of Hunter, "You don't have to be old to be wise. I always thought he was pretty wise. That's the reason I got together with him in the first place."

Hunter recalled, "I wrote 'Ripple,' 'Brokedown Palace' and 'To Lay Me Down' all in about a two-hour period the first day I ever went to England [in May 1970, for the Hollywood Festival]. I sat there with a case of retsina and I opened up a bottle of that stuff, and the sun was shining. I was in England, which I'd always wanted to visit, and for some reason this creative energy started racing through me and I could do no wrong—write, write, write, write!"

"To Lay Me Down," which entered the Dead's repertoire during an acoustic set at the Matrix near the end of July, was another haunting country-flavored love ballad tinged with sadness and longing:

> To be with you
> Once more
> To be with you
> With our bodies close together
> Let the world go by
> Like clouds a-streaming
> To lay me down
> One last time
> To lay me down

"Ripple" is easily one of Hunter and Garcia's best-loved works, though they rarely performed it outside of the acoustic sets the group played in 1970 and 1980. "We were on the trans-Canadian train trip," Hunter said. "Jerry woke up one morning, sat out on the railroad tracks somewhere near Saskatoon and put it to music." "It just seemed to happen automatically," Garcia noted modestly. "Ripple" is another timeless song, a series of gentle aphorisms and, in the case of the chorus, a perfect seventeen-syllable haiku. It sounds as if it might have been drawn from Taoist philosophy:

> If my words did glow
> With the gold of sunshine
> And my tunes were played
> On the harp unstrung
> Would you hear my voice
> Come through the music
> Would you hold it near
> As it were your own?

It's a hand-me-down
The thoughts are broken
Perhaps they're better left unsung
I don't know
Don't really care
Let there be songs to fill the air

Ripple in still water
When there is no pebble tossed
Nor wind to blow

In "Ripple," as in "Uncle John's Band," there is a sense of Hunter speaking through Garcia directly to the listeners, confirming that their situation is our own. One of Hunter's greatest strengths was this rare ability to close the gap between the performer and audience by *including* the audience in what was, in the end, a sort of three-way conversation about life, love, sorrow, joy, mortality and transcendence. The songs represented wisdom, experience and dreams freely and lovingly shared—scattered ideas and images lifted into the air through song, like the wind blowing the hand-scrawled invocations off of a Tibetan prayer flag so the spirits can "hear" them.

In mid-August 1970, shortly after Garcia's twenty-eighth birthday, the group went into Wally Heider's to begin work on the follow-up to *Workingman's Dead*. This was slightly unusual for two reasons: first, *Workingman's Dead* was still rising up the charts, which bands usually use as an excuse to put off making a new record; and second, the entire Grateful Dead sound crew, including their co-producer/engineer on *Workingman's Dead*, Bob Matthews, was out on the road with a strange tour called the Medicine Ball Caravan, which traveled the country in buses like a hippie circus but was sponsored by Warner Bros. Records. The Dead were originally supposed to be one of the main attractions but, dissatisfied by the logistical arrangements and fearing another bust, they dropped out a day before the first show. Their sound crew had already been hired to do the tour, however, so they went ahead while the Dead stayed in the Bay Area. The band had so many new songs they wanted to get down on tape that they simply booked time at Heider's and used staff engineer Steve Barncard instead of Bob Matthews—a move that irks Matthews to this day.

"Generally speaking, *American Beauty* was a very, very live record," Barncard says. "Frankly, I had heard bad stories about engineers' interactions with the Dead and about how they always had a thousand people in the control room and hippies camping out in the studio and massive acid parties. But what I found were a bunch of hardworking guys, a great, tight band who had woodshedded everything, who knew exactly what they wanted to lay down and where they wanted to go with it. The vocals were all ready. There was not a whole lot of experimentation. They had sat around in a circle and rehearsed this record with acoustic guitars, and played most of the songs live, too, I believe, so they were ready to go."

The group recorded the basic tracks on a passel of recent Hunter and Garcia songs, including "Friend of the Devil," "Candyman," "Ripple," "Brokedown Palace" and "Till the Morning Comes." Pigpen had a fine new tune that fit in perfectly with the folk-country direction of much of the rest of the album—"Operator." Weir and Hunter co-wrote a bubbling rocker with country overtones called "Sugar Magnolia," which quickly became one of the Dead's best-loved songs and most exciting live numbers. Weir also handled lead vocals on "Truckin'," a catchy shuffle that was a musical collaboration between Garcia, Weir and Lesh, with words by Hunter. The song gave fans a glimpse of life on the road for this singular rock 'n' roll band—and even included a verse that was explicitly about the Dead's New Orleans bust, which still weighed heavily on them in the summer of 1970:

> Sitting and staring out of the hotel window
> Got a tip they're gonna kick the door in again
> I like to get some sleep before I travel
> But if you got a warrant I guess you're gonna come in
>
> Busted—down on Bourbon Street
> Set up—like a bowling pin
> Knocked down—it gets to wearing thin
> They just won't let you be, oh no

"Truckin' " also contained an exhilarating bridge section that instantly made the song the group's anthem in the eyes of many fans, and which remains to this day Hunter's most-quoted lyric:

> Sometimes the light's all shining on me
> Other times I can barely see
> Lately it occurs to me
> What a long, strange trip it's been

The tenth song on the album was the first on any Dead record to feature Phil as lead singer, and it is one of the strongest Hunter ever wrote, "Box of Rain." "Phil Lesh wanted a song to sing to his dying father and had composed a piece complete with every vocal nuance but the words," Hunter said. "If ever a lyric 'wrote itself,' this did—as fast as the pen would pull."

> Look out of any window
> Any morning, any evening, any day
> Maybe the sun is shining
> Birds are winging or
> Rain is falling from a heavy sky—

What do you want me to do,
To do for you to see you through?
For this is all a dream we dreamed
One afternoon long ago

Though written with Phil and his father in mind, "Box of Rain" took on an extra dimension for Garcia during the recording of *American Beauty*. In the early afternoon of September 8, 1970, Garcia's mother, Ruth, was gravely injured in an automobile accident.

Tiff Garcia recalls the tragedy: "She had a house up in Diamond Heights [in San Francisco] and she had this German shepherd puppy that we'd given her from our litter. She worked the evening shift [as a nurse] at San Francisco General and every day before she'd go to work she'd take the dog up to Twin Peaks and let him run around in the hills up there. It was this gangly little thing, about six months old. The details are still a little sketchy—we tried to get the police reports and all—but what ultimately happened is that when she went to stop the car, the dog got all excited, she didn't set the parking brake and the dog got between the gas pedal and the brake pedal. The car went over a cliff and landed on top of a cypress tree. It just mangled my mom. She had broken bones all over her body and internal injuries. She wasn't in a coma but she was in traction and she was in intensive care at San Francisco General for nearly a month. She knew all the nurses and doctors, and here they were showing her her charts, and she knew what was going on. She was nodding her head. She couldn't talk. She had to write things. It was hard for her to breathe, hard for her to talk, plus there was no air-conditioning in the damn hospital. I was really pissed at the whole system. Jerry and I were always talking about, 'How can we get her out of this fucking place?' But it was the best place for her, of course."

Jerry hadn't seen his mother much since leaving home and joining the army at seventeen, but their relationship was always at least cordial. Ruth hadn't met Mountain Girl until Garcia brought her to the hospital, and Ruth never saw baby Annabelle, seven months old at the time of the accident—Jerry brought a photo of his daughter to the hospital one day and taped it to Ruth's bed so she could see it.

By investing her money wisely, Ruth had managed to live quite comfortably through the years, and in the late '60s she bought a spacious house on Miguel Street in San Francisco that offered a spectacular view of the city and the bay. She cut a slightly eccentric figure in her later years, with her pointy, pastel-colored, rhinestone-studded glasses, fox furs in winter and omnipresent ciggy in a black plastic holder dangling from her lips. She tooled around town in a Mustang, a sporty choice for a sixty-year-old. Friends and relatives agreed she was *always* a terrible driver: "She wrecked every car she ever owned," Tiff says, "but this was one of those freak accidents." Though she rarely saw Jerry, she socialized with Tiff and his wife, Gayle, and she also stayed close to her nieces and nephews—the Clifford clan—in the foothills of the Santa Cruz Mountains.

Although Sara Ruppenthal had remarried, she and Jerry's daughter Heather had remained close to Ruth, who was a doting grandmother. Sara dutifully visited Ruth in the hospital every afternoon, and Tiff and Jerry also made a point of going over often, though Jerry was also busy working on *American Beauty* at Heider's, and in mid-September he had to leave town for about a week for a series of concerts at the Fillmore East. Needless to say, it was a very stressful time for everyone in the Garcia and Clifford families.

"I was living at my grandmother's house [on Harrington Street] and Jerry was in Larkspur," Tiff remembers, "and he'd pick me up every day and we'd go over to see her. She was conscious but you could sort of feel her fading away. Imagine seeing your mom in intensive care every day. To see one of your parents in that kind of condition makes you feel so powerless. You have tears in your eyes when you get in the elevator before you get there; then when you leave, shit, you're emotionally broken. I'm surprised Jerry got any recording done at that time. But maybe he needed to keep busy. I know I felt that way. But there was nothing we could do. It was awful. I think I lost about fifteen pounds. Jerry lost a bunch of weight, too."

At 2 P.M. on September 29, Ruth Clifford Garcia Matusiewicz passed away quietly. As Sara remembers, "I would always call in before driving up from East Palo Alto. One day when I called the doctor told me, 'She's dying,' and by the time I got there she had died. They let me sit with her for a while and I kind of intuitively meditated with the energy there, saying, 'It's okay. You're okay. Go and be well.' I felt like what I was doing was helping her through that transition. Then I called Jerry and asked him to come and be with her and he said, 'What's the point?—she's dead.'

"Tiff and his wife and I did the funeral," Sara says. "It was too emotionally powerful for Jerry to deal with it, so we handled all the papers and found a priest and got the burial together. I remember going to the funeral home and picking out the coffin. Jerry and Mountain Girl came to the funeral at the cemetery in Colma. She had refused last rites in the hospital and did not want a Mass said, so we had to have the funeral at the cemetery rather than in church. After we put the coffin in the ground, I put in a photo of Heather and a rose from our garden and then we drove around in somebody's car smoking a joint, driving around the cemetery and sort of processing this event as best we could."

A few years after his mother died, Garcia reflected on his loss: "I was never really very close to my mother so I felt that, well, *there's* something I was never able to complete. I never was able to say to her, 'I think you did okay.' I was never able to finish that idea. But I don't feel as though our relationship is gone forever. . . . She always respected what I did and liked the fact that I was a musician and she never judged me even through things like involvement with drugs and stuff like that; she was always pretty good. So I don't feel too badly about [her death]. But it's a shock, as things like that always are. But on another level, of course, it's interesting how once your parents are gone, they're *gone;* that's it. On some levels it's liberating and on other levels it's very sad."

Mountain Girl says that Jerry was upset about his mother's passing for quite a while afterward, though, typically, he didn't talk about it very much. Instead he threw himself even more deeply into completing *American Beauty*, although he acknowledged later, "It was raining down hard on us while that record was going on." Perhaps he found some measure of solace in a box of rain:

> *It's just a box of rain*
> *I don't know who put it there*
> *Believe it if you need it*
> *Or leave it if you dare*
> *But it's just a box of rain*
> *Or a ribbon for your hair*
> *Such a long, long time to be gone*
> *And a short time to be there.*

CHAPTER 11
The Wheel Is Turning

n the night of October 4, 1970, less than a week after Garcia's mother died, five of the top groups in San Francisco got together at Winterland for a special concert that was broadcast live in quadraphonic sound on two Bay Area FM stations, and was also shown on the local public television station, KQED. It was the most extensive rock 'n' roll simulcast that had ever been aired. The lineup consisted of a set apiece by the Dead, Jefferson Airplane, Quicksilver, the New Riders and Hot Tuna (Jorma Kaukonen and Jack Casady's blues spin-off from the Airplane). Everything was going along swimmingly until some disturbing information began to circulate backstage during the Dead's set: Janis Joplin had died of an accidental heroin overdose in Hollywood. The news strongly affected both Janis's musician peers and her fans—she was truly beloved, as much for her spirit, pluck and raucous good energy as for her formidable talent. And it was the first major death in the San Francisco music scene. The link between the Dead and Janis was particularly close: they'd gotten to know each other during the Palo Alto folk days; the Dead and Big Brother had spent a lot of time together in Lagunitas in the summer of 1966; they were neighbors in the Haight and then in Marin; and in the summer of 1970 they'd spent that glorious week on the train together.

Shortly after Joplin's death, Garcia commented, "It was just an accident, a dumb fucking accident. [Accidents] happen to everybody—driving a car or walking down a flight of stairs. You see, the payoff for life is death. You die at the end of your life, and it's always appropriate in the sense that no matter how you die, that's it, you're dead. So it really doesn't matter how or when; that's not part of the statement. The statement was the life, the death was the close. I'd describe Janis's life as a good one because she went out when she was happy. She was happy with her new band, happy with her material, she was happy with what she was doing. She was singing better than ever."

Though of course Garcia felt personally sad to see his old friend die, he said that "Janis would've preferred for people to be partying rather than for it be a downer. I can dig that."

The Dead put the finishing touches on *American Beauty* in late September and early October 1970. Though the basic tracks were cut live, there were a number of instrumental overdubs by the band—electric and pedal steel guitars, piano parts by Garcia and Lesh—and several guest musicians helped out: Howard Wales played organ on "Truckin' " and "Candyman," and piano on "Brokedown Palace"; a friend of Phil's named Ned Lagin contributed piano to "Candyman"; David Nelson played electric guitar on "Box of Rain," and the bass on that track was by the man who replaced Phil Lesh as bassist in the New Riders at the end of 1970, David Torbert. This record also marked the first real collaboration between Garcia and David Grisman—his mandolin brightened up two songs, "Ripple" and "Friend of the Devil."

"I was in this [East Coast–based] band, Earth Opera, that was just about on its last legs," Grisman said, "and I came to visit a friend in San Francisco, and I just bumped into Jerry at a baseball game in Fairfax, and he said, 'Hey, you wanna play on this record we're doing?' So I did that session, and I just fell in love with California. I'd never really hung out in San Francisco before, and I figured, 'Wow, I've been out here a day and I got hired to be on a record!' This is the land of opportunity!"

"Some records sort of assemble themselves," comments engineer Steve Barncard, who ended up with a co-production credit on the album. "You do a take and everybody says, 'Yeah, that's it. Let's move on,' and everything falls into place. *American Beauty* was that way. It was a lot of fun; it was like no pain. Even on the vocals, which was supposed to be their weak area, they were brilliant. They walked in and just did it. People don't believe me when I say this."

When *American Beauty* was released in November, *Workingman's Dead* had only been out about six months, and progressive FM radio stations were still playing a number of different cuts from it. Then all of a sudden there was a *new* Dead record to play, and "Truckin'," "Sugar Magnolia," "Friend of the Devil" and "Ripple" became instant radio favorites. If you liked rock 'n' roll in 1970, but didn't like the Dead, you were out of luck, because they were inescapable that summer and fall.

The Dead and the New Riders went on an extensive tour of the Midwest and the Northeast through most of October and November, mainly playing theaters and colleges, large and small. The Dead and colleges were a natural fit in this era: the band was popular enough to draw a good-sized crowd, but not so big that they couldn't play a gymnasium or theater on most campuses; student activities groups had decent budgets and a mandate to book the coolest groups they could; and colleges were filled with kids hungry for action and excitement of every variety. Who knows how many thousands of people had their first significant music, drug and sex experiences in college, safely distant from the protective and watchful gaze of Mom and Dad? As Phil Lesh said in 1970, "Colleges are like islands in the midst of occupied territory, although some of them are occupied territory. But some of them are about the only free ground there is."

Certainly the Dead's reputation as rock 'n' roll outlaws from the Wild West preceded them wherever they went, but their ubiquity on the radio lent them credibility outside of counterculture circles, too. Though together just five years, they were already widely known as "the good ol' Grateful Dead," their image that of high-spirited renegades who left parties in their wake wherever they went. It's not surprising that this scared a number of promoters and local law enforcement officials. In some cities and venues, Dead shows were wide-open, anarchic fun where just about anything was allowed inside. In other cities, security forces wouldn't let the crowd stand up and dance and would leave the auditorium lights on for the entire show so they could keep an eye on everyone, much to the Dead's displeasure.

In a way, *Workingman's Dead* and *American Beauty* were stalking horses for a very different-sounding touring band. Yes, the Dead usually played material from those two albums at their shows, but by no means did they suddenly turn into a group that simply regurgitated its hits, such as they were, onstage. There was still jamming galore at Dead shows, and songs like "Dark Star," "Love Light," "Saint Stephen" and "That's It for the Other One" continued to occupy important slots in the repertoire. Actually, in the case of that last tune, Garcia finally dropped his "Cryptical Envelopment" section, and the band would just charge straight into Weir's segment of the song ("Spanish lady comes to me . . ."), which became known as "The Other One."

Some old-time Dead fans didn't care for the band's turn to shorter, more country-oriented material, and stopped coming to hear the group—for them, the Dead remained frozen in time as the unpredictable fire-breathing acid band that had made *Anthem of the Sun* and *Live Dead*. But by and large the psychedelic veterans accepted this "new" Dead as a natural progression, and the more recent acidheads certainly weren't complaining; the band still visited deep spaces, and there was a new layer of meaning with Hunter's intriguing and quotable lyrics spilling out of the songs and jams. Hunter unleashed a flood of characters, images and feelings that added depth and weight to the Grateful Dead experience. With or without the New Riders on the bill, a Dead concert was considered the perfect setting for psychedelic adventures—long enough to contain the peak hours of an LSD, mescaline or mushroom trip; varied and unpredictable enough to be both constantly entertaining and profound; safe enough an environment that trippers could completely let go, knowing that the band was in control and that by night's end everybody in the gym or theater would be dancing deliriously to some good-time rock 'n' roll tunes. But whereas the 1968 Grateful Dead sound had been so dense, twisted and spacey that it didn't attract many fans who weren't into psychedelics or pot, anyone could dig the 1970 band. And that, as it turned out, began to cause problems for the group.

It wasn't just the drunk frat boys at every show who screamed out loud and long for their favorite songs—" 'Caaaasey Joooones'!" "Play 'Truckin' '!"— not understanding that the Dead would play what they felt like playing and never took requests. Crowds became louder and ruder for a while but didn't fundamentally change the experience of the show. The real trouble came from a rowdy and frustrated element that, unable to get tickets for sold-out concerts, crashed the gates and clashed with security guards and police—or tried to figure out ingenious ways to break or sneak into shows through windows, doors and rooftops. Some defended this activity under the old "music should be free and belong to the people, so let us in" theory, but mostly it was just kids trying to get something for nothing, acting like jerks. The Dead's November 1970 tour was plagued by bad incidents outside their shows, and the band was understandably horrified at this turn of events.

Even Garcia, famous for being Mr. Good Vibes in his dealings with the press, could not contain his anger. A Long Island entertainment magazine called *Good Times* interviewed Garcia the day after a show at Queens College where there had been a rush on the doors, and he was *not* in a good mood: "Last night, if that's an example of what it's going to be like, I'd just as soon fuckin' retire, man. I don't want to make any performances when there's that kind of shit going on; I really don't."

But Garcia was also distraught about the way he personally was being treated on the East Coast now that the Dead were suddenly more popular. He had become—gasp!—a celebrity, hounded by fans every time he left his hotel room, outside gigs, backstage, everywhere. "I liked it when you could just be a musician," he told *Good Times*. "It's like being an artist or craftsman. Nobody mobs a cat that makes nice leather clothes or a guy that does woodwork. Why the fuck should they mob musicians? I mean, it's weird.

"I don't really have anything to say, you know? I mean, that's why I play. I like to avoid adding to that celebrity bullshit. I would rather be playing good music and getting off that way than having to go on all the celebrity trips."

Back in the Bay Area, where, as Garcia put it, he was still "just another freak," there were a few changes afoot. "The lady who owned the Larkspur house put it on the market for $45,000, which to us seemed like an astronomical sum," Mountain Girl says, "so we didn't even think about buying it until it was too late. I think it was Hunter who finally suggested we buy it, so I called the landlady and said we'd like to buy it, and she told us she'd just sold it the previous day. That was my first lesson in the 'one that got away.' It would sell for $500,000 easy now.

"So we looked and looked and looked for a new place and there were already hippies in all the houses and people didn't want to rent to us—'Forget it!' Then we finally found this place in Novato that had been trashed by the previous renters, so we promised we'd clean it up. So we did and we moved in there for a few months and it was pretty bad; it had some bad karma."

The upside of this new rental was that it was located right down the hill from David Freiberg's house in a rural part of Novato, so at least they had a neighbor they liked and could trust. Freiberg says that during this period he and Garcia often drove out to Paul Kantner and Grace Slick's house on the beach in Bolinas, in northwestern Marin County, to get high, hang out and play music.

Another change in Garcia's life around this time came when he started jamming regularly with keyboardist Merl Saunders, first at the Matrix, then at a club in San Francisco called the Keystone Korner. Actually, this was an outgrowth of the Monday night jams with Howard Wales—somewhere along the line, Wales dropped out, and his spot was filled by Saunders. Garcia still played gigs with Wales from time to time, and he helped Wales make a record called *Hooteroll?* which came out in late 1971, but once the quartet of Garcia, Saunders, John Kahn and Bill Vitt got together, that group became Garcia's main musical focus outside of the Dead.

Saunders was several years older than the other guys in the quartet and was already a journeyman musician with extensive experience playing R&B, jazz, blues and standards by the time he hooked up with Garcia. "The chemistry between us was instant," Merl says. "I'd hear Jerry playing and the music was going one way and I'd hear him sort of drifting off in this other much cooler direction, so I'd be right there with him, and we'd sort of smile at each other, like, 'Hey, this is *happenin'*.' If there's two people going one way, even if it's not the regular way, then there's no mistake. And John Kahn was following along with us, too."

In Saunders's memory, his first couple of Matrix gigs with Garcia and Vitt were without John Kahn and *very* loose. But once the quartet started playing together regularly at the Keystone Korner and the New Monk in Berkeley (later renamed the Keystone Berkeley), the music began to go in all sorts of interesting directions. Whereas the gig with Howard Wales was almost completely free-form and all instrumental, the quartet with Merl jammed out on some of his own funk-oriented original songs, Motown and R&B tunes (ususally sung by by Garcia) and jazz standards, which were something new for Garcia.

"That required a whole lot of quick education for me, and Merl was responsible for that," Garcia said. "He really helped me improve myself on a level of harmonic understanding. Playing with him required a whole different style from three-chord rock 'n' roll or even ten-chord rock 'n' roll; it was a whole different thing. But what I was able to bring to that situation was the ability to use odd-length runs in conventional formats. I was able to use ideas that were rhythmically uneven because of working in odd time signatures so much with the Dead."

Garcia said that working with Merl also taught him a great deal about musical structure: "He filled me in on all those years of things I didn't do. I'd never played any standards; I'd never played in dance bands. I never had any approach to the world of regular, straight music. He knows all the standards, and he taught me how bebop works. He taught me *music*. Between the combination of Howard and Merl, that's where I really learned music. Before it was sort of, 'Okay, where do I plug in?' I picked up the adult version of a music attitude from those guys."

In December 1970 Garcia also played several Bay Area club shows in another quartet, this one featuring Phil and Mickey from the Dead as well as David Crosby, who was busy in the fall of 1970 and winter of 1971 working on his first solo album at Wally Heider's, with Steve Barncard engineering. Like Paul Kantner's *Blows Against the Empire*, Crosby's album, entitled *If I Could Only Remember My Name*, was a Bay Area all-stars project that featured most of the Dead and the Jefferson Airplane, David Freiberg, Graham Nash and Neil Young, keyboardist Gregg Rolie and drummer Michael Shrieve from Santana, and Crosby's onetime love Joni Mitchell. In the stoned fantasies of Crosby, Kantner and Garcia, some form of this loose "supergroup"—dubbed the Planet Earth Rock 'n' Roll Orchestra in a moment of Kantnerian grandiosity—would continue to make other records and perhaps even tour together. Night after night, different combinations of players would go into Heider's and jam, just to see what might come of it. Sometimes the musicians would work on specific songs of Crosby's, but they also tackled new songs by the others, a Hunter-Garcia tune called "Loser" among them. Crosby and Garcia also spent hours in the studio jamming on acoustic guitars together—Crosby said they developed a game called "bong-hit telepathy," in which they would toke pot from a water pipe and then immediately improvise on their guitars—to sometimes inspired, sometimes fruitless results.

The album that came out of the hundreds of hours of jamming and goofing around is surprisingly cohesive, considering how unwieldy it could have been. There's a pleasing, mellow consistency to much of the record, and a wonderful feeling of spaciousness and sonic depth to the production, with layers of glistening six- and twelve-string acoustic guitars and sumptuous vocal harmonies dominating a series of dreamlike soundscapes. There's a bit of flashy electric interplay on "Cowboy Movie" and "What Are Their Names" (a song credited to Crosby, Garcia, Lesh, Michael Shrieve and Neil Young), and the gorgeous song "Laughing" contains what is perhaps Garcia's most evocative recorded pedal steel guitar performance. Garcia also rips through an intense electric guitar solo on the otherwise placid "Song With No Words (Tree With No Leaves)." Crosby's record, like *Blows Against the Empire* before it, was attacked by some for its loose hippie vibe when it was released in mid-1971, but those critics overlooked the care that went into its construction and the amazing presence of all the instruments and voices. It was beautifully recorded by Barncard, and despite the lengthy roster of players, it never sounded cluttered for a second.

In *Rolling Stone*'s 1970 year-end issue, the editors named the Grateful Dead "Band of the Year" and also, with tongue partly in cheek, called Garcia the year's "Working-Class Hero." They included a picture of him standing in front of an old Bentley he owned, a big smile on his face. Actually, the Dead *were* working-class heroes then—famous for delivering long concerts, playing benefits and free shows (though not many of the latter after Altamont), supporting a large cooperative family scene and keeping ticket prices reasonable. Salaries were still quite low: about $125 a week for band, crew and office staff, but no one seemed to be lacking. There was food on the table, dope in the stash jar, cars to drive, enough money to buy new instruments and equipment, and the promise of selling even more records and playing larger venues.

Nineteen seventy was the year the Dead finally broke through to a wider audience and established themselves as the quintessential American rock 'n' roll band—steeped in traditional Americana while forging their own distinctive, electrically charged and powered amalgam. They were "Dark Star" *and* "Ripple"; Charlie Monroe's "Rosalie McFall" *and* Buddy Holly's "Not Fade Away"; the trippy playfulness of "China Cat Sunflower" and the earthy melancholy of "High Time"; the acid band in cowboy clothing.

But there was trouble bubbling just below the surface. The Lenny Hart affair had been devastating to Mickey. As he wrote in his autobiography, "I didn't want to play, didn't want to go out on the road. Confused, unbalanced, I wanted to flee and hide, bury my head and cry. I stopped touring with the Grateful Dead in 1971 and went to ground in the Barn. . . . The band didn't blame me for Lenny's thievery; they made that clear. They even kept paying me, treating my departure as a leave of absence that would end whenever I managed to pin to the ground the demons I was wrestling. Whenever I was ready, I was welcome back."

The formal departure occurred after a February 1971 concert at the Capitol Theater in Port Chester, New York, where, as was often the case at the Capitol, members of Mickey's mother's family, the Tessels, could be spotted sitting in folding chairs on the side of the stage. When during the Capitol series Bob Weir was asked by a writer from the *Harvard Independent* about Hart's departure midway through the series, he was vague and evasive: "He's in Long Island at his parents' house; he's under the weather or something, I'm not sure what."

And so, for the first time since the fall of 1967, the Dead were a quintet again. Actually, because Pigpen didn't play as much organ in the early '70s as he did in the pre-T.C. era, opting instead to play congas or cowbell or nothing at all for long stretches during a show, the group was sometimes a de facto quartet during the first nine months of 1971, a very different-sounding (but no less interesting) Grateful Dead. Bill Kreutzmann probably had to make the biggest musical adjustment in response to Mickey's bowing out. The two had been a single eight-limbed rhythm monster for more than three years, and together had been responsible for laying down the foundation for countless big jams. But on some of the lighter country-oriented material the band had started playing in the second half of 1969 and in 1970, two drummers occasionally felt like more percussion than was needed. Kreutzmann frankly believed "at the end of that period [Mickey and I] weren't gelling that much. It's hard to explain what was going on. Those were real complicated times for him and real private times." With just one drummer, Kreutzmann said, "I had the sense that the music became a little more clear. The rhythms and the grooves had a clarity you can hear on tapes from that period."

Garcia's guitar sound changed somewhat during this era, too. He switched from Gibson guitars to a Fender Stratocaster, which "was a vote for articulation," David Gans says. "The Fender was good for fingerpicking and it was suited to a lot of the more country-oriented material Jerry was writing and playing at that time."

As they often did, the Dead used the opportunity of their first big tour of the year to introduce a number of new songs, both originals and fresh cover tunes. That week in February at the Capitol Theater, five new Hunter-Garcia numbers were played for the first time—all of them songs that would still be in the band's repertoire when Garcia died nearly twenty-five years later.

"Bertha" was an immediate crowd-pleaser; a brisk, obviously bluegrass-inspired romp that became a frequent show-opener. It was easy to play (and thus a good song to warm up with), and it got everyone in the crowd up and dancing from the get-go.

Two of the new Hunter-Garcia songs were filled with cardplaying imagery. As Hunter noted, "I liked the way Dylan handled a deck of cards, and it struck me that it was a pretty basic metaphor. Maybe I played a few too many hands, someone suggested at one point." In "Deal," which was initially a slow shuffle, but later became a driving country-rocker, the character appears to be brimming with so much confidence after a streak of winning hands that he feels compelled to offer some advice to his vanquished gambling partner:

> *Since you poured the wine for me*
> *And tightened up my shoes*
> *I hate to see you sitting there*
> *Composin' lonesome blues*
> *It goes to show you don't ever know*
> *Watch each card you play*
> *And play it slow*
>
> *Wait until that deal come 'round*
> *Don't you let that deal go down, oh no*

The gambler in "Loser," however, is in more desperate straits:

> *If I had a gun for every ace I've drawn*
> *I could arm a town the size of Abilene*
> *Don't you push me, baby, 'cause I'm moaning low*
> *And you know I'm only in it for the gold*

All that I am asking for is ten gold dollars
I could pay you back with one good hand
You can look around about the wide world over
And you'll never find another honest man

"Sometimes I sing that song and it's a self-congratulatory asshole, sometimes it's an idiot," Garcia said of this brooding Western ballad. "The lyrics have the guy an idiot, but the idiot's version of himself is, 'Hey, I'm great!' I can ride that either way and there's lots of shading in between where it's both those things at the same time. I love it when a song is ambiguous like that.

"Hunter is able to write that into just about everything—he's able to leave just enough *out*, so that you're not really sure whose side you're on, if it's a matter of taking sides. In 'Wharf Rat' you don't know if you're the guy who's hearing the story or the guy who's telling it. It really doesn't matter in the long run."

"Wharf Rat," which debuted in the same set at the Capitol as "Loser," wasn't from a Western bag particularly, though Garcia's lonesome, lamenting vocal style on the song probably had roots in bluegrass/old-timey singing—indeed, that was in nearly everything Garcia sang. But the droning A chord that rang through the song like a nervous, jagged pulse, and Hunter's opening images of an "Old man down / Way down, down / Down by the docks of the city" immediately placed the song in a much different kind of setting from songs like "Loser," "Deal" or "Candyman." August West, the down-and-out wino in "Wharf Rat," was one of Hunter's most vivid creations—a poor lost soul who'd been kicked around by fate and circumstance:

Everyone said
I'd come to no good
I knew I would
Pearly believed them

Half of my life
I spent doing time for
Some other fucker's crime
The other half found me stumbling around
Drunk on burgundy wine

As Garcia indicated, the song has an interesting narrative structure. It switches from the person encountering August West, to West's own tale of woe and hope for redemption, then back to the person hearing the story, who then wanders the streets pondering, as August West does in the song, whether his own lady love has been true to him. It's completely unlike any other world that Hunter and Garcia ever conjured—as gritty and realistic as a Dorothea Lange portrait, but also both sympathetic and empathetic, for any one of us could become that wharf rat. It's also, of course, a very unusual topic for a "pop" song, which is part of what made it so powerful. Coming after rockers like "Truckin' " and "Not Fade Away," or spacey tunes like "Dark Star" and "The Other One," "Wharf Rat" was like a downpour of cold rain soaking your clothes and putting you in August West's tattered shoes. Garcia's long, open-ended solo on the song would drift out and wander along the docks, each rough-hewn, jangly guitar note a little cry of suffering. Through the years, Garcia usually placed "Wharf Rat" deep in the heart of the second set, a little flash of despair before Weir would send everyone home with some cheery, up-tempo rock 'n' roll song.

The fifth new Hunter-Garcia tune was a subtle and exquisite homage to Janis Joplin called "Bird Song":

> *All I know is something like a bird*
> *Within her sang*
> *All I know, she sang a little while*
> *And then flew on*
>
> *Tell me all that you know*
> *I'll show you*
> *Snow and rain*

Stylistically, the song mixed a folk ballad approach with a little Bakersfield country feeling—the way Garcia would bend the notes in the catchy, flitting eleven-note riff that defined the tune's outer edges was reminiscent of Roy Nichols's playing with Merle Haggard, though the *choice* of those eleven gently bebopping notes was pure Garcia. And the way the song opened up and its jam gradually unfolded, with Garcia slowly but surely leading the band away from the safety of the song's structure out to unsettled and unexpected realms, owed much more to modal jazz than honky-tonk country. It's a fascinating fusion of different ingredients.

Garcia's interest in country also showed up in two cover tunes he introduced in the spring of 1971, "Big Railroad Blues" and "Sing Me Back Home." The former was a peppy old Cannon's Jug Stompers number from the late '20s that Garcia learned in 1965 off of a four-song British EP Eric Thompson owned. The latter was one of Merle Haggard's best-known and most poignant songs, a mournful ballad about a condemned man being led to his execution who asks his prison buddy to "Sing me back home / A song I used to hear / Make my old memories come alive / Take me away and turn back the years / Sing me back home before I die."

To a large extent, the characters who populate the Grateful Dead's universe of songs—both covers and original tunes—are a motley, troubled bunch: loners and desperadoes, gamblers and outlaws, drifters and bad guys on the run. Many of them are folks who have made poor choices in life—usually because of greed or lust or both—and now have to face the legal and/or karmic consequences of their actions. No one gets away with *anything* in this song-world; ironic, since on the surface the Grateful Dead seemed to be getting away with *everything* in the early '70s. They were renegades who were making it, pulling a fast one on straight society. But they were also always on the move, and just a step or two ahead of the sheriff's baying hounds, figuratively speaking. The punishment for living outside of traditional society was some attendant guilt and moral confusion—reflected over and over in the songs—and an almost wistful yearning for the simpler life of a child still under a mother's wing: In "Big Railroad Blues," Garcia sang, "Wish I had a-listened whoa what Mama said / Well, I wouldn't be here tryin' to sleep in this cold iron bed." In "Mama Tried," Weir sang, "Mama tried to raise me better but her pleadings I denied / That leaves no one for me to blame 'cause Mama tried." And in "Brokedown Palace," Garcia, Weir and Lesh wearily sang, "Mama, Mama, many worlds I've come since I first left home."

But Mama isn't around to turn these people in the right direction, so the only other choice is to keep on moving down the road in search of greener pastures, a bigger payday, a longer-lasting love—and indeed, that kind of optimism also runs through the Dead's music: "I'm goin' where the chilly winds don't blow" ("Cold Rain and Snow"); "The sun's gonna shine in my back door someday" ("I Know You Rider"); "I'm goin' where the water tastes like wine" ("Goin' Down the Road Feeling Bad")—every one of these lines borrowed from well-known North American folk songs.

In the spring of 1971 Joe Smith of Warner Bros. Records offered Garcia a $20,000 advance to make a solo album. Smith was genuinely interested in having Garcia make a solo record—after all, the Dead were all of a sudden a money band with a bright future, and Garcia was the most famous member of the group. But the offer was also an attempt to keep Garcia and the Dead happy as members of the Warner Bros. family. Three thousand miles away, Columbia Records president Clive Davis was making no secret of his desire to sign the Grateful Dead; he'd had his eye on the band, and Garcia in particular, for several years. But the Dead were locked up contractually with Warner Bros. As early as 1970 there had been rumblings in the Dead camp that when their contract with Warners was up they might explore starting their own record company. In the meantime, Davis did manage to get a little piece of Garcia onto Columbia: he signed the New Riders of the Purple Sage.

"We got the deal with Columbia because Clive wanted Jerry," John Dawson says. "It's that simple. He wanted Jerry any way he could get him. But that was cool with me. It was a pretty good deal."

Davis was signing a known quantity. The New Riders had cut their debut album at Wally Heider's in December 1970 and January 1971, so Davis essentially bought a finished record that he knew had commercial potential. And in the back of his mind he probably also believed that establishing a relationship with Garcia through the New Riders might pay dividends for him up the line with the Grateful Dead, should they ever be free from their contractual obligations.

As for Garcia's solo album deal, "Twenty thousand dollars seemed like *a lot* of money back then," Mountain Girl says. "It was really the first time we had any money. So I went looking for a place to buy for us, and I looked and looked and looked all over and I finally found this house out in Stinson Beach, which seemed like the end of the earth, but it was this fabulous house—oh God, it was nice!—on the Avenitas Des Farallones. It was an incredible find. It was perfect and it cost $60,000. After what had happened to us with the Larkspur house, we weren't going to pass it up." At the time, M.G. says, Garcia was earning about $2,000 a month—about a teacher's salary—"which was a king's ransom to us—$500 a week; whoa, serious spending power!"

Stinson Beach is a beautiful little village on scenic coastal Highway 1 just a few miles north of where Mount Tamalpais drops precipitously into the Pacific; about forty twisting-and-turning minutes from downtown San Francisco, thirty minutes from the Dead's San Rafael office if the weather was good and the traffic gods were smiling on you. The beach itself is a great white crescent, and the surrounding hills—green in winter, gold in summer—are dotted with a combination of small clapboard beach bungalows and more elegant modern redwood houses, their expansive glass windows taking in the spectacular view of the ocean.

The house that Jerry, Mountain Girl, five-year-old Sunshine and eighteen-month-old Annabelle moved into was high on a hill above the town—not quite as tony as the weekend getaway homes that San Francisco professionals with *real* money owned, but still a beautiful pad with a fantastic panoramic view. "It had eucalyptus trees and cypresses," M.G. says, "and a chicken house that had been converted to a little guest lodge, and then we converted that into a recording studio; George Hunter of the Charlatans, who was an architect, designed it, and Laird Grant built it. Somehow, though, it never felt right to use as a studio—the sea air was kind of thick and there was a lot of fog."

Though Stinson Beach is fairly isolated from the more populated sections of Marin County where most of Jerry and Mountain Girl's cronies lived, they still had plenty of friends to socialize with. Ron Rakow lived in Stinson, Paul Kantner and Grace Slick were just a few minutes up Highway 1 in Bolinas, and of course once Garcia landed on the coast his house became a destination and hangout for people in the Dead scene.

Garcia also spent a lot of time in Stinson with some newfound friends. Mandolinist David Grisman had moved from the East Coast to California in

September 1970, along with Richard Loren, who'd worked on the East Coast as a booking agent and tour manager, and a couple of fresh-faced young singer-songwriters whom Loren was managing, Chris and Loren Rowan, known as the Rowan Brothers. Loren had met Garcia at a September 1970 Fillmore East concert at which Grisman had played mandolin with the Dead during the group's acoustic set. Garcia would often come down to the beach to visit and jam with the Rowans, and vice versa.

Eventually Garcia hired Loren to work as his personal agent to help book gigs for Garcia and Saunders and handle his non–Grateful Dead business affairs, "anything that didn't have to do with the Grateful Dead, that wasn't being taken care of by Sam Cutler or Jon McIntire or those guys," Loren says. Loren rented a series of offices in Mill Valley to accommodate his different businesses—the Rowans' booking and management; his work with Garcia—including one in a house where "Jerry had a room, and I had an offfice," Loren says. "Jerry always had a mattress there. He had a key, I had a key. We used it as an office and kind of like a club. John Kahn would come by, and all of Jerry's friends, most of them apart from the Dead scene, would come by. It was a broad range of people, from Sufis to Hell's Angels.

"I think the Dead viewed all of Jerry's outside bands as a big threat, and it's really a shame because I don't think they were a threat," Loren says. "The Grateful Dead always came first. I used to have a calendar and I'd call in to Cutler's office and say, 'Give me all the dates you're booking for the Grateful Dead. I want to put them in my calendar.' Then we'd work around that. Jerry always insisted, and I completely agreed, that the outside stuff had to be fit around the Grateful Dead, and not vice versa. We would never ask the Grateful Dead to change a date. Unfortunately, the band didn't have the wealth it has today and everybody was making not quite enough to be really comfortable, so I think there were some people who felt that the Dead should play more and that Jerry's solo stuff was getting in the way of them making more; but I didn't see it that way at all. And I think that what Jerry did on the side helped him be a better member of the Grateful Dead, because it stretched him in interesting ways and, above all, it made him happy. But because I worked in an office away from the Dead scene, I think I was viewed by some as 'the guy who's keeping Jerry away from us.' "

That opinion was more common in 1972–73 than in 1971, but the fact is Garcia was doing a lot apart from the Grateful Dead in that year. In addition to the band with Saunders, Kahn and Vitt, which started to play around a lot that year, Garcia was still the pedal steel player for the New Riders, and he continued to do work on other people's records, the best of which was probably Paul Kantner and Grace Slick's *Sunfighter*, which featured several distinctive Garcia leads.

Garcia began his own solo album sometime in July 1971. Unlike the approach taken by Paul Kantner and David Crosby for their albums, Garcia decided early on that he would really make a *solo* album, and play all of the instruments himself, except for drums, for which he brought in Billy Kreutzmann. "Jerry wanted to be very low-key about it," says Bob Matthews, who co-engineered the project with Betty Cantor. "It was Jerry on his own with a couple of people he liked to be creative with—Billy and Hunter and Betty and me. I felt blessed to be one of those people, and it was a real special record for all of us."

The album was recorded over a period of about three weeks in the late summer and early fall of 1971 in Wally Heider's little Studio D, where Matthews posted a sign on the door that read CLOSED SESSION—ANITA BRYANT to keep away curious onlookers. "It worked for the most part," Matthews says, "but there were a few people who just couldn't believe that Anita Bryant [a conservative Republican famous for her anti-gay stance] would be in the middle of the San Francisco rock 'n' roll scene, so they came in anyway. Still, people pretty much left us alone, which is what we wanted."

The way most of the songs on the album were constructed was that Garcia and Kreutzmann initially would lay down acoustic guitar and drum tracks as a guide, and then Garcia would overdub other instruments to his heart's content—bass, of which he had a rudimentary knowledge, pedal steel on a couple of tracks, electric guitars, piano and Hammond B-3.

"I don't want anyone to think it's me being serious or anything like that," Garcia said around the time he began working on the record. "It's really me goofing around. I'm not trying to have my own career or anything like that. . . . In the world that I live in there's the Grateful Dead, which is one unit I'm a part of, and then there's just me. And the me that's just me—I have to keep my end up in order to be able to take care of my part of the Grateful Dead. So rather than sit home and practice—scales and stuff—which I do when I'm together enough to do it, I go out and play because playing music is more enjoyable to me than sitting home and playing scales."

Five of the six conventional songs were previously unrecorded Hunter-Garcia gems from the Dead's live repertoire: "Deal," "Loser," "Bird Song," "To Lay Me Down" and a loping number called "Sugaree" that was first played by the Grateful Dead at the end of July 1971. "Sugaree" was one of the first tunes written by Garcia that was specifically designed to open up to jamming within its fixed rhythmic structure between each verse. Its easy pace let Garcia explore different approaches to structuring his melodic solos—sometimes he'd etch a line with searing, evenly spaced notes; other times he'd break into a double-time attack that worked nicely against the slower time the rest of the band played. Garcia seemed to delight in the predicament presented in the story—his character is trying hard to disassociate himself from Sugaree, who is obviously in a heap o' trouble:

When they come to take you down
When they bring that wagon 'round
When they come to call on you
And drag your poor body down
Just one thing I ask of you
Just one thing for me
Please forget you knew my name
My darling Sugaree

Shake it, shake it, Sugaree
Just don't tell them that you know me

The sixth new Hunter-Garcia song on the album, "The Wheel," spontaneously appeared in the studio one day: "Actually, it was one time through on the piano," Garcia said. "I was playing the piano and I didn't even know what I was doing. Now, the way I approached that side of the album [side two] is that I sat down at the piano—which I *don't* play—and Billy sat down at the drums, which he *does* play. So at least one of us knew what he was doing! And I just played. When I'd get an idea, I'd elaborate on it and then go back and overdub stuff on it. But that side was really almost all one continuous performance, pretty much. When a song would come up in there, or just a progression, we'd play with it and I'd work it through a few more times. And 'The Wheel' came out of that. It wasn't written, I didn't have anything in mind, I hadn't sketched it out."

"The way 'The Wheel' happened was he and Kreutzmann were just jamming," Bob Matthews remembers. "They were out screwing around and I said, 'Hit the machine' [i.e., turn on the recorder] and they were just getting into this groove. 'Hey Bob, you didn't record that, did you?' 'Yes, I did.' They came into the control room and listened to it and we all said, 'Hey, there's a good groove there.' And as we were playing it back and doing some of the overdubs, Hunter was there and he had a big piece of paper and he was writing on it up on the wall. He was writing words while we were listening to one of the playbacks and it turned out to be perfect. It was 'The Wheel.' That song really came from nowhere and just happened like that."

Garcia's music for "The Wheel" almost sounded as if it could have been a country reel, complete with fiddlers sawing away and some old farmer blowing into a moonshine jug. But his approach was much more languorous, with pedal steel crying in the background beneath a steady acoustic guitar rhythm track. Still, the tune had an interesting natural momentum that swung one verse into the next and kept things rolling. The wheel as a metaphor turns up in many different religious traditions: Buddhist, Hindu, Jewish, Christian; a nice ecumenical image that is actually one of Hunter's more easily grasped notions:

The wheel is turning
And you can't slow down
You can't let go
And you can't hold on
You can't go back
And you can't stand still
If the thunder don't get you
Then the lightning will

Won't you try just a litle bit harder?
Couldn't you try just a little bit more?

The remaining compositions on Garcia's solo album were instrumental interludes of varying degrees of weirdness. "Late for Supper" and "Spider-gawd" were both ambitious, dissonant collages that mixed natural instruments with electronically treated sounds and, in the case of the latter tune, a confusing swirl of taped voices from radio and/or TV broadcasts. "An Odd Little Place" was an odd little minute-and-a-half piano and drums duet that served as a transitional segment between "To Lay Me Down" and "The Wheel." "Eep Hour" was the most fully developed instrumental, with its mesmerizing series of chord progressions that Garcia rolled through repeatedly on a series of instruments he stacked to masterful effect: acoustic guitars, piano, organ, fuzzed electric guitar and pedal steel guitar, in addition to bass and drums.

All in all the record was a fine showcase for Garcia's diverse talents. He never sang better than he did on that album; it gave his fans a chance to hear the kinds of bass and rhythm guitar ideas he had away from the influence of Lesh and Weir (Garcia was *much* more conservative than either of his bandmates); and side two of the album served up some of his prettiest and most innovative steel playing.

One reason Garcia had the time to work on so many projects outside the Grateful Dead in 1971 was that the band played only half as many shows that year as they had in 1969 and 1970. "We don't work all that much," Garcia said in late 1970, "because mainly we're into staying high and digging it—enjoying what we're doing. And to work all the time is to make yourself hate it. So we try to balance out the schedule."

What allowed the Dead to play fewer shows was their increased popularity, which led to bigger paydays in larger venues. During 1971 two of the band's most reliable small concert halls, the Fillmore East and Fillmore West, were closed by Bill Graham, who complained that top bands had priced themselves out of venues that size and could only make the money they demanded in larger places. And though the Dead still didn't charge Graham and other promoters as much as most comparable acts—mainly because they wanted to keep ticket prices low for their fans—they did start to play more shows in bigger facilities. In San Francisco the 5,000-seat Winterland became their new home, and on the East Coast, where demand far exceeded the number of tickets available for Dead shows in theaters, they began to experiment with big outdoor shows in places like Gaelic Park in the Bronx and the Yale Bowl in New Haven, Connecticut, where the Dead played a concert to 10,000 fans packed into one end of the giant football stadium.

After having put out two studio albums in quick succession, the band next released a live double album (just two years after *Live Dead*) featuring the post–Mickey Hart quintet recorded on the East Coast and at Winterland in the spring of 1971. Three of the group's new originals appeared on the record— "Bertha," "Wharf Rat" and a promising Hunter-Weir-Hart tune in 10/4 time called "Playing in the Band." The rest of the album consisted of a spacey and varied side-long version of "The Other One" and a slew of covers that showed the breadth of the band's interests and influences: "Big Railroad Blues"; John Phillips's zippy tale of gambling treachery, "Me and My Uncle," sung by Weir; Pigpen's steady version of Jimmy Reed's "Big Boss Man"; "Me and Bobby McGee," which, as sung by Weir and the band, served as a nice tribute to Janis Joplin (who had a posthumous number 1 hit with the song in 1971); Chuck Berry's classic rocker "Johnny B. Goode," also sung by Weir; and the group's big, exhilarating showstopper that year—the combination of "Not Fade Away" and "Goin' Down the Road Feeling Bad," both transformed by the Dead into sing-along anthems.

Warner Bros. executives were thrilled when the Dead informed them that the band would be delivering masters for a live album. *American Beauty* and *Workingman's Dead* were still selling briskly, and quite a few of the Dead's newer fans had dipped back into the band's catalog and bought copies of the first four pre–*Workingman's Dead* albums. There was only one problem for Joe Smith and the high muckety-mucks in Burbank—the album title.

"I was the one who called Joe Smith and said, 'Joe, are you sitting down? The band has told me the next album is going to be called *Skullfuck*," Jon McIntire remembered. "You see, in our contract we had total artistic control, so we actually had the right to do it. Well, Joe came unglued. He just came apart! 'You can't do this to me!' 'It's not me, Joe, it's *all* of us. We're *all* doing it to you!' "

"They were horrified! They were shocked!" Garcia said years later. "They fully believed we were going to do something *awful* if they didn't [let us call it *Skullfuck*], so we finally backed down, but it was more a joke on our part. Aesthetically, it would have been so perfect. It was really a *perfect* name for that record."

In the end, the album was simply titled *Grateful Dead*, and the gatefold cover was adorned with a slick, colorful version of the old skeleton-and-roses design from the classic 1966 Avalon Ballroom poster, updated by artist Alton

Kelley. Through the years, Deadheads have invariably referred to the album as either "Skull and Roses" (after Kelley's round logo for the band, adapted from the larger piece around the same time) or *Skullfuck*, so in popular terms the Dead almost got their way.

Garcia, for one, was very happy with the record. "It's us, man," he said right after the record was released. "It's the prototype Grateful Dead; basic unit. Each one of those tracks is the total picture, a good example of what the Grateful Dead really is, *musically*. Rather than, 'This record has sort of a country, light acoustic sound,' and so on. For a year we were a light acoustic band, in somebody's head. The new album is enough of an overview so people can see we're like a regular shoot-'em-up saloon band. That's more what we are like. The tracks all illustrate that nicely. They're hot."

The band's ever-expanding fan base evidently agreed: *Grateful Dead* became the first Dead album to be awarded a gold record (normally representing 500,000 units sold, but only requiring 250,000 copies for a double LP like this one). It was on the inside gatefold of that album that the Dead blared a clarion call to their fans. DEAD FREAKS UNITE, it said in big, bold letters right next to Bob Seideman's serious photo-portrait of the quintet. "Who are you? Where are you? Send us your name and address and we'll keep you informed."

Within weeks of the album's coming out, the Dead's office—an old wood shingle house in downtown San Rafael—was flooded with hundreds, then thousands of letters from their fans, who were just beginning to be known by the appellation that stuck with them for the rest of the group's history: Deadheads. Initially, Mary Ann Mayer, a woman in the Dead office, was in charge of getting the band's mailing list together, but by early 1972 the volume of mail pouring in was so large that a second person was hired to help—Eileen Law, who had been on the fringes of the scene since the Haight-Ashbury days. Eileen eventually took over the operation and still maintains it today.

By the time the band's loose fan club, called "Dead Heads," began, the Dead already knew that their following was unique in the rock world. "At home, there's always been a certain group of people that don't ever miss a show anyplace we go on the West Coast," Garcia said in 1970. "You know—*every* show. That's the kind of fans we have. It's kind of like symphony fans: they go to see whether or not we get it on, and shit like that. I mean, they know all our trips. And with us it's sort of a thing where we have all the elements, but it's only in special situations where it all works and everything is right. And that doesn't happen all that often."

Garcia often talked about the extreme variability of the Grateful Dead concert experience, and he was a harsher critic of the group than most fans were. Certainly there were some shows when the Dead "got it on" more than others, but if it had been as hit-or-miss as Garcia believed, they wouldn't have developed the sort of fanatical following they did in nearly every city they played repeatedly. The fact that shows were so different from one another was part of the group's appeal. Most rock bands developed *a* show with a fairly fixed song list that they would play basically the same way each night for an entire tour, and then over the years they would make small variations in that show. But Grateful Dead shows could be radically different from night to night because the band's governing aesthetic was to *not* repeat themselves, and to always be on the lookout for new ways to play their songs.

They also constantly introduced new material into their repertoire and made a point of playing it with the same conviction as their well-known songs. Typically in rock 'n' roll a band might highlight a few songs from their new album on a tour designed to support that record, but by the next tour they'd drop all the new songs except for the ones that were considered hits. Not so with the Dead. They usually introduced new songs *months* before they recorded them, and they kept playing them based on their own whims— whether the songs were working for them as a group or not. They rarely made concessions to a song's popularity—there was never a guarantee they'd play their radio hits at a given show—and by the early '70s they had so many different songs to choose from that it usually took going to a couple of shows in a row to see the full range of the Dead's material. (It wasn't until quite a bit later that the Dead consciously tried to avoid repeating any songs for three or four nights.)

By the Dead's second trip to New York in 1967, they discovered that they had supporters there who were coming to see them several nights in a row, and even a hearty few who followed them to other East Coast cities. Once they started playing the Fillmore East regularly, that venue became a mecca for Deadheads. It was one place the Dead always played well, so fans would go on multiple nights. And then, from 1969 to 1971, the band played so many colleges in the Northeast that were close to each other that people began traveling along with the tour. It was no big deal for students to cut a few days of classes and go from Bucknell University in Lewisburg, Pennsylvania, one night, to Allegheny College in Meadsville the next night; Princeton, New Jersey, two nights later and the State University of New York at Cortland the night after that. For many people, seeing the band in new places became part of the adventure of being a Deadhead. If the shows were the sacrament for Deadheads—rich and full of blissful, transcendent musical moments that moved the body and enriched the soul—then getting to the shows, buying tickets, finding a place to crash and people to hang out with was part of the pilgrimage.

When the Dead started Dead Heads (the fan club) they were inundated by long, thoughtful letters from people articulating what the Dead experience meant to them, as well as poetry and artwork inspired by the Dead. The band responded by creating a fanciful (nameless) newsletter that they sent out to their ever-growing mailing list every few months (irregularly, of course). Hunter and Garcia were the guiding lights of the newsletter, which in addition to providing information about upcoming projects and tours also contained bits of Hunter's poetry (usually commenting obliquely on the state of things in the Dead's world) and surreal doodles by the two of them. The Dead Heads newsletter even had its own resident Zen-clown character, St. Dilbert the Arch, a Hunter creation who was the subject of a series of barely fathomable parables allegedly designed to elucidate an anarchic pseudophilosophy called Hypnocracy:

> When asked the meaning of life, St. Dilbert is said to have replied, "Ask rather the meaning of hypnocracy." When asked the meaning of hypnocracy, St. Dilbert replied, "Is not hypnocracy no other than the quest to discover the meaning of hypnocracy? Say, have you heard the one about the yellow dog yet?"

And if that wasn't clear enough, there was always the explanation from another one of the newsletters:

> *Hypnocracy for the Dozens*
>
> watch for it
> don't miss it
> it's comintagetcha
> it's gone
> What was it?
> Was what?
> Hm?
> Ah!
> Oh—mmhmm.

But mostly the Dead Heads newsletter was a communiqué between the Dead and their fans that spoke honestly about the big issues the band faced in the early '70s—the growth of their fan base, the move into larger venues, the group's increasing overhead. The newsletters talked to the Deadheads as if they were family—even detailing how the organization's income was spent, for example—and this made the bond between band and fans even stronger and more intimate.

"We hope you will continue to turn us on to what's happening where you are and where you're at," an early 1972 newsletter concluded. "Thank you all for all the far-out letters and drawings you've sent us; we've all really enjoyed them, and we hope to hear from you again. Don't give up on us; we will be in touch with you again, but we can't promise when. Take care, have fun, stay high—The Grateful Dead."

Twenty-seven years later, the letters and drawings still flow into the Dead's San Rafael post office box. And the occasional newsletter, now called *The Grateful Dead Almanac*, is still published and mailed to every Deadhead on the mailing list.

CHAPTER 12
Wait
Until That Deal
Come 'Round

igpen's role in the Grateful Dead had been gradually diminishing through the years, to the point where he usually sang only two or three songs each show, and maybe added a little organ and percussion when he felt like it. Still, Pig-sung tunes like "Love Light," "Good Lovin' " and Otis Redding's "Hard to Handle" were always popular with the crowd, and the jams in those songs gave the band a chance to thoroughly explore their R&B side—an important part of their roots but somewhat subsumed by the country influences in the early '70s. During parts of 1970 Pigpen's health had been shaky, but in the middle of 1971 he actually became desperately ill with what doctors diagnosed as advanced liver disease. His years of drinking cheap sweet wines had finally caught up with him, and at twenty-five he was in perilously poor shape.

"He's pretty sick," Garcia said around this time. "But he's living. He was really, really *extremely* sick. I don't really know *how* sick, because I never hung out at the hospital that much, although I did give him a pint of blood. We all did. He was really fucked up and his liver was full of holes, and then he had some kind of perforated ulcer—just all kinds of bum trips from juicing all those years. And he's a young dude, man. He's only twenty-six.

"From juicing! He survived it and now he's got the option of being a juicer or not being a juicer. To be a juicer means to die, so now he's being able to choose whether to live or die. And if I know Pigpen, he'll choose to live. That's pretty much where he's at. For the time being he's too sick to go out on the road, and I wouldn't want to expose him to that world. It would be groovy if he could take as long as it takes to get him to feelin' right."

Pigpen stopped touring with the Dead at the end of August 1971 and stayed in California to recuperate until the group's December '71 tour. He did, in fact, stop drinking completely and developed healthier eating habits. In the meantime, the band hired a new piano player, a taciturn, somewhat withdrawn fellow named Keith Godchaux. Keith's background was mostly in jazz, but he and his wife, Donna—a former backup singer from Muscle Shoals, Alabama—were Deadheads, and Donna managed to talk Garcia into letting her shy husband audition for the keyboard slot.

"The Dead were having a rehearsal and Jerry had told us to come on down, so we did," Donna recalled. "But the band had forgotten to tell Jerry that the rehearsal had been called off, so Jerry went down there by himself. So Keith and Jerry played, and we played him some tapes of songs that I had written and was singing on. Then Jerry called Kreutzmann and got him to come down, and the three of them played some. Then the next day the Dead practiced, and by the end of that day Keith was on the payroll."

After a few rehearsals, Keith's first tour with the Dead began with a gig at the University of Minnesota in Minneapolis on October 19, 1971. From the first moments of the opener that night, "Bertha," it was obvious that Keith was a good choice for the band. For a guy who had limited rock 'n' roll experience, and even less playing country, he eased into his role with fluid grace. On the uptempo rockers he could pound away like Johnny Johnson or Jerry Lee Lewis. On country songs he had just enough Floyd Cramer and Glenn D. Hardin in him to be convincing. And when the music went outside, as it did during "Dark Star" at the Auditorium Theater in Chicago two nights after his debut, some of Keith's jazz chops came to the fore. His presence in the band freed the other players in ways that no one could have expected: Billy Kreutzmann now had a solid rhythmic partner to help him anchor the music, leaving Billy more room for ornamental accents. With Keith's piano now occupying so much of the harmonic midrange, Weir was able to move his guitar comfortably into higher and lower registers and even further away from strictly chordal lines. And Garcia and Lesh could go farther afield in their intricate melodic and tonal pas de deux, knowing that a firm center would usually be as close as the new guy at the grand piano. Though there were a number of fine shows throughout the first three-quarters of 1971, there was a certain tentativeness to some of the playing as the band adjusted to Mickey Hart's absence and struggled a bit to reinvent itself. With Keith Godchaux's arrival, whatever might have been missing was suddenly there, and the fall tour found the band playing both more confidently and more adventurously.

Once again there was a healthy infusion of new songs into the repertoire for the tour. Six new tunes were introduced that first night in Minnesota, three by Hunter-Garcia and three by Weir—one written with Hunter, one with Bob's old friend from prep school, John Barlow, and one by himself.

Two of the three Hunter-Garcia songs were among the most whimsical tunes the pair ever wrote. "Tennessee Jed" and "Ramble On Rose" don't actually sound that much alike, but they are cousins musically. Both are based around rhythmically irregular, herky-jerky guitar lines that give the songs an old-time quality. Like so many of Hunter and Garcia's songs from this period, they sound like they could belong to any time in the past hundred and fifty years. Certainly the 1890s didn't produce anything quite like them—weird, stumbling tunes that lurch forward like happy drunks. But "Tennessee Jed" sounds as if it evolved from some fine old mountain tune, and "Ramble On Rose" sounds as if it were recovered from a player piano roll in a turn-of-the-century Storyville whorehouse.

As far as the musical antecedents for songs like "Tennessee Jed" and "Ramble On Rose" are concerned, Garcia once noted that "I haven't the slightest idea. They just come out of my mind. Sometimes I think, 'Yeah, this is kind of like a record I once heard somewhere,' but I never find 'em! The rhythms come from my background in rhythm and blues more than anything else. But they also come from a kind of rhythmically hip country and western style—like Jerry Reed and people like that. Memphis more than Nashville. Some of the old California country and western stuff—old Buck Owens—had some nifty rhythmic ideas in it, as opposed to the old 4/4 stuff, just plunking away. 'Tennessee Jed' is a cop from that world, although not consciously and it's not from any specific tune. Just the feel."

Both tunes were crowd-pleasers from the start—great to dance to and fun to sing along with on the choruses, which *begged* for audience participation. These songs also served as light stepping-stones in sets that were already crowded with heavy songs.

And speaking of heavy songs, the third new Hunter-Garcia composition was an achingly slow, country-tinged ballad called "Comes a Time," in which a character who has become desensitized to life's emotional nuances is offered a glimmer of hope:

> *Been walking all morning*
> *Went walking all night*
> *I can't see much difference*
> *Between the dark and light*
> *And I feel the wind*
> *And I taste the rain*
> *Never in my mind*
> *To cause so much pain*
>
> *Comes a time*
> *When the blind man takes your hand*
> *Says, "Don't you see?"*
> *Got to make it somehow*
> *On the dreams you still believe*
> *Don't give it up*
> *You've got an empty cup*
> *Only love can fill*

Garcia didn't play "Comes a Time" a lot in the early '70s—only about a dozen times each in 1971 and 1972—but when he did, it was always an emotional event, for both the crowd and Garcia, who sang the song passionately, as if it described a moment he knew all too well.

The fact that Weir introduced three new songs at once reflected his emergence as an important songwriter and frontman for the band, just as Pigpen was receding into the background and Garcia was looking to have some of the weight of the band lifted off him. Garcia's songs dominated the Dead's repertoire in the late '60s simply because he was so prolific during that period. But in the early '70s the Dead began consciously to alternate between Garcia-sung tunes and numbers sung by Weir and Pigpen. At first, most of Weir's songs were country cover tunes, such as "Me and My Uncle," "Mama Tried," "Me and Bobby McGee" and Marty Robbins's "El Paso," or Chuck Berry songs like "Johnny B. Goode" and "The Promised Land." But by the end of 1971 he also had an impressive collection of songs he'd written: "Sugar Magnolia," "The Other One," "Truckin'," "Playing in the Band" and the three unveiled in Minneapolis—a gunfighter polka (!) called "Mexicali Blues," written with John Barlow; a supercharged Chuck Berry–style rocker, "One More Saturday Night," which was every bit as good as the songs it imitated; and, best of all, the dynamic Western tune "Jack Straw," Robert Hunter's sprawling, cinematic tale of treachery, deceit and doomed outlaws on the run.

No longer "the kid," Weir grew comfortably into his expanded role, with Garcia encouraging him every step of the way: "He's like the devil's pitchfork—'You go out there and tell them a story,' " Weir said, mimicking Garcia. And while the audience's interest in and affection for Garcia did not diminish with Weir's ascension, a whole new level of Dead fan was attracted to the scene—Weir followers and groupies, who ranged from hippie girls (and a few boys) smitten by his good looks and appealing space cowboy persona to people who dug his songs, his singing and his confident command of his instrument and the stage in general. And by and large, the folks who initially came to the Dead through Weir all became ardent fans of Garcia and the other bandmembers, too.

The fall 1971 tour also marked the end of Garcia's membership in the New Riders of the Purple Sage. He was aware that it would be impossible for him keep playing with the Riders and the Dead without eventually burning out and shortchanging both groups. And, as he noted in mid-1971, "The New Riders are actually too good for me to be playing steel with. What they need is a regular, good guy who's been playing since he was three."

David Nelson recalls: "Finally we said, 'Look, Jerry, we want to be a band. We know you're not going to leave the Dead.' My feeling was that I was so thankful that he was so graceful about it. He was ready to go on if we needed him to go on, or stop now if we needed him to stop now. It was all in deference to us. So I said, 'Let's wait until we find the killer guy, the guy who really fits in with us.' Then, on the Festival Express, [Sam] Cutler was taking me through this stadium in Toronto and I couldn't even see who was onstage but I heard this steel player who was jamming, just *kickin'* it, playing some shit. I wondered, 'Wow, who's *that?*' It was Buddy Cage of Ian and Sylvia's band.

So later when it came down to it, I said, 'Can we try to get him?' " By that time Cage was working with pop singer Anne Murray and was happy to hitch his wagon to the Riders.

There was no drop-off of interest in the New Riders when Garcia split from the group, and now they were free to go on tours of their own and not be beholden to Garcia's schedule. Cage *was* the perfect replacement, and his presence tremendously energized the group at that critical juncture. It helped, too, that the New Riders' excellent debut album (featuring Garcia, Lesh and, on two tracks, Hart) had just been released and was an enormous success, selling 70,000 copies in the first week alone. The Dead and the New Riders remained close, however, and still toured together periodically. And Garcia played some banjo and piano on the New Riders' strong second album, *Powerglide*, and later produced their first live album, *Home, Home on the Road*.

Though later in life Dawson and Garcia rarely saw each other, they were quite chummy during this period, and Dawson has some interesting observations about watching Garcia with the Dead night after night in the early '70s:

"Garcia led people by the mind, by the ears. When he was playing great—and he almost always did in those days—he would play with your brain, in that he'd be noodling around and then he'd figure out that you're trying to anticipate what he's going to do next, so then, of course he'd go and play some completely different phrase or idea; he'd throw a curveball at you. He loved doing that; that was one of his fine pleasures. And when it worked, you could see what it would do to the crowd. There'd be this big 'Yeaaah!' and everyone felt it; you couldn't miss it.

"He loved to take musical chances. If you're going to take chances and go out on a limb . . . well, Garcia lived in the twigs. He'd go out there and sometimes he'd make it back and sometimes he wouldn't. But he had this sense of how to catch himself on the the next branch on the way down and eventually end up on his feet at the end. It's a thing that when you're hearing it, you can follow in your head and actually see where he tried and he either made it or he didn't, but you're with him the *whole way*. And then you add to that the ability of *all six* of them to move on to something new in a moment—like a school of fish or a flock of birds—and you understand why so many people thought they were amazing."

The Dead decided to try an interesting experiment in an attempt to satisfy the tremendous demand for tickets on the November–December 1971 tour and to avoid the nasty gate-crashing incidents that had plagued some of their East Coast shows since the fall of 1970. They arranged with FM stations in nearly every city they played to broadcast the concert, or if there were two shows in a city, to broadcast one of the two concerts. This strategy worked for the most part, encouraging the ticketless hordes to stay home and listen to the Dead on the radio. (In the early '70s there was not yet a hippie marketplace scene outside Dead shows; that was an '80s phenomenon.) The broadcasts served the Dead in two other ways as well. They allowed thousands of people who had never listened to the Dead, or never heard anything but their records, to hear the band in their true element—onstage, live, playing two generous sets spanning nearly every style of twentieth-century American popular and folk music, and jamming to their heart's content; also, the radio shows from this tour were widely taped at home and freely disseminated. These reel-to-reel recordings were many Deadheads' first tapes of the group.

"We've always been into free concerts," Garcia said that fall, "and the broadcast was kind of a free concert without any hassles. Ever since Altamont, everything has been so sticky when you try to do a free show. With us, the whole trip is to make music available."

Pigpen returned to the Dead lineup in December 1971, paler and thinner than before, his role reduced even further now that Keith Godchaux was in the band. Still, he added percussion and B-3 to some songs, occasionally giving the group a full-sounding double-keyboard attack, and his spirit was still strong. Generally speaking, he steered clear of the numbers that required a lot of his energy—big vocal improv songs like "Good Lovin' " and "Love Light"—but he gave his all on his shorter tunes, and he even had a fun new cover song for the Christmas season: Chuck Berry's "Run Rudolph Run." Everyone agreed that Pigpen at less that full capacity was still better than no Pigpen at all.

"It was okay for Pigpen to lay out," Phil said. "We kept wanting Pigpen to be there because he was *one of us.* He really was. But he would lay out and that was okay, too. He didn't mind. We didn't mind. There was no ego problem there."

The Dead stayed off the road from mid-December 1971 all the way until the last week of March 1972, with just three shows at Winterland in between. Which is not to say that the band was inactive during that period; far from it. The group spent much of that time helping Bob Weir record *Ace,* his first solo album for Warner Bros.

"I pretty much knew in the back of my mind what would happen," Weir said in mid-1972. "I go and get the [studio] time booked and start putting the material together. Everybody gets wind of the fact that I got the time booked, and I may be going into the studio. So, one by one, they start coming around. Lesh and Garcia—'Hey man, I hear you got some time booked at Wally Heider's. Need a bass player? A guitarist?' etc. It's kind of like the Tom Sawyer routine with the fence. And I say, 'Wel-l-l, I wanna be careful and get just the right musicians for the record, you know.' Of course I ended up with the Grateful Dead on the record, which I figured up front. I don't have any reason to believe anybody thought it'd be any different. And we had a great time making the record."

The album contained several songs the Dead had performed for a while, including "One More Saturday Night," "Mexicali Blues" (both augmented by the Tower of Power horns on the record), a driving rocker called "Greatest

Story Ever Told," with lyrics by Robert Hunter, and a studio version of "Playing in the Band" that *far* surpassed the crude early live reading on "Skull and Roses." It still stands as one of the Dead's finest recordings; that rare studio track that is both powerful and spacey and shows off the band's formidable control of dynamics. Two other songs on *Ace* also found their way into the Dead's repertoire. The syrupy but powerful ballad "Looks Like Rain" debuted in the spring of 1972; and the lovely, folk-flavored "Cassidy" came alive onstage beginning in 1976. In the latter, lyricist John Barlow deftly interwove flashes of Neal Cassady's life and the birth of Eileen Law's daughter—named Cassidy—at Weir's house in West Marin in early 1972.

Ace also marked the first time Donna Godchaux sang with the band—in typical Marin hippie-speak, she's credited on the album with "harmony, the chick vocals." There was obvious chemistry between Donna and the band during those sessions, so it was not at all surprising that when the Dead next went out on the road, Donna joined them. She sang onstage for the first time at a March 1972 benefit concert for the New York chapter of the Hell's Angels at the Academy of Music in New York City. At first she sang harmony on just a few songs, but by the fall 1972 tour Donna was completely integrated into the lineup (though there were still long stretches when the band would jam and she would leave the stage).

Garcia's first solo album, entitled simply *Garcia*, was released near the end of January 1972 and, predictably, Deadheads snapped it up by the thousands. A number of FM radio stations played different songs from the record, mainly "Deal," "Sugaree" and "The Wheel." Warner Bros. even released a single of "Deal" backed with "The Wheel," though it was not successful in that format.

Garcia was also prominent on another album that came out in the winter of 1972, Merl Saunders's *Heavy Turbulence*, on Fantasy Records. The album gave a fairly good picture of their club band from this era. The core lineup for part of '71 and '72 included former Creedence Clearwater Revival member Tom Fogerty on rhythm guitar in addition to Garcia, Saunders, Kahn and Vitt. On several cuts, Merl's friends the Hawkins Family singers and saxophonist Bob Drew joined in, too. The record mixed original songs by Merl with cover tunes the group played live, such as the Band's "The Night They Drove Old Dixie Down" (sung by Garcia) and an instrumental version of John Lennon's "Imagine."

The Saunders-Garcia group was loose enough during this era that musicians came and went freely without there being a huge impact on the group's overall sound. Bill Kreutzmann sometimes played drums instead of Bill Vitt, Tom Fogerty was in and out, and during March of 1972 Santana's Armando Perazza played percussion. As Merl says of Perazza's addition, "He fit right in. Our music didn't change. It was just like adding a little pepper to it." It was that way with nearly all of the support players who floated through Garcia's bands over the years.

The group's live repertoire was a mixture of the material on *Heavy Turbulence* and songs such as "That's All Right Mama," Motown tunes like Marvin Gaye's "How Sweet It Is" and Stevie Wonder's "I Was Made to Love Her," J. J. Cale's "After Midnight," Dylan songs like "When I Paint My Masterpiece" and "It Takes a Lot to Laugh, It Takes a Train to Cry" and Ray Charles's "Lonely Avenue." Every song the group played was an excuse to stretch out and jam—few songs clocked in at under ten minutes, and most were considerably longer. To the very end, Garcia's solo bands always retained some of the flavor of the original Matrix and Keystone Korner jam sessions.

Not surprisingly, the more the band played, the bigger the following they attracted, even though they stuck to small clubs exclusively. As Merl put it, "The first few times we played, there would be between twenty and thirty people there and we'd split maybe fifty dollars between us at the end of the night. And that was fine. Jerry's really the guy who taught me the value of money— it don't mean a fuckin' thing. Having *fun* is what's important. Anyway, from there it got to be a couple of hundred people at every show, and eventually it was, 'Hey, I just flew in from Boston to see you guys,' " he says with a laugh.

Garcia also found time to play a handful of shows on the East Coast in the winter of 1972 with Howard Wales's new group, in part to help promote the record of jazz instrumental jams they'd made together during 1971, *Hooteroll?* Though he was billed only as a "special guest" on the tour, Garcia was obviously the main attraction for many of the fans who turned out for the shows, some of whom became disgruntled when Garcia only played on a few songs during each concert.

"I didn't really go on the road that time to play," Garcia said a couple of years later. "The thing was really misrepresented. I just wanted to get Howard out playing and the band had a nice thing going which really didn't have much to do with me. I was just there fucking around."

That experience probably influenced Garcia's decision not to take his club band with Saunders out on tours beyond the West Coast. Hell, that band didn't even have a name—usually they just went by "the Group." "It's like a low profile is more desirable to me," Garcia explained. "The Dead and the Group are two different trips. And [the Group] has a lot less pressure associated with it because we haven't made an effort to get famous at it. That's one of the things that makes it possible. I couldn't take the pressure of being a double celebrity. It's a drag just being it once."

The Dead's highly anticipated Great Tour of Europe had first been planned in the spring of 1968 and was talked about every year after that. It finally became a reality in the spring of 1972—at last, the tour made economic sense for everyone involved. The Dead were out of the hole financially and could afford to take a few smaller paydays on their way to (they hoped) building a strong

European fan base. Warner Bros., now suddenly in love with this band that actually sold a lot of records, had three albums to promote in Europe—"Skull and Roses," *Garcia* and Weir's *Ace*. And the Dead agreed to bring their sixteen-track recorder on the road and deliver another relatively inexpensive live album to Warner Bros., a plan that would justify sending more than forty people—band, crew, managers, office staff, wives and girlfriends—on a seven-week, twenty-two-concert working vacation.

"We hoped that we'd play to enough people every night to make it worth our while," Phil Lesh said. "It turned out to be fairly successful, if I remember correctly. I mean, the halls weren't sold out, but it wasn't like some places we played in the States where we'd play in a basketball-sized arena and there'd be 300 people down front. Maybe we were trying to prove something to the few people that were interested enough to come see us."

Actually, the tour was quite well attended, especially in England and Germany. The band's first shows in cold and rainy London at the beginning of the tour were rapturously received by 8,000 British (and a few American) hippies each night, and warmly reviewed by the British rock press, which wasn't nearly as hostile and jaded in those days as it is today. After a disappointing show in Newcastle, before what Weir called "the coldest, stiffest audience I've ever played for," the Dead took an overnight ferry to the Continent, and that's when the adventure really began. The entire Dead retinue traveled in two buses, one of which was designated the Bozo bus, the other the Bolo bus.

"The Bozo bus was for people who wanted to be tripping out and raving all the time," Bob Hunter said. "The Bolo bus was people who preferred to sink totally into their own neuroses, or just sleep."

The happy wanderers managed to smuggle quantities of pot, cocaine and LSD into Europe. Of course their reputation preceded them, so they were able to score dope on the road, too, much to everyone's delight. Some folks took to wearing clown masks from time to time, just for absurdity's sake—the band even wore them onstage once or twice. They were loose and wild on the road, yet their itinerary took them to luxury hotels, expensive restaurants and a few venues, such as Vienna's Concertegebouw, that had hundreds of years of staid tradition behind them.

"We were something of an invasion," Rock Scully said. "Because there were so many of us we could just take over a hotel or a restaurant. That's the meaning of the big American shoe coming through the rainbow on the cover of *Europe '72*. Most of the people had never been to Europe before, and it was also the longest Dead tour ever, so a group consciousness developed that tended to exclude the surroundings." Which is a nice way of saying that the Dead family marauded through Europe like Huns, partying instead of pillaging.

Musically, the Europe tour was one of the Dead's strongest ever. "We played great," Phil said many years later. "Keith was just coming into his own, really. And I gotta say that Billy played like a young god on [that] tour. I mean, he was *everywhere* on the drums, and just kickin' our butts every which way, which is what drummers live to do."

The wide-open jamming tunes like "Dark Star," "Truckin'," "The Other One" and "Playing in the Band" went to spaces they'd never been to before, as the group fearlessly deconstructed rhythms and melodies, broke down familiar forms and then reassembled the individual components of their sound in fresh ways. With Keith banging out unusual, blocky chord clusters that sounded as if they were straight out of Sun Ra or Cecil Taylor, and Garcia sometimes riding his wah-wah pedal to create bizarre, growling crescendos, the Dead delved deeper into dissonance than ever before—the twenty-five-minute versions of "Dark Star" from 1969 sounded like mellifluous poetry compared with the edgy cacophony of so many of the 1972–74 versions. Still, the group never abandoned its fundamental lyricism. Out of the noisy chaos would eventually come form and consonance, and at this point the band was always able to play music of amazing delicacy as well.

Two new Hunter-Garcia songs were premiered on the European jaunt. "He's Gone" was a slow shuffle Garcia composed just before the trip. "I remember working on it in a little apartment I had in in the city [San Francisco]," he said. "It's when I was playing lots and lots of shows with Merl at the Keystone Korner. I had an apartment where I could hang out on nights I didn't feel like driving all the way back to Stinson Beach." Hunter said of his lyrics for the tune, "It was considerations of Lenny [Hart] that kicked off the [opening lines]":

> Rat in a drain ditch
> Caught on a limb
> You know better but I know him
> Like I told you
> What I said
> Steal your face right off your head

"So the song started that way, but later on it became an anthem for Pigpen, and it's changed through the years," Hunter said. "These songs are amorphous that way. What I intend is not what a thing is in the end."

"Me neither, for that matter," Garcia added in the same joint interview. "We don't create the meanings of the tunes ultimately. They re-create themselves each performance in the minds of everybody there."

The other new Hunter-Garcia song was an unclassifiable slice of vintage Americana (old-timey rock?) called "Brown-Eyed Women," which served up some colorful characters and vignettes from America's not-too-distant past:

Delilah Jones was the mother of twins
Two times over and the rest was sins
Raised eight boys, only I turned bad
Didn't get the lickings that the other ones had

Brown-eyed women and red grenadine
The bottle was dusty but the liquor was clean
Sound of the thunder with the rain pouring down
And it looks like the old man's getting on

While he was in Europe Garcia also put music to a set of lyrics that Hunter had written in New York's Chelsea Hotel in mid-1970. "Stella Blue," which debuted at the Dead's first concert after the European tour—a June show at the Hollywood Bowl—is one of the duo's most powerful ballads, with music that sounds almost as if it could be from the songbook of Billy Strayhorn, and lyrics filled with a world-weary loneliness and melancholy; a "brittle pathos," as Garcia once described it:

All the years combine
They melt into a dream
A broken angel sings
From a guitar
In the end there's just a song
Comes crying like the wind
Through all the broken dreams
And vanished years

Stella Blue

Garcia said that "Stella Blue" was "a good example of a song I sang before I understood it. I understood some sense of what the lyrics were about, but I didn't get into the pathos of it. . . . Originally I was taken with the construction of it, which is extremely clever, if I do say so myself. I was proud of it as a composer—'Hey, this is a slick song! This sucker has a very slippery harmonic thing that works nicely.' That's what I liked about it. It wasn't until later that I started to find other stuff in there."

The song managed to stay fresh and vital until the end; in fact, it became *more* powerful and Garcia sang it with greater conviction as the years went by. In a way, it was a song about the *end* of life and was better suited to the tired and broken Garcia of fifty than the strong, confident man of thirty who first sang it.

Pigpen was still three years shy of his thirtieth birthday when he played what turned out to be his final show with the Grateful Dead—that same

Hollywood Bowl concert three weeks after the end of the European tour. The trip to Europe had been hard on him, even though he conscientiously avoided booze the entire time, which was no easy feat in Germany and France.

"When they came back from Europe, the rest of the band would go on tours," Eileen Law said. "Keith went out and Pig stayed home. Pig would call the office—it was just a skeleton crew—and he was really having a hard time with the band on the road and him being out of that. He would call and just want to talk. We all felt really bad for him because here was this person that I once thought was a Hell's Angel, and now he was this little thin person. It was like seeing someone get cancer and then just deteriorate. He had this thin, thin face, but he'd still have his little hat on."

The Dead kept on rolling along without Pigpen, though at most stops on their tours in 1972 Weir or Lesh would mention from the stage that Pigpen was sick back in California and "we'll all send your best wishes back to him," or words to that effect.

By the middle of 1972 the Dead had pretty much decided to leave Warner Bros. Records and explore the possibility of starting their own independent label. This is something the bandmembers, and Garcia in particular, had been thinking about for years, but it was Ron Rakow, an associate of the group's since the Haight-Ashbury days, who came up with the plan to make the dream a reality.

The problem with Warners, as Rakow and the Dead saw it, wasn't just that it was a straight company. They believed the label was inefficient at marketing the Dead's records, and that a group with such a devoted nonmainstream following would be better served by specialized promotional methods that were beyond the grasp of a conventional record company. And Warner Bros. was even considered the hippest of the major labels in the late '60s and early '70s—the company was home to such idiosyncratic artists as Frank Zappa, Neil Young, Ry Cooder, Randy Newman and Joni Mitchell.

On July 4, 1972, at a meeting at Billy Kreutzmann's house, Rakow presented the band with a ninety-two-page document called "The So-What Papers," outlining his findings about the feasibility of the Dead starting their own record company. Rakow was nothing if not an enterprising schemer. For instance, his original vision was that the Dead would get the capital to launch their label from the Minority Enterprise Small Business Investment Company Act (MESBIC). "I had hippies declared a minority," Rakow says. "They were going to give us the money."

In October 1972 Alan Trist, Garcia's buddy from the early Palo Alto days, who'd come back to America from England in the fall of 1970 and stepped into the Dead's somewhat amorphous management structure, presented the group with a summary and analysis of different options facing the band. These included Rakow's plan for total independence from the straight music industry by setting up a Dead-controlled franchise distribution and mail-order system;

a scenario favored by Owsley to have Deadheads buy an annual "subscription" to the Dead's records; and, the most conservative option, starting a custom label within a major record company, along the lines of the Beatles' Apple Records or the Jefferson Airplane's Grunt Records.

In the end, the band decided to take the big step and go completely independent, which is the option Garcia favored strongly from the beginning. Rakow finagled a deal with Atlantic Records boss Jerry Wexler, selling the foreign distribution rights for the Dead's albums for the $300,000 that was needed to start the company. By the spring of 1973 a company structure was in place, with Rakow installed as president of the fledgling label.

But before any of that could happen, the Dead still had to fulfill contractual obligations to Warner Bros. In the late fall of 1972 Warners put out the three-record live set *Europe '72* (the group's third live album in four years), and it raced up the *Billboard* charts to number 24 in a matter of weeks, easily justifying the tremendous expense of the tour for Warners. The album's six sides painted an even better picture of what the Dead were all about than "Skull and Roses" had. There were old and recent concert favorites like "Morning Dew," "Cumberland Blues," "Sugar Magnolia," "China Cat Sunflower" > "I Know You Rider" and "Truckin' "; two long, spacey jams; Garcia's cover version of Hank Williams's "You Win Again"; and nearly an album's worth of previously unrecorded tunes—"Ramble On Rose," "Tennessee Jed," "Mr. Charlie" (a rollicking Hunter-Pigpen song), "Jack Straw," "He's Gone" and "Brown-Eyed Women."

The band saved themselves a lot of time and money by putting new songs on both "Skull and Roses" and *Europe '72*, but in later years both Hunter and Garcia said they were sorry the band never tackled those songs in the studio. "To me, all that material was sort of the kicker follow-up album to *American Beauty*," Hunter said. "Instead we put out this three-album package that sounds wonderful, but it spread out the material so much we never got a chance to hear what those songs would have sounded like as a package. I personally would've liked to hear those songs on an album of their own."

Another new Hunter-Garcia song that would have fit perfectly on that mythical studio album was "Mississippi Half-Step Uptown Toodleoo," which the Dead first played in the summer of 1972. It was a playful country-flavored song that felt like an old-time fiddle tune with a dash of early jazz thrown in—Duke Ellington had cut a song called "East St. Louis Toodleoo" with his group in 1926. Lyrically, the song offered an intriguing pastiche of allusions and metaphors, from Bible figures to gambling to seamen's lore. Once again, the main character is a troublemaker on the move, cursed by destiny and fate:

> *On the day that I was born*
> *Daddy sat down and cried*
> *I had the mark just as plain as day*

Which could not be denied
They say that Cain caught Abel
Rolling loaded dice,
Ace of spades behind his ear
And him not thinking twice

Songs like this wouldn't have had the kind of resonance they did if Hunter hadn't been able to somehow connect them to Garcia's real-life persona. Hunter was able to write songs for Garcia that weren't usually autobiographical, yet attitudinally they fit him to a tee. Garcia could play the reprobate in these songs because that's how he viewed himself to a degree—a fuckup who'd succeeded against all odds.

Still, Garcia once noted, "I don't really very often relate to the characters in the songs. I don't feel like 'Okay, now this is *me* singing this song.' . . . Actually, I relate better to Dylan songs more often than not. Sometimes I feel like I'm right *in* those songs; that is to say, that it's *me* speaking. . . . That rarely happens to me with Hunter's songs, but something *else* happens to me with Hunter's songs that I think is more special. And that's the thing of them coming from *a world*—some kind of mythos or alternate universe that's got a lot of interesting stuff in it. And I feel like I'm in that world and of it somehow; or at least I know it when I see it, and I feel like I have something to say about it and I'm participating in it, but in a different sort of way. It's participating in the mythos."

And the songs were open-ended enough for the audience to enter into that world and imagine that it was also *their* strange universe of real and imagined people, places, feelings and dreams.

CHAPTER 13

Line Up a Long Shot, Maybe Try It Two Times

tarting an independent record company was a gamble, but at least it was a bold move taken from a position of strength. All through 1972 the Dead's popularity was rising. Though they still performed mainly at 2,500- to 3,500-seat theaters, they were increasingly booking civic auditoriums, small stadiums, college sports venues and professional basketball and hockey arenas. In the New York area, where ticket demand was always intense, they now played just across the Hudson River in Roosevelt Stadium, a decaying minor-league baseball park in Jersey City that could accommodate 23,000 fans. In Philadelphia, also rabid Dead territory, the band played its first show at the 17,000-seat Spectrum in September 1972.

Garcia viewed the Dead's steady rise in popularity with some measure of alarm. It's not that he didn't want his work to be enjoyed by large numbers of people; on the contrary, he was proud that the Dead had been able to amass such a following without consciously making concessions to mainstream commerciality. But playing in larger places made it more difficult to feel as if he was connecting with everyone in the audience. The Acid Tests and psychedelic nights at the Fillmore Auditorium had been models of how high a band and crowd could get *together*. Playing a 20,000-seat venue made the energy exchange between group and audience completely different. As Garcia noted in the early '70s, "A lot of times people who don't know how to get it on way outnumber the people who do know how to get it on." But Garcia also recognized that with a big crowd you also have even greater potential to get the *big rush*—when *everyone* is locked in on the same wavelength as the band, and the room becomes a single, undulating celebratory organism.

To their credit, the Dead did everything they could to make the experience of going to large concerts more pleasant for the audience. The band had always invested lots of time and money into developing loud and clear sound systems. It had been part of Owsley's original vision for the band, and the mantle had been taken up by Dan Healy, Bob Matthews and everyone who was a part of the group's technical support staff. In the late '60s, it even led to the formation of a separate sound entity, Alembic, which was dedicated to producing outstanding sound reinforcement systems, recording electronics and musical instruments. The loose group of hi-fi wizards took its name from the world of alchemy (one of Owsley's areas of interest)—an alembic is an instrument used to refine, purify and transform. The Dead helped support the Alembic technical brain trust and workshop, and in return got a sound system that was the envy of everyone in the touring music industry and which allowed the band to feel good about playing the occasional monster gig.

The larger sound systems the Dead introduced in the early '70s required a bigger road crew to move and assemble the mountains of equipment, which put even more financial pressure on the band to play bigger shows. By the end of 1972 the Grateful Dead "family" was more than seventy-five people, with about thirty on the payroll, and playing in 2,500-seat halls wasn't going to bring in enough money to cover a group that big. In this regard it became the typical American success story, and it led to some of the usual pitfalls: earning more money encouraged people to buy homes and better cars, which led to mortgages and term payments that had to be maintained month after month. Not that anyone in the scene was living ostentatiously—these people were still on the lower end of the economic scale in Marin, and, considering the Dead's popularity, on the lower end of the economic scale in big-time rock 'n' roll, too.

If anyone in the organization had a plan that was going to make the scene cooler or more efficient in some way, he or she could usually get the money to try to implement that idea. However, nothing happened unless all the bandmembers agreed that it should. If one person in the band *really* didn't like an idea, he could block it. And the band also listened carefully to the opinions of the road crew, so if one of them or a couple of them were strongly against something, a member of the band might join them and defeat a proposal. That said, though, everyone in the organization generally gave one another latitude for their ideas to blossom. Indeed, the major upside of success was the freedom to try new things and increase their autonomy in the music business. So at the same time the record company was starting up and development money was being funneled to Alembic, the Dead also sunk some money into starting their own booking and travel agencies in an audacious attempt to control nearly every aspect of their working life. And for a few years it worked.

Garcia, says Alan Trist, had strong opinions on how to conduct the business of the Grateful Dead. "He said, 'Okay, let's not fall into the traps that are out there.' So one response is to have your own people around you, and that's an aspect of the social and business world of the Dead that was consistently upheld by Jerry. And that was a real necessary protection against what the world would do to you otherwise. He was constantly making sure that business decisions and strategies were *righteous,* in the old sense of that word. So instead of pursuing a path that would make more money and doing all the things it was possible for them to do along that road, they chose to go in the opposite direction, because it was clear they were not going to buy into that culture of money and fame and fortune in the traditional way. They rejected the easy options, and to me that was an extremely attractive and courageous way to go."

At the Dead's first show of 1973, in Stanford University's Maples Pavilion, the band unveiled seven new Hunter-Garcia songs, the biggest batch they'd ever introduced at once. The songs were all over the map musically and lyrically, and none of them much resembled any songs the two had written before. Generally speaking, they were less folk- and country-influenced.

Two of the new songs—"They Love Each Other" and "Row Jimmy"—showed Garcia's infatuation with reggae, the spirited, highly rhythmic Jamaican music form that got its first wide American exposure through the soundtrack album for the 1972 film *The Harder They Come*, featuring Jimmy Cliff, Toots and the Maytals, Desmond Dekker and others. Garcia liked the title song so much that he began playing it with his solo band in mid-'73. And he was sufficiently intrigued by reggae that he attended one of the first American appearances by Bob Marley and the Wailers—then virtually unknown outside Jamaica—in a small Bay Area club later that year. Typical of Garcia, when he decided to borrow from the idiom in his own songs, he modified it considerably. "They Love Each Other," a sprightly paean to the glories of a blissful romantic union, added some interesting little rhythmic tricks within the basic beat. "Row Jimmy," with dreamy and obtuse Hunter lyrics, slowed down a reggae beat to the point where each component note and counter-rhythm was clearly discernible and the tune as a whole moved along like a lazy river.

The humorous R&B-flavored romp called "Loose Lucy" found Garcia in an unusual role—accused cad and submissive plaything of the intimidating title character. "Wave That Flag" was also a lighthearted number, a fast shuffle consisting of several stanzas of short, playful, seemingly unconnected rhymes that Garcia had great difficulty remembering in the correct order—not that it mattered to the overall feeling of the tune, where the rhythm of the words was as important as their literal meaning. This is the song that, a year later, was tightened up lyrically to become the much more successful "U.S. Blues."

Garcia admitted that "Here Comes Sunshine" was inspired by songs from the Beatles' *Abbey Road* album such as "Sun King" and "Here Comes the Sun." This was particularly evident on the choruses, which taxed the group's harmony chops to the limit. But even the main motif, a lilting melodic line with a cadence almost like a music box, owed something to "Here Comes the Sun." Hunter's elliptical words were inspired by childhood memories, as he later noted in his book of lyrics: "Remembering the great Vanport, Washington, flood of 1949; living in other people's homes; a family abandoned by father; second grade." Yet the tone of the lyrics was actually optimistic, and Garcia's music was so buoyant and affirmative that the song always felt like a joyous celebration of life, as well as perhaps a message to the Dead:

> *Line up a long shot*
> *Maybe try it two times*

Maybe more
Good to know
You got shoes
To wear
When you find the floor
Why hold out for more?

Here comes sunshine
. . . Here comes sunshine!

This song opened up to jamming easily. It provided a mellow framework to work within, and the band usually managed to stretch out quite far within the groove, slowly building crescendos piece by piece without straying too far from the main melodic figure.

Hunter said his original title for the haunting ballad "China Doll" was "The Suicide Song," and a look at the first two verses shows why:

A pistol shot at five o'clock
The bells of heaven ring
Tell me what you done it for
"No, I won't tell you a thing

"Yesterday I begged you
Before I hit the ground—
All I leave behind me
Is only what I've found . . ."

"It's almost like a ghost voice: 'Tell me what you done it for / No I won't tell you a thing,'" Hunter said. "It's a little dialogue like that. I think it's a terrifying song. And then it's also got some affirmation of how it can be mended somehow. There's a bit of metaphysical content in there which I leave open, not that I subscribe or don't subscribe to it. At the time it resonated right. The song is eerie and very, very beautiful the way Garcia handles it."

Perhaps the most instantly popular of the seven new Hunter-Garcia tunes was "Eyes of the World," a fresh, breezy, wide-open song with a distinctive samba feel. "It was kind of a Brazilian thing," Garcia said, and indeed, it almost sounded like some jazzy horn number you might hear being played by an *orchestre tropicale* in a seaside Rio nightclub. The song became one of the Dead's liveliest jamming tunes, offering the band lots of room between verses, and also many different possibilities for connecting it to other tunes, since it had no formal ending—after the final chorus the band usually played around the central riff for a while longer, then Garcia or Lesh would signal a key change at some point and it would slip off in another direction, sometimes coming back to an "Eyes" riff, other times leading to a different song or groove. "Eyes" was another song Garcia never tired of. Though it went through small changes over the years, usually related to tempo, its essence remained unchanged.

After a very successful eight-show tour of the Midwest, where the smallest hall the band played had 7,500 seats, the Dead returned to the Bay Area for a couple of weeks in advance of an East Coast tour of basketball arenas, including three consecutive nights at the 17,000-seat Nassau Coliseum (on Long Island) and concerts at the cavernous Boston Garden and the Philadelphia Spectrum. It was hard to believe that two years earlier the band had been playing the relatively tiny Boston Music Hall (drawing so many people outside that there was a near-riot).

On the night of March 8, a week before the tour, Pigpen was found dead in his Corte Madera apartment, a victim of what the Marin County coroner ruled a "massive gastrointestinal hemorrhage." His liver showed acute signs of disease and his spleen was also enlarged. Though Pigpen had been sick for a long time, his death still stunned nearly everyone close to him. "It was very shocking and very sad, and so untimely," said Sue Swanson. "I mean almost nobody was even thirty at that point, so to lose someone was almost unthinkable."

"When he went to the hospital in '71 and we all gave him blood," Garcia said years later, "they were saying, 'That's it, he's not going to make it,' so in effect we went through it—we went through the pain. Then he came out of it for a while and it was great. And actually I thought he was doing pretty good. When he died he just snuck away. I guess the stress on his system was just too much for him."

On March 12 a traditional Catholic funeral at a mortuary in Corte Madera was attended by about two hundred people, including the whole McKernan clan, members of the Dead family and various Merry Pranksters and Hell's Angels. Pigpen was laid out in an open coffin, wearing his trademark leather jacket and a cowboy shirt, his hat on the pillow. "It was a bummer," Garcia commented the next day. "They had an Irish Catholic priest to say kind words, but it was for the straights."

"I just remember the funeral as totally depressing," Rock Scully said. "I was just totally brought down. I'd never seen Jerry more unhappy, ever. God, he was devastated; we all were."

"It was pretty sad," Laird Grant said. "There are a lot of funerals you go to and you feel okay about it—the guy's been dying for six months and everyone expects it—but with Pigpen it was sort of like: Okay, here's *this* one. Hang on to your hats, kids! You ain't seen shit yet! Here goes Pigpen. *Now* what happens?"

What happened was the Dead went out on that East Coast tour two days after the funeral. "We'd been getting used to it [Pigpen's absence] all along, so it wasn't a sudden change when he died," Weir said. "It was a very gradual change that became formal when he wasn't here anymore at all."

"Still, after he died you'd go out there [onstage] and it'd be like, 'Where's Pig?' " Garcia noted. "And we missed all those songs. It was like operating with a broken leg. So we went to our next strong suit, which was kind of a country feel; the American mythos, the Hunter songs. And our other strong suit was our [musical] weirdness. So we went with our strong suits that didn't involve Pigpen."

On the third night of the East Coast tour, at Nassau Coliseum, the Dead played "He's Gone" as the second song of the night, and many in the audience took it to be a memorial to Pigpen and lit matches to honor his memory. It's a ritual that was repeated in other cities that year, too. Even though the Dead had thousands of new fans in 1973 who had never seen Pigpen perform, his legend loomed large and the affection that everyone in the Dead scene felt for him was well-known.

"It's hard to say what it was about him that people really loved," Garcia said in 1988. "But they loved him a lot. I know I loved him a lot, and I couldn't begin to tell you why. He was a lovable person. Really, it hasn't felt right since Pigpen's been gone, but on the other hand he's always been around a little, too. He hasn't been entirely gone. He's right around."

Ronald C. McKernan's gravestone at Alta Mesa cemetery in Palo Alto reads: "Pigpen was and is now forever one of the Grateful Dead."

While the Dead's following seemed to grow with each passing month, Garcia continued his low-key involvement with his club group, and in the winter and spring of 1973 he also plunged into a new side project—a bluegrass group called Old and in the Way, featuring Garcia on banjo and vocals, John Kahn on string bass, David Grisman on mandolin and vocals, fiddler Richard Greene and guitarist-singer Peter Rowan, the older brother of Chris and Loren Rowan.

"Old and in the Way was basically David Grisman's trip," John Kahn recalled. "There was no fiddle player in the group at first. It was me, Peter Rowan, Grisman and Jerry. We'd get together and play at Jerry's house in Stinson Beach, or at my house in Forest Knolls, and then we started playing some real small gigs informally, like at the bar in Stinson Beach. It was this tiny place and the audience was louder than the band. It was all these big hippies dancing with these big hiking boots with the big flaps bouncing up and down. They'd start clapping and you couldn't hear us at all. Even *we* couldn't hear us!"

"You know Jerry—if he thinks something is worth doing, he'll just take it out there right away, which is good," Grisman said. "He said, 'Let's play some gigs!' and he had the gigs lined up! We started playing in clubs and then he booked a tour. It was a real informal thing."

Richard Greene came on board at a benefit concert at the Stinson Beach firehouse and played fiddle for the first few months the group was together. An alumnus of Bill Monroe's group, and later the progressive-rock band

Seatrain, which also included Peter Rowan, Greene hadn't played with Garcia since the mid-'60s.

"When I played in Old and in the Way I got to see more of the 'star' Garcia," he says. "Not that he acted that way; but in terms of how people in the audience related to him. Do you know about the checks in the glove compartment of his car? He was just like he was in the '60s when I knew him, only now it's the '70s and he's getting rich and famous and everything. Jerry was receiving a lot of money from all sorts of sources and he'd get a check and just throw it in the glove compartment of his car, and eventually, thousands of dollars were sitting in there that he completely forgot about. He just didn't pay attention to money; he was a true hippie in that way. That was symbolic for me."

Greene was living in Los Angeles the whole time he was with the group and was in the process of launching his own band, the Zone, so eventually he dropped out of the band and was replaced by Vassar Clements, another veteran of Bill Monroe's band (as well as groups with Earl Scruggs, Jim and Jesse McReynolds and John Hartford), and widely regarded as one of the best fiddlers anywhere. "I thought he was the best of all of us," John Kahn commented, "and easily one of the best players I've ever worked with. He could've played jazz with Coltrane. He could play anything."

Much of the group's repertoire came from traditional bluegrass—Monroe, the Stanley Brothers, Jim and Jesse, et al. But Old and in the Way also incorporated a handful of excellent original tunes by Grisman, Clements, Peter Rowan—the ostensible lead singer in the group and author of "Midnight Moonlight," "Panama Red," "Land of the Navajo" and "Lonesome L.A. Cowboy"—and even a few pop songs rearranged bluegrass-style by Garcia, such as the Rolling Stones' "Wild Horses" and the Platters' '50s hit "The Great Pretender." In Grisman and Clements the band had two exceptionally good soloists, and though Garcia was no longer the red-hot five-string banjo picker he had been in the mid-'60s, he brought his characteristic spunk and good taste to everything he played on the instrument.

"Jerry worked real hard at playing the banjo," Vassar Clements says. "Anything he tried he worked hard at. And the way it was with him, if he didn't feel pretty sure of himself, he wouldn't go out and play. What I liked about this playing is that it was different. You could tell he wasn't a guy who'd been playing banjo all his life, but the groove was always there and he had good ideas. It sounded great to me."

Old and in the Way played sporadically through 1973 in between Grateful Dead tours, and even cut an album at Mickey Hart's studio, though it was never released. "We weren't too happy with it," Grisman said. "It was kind of rushed. It didn't seem to equal what we were doing live." A live album recorded by Owsley at the Boarding House club in San Francisco came out in 1975 and went on to become one of the best-selling bluegrass albums of all time. But by the time that record was released the group had long since disbanded, a victim of squabbling between Rowan and Grisman and the difficulty of trying to work around Garcia's always hectic schedule.

Garcia's memories of the group were nearly all positive, and shortly before he died he even talked about getting the band together again. "We were supposed to go out on a tour in the fall of '95," Clements says wistfully, adding, "Shoot, I wish he'd lived to be a hundred and twenty."

"Playing with Old and in the Way was like playing in the bluegrass band I'd always wanted to play in," Garcia said. "It was such a great band and I was flattered to be in such fast company. I was only sorry my banjo chops were never what they had been when I was playing continually, though they were smoothing out near the end."

To give a sense of the double life Garcia was leading in those days, on May 18, 1973, Old and in the Way played a show at a small Palo Alto club called Homer's Warehouse, and then two days later he strapped on his electric guitar to play with the Grateful Dead in front of 40,000 people at Kezar Stadium in San Francisco—the Dead's first big stadium show. Four nights later he was back playing banjo with Old and in the Way at the Ash Grove in L.A., followed by one-nighters in Boston and Passaic, New Jersey, before joining the Dead in Washington, D.C., for two enormous gigs at RFK Stadium with co-headliners the Allman Brothers Band.

The Dead and the Allmans had been friends and mutual admirers for several years. The Macon, Georgia–based Allmans cited the early Grateful Dead—particularly the *Anthem of the Sun*–era band—as one of their influences. Indeed, that album was the source of the Allmans' famous "Mountain Jam": the theme from Donovan's "There Is a Mountain" appeared in the middle of the jam on "Alligator" on *Anthem*. The Allmans had the same instrumental lineup as the 1968 Dead—including two drummers—and like the Dead the Allmans had paid dues in the psychedelic world, tripping and jamming for hours on end. But whereas much of the Dead's music had been informed by country sources, the Allmans drew more from blues and R&B. The group's distinctive sound came from the blending of Duane Allman's and Dickey Betts's guitar styles with Gregg Allman's sturdy B-3 work and a relentless powerhouse rhythm section. Their music never had the loose, slippery, unpredictable quality that the Dead had in spades, but what they did have was the ability to play incredibly complex, bebop-inspired unison lines that exploded into jams which invariably led to other fiery crescendos. These guys had *serious* chops, but the veneer was still that of a simple electric blues band.

The Dead and the Allmans had shared a bill at the Fillmore East in February 1970, and then in April 1971 Duane played slide on three songs with the Dead during the group's final series at the Fillmore East. Tragically, in October of that year Duane was killed in a motorcycle accident. But the Allman Brothers had so much momentum following the release of their incendiary

LEFT: Sitting in the empty Boston Music Hall during a sound check, November 30, 1973. *(Randy Berge)*

ABOVE: Backstage at the Golden State Bluegrass Festival in San Rafael, California, April 27, 1974. This show was the final gig for Old and in the Way. *(Jon Sievert)*

LEFT: In front of the Wall of Sound in Reno with his first Doug Irwin custom guitar, May 12, 1974. *(Bruce Polonsky)*

ABOVE: Garcia, Weir and Lesh at Winterland, October 1974—the "retirement" shows. *(Bruce Polonsky)*

ABOVE: A free concert in Golden Gate Park, September 28, 1975. Jerry's playing a Travis Bean guitar. *(Bruce Polonsky)*

LEFT: Jerry enjoys a joint and some red wine during a photo session for the cover of *BAM* magazine, November 1977. This was the day the author first met Garcia. *(Jim Marshall)*

Stockton Civic Center, January 18, 1978. *(Bruce Polonsky)*

BELOW: Acoustic Dead at the Warfield Theater in San Francisco, October 1980. *(Jon Sievert)*

Two views of the Dead at the Greek Theater in Berkeley, 1982 (inset) and 1983. Keyboardist Brent Mydland is on the right in the wide shot. Tie-dyes by Courtney Pollack. *(Clayton Call)*

A Robert Hunter recording session at Club Front, fall of 1981. John Kahn is playing the stand-up bass. *(Herb Greene)*

Jerry on the comeback trail, jamming with Los Lobos' Cesar Rosas at New George's in San Rafael, California, November 1986. *(Bruce Polonsky)*

Backing Dylan in Eugene, Oregon, in 1987. *(Jay Blakesberg)*

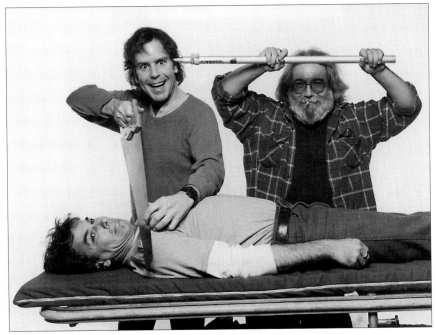

Mickey, Bob and Jerry, clowning in the band, 1987. *(Herb Greene)*

The Jerry Garcia Acoustic Band on Broadway, Halloween 1987. *Left to right:* Kenny Kosek, John Kahn, Sandy Rothman, David Nelson, JG. *(Jay Blakesberg)*

live album *At Fillmore East* that they were able to stay together and actually increase their following on subsequent tours. In July 1972 Dickey Betts, bassist Berry Oakley and drummer Jaimoe joined the Dead for a few songs at Dillon Stadium in Hartford, Connecticut, and the following night Garcia, Weir and Kreutzmann returned the favor by jamming with the Allmans at Gaelic Park in the Bronx. By 1973 the Dead and the Allmans were the most popular touring bands in the country, and really the last true-blue proponents of the Big Jam left in American rock 'n' roll.

So there was history and momentum going into the June RFK concerts, which attracted 110,000 people over two days (okay, it was a lot of the same people twice). The Allmans headlined the first of the two shows, both of which were played in sweltering heat and crippling humidity. The second day the order was reversed and the Dead closed the show with a three-set extravaganza, the last featuring the Dead and Allmans together for a set of rock 'n' roll tunes that included "That's All Right Mama," "Not Fade Away," "Goin' Down the Road Feeling Bad," "The Promised Land" and "Johnny B. Goode."

But the RFK shows were really just a taste of what was yet to come. A month and a half later, the Dead, the Allman Brothers and the Band drew 600,000 people to a concert at the Grand Prix Racecourse in Watkins Glen, New York, in the beautiful Finger Lakes region.

The promoters had expected a crowd of about 150,000 to show up—just a few thousand more than typically came to see the annual United States Grand Prix race there—but there were that many people camped outside the gates two days before the show. Bill Graham, who had been hired to stage the concert, persuaded the promoters to open the gates four hours earlier than planned, and by midday Friday—a day before showtime—the area was packed nearly half a mile from the stage, while hundreds of thousands more streamed toward the site on foot, since traffic was backed up for twenty miles in every direction. As had happened at Woodstock and virtually every other humongous festival, tickets eventually stopped being collected and then the masses really poured into the area. The early arrivers were rewarded for enduring a torrential downpour the night before the gates opened—the Dead played two short sets as a "sound check," the Allmans played for ninety minutes, the Band an hour. There were people in the woods and covering the hillsides for miles around, and most didn't seem particularly concerned that the sound couldn't possibly travel to the far reaches. They just wanted to *be* there. Dan Healy arranged to have the concert broadcast on a frequency that could be picked up by radios within a few miles of the site. It was a mellow crowd, content to hang out and party with each other for the most part.

Most agreed that the Dead's two sets on Saturday afternoon were not their best—not in any way *bad* like at Woodstock, but not as consistently powerful as most of their 1973 shows, including the RFK concerts. At least this time the Dead missed the rains, which nearly washed away the Band during their set. The day really belonged to the Allman Brothers, whose music had more of the grand sweep needed to communicate to people half a mile away. There was another nice Dead-Allmans jam session at the conclusion of the Allmans' set around 2:30 Sunday morning, and the thousands who could actually hear the music seemed to enjoy it thoroughly. There were a few drug arrests, the usual scattering of bum trips and overdoses, and several highway fatalities miles from the site before and after the concert, but considering the size of the crowd and the scarcity of food and other amenities, things went extremely well. It helped that it was only a one-day event.

Garcia didn't have much time to savor the triumph of Watkins Glen. In fact, he helicoptered directly from the concert site to Mount Holly, New Jersey, where he was facing charges stemming from a March 29 bust on the New Jersey Turnpike. Garcia and his passenger, Bob Hunter, had been driving from a gig in Baltimore to one two nights later in Springfield, Massachusetts, in a rented 1973 Chevrolet when they were pulled over because Garcia was driving 71 mph in a 60 mph zone. A search of Garcia's briefcase (which he opened to retrieve his driver's license) turned up small quantities of pot, LSD and cocaine, so Garcia was arrested and later released on $2,000 bail. Hunter was not charged.

If Garcia was worried when he went to court following the Watkins Glen show, it didn't show. He cheerfully signed autographs for well-wishers in the courtroom and chatted amiably with reporters on the scene. Probation officials at the hearing described Garcia as "a very likeable person," and one county official revealed that the state trooper who had arrested Garcia had said, "He was such a nice guy, we hated to bust him." After an attorney for Garcia presented a psychiatrist's report stating that Garcia was not addicted to drugs, was "a good family man and a creative individual," the Burlington County court judge gave Garcia a suspended one-year sentence, with the charges to be dropped after that period provided Garcia was not named in another criminal offense. Two days later Garcia was back with the Dead for two sold-out shows at Roosevelt Stadium (with the Band opening), the second of which fell on Garcia's thirty-first birthday.

The Grateful Dead spent most of August ensconced in the Record Plant, a cushy state-of-the-art recording studio in Sausalito, recording *Wake of the Flood*, their first album for Grateful Dead Records. Four of the seven Hunter-Garcia songs introduced in February made it onto the record: "Here Comes Sunshine," "Mississippi Half-Step Uptown Toodleoo," "Row Jimmy" and "Eyes of the World," plus the earlier "Stella Blue." Keith Godchaux sang lead on an R&B/gospel-tinged song he and Hunter wrote called "Let Me Sing Your Blues Away" (it would be Keith's only vocal appearance on a Dead record), and Weir contributed the three-part "Weather Report Suite," featuring sections co-written with folk songwriter Eric Anderson and John Barlow. The Weir-Barlow section in particular, "Let It Grow," showed perhaps the greatest compositional sophistication of any Weir tune to date, mixing Spanish-influenced passages with furiously fast jamming and dynamic shifts that took the piece from thundering stepped riffs to a soft, graceful lilt within a matter of seconds.

With the exception of Keith's song, all of the tunes had been road tested, so recording them was mainly a matter of engineers Bob Matthews and Betty Cantor getting good performances on tape. A few songs featured outside players: Vassar Clements's fiddle snaked through "Mississippi Half-Step"; a small horn section added peppery blasts to "Let Me Sing Your Blues Away" and "Let It Grow"; Doug Sahm, former leader of the Sir Douglas Quintet, played twelve-string on a track; and helping on background vocals was a singer named Sarah Fulcher, who had also had a brief tenure with the Saunders-Garcia group earlier in the year.

On the Dead's September East Coast swing following the completion of the album, two of the horn players on the record—saxophonist Martin Fierro and trumpeter Joe Ellis, both from Doug Sahm's band, who opened every show on the tour except one—joined the Dead for a couple of numbers at each concert, to mainly negative reviews from the Deadheads. "To be honest, the fans didn't like the horns, so the Dead finally said, 'Fuck it!' " Fierro says good-naturedly. "But we had a great time; it was wonderful. We rehearsed, but we didn't have written arrangements. We had head arrangements. And sometimes it sounded pretty good and sometimes it was a little rough." After this tour, Fierro started dropping in regularly with the Saunders-Garcia group, too.

Wake of the Flood was released in mid-October through a network of independent record distributors. As in the later Warners days, the band sold about 450,000 copies in the first four months and after that sales tapered off rapidly. "I think some people believed that we were going to instantly go out and sell a million copies of our record because Warner Bros. had done such a lousy job and now we were in control," Ron Rakow says. "Then, when it didn't sell a million copies some people thought I was fucking with them. See, there was this attitude in the Dead that the record company is for fucking with. I thought it was just because it was Warner Bros., but once *I* became the record company, I found out it was whoever had the gig. So some people in the band didn't believe our fans were buying it quickly and that there were only that many of them, which was Garcia's theory, and what Warner Bros. always said. So when the same thing happened to us they thought I was fucking with them."

Even if sales weren't up dramatically, the amount of money the band made from album sales was. "We were making about thirty-three cents an album" with Warners, Rakow told the *Wall Street Journal* in 1974. "Now we make about a dollar twenty-two an album."

By controlling every aspect of an album's production, manufacturing and distribution, Rakow was also able to devise creative ways to make and save money for the band. For example, when *Wake of the Flood* came out, Rakow learned that the price for printing two million covers was only five thousand dollars more than printing the million they actually needed, so he ordered the extra covers made. "Then, a few years later, when we needed money," Rakow relates, "I ordered the records to fill the covers from our pressing plant in Santa Maria at a special rate. I had the records drilled as cutouts [overstock] before they were even shrink-wrapped, and then I sold them all to a cutout operation in Philadelphia for ninety-five cents apiece and made five hundred thousand dollars in one day. They sold them in stores for two dollars apiece, so in the end almost two million copies of *Wake of the Flood* were sold."

According to Rakow, Garcia was fascinated by these kinds of financial machinations. "I've heard people say that Jerry was impressed with me because I had Wall Street experience. That's bullshit. Jerry wouldn't know Wall Street if it fell on him. He never owned a stock in his life, at least when I knew him. But I regarded business as an art form and a game and he loved that, and that's why I intrigued him. We weren't just doing a business; it was a way to employ people—our friends. It was to answer a question that we asked ourselves often: 'Who are we and what are we? Are we dessert on an already maggot-ridden, decadent capitalist table, or are we appetizers on the banquet of the new form?' I phrased it one time stoned on acid, and we asked it to ourselves over and over and over for ten years."

Not everyone in the Dead organization was thrilled with Rakow's crafty gamesmanship or the strong influence he apparently had over Garcia. Rakow was a schemer and a dealmaker—he bragged about his exploits—and a couple of bandmembers were privately nervous about where Rakow might lead them. Dave Parker, who had helped lead the band out of their financial hole and handled some of their day-to-day business affairs, was among those who were suspicious.

"Rakow was very sharp and very adept at getting people's confidence," he says. "He became close to Jerry and things took a different direction after that. I can't say I was comfortable with it.

"Jerry was always willing to go along and trust somebody who maybe other people wouldn't have trusted. You know how it is in the rock 'n' roll world—there are all sorts of characters. A good rap was presented to Garcia, he was sold on it and he made the decision to trust that it was going to happen and happen right."

"Rakow had lots of great energy for a lot of things, and then terrible energy for other stuff; it was a strange, unpredictable mixture," Mountain Girl says. "But it was energy that the group seemed to need—that Pranksteresque business. He was utilitarian, practical, but crazy. He seemed harmless at the time. He was an element, a character, another escapee from New York."

The Dead played its final shows of 1973 in mid-December (it was one of the few years the group didn't play on New Year's Eve), and shortly after returning to California, Garcia began work on his second solo album, which would be one of the first releases on a new Grateful Dead subsidiary label, called Round Records, designed to put out solo projects by the bandmembers. (Rakow says the reason the Dead's record companies had such "lame, unimaginative" names was "nobody could ever agree on *anything*. 'Okay, records *are* round.' That they agreed on.") Whereas Grateful Dead Records was a partnership involving ten people—the six bandmembers, Rakow, Jon McIntire, Rock Scully and Alan Trist—Round was owned entirely by Garcia and Rakow because "some of the Dead don't want a risk," Rakow told *Rolling Stone* at the time. "Garcia likes risks, likes worries, so he can always be on the edge."

The approach Garcia took on his second album was the polar opposite of the way he'd made the first one: he put it almost entirely in the hands of John Kahn, allowing his friend to help choose material and select the musicians who would be on the record. "He was game to try something different," Kahn said, "and it was almost like he didn't want to be the boss on it.

"We picked out the songs together. I would present him with a bunch of ideas, he'd take the ones he liked and work on those. It was mainly stuff that he wouldn't ordinarily have thought of, and I think that was part of the challenge for him—to try something that was really new to him, he chose [Irving Berlin's] 'Russian Lullaby.' He had a record of Oscar Aleman doing it in this weird guitar trio. Jerry told me it was Hitler's favorite song."

A few of the songs the pair chose included Smokey Robinson's "When the Hunter Gets Captured by the Game," Chuck Berry's "Let It Rock," the Stones' "Let's Spend the Night Together," Van Morrison's "He Ain't Give You None," Dr. John's "What Goes Around," Peter Rowan's "Mississippi Moon" and a Hunter-Kahn original called "Midnight Town." It was a very broad range of styles, and Kahn "cast" every song differently. Several songs had horn arrangements, "Mississippi Moon" utilized a full string section, and on a few tunes Kahn brought in the ace L.A. session guitarist Larry Carlton to play rhythm guitar. Merl Saunders appeared on several cuts, Richard Greene fiddled on two, and this was the record where Garcia and Kahn first encountered Ron Tutt, Elvis Presley's outstanding drummer, who joined Garcia's solo group later.

While the various bandmembers were engaged in solo pursuits of one kind or another at the beginning of 1974, the Dead's sound wizards were busy developing the famous "Wall of Sound"—a sound reinforcement system larger than any ever built before, expressly designed to deliver clean, loud audio in large venues such as stadiums and basketball arenas. It was the culmination of theories that the Dead's technical gurus had been exploring and refining for years. As Dan Healy put it, "We became used to a quality of sound that was just not attainable via rental systems. We realized that if we didn't do it ourselves, it wouldn't sound good. We thought, 'For the prices we're paying to rent equipment that sounds shitty, we could develop our own stuff,' so we did."

The original idea for the Wall of Sound was probably Owsley's, though it stemmed from hours and hours of conversations with sound and electronics experts like Ron Wickersham, Rick Turner, John Curl, Bob Matthews, John Meyer, Dan Healy and others. Owsley believed that they could "build an integrated system where every instrument has its own amplification, all set up behind the band without any separate onstage monitors," he said in 1991. "It's a single, big system, like a band playing in a club only larger, and the musicians can all adjust everything, including their vocal level, by having a single source; by using this point-source thing."

The system debuted on March 23, 1974, at the Cow Palace in San Francisco—a concert formally dubbed the Sound Test. It was the Dead's first arena show in the Bay Area, where they normally played at the 5,000-seat Winterland, and more than a few local Deadheads didn't like this development at all—they saw the Wall of Sound as a sellout by the Dead—an excuse to play larger venues, rather than a response to the necessity of doing so. Still, nearly everyone agreed that the system delivered incredibly clear sound to almost every nook and cranny in the notoriously bad-sounding arena, and fears that the Dead would now play only giant shows proved unfounded—their next Bay Area shows were back at Winterland.

Rising more than 30 feet at the rear of the Cow Palace stage, the Wall of Sound incorporated 480 loudpeakers stacked in columns behind the band. By July, there would be 640 speakers powered by 48 amplifiers in the setup. It required a crew of 16 to transport and maintain it, adding tremendous overhead to an already expensive road operation—and this at a time when the Grateful Dead were trying hard to keep their ticket prices low.

"It was highly impractical to try to move it around—set it up, tear it down and move to the next city," Dan Healy recalled. "We had two complete stages and they were *extremely* complicated; it cost close to $200,000 for the two stages. So when we went out on tour, the stages would leapfrog. We'd set one up in this city, while the other one went to the next city. You talk about out of hand . . ." (The practice of having two identical setups became common with stadium acts like the Rolling Stones and Pink Floyd in the late '80s.)

"But the bottom line was it sounded *great*," Healy added. "I think it raised the consciousness of the [touring sound] industry and set new standards and exemplified the direction it really should be going in. I think it changed the whole face of the audio world. I know for a fact that a lot of major sound companies changed their designs and changed their array theories after we did that. It was an experiment. But it was magnificent in its glory, and I loved every second of it."

By this time, too, Garcia had changed his guitar sound again, moving away from Fender Stratocasters to a custom guitar made by a Northern California luthier named Doug Irwin. Garcia said he liked Irwin's axes because they combined some of the best sonic elements of Gibson and Fender electrics while also having their own character. "His guitars have great hands," Garcia noted. "My hand falls upon one of them and it says, 'Play me,' and it's one of those things not all guitars do." Garcia played Irwin guitars from 1973 on, with just a couple of short periods trying other models.

As usual, the Dead introduced several new songs at the beginning of their touring year. In late February at Winterland, Garcia rolled out three songs he'd written with Hunter, who was now splitting his time between Marin County and England.

"U.S. Blues" represented a serious reworking of "Wave That Flag," which had quietly slipped out of the repertoire in June of 1973. It retained the original song's quick rhyming scheme: "Back to back / Chicken shack / Son of a gun / Better change your act . . ." But it added an opaque commentary about the Dead's place in an America that was being ripped apart by the Watergate scandal, which was escalating almost daily, steaming inexorably toward Richard Nixon's resignation in August 1974:

> I'm Uncle Sam / That's who I am
> Been hiding out / in a rock 'n' roll band
> Shake the hand / that shook the hand
> Of P. T. Barnum / and Charlie Chan . . .
>
> Wave that flag
> Wave it wide and high
> Summertime done
> Come and gone
> My oh my

Though there was a cynical edge to "U.S. Blues," the music was exuberant and the song quickly became an anthem of sorts for the Dead—a declaration that their traveling circus was as American as apple pie.

The ballad "Ship of Fools" also worked well as oblique reflection on the U.S. political situation or the confusing state of affairs in the Grateful Dead or any other organization, for that matter.

> The bottles stand as empty
> As they was filled before
> Time there was a-plenty
> But from that cup no more
> Though I could not caution all
> I still might warn a few:
> Don't lend your hand to raise no flag
> Atop no ship of fools . . .

Musically, it was one of Garcia's most conventional tunes—George Jones could easily have sung "Ship of Fools." When Elvis Costello did cover the song in the late '80s he played up its honky-tonk side to great effect.

"It Must Have Been the Roses," with words and music by Hunter, also had a country feel, though the lyrics came straight from the mythic world Garcia described earlier. As in "Ship of Fools," there's a sense of nonspecific place and time, the past and present floating in the air like vapors, secrets revealed yet others barely hinted at remaining hidden. Hunter once described "Roses" as "my Faulknerian song."

The third new Hunter-Garcia song was "Scarlet Begonias," a bright and infectious polyrhythmic tune that "definitely has a little Caribbean thing to it, though nothing specific," as Garcia noted. Hunter's lyrics playfully tell the story of a chance encounter with a free-spirited girl in London—a giddy mix of images about fate, desire, temptation, memory and expectation. Do they or don't they? That is the question. Hunter, ever the teasing obscurant, provides no answers.

With its irresistible rhythmic momentum, generous space for melodic guitar solos, and long, spacey instrumental coda, "Scarlet Begonias" fast became a favorite of most Deadheads, as eagerly anticipated as songs like "Uncle John's Band," "Sugar Magnolia" and "China Cat Sunflower," to name three sure-fire crowd-pleasers. The fans seemed to particularly enjoy the spirit of the song's final verse, which many took to be an affirmation of the magical bond between the Dead and Deadheads at a show:

The wind in the willows played "Tea for Two"
The sky was yellow and the sun was blue
Strangers stoppin' strangers
Just to shake their hands
Everybody's playing
In the Heart of Gold Band
Heart of Gold Band

Although the Dead's sound changed noticeably from year to year during their first decade—either because of personnel changes or additions and/or subtractions to and from the repertoire—the essential musical character of the 1973 and 1974 shows was similar. In those years the band scattered plenty of short tunes in their sets, but there were probably more jamming songs those years than any since 1968. And the sheer number and variety of songs that took the band into interesting jamming spaces was unequaled in their history before or after: "Eyes of the World," "Scarlet Begonias," "Truckin'," "The Other One," "Here Comes Sunshine," "Weather Report Suite," "China Cat Sunflower" > "I Know You Rider," "Dark Star," "Playing in the Band"—any one of those, each different from the other in almost every way—was a guaranteed thrill ride that was unique every time and showed the Dead at their improvisational best. There is a large contingent of Deadheads who argue fairly persuasively that 1972 to 1974 was the Dead's most exciting and creative period. Even vaultmaster Dick Latvala, the acidhead keeper of the spirit of '68, says, "Though in my soul I'm an *Anthem*-era man—'That's It for the Other One' and 'Dark Star' and 'China Cat'—I think '73 was the best year the Dead ever had. There were so many unique vehicles for jamming that year. They *always* kept a space where they could express that psychedelic side."

After the Sound Test in late March, the Dead went into CBS Studios in San Francisco to record a new album, *Grateful Dead from the Mars Hotel* (the Mars Hotel was a transients' hotel near the studio). As with *Wake of the Flood*, the band recorded their basic tracks live and then added overdubs—and since they were able to synchronize two sixteen-track machines, they had plenty of room for textural elements to give the songs more depth. Garcia had five tunes on the album: "Scarlet Begonias"; "China Doll," which was put in a mainly acoustic setting, with an exquisite harpsichord part by Keith Godchaux; "U.S. Blues," which was the album's radio hit; "Loose Lucy" and Ship of Fools." The remaining three songs had never been played live before: Weir and Barlow's "Money Money"; and two songs by Phil and Bobby Petersen, featuring Lesh's first lead vocals since "Box of Rain"—the country tune "Pride of Cucamonga" and "Unbroken Chain," which contained the best jamming the Dead had put on a studio record since the *Ace* version of "Playing in the Band."

The album was all over the map stylistically—like a Dead show—but the performances were superb, the vocals strong and it was loaded with imaginative guitar effects, nifty percussion parts and *many* different keyboard sounds—this was the album where Keith Godchaux really came into his own as a studio player. Guests included John McFee of the Marin-based country/R&B band Clover on pedal steel guitar (Garcia deemed himself too rusty to handle any steel parts) and Ned Lagin on synthesizer. (Lagin also occasionally played electronic space music in duets with Phil onstage at a number of '74 Dead concerts, usually as a miniset between the first and second Dead sets.)

From the Mars Hotel was one of three albums to come from the Dead camp in June 1974. The other two were the first releases on Round Records—Robert Hunter's impressive debut, *Tales of the Great Rum Runners*, recorded at Mickey Hart's barn studio with a slew of Marin County musicians and Garcia helping out on the mix; and Garcia's second LP, inexplicably titled *Garcia*, like his first album. (It later became known as *Compliments of Garcia*, after a sticker that was put on radio station promotional copies; the currently available CD is simply called *Compliments*.) *Mars Hotel* sold briskly as expected, but Garcia's record was a commercial disappointment. FM radio largely ignored it, and Deadheads gave it mixed reviews—the most common complaints were that there were no extended guitar solos (nine of the ten songs were under four minutes), and since the instrumentation on the record varied so much from track to track, it didn't feel as if it had been made by Garcia's group. Still, there were a few standout tracks. A funky reading of Little Milton's "That's What Love Will Make You Do" contained a crisp Garcia solo; Albert Washington's "Turn On the Bright Lights" gave Garcia room to lay down a scorching guitar line that soared above the beefy horn arrangement; and "Russian Lullaby" featured Garcia's only recorded work on classical guitar.

Deadheads hungry to hear Garcia really cut loose and jam bought copies of a double LP by the Saunders-Garcia-Kahn-Vitt club band called *Live at Keystone*, recorded in Berkeley in July 1973 but released in the spring of 1974 as part of Merl Saunders's deal with Fantasy Records. The album marvelously captured the spirit of that quartet at its peak (before Vitt left to join the Sons of Champlin), as they roamed through myriad genres in their typically relaxed but still intense fashion. There was an eighteen-minute workout on "My Funny Valentine" that would have had Rodgers and Hart scratching their heads; an ultra-funky version of Lightnin' Hopkins's "Someday Baby"; extended takes on "The Harder They Come" and Dylan's "Positively 4th Street" (with David Grisman helping out on mandolin); and what remains one of Garcia's most moving performances, "Like a Road," the Dan Penn–Don Nix tune originally cut by Albert King.

The Saunders-Garcia group in the first half of 1974 found Bill Kreutzmann in the drummer's seat and Martin Fierro playing reeds occasionally, sharing the solo spotlight with Jerry and Merl. In the spring of 1974 Garcia also played banjo and guitar with a short-lived, eclectic acoustic group called the Great American String Band, whose membership variously included David Grisman, Richard Greene, Taj Mahal on bass and vocals, Sandy Rothman on guitar and vocals, guitarist/singer David Nichtern and bassist Buell Neudlinger. Despite the presence of three Old and in the Way alumni, the band played very few bluegrass tunes. Mainly they dabbled in blues, old-timey and Djangoesque swing jazz. Garcia played only about a dozen gigs with the group—including one where they opened for the Grateful Dead in a stadium at the University of California at Santa Barbara—"and then we went into all sorts of different groups without Jerry," says Richard Greene. "One of them was the Great American Music Band, which later evolved into the David Grisman Quintet."

Beginning in July 1974 the Saunders-Garcia band had a slightly altered lineup—with Kahn, Fierro and jazz/R&B drummer Paul Humphrey—and, for the first time, a name: the Legion of Mary. "The name was my idea, but it backfired on us," Kahn said. "We played our first gig under that name at the Keystone Berkeley and these people showed up who were really part of this religious group called the Legion of Mary. I thought I'd made it up! They were a pretty obscure group. They had a brochure that had this picture of these medieval people and then some guy in a suit. I'm not sure what that was all about. Anyway, they came to listen to us and they ended up liking us so they let us use their name. At the same time, we realized we probably didn't want to go under that name *too* long; it was a little weird."

The Legion of Mary's music was a slight departure from the past Saunders-Garcia bands in that Martin Fierro's role was expanded and the jams sometimes took jazzier turns. Fierro also brought in a few new songs. Despite Garcia's earlier pledge to keep his solo groups local, he took the Legion of Mary out on a Northeastern tour in the fall of 1975, but stuck to clubs and small theaters exclusively in an attempt to keep it low-key. It was at one of those shows, at a trendy New York rock club called the Bottom Line, that Garcia got to meet one of his favorite musicians, former Beatle John Lennon.

"He came backstage and Jerry introduced him to us and I couldn't speak, man," says Fierro. "My voice left me. He was one of my biggest heroes and I couldn't talk. I was like a drugstore Indian. Then he came back with us to the hotel in the limo. No guards, no Yoko, just him. And he partied with us for a while."

John Kahn's memory of the evening was less starry-eyed, however. "My perspective was a little off-base because I'd dropped a TV set on my hand that morning and I'd gotten a pain pill from the Hell's Angels," he said. "So I wasn't in the best shape. Lennon was sort of in disguise and he was with this really weird guy I didn't know. I heard from Richard Loren, I think it was, that Lennon asked if there was a guitar there that was louder than Garcia's. He wanted to sit in. Well, that got back to Jerry, and Jerry said, 'No, fuck him.' Later, Lennon came down to the dressing room and was there for a long time; a couple of hours. He was real drunk and was a little belligerent. He kept referring to Jerry as 'J.C.,' which I took to mean Jesus Christ, like making fun of Jerry. That night Lennon ended up with the Hell's Angels and we had a particularly sleazy, motley group of Hell's Angels with us. Years later I got asked to play with him by a guy in his band, Jesse Davis, but it didn't work out. I would have liked to. I liked his music a lot. And basically I thought he was really cool, even though he was not cool when we met him. But I'm sure that sort of thing happens all the time. You meet a guy under the wrong circumstances . . ."

Meanwhile, the Grateful Dead juggernaut kept on rolling, packing stadiums and arenas from the middle of May through the beginning of August— just twenty-four shows, with plenty of breaks in the schedule. Everywhere the tour went, the Wall of Sound drew rave reviews from Deadheads for both its clarity and its impressive and imposing physical presence. But traveling with the Wall of Sound turned out to be enormously expensive and the band quickly found that their coffers were being depleted almost as fast as they were filled. Off the road, expenses were rising, too. Salaries continued to escalate, as did the size of the payroll. The two record companies needed money to pay for studio time and product manufacturing, and everyone in the group seemed to have personal needs that required money, whether it was Weir building a recording studio adjoining his sylvan house on the slopes of Mount Tamalpais, or a new car for Billy.

There was also another significant drain on the Dead's resources that didn't have anything to do with concerts, the record company or the handful of auxiliary businesses the Dead were supporting, and that was cocaine. When coke first came into the Dead's world in the late '60s it was viewed as an exotic delight, a perk of the rock 'n' roll lifestyle; a pick-me-up—a beneficial road tool. But through the early '70s, more and more coke came into the Dead scene, some of it brought in by various millionaire Dead fans (a few of whom also got into heroin later). By 1974 it was a big problem. Not only was the white powder very expensive, it was so psychologically addictive that most of the people in the Dead scene who got into using it regularly used too much of it, and it made many of them irritable and paranoid. And it attracted a sleazy element to the Dead's backstage that wasn't eradicated for many years—most coke dealers were *not* cool people.

Unfortunately, Jerry Garcia *loved* cocaine.

"At first it seemed like this *neat shit,* man," John Dawson says. "It cost a whole lot of money and it was really subtle. It was one of those things where you didn't particularly notice it until you'd had too much of it, and then it was like having a hand grab you at the back of the neck. In the beginning it was a treat when it was there and it wasn't a big deal when it wasn't there—'Oh man, you've got some cocaine? Far out! Wow, thanks!' You'd snort it and go on your merry way."

"I first noticed it in '69 or '70," Mountain Girl says. "It was shown to me with considerable excitement: 'This stuff is really great!' I tried it and it didn't do a thing for me at all. It made me so grouchy I couldn't stand myself. I really got unfriendly. It's bad enough being me without that. I'm already rude and sharp-tongued enough without having to get into actively disliking everyone! Compared to LSD or pot, it just had no life for me.

"But Jerry and Hunter liked it, and the crew guys liked it, and it pretty much fell on gender lines for a long time. The guys were sneaking off and snorting coke and the gals were home. The guys had always pretty much been in charge of the procurement, so it also bypassed me.

"Of course in those days we didn't know as much about it as we do now," she continues. "Medical professionals said it wasn't so bad, and various Indians do it every day and live to be ninety-five years old and have legs like gazelles, so they rhapsodized about it that way."

"Cocaine definitely did change things in the scene," comments Richard Loren. "If you're a greedy person, it's only going to make you more greedy. It's like Robin Williams said: 'Cocaine is God's way of telling you you're making too much money.' What happened during that period is a lot of money went to cocaine, and some decisions had to be made based solely on money that wouldn't normally have been made if a lot of money wasn't needed. A lot of money went out and it needed to be replaced. How is that money replaced? Play bigger gigs, put more stress on the managers to make more money. 'Why do you need more money? Five years ago things were good: Okay, you had a broken-down car, but you got high, the sun was shining; it was wonderful.' That's not to say that cocaine was all bad. It kept people awake a lot longer. It got people's minds thinking. I think at first it was a genuinely communicative drug. But it was a double-edged sword."

"Cocaine really subverted a lot of good people and fucked up the '60s in a major way by creating a lot of chaos and sickness," Mountain Girl says. "I hated it! It really ruined our lives. If anything ruined our lives it was cocaine. Jerry and I had fights about it. Coke makes you think you know it all and it makes you shoot your mouth off and it makes you hate everybody the next day. It was the end of the open heart. Instead, everybody went into the bathroom [to snort it]. People got greedy about it and it never had that warm, social thing that pot had. It was so subtle at first but it got to be so pervasive; it was *everywhere*."

Bandmembers, managers, crew, girlfriends—everyone was touched by cocaine to some degree. Some people handled it okay, others were pitched into a downward spiral because of it. It's difficult to assess how cocaine affected the Dead's music in the early '70s, because there wasn't a time in that era when most of the band didn't use it. Did they play faster? Did it give them the energy they needed to play four-hour shows? Did it affect the direction of the songwriting at all? We'll never know. Garcia always maintained that *none* of the drugs he took after his early LSD days had much of an effect on his music.

If we're to believe Rock Scully's fascinating but factually dubious memoir, *Living with the Dead*, the cocaine issue came to a head when the Grateful Dead went to Europe in September 1974. According to Scully's lively account, when they got to England a few days before the first concert at the historic Alexandra Palace, they were offered *mounds* of cocaine by their wealthy British hosts, which, on top of the LSD that was also going around, made things a little crazy. Finally, Scully writes, Rex Jackson, one of the Dead's senior roadies, who'd been with the band since 1968, laid it on the line backstage at a sound check before the first London show. He challenged everyone to give up cocaine and to dump out their stash in a pile *right there*. The band and crew grumbled but agreed, and eventually they burned the snowy mountain.

To what degree this colorful tale is accurate is hard to say without corroborating eyewitness accounts (we'll have to wait for the *crew* memoirs). But Steve Brown, who was on the tour working for Grateful Dead Records, says, "A lot of that stuff in Rock's book is true. There was a very heavy scene that went down when we got over there initially. We sent a lot of marijuana over there in the speakers; it was made available to us for both use and trade for whatever else we might want. Then, when we got over there, people were being pulled on right away to go out and party and to hang out with certain crowds. Right away it was like, 'The Grateful Dead from San Francisco are here: Let's party!' But there was also a thing of various people being uptight and strung out with their own drug habits at that point. And the cocaine was definitely a problem.

"I think what they went through," Brown continues, "is something that had to happen at some point, whether it was the sacrificial bonfire or the massive flushing of the toilets, getting rid of stuff that way—I remember hearing people in the rooms shouting, 'Flush it! Flush it!' It was like an early intervention on themselves brought on by their own paranoid delusions or whatever. It was a strange little moment in time. And this was the *beginning* of the tour. This isn't the end when you've had enough and you're ready to go home. This is when you're just getting started."

In any case, the Dead played three outstanding shows at the Alexandra Palace, as documented on *Dick's Picks Volume Seven,* a three-CD set released in 1997. The rest of the tour, which consisted of just one show in Germany and three in France, was considerably calmer than those first days in London. Some people were still doing coke (it was hard to stay away from those dealers who wanted to *give* it to them), but it was curtailed considerably. Because they were carting the thirty-eight-ton Wall of Sound around, the band played larger venues than on the 1972 tour, but the tour didn't draw huge crowds, so it ended up costing the Dead quite a bit—and of course this time Warner Bros. wasn't there helping to foot the bill. (This time, too, the Dead left the family at home. That may be another reason things spun out of control—too many unsupervised guys on the prowl.)

The Dead's original plan for 1974 called for them to tour through the autumn and into the first weeks of 1975, but at some point they decided they'd had enough. The cost of keeping the Wall of Sound on the road was prohibitive, the venues the band was forced to play to sustain their scene were getting bigger and bigger, people were feeling burned out from ten years of nearly constant touring and too many people had attached themselves to the humongous Grateful Dead touring machine—"the Grateful Dead tit," as John Kahn referred to it. So they made a decision: they would stop performing for an indefinite period, take some time to work on individual projects, make a record without the pressure of having to go out on the road every few weeks, and assess where they'd been and where they were going to see if they could bring the beast under control—get away from "the mega-gig, the huge stadium," as Garcia later put it.

"That represented the end of the line, developmentally, of what's there in America," he said. "You can't go anywhere else; you can't get any bigger. So what we would like to do is improve the quality of the experience both on the level of what we're doing amongst ourselves and how we interact with the audience, and what the audience experiences when we're there. In that sense we're the Don Quixotes of rock 'n' roll. We're doing something nobody else cares to do, which is trying to figure out how to make the experience we value and which our audience values something that's more in line with what it feels like, which is a sort of positive outpouring of good energy. That's the reason we stopped—to think about it."

In another interview he said, "Fame and success are human-eaters. They'd like for you to go for it. They love it when you go to Hollywood and get your-self a comfortable pad and a swimming pool and get into the pleasure palace trip. And either you go for it or you say, 'No, I don't want that.' "

Plans for a late fall/winter tour were abruptly scrapped, and instead the Dead booked five consecutive nights at Winterland, October 16–20. Tickets for the final show of the series were ominously stamped with the words THE LAST ONE, and while optimistic Deadheads fully believed the break from perform-ing was a hiatus rather than a retirement, no one knew for sure whether the Dead would ever come back.

Because the future *was* unclear, the Dead decided they should document the shows somehow, so they turned to a New York filmmaker named Leon Gast to assist them. Gast, who won an Oscar in 1997 for *When We Were Kings*, his documentary about the 1974 Muhammad Ali–George Foreman heavyweight championship match in Zaire, first contacted Garcia and Ron Rakow in early 1973 to see if they would help finance a documentary he'd been working on about the Hell's Angels. Sandy Alexander, president of the New York chapter of the motorcycle club, introduced Gast to Garcia and Rakow, "and we hit it off," Gast says. "Jerry came by one day, all alone, to look at what we had. I showed him maybe an hour of material and he loved it. Rakow loved it, too, and he said, 'Well, what do we do?' We shook hands and that night we made a deal and they agreed to provide the financing to com-plete the film, which I believe was about $300,000." Garcia also agreed to ap-pear in the film, speaking on camera about the Angels and playing with the Saunders-Garcia band during a September '73 Hell's Angels "Pirate Party" aboard the ferryboat SS *Bay Belle* circling around Manhattan—it was that band's first appearance outside of the Bay Area.

When Rakow and Garcia originally approached Gast about shooting the October '74 Winterland shows, "They were talking about doing a video shoot," Gast says. "They wanted to document these shows, because, as I understood it, they were breaking up. But I said, 'Why do a video? Let's do a film thing.' So I showed them some James Brown footage that I'd just shot in Africa [which ended up in *When We Were Kings*] and they were impressed. So we went from doing a $40,000 video to a $1.2 million film. Film shooting was budgeted for $250,000 and it came in right there."

Gast assembled a crew of nine cameramen to cover every aspect of the shows, from people waiting in line outside to Deadheads dancing in the hall-ways or buying snacks during the show to family, friends and crew members hanging around backstage. There were a couple of fixed cameras in the audi-ence shooting the action onstage, one mounted on a crane on one side of the stage, and also cameramen dressed head to toe in black wandering around the edges of the stage to capture close-ups of the bandmembers.

"Jerry's big thing was that he wanted the cameras to be as unobtrusive as possible," says Emily Craig, who was married to Rakow and who worked on the postproduction of the film. "He didn't want the film to get in the way of people having a good time and feeling like they were at a regular Dead show, and I think that if you look at the movie, what's there *is* like a regular Dead show." (That said, many who attended the shows did find the cameras and lights on the audience rather invasive.)

Predictably, the Dead made no real concessions to the presence of the film crew. They just went out and played five strong shows so there would be lots of good material to put into the film. And for their part, the Dead's stage crew made a point of giving the cameramen a taste of Grateful Dead craziness: "I think almost everybody got dosed [with LSD] every single night," Gast says with a laugh. "I spoke to the Dead and said, 'I don't know who's going to be able to handle it and who won't, but you're paying a lot of money to do this, so don't fuck around.' Okay, night number one it was very easy to determine when people got dosed, because it was in the coffee urns and the punch bowl. There was a little army of dosers going around. Second night they took the paper cups out of the coffee machine and put a little drop in each one and put them back. Another night they put it in oranges and bananas with hypodermic needles. The last night they had big buckets backstage filled with Coca-Cola and beer, and supposedly there was acid in the bottom of the barrels so you'd get dosed when you put your arm down into it. The last night, too, [roadie] Steve Parish had the 'L' and you had to lick a drop to get onstage. I remember being on the the headset and calling for Don [Lenzer, one of the on-stage cameramen], 'Oh Don! Don, can you . . .' and I looked up and Don was just sitting on the stage with his camera in his lap, listening to the music. It was quite an experience, but everybody did a great job considering."

The final night was a three-set extravaganza in which virtually every member of the Dead family—including the band—and a large segment of the audience took acid; after all, that was an essential part of the Dead's roots. And for old time's sake Mickey Hart rejoined the band for part of the show and smashed away at his kit as if he'd never left. Sometime after two in the morning, the band assembled onstage to sing a final a cappella version of the old Bahamian spiritual "We Bid You Goodnight," and then it was over. A shower of roses were flung onto the stage and thousands of Deadheads began to file out of Winterland, while hundreds more stuck around as long as they were allowed to, soaking up the vibe of the Dead at Winterland as long as they could, and watching the road crew begin to dismantle the Wall of Sound for what might be the last time.

CHAPTER 14

Beneath the
Sweet Calm Face
of the Sea

Jerry and Mountain Girl's second baby girl, Theresa (aka Trixie), was born in September 1974 while the Grateful Dead were on tour in Europe. This should have been a cause for grand celebration, but by the fall of 1974, the pair's relationship had deteriorated considerably and Jerry was spending more and more time out of the house, mostly working on one musical project after another. M.G. knew that Jerry had been unfaithful to her at different times during the previous couple of years—"catting around," she calls it—but she chalked that up partly to the vicissitudes of the rock 'n' roll lifestyle. And most of Garcia's romantic conquests weren't relationships per se.

Still, M.G. says, "He was sleeping and eating and changing his clothes at home; hanging out for a few hours during the day. That was his routine. It was comfortable and easy. I didn't expect him to take out the garbage. And he was great with the kids. He would hang out with them. He used to sing to them. I remember he worked out 'Russian Lullaby' in front of them."

Around the time of the Europe tour, however, "I knew something was wrong because he started being brief with me," M.G. says, "and then he'd come home and say some of the weirdest shit—anti-family things like, 'Having a family is probably going to ruin my artistic career.' He didn't mean it; he was just trying it out. He'd make these weird statements and then he'd watch me to see what I said. So I'd either refute it or be so startled by it I'd be undone by it."

What M.G. didn't know was that Jerry was falling in love with another woman, an aspiring filmmaker named Deborah Koons. She was a few years younger than Jerry, the daughter of wealthy Cincinnati professionals—John Fletcher Koons III was a successful businessman and his wife, Patricia Boyle, was a lawyer. Deborah's grandfather, John Koons Jr., had made his fortune heading the local Burger Brewing Company and a Pepsi bottling concern, and he was also active in various civic affairs. In 1949 the Koons family was listed in Cincinnati's Blue Book social register for the first time. Deborah, her brother, John, and sister, Christina, were brought up in one of the city's toniest neighborhoods. She attended private schools, and after graduating from Hillsdale prep school she went to the University of North Carolina at Chapel Hill from 1967 to 1971, majoring in radio-TV-film. Early on she had set her sights on a career in filmmaking.

She first saw the Dead in the late '60s and didn't like them. But in March 1973 she attended a concert at the Nassau Coliseum and, after that show, "someone suggested that I ride back to Manhattan with the band and crew on their bus, and so I got on and sat next to Jerry and we had a conversation and struck up kind of a friendship. I mentioned that I was leaving in a few days to go to Europe for a year and when we parted he gave me his address [actually, the Dead's post office box] and asked me to write him."

She says the two exchanged half a dozen letters while Deborah was in Europe, and when she moved back to the United States around the middle of 1974, settling in New York, she contacted Jerry again, and shortly after that the two began a clandestine relationship. Deborah then moved to California and the pair started seeing each other regularly, though Jerry was still nominally living at the Stinson address. She traveled with Garcia during part of the September 1974 European tour, and the guitarist made sure that when postproduction on the Grateful Dead movie began, Deborah had a role to play—she's listed in the credits under "Script Assistance."

Almost immediately following the Dead's October '74 series at Winterland, Leon Gast had begun to wade through the hundreds of hours of film that had been shot by his nine cameramen. However, when it became clear to him that the Dead, and Garcia in particular, wanted control over editing the film, Gast bowed out of the project and the job of editing fell to Susan Crutcher, who had originally been hired as an assistant editor on the project.

While the long, tedious job of synching the film to audio was going on at a rented Mill Valley house that served as headquarters for the movie's postproduction (the film company was dubbed Round Reels), the Dead began work on their next album at Bob Weir's new home studio. Previous Dead studio records were dominated by songs that had already been played live. For this album—eventually entitled *Blues for Allah*—the band took a new approach: it was built up from nothing in the studio. "We kind of made a ground rule for that record: 'Let's make a record where we get together every day and we don't bring anything in [in advance],' " Garcia said years later. "The whole idea was to get back to that band thing, where the band makes the main contribution to the evolution of the material. So we'd go into the studio, we'd jam for a while, and then if something nice turned up we'd say, 'Well, let's preserve this little hunk and work with it, see if we can't do something with it.' And that's how we did most of that album."

"I would say that it's musically the most adventurous album we've done in a pretty long time," Garcia remarked in an interview during the making of the album. "Our development [historically] has been to synthesize various forms, like playing jazz, playing country and western, playing rhythm and blues and forming combinations of those genres and styles within what we're doing, within our instrumentation. Now we're working on *creating* styles rather than just being eclectic or synthesizing other styles. Thus, it's a little bit more difficult, and considerably more experimental. It's still questionable as to whether the things will be successful musically, but we're sort of into defining new spaces for ourselves musically to go to."

As Phil noted after the album was released, "We wanted to free ourselves from our own clichés, to search for new tonalities, new structures and modalities. I think we succeeded."

Because the band was recording at Weir's house, they didn't have to worry about paying for studio time or hurrying because some other group had a session booked. They were able to dig in and work as long as their stamina (aided by copious amounts of cocaine) allowed—at one point, according to Garcia, they worked fifty hours straight. Of course even recording in a home studio isn't exactly *free:* tape expenses alone ran into many thousands of dollars. But whereas with *Wake of the Flood* and *Mars Hotel* the group rehearsed outside the studio so they could then go in and get good, strong takes right away, the whole point of the *Blues for Allah* experiment was to allow the entire process of musical evolution—from germination to tracking to overdubbing—to occur in the studio environment in a natural way, at its own speed, without the meter running, so to speak.

At the same time that the *Blues for Allah* sessions were taking place in the winter of 1975, four other albums were being readied for release on Round Records, and Garcia played on all of them.

Keith and Donna was the first album by the Godchauxs, and it was literally a homegrown product—"Almost all of it was recorded at our house in Stinson Beach," Donna says. "Bob Matthews brought in a Neve board [recording console] and we had our nine-foot Steinway there and we had our whole living room set up as a recording studio for a while. Jerry was just a couple of minutes away, so it was real easy to get together and work on it."

Keith and Donna wrote almost all the songs on the album—except "Showboat," written by Keith's younger brother Brian, and the rather torpid cover of "River Deep, Mountain High"—and it reflected their passion for gospel music and good-time rock 'n' roll. Naturally Keith's keyboard work infused every track, but Garcia was actually the principal soloist *and* colorist. He played his guitar through several distinctive pedal effects, and on "Every Song I Sing" he laid down his longest slide guitar solo on any studio album. Garcia's singing was also prominent on a pair of songs that hearkened back to the spirit of the great black gospel groups of the '40s and '50s: "Showboat," sung by Keith, was written in the style of an old Golden Gate Quartet or Swan Silvertones number; and the traditional spiritual "Who Was John" found Keith, Donna and Garcia harmonizing quite effectively a cappella.

"There was a period there when Garcia and Keith and I just spent hours and hours and hours listening to tons of different albums of old gospel music— Dorothy Love Coates and the Blind Boys of Alabama; real funky, real spiritual gospel music," Donna says. "We did that for a *long* time, and 'Who Was John' came out of that, though I can't remember who did that before us. We were just in that world all the time for a while. Jerry loved those kind of harmonies."

Old and in the Way was a live album by the defunct group, recorded in October 1973 at the Boarding House by Owsley. Garcia sang lead on two cuts—"Pig in a Pen" and the traditional bluegrass spiritual "White Dove"—and played banjo and sang baritone harmony throughout. The album went on to become a surprise best-seller in the bluegrass community (as well as among Deadheads), which was ironic since Garcia had never been able to sustain a commercially successful bluegrass band in the days when he was more serious about it—Old and in the Way was never more than a sideline for him.

Garcia produced, arranged and played electric and acoustic guitars, pedal steel and various keyboards on Robert Hunter's slicker and more focused second effort, *Tiger Rose.* "I like Garcia's arrangements and production on it, and I like the songs," Hunter said in 1984. "The only thing I can't stand is the vocals on it. I played it for the first time in years the other day and I was horrified." So much so that in 1988 he recut all the lead vocals on the album. In addition to Garcia, the album featured an impressive roster of friends, including Mickey Hart, David Freiberg, Starship keyboardist Pete Sears, David Grisman and New Riders bassist Dave Torbert.

Phil Lesh and Ned Lagin were the driving forces behind *Seastones,* an ambitious and altogether difficult album of electronically treated instrumental and vocal performances. Along with Garcia, the album also featured Grace Slick, David Crosby, David Freiberg, Mickey Hart and Spencer Dryden (the usual suspects), but most of the record was a soft, subtle electronic wash with barely distinguishable parts—sort of a cross between a Grateful Dead "space" jam and the proto–New Age experiments of Brian Eno and Harold Budd. The thirty-six-minute piece that came out as *Seastones* was recorded in February 1975. The CD version, released in 1990, contains a second, even more challenging composition that was recorded in November 1975.

Though the Dead were still "in retirement," in mid-March 1975 Bill Graham coaxed the band into performing at a huge, star-studded benefit concert at Kezar Stadium for the San Francisco Public Schools' cash-strapped sports and music programs. The Dead, billed as Jerry Garcia and Friends, shared the bill with some heavy company—Bob Dylan with Neil Young and three members of the Band, Santana, Jefferson Starship (in one of their first local appearances since the Jefferson Airplane's demise), Tower of Power, the Doobie Brothers (who were hugely popular in the Bay Area at the time), Joan Baez and a few others. Not bad for five bucks at the gate. Marlon Brando spoke, various local sports heroes were introduced, to appreciative applause, and the Grateful Dead played the strangest set of music imaginable, stunning even their most ardent fans with their odd and thoroughly spacey presentation.

They opened their forty-minute segment with an instrumental version of the tune that would later acquire lyrics and be named "Blues for Allah." It was built around a slow, strange, ominous-sounding sequence of notes which then led to other related progressions that were filled with a sort of lumbering drama that fell somewhere between being genuinely fascinating and actually kind of nerve-grating. Much of the mostly non-Deadhead audience didn't know what had hit them—could this really be San Francisco's original good-time party band?—and sort of stood and sat around looking puzzled and bored. That tune then led into another instrumental, written by Phil, called "Stronger Than Dirt," that had some interesting tempo changes and a Latin feel in places—it's one of the jazziest pieces the Dead ever recorded. That piece was split in two by a drum solo by Mickey and Billy—a clear signal that Mickey had come back into the fold—and eventually wound up back at the "Blues for Allah" theme again. The band left the stage to light applause, then returned and played "Johnny B. Goode," which couldn't have been more different from what they had just played—but was exactly what the crowd wanted to hear. All in all it was a rather peculiar afternoon for the Dead in their first appearance since their hiatus began. They certainly couldn't be accused of pandering; quite the opposite.

Garcia spent the first three weeks of April on an extensive tour of the East Coast (and three shows in the Midwest) with the Legion of Mary, which now included Ron Tutt on drums, replacing Paul Humphrey. "Ron Tutt was the Rolls-Royce of drummers," Merl Saunders says. "He said that he didn't know how to play jazz but I thought he could play anything."

At first, playing in theaters and clubs with the Legion of Mary was a nice change of pace for Garcia after the last couple of years of huge gigs with the Grateful Dead. But after a while even that scene got to be fairly crazed. Merl Saunders says that crowds of people approached Garcia wherever he went, which started to wear on him. Eventually Garcia just holed up in his hotel room when he wasn't onstage.

"I'm a person who really likes to be connected to people," Saunders explains. "Jerry liked people, too, but he also sometimes became very distant, and other times he'd be very spacey. He would also sometimes get very angry. You could never tell this when he was playing, because he seemed to always be happy when he was playing, but offstage he'd go through these dramatic changes, like getting in the limo: 'Fuck it. In the car, Merl! Roll up that window! Driver, just drive right through the crowd!' And I'm like, 'Hey man! Cool it!' It bugged him that these people wouldn't give him his space. It became very annoying to him. The people were always well-meaning and all, but he just didn't want to have to deal with it a lot of times. He wanted to play his music and then just be himself. Some days he accepted it, some days he didn't. Some days he had the bullies [his road crew] in front of him to keep people away from him."

The Grateful Dead resumed work on *Blues for Allah* at Weir's studio in early May and continued until the beginning of July. In the middle of that period, the Grateful Dead played their second concert since their "retirement," a benefit concert at Winterland to raise money for the family of San Francisco poster artist Bob Fried, who had died that spring. The top-billed act at "The Bob Fried Memorial Boogie" was supposed to be Jerry Garcia and Friends, but everyone there knew who was really playing that night, and the place was electric with anticipation. There were opening sets by Keith and Donna's band (which included Garcia) and Kingfish, a rock/R&B band featuring Weir, Dave Torbert and an excellent guitarist in the Garcia mold named Robbie Hodinott. Then the Dead came out and opened up with a new Hunter-Garcia song called "Crazy Fingers." Garcia said that in his original setting the song was almost heavy metal, but by the time it reached the concert stage it had been transformed into a floating, lyrical, slow reggae tune that perfectly matched the feeling of the words, which Hunter described as "a collection of haiku-style verses, mostly seventeen syllables, some more successful than others, with no connecting link other than similarity of mood."

> *Your rain falls like crazy fingers*
> *Peals of fragile thunder keeping time*
>
> *Recall the days that still are to come*
> *Some sing blue*

The band ended their first set with a sequence of three new songs that were linked to one another—"Help on the Way" (by Hunter-Garcia, though at this Winterland show it was played without vocals), an intricate instrumental connector by the whole band called "Slipknot" and Hunter-Garcia-Kreutzmann's "Franklin's Tower."

"Help on the Way" was written around one of the jazziest progressions Garcia had ever conceived. It was a little sharp-edged and dissonant, and Hunter's dramatic lyrics matched the urgency of the music:

> *Paradise waits*
> *On the crest of a wave*
> *Her angels in flame*
> *She has no pain*
> *Like a child she is pure*
> *She is not to blame*
>
> *Poised for flight*
> *Wings spread bright*
> *Spring from night*
> *Into the sun*
> *Don't stop to run*

She can fly like a lie
She can't be outdone

"Slipknot" opened and closed with a spidery unison line that had a slightly bebopish feeling, but in the middle it opened up to a jam that ascended noisily in steps and then cruised to other plateaus before finding its way back to the unison line and then falling into "Franklin's Tower," which bounced along happily like a spry bluegrass tune on a chord sequence that Garcia admitted he'd purloined from the "colored girls" section of Lou Reed's "Walk on the Wild Side." The verses consisted of couplets that were rich in metaphor.

Some come to laugh their past away
Some come to make it just one more day
Whichever way your pleasure tends
If you plant ice, you're gonna harvest wind

Roll away the dew
Roll away the dew

The song "Blues for Allah" eventually became a three-part suite in the studio, and it "was a bitch to do," Garcia said. "When we got toward the end of the album, we had some time restrictions and we started working pretty fast. But up until then we'd been pretty leisurely about it. That song was another totally experimental thing. In terms of the melody and the phrasing and all, it was not of this world. It's not in any key and it's not in any time. And all the line lengths are different."

Most of the nearly thirteen-minute "Blues for Allah" suite was instrumental, and the middle section, entitled "Sand Castles and Glass Camels," contained some of the freest playing the Dead ever did in the studio. The Lesh instrumental introduced at Kezar in March was fleshed out and tightened up to become something called "King Solomon's Marbles," and Weir had two songs on the record, a delicate guitar instrumental called "Sage and Spirit" (named for Rock Scully's daughters) and "The Music Never Stopped," a gospel-tinged rocker with John Barlow lyrics that seemed to be about the Dead themselves:

There's a band out on the highway
They're high-steppin' into town
It's a rainbow filled with sound
It's fireworks, calliopes and clowns
Everybody's dancin'

The album as a whole had an intimate feeling to it, and though it took a long time for the tunes to emerge from the jams and become songs, the finished record sounds remarkably like performances of the songs rather than some layered studio product. Dan Healy engineered the disc and managed to capture the interaction between the players in a more immediate and obvious way than some of their studio records had. If the record was lacking anything, it was the warmth and confidence that the band drew from playing songs in front of people for a while before recording them.

While the band was finishing up *Blues for Allah*, Garcia was also putting in long hours in Mill Valley overseeing the construction of the Grateful Dead movie, working closely with Susan Crutcher to determine the shape of the behemoth. "It was fascinating to see what six camera people were doing at the same moment at the same point of a song," Crutcher says of the process of viewing the unedited footage. "We had great camera people so it was almost all really high-quality work. A few of them had never seen a Dead show, so that was quite an experience for them. Since we had five nights of concerts, we had a couple of versions of some favorite songs, and then we had a lot of one-version songs—like 'Uncle John's Band' we had only one version of, which didn't make it because Jerry's view was that even if something was very strong visually, if he wasn't completely happy with it musically, he didn't want to use it. It also took him a while to get used to looking at himself on camera. But actually he was good about that; a lot better than a lot of people I've worked with. He was more concerned with his playing."

Crutcher says that Garcia was perhaps most fascinated by the hours of Deadhead footage, since it gave him a glimpse of something he'd never seen—his fans before, during and after a show. "There was so much funny and weird stuff," she notes. "We named everybody: There was 'Moosegirl,' the girl who makes that noise that sounds like a moose call. There was 'Iggy,' who recites this poem in the movie—'Mama Hated Diesels So Bad.' We had names for the dancers. It was fun, because it personalized it for us, and we got to know them. Jerry loved that part of it."

Garcia's creative juices were certainly flowing in mid-1975, but his personal life was in a shambles. "He was gone more than he should have been during that period when he was working a lot on the movie," Mountain Girl says. "I'd go over there to the movie house and people just didn't talk to me; literally didn't talk to me. The vibe was very cool. I had no idea about Deborah or any of that stuff. They all knew and they weren't sure if I knew or not. Nobody had told them. So there was a weird vibe and I didn't go over there much. Plus the kids couldn't really hang out there because there was film and equipment all over the place."

"It was a little awkward for me," Crutcher says, "because Deborah was Jerry's girlfriend but he was still [living] with Mountain Girl. Mountain Girl would come over and put rock salt in the corners of all the rooms to eliminate the evil spirits, and that kind of thing. I think it was a sort of magic thing. It was her way of saying that she knew, without confronting anybody. Then ultimately she did, of course."

Then, M.G. says, "Jerry just kind of vanished with no explanation. I found out where he was and I ran into him. It was very upsetting. Then he came back for a while and he was kind of going back and forth." What was his explanation? "He needed some space. That was actually possible. Home life was getting a little crowded. We had three kids in a two-bedroom house. And I was stubborn. I just stuck to my spot and waited for him to show back up again. I didn't chase him over the hill. A couple of times I sort of chased him down and tried to talk to him, but he was evasive. But then he'd show up at the door and spend some time. He seemed to think he could have it both ways. And he got away with it for a long time.

"I think it was a terrible strain on everybody. I couldn't believe it; it was a nightmare. It was also difficult to find out that everybody knew and hadn't told me."

Eventually Jerry and Deborah moved into a duplex in Tiburon, an upscale Marin community spread along a peninsula that juts into San Francisco Bay near Mill Valley, and Mountain Girl was left to fend for herself and the three girls in Stinson. Steve Brown, who helped move some rented furniture into the Tiburon house, says that Garcia and Deborah seemed to be very happy together. "I think the reason it seemed to work was that Deborah stayed away from the Grateful Dead scene pretty much. I liked Deborah. She was very nice to me and was a very pleasant person to be around. There was definitely that kind of puppy love thing of when people are first together; they were a cute couple and there was a lot of affectionate goo-goo eyeing and stuff. They were into a lot of the same things; some of the same writers and science fiction and film, of course. But she was pretty smart and stayed out of any real obvious situations that would cross any of the other old camp of Mountain Girl family people; women particularly. She kept a pretty low profile."

"She was a strange bird," comments Donna (Godchaux) MacKay. "There was kind of a seductive mystery about her, but it was really no mystery—she was just very inward. Everything that was in Jerry that was secretly very inward was attracted to that. He might have been very outgoing, but that's when he wanted to be. When he didn't want to be, we all know, Jerry could be very . . . 'I don't want you to be in my world and don't you *dare* try to get in!' He wouldn't say that, of course, but he'd get that look on his face. He could slam that door absolutely shut. That's just the way it was. And I think that was part of his attraction to her. So much of his world was the other [outgoing side] that she was a 'safe place' to be inward with." Donna, too, remembers that the couple "kept to themselves most of the time."

However, as M.G. notes, "There were a number of confrontations. We had a scene in Weir's studio on Jerry's birthday [in August 1975]. Annabelle wanted to give Jerry a birthday present, so I pulled myself together and went over there with Annabelle and Trixie either on his birthday or the next day. I'd been pretty freaked out for a while. So I showed up and I was talking to Jerry, and Deborah came into the room and sat down and smiled at me, and I just *lost* it. There was something about her that really made me upset. The stakes just seemed so high all of a sudden and I grabbed her and threw her out of there and broke the door off the hinges in the process. I created a huge hysterical scene."

The Grateful Dead made two more appearances in 1975. On August 13 they played a private, invitation-only party at the 650-seat Great American Music Hall to celebrate the release of *Blues for Allah*. This was the smallest show the Dead had played since the late '60s. The concert was broadcast nationally a couple of weeks later over the Metromedia radio network, so the Dead got some excellent publicity for their new record. The new songs were different from any the band had written before, yet they still sounded completely natural surrounded by other Dead tunes like "Eyes of the World," "Sugaree," "The Other One" and "U.S. Blues." The evolutionary path was clear.

A month and a half later, on September 28, the Dead and the Jefferson Starship got together and put on a free concert, announced the day of the show, that drew 25,000 people to Golden Gate Park's Lindley Meadows on a cold and foggy Sunday afternoon. The Dead played one long set that day, mostly showcasing their new material, but also revving up the crowd with favorites like "Truckin'," "Not Fade Away" and "One More Saturday Night." Four appearances during their first year away from touring? It was ample indication that this band was not about to retire. On the contrary, they seemed more energized at each successive appearance. There was still no indication that the hiatus would end anytime soon, but most Deadheads believed it was only a matter of time before the Dead would succumb to the lure of the stage again.

The lack of touring certainly had an adverse affect on the Dead's financial situation. After all, that had always been their main source of income. Yes, there was the $300,000 Rakow had managed to snag from Atlantic Records for the Dead's foreign distribution rights, but by mid-1975 that money was long gone. Grateful Dead Records turned a tidy profit with each Dead album, but the Round Records projects were not nearly as successful, particularly *Seastones* and *Keith and Donna*. Moreover, manufacturing costs had soared on the last few record projects because of a vinyl shortage caused by political turmoil in the Middle East's oil-producing nations. But the real money drain was the movie, which ate up hundreds of thousands of dollars. That was Garcia's baby, and the rest of the band recognized that the movie had the potential to be a tremendous artistic statement by and about the band. They trusted Garcia's vision of the project and the postproduction crew's regimen, which turned out to be slow and methodical. Garcia had hoped that the movie would be in theaters by Christmas of 1975; as it turned out, work on the film continued all the way into early 1977.

"What we really need is a subsidy," Garcia joked in 1975. "The government should subsidize us and we should be like a national resource."

In mid-1975 Rakow and the band agreed that it was time to end the great independent record company experiment, so they signed a distribution deal with United Artists Records—not exactly an industry giant—to handle Grateful Dead albums and the solo discs on Round Records. The Dead organization got a much-needed infusion of cash to keep the various recording and film ventures going (the *Hell's Angels Forever* movie project was still eating up money, too), and for the first time in a couple of years, Garcia, Rakow and company didn't have to worry about the endless minutiae of record manufacturing and distribution.

"The independence we had with Grateful Dead Records really isn't that important," Garcia said a year later. "I felt as though it was something we tried to do, but the time it happened was just the worst possible time to do it. It was the time when there were incredible vinyl shortages and all that stuff, and here we were, starting our little record company in the midst of 'the collapse of the record industry.' It was like swimming upstream.

"But it doesn't bother me if some plan doesn't work. They have lives of their own after a while. If they work, they deserve to. If they don't, the heck with it. No sense worrying about it."

Garcia gigged with Keith and Donna's group, which also included Kreutzmann and three other players, for about four weeks in August and September 1975. The band played a combination of songs from the *Keith and Donna* album, Memphis soul tunes like "Knock on Wood" and "I Can't Turn You Loose," and even a few Garcia-sung covers. When he returned from the Keith and Donna tour, Garcia abruptly kicked Merl Saunders and Martin Fierro out of the Legion of Mary and hired British rock 'n' roll piano wizard Nicky Hopkins— who'd played with everyone from the Rolling Stones to Quicksilver—for the newly named Jerry Garcia Band (which also included John Kahn and Ron Tutt).

John Kahn said the decision to go in a different direction with the group was made for purely musical considerations: "It didn't seem to be headed anywhere for us. It was stuck in a bag. Without putting anybody down, it was just a period of nongrowth musically, I thought, and Jerry thought so, too. We dealt with it like Jerry dealt with a lot of things—we just sort of ditched it. We hid and just didn't have any gigs for a long time, and then we started another band. It wasn't very well done. Since then I've been more careful making sure that sort of stuff was done properly. Jerry was supposed to do that one himself, because I'd been the guy who fired Kreutzmann to get Tutt. So it was his turn, but of course he wouldn't do it."

Whatever the grisly details, the change in the fall of 1975 did represent a new direction for Garcia's band. Hopkins was an amazing technician on the piano, equally capable of providing florid ornamentation, spare melodic filigrees and deft rhythmic pounding. The music lost some of its jazzy flavor when Saunders and Fierro left and took on more of a rock 'n' roll personality. A raft of fine new songs came into the repertoire around this time, too, including "Catfish John," a contemporary country tune that Old and in the Way had performed bluegrass-style; several numbers written by Hopkins, such as "Lady Sleeps" and "Edward, the Mad Shirt Grinder," which he'd originally recorded with Quicksilver on their *Shady Grove* album; "I'll Take a Melody," a little-known song by New Orleans songwriter-producer Allen Toussaint; three tunes from the Grateful Dead's songbook—"Sugaree," "They Love Each Other" and "Friend of the Devil"; and a new Hunter-Garcia composition called "Mission in the Rain," which Garcia described as "a song that might be *about* me. It's my life; it's like a little piece of my life. Hunter writes *me* once in a while."

Not that any real information about Garcia is imparted in the song. But the setting—San Francisco's Mission district—is from the attic of his life. And Hunter's as well—when he first moved to San Francisco during the Summer of Love he lived at 17th and Mission Streets, "and that [song] was very much a portrait of that time—looking backwards at ten years," Hunter said.

> Ten years ago I walked this street
> My dreams were riding tall
> Tonight I would be thankful
> Lord for any dream at all
> Some folks would be happy
> Just to have one dream come true
> But everything you gather
> Is just more than you can lose
>
> Come again
> Walking along in the Mission
> In the rain . . .

The Jerry Garcia Band (henceforth the JGB) toured quite a lot in October and November of 1975, and also found time to record a few songs for the Garcia solo album that became *Reflections*. "That album was supposed to be a Jerry Garcia Band album but it sort of fell apart in the middle, so it ended up being half that band and half Grateful Dead," John Kahn said.

The problem, alas, was Hopkins, who besides being a major cokehead—not an issue where Garcia and Kahn were concerned—also had a severe drinking problem. This is why he occasionally rambled on incessantly between songs onstage, muttering incomprehensibly in his thick British accent, and why by year's end he was out of the group.

"He was an incredible player," Kahn said, "like the Chopin of rock 'n' roll. He was bluesy but he also had this beautiful tone and touch that complemented Jerry's playing really well. That was the idea, and then Tutt and I would lay down this really fat, well-defined bottom sound. But it didn't work out. That wasn't Hopkins's best period. Frankly, he didn't even remember any of the gigs. Later, he asked me if we ever had any fun. I said, 'Yeah,' and he said, 'Then it must've been all right.' Tutt really didn't like Hopkins, and after a while he blew Jerry out, too, because he was just too over the edge; he was too fucked up to play music. That's the line where you've gone too far. At this Winterland show [in December 1975] he was on another planet, playing in the wrong key, and you just couldn't get to him. He sort of wrecked that whole gig. Tutt was really mad."

Hopkins's last gig with the band was a New Year's Eve show at the Keystone Berkeley. Shortly after that the JGB debuted another new lineup at the Keystone Berkeley, and this one stuck for a while: Garcia, Kahn, Tutt and Keith and Donna Godchaux. "Keith was an interesting player," Kahn said. "He didn't have the same background as the rest of us. Like, he wasn't well rooted in blues, but he picked stuff up real fast. He was an amazingly quick study. We'd teach him about some style one day and he'd have it down the next. He picked up the New Orleans stuff real fast. That was a real good band for a long time; definitely one of my favorites."

Not surprisingly, bringing in Keith and Donna added a gospel feeling to much of the material the band played, and they even tackled some straight gospel numbers, such as the traditional "Who Was John," the Sensational Nightingales' "My Sisters and Brothers" and the Mighty Clouds of Joy's "Ride Mighty High," as well as gospel-influenced songs like Dylan's "Knockin' on Heaven's Door" and the reggae classic "Stop That Train."

Garcia's solo album *Reflections* came out in February 1976, and offered quite a potpourri of musical styles. Four songs featured the JGB (with Hopkins) augmented by Mickey Hart on percussion, and keyboardist Larry Knechtel (who had also played on Garcia's second solo record): "Mission in the Rain," which also had an effective synthesizer line by Kahn; "I'll Take a Melody"; Hank Ballard's driving "Tore Up Over You"; and "Catfish John." And on two of the four, Donna and Bob Weir sang background vocals.

The other four songs on *Reflections* were performed by the Grateful Dead, including Mickey Hart, who was formally back on board. "It was a continuation of what we were doing with *Blues for Allah*," Garcia said. "We were having fun in the studio is what it boils down to, and that's pretty rare for us. The energy was there, and I thought, 'I've got a solo album coming up. Let's cut these tracks with the Grateful Dead. I've already taught them the tunes.' "

Three songs were ones the Dead had played for a while but never recorded: "Comes a Time," "It Must Have Been the Roses" and "They Love Each Other." The fourth was an exuberant new Hunter-Garcia rocker called "Might As Well," about the Festival Express train trip across Canada in 1970.

Sometime in early 1976 Garcia moved into an old Victorian house in Belvedere, a posh, old-money enclave on a small island off Tiburon. "I went and visited him and Deborah there a couple of times," John Kahn said. "It was a *really* nice place."

Around the same time, Mountain Girl says, "Jerry said he was going to cut me loose, so I was cut loose." Garcia agreed to give her a thousand dollars a month plus the house in Stinson Beach. "I stayed in Stinson until mid-1976, but I was very unhappy. It was like a bomb had gone off. The kids were unhappy.

"So I went up to Oregon for a year," she continues. "I bought a place out on the coast, in Port Orford, with money I'd made from my book [a popular guide to cultivating marijuana], and I kind of went up there and hid. I was really lonely. I got tired of Port Orford in a hot second. I lasted there about fourteen or sixteen months. The kids did a year of school there that was just hell. It was really boring."

Another change occurred in the scene during this period: the arrival of freebase cocaine, which instead of being snorted was smoked and thus was introduced into the bloodstream much quicker and with a more dramatic—some say nearly orgasmic—head and body "rush." This technique used up cocaine faster and it was much more psychologically addictive. Years before crack cocaine laid waste to thousands of inner-city adults and kids, freebase ravaged the Grateful Dead's world.

"The weaker ones really fell by the wayside with that drug," Steve Brown observes. "People who had more to lose started to really go downhill when that started happening. That one sucked a lot of people under, and some people never really got out of it. A lot of them eventually went from freebasing to also smoking heroin—it was a marriage made in hell."

Ironically, "Garcia was totally healthy-looking back then," Brown continues. "He was lucid. He was funny. Most of the time you could never tell with him. And that lasted all the way up to the late '70s. He just had a very high tolerance, I guess."

John Kahn agreed. "He never got so fucked up he couldn't play or carry on a normal conversation. We played some of our best shows during that period." And like many drug users, Garcia went through relatively clean periods followed by periods in which he binged.

By the late winter of 1976 the Dead had decided to begin touring again, but on a much more scaled-down level than before. "We're horny to play," Garcia declared. "We all miss Grateful Dead music. We want to be the Grateful Dead some more."

The Wall of Sound had been taken apart and dispersed: "There are probably twenty-five little bands running around that got outfitted by that system," Dan Healy said in the mid-'80s. "So when we went back on the road we decided no more albatrosses. We had a year to miss touring, and we had time to reflect on what a truly valuable, precious thing we had. And we wanted to keep it economical so we'd survive."

The road crew was winnowed down from twenty to just six—"The core nucleus stayed," Healy said. "It was the same people who were there originally, no more, no less"—and Healy went back to renting equipment, which was then configured in ways that were consistent with some of the audio principles that had emerged from the Wall of Sound experiment.

During the time the band was off the road, all sorts of different ideas about how to make the Grateful Dead concert experience more manageable for both the band and crowd had been explored—from looking into the feasibility of televising concerts to having Buckminster Fuller work up plans for a permanent, customized geodesic-domed performance venue in the Bay Area, where the group could stay put and concertize most of the year. In the end there simply wasn't enough money for anything so grandiose. But in a noble attempt to reestablish some sense of scale to their operation, the band played in theaters rather than arenas and stadiums on their first tour after the hiatus, with the first crack at tickets going to the 45,000 people on the Dead Heads mailing list.

"Basically, us returning to performing is a compromise," Garcia said in March 1976, two months before the tour. "It isn't a totally satisfactory move. The way we're gonna do it is gonna be different from the way we've done it. But it's retrograde rather than moving on with the idea. We're actually backing up because there are literally no alternatives. We're trying to bluff an alternative into existence. But that doesn't mean there is one. We haven't succeeded on that level yet."

Still, Garcia said that his year and a half in the Deadless wilderness had left him feeling that "the thing I'm most into is the survival of the Grateful Dead. I think that's my main trip now. . . . I feel like I've had both trips now—I've been with the Grateful Dead for ten or twelve years, and I've also been out of it, in the sense of going out in the world and traveling and doing things under my own hook. And really, I'm not that taken with my own ideas. I don't really have that much to say, and I'm more interested in being involved in something that's larger than me. . . . So, sometime in the last year I decided, yeah, that's it—that's definitely the farthest-out thing I've ever been involved in, and it's the thing that makes me feel the best. And it seems to have the most ability to sort of neutrally put something good into the mainstream. It's also fascinating in the sense of the progression. The year-to-year changes are fascinating."

Work on the Grateful Dead movie continued all through the winter and spring of 1976, with Susan Crutcher and her team putting in long hours at the Mill Valley film house assembling a massive rough-cut version—the first one ran nearly five hours, long even by Grateful Dead standards. Another expensive and time-consuming element was added to the film when it was decided to open the movie with a short, trippy animated sequence by a young San Francisco filmmaker-animator named Gary Gutierrez. Those seven mind-blowing minutes ended up costing $250,000.

The Dead had been in fairly dire financial shape for a while, and their return to the road, scheduled for June, wasn't going to do much to rectify that. After all, they had decided to play multiday runs in small theaters in just a few select cities. The movie was getting closer to completion but it still needed more cash. Mickey Hart had gone way over budget on an album he was making with the Diga Rhythm Band, a wondrous all-percussion ensemble he was a member of. There was pressure in many different sectors of the Dead organization to find more money, and in some circles there was the belief that Ron Rakow's wheeling and dealing was no longer helping the Dead; a few even suspected that he had been lining his own pockets, an accusation that was never formally made or proven.

"Everybody wanted to trust Rakow because Jerry did," says Emily Craig, who was Rakow's wife at the time. "Jerry's vote was greater than the sum of everybody else's. If he wanted to do something, that's what was happening. But nobody ever really trusted Rakow, and rightfully so."

"The big mystery to me is how he was able to gain Garcia's trust and somehow form an alliance with him," Dave Parker says. "That was the single most negative event that happened to me in the whole time I worked for the Dead—having to deal with that fact; that Rakow and Garcia essentially became partners, and there was a kind of separation between Jerry and the rest of the band at that point."

The friction between Rakow and certain bandmembers and key players in the Dead organization came to a head in May 1976 when Rakow went down to Los Angeles to collect a $275,000 recording advance check from United Artists. Instead of turning the money over to the Dead, Rakow put the check in his own account and split the Dead scene completely. It's an event that still draws emotional responses from the participants twenty years later.

"There was a sizable check that Rakow had gotten from the record company, and he had some kind of manipulation that he was going to do with the money," Parker says. "I basically was instructed that I had to trust Rakow with this money. It was at Jerry's insistence that he be given this level of trust. There were some meetings with the band [before Rakow got the check] and a couple of bandmembers had expressed concern to me about what Rakow was doing. Billy was probably the most concerned. Phil was very concerned as well. They all were to a degree, but essentially the way it came down was that Jerry said, 'This is the guy I want to be doing this stuff. I just want it that way.' It was like an ultimatum. I felt very strange about that."

In Rakow's telling of the story, he was in the offices of United Artists' Mark Levinson picking up the check when a phone call came through from

Rakow's lawyer telling him that the Grateful Dead's attorney said that Rakow had been fired. "I told my lawyer that the call he got has no status and this call does not compute," Rakow says, so he took the check. From his perspective, it was money that was owed him for long and faithful service, plus he had obligations he had to take care of:

"What nobody knows is that the movie was being made partly by money that I had personally borrowed from a very heavy connection of drug dealers," Rakow says. "Now, I wasn't going to leave that scene and not pay back that bread before I left. The Grateful Dead had a friend named Cousin David—it was a cover name—and he ran a boutique smuggling operation from Mexico. By boutique I mean he had three or four small planes with seven or eight guys; a real buccaneer when drug smuggling was a small business run by really soulful people who had strong feelings. And he was interested in helping us get that movie out. And our cash flow was terrible—nobody was working. They stopped working October 21, 1974. I left in May 1976. The day I left, we owed Cousin David $47,000, which we had used to make payroll at the film house. The only one that knew what my particular thing was, was Jerry. He knew I owed this guy forty-seven grand. We talked about it. I wasn't going to leave and depend on somebody like Hal Kant [the Dead's lawyer] to see that my personal debts were paid."

Rakow says he put another $40,000 toward completing costs for *Hell's Angels Forever* and "I helped the Rolling Thunder guys buy some land in Ruby Valley that the Native Americans live on." He also bought (for himself) a sizable collection of original copperplate negatives of photographs by Edward S. Curtis, the premier photodocumentarian of Native Americans in the nineteenth century.

"I'm not a lawyer, and I never looked at the books, but it seemed pretty illegal to me," says Richard Loren. "Rakow says the Grateful Dead owed him money, and that's probably true, but if you can't convince them to give it to you, then is it okay to steal it?"

A year and a half after the imbroglio, Rakow told a writer, "I didn't like the way they treated me. I felt ripped off and I wanted to make sure they felt totally ripped off, and I think they did."

"He bragged about it to me extensively," Mountain Girl says. "He thought he'd really run a big score. I was shocked."

Not surprisingly, Rakow's departure had a devastating effect on everyone in the Grateful Dead organization. Not only did it mean the loss of critically needed income, it created a rift between Garcia, who was Rakow's greatest supporter, and the rest of the band.

"Jerry had gone to bat for Rakow in a way, and he'd never say it, but it must have affected him," Loren says. "He had to look the band in the face after Rakow was gone. You're sitting down with the other musicians and it was like a 'He was your guy' kind of attitude."

"Ultimately, nobody wanted to go as far as suing about this," Parker says.

"Some of the band and some of the rest of us didn't feel that what had happened was right, but Garcia had a certain ambivalence about it, and if he had come down strongly one way or another it might have made a difference. But as it turned out there was some going back and forth among lawyers and the way it finally came down is the band decided not to go after him for the money legally. Basically to accept his claim that he was somehow entitled to it. I think they didn't want to get involved in a big legal showdown—going to court, getting all that publicity. It just kind of faded away. And Rakow got away with it."

This sort of crisis might have broken up less stable groups, but the bond between the Grateful Dead members was such that they just kept plugging along, no doubt feeling battered, bruised and pissed-off. The anti-Rakow forces were happy to be rid of him, and now the focus could switch completely to the band's imminent return to the concert stage.

The Dead rehearsed extensively before the tour began in early June. After all, they needed to get used to the idea of playing together regularly again after a year and a half in separate orbits. They also had to bring Mickey Hart up to speed—though he'd played with the group at the four gigs in 1975, he still had five years of the band's evolution to absorb, and the band had to adjust to Mickey's being back in the group, too. Weir said that with two drummers in the band again it became a little harder to "turn the corner" in jams, and Kreutzmann noted, "Things maybe didn't flow quite as easily for a while. It was a little more cumbersome, which I think you'd expect, but it smoothed out over time."

"Everyone was playing slow," Mickey said. "The songs had slowed down and then we started to build up steam again. I was out of shape. Billy and I hadn't really played together for years. This looks easy to some people, but the reason you don't see two drummers playing together very often is because it's not easy. It's not just being good, and it's not just putting two drum sets up on the stage."

The band's sound on that first tour was quite a departure from the wide-open approach the group took in 1973–74. Sets were shorter, there wasn't nearly as much free-form jamming, the tempos *were* slower for the most part and there was almost no real "space" music. Deadheads weren't complaining, however. They were happy to have the band back on the road, and there were lots of new songs to enjoy: all the material from *Blues for Allah*, which hadn't been played outside the Bay Area; revivals of old Dead songs like "Saint Stephen" and "Cosmic Charlie" in different, slower arrangements; cover tunes like Reverend Gary Davis's "Samson and Delilah" and a completely reworked disco arrangement of "Dancing in the Streets"; and numbers from Garcia's and Weir's solo albums and band repertoires, such as "The Wheel," "Mission in the Rain," "Might As Well" and Weir's "Lazy Lightning" and "Supplication" (which he'd played with Kingfish).

There were many popular Dead tunes that *didn't* immediately follow the group out of retirement, too: "Dark Star," "China Cat Sunflower" > "I Know You Rider," "Uncle John's Band," "Jack Straw," "China Doll" and "Casey Jones." But they all reappeared over the course of the next three years.

In the fickle, transitory world of conventional entertainment, a year-and-a-half layoff is a long time—enough for some people to assume that the act is washed up, or to forget about them altogether. It's the "What have you done *lately*?" syndrome. But with the Grateful Dead the opposite happened: the intense loyalty of their fans actually increased during the band's time away from the road, as people came to realize just how important the group was to them. In addition, during the Dead's hiatus the underground Grateful Dead tape-trading network had blossomed and, in effect, gone public when a few New York–area Deadheads started a newsletter/magazine called *Dead Relix* (later simply *Relix*), devoted to disseminating information about Grateful Dead tapes and taping.

Surreptitious taping from the audience on recorders smuggled into concerts had been going on at some Dead shows since the late '60s, but the number of tapers increased each year, and the quality of the tapes improved as well. Between audience-made concert tapes and the numerous Dead shows that had been recorded from FM radio broadcasts, there were many tapes in circulation among traders by the mid-'70s. This encouraged more people to collect tapes and to become tapers themselves. Since every show was different and certain nights were unquestionably magical, why not try to capture that magic? Though bootleg albums occasionally turned up on the black market, the great majority of tape transactions in the Deadhead world were trades only—a code of honor specifically prohibited the buying or selling of Dead tapes. This ethical standard remains in place today and has spread into non–Grateful Dead taping circles.

Garcia, for one, was always sympathetic to the tapers, having been a bluegrass taper himself in the mid-'60s. "I think it's okay," he said in 1975. "If people like it they can certainly keep doing it. I don't have any desire to control people as to what they're doing and what they have. There's something to be said for being able to record an experience you've liked, or being able to obtain a recording of it. Actually, we have all that stuff in our own collection of tapes. My responsibility to the notes is over after I've played them. At that point I don't care where they go," he added with a laugh. "They've left home, you know."

Five of the twenty-five shows on the Dead's June–July '76 "comeback" tour were broadcast on FM stations, and tapers at the shows generally found the Dead turning a blind eye to their activities. There were occasional confiscation sweeps through the tapers' ranks by less sympathetic members of the Grateful Dead road crew, but by and large Dan Healy condoned the practice; in fact, he took an interest in how the tapes sounded, because in a sense they reflected on his work mixing the band. In 1976 there were only a handful of tapers at most shows, but it seemed their numbers increased exponentially each year.

As it happened, the early-summer theater tour turned out not to be a sign that the Dead were returning to smaller venues on a permanent basis. By August they were back to playing small stadiums and giant arenas—in early October they even played two shows at the enormous 55,000-seat Oakland Stadium (which they did not sell out) on the same bill as the Who. Except for a New Year's Eve concert at the Cow Palace, the group took a break from touring from the middle of October through the third week of February 1977. (At one point they had hoped to go to Australia, New Zealand and Hawaii in the late fall, but once again it was deemed financially unfeasible.) Which isn't to say they were inactive. Garcia, naturally, was busy almost constantly, gigging on the West Coast with the JGB, working to complete the film and, beginning in January, recording the next Grateful Dead album.

The Dead's commitment to United Artists ended when the band formally dissolved Grateful Dead and Round Records in the fall of 1976. At that point the Dead started shopping for a major record label that would pay them big bucks and grant them complete artistic freedom in exchange for the next few Grateful Dead albums. Waiting in the wings for just such a moment was Clive Davis, departed from Columbia Records and now boss of his own New York–based label, Arista. Davis had wanted the Dead to record for him since the late '60s, so when they were ready to sign with a major label again, he courted them heavily, earning points with the Dead's managers—particularly Richard Loren, who'd worked with Davis on the Rowan Brothers' Columbia discs—and John Scher, who, beginning with the Dead's return to the road in mid-'76, acted as a business advisor to Garcia and the Dead, and produced or co-produced nearly all of the group's shows east of the Rockies.

"The prior period had been the culmination of that process of taking on everything and doing it all ourselves—the record company, the Wall of Sound, booking, our own travel agency," Alan Trist says. "There was nothing, with the exception of tickets, that we weren't doing in-house, and of course we did that later. Then, after the hiatus, the philosophy that Richard and Jerry and myself were in accord on was completely different: 'Okay, let's just do what we do best—be a band, and we'll get other people of our own choosing to do everything else.' So we hired producers to do the records, hired John Scher to do the booking on the East Coast, Bill Graham to do the West Coast, let Arista do publicity. But it didn't mean that the basic Grateful Dead head had changed. We'd just learned some lessons about taking on too much."

CHAPTER 15
Some Rise, Some Fall,
Some Climb...

uring the first week of December 1976 Robert Hunter had a flash of inspiration: "I wrote 'Terrapin, Part One,' at a single sitting in an unfurnished house with a picture window overlooking San Francisco Bay during a flamboyant lightning storm," he recalled in his book *Box of Rain*. "I typed the first thing that came into my mind at the top of the page, the title: 'Terrapin Station.' Not knowing what it was about, I began my writing with an invocation to the muse and kept typing as the story began to unfold."

> *Let my inspiration flow*
> *In token rhyme suggesting rhythm*
> *That will not forsake me*
> *'Til my tale is told and done*

"On the same day, driving to the city," Hunter continued, "Garcia was struck by a singular inspiration. He turned his car around and hurried home to set down some music that popped into his head, demanding immediate attention. When we met the next day, I showed him the words and he said, 'I've got the music.' They dovetailed perfectly and 'Terrapin' edged into this dimension."

The suite of songs and instrumental interludes that became known as "Terrapin, Part One" represent a culmination of sorts for the Hunter-Garcia writing partnership—a place where their deep folk roots blossomed into a mythic dimension outside of time, space and place; ancient yet eternal; a swirling galaxy of images, ideas and archetypal characters.

The opening section of the suite, "Lady with a Fan," established the character of the storyteller, who spins the centuries-old tale from the British folk ballad "The Lady of Carlisle" (which had been sung in Appalachia at least since the nineteenth century, and was popularized in late-'50s folk circles by Mike Seeger and the New Lost City Ramblers). The story of "The Lady of Carlisle" is a simple one—a lady is torn between loving a brave army lieutenant and a brave sea captain. To choose between them she throws her fan into a lion's den, saying whoever retrieves it will "gain a lady." The lieutenant declines. The sailor fearlessly goes in among the lions, picks up the fan and returns it to the lady. As she offers herself to him, she says, "Here is the prize that you have won."

In Hunter's deft, poetic retelling, the characters are summoned up out of the storyteller's fire (around which we are all presumably huddled) like visions:

> Shadows of a sailor forming
> Winds both foul and fair all swarm
> Down in Carlisle he loved a lady
> Many years ago
>
> Here beside him stands a man
> A soldier by the looks of him
> Who came through many fights
> But lost in love
>
> While the storyteller speaks
> A door within the fire creaks
> Suddenly flies open
> And a girl is standing there

Upon throwing her fan in the lion's den, the lady asks the essential question:

> "Which of you to gain me, tell,
> Will risk uncertain pains of hell?
> I will not forgive you
> If you will not take the chance."

The message is clear—love and life are filled with danger and uncertainty, and sometimes the greatest rewards require the greatest risks. In this case, the sailor triumphs and claims his lady love, but Hunter refuses to judge whether his is the smart path: "You decide if he was wise," he tells us, adding:

> The storyteller make no choice
> Soon you will not hear his voice
> His job is to shed light
> And not to master

There, in a nutshell, is an elucidation of Hunter's role as a poet/lyricist and as the voice of the Grateful Dead—offering nuggets of wisdom in shards of verse and elegant metaphor, but never telling us what to believe or how to think. One could go on to say that this song summed up the Grateful Dead itself. The band's course was filled with tests, and time after time they ventured into the lion's den. These experiences defined the band, but did they always take the wise course? Perhaps; perhaps not. Many who chose the more dangerous and mysterious path—Garcia included—did not survive as long as they might have.

Garcia set "Lady with a Fan" to one of his prettiest folk melodies—it could have been played as easily on lutes and flutes as on electric guitars. The next section of the song cycle was a brief instrumental passage that serves as a transition between the telling of the tale and a return to the storyteller, who invokes his muse again as the music rises to a new peak:

> *Inspiration move me brightly*
> *Light the song with sense and color*
> *Hold away despair*
> *More than this I will not ask*
> *Faced with mysteries dark and vast*
> *Statements just seem vain at last*
> *Some rise, some fall, some climb*
> *To get to Terrapin*

What and where is Terrapin? Is it an elusive Holy Grail for which we search our entire lives? A metaphor for heaven and/or nirvana? Is it death and resurrection, or the purgatory of an unending quest for meaning? "I can't figure out if it's the end or beginning," Hunter writes in the song, "but the train's put its brakes on and the whistle is *screaming: 'Terrapin'*!" In "At a Siding," a short following piece in the suite, Garcia sings, "The sullen wings of fortune beat like rain / You're back in Terrapin for good or ill again," as if this is a destination fraught with real or psychic peril.

"Jerry favors a certain type of folk song," Hunter said when I asked about his and Garcia's affinity for the kind of timeless folk themes that crop up in "Terrapin." "He loves the mournful, death-connected ballad, the Child ballad stuff. This is a venerable source that has always spoken to him, and to me as well, which is one reason we got together writing songs—because of that haunting feel that certain traditional songs have. I just eat them up and so does he. It's a point of absolute mutual agreement. 'Terrapin' gets that in spades. 'Terrapin' was our attempt to entirely surrender and go in that direction. That's our little temple of that. It's full of ghosts.

"It's archetypal. It hearkens to something in us that is built into us partly genetically and partly by the culture we assimilate, the values built into popular songs. I try to go for something real basic when I write a song. It's got to have these resonances to me or it's not right. Unless, maybe, I'm trying to write a rock 'n' roll song, and then I'm looking for rock 'n' rollish resonances. But I'm generally deep-sea diving in imagery and getting things that sometimes— as in folk music—you don't know quite what it means, but it's resonant."

"Terrapin Station, Part One" would form the backbone and provide the title for the Grateful Dead's first Arista album, which they started recording sometime in January 1977. (It was "Part One" because Hunter wrote several other thematically connected songs for the suite, but Garcia elected not to set them to music. Hunter has performed other sections of the suite himself through the years, and the lyrics for the full work are printed in *Box of Rain*.) At the urging of Clive Davis, who felt that the Dead had the potential to make a great commercial album, the band agreed to work with an outside producer for the first time since a very frustrated Dave Hassinger was driven away from the *Anthem of the Sun* sessions in early 1968.

"When we went with Arista," Garcia said, "we went with a spirit of co-operation, thinking, well, we've tried things our way; we've had our own record company, we've produced ourselves—we've done it a lot, in fact—and it'd be interesting to try somebody else's approach totally and see where it takes us, because of the fact that our records—as records—have always been neither here nor there. They haven't been relevant. We wanted some fresh ears—that was part of the reason it didn't seem outrageous to us. . . . We're very conscious of how easy it is to get into your own trip so much that you just don't have any sense of it, no objectivity at all. It's easy to do."

Davis made a number of different suggestions from the ranks of top producers of the day, including a young producer based in Los Angeles named Keith Olsen, who was red-hot in the industry after producing a superb, multi-platinum pop album for Fleetwood Mac.

Garcia and Weir in particular liked Olsen, and at this point in the Dead's history, with the smoldering, twisted ruins of Grateful Dead Records still vivid in the rearview mirror, the notion of making a more "commercial" record was fairly attractive. Besides, it's not as if they were remotely close to going "pop"—neither the grandiose "Terrapin" nor "Estimated Prophet," Weir's strange new reggae tune in 7/4 time, were going to be AM radio fodder; far from it. But if Olsen could smooth some of the group's notoriously ragged edges so that more radio stations might find the Dead palatable, perhaps it was worth a shot. So they agreed that Olsen would produce the record at his own Sound City studio in Van Nuys, northwest of Los Angeles. That worked out nicely for another reason, too: at the same time that those sessions were going on, Garcia and Dan Healy, aided by Susan Crutcher, could complete the sound work on the final dub of the Grateful Dead movie at Warner Bros. studios in nearby Burbank. The band, managers and a few Grateful Dead family types took over a wing of the inexpensive Van Nuys Travel Inn for nearly two months, and Garcia worked almost around the clock the entire time he was in Los Angeles.

Olsen had the band rehearse extensively before they began cutting basic tracks for the album, and he quickly learned that after years of improvising together and staying loose enough to follow the music that unfolded before them, the Grateful Dead had a lot of ingrained musical habits—some good, some bad—from his perspective.

"The cutting of tracks in general was very difficult because I was trying to get them to be tight," Olsen says. "Mickey Hart is a real good drummer but he has a tendency to lean forward on the beat, and Bill Kreutzmann is a real laid-back guy and he lays back on the beat. So where's the beat? Every single bass and snare drum beat, when you'd hear them together, would sound a little off to me. It was a mess. Mickey has the fire, Billy has kind of a groove. So I said, 'Why don't we orchestrate the drum parts? Okay, Billy, you get the hi-hat, kick [bass drum] and snare and an occasional cymbal. Mickey, you get all the tom fills, all the flash, all the color.' And they did it. That's the way we recorded.

"Garcia and Weir were both really good," Olsen continues. "Garcia always played really cool stuff. He never played something the same way twice, but almost everything he came up with was cool. He just had endless ideas about *everything*. Weir is a real interesting guy in general. I spent seven months with him [recording *Terrapin Station* and then a solo album with Weir called *Heaven Help the Fool*]. He's a sweetheart. He's very talented in his own way, but definitely only in a Bob Weir kind of way. It's like all the guys in the Dead are talented in a Dead kind of way. They can't really run out and do that many other things because outside of that idiom they get lost."

Olsen says the basic tracks took about six weeks to record, "and we didn't get one basic for the first three weeks we were there. I kept throwing them away, saying, 'It ain't good enough, guys.' Garcia would say, 'Really?' And I'd say, 'No, Jerry, it's not good enough.' Bobby would say, 'But we don't play any better than this.' And I'd say, 'I'm going to make you play better. It isn't too late!' "

The overdubbing process also took a long time, because Olsen was such a stickler for mistake-free playing. But, he says, "Garcia had so much fun. He'd be giggling in the control room. When we were doing this double-speed guitar stuff [speeding up the guitar electronically] and these double-speed harmony parts on 'Terrapin,' he was just laughing. I never heard anybody laugh so much when they were working. Garcia loved playing more than anything and he sat there and laughed while he was playing. It was great."

During the period the Dead were recording the album, they played just five concerts—two in Southern California in late February, three at Winterland in late March—and at each of them they played both "Terrapin" and "Estimated Prophet" to universally fantastic reviews from Deadheads. Here were two new songs completely unlike any other in the Dead's repertoire: "Estimated," which appeared to portray the thoughts of some delusional messianic zealot—"a guy I see at nearly every backstage door," Weir said—juxtaposed a dark, ominous, minor-chord reggae feeling with bright, major-chord progressions that were nearly as sunny and triumphant as those in Weir's "Sugar Magnolia" jam. Garcia got to try out a new pedal effect for his guitar on this song—an envelope filter that gave each note he played a wah-wah-like *thwack*, depending on his picking intensity. And "Terrapin" was a complex and involved world of its own, moving from the timeless balladic opening to a stirring buildup that had almost martial overtones, finally leading to an explosion of nearly baroque-sounding unison lines and counterpoint that the band would play again and again, changing timbres and tones with each pass, the music swelling to heroic proportions and pulling back unpredictably.

Garcia introduced another major new song at the first of the March Winterland shows, though he didn't actually have a hand in writing it. "Fire on the Mountain" had been written by Mickey Hart and Robert Hunter for the aborted follow-up to Hart's first solo album, *Rolling Thunder*. "That was another Mickey Hart rhythm extravaganza with no melody," Hunter said of the song's origin. "He just gave me this track—bop, bop bopbopbopbop . . . —and said, 'Make this a song, Uncle Bob.' So I wrote 'Fire on the Mountain' to it and recorded over the tracks. I still think he did the best version of it years before the Dead got to it." There was a literal fire on the mountain that inspired the song—a fast-moving wildfire that threatened Hart's ranch. The pre-Dead versions with Mickey rapping through verse after elliptical verse were frenzied and ragged but actually suited Hunter's lyrics perfectly. When Garcia finally tackled the song, he fashioned a melody of sorts for the verses but elected to sing only three, including this evocative middle verse, which, as usual, has metaphorical implications relating to the Grateful Dead:

> *Almost ablaze, still you don't feel the heat*
> *Takes all you got just to stay on the beat*
> *You say it's a living, we all gotta eat*
> *But you're here alone, there's no one to compete*
> *If mercy's in business I wish it for you*
> *More than just ashes when your dreams come true*
>
> *Fire, fire on the mountain . . .*

The main riff was an infectious repeating groove that had a slight Afro-Caribbean bounce to it. Half a year before Garcia started singing it, the groove turned up as an instrumental track he played on called "Happiness Is Drumming" on the extraordinary Diga Rhythm Band album. "Fire on the Mountain" was another song on which Garcia used the envelope filter to great effect. Every note had its own round, fat shape—you could hear the attack and decay—as the lead guitar line danced around, inside and on top of the big groove that the other players created with their own pounding instrumental voices. There are versions in which the envelope filter allows Garcia's guitar to take on some of the character of steel drums, and others where there's a hint of viola or French horn. Except for just a few versions over the years, "Fire on the Mountain" was always attached to the similarly driving and polyrhythmic "Scarlet Begonias." "Scarlet-Fire," as the sequence was called in

Deadhead slang, became one of the Dead's most popular song combos, perhaps even *the* most popular.

Many Deadheads regard the Dead's spring 1977 East Coast tour as one of their finest, and it's easy to see why. The infusion of new material—three of their all-time best songs—took the music in exciting new directions at the same time that the most successful tunes from *Blues for Allah*—"Crazy Fingers" and the triumvirate of "Help on the Way" > "Slipknot!" > "Franklin's Tower"—were reaching new levels of maturity. On that spring tour, too, the group continued to reintroduce songs that hadn't been played since the hiatus; major songs like "Jack Straw," "Brokedown Palace" and "China Doll." And Garcia introduced two very different cover tunes. "Jack-A-Roe," a peppy old British sea-song about a woman who dresses up like a male sailor so she can go to war at her loved one's side, had been popularized by Joan Baez during Garcia's folk days. The rubbery, syncopated "Iko Iko" came from New Orleans's Mardi Gras Indian (actually, African-American) culture. Sugarboy Crawford cut the song as "Jockomo" in the late '40s; the Dixie Cups had a fluke hit with a nearly a cappella version of "Iko Iko" in the '60s; and Dr. John put the song on one of his albums in the early '70s. It was that version that inspired Keith Olsen to suggest that Garcia cover the song with the Dead.

Working to tighten up their sound under Olsen's benign whip had a tremendous influence on the Dead. During the spring 1977 tour the playing was crisp and rhythmically assured, as if they'd discovered some new source of power within themselves. Brimming with confidence gained from playing so powerfully, the band was then able to relax enough to open up their jams more in 1977, too. Songs like "Saint Stephen," "Dancing in the Streets" and even "Not Fade Away" became springboards to all sorts of fascinating and inventive grooves that the band explored with tremendous zest and imagination.

Another reason Garcia seemed so exuberant on the tour was that the Grateful Dead movie—rather unimaginatively titled *The Grateful Dead*—was finally completed just before the band went out on the road, ending what he called at the time "two years of incredible doubt, crisis after crisis, as the movie was endlessly eating bucks. Every time I thought of something, my mind would come back to the film and I'd get depressed. It's boiled down to about two hours and ten minutes now, but it sure took a lot of energy."

The film opened with great fanfare at the giant Ziegfeld Theater in Manhattan on June 1, 1977. Predictably, Deadheads loved it and everyone else pretty much ignored it, though it did get a handful of positive and negative reviews in the mainstream press. In some ways the film represents Garcia's most fully realized tangible work of art. He spent longer on the project than on any other, and it stretched him in many new directions as he was forced to ponder how to communicate the totality of the Grateful Dead experience in both visual and musical terms. How do you *show* how the Grateful Dead interacts musically onstage? How, without a voice-over narration, do you explain what Deadheads are all about? How do you give some sense of both the tactile trippiness and the transformative power of the music? Imagine what it must have been like for Garcia to wade through all that raw footage that showed him every imaginable perspective of a Dead concert, when he'd only seen it from his own vantage point onstage for ten years—dancers in the audience spinning like gypsies; straight union vendors selling hot dogs in the cramped Winterland hallways; Billy Kreutzmann in action close up as seen over his left shoulder; a security guard dealing with kids trying to talk their way into the show; a wild nitrous oxide party backstage during the concert.

Working on the film "changed my outlook towards the whole thing," Garcia said shortly after the film opened. "It gave me a greater sense of the unique value of the Grateful Dead, which is something of which I've been aware but haven't known how to express effectively and don't care to. It either is, or it isn't.

"The film works very well on the contour of it—its energy is a good example of the Grateful Dead experience. It's a translation of that idea, both coming from what it's like for me—in my head, as abstract ideas, nonspecific images—and what it's like for anybody."

What's striking, too, is that even though the film was already "out of date" in a sense when it was released—by 1977 Mickey was back and the group really had a very different sound—it was fundamentally *true*, and more than twenty years later it still communicates the essence of the music and the experience better than any other single work. What it said about the music and the crowd, in its own impressionistic way, is no less valid today than it was in 1977. Garcia could be a very tough critic of his own work, given to sometimes harsh revisionism, but he always spoke fondly of the movie. He remained rightfully proud of it for the rest of his life.

As usual, Garcia didn't really have any time to savor the completion of the film. "He segued from the Dead movie to mixing *Terrapin Station*," says Emily Craig, who worked as assistant to Garcia during the mixing sessions, "and I thought the song 'Terrapin Station' had a very filmic approach. They were physically cutting sixteen-track tape in between some very rapidly played guitar notes. It was really exciting and slightly bizarre. They were taking movements of music and treating them as if they were scenes. I think there was a lot of film influence in how that particular song got approached."

The final overdubbing on the *Terrapin Station* album had been completed during the spring tour: "I remember working in New York [at Automated Sound]," Olsen says. "They were working at the Capitol Theater [in Passaic, New Jersey] or someplace doing shows and they couldn't get back in the city until midnight. So we'd start to work at midnight and go from midnight to 9 A.M. Actually, it worked out well—they were ready to roll then. John Belushi [of the TV comedy hit *Saturday Night Live*] was there a lot, but after he passed out on the floor I barred him. I remember having to step over him when he was passed out."

After the tour left the New York area, Olsen flew to London to work with the renowned British arranger Paul Buckmaster on orchestral parts for "Terrapin" and Donna Godchaux's moving ballad "Sunrise," which had been inspired by the death of Grateful Dead road manager Rex Jackson in an automobile accident in September 1976. "The orchestrations were written after the vocals were done because I wanted to complement the Dead instead of have the Dead complement some orchestration," Olsen says. "So I took the tapes and went over to England. Buckmaster, being quite well-to-do for a string player, owned this house [in London] but he had put no furniture in it. So we had a tape deck on one side of the room and a remote control and charts all over the floor, and we were on our hands and knees on the floor writing out this part and that part."

The orchestrations proved to be the most controversial element on the album, and Mickey Hart in particular hated Buckmaster's light and breezy orchestrations on the otherwise furious drum duel known as "Terrapin Flyer." Olsen says, "I told Garcia and Weir exactly what I planned on doing with the orchestrations and they gave me the go-ahead. I said, 'Do I have to go through every member of the band?' They said, 'No, we'll take care of it.' But I don't think they ever told anybody."

The strings, a five-piece recorder consort, a horn section and a choir (for the last section of "Terrapin") were recorded at three different London studios, and then Olsen brought the tapes back to California and he and Garcia mixed the record in a number of marathon sessions.

"It was a slightly strange time because almost nobody else was around or allowed in," Emily Craig says. "The other bandmembers were in and out. Mickey drove off a cliff and was laid up for a while. And Deborah was persona non grata."

The relationship between Garcia and Deborah Koons had started to unravel a bit as early as mid-1976, and by the beginning of 1977 Garcia had moved out of his Belvedere home and into a room in Richard Loren's Mill Valley management office, which was in a nice house on a hill. By most accounts, the breakup was long and messy. Garcia was famously unassertive and non-confrontational in relationships. He preferred ducking and hiding and allowing others—crew members, friends—to build an impenetrable wall around him to protect him from unpleasantness. It didn't always work. In one incident, recounted by a witness, Deborah threw a container from a water dispenser through a window at Loren's office after Garcia and a couple of his cronies repeatedly refused to unlock the door to let her in.

Rock Scully and others have suggested that the Grateful Dead crew was instrumental in destroying Jerry and Deborah's relationship. But Richard Loren maintains, "Jerry drove her away as much as the crew drove her away.

If Jerry wanted to have her by his side and the crew didn't want it, she would have been there. So that doesn't give Jerry credit for having a say in his love life. I think it was much deeper than that. Jerry was such a complex person that no woman was going to be part of all of his life. I think what part of him that she had was precious to her and vice versa."

In Deborah's telling of the relationship's demise, she broke up with Garcia in November 1977, many months later than others claim. "I had been traveling with Jerry for about three years," she said, "and I'd moved to California to live with him, and what I realized after those three years is that I felt that I'd lost my identity in Jerry's life. I felt like I kind of dissolved myself in his life. And I wanted to not have to go everywhere with him and do everything with him—basically live his life. So I told him I didn't want to travel with him anymore and I wanted to kind of pull back, and he got angry about that and we just reached a rocky place. I think that if we'd been able to be left alone, we could've worked it out, but such was the nature of Jerry's life that there were a lot of people around him and they jumped in and started interfering and kind of taking over."

Mountain Girl returned from her self-imposed exile on the Oregon coast to the Stinson Beach house in August 1977. She enrolled Sunshine and Annabelle in a public school in Bolinas, and then a few weeks later "Jerry showed up and said he was moving back in if that was okay with us," she says. "We all stood there with our mouths hanging open. 'Oh, okay.' The bad part was I had come back and put the house on the market because I decided it had too many ghosts for me—I literally sold it the night before he came home. Anyway, he came back and it was a very nice moment for all of us, and we got to stay there for three or four months before the sale went through."

Meanwhile, back in the corporate record business world, Arista Records boss Clive Davis directed his company to make a concerted promotional push for *Terrapin Station* when it was released in the middle of the summer of 1977, and the album did sell more in its first few months than the previous studio album on Grateful Dead Records, *Blues for Allah*. Still, there weren't many radio stations willing to take the plunge and play the entire eighteen minutes of the "Terrapin" suite. "Estimated Prophet" garnered much more radio play (and does to this day), but Arista failed to break a hit single from the record. First they considered releasing a remixed version of "Dancing in the Streets," augmented with horns; then they switched at the last moment and put out "Passenger," a propulsive rock tune written by Phil Lesh and Peter Monk and sung by Weir and Donna Godchaux. It failed to catch on, however.

Reaction to *Terrapin Station* among Deadheads was decidedly mixed. Many were simply unwilling to accept a Grateful Dead slicked up by an L.A. producer using horns and strings. The record was also characterized by an odd sort of perfection—never a Grateful Dead quality. "It actually sounds like a record," Garcia crowed at the time. "People won't believe it's us."

The Dead were not exactly considered to be a band on the cutting edge in 1977; quite the contrary. That was the year punk and new wave hit with a vengeance, and with them the beginnings of a serious anti-hippie blacklash in the youth culture. With an amazing array of British acts crossing the Atlantic—the Clash, Elvis Costello, Graham Parker—and a new breed of U.S. groups tearing up the clubs—Blondie, the Ramones, Mink DeVille, Talking Heads—the Dead were suddenly regarded as terribly passé in rock-critic circles. Bands that jammed and played eighteen-minute songs were regarded as bloated, antiquated relics of rock's past. Better to pogo furiously for the two minutes of the Ramones' "Blitzkrieg Bop" than to wiggle in your seat to eleven minutes of "Peggy-O." (For his part, Garcia professed to liking the Ramones, Elvis Costello and other new wave bands.) Pot was derided as a brain-rotting soporific; psychedelics were considered more '60s detritus. Speed, cocaine and heroin were the preferred drugs in the punk/new wave world.

The Dead scene didn't discriminate against *any* drugs, and by the end of 1977, cocaine and, to a lesser degree, heroin use were on the rise. When Mountain Girl first heard reports that a form of smokable heroin known simply as "Persian" had entered the scene, "I didn't believe it. We associated heroin with crummy, dirty junkies on the street; the downward chute, where you're flat on your back within two weeks. I thought it was totally antithetical to what I felt we were all about. Heroin is just such a dead-end drug. It doesn't lead you anywhere but down. There's no special enlightenment to be gained from it. It's sheer wastage, beyond cocaine. Cocaine at least you get some work done, even if it's not very good work."

Heroin had been on the fringes of the Dead's world since the '60s. Some members of the extended Diggers family had been into smack, and it was used by a number of people in San Francisco bands, including Big Brother and Santana. Members of both of the Dead's Watkins Glen mates—the Band and the Allman Brothers—had had problems with heroin, and the drug even gained a foothold at Mickey Hart's ranch for a while. In his book, Rock Scully says that French concert promoters on the Dead's 1974 Europe tour gave the band some potent China White heroin, and Ron Rakow admits that one Christmastime, on a whim, he took it upon himself to score some of the powder for himself and Garcia. But even in a world that embraced drugs the way the Dead did, heroin was widely regarded as the one true no-no. That is, until Persian came into the scene.

"When it first came around it was not called heroin; it was known as Persian opium," says Alan Trist. "Of course it turned out to not really be opium, which is somewhat benign, at all, but a form of processed heroin. At first it was an experience of an energizing drug. Eventually, of course, you sort of fall down or get slopped out on it, but initially it isn't like that—it's energizing, particularly if you combine it with cocaine. It was in some respects ideal for the situation that Jerry was in. It allowed him to do a tremendous amount and not be bothered by all the pressures. Eventually, of course, it turns on you and it has the opposite effect, which is perhaps not that recognizable to the user, but is to others."

"When you're a guy like him," Richard Loren says, "you're in the center of a maelstrom, a whirlwind. Everybody's asking questions, everybody wants you to give a decision on things, everybody wants help, everybody needs you *just for a second*. Plus you've got to play good music. Everybody's dependent on you. You're one large breast and nipple. So you've got all these demands on your time, so you're taking more coke to be able to do more things and then all of a sudden you're 'burned out from exhaustion, buried in the hail,' as Dylan said [in "Shelter from the Storm"]. And when the Persian came in it was like 'Phew!' I saw that it relaxed him."

Richard Loren adds that because Garcia was wired on cocaine so much of the time, "his body needed the tranquility that heroin offers, without damaging the liver the way alcohol does. It was something that relaxed him. I think he might have died sooner of a heart attack if he hadn't done heroin. Because on coke you're racing, racing, racing."

For a considerable period, Garcia's involvement with opiates was relatively light and didn't seem to be a significant problem. He wasn't lacking in energy, he was still mostly his genial self, and his creative drive was definitely still intact. So much so that in the second half of 1977 and the winter of 1978 he and the Jerry Garcia Band spent hundreds of hours in the Dead's Club Front rehearsal space cutting an album of completely original material—*Cats Under the Stars*.

"We put so much blood into that record," John Kahn said. "That was our major try. It was all new material and we did it all ourselves. We spent so many hours in the studio. When we were inside there we didn't know if it was day or night except for this one little crack in the ceiling that would allow you to see if it was dark or light. I remember one stretch where it changed three times before I left the studio."

"I worked real hard at it and was very diligent and almost scientific about it," Garcia said. "There was a lot of heart in it, you might say."

Though a few of the songs were performed on the East and West Coasts in the late fall of 1977, the songs were mostly unknown to Deadheads around the country when the record came out in April 1978. The album accurately captured the gospel vibe of that version of the JGB with Keith and Donna and Ron Tutt, and the songs wore well through the years, developing nicely in concert.

The opener, "Reuben and Cherise," was a favorite of both Hunter and Garcia. Musically and lyrically, the song was somewhat reminiscent of parts of the "Terrapin" suite: like "Lady with a Fan," it was a linear story with mythic overtones dealing in part with true and transcendent love, and laced with symbolism. (Hunter acknowledged that the song was influenced in part by *Black Orpheus*, Marcel Camus's 1960 film that retells the Orpheus myth in a Brazilian *Carnaval* setting.) And like the instrumental track "Terrapin Station," the jam at the end of "Reuben and Cherise" revolved around a clever melodic figure that changed subtly over the course of many repetitions. Using the envelope filter on his guitar, Garcia elicited a hornlike tone that gave the song an almost regal quality, as if it were being played by some troubadour before a king centuries ago.

> *Cherise was brushing her long hair gently down*
> *It was the afternoon of Carnival*
> *As she brushes it gently down*
>
> *Reuben was strumming the painted mandolin*
> *It was inlaid with a pretty face in jade*
> *Played the Carnival Parade*
>
> *Cherise was dressing as Pirouette in white*
> *When a fatal vision gripped her tight*
> *"Cherise, beware tonight"*

Garcia's double-tracked acoustic rhythm guitar line propelled the song briskly, and Keith Godchaux contributed some of his boldest playing on this standout tune. One could imagine that "Terrapin" might have sounded something like this had Garcia, rather than Keith Olsen, produced that record.

From that dense but powerful opening song, the album progressed through a number of different interesting moods. "Love in the Afternoon," by Hunter and Kahn, was a light, easygoing tune that fell somewhere between reggae and a samba. "Palm Sunday" was one of Garcia's shortest songs—just a little more than two minutes long—but it's one of his prettiest. For the first minute of the tune, Dave Burgin plays a lovely line on the chromatic harp while Garcia plays acoustic guitar underneath. Then Garcia and Donna Godchaux sing a beautiful gospel-inflected unison duet on the song's lone verse:

> *The river so white*
> *The mountain so red*
> *And with the sunshine*
> *Over my head*
> *The honky-tonks are*
> *All closed and hushed*
> *It must be Palm Sunday again*

"I really loved that tune," Donna says wistfully. "Every Palm Sunday after that I would call Jerry and say, 'Hey Jerry, looks like Palm Sunday again,'" she laughs.

Both "Cats Under the Stars" and "Rhapsody in Red" allowed Hunter and

Garcia to address their mutual love of music itself. In the former, Garcia worked through what sounded like a quirky blend of New Orleans funk and '30s pop and jazz styles, while Hunter, who said he based the lyrics on a doodle he drew, depicted a world for the musicians in the JGB to jam in:

> *Cats on the bandstand*
> *Give 'em each a big hand*
> *Anyone who sweats like that*
> *Must be all right*

"Rhapsody in Red" sounded like a midtempo Chuck Berry song as John Lennon might have rewritten it. Garcia played a piercing electric guitar line through the entire song, and this is one of several tunes on the record that benefited from a sympathetic organ overdub by Garcia's old compadre Merl Saunders.

The longest track on the album was "Rain," a somewhat Beatlesesque tune written and sung by Donna, and with a lush orchestration by John Kahn that featured Keith's brother Brian and sister-in-law Candy on violins. Kahn's instrumental "Down Home" had no lyrics at all: It was just Donna singing wordlessly above a nicely arranged backup chorus of stacked "oo-oo" vocals and an acoustic bass line; a serene but slightly melancholy Southern gospel interlude that one could imagine hearing in a film like the black musical *Cabin in the Sky*. Then, with barely a break, "Down Home" rolls into a lazy shuffle called "Gomorrah," a Sunday school parable (with a dash of irony delivered by the Reverend Garcia), to end the album.

"As far as I'm concerned," Garcia said in the early '90s, "*Cats Under the Stars* is my most successful record—even though it's my least successful record! I've always really loved it and it just never went anywhere."

Garcia admitted he was disappointed that both rock radio and so many of his fans ignored the record. It *was* a beautifully made album loaded with strong melodies and sure rhythms. In a way it felt like a continuation of the "Terrapin" vibe, though perhaps lacking that work's deep, heartfelt passion. There was no great revelatory moment—no "inspiration, move me brightly"—where Garcia's and Hunter's souls clearly merged in mystical union and sang with one voice. But the album stands as one of the most cohesive and fully realized projects Hunter and Garcia worked on together; and it represents the last great studio collaboration between Garcia and John Kahn.

By the time *Cats Under the Stars* came out in April 1978, Ron Tutt had left the group, replaced by L.A. drummer Buzz Buchanan; and Maria Muldaur, who was John Kahn's girlfriend, had been added as a second harmony singer. (She appeared on two songs on the album.) The combination of Donna and

Maria boosted the JGB's gospel quotient, but Buchanan, though talented, didn't have the supple touch that Ron Tutt is so revered for.

"That version of the group with Maria sounded really good," Kahn said, "but it didn't end up being a good idea to have two couples in the band. There would be huge fights. Let's face it—it's an abusive lifestyle. It's not the best way to have a relationship." Still, Kahn said of the group at the time, "We've really become a band. It's not just something Jerry does in his spare time or that I do in my spare time or anything like that."

"Not only is it a band," Garcia enthused, "but it's a band that has this thing of consonance. . . . This band represents an amazing agreement. By contrast, the Grateful Dead represents amazing disagreement in terms of everybody having tremendously different ideas about music. But that's interesting for other reasons. This gets us all off in the same way. When the Grateful Dead gets off, everybody gets off differently."

By mid-1978 Garcia, Kahn and Keith were all sliding toward heavier drug dependency, and Keith in particular seemed to be completely wasted much of the time onstage with both the Jerry Garcia Band and the Grateful Dead. His playing, once full of life and overflowing with imaginative ideas, often became blocky and monochromatic during this period, and he wasn't nearly as responsive to the other musicians.

"Unfortunately, Keith was determined to do all the bad things that everybody else did," Mountain Girl observes. "That was one of the goals—to get messed up. He really liked to get trashed, and I think he was also an influence that way. He didn't really care how rubbery he got, and because he wasn't right out front in the band he could afford to get more rubbery.

"But I actually really enjoyed Keith," she continues. "He was a trip and sometimes he was very sweet. He definitely fit for a while. I thought he had a number of different talents."

By the end of the year, though, Garcia had dissolved the Jerry Garcia Band, and his relationship with Keith was strained. "Jerry caught him stealing something inside his briefcase; his drugs or something," John Kahn said. "He was inside Jerry's briefcase and then he was gone [from the JGB] right after that. I'm sure he would have been gone anyway. It was in the works that they were going to split up. But Keith would burn me and Jerry out of drugs all the time. He made Jerry mad for a period of time and it culminated in that."

Garcia was beginning to have his own problems with the Persian, too. "Jerry had been kind of quiet, but at least he'd been home," Mountain Girl says. "But he was definitely a little subdued, so I guess he was getting into some stuff. At that point I didn't see it at home really; that came a little later, but I could tell something weird was happening."

Deborah Koons said that she hung out with Garcia again in the spring and summer of 1978 and found him "very unstable. He was bouncing around, staying different places." By this time Deborah had enrolled at the San Francisco Art Institute, which took up a lot of her time, "and the farther away I got from that whole scene, the better I felt, so I just kept going. I didn't see him again for fifteen years."

Again, it's difficult to gauge the effect Garcia's drug use might have had on his playing at this time—there is no noticeable drop-off in the quality of his performances. Shows were generally a bit shorter than they had been, but they were not lacking in focus or energy. Indeed, in the few videos from 1978 that are in circulation among traders, Garcia is tremendously animated. In a black-and-white video of the Dead at Duke University in April 1978, Garcia is smiling, gesturing, doing Pete Townshend "windmills" on his guitar, even joining in on the drum solo as if he's been possessed by the spirit of Gene Krupa. And the one cover tune Garcia introduced in the spring of 1978 showed that his puckish spirit was intact. The Dead's version of Warren Zevon's playfully macabre "Werewolves of London" (which had just come out on Zevon's second album) was a howl—literally.

The band continued mainly to play large gigs—including stadium shows in Santa Barbara (where Zevon was among the opening acts), Kansas City and Eugene, Oregon—but in the summer of '78 they also played their first shows at the 9,000-seat Red Rocks Amphitheater, outside of Denver, which would become one of the Dead's magical "power spots" over the next decade. Set high on a hill amid towering rock slabs, with a magnificent view of Denver across the distant plain, Red Rocks was right out of a Zane Grey novel—it was the most overtly *Western* environment the Dead played in; the perfect place for a band that sang about outlaws, saloons and gamblers. It was its own world, completely cut off from civilization, and for band and Deadheads alike it was both haven and heaven.

Shortly after the Dead's first shows at Red Rocks in July 1978 the band started working on their second album for Arista, *Shakedown Street*. It was Garcia's idea that they work at Club Front—he had enjoyed making *Cats Under the Stars* there. No one was anxious to go to Los Angeles after their experience making *Terrapin Station*. At Club Front they'd be close to home; it was *their place.*

The band agreed to use an outside producer again, but this time they went outside traditional production circles and selected a musician who had also produced a couple of his own band's records—Lowell George of Little Feat. "We chose Lowell George because we wanted someone who understood band mechanics," Garcia explained in 1978.

Lowell George was truly one of rock music's great spirits—a big furry bear of a guy who always seemed to have a smile on his face. He was also one of the finest slide guitar players of all time, a soulful and expressive singer with a gruff, bluesy voice, and a gifted songwriter with a truly warped and unusual perspective on the world. Little Feat and the Grateful Dead were simpatico in the same way that the Allman Brothers and the Dead were: they loved to jam, they drew from many of the same musical sources and they enjoyed getting high and playing for dancing crowds. But whereas the Dead and the Allmans seemed to connect most on some mutual psychedelic plane, the Dead and Little Feat met on a polyrhythmic plane: No one played funky, syncopated N'awlins-style rock 'n' roll better than Little Feat, and they also had their share of quirky shuffles—a little like the Dead, but with a bluesier edge.

"I really liked Lowell a lot," Bill Kreutzmann said. "Whereas Keith [Olsen] always wanted to be the director-producer type and wear the higher hat—to work in the upper office, so to speak—Lowell was really like a member of the band more. If we were working on a song and he didn't feel it was going right, he'd just grab a guitar and come into the studio and show us how he felt it. That was one of the ways he'd communicate, and it worked great. I had a tremendous amount of respect for him."

Most of the songs on the record had never been played live by the Dead. The exceptions were "Fire on the Mountain"; Weir's Latin-flavored retooling of the old Pigpen vehicle "Good Lovin' "; and a revamped version of "New Minglewood Blues" that Weir called "All New Minglewood Blues" (though it actually wasn't so new).

Garcia had three new songs to contribute to the album. "Shakedown Street" was the Dead's original contribution to the age of disco—after all, 1977–78 was the heyday of Donna Summer, the soundtrack mega-hit *Saturday Night Fever* and dozens of one-hit wonders who lit up the disco dance floors with a song or two and then were never heard from again. Conversely it was also the era of "disco sucks," and more than a few Deadheads were horrified when they heard "Shakedown Street" for the first time, particularly coming on the heels of the group's lamentable disco version of "Dancing in the Streets." The disco-haters needn't have worried, however. Just as the "disco" "Dancing in the Streets" became a fascinating vehicle for some intense rhythmic jamming when the band played it live, "Shakedown Street" developed far beyond its steady rhythmic pulse in concert. It gave the band a chance to explore the funky R&B side of their roots, which had been nearly dormant since Pigpen's departure. The big jam in the last third of the song would've done Parliament/Funkadelic proud.

"If I Had the World to Give" was perhaps the most straightforward love ballad that Hunter and Garcia ever wrote together. On the surface it seemed almost like a traditional pop love song from the '40s or '50s, but Garcia's musical setting was salted with some chord choices that lent the piece a certain sadness, and lyrically there was a hint of darkness amid the bliss. The Dead played the song live only three times, possibly because Garcia had considerable difficulty negotiating its difficult vocal leaps. That's a shame, because all three versions packed a powerful emotional charge, with Garcia reaching deep down in his soul during his raw, screaming guitar breaks. The version on *Shakedown Street* was technically very strong—Garcia felt it "came out really nice"—but it didn't quite have the visceral quality the song had live. Who knows what it might have become if Garcia had kept playing it through the years?

"Stagger Lee" was a tune that worked well both live and on the record. Like "Dupree's Diamond Blues" and "Casey Jones," it was a case of Hunter and Garcia embellishing a venerable song tradition. There are "Stag-O-Lee" and "Stack-O-Lee" songs dating back more than a hundred years, and everyone from Mississippi John Hurt to Doc Watson to Dr. John covered versions of the story/song through the years. In most of the different "Stagger Lee" songs, the title character is a bad dude who kills a fellow named Billy Lyons after Billy steals Stag's Stetson hat.

Hunter's telling of the story is wonderfully colorful. His setting is "1940 Xmas eve with a full moon over town," and instead of stealing Stagger Lee's hat, Billy DeLyon wins it in a dice game and then gets blown away. Hunter adds an ineffectual policeman named Baio to the tale, but the central character is really Billy's wife, Delia, who is bent on revenge.

> *As Stagger Lee lit a cigarette she shot him in the balls*
> *Blew the smoke off her revolver, had him dragged to City Hall*
> *"Baio, Baio, see you hang him high*
> *He shot my Billy dead and now he's got to die"*

"Stagger Lee" was Hunter and Garcia's last stab at bringing the oral tradition of narrative storytelling into the present day. It was also one of their most successful attempts.

The other new songs on the album were Weir and Barlow's humorous testosterone-fueled rock rave-up "I Need a Miracle," another wispy, romantic ballad by Donna called "From the Heart of Me" and a strange little percussion excursion titled "Serengetti."

The sessions for *Shakedown Street* were—like Lowell George himself—extremely loose, especially compared with Keith Olsen's demanding studio regimen. (Which is not to imply that Olsen didn't like to party with the band; he did, but he also asked more of the group than Lowell did.) There were many long, unproductive days and nights in the studio—sessions that were frittered away getting high. Lowell and Garcia were each independently using both coke and heroin (mainly lots of the former), and the band as a whole was in a bad period in terms of substance abuse.

The band fell behind schedule making the album and because of commitments to tour with Little Feat, Lowell was unable to work on the record after the basic tracks were recorded. This may have actually been a good development. Midway through the project Garcia told a writer, "Really, it's better to work without a producer at times. I'm not happy with all the basic tracks on this—but I'm never completely happy."

The group had hoped to have the record completed by the end of August, because looming in mid-September was the Dead's greatest adventure yet: a trip to Egypt for three concerts at the foot of the Great Pyramid and the Sphinx. The album could wait.

CHAPTER 16

The Desert Stars
Are Bright Tonight

T he notion of the Grateful Dead playing at the pyramids had been tossed around in stoned conversations almost since the band started. The fantasies didn't stop there, either: Why not play Machu Picchu and Easter Island and the Great Wall of China and Stonehenge? Imagine what it would be like if the Dead brought their music to ancient, spiritually high places! Perhaps they could tap into the mysterious power of those spots, stir up a few ghosts from the collective consciousness— channel an Inca healer or Druid priest or Egyptian king. At the very least it would be a blast for the band and family and the hearty fans who were willing to make the long journey.

"I'm into the psychedelic archaeology of the ancient world," Phil explained, "the structures that mark the channels of earth energy and places of power. No matter what anyone thinks they might be, there is definitely some kind of mojo about the pyramids. When you get there you find out there *is* power."

The idea inched toward becoming reality after Richard Loren visited Egypt in 1975. As he explains, "When I lived with Marty Balin for the first three weeks that I came here [in 1970], Marty was an avid reader and an avid fan of Egypt. He introduced me to Egyptology and Egypt as a country, and I fell incredibly in love with it. I read all Marty's books about it and it became a real hobby for me. The first chance I had to take a vacation from the Grateful Dead I went to Egypt for three weeks. Then I went a second time the next year. I was on a horseback ride with a friend near the Great Pyramid and the Sphinx and I remember riding along and then all of sudden I turned around and I saw this stage to the left of the Sphinx and I saw the pyramids and it dawned on me, 'Wouldn't it be great if the Grateful Dead could play in Egypt?' I brought the idea back with me and I took it to Jerry first. He thought it was a great idea and that we should go for it, so I presented it, with Jerry, to the Grateful Dead. 'Yeah, man, that's far-out. Great, great, great!' We put together a committee to try to make this happen, and that committee was comprised of Alan Trist and myself and Phil Lesh, who was the band's representative. Jerry got totally into Egyptology and the mysteries of the pyramids, of course. And my office *became* Egypt for that period. It took two years to get there from when the idea came up in January of 1976."

No rock 'n' roll band had ever played at the Sound and Light Theater in

Giza before—it was used mainly for a dramatic tourist show about the pyramids and the Sphinx, and occasionally for concerts of Egyptian music. But there was a stage and seating for about a thousand people, and that's what had caught Loren's eye. The Dead faced numerous obstacles in gaining permission to play the gigs there, but early in the process they managed to find a couple of allies in American diplomatic circles who wrote letters to the Egyptian ambassador in Washington and the minister of culture in Cairo to lay the groundwork for a formal request.

"Then Phil and Richard and I got on our suits and we flew to Washington and went to the Egyptian embassy and we had a big meeting there with the ambassador," Trist says. "This was our big hurdle—if the Egyptian ambassador in Washington said it was okay, then we could go on to the next step. The meeting went very well, and the thing that pulled it off really was Phil. The Egyptian ambassador had a crucial qustion in his mind which was very simple: 'Why do you want to play there? You're a rock 'n' roll band—what's this all about?' And Phil's answer was, 'Because as musicians we have learned that playing in different places and in different cultures influences our music in ways that we treasure.' Well, you could see the ambassador light up and smile. He loved that answer, because it was so genuine. It was totally from a musical perspective and not loaded up with political stuff or cultural stuff or commercial stuff. It was very pure. And it *was* pure. Our wanting to go there had nothing to do with money or detente or any of that.

"So after we had the ambassador's blessing, the three of us went to Cairo and we spent two or three weeks there seeing the minister of culture, the minister of information, the director of the Sound and Light Theater and all these other officials. It took *forever* to get all these appointments done. The minister of culture would say, 'I'm having a sauna at four o'clock. Meet me there.' And we'd go there and he'd already have gone off somewhere else. It took days to get anything done. Then Richard and I went back to Egypt two more times after that trip to work on logistical things."

Finally, the Dead won over everyone they needed to, and the gigs were scheduled for September 14, 15 and 16, 1978. As part of their agreement, the Dead could not take any money out of the country after the shows—all proceeds from the concerts went to the Department of Antiquities (which was involved in the protection and restoration of ancient sites in Egypt) and to the Faith and Hope charity for handicapped children, a pet project of the wife of Egyptian president Anwar Sadat, who, as fate would have it, would be in America trying to negotiate a peace agreement with Israel at the time of the shows. Arista Records agreed to contribute some money for the trip, and paid for multitrack recordings to be made for a live album.

The band warmed up with two shows at Red Rocks at the end of August (where they debuted "I Need a Miracle," "Stagger Lee," "Shakedown Street," "If I Had the World to Give" and "From the Heart of Me") and then a big moneymaking concert at Giants Stadium in northern New Jersey to help defray some of the costs at the Egypt trip. Of course if a rock band made an excursion like that today, the venture would probably be underwritten by some corporation in conjunction with MTV or a cable television channel, but that was not the Dead's way of operating, then or later. In fact, everyone in the Dead family paid most of their own way there. And a tour of Europe was booked for after the Egypt trip to make the trip east even more worthwhile.

On September 4, more than two hundred Grateful Dead family and friends flew on a chartered jet to New York, where they picked up the band and crew, and then made their way across the Atlantic to Paris and on to Cairo. For nearly two weeks the Dead and their friends took over the Mena House hotel, a luxurious (for Giza) four-story building a stone's throw from the Great Pyramid. Days were spent wandering ancient sites in small groups, learning to ride camels, lounging by the Mena House pool, dining on local specialties, smoking hashish and preparing for the shows. Quite a collection of fellow travelers were along for the ride: Owsley, Kesey, Babbs and assorted Merry Pranksters, Deadhead basketball star Bill Walton, writer-humorist Paul Krassner, David Freiberg, John Kahn (who was in charge of recording the shows), Bill Graham (there as a tourist instead of a promoter for a change) and a few hundred fans from all over who'd scraped together enough money to make the trek. Among the Dead family no-shows were Rock Scully, who had been out of the scene for a while, and Robert Hunter, who Garcia joked was "too mean" to go. "That rat," Garcia said. "He was too stingy to buy a ticket. He convinced himself it wouldn't be important."

"It was probably the most exciting thing a lot of us had done," Mountain Girl says, "because it was really, really different. Europe at least you can be assured of certain things, but in Egypt, forget it. It's a really different culture. It was truly the third world, with salesmen on every corner and donkey dung underfoot, bad water and great hash from the taxi drivers at really high prices. There was a lot of sexual harassment for the women. Lots of petting and fondling and grabbing. I had men stop me on the street and ask, 'How much do you weigh?' Because there, the bigger you are the better; big gals are *in*," she laughs.

"It was overwhelming," Trist says. "There wasn't one minute that we weren't naturally on a high day after day. People could hardly sleep because the energy was so intense. So that was the context of the gig. On top of all this, the music was almost incidental; or certainly the context of other things going on was much greater than any other gig I'd ever been to."

It's probably going too far to say that the shows themselves were anticlimactic, but nearly everyone agreed that the Dead had played much better. The band was hampered by a number of factors. Bill Kreutzmann cracked a bone in his wrist in a fall from a horse and could only play with one arm. ("When asked by the Egyptian press what it was like playing with one arm,

Billy said, 'In the land of the limbless, a one-armed drummer is king,' " Trist notes with a laugh.) The piano tuner who was supposed to go to Egypt with the band backed out at the last minute, so Keith's piano was horribly out of tune all three nights. John Kahn severely sprained his ankle in a tumble down the stairs of the recording truck, and then he and Garcia spent much of the time doped up on prescription pain medication, since there was no Persian to be found there. "John and Jerry were taking these painkillers and snoozing their way through Egypt basically," M.G. says. "That's when I really began to associate snoozing with drug use. That had never been a problem before, but the long snoozes got longer and longer and more and more frequent."

"Jerry wasn't in the best of spirits; he was having some difficulties with things," Richard Loren says. "The Dead are a collective and they're not going to put on a great show if they're not all feeling good. They were happy to be there and everything was wonderful there, but there was a lot of personal angst and anxieties going on amongst themselves."

"Jerry was definitely going through something, but I couldn't tell you what it was," John Kahn corroborated. "Even though I spent a lot of time with him, sometimes he'd shut me out, just like he shut out other people, and he just wouldn't talk about stuff. I didn't push him; I figured when he wanted to talk about something he would. The rest of the time I gave him his space, which is one reason I think he liked to hang out with me.

"I know he wasn't entirely happy with how *Shakedown Street* was going. I know he was unhappy with certain things about the Grateful Dead at that time—Keith was kind of out of it; Jerry and Phil were kind of distant in that period. I think there was also some weird fallout in his personal life—the thing with Deborah was over and here he was in Egypt, and M.G. was there, but not really 'with' him. It was a little weird, but even so, I think he would tell you he had a great time. Everyone did. We talked about little things that happened on that trip for years. We even talked about it a little the last time I saw him, just before he died."

The concerts attracted 1,000 to 1,500 people a night. About half were Americans and Europeans, half Egyptians. Madame Sadat and a number of other government dignitaries were on hand for the first night's performance. Each concert opened with a set by Hamza el-Din, a Nubian friend of the Dead's who had been a sort of one-person ambassador for traditional Egyptian music in America since the '60s, well-known in world music circles years before his association with the Dead. At the shows, Hamza was joined by a small troupe of Nubian friends playing ouds and tars (a tar is a deeply resonant single-membrane hand drum that looks like a giant tambourine), singing and clapping their hands rhythmically in a set of Egyptian folk songs. Then the Dead came out and joined forces with the Nubians on a rhythmic improv, with Garcia's guitar singing sweetly above the clapping and drumming. The first night that cross-cultural jam eventually segued into the Dead playing "Not Fade

Away." The second night it was "Deal." The third night it was "Fire on the Mountain." Otherwise, the Dead played the same kind of material they played in San Francisco and Des Moines and Boston: cowboy tunes, Chuck Berry rock 'n' roll, "Stella Blue" and "Terrapin," "The Other One" and "Shakedown Street."

The final night was the magic night. The concert coincided with a total eclipse of the full moon, and nearly everyone in the Dead's extended family decided to throw caution to the wind and trip for the occasion. Kesey had brought a Murine eyedrop bottle filled with liquid LSD, and he nearly emptied it that night putting drops on eager tongues.

"Take a perfect setting," Garcia said later. "What could be better? What could be more amazing? A total eclipse, a full moon, the Great Pyramid; everything perfect and we went and played shitty. It didn't really matter. We had a wonderful time, man, we really did. We got a lot out of it. We got off like bandits. It was great."

"Maybe the whole thing was just a little overwhelming," Donna Godchaux observed in the mid-'80s. "Our expectations were so high I think we were a little disappointed we weren't 'beamed up' or something. It's definitely something I'll never forget, a real highlight in my life."

To the dismay of their British fans, the Dead abruptly canceled the shows they'd scheduled for London's Rainbow Theatre following the Egypt trip, in order to finish *Shakedown Street* and have it come out before their November U.S. tour. Back in America, Garcia listened to the multitrack tapes of the Egypt shows and his worst fears were confirmed: the performances weren't good enough to put out as an album. The Egypt trip had cost about half a million dollars, and there was no "product" to show for it.

Since Lowell George was not available to work on overdubs or mixing for *Shakedown Street*, Garcia brought in John Kahn to help the band finish the album, but "nobody seemed to be that into it," Kahn said. "They just wanted it to be done. It was a horrible experience; a pain in the ass doing it. They're all so difficult. There are so many of them and they have pretty much an equal voice. You have Mickey making sure that every track is filled with some kind of percussion sound, and at the same time you're having to make sure everyone else gets heard, too. It was just tedious; it was real hard work. I ended up playing a lot of the keyboards on it because Keith would ditch the sessions a lot. I was down in L.A. when they were doing *Terrapin Station* and I remember he missed a lot of those sessions, too. I ended up playing most of the Hammond organ on *Shakedown Street*—that's me on 'I Need a Miracle' and 'Good Lovin'.' But everybody seemed kind of scattered then, including Jerry."

By this time, Jerry, Mountain Girl and the kids were living in a house in Inverness, a remote but beautiful little community by the sea in west Marin. M.G. had bought a small business, the Foggy Mountain Bakery, to occupy some of her time, and Jerry was spending endless days and nights at the studio. According to M.G., after the Egypt trip Garcia's drug use began to escalate noticeably. "That was when I really saw that he was into something that was addictive and weird," she says. "He was smoking this stuff on tin foil, and that was the first time I caught on that something was wrong. He told me it was opium, so it was okay. I said, 'I don't really like opium much; it makes me dizzy.' It's fine if you want to get to sleep, but I had to do the dishes and keep the house together and all this other stuff.

"I tried [the Persian] one time by accident, Jerry had left a bunch of this stuff around the house and I didn't really know what it was. He left some out on the tin foil and I smoked it and I passed out and threw up the whole thing! I said, 'Wait a minute, this is *not* opium! I know opium and this isn't it.' So I confronted him about it. I was really, really upset. And he admitted he was strung out. And I ranted a bit and he stalked away. Basically I told him he had to choose between that and us; our scene. And that scared him. A couple of days later he came back and said he was going to kick; that he was kicking. I didn't know what to do. I had to go to work. I didn't know anything about kicking. I didn't want to call Synanon or some place like that. I couldn't think what to do or who to call. So he kind of gruffed around the house for a couple of days and then split again."

Shakedown Street was completed in time to hit the stores in the beginning of November, as hoped. A single of "Good Lovin' " backed with "Stagger Lee" was released but didn't sell many copies. The album itself sold fairly well—actually, better than *Terrapin Station* had initially—and both the title song and "I Need a Miracle" became popular songs on FM radio for while.

The band's tour kicked off on a high note with an appearance on *Saturday Night Live* before the largest viewing audience they'd ever played for—an estimated fifteen million viewers. Garcia had long proclaimed his distaste for playing on television, which he once said was "just the wrong form for the Grateful Dead. I mean, it's about enough time for us to tune up. Also television is kind of reductive. The band playing on television seems reduced. It doesn't come through." Nevertheless, *Saturday Night Live* in 1978 was much hipper than "regular" TV, with some cast members and writers nearly as enamored with pot and cocaine as the Grateful Dead, and it was probably the most popular program on television with the Dead's core demographic audience. The group played three songs on the show—"Casey Jones," appropriately enough, and a medley of "I Need a Miracle" and "Good Lovin'." Outwardly they seemed to be having a ball on the show, and Garcia in particular seemed to play to the cameras more than the others. He might not have *liked* television (though that is debatable), but he understood its power and he almost always played well on TV.

The rest of the tour, which stretched from the second week of November 1978 all the way to mid-February 1979 with just a few short breaks, was reasonably solid musically, but fraught with personal crises. In late November

Garcia came down with a severe case of bronchitis, no doubt exacerbated by smoking Persian and freebasing cocaine (not to mention his usual chain-smoking of unfiltered cigarettes), and he was hospitalized for a couple of days. Keith was barely a factor onstage at this point, and offstage he could be surly and even more uncommunicative than usual.

"Keith's and my personal life then was so horrible," Donna recalled, "and in the band as a whole the feeling was, 'The music stinks. Every concert stinks.' Things got to a point where on every conceivable level things were so bad I went to the road manager and said, 'I've gotta go home.' And I did. I left and missed the last couple of dates [in Buffalo and Detroit in January 1979]. Then Keith and I did one more tour, discussing all along the way how we could get out of it. It was horrible, because we weren't quitters."

At the same time, the band was wondering how they could relieve the Godchauxs of their duties. Keith had been a problem for a long time, and Donna, though obviously talented, had trouble hearing herself onstage amid the loud instruments and frequently sang off-key. There was no way one could be fired and the other retained, so it was decided both had to go.

According to Donna, "What happened was after I left that tour, then Keith and I decided we wanted to get out and start our own group or do something else—*anything* else. So we played that benefit concert at the Oakland Coliseum [February 17, 1979's Rock for Life benefit to end environmental cancer], and then a few days later there was a meeting at our house and it was brought up whether we should stay in the band anymore. So we discussed it, as a band, and we mutually decided we would leave. I'll tell you, I instantly felt like about a billion pounds had been lifted off me." Tragically, Keith was killed in an automobile accident a year and a half later.

By the time Keith and Donna left the Dead, the group had already decided on a replacement: Brent Mydland, who was the keyboardist and backup singer in Bob Weir's solo band. Brent recalled, "Bob gave me a call one night out of the blue and said, 'Would you be interested in being in the Dead? It's not for sure, but Keith and Donna might be leaving soon, so you ought to check out some of this stuff,' and he gave me a list of some tunes to listen to—fifteen or twenty songs.

"I knew quite a few of them. I'd liked the Grateful Dead when I was younger, though I kind of lost track of them in the early '70s. In fact, when I first met Bobby, I didn't even know the Dead were still together."

Brent and the Dead had about two weeks of rehearsals at Club Front before their first gig together at San Jose's Spartan Stadium on April 22, 1979. Sitting behind a Hammond B-3 organ with his long blond hair and bushy beard, Brent looked a lot like the young Gregg Allman. It was immediately apparent that he was a much more physical player that Keith—he really threw himself into his playing—and because he played a broader range of keyboards, he drew from a wider sonic palette than his predecessor. Whereas Keith had always been an acoustic piano man first and foremost (with occasional periods of investigating the Fender Rhodes electric piano), Brent's heart was in the B-3, and he was also adept at synthesizer. Coming into a band that was already fourteen years old, with the kind of history the Dead had, must have been intimidating, but Brent was a quick study and a reasonably confident player.

"What we wanted was a keyboard player who wasn't a pianist," Garcia explained in early 1981. "The whole thing was that with piano, guitars, bass and drums, what you've got is an all-percussion band. What we wanted was a keyboard to provide color and sustain and some of those qualities that guitars don't provide, and Brent has been real good at that. He's been adding a lot of texture and color and he's also a fine singer, probably the best of all of us, so our trio singing is real nice."

Indeed, the most noticeable change when Brent came into the Dead was the improvement in the band's vocal quality. Garcia was always the surest, most pitch-conscious singer in the group, while Weir and Donna tended to slide around notes, which made for some awkward harmony blends. But Brent's craggy tenor was steady enough to nail the high end in a harmony, and combined with Garcia's vocal, it set up an easy pocket for Weir to slip his part into. Garcia seemed visibly elated and energized by the band's new vocal power. Songs with prominent three-part harmonies like "I Know You Rider," "The Wheel," "Mississippi Half-Step," "Eyes of the World" and "Truckin' " sounded better than they had in a while, and the vocal combination of Brent and Bob on songs like "Mexicali Blues," "Playing in the Band" and "Cassidy" brought out new subtleties in those tunes.

The first tour by the new band in the spring of 1979 was very well received by Deadheads. Not surprisingly, some of the jamming was a bit tentative, as Brent adjusted to his role and the band got used to him, but it caused only a minor disruption in the band's evolution.

The other exciting development on that tour was the addition of "the Beast," a massive new setup of drums behind Mickey and Billy. The Beast had evolved out of Mickey's work on the soundtrack for Francis Ford Coppola's moody, impressionist Vietnam epic *Apocalypse Now*. When Coppola asked the drummer to contribute an all-percussion score that could be used in different parts of the film, Mickey collected dozens of drums and percussion devices and even had some new drums built to be able to convey the feeling of the jungle and the horrors of war. There were other influences affecting the drum solos around the same time, too: Mickey studied Japanese taiko drumming with a troupe called On-Deko-Za, and he brought some of that music's precision and articulation into his solos; Billy began playing the African talking drum regularly; and Mickey brought the Egyptian tar into his arsenal. Over the next few years, the drum solo became more exotic and compelling as Mickey introduced instruments with distinctive and unusual timbres, such as the marimbalike African balafon, a one-stringed South American drone instrument called the berimbau, and resonant bronze Tibetan bowls that ring like temple bells when flicked lightly with a fingertip.

Garcia's ongoing involvement with heroin and cocaine was exacerbated by the return, shortly after the Egypt trip, of Rock Scully. The onetime Grateful Dead manager had drifted off during the band's performing hiatus (and even spent time in prison for drug possession), but had now finagled a position as the press liaison for the group, and in no time was back in the thick of things. Garcia moved into a downstairs bedroom in the house at 84 Hepburn Heights in San Rafael where Scully and his wife, Nikki, lived, and he and Scully became partners in Persian; indeed, Scully became one of Garcia's main procurers.

John Kahn was also wrapped up in this increasingly dark circle of coke and Persian users. Like Garcia, though, he continued to be quite productive musically. In December 1978 he formed a group called Reconstruction around Garcia and a quartet of jazz players—drummer Gaylord Birch, reeds player Ron Stallings, trombonist Ed Neumeister and organist Merl Saunders.

"Reconstruction was going to be a band that would do more jazz, explore that avenue on a deeper level than the old Merl and Jerry thing," Kahn recalled. "It was supposed to be a thing where if Jerry was going to play in the band, which he ended up doing, we could still do work when he was out of town with the Grateful Dead. That was the point. In which case we'd have another guitar player. It was supposed to be something I could do when Jerry was away with the Grateful Dead, which seemed to be more and more of the time. I actually did it a few times—I did some gigs with Jerry Miller of Moby Grape. He was a really good guy and a great player. I wasn't really planning on Jerry being in the band originally, and then when he was in the band it sort of changed everything from what the plan was. Then, when he left for Grateful Dead tours, we were never able to really get anywhere because everyone expected to see Jerry in there. But it was fun for a while; we had some nice gigs. It was fun making Jerry play those real difficult songs. The horn players used to make fun of Jerry and me for being late or taking drugs or whatever— the same old stuff—and then I'd listen to tapes and we were the only ones who could play the songs right!"

The group had a different repertoire from any of Garcia's other solo ventures. While there were some holdovers from the Jerry Garcia Band, like "Someday Baby," the Beatles' "Dear Prudence" and "That's What Love Will Make You Do," most of the tunes were new to Garcia—Horace Silver's "Freedom Jazz Dance," Jimmy Cliff's "Struggling Man" and various recent Merl Saunders tunes. And this time out there were four soloists in the band: the two horn players, Merl and Garcia.

The approach was to play jazz and rock together but still be danceable," Merl comments. "It was a great band for a while. Jerry liked that it gave him a totally new structure to work with, with these great horn players and a different set of tunes. These were really excellent musicians. And because they came from outside the Grateful Dead world, they related to Jerry as just another player, not a 'star.' "

Reconstruction stayed together for only nine months, and except for three shows in Denver in April 1979, they never left the Bay Area. Merl believes that Garcia's increasing drug dependence played a role in the dissolution of the band. "He seemed pretty clean at first," he says, "but then I saw him start to slip, and then there was a night when he didn't show up for a gig, which was done purposely, I think. It was sabotaged. [Saunders won't say by whom.] They didn't tell him there was a gig to get to. And shortly after that he and John started a different group and I sort of lost touch with him."

In mid-1979 the Grateful Dead returned to Club Front to begin recording *Go to Heaven*, their first album since Brent Mydland joined the band. Though no one in the group had been particularly happy, in retrospect, with either *Terrapin Station* or *Shakedown Street*, they agreed once again to enlist an outside producer. They remained convinced that with the right producer they might actually turn out a bona fide hit single. As the years went on Garcia seemed increasingly unwilling to shoulder the responsibility for running the Dead's recording sessions, so they looked outside their ranks for a firm but sympathetic hand. This time they settled on a British producer who'd already struck gold and platinum working in America—Gary Lyons, who was best known for working with the hard rock group Foreigner.

"I guess I was considered sort of a hot producer at the time," Lyons says, "and the Dead had the reputation as being the Bermuda Triangle for producers."

Garcia had only three original tunes to offer for the sessions. His songwriting output had been on the decline since he started smoking Persian regularly, the *Cats Under the Stars* material in 1977 being his most recent burst of solid collaboration with Hunter.

"Alabama Getaway" was a rare rock 'n' roll tune from Garcia, a catchy bit of Chuck Berry–inspired riffing, with lyrics that sounded as if they could've been matched to an old prison blues.

"Althea" was back in the vein of other Garcia midtempo shuffles, but lyrically it was something new—a sly evocation of a powerful woman; "the helpful lady, big sister kind of," Garcia said. "Minerva," Hunter suggested, referring to the Roman goddess of wisdom, invention and martial prowess. In the song, Garcia's character looks to Althea for advice:

> *I told Althea I was feeling lost*
> *Lacking in some direction*
> *Althea told me upon scrutiny*
> *That my back might need protection*
>
> *I told Althea that treachery*
> *Was tearing me limb from limb*

Althea told me: "Now cool down boy—
Settle back easy, Jim"

Althea continues to outline the faults of the main character, who is "loose with the truth" and "honest to the point of recklessness / self-centered in the extreme." But in a clever twist at the end, the singer reveals his true colors:

I told Althea
I'm a roving sign—
That I was born to be a bachelor
Althea told me: "Okay, that's fine"
So now I'm trying to catch her

The band cut basic tracks on a third Hunter-Garcia tune called "What'll You Raise," which was overflowing with gambling metaphors, but Garcia said, "I wasn't too happy with it. It was too much like what we've done and so I dumped it." He did have one other lead vocal on the album: a lively re-arrangement of one of the group's oldest cover songs, "Don't Ease Me In," the A side of the Warlocks' first single in 1965.

Go to Heaven was the first Grateful Dead album since *Anthem of the Sun* to contain more original songs written by Weir than Garcia. And Weir's three new tunes, all with lyrics by John Barlow, showed his continuing maturity as a songwriter. "Lost Sailor" was an odd but appealing ballad about confusion and wanderlust, filled with unusual, clashing chords. The lost sailor's dilemma was resolved in the rollicking, optimistic "Saint of Circumstance" (the two songs were connected in performance for many years), which concluded with an anthemic sing-along that seemed to speak for both the Dead and their fans: "I sure don't know what I'm going for / But I'm gonna go for it for sure." The third Weir-Barlow song, "Feel Like a Stranger," was very much a song of the '70s—an emotionally icy funk tune about lust and alienation on the disco floor. (Some have also suggested that "Feel Like a Stranger" reflected some of Weir's alienation during this period, when Garcia was increasingly withdrawn.)

"When I first started working with them on the record," Gary Lyons remembers, "they had the songs but they hadn't had the chance to develop them much onstage at that point, which I gather is not the way they generally worked. So they'd come in and everybody would have all sorts of suggestions for tempos and feel. Jerry more or less had his things worked out, so it became a question of capturing that magical moment, which was not easy—'Althea' was a tune we must have recorded a hundred times. We'd do it ten or fifteen times and then go on to another song, and come back to it later or the next day or whatever. Eventually it fell into place and it came out quite nicely.

"Jerry always had a good idea of what he wanted on a song. With Jerry's main tunes on that album, 'Alabama Getaway' and 'Althea,' the band was riding on Jerry's rhythm completely, so it had to be right in the groove or it wouldn't work. Otherwise it sounded very sloppy. Sometimes in the studio it took a while to get that groove, but when he heard it he knew it right away."

As with both *Terrapin Station* and *Shakedown Street*, eventually work on *Go to Heaven* bogged down. During their fall 1979 East Coast tour the Dead found themselves working on overdubs for the record at New York's Media Sound studios during the day and then playing at Madison Square Garden or Nassau Coliseum at night, in an attempt to meet Clive Davis's pre-Christmas deadline. Despite the heroic effort, they missed that deadline and the record was finally released in April 1980.

The album itself was a mixed bag—technically well-recorded and -mixed but curiously uninvolving. All of the songs on the record would develop more as they were played in concert over the next few years, particularly Weir's songs, which were a bit stiff on the record. Actually, this was typical of Weir's material through the years—his songs evolved much more slowly than Garcia's did. They were also much more difficult to play, with strange tempo shifts, peculiar instrumental voicings and sometimes elusive melodies. (Those were their strengths, too, and why Garcia liked them so much from a player's perspective.) Garcia rarely strayed far from his folk, country and R&B roots in his writing, though he certainly created his own oeuvre from those strains. Weir's writing was always quirkier and less tied to specific genres; more purely "original," for what that's worth.

On June 7 and 8, 1980, the band marked their fifteenth anniversary (which they measured from the week in June 1965 when Phil moved to Palo Alto to join the Warlocks) with a pair of concerts at Folsom Field in Boulder, Colorado, long a hotbed of Deadhead activity. Then, after a few shows in the Pacific Northwest, the Dead flew up to Anchorage, Alaska, for three concerts in a high school auditorium. At first there was a notion to go to Japan after the Alaska shows, but it was financially prohibitive and there were serious concerns that Garcia might end up in a Japanese jail if he didn't stop using drugs—which was not likely. Most of the band and entourage took advantage of their time in Alaska to check out the state's natural splendor, and Mickey even went on a little recording expedition in the northern part of the state, looking for native drummers as he had in Egypt. Garcia, however, stayed in his room the whole time; "He didn't do anything," Richard Loren says, disappointment in his voice. The concerts themselves were generally quite good, and the third show had a special vibe because it took place on the night of the summer solstice, when the sun shines for twenty-four hours in Alaska.

When Bill Graham heard that the Dead had celebrated their fifteenth anniversary with shows in Colorado, he approached the band about doing something special to mark the occasion in the Bay Area, too. They settled on an extended series of shows at the relatively intimate 2,000-seat Warfield Theater. It started out as nine concerts, but eventually stretched to fifteen.

Around the same time, the Dead decided that their next album for Arista would be a live one—their first since the early '70s—and that at the Warfield they would not only play (and record) their standard two electric sets each night, but a full acoustic set as well (for the first time since 1970). The band also booked this three-set extravaganza for two nights in New Orleans following the Warfield series, and then for eight nights (also recorded) at New York's 8,000-seat art deco showplace Radio City Music Hall, with the final concert on Halloween night. Upping the ante, the Dead, at the suggestion of Richard Loren and concert producer John Scher, decided to televise the Halloween show live to sixteen East Coast and Midwest theaters that would be specially equipped with rock 'n' roll sound systems. This was the first rock 'n' roll closed-circuit telecast of this sort.

"We thought that on the East Coast, where we have a problem of sort of too large of an audience, maybe it would be a good way for us to be able to play fifteen places in one night, and maybe there would be something to that," Garcia said. "It was really an experimental idea top to bottom. . . . We did it mostly as a gesture to our audience to see if there wasn't something we could do apart from living on the road—something that would maybe allow us to be a little bit more selective—and also to see if the experience would have any value to the concertgoer. So it was an interesting experience for us, and it paid for itself."

To direct the live telecast, make a separate Showtime cable TV special *(Live Dead!)* and, later, a commercial video *(Dead Ahead)* edited from videotapes of the last three shows of the Radio City series, the Dead hired Len Dell'Amico, a graduate of New York University's prestigious School of Film and Television. Dell'Amico came to the project with extensive experience directing live music video shoots for John Scher's company—in fact, Dell'Amico first shot the Dead for Scher in 1976, and he was also the director of a 1978 Capitol Theater telecast during which Garcia was so sick he could barely sing. But Dell'Amico didn't actually meet Garcia, whom the director described as "the point man on all things visual" in the Grateful Dead, until he was flown out to the Bay Area in late September 1980 to discuss the Radio City telecast, a little more than a month away.

At the time of their meeting, almost nothing had been conceptualized about what the telecast would consist of besides the concert itself. After all, there was lots of nonmusic airtime to fill: the pre-show and then two thirty-minute-plus breaks between sets. "When I got there," Dell'Amico says, "we had zero, and when I left a week later we had brought [*Saturday Night Live* writer-comedians] Franken and Davis out, wrote the comedy out, rehearsed it and shot it. Money was no object whatsoever, which was alarming. I mean, to shoot all the comedy just to see if it would work? And then redo it all at Radio City? At Radio City, the union bill alone was several hundred thousand dollars, which in today's dollars would probably be about half a million."

The choice of Al Franken and Tom Davis as hosts for the telecast turned out to be perfect. They were already famous for their dark, deadpan, politically and culturally hip humor, and they loved the Dead to boot. The band appeared in various backstage skits that were shown during the set breaks at the concert. The supposed theme of the night was a telethon to raise money for "Jerry's Kids"—a takeoff on Jerry Lewis's annual muscular dystrophy fund-raising event—with down-and-out hippies vying for our sympathy and pledge dollars. In one segment, Garcia—looking at once nervous, bemused and a little coked up—tried to auction off his missing finger, which he presented to the TV cameras in a nice little box. At another point, Davis went up to Garcia and in his endearing/annoying way asked the guitarist if he had any cocaine. Steve Parish played his tough roadie role to the hilt, throwing Davis to the ground. And in one of the evening's best skits, Davis interviewed former secretary of state Henry Kissinger (actually, Franken in a superb $2,000 makeup job) about his love of the Grateful Dead. All goes well until Davis is shocked to discover that Kissinger is secretly recording the concert with equipment he'd smuggled in. Franken and Davis also got the closed-circuit audience involved in the fun by periodically mentioning incidents that were reportedly happening in the different closed-circuit theaters.

All in all, the comedy part of the event showed conclusively that the Dead had a sense of humor about themselves, and that they were also on the same wavelength as their audience and understood who they were—of course that was evident from the Dead movie as well. The stoned, tripping, Halloween-costumed crowds at Radio City and watching the telecast live in theaters cheered wildly for every routine, no matter how bad the acting by the bandmembers, who seemed to thoroughly enjoy poking holes in their own myth. (The show turned out to be educational, too. Quiz question posed to Deadhead: "Who dosed President John F. Kennedy?" Correct answer: "Lee Harvey Owsley.")

The Halloween telecast was the wild capper to the Dead's twenty-five-show run of three-set concerts celebrating their fifteenth anniversary. But what was most thrilling for the thousands of fans lucky enough to get tickets for the shows was the opportunity to see the Dead in more intimate surroundings. Not that Radio City is like Carnegie Hall, but since the days of Fillmore East the Dead had played in the New York area primarily in stadiums and arenas. And Radio City was a trip in itself.

The great musical treat was the acoustic sets, which were much more interesting than their 1970 counterparts. Unlike the '70 sets, which were mostly just Garcia and Weir playing as a duet, with an occasional appearance by Lesh or Pigpen, the '80 acoustic sets involved the entire band playing in close proximity onstage. Brent played mainly acoustic piano, the drummers played small kits or little percussion instruments and Phil's bass was turned down in proportion to the level of Weir's and Garcia's guitar volume. The repertoire for this remarkable acoustic ensemble was typically eclectic and came from "our collective musical background," as Garcia put it. It included old and more recent folk, country and blues tunes, such as George Jones's "The Race Is On," Elizabeth Cotten's "Oh Babe It Ain't No Lie," the Memphis Jug Band's "On the Road Again," "Deep Elem Blues" from Texas in the '20s and Jesse Fuller's "The Monkey and the Engineer."

The real revelation of the acoustic sets, though, was the Grateful Dead tunes, most of which had never been played acoustically before. "China Doll," with Brent on harpsichord, was imbued with a fragility that made the song extra-chilling. "It Must've Been the Roses" and "To Lay Me Down" allowed Garcia, Mydland and Weir to flex their vocal chops and explore the delicacy of the melodies. The surprising power of jamming tunes like "Bird Song" and "Cassidy" demonstrated that the band's deft interplay did not require loud electric instruments. In fact, the relationship between the instruments sounded virtually the same as in the electric band, stripped down to a more elemental level.

Every acoustic set ended with "Ripple," which the band hadn't played since 1971. Just about everyone in the theaters would sing along on the song, which just ten years after it was written somehow felt ageless, as old and wise as the disparate songs the Dead had plucked from long-gone pickers and singers. It was quite moving to hear Garcia sing "Ripple"—a slight smile peeking through his beard, which was just beginning to show flecks of gray then—because in that setting the song seemed like an affirmative and empathetic transmission from his soul to every person in the audience.

"[Playing an acoustic set] was a nice way to start the show," Garcia noted. "It kind of changed the emotional paper of the show, since the acoustic set we did had a real intimate quality; it wasn't a high-energy thing. It was a kind of relaxing and intimate experience for both us and for the audience."

Some of the electric sets were a tad subdued, compared to the tours directly before and after the three-set shows, but no one was complaining—everyone knew that the Warfield, New Orleans and Radio City series were rare and special events. The band knew it, too, and stayed relaxed but focused throughout the month-plus of marathon shows. Garcia was definitely in the best condition he'd been in for quite a while, both physically and mentally, and this burst of positivity carried through a fine three-set affair New Year's Eve at the 7,500-seat Oakland Auditorium (the de facto successor to Winterland, which closed after New Year's Eve 1978) and into the first part of 1981, when Garcia and Len Dell'Amico worked on the *Dead Ahead* video together.

"At the time of *Dead Ahead*, as everyone pointed out to me much later," Dell'Amico says, "Jerry had gotten himself into a very healthy position, apparently for the sake of doing this project. So I came away from it with a distorted view because he was so acute and in such good shape. I couldn't imagine him *not* being in good shape."

During that fall of 1980 the mood of the band and the crowds seemed so high it was easy to forget that there was an insidious malaise creeping across the Dead's world, and that Garcia's drug dependency was only arrested, not stopped. Darker days were still to come.

CHAPTER 17

This Darkness
Got to Give

ifteen years is the chronological middle of the Grateful Dead's performing career, but there would be few radical musical developments in the group's sound after that point, and the basic format of a Dead show would never change again.

First sets consisted mainly of shorter songs with relatively fixed arrangements—Weir-sung cowboy tunes and blues, lighter Garcia numbers like "Bertha," "Sugaree," "Tennessee Jed," "Dire Wolf" and "Ramble On Rose"— and one or perhaps two extended numbers toward the end of the set, but rarely anything that matched the long, exploratory versions of "Playing in the Band," "Here Comes Sunshine" and "Scarlet Begonias" that had graced many a first set in the early '70s. With the exception of "Bird Song," most of the so-called first-set tunes that opened to extensive improvisation were Weir's: "Cassidy," "Feel Like a Stranger," "Let It Grow," "The Music Never Stopped," "Lazy Lightning" > "Supplication" and the combination of "Lost Sailor" and "Saint of Circumstance." Garcia had a handful of knock-'em-dead set-enders like "Deal," "China Cat Sunflower" > "I Know You Rider" and "Might As Well," but he always saved most of his heavier material for the second set. First sets were usually about ten songs and a little over an hour, a far cry from the marathon fourteen- to seventeen-song first sets that were common in 1972–'74. Garcia often talked of the first set as being a "warm-up" for the second set. That became increasingly true in the early '80s.

The structure of the second set became fairly fixed as well, though certainly there was tremendous variation within the formula. The set-opener was usually an untempo tune like "Samson and Delilah," "Shakedown Street" or various combinations that lent themselves to jamming, like "Scarlet Begonias" > "Fire on the Mountain" and "Feel Like a Stranger" > "Franklin's Tower." ("Help on the Way" and "Slipknot" had been dropped in the fall of 1977.) With "Dark Star" essentially out of the repertoire since 1974 (save for two versions in 1979 and one each in 1978 and 1981), "Playing in the Band" was the most open-ended song the Dead performed with any regularity. By 1981 the song appeared only in the first half of a second set, with a reprise of the tune often coming near the end of the set. Songs like "Estimated Prophet," "Eyes of the World," "Ship of Fools," "He's Gone" and "Terrapin" were slotted in the first half of the second set as well.

Four or five songs into the second set, usually at the end of a jam, the guitarists and Brent would leave the stage and the drummers would take over for an extended percussion workout. Then, when Garcia and Weir returned, Mickey and Billy would slip away and the two guitarists would engage in some free-form sonic weirdness colloquially known as "space." The other bandmembers would eventually return, and out of the often cacophonous but sometimes amazingly lyrical "space jam" would emerge a riff or a theme or a beat that would slowly blossom (or on occasion *explode*) into songs like "The Wheel," "The Other One" or "Not Fade Away." Then, typically, Garcia would bring the energy down again for one of his powerful ballads—"Wharf Rat," "Black Peter," "Stella Blue"—before Weir whipped everyone into a frenzy one last time with some high-octane rocker like "Sugar Magnolia," "Around and Around," "Good Lovin' " or "One More Saturday Night." The encore was usually something fast and simple: "U.S. Blues," "Don't Ease Me In" or the band's clunky but fun version of the Stones' "Satisfaction." If Garcia was feeling introspective, he might close with "Brokedown Palace" or Dylan's "It's All Over Now, Baby Blue"—songs that sent the crowd home floating instead of charged up. Second sets were usually close to an hour and a half, though about a third of that time was taken up by "drums" and "space" rather than conventional songs.

The band's repertoire was extensive enough that they could play three consecutive shows without repeating a song if they were so inclined (though they tended to repeat their newer material more often). And though the format was more fixed than it had been previously, there was actually more variety to the sets than there had been in 1976–78, when fewer songs were in the rotation.

While Garcia and Weir, the lead vocalists, seemed content with the state of affairs in the band in 1980, the ever-critical Phil Lesh told a writer he felt the Grateful Dead were "in a holding pattern. We're still at the same altitude, but we're circling." He noted that he was "kind of bored writing for the Grateful Dead. That period around *Live Dead*, when the music was a little more complex, was the peak for me." But he added, "I'm not bored being *in* the Grateful Dead. To me the Grateful Dead is life—the life of the spirit, and the life of the mind, as opposed to standing in line and marking time in the twentieth century."

"The whole thing with the Grateful Dead is a challenge to get something new happening, even when you don't feel like doing anything new or feel anything new lurking around the corner," Weir said in 1981. "To find something new in either a given treatment of a particular song or some totally new unexplored territory in one of our jams or something. We actually try to go for that every night, and to be together enough and responsive enough to do that sort of stuff, you have to really keep your wits fairly sharp and your chops together. And the band has to be a working, functioning unit. You always have to work at that, like they say you always have to work at making a marriage work. It's a whole lot like being married."

The fundamental musical relationships in the band had not changed significantly through the years, though each player went through periods of greater and lesser commitment to the group, as happens with every band. However, their collective musical vocabulary seemed to broaden a bit more every year as they developed as players both together and apart. Beginning with the introduction of the Beast, Hart and Kreutzmann took the concept of a drum solo places no one had ever been. And by the early '80s Weir had evolved into an extraordinarily inventive and colorful guitarist, so much more than his inadequate "rhythm guitar" label suggested. Weir will probably never receive the credit he deserves for being a truly outstanding and original guitarist because he toiled in Jerry's immense shadow. By the late '70s, however, he was clearly stepping out as a player and a songwriter and it's not exaggerating to say that his emergence helped the band immeasurably during periods when Garcia was not at his best.

By 1980–81 hippies were almost as scarce in America as they had been in 1965–66. Most of the original flower children had long since grown up and landed jobs in straight society. Long hair on boys and men was more common among Southern rednecks than Northeastern city-dwellers, and more common among fans of hard rock than any other musical genre. With the punk/new wave movement had come short hair, black clothes, skinny ties and a dislike of hippies. Yet the Dead's following continued to grow slowly each year, as friends turned other friends on to the band through live tapes or by taking them to concerts. Grateful Dead shows became just about the only place outside of Haight-Ashbury and Santa Cruz where tie-dyed clothing was common. And though the percentage of longhaired guys at Dead shows wasn't as high as it was in the mid-'70s (when even some television news anchormen had longish hair and sideburns), it was still much greater than at any other kind of concert except hard-core reggae shows, which always attracted lots of hippies.

"The crowds haven't changed that much," Garcia said in 1981. "Really, *we've* changed more than the crowds have, I would say. But 1980 and 1981 is definitely *this time*, now historically, and the '60s were the '60s. There are those kinds of differences—just the differences of the world at large. But in terms of people and why they come to our shows and what the audience is about and what the music is about, what the whole event is about, I think that situation has stayed pretty much the same. People are coming basically for the same sort of experience. And that's kind of a nice thing. It's an ongoing thing. We've seen our audience get younger, or maybe what it really means is we've gotten older. Our audience has maybe stayed the same age as when we started; maybe it's gotten a few years younger."

Since the late '70s the number of college-age Deadheads who followed the band from city to city for part or all of a tour—usually staying in cheap motels or crashing with friends—had been increasing every year. In fact, it became something of a rite of passage for kids and young adults to be able to master the logistical, financial and pharmacological demands of partying for an entire tour. The close bonds among Deadheads that were formed on long, sometimes uncomfortable road trips added to the already strong communal feeling of the concerts, as the same Heads would see each other in different locations, months or years apart.

Another interesting phenomenon that became much more noticeable in the early '80s was the number of older Deadheads, many of them successful professionals, who went on tour with the Dead, often staying in luxury hotels and eating in fine restaurants along the way. For these white-collar Deadheads, going to shows became a way to get in touch with a freer, looser, some might say more *authentic* version of themselves. By the late '80s there were thousands of people in this category who found ways to juggle their busy work schedule to periodically take a week's vacation away from the law firm or computer company or hospital to follow a Dead tour to a few cities. They'd go back to their workplaces tired but with their souls enriched and their spirits replenished, and most of them firmly believed it made them better, happier workers.

If Grateful Dead shows were among the few remaining bastions of hippies and ex-hippies in the early '80s, they were also integral to the survival of the psychedelic drug culture. Pot and psychedelics remained by far the most common consciousness-altering substances at Dead shows, though cocaine and, to a much lesser degree, heroin made inroads in some segments of Deadhead society, and dealers could usually be found easily near any tour stop. It was not a coincidence that after the Dead played a show in New Haven or Des Moines or Salt Lake City the local drug undergrounds in those communities were at their most active. In the early '80s this was not really a problem in most cities, because the number of people using psychedelics was relatively small, mainly confined to those who already had some experience with those kinds of drugs and had, in a sense, been socialized in the generally safe and supportive Grateful Dead show environment. But in the late '80s and early '90s, when the scene surrounding Dead shows got so big that every concert attracted thousands of people—including many non-Deadheads—who hung around the bizarre bazaar outside the venues, the volume of drugs and attendant negative drug-related incidents in cities along the Dead's tour route became alarmingly high. The early '80s look positively quaint in comparison.

"What fascinates me is how Deadheads improvised a tradition around psychedelics and created a grassroots and extremely homey and unpretentious way of getting tens of thousands of people at a time off on pychedelics," says Steve Silberman, author of *Skeleton Key: A Dictionary for Deadheads.* "There were those shows in the '70s and the '80s, especially a Saturday night, when you'd walk around and it seemed like everyone was tripping; if not everyone, maybe two-thirds or three-quarters. And to think there's that much intense experience going on with no chaperone—Mom's not around, and they're not passing out copies of Leary's books in the hallways.

"I think it's too contrived to say that going to Dead shows became some sort of an ersatz peyote ritual for kids," Silberman continues. "But another ancient archetype they reiterated was something more like a kid going off into the wilderness, and because there isn't much real wilderness anymore, the 'wilderness' could be hitchhiking from one town to another with very little money in your wallet, sleeping on the floor of a motel with twelve other people you just met, having sex with someone you just met, getting a ticket somehow—bartering, whatever. A lot of the kids who were doing that were children of relative privilege, so to leave a zone where they were assured of physical comfort to enter a zone where there really were wolves—DEA agents and people with really weird or even bad vibes—was quite a step.

"Deadheads gave each other a tremendous amount of freedom of literal physical movement and deportment and that ended up being a very good thing for the psychedelic experience, because if you needed to lie down on your back, even though it was a concert, even though the show was going on, it was okay if you weren't engaged in the spectacle. The spectacle was you and all of us and wherever you were at. There was a tremendous amount of tolerance for people who were in different places than you psychically."

Musically, too, it could be argued that the Grateful Dead had been born of and designed for the psychedelic experience. Garcia said as much: "Our second half [the second set] definitely has a shape which, if not directly, at least partially is inspired by the psychedelic experience as a waveform: The second half for us is the thing of taking chances and going all to pieces and then coming back and reassembling. You might lose a few pieces, but you don't despair about seeing yourself go completely to pieces; you let it go."

"The secret that ties Grateful Dead music to psychedelics," Silberman says, "is when you take psychedelics, when you start and you're sober, you're starting in a familiar place—your ordinary mind. Then, as the psychedelic comes on, you leave the realm of familiar thought and familiar experience, and you go to a place where there are all these other less familiar, chaotic experiences. Well, the music would parallel what your mind was doing. It would start in a familiar place, with lyrics and a melody, then it would get more and more open to the winds of inspiration and the winds of chaos. Then, at the most extreme point of out-there-ness, Mickey and Billy would play the oldest instruments on earth, so you would hear the drums that are the traditional accompaniment to psychedelic experience on planet Earth. You would hear these instruments that spoke to the earliest roots of humanity and the roots of performance in shamanistic experience; the roots of rhythm and the roots of collective ritual.

"So in the middle of this chaos, you're presented with this ancient signpost, and then you would come back from there, after being, you could say, primitivized or stripped of the random programming of contemporary culture—you momentarily forget the sitcom you watched the night before, and your job—and you'd be returned to this primordial human state. Then you would journey back through chaos ["space"] to some statement of philosophical reflection—'The Wheel,' 'Stella Blue.' They seem to offer you a plateau from which you can observe everything else. They seem to occur in the stillpoint of the turning world, so you can inhabit them with Jerry for a while and look out at the wheels of fate, which included your future and your past and maybe even your death. And it would also make you aware of the ephemeral nature of all the people in the room with you, including the band."

"You'd laugh and you'd cry and you'd dance and you'd sing and you'd be terrified and you'd feel, 'Oh my god, what's coming next?' " says Peter Toluzzi, a keen observer of the latter-day Dead. "You'd feel awe, you'd feel that great rescued feeling that no matter how far out you were taken, you were always brought home and put back together pretty decently. So it became known as a safe place to let go and just allow your emotions to go through their flow. And I think that's a very cleansing experience emotionally, even more than mentally. After a while people learned that they could do this and it became a safe, comfortable avenue that provided the stimulus for a familiar enough path that you could have variations on this experience again and again. And each time it would be personally revelatory in a different way, just as the music was different every time, too."

Mickey Hart said that the Grateful Dead weren't in the music business, they were in the *transportation* business. And it's true that for many Deadheads, the band was a medium that facilitated experiencing other planes of consciousness and tapping into deep, spiritual wells that were usually the province of organized religion in this country. Psychedelics and even pot intensified the experience, but thousands upon thousands of fans "got" the cosmic connection without drugs, too. It's been simplistically stated by some that the Grateful Dead *were* LSD—that the way their sets unfolded and the places the music went and the messages the lyrics proferred were so imbued with lessons learned on the psychedelic edge that the experience went beyond mere metaphor and became the real thing. This much is certain: the Grateful Dead got people high whether those people were on drugs or not. Certainly the musicians recognized this from day one and played into it, because Dead shows were their spiritual launchpad, too.

"I've always felt from the very beginning—even before the Acid Tests," Phil said in 1982, "that we could do something that was not necessarily extramusical but something where music would be only the first step. Something even close to religion—not in the sense of that 'The Beatles are more popular than Jesus' [John Lennon's controversial 1965 remark], but in the sense of actually communing. We used to say that every place we play is church. Now it's not quite so all-encompassing; it's not quite so automatic. . . . The core of followers is not the reason it feels like church. It's that other thing, 'it.' "

"In primitive cultures that state of the shaman is a desirable state," Garcia noted. "In our society, we are somehow trying to not have that. That's a real problem. We need the visions. A lot of what we do is already metaphors for that—movies, television, all that stuff. We want to see other worlds. Music is one of the oldest versions of it.

"In a sense, the Grateful Dead experience is that metaphor, too. It's like, 'Here's the ritual that we have been missing in our lives.' We don't go to church anymore. We don't have celebrations anymore. The magic has even been taken out of the Catholic Mass. English? Sorry, it doesn't have that boom—it doesn't have that scare."

For a fairly sizable segment of Deadheads, however, the Grateful Dead were simply a supreme kick-out-the-jams party band that played some terrifically involving rock 'n' roll. Some people weren't interested in the existential tenderness of "Stella Blue"; didn't want to hear twelve minutes of jamming after the song part of "Playing in the Band" had evaporated; and used the always challenging, constantly unpredictable "drums and space" section of the show as a time to hit the snack bar or the bathroom. It didn't mean they weren't true Deadheads; rather, it showed the range and power of the Dead experience. And the group was always more than willing to be the party band for those fans. It was part of who they were, too. As Garcia put it in 1980, playing in the Grateful Dead was "sort of like *being* New Year's Eve; every place you go there's a big party. But five New Year's Eves a week is kind of a lot," he chuckled, "so I try to lead a pretty sane life on the road. I don't party every night or anything like that."

By mid-1981, though, Garcia's coke and heroin problem was escalating again. In the winter, when he had been working on the *Dead Ahead* video and helping put together the first of two double-LP sets from the Warfield and Radio City series—the excellent acoustic album *Reckoning*—Garcia seemed to be in fine form. But in *Living with the Dead* Rock Scully writes that by spring Garcia was reluctant to tour Europe with the Dead because he was concerned about being able to score his beloved Persian on the road. As it turned out, this was not a problem—if we're to believe Scully, friends of the Who's Pete Townshend made sure Garcia (and Scully) were taken care of in that regard. Though he was clearly strung out, Garcia still managed to play fairly well on the tour, which was just a week long—four nights at the Rainbow Theatre in London and a televised concert with the Who in Essen, Germany, where Townshend even joined in on a few numbers. Garcia also managed to be his usual, cheerful self for the obligatory round of interviews with the British rock 'n' roll press.

Writer David Gans and I interviewed Garcia twice in the first half of

1981—at the end of April and during the second week of June—and he seemed incredibly charming, vibrant and together. Of course this impression bore no relation to what Garcia's drug use was at the time, but it indicates that at the very least he was capable of appearing "normal," which for him meant being funny, curious, engaging, self-effacing and very articulate about both the philosophy behind and the structural mechanics of the Dead's music.

Appearances aside, there's no question that Garcia's drug use drove a wedge between him and the rest of the band during this period. He and Scully were in their own world to an extent, and about the only time Garcia would get together with the other bandmembers was at gigs. In 1980 and '81 the Dead didn't do any recording at all; in fact, these were the first years since the Dead started that the band introduced no new original songs. That made it a rough time for Robert Hunter, too, who more or less lost his writing partner to a Persian haze. The two were not particularly close during this period, when Garcia was spending nearly all his time getting high in his dark room in the downstairs of the Hepburn Heights house, or touring with the Dead or the many incarnations of the Jerry Garcia Band, where John Kahn was always a waiting co-dependent.

The Garcia Band went through numerous permutations between the fall of 1979 (after the dissolution of Reconstruction) and the fall of 1982—seven groups of varying membership and musical quality, with John Kahn the only constant in all of them. From the fall of 1979 until the fall of 1980 Garcia's main musical foil in the band was a talented keyboardist-singer named Ozzie Ahlers, who had worked with Van Morrison, Jesse Colin Young, Robert Hunter and others through the years. In December 1980 he was replaced by two keyboardists who were polar opposites. Electric pianist Jimmy Warren was, to put it delicately, sympathetic to Kahn's and Garcia's offstage behavior, while organist Melvin Seals, who would play in the Jerry Garcia Band for the next fourteen years, was a straitlaced man of the church. Most of the material the Garcia Band played between 1979 and 1982 had been in the repertoire for several years, and the quality of the shows varied widely. On the road, where much was expected of them, they usually played fairly well. In the Bay Area, sets and entire shows often dragged and seemed unfocused. Rock Scully suggests that the main reason the Garcia Band played as often as it did during this period was to support Scully's, Kahn's and Garcia's drug habits—which could cost several hundred dollars a day. But in truth they performed many fine shows then, and one of the 1981 lineups, with the two keyboardists, drummer Daoud Shaar (another Van Morrison band alumnus) and singers Essra Mohawk and Liz Stires, played a number of exceptional dates. Still, even John Kahn admitted that "things got kind of out of control around then. Jimmy Warren was just sort of a friend. It didn't work out and it went on too long; it wasn't one of our better bands."

Kahn believed that most people had a mistaken impression of his and

Garcia's drug use: "It wasn't a way for us to hang out; it was quite the opposite. It was an *anti*social thing. It's not something you do with a lot of people; it's sort of private. In fact, that's the thing that kept me and Jerry apart more than anything. It wasn't a shared thing; it was always real private. 'That's your stash and this is my stash.' He'd be uncomfortable because he wouldn't do it while I was around, because he'd think he'd have to give me some or something like that. It wasn't a great time for anybody. It's just something that happened."

Like Garcia, Kahn also believed that the Persian didn't affect the music much. "Not in any obvious way, like the tempos didn't get slower or anything," he said. "The breaks got longer and we started later. I really don't believe that drugs were as important a thing as it's probably perceived. Everything would have been the same. We would have had a band. We would have played the same kind of music. Our relationship didn't have to do with that [drugs] and our band didn't have to do with that. Without Scully I don't think it would have had any influence at all on anything. *He* was the one who propagated it on a larger scale. You have a manager saying, 'They won't go on until they have a snort,' not musicians saying, 'We won't go on until we get a snort.' That's the truth. So I don't think it's as important as it's played up to be. But peripheral things are: what it did to certain relationships and things it brought out in people—how people would fold when things got tough; how people would cop out on you and act like they weren't your friend because it got too difficult for them. But everything would have happened regardless of whether the drugs existed. We still would have gone to Front Street all those nights and we would have made all those records."

In Grateful Dead circles there was tremendous concern over Garcia's drug habit, but who was in a position to say anything to him? Others were strung out on junk and cocaine, too, and some of those who weren't had other problems—Phil Lesh once described this period of his life as "the Heineken years." Plus there was a sort of unwritten rule in the Grateful Dead that you didn't tell other people in the organization how to behave. Part of the reason the Dead had succeeded artistically through the years was that the bandmembers had been able to follow their creative muses to their heart's content, and if that involved drugs, so be it.

"Classically, the band has had a laissez-faire attitude in terms of what anybody wants to do," Garcia said. "If somebody wants to drink or take drugs, as long as it doesn't seriously affect everybody else or affect the music, we can sort of let it go. We've all had our excursions."

However, Steve Brown notes, "I think the noninterference idea was a cop-out in a lot of ways, to be able to not have to deal with stuff that maybe needed dealing with. That's because they were an alternative, risk-taking kind of an entity, they were allowed to get away with this stuff—'We're not going to tell people to do anything.' That whole philosophy came from Garcia as far as I can tell. I think he was the one who instilled it into the Grateful Dead body as the ethic of you don't tell how people how to behave, because *he* was the guy who didn't want to be told how to behave. That kind of ruled for a long time, and then it was too late by the time people started mentioning stuff."

And even if people in the band and organization weren't talking directly to Garcia about his problem in the early '80s, they were talking among themselves and to each other behind his back. "People were always talkin' to me about Jerry's dope problem," says Richard Loren. "And I was as much enmeshed in it as Steve Parish was. He and I were driving him to places to get clean; to doctors who could help. We saw the man suffer through withdrawal."

Was Garcia embarrassed by his addiction? "Not at all," Loren says. "He didn't have fear and he didn't have guilt. He was never a guilt-ridden person and he wasn't intimidated by what other people thought. He knew what he was doing when he was doing it, and he was smart enough to know about it. But eventually, of course, you start needing a whole lot of it, and it gets to be a monkey on your back. It takes pleasure away, too, and you're in pain, like if you have the DTs."

The great majority of Deadheads were blissfully unaware of Garcia's drug problems during this period. Some heard ugly rumors but discounted them— "Not Jerry!"—while others were simply out of the information loop. The extended Grateful Dead family was so numerous that there were always plenty of people who did hear the dirt about Garcia and others, and they in turn spread the gossip freely. But by and large the news didn't filter out to the rank-and-file Deadheads, who continued to show up in droves at every Dead and Garcia Band appearance and dance deliriously the way fans had since 1965.

And the truth is the shows themselves were the best thing about the early '80s Dead scene. In California in 1981 and '82, the Dead began playing at some midsized outdoor venues that were positively magical and made every show feel special. The 9,000-seat Greek Theater in Berkeley was a wonderfully intimate cement amphitheater surrounded by eucalyptus trees, where everyone could see each other and the band played in front of bas-relief Greek columns (and for the first couple of years there, beautiful tie-dyed hangings made by Courtney Pollack, famous for his dyes since the early days of the art form). Frost Amphitheater, on the campus of Stanford University in Palo Alto, was a genteel oasis of terraced grass enclosed by a perimeter of California trees and shrubs—incredibly beautiful and serene. It comfortably accommodated 9,000 fans, who would park and party in adjoining eucalyptus groves. And down the California coast an hour north of Los Angeles was Ventura's dirt-floored rodeo stadium/fairgrounds, just a few hundred yards from the blue Pacific Ocean.

Between shows in those places and venues like Red Rocks, Oakland Auditorium (site of the Dead's New Year's bashes from 1979 to 1982), sumptuous Alpine Valley in Wisconsin, Compton Terrace in Arizona and the large but beloved Madison Square Garden, Deadheads were able to enjoy the band in some exceptional environments. No wonder so many more Deadheads hit the road to follow the band in this era.

In the midst of all this endless touring and craziness, and in some quarters, consternation, Garcia unexpectedly married Mountain Girl in a brief ceremony backstage at the Oakland Coliseum on New Year's Eve 1981–82. According to M.G.'s account of the event in Robert Greenfield's *Dark Star*, she and the kids had gone down to the Bay Area from Oregon around Christmas, and as soon as he she saw Jerry, "I knew that he was playing with dangerous stuff," she said. "I realized that he could die at any minute. I said, 'Look, you know you're probably going to croak here or something bad might happen. I would feel better if we were married.'

"We still loved each other very much, but by now it was through this incredible series of impediments. I had taken the high moral ground and couldn't come back because I couldn't do what he was doing. And he couldn't step out of what he was doing because by now he was really into it."

Though Mountain Girl said she had fantasies about the two of them getting back together and living as a family with the kids, Jerry quickly put that notion to rest, saying he still wanted to live apart. There were tax reasons that made getting married advantageous to both Jerry and M.G., and that's one reason it was important for the wedding to take place that New Year's Eve, before 1981 became 1982. So right after the Dead had played a set backing Joan Baez (who was involved with Mickey Hart at the time), Jerry and M.G. were married in Jerry's dressing room by a Buddhist monk friend, who performed the ceremony in Tibetan as the couple's daughters, Steve Parish and a few others looked on. Shortly after the ceremony, Garcia strapped on his electric guitar and went out onstage for the first of three Dead sets that night. One has to wonder if Garcia's second song choice that set was meant to be serious, ironic or funny—it was "Cold Rain and Snow," which opens with the lines "I married me a wife / She's been trouble all my life / Run me out in the cold rain and snow." Whatever was going through Garcia's head that night, he played a magnificent show, even pulling out "Dark Star" for the first time in three years to open the Dead's last set sometime after two in the morning.

M.G. stayed for a few days at Hepburn Heights after the New Year's shows but, as she told Greenfield, "Things were so strange and uncomfortable that I couldn't wait to get out of there. I remember jumping up and saying, 'Oh, it's time to go. I've got to go,' and I was thinking, 'Poor Jerry, he has built this for himself and it's not very nice.' Back we went to Oregon. Jerry would come through on tour or we would go down there to see him, but we didn't see very much of him at all. Jerry and I got married but it didn't change a god-damn thing. It didn't make a damned bit of difference."

From a strictly musical standpoint, 1982 started out quite promisingly with a pair of fine benefit shows (for eleven mainly local nonprofit groups) in mid-February at the Warfield Theater in San Francisco, followed by concerts in Los Angeles and San Diego. The first three weeks of April they played more strong shows on an East Coast swing that took them to two Southern states that were proving to be rabid Dead Country—North Carolina and Virginia—and some of their oldest proven markets—Philadelphia, Long Island, northern New York state, Hartford, Providence and Baltimore. Halfway through the tour Garcia and Weir appeared on *Late Night with David Letterman* for the first time. They performed "Deep Elem Blues" and "The Monkey and the Engineer" on acoustic guitars and chatted amiably, if nervously, with Letterman.

That spring of 1982 also marks the beginning of Garcia and John Kahn playing shows as an acoustic duet. Actually, the first acoustic show, which took place at the Capitol Theater on a night between two Dead shows, featured Garcia alone—the only time since his folk days that he had played without supporting musicians. And he hated the experience. He looked nervous and was somewhat sheepish in both his singing and playing.

John Scher, who had persuaded Garcia to play solo shows, remembers, "He went out there and he played a short first set and he came off just freaked and pissed at me, which was unusual—I could count on one hand the times he was even annoyed with me. I followed him into his dressing room and he was just fuming. I said, 'Aw, come on. It's not so bad.' But he just did *not* enjoy it; he didn't like playing alone. By the next night we had John Kahn out there."

It was in fact eleven days between the first night at the Capitol and the next acoustic shows, at the Beacon Theater in Manhattan, two nights after the end of the Dead's tour. With Kahn backing him on stand-up bass, Garcia was much more confident, though frankly he never looked completely at ease playing in an acoustic duo. For Deadheads it was a chance to hear a different repertoire, one that included many of the same cover tunes and Dead songs that he'd sung during the 1980 acoustic sets, as well as a few numbers from the Garcia Band songbook—"Gomorrah," "Reuben and Cherise," Dylan's "Simple Twist of Fate" and "It Takes a Lot to Laugh, It Takes a Train to Cry"—and rarities like Merle Haggard's "Sing Me Back Home," which he hadn't sung since the early '70s. Because he hadn't really kept up his acoustic guitar chops, Garcia's playing could be a little clunky and imprecise. But when he and Kahn were clicking and the music flowed, the acoustic sets were quite powerful, especially on ballads, where the spare arrangements took on a haunting, fragile intimacy.

Back on the West Coast, the Jerry Garcia Band, with the two keyboardists, two women backup singers and Bill Kreutzmann on drums, played sporadic gigs in Northern California and Oregon in the spring. Then, beginning in mid-June, they went on a three-show Northeast tour with Bob Weir's solo band, Bobby and the Midnites, followed by more East Coast dates and then eleven shows by Garcia and Kahn acoustic that took the duo from Washington, D.C., out to Boulder, Colorado. It did not escape the notice of those who were concerned about Garcia's and Kahn's drug use that these acoustic concerts netted the musicians much more money than regular JGB gigs, where the night's take was always divided evenly by what was then a septet; all the better to feed their increasing habits. In fact, some suggested that was the main reason they played the acoustic concerts. Many of the sets they played were very short—at least by Grateful Dead standards—but in general Deadheads seemed to enjoy seeing Garcia's playing in this stripped-down context.

Garcia and Kahn also put together a Garcia solo album over the course of spring and summer. *Run for the Roses* (released in early October 1982) was a rather uneven collection of material. Two songs were leftovers from the 1974 sessions for Garcia's second album, with new lead vocals added: Clyde McPhatter's "Without Love" and one of the must puzzling covers Garcia ever attempted, a reggae version of the Beatles' "I Saw Her Standing There." There were two new potent Hunter-Garcia songs. In the bluesy "Valerie," which chugged along in a loping cadence somewhat similar to "Sugaree," Garcia's character is desperate to prove his love for a hard-hearted two-timing gal who won't give him any satisfaction. In one verse, at Valerie's command, "I went downtown with my pocketknife / Cut your other man but I spared his life." In another, "I shot my dog 'cause he growled at you / Valerie, won't you be good to me." Tragic stuff, but Garcia's delivery usually brought out the humor in Hunter's hapless, *whipped* hero. It's one of the neglected gems of their partnership.

The title cut, "Run for the Roses," was a common set-ender for the JGB in the second half of 1982, a bouncy melodic number in the tradition of "Bertha." It's littered with several different metaphors, bits of advice, observations—a typically playful and sage Hunter hodgepodge that could be autobiographical or directed at Garcia or aimed squarely at the audience:

> *Reach for the rose*
> *Get caught on the briar*
> *You're warming to love*
> *Next thing there's a fire*
> *The trouble with love*
> *Is its other face*
> *You just want the cup*
> *You don't want the race*
> *No, you don't want the race . . .*

The most interesting song on the album was a Hunter-Garcia-Kahn composition called "Midnight Getaway," which painted a vivid noirish picture of a man lying in bed and listening to his lover slip out of the house for a secret rendezvous. There are few rhymed lines, just bursts of near-prose:

> Heard you stop and turn back once
> Then I thought I heard you sigh
> Or maybe it was the breeze
>
> Heard the jingle of your keys
> Then you stumbled and cursed the cat
> That was sleeping on the stairs under the stars

Garcia played acoustic guitar on the song, which closed with a nicely executed, open-ended jamming coda. The JGB never performed the song live.

The album's remaining tunes were a rather turgid reading of Dylan's "Knockin' on Heaven's Door" (which was even deadlier in a JGB second set at one-thirty in the morning in some sweaty club) and Hunter and Kahn's "Leave the Little Girl Alone." All in all, a rather erratic collection that was also a commercial failure.

"That was *not* our greatest work," Kahn said in 1996. "That was a bad time. Right after that record I moved to L.A. for two or three years. The scene had become such a drag. I couldn't stand it anymore, with Scully and Alan Trist and that whole thing up at the house. I couldn't stand Jerry's thing with Rock, so I needed to get away for a while. The band stayed in existence; we played some gigs; not a helluva lot. I got a place in Westwood, but I hated it. I was hoping to work down there and get into my own thing again doing sessions, but it just never happened. I never met anybody interesting; I never ran into anybody. I was happy to move back up here when I did. But it was something I had to do at the time; I wouldn't undo it.

"I had to get my own self together; that was part of it," he continued. "First of all, I didn't make nearly enough money to be carrying on with Rock and Jerry at their level. When I moved to L.A. there was no way I could keep it going so I just stopped doing [heroin]. I was sick for a while and then I was better, and that lasted a long time—two or three years."

In late August 1982, at a Dead concert at the Oregon Country Fair in Veneta, Oregon—Prankster country—Garcia introduced two new songs he'd written with Hunter. "West L.A. Fadeaway" was a musical and lyrical departure for Hunter and Garcia. In form it was a fairly straight blues shuffle, but the main character was a creation far removed from Hunter's or Garcia's worlds: a small-time mob hustler on the lam. The song always had a dark, creepy edge to it that was heightened by Garcia's ripping fuzztoned solo in midsong. "Keep Your Day Job" was musically reminiscent of both "Deal" and

"U.S. Blues," the rare Garcia song that sounded a bit like a retread. Hunter's lyrics were undeniably clever, but the message of the song—"Keep your day job until your night job pays"—was not one most perennially free-spirited Deadheads wanted to hear.

"Day Job" was one of the few Hunter-Garcia songs to be actively disliked by a large segment of Deadheads. It was played fairly often as an encore from the summer of 1982 until the end of 1986, and it *always* sent many fans scrambling for the exits. Why? My conjecture is that the lyrics essentially endorsed attitudes of the straight world, a perspective that clashed with the sort of mythic universe that was constructed song by song over the course of a typical Dead show. "Day Job" was, to use the hippie colloquialism, a "buzz crusher." In his book of lyrics, Hunter wrote, "This song was dropped from the Grateful Dead repertoire at the request of fans. Seriously."

On that same summer tour Garcia revived three songs that hadn't been played in a few years: "Stagger Lee" (missing since 1979), "Dupree's Diamond Blues" ('78) and, most exciting of all, "Crazy Fingers" (absent since 1976), which magically appeared during a second set at the Ventura Fairgrounds.

On the East Coast tour that fall Garcia introduced another new song, "Touch of Grey," which had been intended for a Hunter solo album that Garcia, Hunter and John Kahn did some preliminary work on in the fall of 1981. (Hunter wrote the first draft of the lyrics in September 1980.) That project never got off the ground, but Garcia liked the lyrics enough that he asked Hunter if he could reset them to his own music. Garcia's music was bright and tuneful, with a steady percolating rhythm that made the song a cousin to romps like "Bertha" and "Scarlet Begonias." Hunter once said that the lyrics were an expression of his own "intense alienation" from a Grateful Dead scene riddled with personal and financial problems, but what is communicated is a message about perseverance in the face of the negativity that bombards us from all sides every day. Hunter wants to view the cup of life as half full:

> *I see you got your list out*
> *Say your piece and get out*
> *Yes, I get the gist of it*
> *But it's all right*
> *Sorry that you feel that way*
> *The only thing there is to say*
> *Every silver lining's got a*
> *Touch of grey*
>
> *I will get by / I will get by*
> *I will get by / I will survive*

Coming from most writers, this sort of sentiment might be viewed as passive resignation, but everything about the music and the way Garcia sang "Touch of Grey," with Weir and Brent joining in on the chorus, made it feel like an anthem of triumph. And then on the final chorus it switched from "I will get by / I will survive" to "*We* will get by / *We* will survive." That took the song from being a seemingly personal declaration of faith and commitment from Garcia as he hit forty—"Oh well, a touch of grey / Kind of suits you anyway / That was all I had to say / It's all right"—to something much more inclusive, as if the "we" were all Deadheads, or all humanity.

Though Garcia had said at midyear that the next Grateful Dead album would be out by Christmas 1982, the group never even got together to record any of their new material. In fact, it would be five years before the Dead made another record. The group's year-end shows at the Oakland Auditorium were uneven and only occasionally inspired, though the band's third set New Year's Eve was a keeper. Rhythm and blues legend Etta James fronted the Dead— whom she labeled "the baddest blues band in the world"—for a set of tunes that included three songs Pigpen used to sing: "Love Light," "Hard to Handle" and "Midnight Hour."

Nineteen eighty-three was an odd year for the Grateful Dead. Garcia's drug addiction made him more insular with each passing month. When he was off the road, he almost never left Hepburn Heights. Band meetings were few and far between and usually had to take place at Garcia's house, because he no longer came to the Dead office at all. His onstage demeanor gradually changed, too. Whereas in 1980 and 1981 Garcia had still smiled quite a bit while he played and he seemed physically aware of his surroundings—interacting with the other bandmembers and occasionally acknowledging the dancing throngs in front of him—by the middle of 1983 he barely moved onstage at all; he played with his head down staring forward at nothing in particular. He rarely looked at his bandmates and he completely ignored the audience. He looked terribly unhealthy—he had put on quite a bit of weight and his skin was a pallid grayish-white, similar to the color becoming dominant in his beard and hair. Sets got a little shorter, and in the pre-"drums" portion of the second set Garcia often bolted from the stage without jamming after the song that led into Mickey and Billy's segment. The sets at Garcia Band shows, particularly the ones in Bay Area clubs, shortened dramatically, usually consisting of just five songs. Following a shaky set of Grateful Dead shows in Ventura in late July, a brief Garcia Band tour was canceled because of an infected insect bite on one of Garcia's feet; when he returned to the stage in late August with the Dead he was perkier than he had been in a while, though still pastyskinned and overweight. At gigs he almost never left his dressing room, and he raced through hotel lobbies to avoid having to stop and interact with Deadheads. When he did stop, though, he was unfailingly courteous to his fans.

"In the '80s, things sort of closed up around Jerry," says Susan Crutcher. "You couldn't just go backstage and say hi. It got a lot darker, and as someone who hadn't really kept up that much, I didn't really know why. So I basically stopped going. Then, if I did go, I'd hang out with Healy, who I always liked a lot." But Healy, too, got swept up in the rising tide of opiate use.

"There was a time in the '80s when Jerry was really reclusive, and I was pretty worried about him," Tiff Garcia says. "I'd go see him and he'd be in this big house, downstairs in this small, dark room, and he'd never leave. He had everything he wanted in there—a stereo, headphones, a guitar—but he would never leave that fuckin' room. People would come visit him and they wouldn't go down there; they'd be afraid to go down there because they'd feel like they were invading his privacy. I almost felt guilty because he was talkin' to me, 'cause all these other people wanted to talk to him and he wouldn't talk to anybody. I felt like saying, 'Jer, c'mon, these people have been part of your life for a long time. Respond to them somehow. Give 'em some feedback. Yell at 'em or something!' He wasn't lookin' good at all."

"There was definitely a wall around Jerry," remembers his old friend Laird Grant, "but I could walk through it with no questions. There were times when it was difficult, especially at shows, but on the day-to-day, I had no problem going to my friend's door and walking in without even having to knock. Naturally, when I saw what was going on with him, I was concerned. I knew what it was; I held his hand a couple of times, and we talked about it: 'What the fuck are you doin', man? Didn't you read the story about Billie Holiday?' And like everyone who's in it, he'd say, 'Man, I can take it or leave it. At this point I'm takin' it.' It's like what Mark Twain said about quitting smoking: 'Hell yeah, I can quit smoking. I've done it thousands of times—every time I put out a cigar.' "

Despite Garcia's plainly visible malaise, the Dead played better in 1983 than they had in 1982. In fact, they improved each year through the first half of the '80s, as if Garcia's deteriorating physical condition almost didn't matter. In the early part of the year, to the delight of Deadheads everywhere, he reintroduced "Help on the Way" and "Slipknot" after not having played them since the fall of 1977. The band's late-summer tour, which hit Washington, Oregon, Idaho, Colorado, Utah, New Mexico and Texas, was loaded with strong and energetic shows. And at Madison Square Garden in the fall, Garcia brought back "Saint Stephen" after a five-year absence, in an arrangement closer to the late-'60s version than the late-'70s variant. (Alas, the song was played only three times that fall before going into dry dock again, this time permanently.) Garcia also tried out an unusual new cover tune: "Revolution," by John Lennon. Predictably, Garcia opted to sing the slow version of the song ("Revolution #1" off the Beatles' "White Album"), but could never quite learn all the words—he'd simply mutter his way through most of the verses until he got to the part of the song that clearly appealed to him, the refrain: "You know it's gonna be all right."

By 1984 there was widespread concern in the Grateful Dead organization over Garcia's worsening physical condition. He had ballooned to close to three hundred pounds, and it wasn't just a fat stomach, though he certainly had that. His legs and ankles became swollen from edema. In *Living with the Dead*, Rock Scully talks about how during this period, Garcia almost never slept in his bed—he'd just grab a couple of hours here and there sitting in his chair smoking Persian and base cocaine and watching television or doing nothing. His cigarette ashes burned holes in all the furniture in Hepburn Heights, and even his trademark black T-shirts had burn holes in them. He rarely showered—as his greasy hair, black elbows and strong body odor showed—and his diet consisted mostly of ice cream and other junk food. Scully's account on this subject is probably spot-on—he witnessed it and was in his own degraded state at the time.

Len Dell'Amico recalls, "In '84 I started hearing some rumors that I found hard to believe, because they didn't correspond to what I knew in '81. I was disturbed and in denial, and one day I realized I really cared a lot about this guy and I had to do something. It was one of those things where I didn't feel like I had any choice. Coincidentally, he had Sue Stephens send me some tapes from the '84 Greek shows, and I thought, 'This is great!' So I went to see him in Pennsylvania on a JGB tour and then I saw him in Long Island with the Dead in mid- to late '84. And the rumors were true. And I was scared to death. It was a turning point for me. Now what—you wanted to find out, now you know, now what are you going do? Among other symptoms, he had some edema. When the toxins in your body reach a certain point, your tissue begins to swell. You'll see that in an ICU ward—usually you've got weeks or, if you're lucky, months.

"My analysis was that his problem essentially was boredom and that he had this amazing mind that had evolved in an unprecedented way, plus a passivity bred by being a rock star: 'Everything comes to me so I don't have to decide what I'm going to do. The people in the family make demands and I fulfill demands, like a Papa— We need the JGB tour. We need this . . . We need money.' And there's no point at all in telling someone superintelligent that if they do continue with the substance abuse they're going to die. They *know* that. So I started proposing activities: 'Why don't we do a Garcia Band video?' he said, 'Okay, but first we'll do the Grateful Dead, for political reasons.' I said fine, and that started the seven-year haul that produced the *So Far* video, two pay-per-view events, a bunch of network appearances, the rain forest benefit, the AIDS benefit . . . And we never got to do the Garcia Band project."

Others confronted Garcia more directly about his addiction, but he was always dismissive, sometimes even hostilely so. There were also attempts to rid Garcia's inner circle of people who were deemed bad influences. In late

1983, Alan Trist, who was a serious cocaine abuser, was let go. Rock Scully was forced into rehab the following year, and even after kicking heroin he became a pariah in the Dead scene. Though he claims he was given the option of coming back to work for the band, he drifted off into other things and never returned. Unfortunately, the departures of Trist and Scully didn't have much of an impact on Garcia's drug use. (Trist was rehired in 1994 to help with the administration of Ice Nine Publishing, a job he holds to this day.)

In 1992 Jerry's daughter Annabelle remembered 1983–84 as being particularly painful for her: "It got to the point where he'd call me up on the phone in Oregon and nod off while he was on the phone. There was nothing I could do except wait till he woke up and then finish the conversation. That kind of stuff is naturally really disturbing. It was a long period of time my father wasn't himself at all. I'd go visit him and nothing would happen—I'd just sit there and watch him burn holes in things with cigarettes and fall asleep and then wake up, do some more drugs, and then fall asleep and wake up and do some more. It was really awful; really super-awful.

"When he was doing those drugs, there wasn't much I could do," Annabelle continued. "I felt really young and real small and he was so grumpy at those times anyway, I was half-scared of him a lot of the time—not scared for my life, but of a presence. I realized that most of the reason he was doing it was because he was so damn bored. He had his music, but that was about it. He couldn't go outside anymore because so many people bugged him.

"But the biggest problem I had with that whole time is everybody else in the band and the roadies and all the women would say, 'Well, why don't you say something?' And I'd say, 'I'm sorry, but I don't want to sever any bonds with my father. I'm afraid that if I say anything to him, he won't want to see me anymore.' That was my big fear at thirteen or fourteen years old.

"That whole period of time has a real dreamlike quality and a real strange, surreal quality for me, and for everybody else, too. Because everybody felt they were walking on eggshells around him. And there were always creepy people coming on tour and making sure my dad was going to live through the tour. It was the epitome of the rock star's mistake—the worst you can do and still not die."

Mountain Girl, who at the time was living in Oregon "in relative poverty," says she received panicky phone calls about Jerry: "The bandmembers would call me and say, 'God, M.G., you've gotta do something.' So I'd drive down there and try to do something and it was just extremely difficult because he didn't want to do anything about it. He was really strung out for a long time."

"I was pretty out there," Garcia said in the late '80s, "but I was still mainly a maintenance junkie. I never enjoyed sitting around smoking freebase. If I didn't have heroin and freebase, I didn't want freebase. For me, I liked the heroin much better, but I liked to be able to stay awake to enjoy it. So the heroin and freebase thing was about right for me, but I never got that high. I just developed a huge habit; but it was still a maintenance habit.

"The drugs I was taking were escape drugs. It was like a long vacation. It worked good; I mean, I got my 'vacation.'

"For a long time there I sort of lost heart. 'I don't know if I want to do this. I don't know what I want.' It was that thing: 'Fuck. Is this right? Is this good? Is this the thing I should be doing?' For a long time—about eight years—I felt like I wanted to get away from everything somehow. But I didn't want to just stop playing, or have the Grateful Dead stop because that's what *I* wanted to do. And I didn't even know consciously that that's what I wanted. I don't think I really realized it until lately [late '80s]. Looking back on it I see certain patterns.

"Part of my nature is deeply pessimistic. And it's something I have to fight with a lot. Part of me is overconfident, too, so it's these two polar opposites."

In another late-'80s interview Garcia noted, "Drug use is kind of a cul-de-sac. It's one of those places you turn with your problems, and pretty soon all your problems have become that one problem. Then it's just you and the drugs.

"I was never an overdose kind of junkie. I've never enjoyed the extremes of getting high. . . . For me, it was the thing of just getting pleasantly comfortable and grooving at that level. But of course that level doesn't stay the same. It requires larger and larger amounts of drugs. So after a few years of that, pretty soon you've taken a lot of fucking drugs and you're not experiencing much. It's like a black hole, really."

But life went on apace, and the summer '84 Grateful Dead tour contained a number of powerful shows. Weir reintroduced the band's late-'60s (non-disco) arrangement of "Dancing in the Streets" and sang "Love Light" for only the second time since Pigpen's death. "Dark Star" made a rare appearance at the Greek Theater in July—played as the encore, as slides of space scenes were projected on screens behind the band. At a few shows, Phil gamely attempted to sing Paul McCartney's raucous "White Album" novelty "Why Don't We Do It in the Road?" with hilarious results. And at Red Rocks, Brent and Garcia sang Traffic's "Dear Mr. Fantasy" for the first time, and the words sounded as if they could've been written for Garcia:

> Dear Mr. Fantasy, play us a tune
> Something to make us all happy
> Do anything, take us out of this gloom
> Sing a song, play guitar, make it snappy
> You are the one who can make us all glad
> But doing that you break down in tears
> Please don't be sad if it was a straight life you had
> We wouldn't have known you all these years

Former road manager Jon McIntire had been away from the Dead scene for several years and was living in St. Louis when a friend persuaded him to go see the band's show in Kansas City that July. He hadn't spoken to anyone in the organization for more than a year, but reports of Garcia's condition had made it to him. McIntire said he found the concert "very depressing. I felt there was a great deal more energy coming from the audience to the stage than there was from the stage to the audience. I didn't think there was anything new going on. It was wonderful seeing my old friends again, but the actual concert was disturbing to me."

The next night at dinner, Weir asked McIntire if he would come back to work for the band because Danny Rifkin was planning to take some time off to be with his wife and the baby they were expecting. McIntire was nervous about getting involved, as the band seemed to be in such desperate straits, but a couple of months later, after talking to Phil, longtime road-crew chief Ram Rod, Rifkin and Hunter—all of whom said that things seemed to be taking a turn for the better—he agreed to return as road manager, beginning with the fall '84 tour. Once McIntire got out on road again, he quickly glimpsed the Dead's dark underbelly, and like everyone else was heartsick about Garcia's condition.

In November 1984 Garcia and Kahn and opening act Robert Hunter played a ten-show acoustic tour of the East Coast. According to Hunter, "The Grateful Dead were on the financial skids in '84 and things were not looking like they were going to get better. No new album for many years; [Jerry] wasn't interested in writing. This tour looked like a moneymaker with no appreciable overhead—just Jerry, John and me traveling by bus with a skeleton crew." But ten days before the tour began, Hunter had been part of a meeting where Garcia's drug problem was discussed at length, and the specter of doing an intervention on him—in which the band and roadies would confront him and insist that he get treatment—was raised. "Hard to know what to do. Hard to know what not to do," Hunter wrote in his journal at the time. "Hard, hard, hard. Classic conundrum. Personal paradox."

Hunter said he undertook the acoustic tour with Kahn and Garcia "with misgivings, persuaded by many who thought I might be the only one able to get through to Jerry. I wasn't so optimistic. Phil called the morning I left and wished me 'Godspeed' in the mission."

Alas, near the end of the tour Hunter wrote that he'd had almost no contact with Garcia during the entire two weeks and that "the humanitarian side of this venture is a total failure. He goes in his compartment at one end of the bus journey and stays there till the destination. At least I've seen with my own eyes what has been told me.

"There is no cry for help here—just a powerful individual doing what he damn well pleases. The loyalties he commands are staggering. He is, of course, more than a person—he's an industry."

Even Garcia's most ardent admirers acknowledged that the tour was uneven at best, with the moments of leaden and uninspired playing outweighing the good parts at several shows. John Kahn said he talked to Garcia about his drug use during this period, "and he'd say, 'Leave me alone. I'm fine.' But I had to say it anyway. People said that to me at one time or another, and I said 'Fuck you' to them, too. He felt people should stay out of his business. And I agree."

By January 1985 the die was cast, and the band decided to proceed with the intervention. In Garcia's rosy telling of the event later, "everybody came over to my house and said, 'Hey Garcia, you got to cool it; you're starting to scare us.' " Hunter's recollection, in his on-line journal in 1996, is probably closer to the truth: "We went en masse to Jerry's house. Knocked. He opened the door and said, 'Get the fuck out of here!' We refused. Into the lion's den we boldly entered, steeled to the deed to be done. He listened, anger slowly relenting. . . ." Garcia was told that he had to choose between drugs and the band and that if he didn't get help the group would disband or go on without him. They tried to persuade him to enter a program immediately, but Garcia managed to convince them that he would go in for treatment in a few days.

"It was really organized and everybody participated," Mountain Girl recalls. "We got twelve people to go over there. A lot of people didn't want to do it, but we talked them into it. I remember how awful it was, and how he ducked it. We were trying to get him into this program over at Lake Merritt [in Oakland], because that seemed like the most humane program in the Bay Area; I checked them all out. I had spent four or five days making all these calls, using a phony name, finding out about different treatment programs and what they cost and all that."

On January 18, a few days after the intervention and the day before he had said he was going to enter a rehab program, Garcia was busted for possession of heroin and cocaine in Golden Gate Park. He was sitting in his BMW near Metson Lake, off Middle Drive, adjacent to the Polo Fields, smoking some Persian, when a policeman happened by and saw that the registration tags on the car had expired. When he approached the car he smelled something burning, and he found Garcia holding "a piece of tin foil paper which had a brown sticky appearing substance on it," the officer wrote in his report. Garcia quickly shoved the foil under his seat. There were more pieces of tin foil with burned brown residue on them sitting in an open briefcase, along with twenty-three paper bindles—some empty, some containing small amounts of heroin and cocaine—assorted drug paraphernalia, lighters and, for a reason we'll probably never know, a seven of hearts playing card.

Garcia was arrested and briefly jailed in a downtown San Francisco precinct. A few hours later, bail of $7,300 was paid for him and he was released on his own recognizance. Of course the story was immediately all over the local television news, and a photo of Garcia being arraigned appeared prominently in the next day's paper.

Many Deadheads had been aware of Garcia's drug addiction for some time, but many thousands had no idea Garcia was a junkie, and the distressing news of the bust was the first they heard of it. "I think after the bust he got really embarrassed and he suddenly realized, 'Wait a minute, I'm not invisible. People are looking at me,' " M.G. says.

"I'm the sort of person," Garcia said later, "that will just keep going along until something stops me. For me and drugs, the bust helped. It reminded me how vulnerable you are when you're drug dependent. It caught my attention. It was like, 'Oh, right—illegal.' And of all the things I don't want to do, spending time in jail is one of those things I least want to do. It was as if this was telling me it was time to start doing something different."

CHAPTER 18
If Mercy's in Business, I Wish It for You

month to the day after his bust, Garcia was back onstage with the Grateful Dead at the Oakland Auditorium (newly refurbished and renamed the Henry J. Kaiser Convention Center) for three shows celebrating the Chinese New Year. The bust was Topic A in pre-show conversations among Deadheads, and there was a palpable tension in the air. Some of that tension evaporated the minute Garcia came onstage the first night of the series. He looked the best he had in some time—perhaps ten pounds lighter—and in a move that was noticed by every veteran Dead-watcher on the scene, Garcia had replaced his trademark black T-shirt with a more festive reddish-maroon one (immediately giving rise to TROUBLE AHEAD, JERRY IN RED bumper stickers, playing off a line in "Casey Jones"). The shows were raggedly played, but Deadheads took delight in the obvious changes in Garcia's stage demeanor. Rather than standing stock-still and staring blankly ahead as he had at most 1984 shows, he bopped around and even broke into grins from time to time. The most cathartic moment of the three-show run came during the second night when, during a second set-opening version of "Truckin'," the band came to the lines "Busted down on Bourbon Street / Set up like a bowling pin . . ." With every eye in the arena fixed squarely on Garcia, the crowd screamed out the lyrics. Garcia smiled slightly and the crowd roared, then he backpedaled to his amp, shook his head and grinned broadly after the line "They just won't let you be . . . oh, no."

Although he was still addicted to heroin and also using cocaine regularly, Garcia had begun what would be a fifteen-month incremental process of stepping away from those drugs completely. Rather than going into a drug rehabilitation program, Garcia was able to convince the judge in his case, Raymond Reynolds, that he would seek the treatment he needed independently. Additionally, he agreed to attend a Narcotics Anonymous–like drug diversion program just a couple of blocks from his Hepburn Heights house, and to perform a benefit concert for the Haight-Ashbury Food Project.

The changes came slowly at first—sometimes he'd even duck out of his diversion sessions during a break to go home and get high. But by the spring Garcia had made a commitment to change his lifestyle, aided considerably by his housemate, Nora Sage. Nora had worked as a cook in the household since the early '80s, when she lived down the street. She moved in following Rock

Scully's departure in 1983 and acted as a de facto housekeeper, too, all the while attending law school in San Francisco. In fact, the day he was busted, Garcia had driven Nora to school, which was highly unusual for him, and then gone on to the park and gotten busted. In the weeks after the bust, Nora, in consultation with Jerry, conceived of an unorthodox method of weaning him from drugs that would be less radical than enrolling in a live-in facility.

The first stage was to get Garcia to openly admit he was a junkie and thus stop the elaborate subterfuge and sneaking around to score dope. Part of the household budget was set aside for his drug habit, but it was up to Nora to ration the drugs, cutting Garcia's usage little by little over a period of about a year. She also tried to get Jerry involved in as many activities as she could to keep him busy. She encouraged him to get into painting for the first time since his art school days, and she also bought him various model kits, because he loved doing projects with his hands. During this time Garcia built seven remote-control cars, which he would take down to a nearby park and race around. He also put together a number of model guns from kits, including an Uzi submachine gun. (Garcia's love of guns is something he rarely talked about, but at various times from the mid-'60s on he owned a number of different kinds of pistols, including a James Bond–style Beretta.)

"If it wasn't for Nora Sage," Tiff Garcia says, "Jerry probably would have been dead a lot earlier. She really tried to take care of him. She turned him back on to art, got him an airbrush outfit and various things, and tried to get him to eat a little healthier. And yeah, she got dope for him, too, if he needed it, but she was really the one who was most responsible for his turnaround."

Not everyone in the Dead scene was thrilled with Nora or the stepping-down program, which one skeptical member of the Dead organization termed "a junkie's solution, where Jerry had all the power and could do whatever he wanted." There were those who felt Nora was excessively controlling and made too many decisions about who could have access to Garcia—always an issue, since so many people wanted or needed to talk to him. Others correctly noted that without some professional guidance and the aid of therapists who could help Garcia understand the root causes of his craving for drugs, he was a poor candidate for long-term addiction recovery. After all, Jerry was someone who was *famous* for giving in to his appetites—what would change that behavior in the long run?

Nevertheless, even skeptics had to be impressed by Garcia's gradual transformation from an emotionally closed-off physical wreck, content to while away the hours getting high and watching TV, to someone who enjoyed hanging out with people again and working on different musical projects.

In the spring of 1985 there was still no sign that a new album was forthcoming from the Grateful Dead. The band's one attempt in the studio since the making of *Go to Heaven* in 1979 had come during the darkest days of Garcia's addiction in '84. It had produced nothing but anxiety over Garcia's utter lack of interest in the sessions, and, in the case of the drummers, over Bob Weir's using a drum machine as a click track in hopes of establishing surer rhythms for his songs. There was some talk about trying to delay recording and waiting until Arista threw up their hands and released the Dead from their contract, thus enabling them to sign with a new company for more money. But Clive Davis was always patient and encouraged the group to take their time and record when they were ready to.

Instead of working on the new album, the band decided to make a long-form video (many songs as opposed to just one) with Len Dell'Amico once again directing, aided closely by Garcia. Shortly after a very spirited and successful East Coast tour at the end of March and the beginning of April (marred only by nagging vocal trouble for Garcia caused by a persistent case of his old nemesis, bronchitis), the band secretly gathered in the intimate, 2,000-seat Marin County Veterans Auditorium in San Rafael for three long days of videotaping and multitrack recording without an audience. The group had played superb shows there in 1983 and '84, so it was a familiar room, and, miraculously, word about the sessions didn't leak out to the public. Dell'Amico had the band set up as if they were playing a gig, except with Weir facing back toward the drummers, and Garcia and Brent turned more toward each other. A full video crew shot the group from many different angles, while John Cutler, who had been part of the Dead's sound crew for a number of years, captured the performances in a mobile recording truck parked outside the auditorium. Over the course of three days the Dead ran through most of their recent unrecorded songs, as well as classic Dead tunes like "Terrapin," "Playing in the Band," "Uncle John's Band," "Cassidy," "Comes a Time" and "Jack Straw." There were oddities like "Hi-Heel Sneakers" and Booker T.'s "Green Onions," and chilling versions of a new Dylan cover tune Garcia had played once on the spring tour, "She Belongs to Me." Because there was no audience, the band could start and stop songs when they pleased and play multiple versions of the same song if they wanted. They taped for three days in April and three days in November, hoping to get enough good performances to provide a skeleton frame for the video; from the outset the intention was to combine the Marin Vets footage with other, more conceptual video approaches.

"There was a year of all these different possibilities being explored," Dell'Amico says. "For example, we wrote an entire script with dialogue, scenes and action involving animated creatures. And an outgrowth of that was an idea of having Jer do the artwork, so we pursued that a bit. He did a lot of drawings, we went to an effects house and animated them. Then, one day, the band decided they didn't like that approach anymore. For me it was like, 'Oh, okay. Maybe something else,' " Dell'Amico said with an amused shrug.

Garcia was involved in another prospective film project around the same time. Several years earlier he, Richard Loren and John Kahn had acquired the movie rights to Kurt Vonnegut's science fiction novel *The Sirens of Titan*, and through much of 1984 Garcia had been in close contact with Tom Davis as the writer/comedian prepared the first draft of a script. According to Garcia, *The Sirens of Titan* "occurred to me as a real cogent cinematic experience in my mind's eye." By early 1985, Gary Gutierrez, the skilled animator who had worked on the Grateful Dead movie, was preparing detailed storyboards for the film-to-be, which would be directed by Garcia.

"If I'm going to make movies," Jerry said in March 1985, "I'm going to make them on my terms. I'm not going to become a filmmaker as a career. I'll do it like Jean Cocteau—do a couple of tasty movies and that's it. I don't know if I could do somebody else's ideas, for one thing. I don't know if I'd want to. And making a film is a hassle. You have to live with an idea for an awful long time, which means the idea has to have great power. You have to love it a lot or else you have to be really tolerant.

"For me, ideas lose their sheen, lose their exterior real fast; and it's only the power and longevity of some ideas that have made me want to stick it out to that extent. *Sirens* is one of those long-lived ideas that has stayed good no matter how much I've thought about it and how much time has passed. That kind of freshness, that kind of real love for a piece, is the only thing that would make me want to make a film of a piece."

In June 1985 the Dead officially celebrated their twentieth anniversary with three shows at the Greek Theater in Berkeley, which after four years of great Dead concerts there had become many Deadheads' favorite place to see the band—a mecca worth traveling to; ground zero. This momentous occasion did not escape the notice of the mainstream media, either. Beginning with the Dead's spring tour, newspapers and magazines around the country had started to take note of the impending anniversary, with one perplexed reporter after another sent to wade into the tie-dyed throngs in the parking lots outside Dead shows to explore and then try to explain the mystery of the Dead's allure. Hippies, in 1985? So the intrepid scribes would find a flaxen-haired young hippie girl named something outlandish like Rainbow Starcloud, selling veggie burritos, and a grizzled, gray-bearded Haight-Ashbury acid casualty sitting by a dilapidated VW van, and those two people would be used to represent all Deadheads. This same type of story, with minor variations in the cast of characters, was written hundreds of times in cities big and small. The American press loved writing about the Dead from the mid-'80s on, mostly because the bandmembers were perceived as leaders of a strange hippie cult dedicated to keeping the supposedly outmoded ideals of the '60s alive. In 1985 the Dead and the Deadheads were the antithesis of what was considered hip. At best, writers treated them as colorful anachronisms; more often the tone of the writing about both was condescending or downright insulting. There was rarely much intelligent writing about the band's music, and the rock press, including the once-friendly *Rolling Stone*, largely ignored the Dead altogether.

But the twentieth anniversary perked up a lot of people's interest. Twenty years *was* an achievement in the world of rock 'n' roll bands. Who else could boast such longevity? The Rolling Stones, but they survived only because they had gone through long periods when they didn't tour or even see each other. The Dead had toured solidly for twenty years, even gigging during their hiatus. The Beach Boys? By 1985 they had been strictly an oldies act for ten years, cranking out the same twenty hits every night. No, in the mid-'80s the Dead could rightfully claim to be the most successful touring rock band in history, and though they had not put out a record of new material in five years, their following continued to grow across the country, particularly in the South and the Northeast, where they could now sell out more than one show at a time in sports arenas in several different cities.

"The years are starting to pay off," Garcia commented to one writer that spring when asked about the band's durability. "It's like the Budapest String Quartet or the Duke Ellington Orchestra, which had the same horn section for more than twenty years. It matters. Those horn blends are legendary.

"We're not family," he went on. "We're far closer than family could ever be. No matter what we do, the Grateful Dead will always be something we're involved with. At this point, it's reflexive."

The anniversary concerts themselves had an unusually festive air about them. Behind the stage hung a giant banner designed by Rick Griffin depicting a skeleton minuteman holding Garcia's guitar instead of a musket and standing in front of an American flag. Under the Dead's name it read TWENTY YEARS SO FAR in ornate Griffinesque lettering. T-shirts bearing Griffin's design were top sellers throughout the summer and fall Dead tours.

As the band came onstage on the first night of the three-show series, Dan Healy cranked up the opening of the Beatles' "Sgt. Pepper's Lonely Hearts Club Band" through the PA: "It was twenty years ago today, Sergeant Pepper taught the band to play / They've been goin' in and out of style, but they're guaranteed to raise a smile. . . ." The Dead kicked off the show with a tune from their early days, "Dancing in the Streets," and the Greek was a blur of color, motion and white, toothy grins in the late-afternoon sun. Three songs into the set, though, there was a malfunction in the sound system and the band had to leave the stage for a time while it was fixed. How *very* Grateful Dead for something to screw up on their big day!

Once the gremlins had been chased away, however, the Dead responded by playing three excellent shows packed with neat surprises, including Derek and the Dominoes' "Keep On Growing," sung by Phil and Brent, remarkably apt for the occasion; the first version of the "Cryptical Envelopment" section of "That's It for the Other One" in fifteen years; and the return after five years of "Comes a Time." Garcia's singing on that last tune was particularly emotive and affecting, no doubt because the words mirrored his own experience of the previous few years so well:

> Day to day just lettin' it ride
> You get so far away from how it feels inside
> You can't let go, 'cause you're afraid to fall
> But the day may come when you can't feel at all

> Comes a time when the blind man takes your hand
> Says 'Don't you see?' . . .

The Dead's tours that summer and autumn were unusually strong, with especially varied set lists, crisp and purposeful jamming and a higher level of energy onstage than anyone had seen in quite a while. From outward appearances, Garcia was a different person than he'd been a year earlier, and his more open and ebullient stage personality clearly affected the other bandmembers—particularly Phil, who was now happily married and the most sober he'd been in years. The Deadheads, in turn, could see the obvious shift in the onstage dynamic, and that contributed to a more upbeat environment in the audience, as the widespread concern for Garcia's well-being in the wake of the January '85 bust was slowly replaced by an almost giddy optimism. "We will survive," indeed.

The downside of the Dead's renaissance is that on many tour dates, especially on the East Coast, the shows started to attract large crowds of people who didn't have tickets for the sold-out concerts and who were content to hang around outside the venues, trying to score spare tickets (or spare change), partying with each other and occasionally trying to storm the doors to get in free. In Richmond, Virginia (very strong Dead Country), in early November, gate-crashers ran up against mounted police outside the Coliseum, resulting in a number of arrests and minor injuries. A week later, outside the Brendan Byrne Arena in northern New Jersey, ticketless hordes, aided by drunken, rowdy New York Giants fans who'd attended a football game next door at Giants Stadium, broke through a tight security cordon and clashed with the arena's security forces. These sorts of crowd-control problems would dog the Dead intermittently for the rest of their days.

Still, this hopeful and regenerative year ended on an up note, as the Dead played their traditional New Year's Eve concert for one of their largest audiences ever. The second set (the "midnight set") of the concert from the 14,000-seat Oakland Coliseum Arena was broadcast live nationwide over the fledgling USA cable television network. For East Coast Deadheads, the telecast began at 2:30 in the morning, but it offered them a rare chance to witness one of the sacred rituals of Grateful Dead culture since the late '60s—a New Year's Eve show.

Because Garcia was so heavily involved in Grateful Dead–related activities for much of 1985, the Jerry Garcia Band didn't play as often as they had in '83 and '84, when they had undertaken several tours outside of California. Still, the JGB definitely benefited from Garcia's improved health and disposition. The core lineup of Garcia, John Kahn (who was still living drug-free in Los Angeles during most of 1985), organist Melvin Seals, drummer David Kemper (also a successful L.A. session player) and singers Gloria Jones and Jaclyn LaBranch slowly developed into a formidable unit that carried forward the tradition established by Garcia's best late-'70s groups, but with even stronger gospel underpinnings. Melvin was more than just a gospel foil for Garcia, however. He had strong rock, R&B and blues chops from playing in Jon Hendricks's long-running musical *Evolution of the Blues*, and as a member of Elvin Bishop's rockin' boogie band for six years.

"Jerry was so happy when we got to that lineup with Melvin, Jackie and Gloria," Kahn said in 1996. "They were so easygoing and always in a good mood and they were up for anything. We'd try all these weird songs in rehearsal, every style you can imagine—Beatle songs, Dylan songs, old R&B— and they'd be right on it, even though most of them were songs they didn't know."

By April 1986 Garcia had stopped using heroin and cocaine altogether— suffering through a rough withdrawal immediately after kicking—and his transformation back to the ebullient "old Jerry" was complete, much to the delight of his fellow bandmembers, friends and everyone in the crowd, who couldn't help noticing the change. That said, the Dead's shows in the first half of 1986 were more erratic than they had been in the second half of 1985. The concerts were full of spirit, to be sure, but there didn't seem to be as much thought put into the transitions between songs in the second set as there had been six months earlier, and there was not as much jamming in general; it's not clear why that would be true of this period, and one didn't hear many complaints—it was enough to watch the happy Garcia.

"By April of '86 he was straight," says Len Dell'Amico, "and the ripple effect that this had in their tribe was amazing to see. Think about how hard that must have been for him—being addicted to those substances on that level, and gradually stepping away from them; and the sense of sacrifice to achieve that and how strong, leonine and leaderlike and positive that was. So this flowering was taking place and there was a very uplifting sense of possibilities in the scene."

When he wasn't on the road playing with the Dead, Garcia spent much of his time with Dell'Amico choosing songs from the Marin Vets video sessions to be included in their forthcoming long-form video and working on edits of the performances. By the spring of 1986 they had it whittled down to two hours, but another hour would be eliminated before the video was completed in the spring of 1987.

The Dead's summer tour that year generated more interest than usual outside of Deadhead circles, because five of the shows—all in football stadiums—paired the Dead on a bill with Bob Dylan and Tom Petty and the Heartbreakers, who also acted as Dylan's backup band. Garcia had attended a Dylan-Petty show at the Greek Theater that spring and had spent considerable time chatting with Dylan backstage; though Garcia had played with Dylan at the Warfield Theater in 1980, it was this night at the Greek and on the following summer tour that cemented their close personal relationship. They were mutual admirers who shared similar roots in American folk and blues. And they had both carried heavy loads since the '60s—Dylan as the de facto poet laureate of American music; Garcia as the embodiment of the libertine Haight-Ashbury ethos—and had attracted more than their share of fanatics and devoted followers who placed them on uncomfortable pedestals. Garcia had more Dylan tunes in his repertoire than did any other major American singer: Just in 1985 and 1986, between the Dead and the JGB, Garcia sang "She Belongs to Me," "It's All Over Now, Baby Blue," "Visions of Johanna," "It Takes a Lot to Laugh, It Takes a Train to Cry," "When I Paint My Masterpiece," "Knockin' on Heaven's Door," "Tangled Up in Blue" and "Simple Twist of Fate."

Expectations for the tour ran high, with most Deadheads hoping that Dylan and the Dead would find a way to play together. At the first concert in Minneapolis, they didn't join forces. But at the Rubber Bowl in Akron a week later (after the Dead had played several shows alone in the Midwest), Dylan joined them during their first set and played some typically odd, off-time rhythm guitar on a version of the blues standard "Little Red Rooster," and then led the band through stumbling versions of his own "Don't Think Twice, It's Alright" and "It's All Over Now, Baby Blue." This was a period when Dylan's singing was particularly nasal and unmelodic, and the Dead had a difficult time following his unpredictable phrasing. Still, there were hints that the partnership could produce something interesting.

Unbeknownst to the rest of the band, Garcia began smoking heroin and cocaine again on the tour, using old contacts to secretly score drugs for him—and there was never a shortage of people wanting to get Garcia high, even in the middle of the night, usually in exchange for a backstage pass for the next show or some such perquisite. Why did Garcia slip back to his old ways on the tour after having worked so long and courageously to get clean? Nora Sage, who was on the tour and suddenly found herself frozen out of Garcia's life—perhaps because he knew she would not approve of his drug use—suggests that he felt a lot of pressure because he was unaccustomed to playing in stadiums, and being on the same bill with Dylan added a layer of weirdness to the proposition. And there was his physical discomfort: In Ohio he was bothered so much by an infected tooth that he had to go to a dentist, who prescribed large dosages of codeine, a narcotic itself.

Two days later, on Independence Day, the tour reached Rich Stadium in Buffalo, and Garcia wasn't feeling well. The codeine had laid him low; he bowed out of a planned dinner at Len Dell'Amico's mother's house and stayed in his motel instead, feeling groggy. He was having kidney problems as well. In the record heat and humidity that had followed the entire Midwest swing of the tour, Garcia had suffered from dehydration, while at the same time he kept feeling the need to urinate, a very uncomfortable sensation he couldn't shake for days.

Still, Garcia managed to gather enough strength to play an excellent show in Buffalo, including a half-hour segment of the second set that was telecast live across the country as part of Farm Aid, a benefit concert country music superstar Willie Nelson had put together to raise money for financially strapped farmers. During the Dead's televised portion, Garcia sang fine versions of "The Wheel" and "Uncle John's Band" and successfully concealed his physical distress. The Farm Aid broadcast also showed a portion of the Dylan-Petty set; Dylan and the Dead didn't play together at this show.

The Dead-Dylan-Heartbreakers minitour ended with two concerts played in steambath conditions at RFK Stadium in Washington, D.C., site of the famous Dead–Allman Brothers concerts more than a decade earlier. At the second of those two shows, July 7, Dylan once again ambled onstage during the Dead's first set and joined the group for tentative versions of "It's All Over Now, Baby Blue" and "Desolation Row" (which Weir seemed to know much better than Dylan).

"I found myself in the weird position of teaching Dylan his own songs," Garcia said with a chortle. "It's just really strange! It was funny. He was great. He was so good about all this stuff. Weir wanted to do 'Desolation Row' with him, y'know, and it's got a million words. So Weir says, 'Are you sure you'll remember all the words?' And Dylan says, 'I'll remember the important ones!' "

Though outwardly Garcia's demeanor at the concert was upbeat, it was clear that something was not right with him physically. On a couple of occasions between songs he left the stage—including during the jam on "Playing in the Band" in the second set. Both sets were much shorter than usual, not surprising since the temperature was in the high nineties even late in the evening.

An exhausted Garcia flew back to California the next day, happy to be heading back to Marin County's more temperate climate. On the afternoon of his second day back, July 10—a day before the band was set to go down the coast to Ventura for their annual shows at the beachside County Fairgrounds—Garcia became delirious, and eventually passed out in the bathroom of his house, where Nora Sage discovered him. She immediately called an ambulance, but by the time he reached Marin General Hospital in Greenbrae, Garcia was in a deep coma with a perilously high temperature. The doctors put him on a bed of ice to bring his temperature down, and Nora spent the night rubbing his feet, trying to keep his circulation going. Though he was basically comatose, at one point Garcia came to long enough to yank the tubes from his nose and throat, so nurses shot him up with Demerol to sedate him.

"I felt better after cleaning up, oddly enough, until that tour," Garcia said a year later. "And then I didn't realize it but I was dehydrated and tired. That was all I felt, really. I didn't feel any pain. I didn't feel sick. I just felt tired. Then, when we got back from the tour, I was just really tired. One day, I couldn't move anymore, so I sat down. A week later I woke up in the hospital, and I didn't know what had happened. It was really weird."

What had happened, according to the Dead's own statement at the time, was that Garcia had slipped into a coma as a result of "the sudden onset of diabetes and a general systemic infection as a result of an abscessed tooth and exhaustion following a road tour." Although he had no history of diabetes, his notoriously poor eating habits—lots of ice cream and other junk food—coupled with his chain-smoking of cigarettes, his years of serious drug abuse and the process of weaning himself of his heroin addiction contributed to his precipitous decline. He was teetering near the brink of death when he arrived at the hospital, and for the next five days his fortunes went up and down.

"It was adrenal exhaustion which led to a diabetic episode," says Mountain Girl. "It was really, really hot on that tour; a sweatbath. It was a hundred and four, a hundred and seven; just wretchedly hot. If any medical people had been looking at him they would have caught it. But nobody was there for him. He got into peeing and peeing and peeing and you just start wasting away and dehydrating. But nobody got him to the doctor and nobody called the doctor to say, 'Gee, Jerry's having to stop the music and pee every twenty minutes.' It was driving him nuts. He didn't know what was happening to him. And that was the beginning of the breakdown. He came home and fell apart."

M.G. was home in Oregon when she got the news about Jerry's collapse. "I jumped on a plane at six-thirty the next morning and took the airporter up to the hospital and I got there and the doctor was saying, 'We're not sure he's going to live through the hour.' They were saying, 'We're readying him for a tracheotomy to help his breathing.' I said, 'A *what*? No, you're not!' I told them I thought that was a really bad idea. Obviously if it was absolutely necessary as a last resort to save his life that would be one thing, but . . .

"At first they wouldn't let me see him. He was a little bit wakey when I went in at about one-thirty. He was just sort of coming to, and he was really glad to see me. He was in pretty serious shape and they shooed me out of there really fast. He was going in and out. He was having a lot of breathing problems. What it was is they'd given him thirty milligrams of Valium IV—

he claims to have been allergic to Valium so it stopped his heart and his respiration; it shut his whole body down. His chart is how I found out about that. The doctor admitted to me that when they took him in they didn't know what was the matter with him and they couldn't figure it out so they decided to give him a CAT scan and he was sort of thrashing around and moaning during the CAT scan. . . . It was a diabetic coma, for Christ's sake; how hard is that to diagnose? Any paramedic should have picked that up, but they didn't look at it until the middle of that afternoon when they checked his blood sugar and it was just sky-high; it was off the charts. 'Oh, is *that* what it is!' So no tracheotomy, no more heroic measures.

"So the scene in the hospital was a lot of people trying to defend Jerry from the doctors; at least that's the way it felt to me. Yes, they had him very carefully suspended, but the slightest little thing would set it off, and he had a number of close calls. He had a systemic candida infection that put him back in ICU for four days. It's a yeast infection of some sort that you can get in the hospital. It comes into your whole body. It's a very dangerous systemic fungus infection. It was growing in his mouth and throat—this white stuff. Oh, man, it was really bad.

"They had to do all this emergency dialysis and that was unbelievable. And bloody. He had a complete kidney shutdown for ten days. He didn't pee for ten days. So they did this big emergency dialysis every couple of days. And he was not getting any better and every time they do it it's very dangerous."

Garcia was in and out of a coma for four days, and during that period it was not clear that he was going to live. He had a fever of 105 degrees for several hours and his system fluctuated erratically for several days.

"The doctors said they'd never seen anybody as sick who wasn't dead," Garcia said just two months after the episode. "So if that's any indication, apparently I was real sick. Although I gotta tell you, I didn't experience any pain or discomfort, really, apart from being wired and having tubes and holes and all kinds of things in me."

"I must say, my experience never suggested to me that I was anywhere near death," he said in another interview. "For me, it had just been this weird experience of being shut off. Later on, I found out how scary it was for everybody, and then I started to realize how serious it all had been. The doctors said I was so dehydrated my blood was like mud."

Garcia's delirium took on a weird, science fiction quality: "My main experience was one of furious activity and tremendous struggle in a sort of futuristic spaceship vehicle with insectoid presences. After I came out of my coma, I had this image of myself as these little hunks of protoplasm that were stuck together kind of like stamps with perforations between them that you could snap off," Garcia recounted with a laugh. "They were run through with neoprene tubing, and there were these insects that looked like cockroaches which were like message-units that were kind of like my bloodstream. That was my image of my physical self, and this particular image lasted a long time. It was really strange.

"It gave me a greater admiration for the incredible, baroque possibilities of mentation. The mind is so incredibly weird. The whole process of going into the coma was very interesting, too. It was slow onset—it took about a week—and during this time I started feeling like the vegetable kingdom was speaking to me. It was communicating in comic dialect in iambic pentameter. So there were these Italian accents and German accents and it got to be this vast gabbling. Potatoes and radishes and trees were all speaking to me. It finally just reached hysteria and that's when I passed out and woke up in the hospital."

Word of Garcia's calamity spread quickly through the Deadhead community. At first, representatives from the Dead organization called a few well-connected Deadheads to say that someone in the band—they wouldn't confirm who it was—had fallen desperately ill and that the Ventura concerts that weekend would be canceled, so spread the word—and pray. Of course it wasn't long before it became known, through sources at hospital, that it was Garcia who had been stricken, and the news went across the phone lines all night long on July 10, as worried fans broke the news to friends far and near. Unfortunately, the dire news didn't reach everyone who needed to hear it—more than a thousand Deadheads, many of whom had driven from the East Coast and were expecting to camp outside the venue, arrived in Ventura on Friday afternoon and Saturday morning expecting to see a concert. They were turned away at the gates and had to find other places to camp up and down the California coast. The cancellation was a disaster for Ventura's many hotels, too: the annual Dead concerts there had become the city's busiest tourist weekend.

Given Garcia's well-publicized drug bust in 1985, it was not surprising that there were lurid rumors that the guitarist had OD'd on heroin. The Grateful Dead said nothing publicly about the illness the first day. The following afternoon they released a fairly detailed statement to the press and also put a message about Garcia's condition on the band's telephone "hotline," which usually carried information about upcoming concerts. That first weekend alone, the hotline received more than ten thousand calls from concerned Deadheads, and as the days passed the message was updated periodically with medical reports. Northern California newspapers and television stations gave the story significant play, and by and large the press coverage was very sympathetic. Garcia was that rare local figure whose popularity transcended his actual following. Even people who had no interest in the Grateful Dead knew him as the smiling Haight-Ashbury veteran who was still rockin' on the road and selling out a dozen or more local concerts every year, the most visible and vocal member of the group.

The first few days after the collapse it was difficult to obtain reliable information about Garcia's condition. News spread that he had lapsed in and out of the coma several times and didn't seem to be improving. This led to considerable conjecture that even if Garcia didn't die from the diabetic episode, he might have suffered brain damage or developed a permanent kidney condition that might require regular dialysis or perhaps even a kidney transplant.

Len Dell'Amico, who was working in Texas when he heard about Garcia's collapse, says, "When they said the word coma I was stricken pretty bad, because most times that doesn't have a good outcome—you either stay there or you're damaged. And the idea of a damaged Garcia was really, really repellent because you're talking about somebody who's much more interesting and evolved and beautiful than most people. That was not a happy idea."

"At one point the doctors said Jerry might not walk again," Mountain Girl says. "There was talk about nerve damage and heart problems and all sorts of other bad stuff. It was very confusing for a while. Nobody seemed to know what was going to happen."

Eventually, she says, Garcia came out of the coma and suddenly announced, "I'm not Beethoven," meaning, "I'm not deaf. I can hear what you're saying." After that, "I was pretty scrambled," Garcia said. "It was as though in my whole library of information, all the books had fallen off the shelves and all the pages had fallen out of the books. I would speak to people and know what I meant to say, but different words would come out. For the first few days it was mostly sort of Joycean inversions of language, and then after a while I started to remember how it worked. But I had to do that with everything. They had to teach me how to walk again. . . . The bits and pieces were there, but I didn't have ready access to them."

Once he was out of immediate danger, Garcia was allowed to begin having visitors, and a steady stream of faces from his past and present stopped by to offer their love and support—band, crew and office members; picking mates like David Nelson and Sandy Rothman; his old childhood friend Laird Grant; brother Tiff; his daughters with M.G., Annabelle and Trixie; and his ex-wife Sara and daughter Heather, whom he hadn't seen in many years. Sara says Jerry cried when he saw Annabelle and Heather standing together by his bedside.

"I got to see him, I'd guess, sometime within a week," says Len Dell'Amico. "His brother was there. It was very dark in the room. And he and Tiff were reminiscing about their dad and other things from their childhood. It was a process of reconstructing memory. He was free-associating and they seemed very close. I was teared up anyway, but this was just so great to see. So I had a very warm visit with him and I was encouraged. Then I visited again a couple of weeks later when he'd moved to the cardiac ward. I believe in the power of prayer and he expressed that he had felt the influence of hundreds of thousands of people putting their energy with him; it's a feeling I don't think you or I will ever experience."

Indeed, Garcia said, "I'm not a believer in the invisible, but I got such an incredible outpouring. The mail I got in the hospital was so soulful. All the Deadheads . . . it was kind of like brotherly, sisterly, motherly, fatherly advice from people. Every conceivable healing vibe was pouring into that place. I mean, the doctors did what they could to keep me alive, but as far as knowing what was wrong with me and knowing how to fix it—it's not something medicine knows how to do. And after I'd left, the doctors were saying that my recovery was incredible. They couldn't believe it.

"I really feel that the fans put life into me, and that feeling reinforced a lot of things. It was like, 'Okay, I've been been away for a while, folks, but I'm back.' It's that kind of thing. It's just great to be involved in something that doesn't hurt anybody. If it provides some uplift and some comfort in people's lives, it's just that much nicer. So I'm ready for anything now."

Garcia called the episode "another one of those things to grab my attention. It was like my physical being saying, 'Hey, you're going to have to put in some time here if you want to keep on living.' Actually, it was a thought that had never entered my mind. I'd been lucky enough to have an exceptionally rugged constitution, but the thing of getting older, and basically having a life of benign neglect, had caught up with me. And possibly the experience of quitting drugs may have put my body through a lot of quick changes."

Two days before Garcia was released from the hospital—on his forty-fourth birthday, August 1—Nora Sage was informed by Jon McIntire that Garcia had decided he wanted her to move out of the house, and she was given twenty-four hours to clear out her things. Though earlier in his convalescence Garcia had told several people that he didn't want to live with Mountain Girl again, M.G., McIntire and and a few others convinced Jerry that it would help his recovery and be good for his spirits if M.G., Annabelle and Trixie moved into the house to help him.

"When he got out of the hospital, Jerry was feeling really, really cheerful," M.G. says. "Some of his confidence was coming back. Things were looking really bright—he wanted to go for long drives; he wanted to get out. He wanted to eat something besides sandwiches with no mayonnaise. He was ready for life again. But he was pretty weak physically, so it took a while for him to get his strength back again."

In the third week of August, about six weeks after the collapse, M.G. says, "We went up to Oregon together to get my stuff, and he looked around my place in Oregon and said, 'Jeez. This is great. Why are we leaving here? Why don't we stay here for a while?' So we stayed there for about a week and it was great. We also stayed for a weekend on a houseboat on Lake Shasta at the tail end of that. We met Big Steve [Parish] and Robbie [Taylor, of the road crew] in Packer's Bay and rented a houseboat. We swam in the warm water. At that point, Jerry hadn't really played the guitar yet. Steve brought Jerry's banjo down to the boat and Jerry tried to play a little bit, but it hurt his hands. His calluses were gone. He definitely had a long, long way to go."

"When I was in the hospital," Garcia said later, "all I could think was, 'God, just give me a chance to do stuff. Give me a chance to go back to being productive and playing music and doing the stuff I love to do. Shit, man, I'm ready.' And one of the first things I did—once I started being able to make coherent sentences—was to get a guitar in there to see if I could play. But when I started playing, I thought, 'Oh man, this is going to take a long time and a lot of patience.'"

Interestingly, it was not a member of the Dead but Merl Saunders who, at M.G.'s urging, took on what looked to be a Herculean task of helping the physically weak and mentally scattered Garcia recapture his musical abilities. Even before he was ready to attempt to play, Merl helped him get some of his strength back: "I'd take him for a walk. We'd take ten steps, then take ten steps back. His attitude was great. He wanted to get better, but he was scared, too. He got tired very easily, but he never really got discouraged. The most he'd say would be, 'Oh man, this is harder than it looks!'"

Once Garcia picked up a guitar, "It came back very slowly," Merl says. "He had to learn chords all over again and he had a lot of trouble remembering how to do even the simplest stuff. And I didn't want to push him. 'Man, I'm tired.' He'd been playing for five minutes. 'Okay, that's fine. Put it down. Let's go for a walk.' And we'd do that for a few minutes until he'd get tired. We'd talk about music. I'd tell him about songs I was working on and that would get his mind going. We'd talk in musical terms. And slowly he started to get his strength back. But it sometimes took an hour or two for him to get even a simple chord down. Then, as we got farther into it, some things started to come back to him a little, but it took a lot of work. The first song he wanted to learn again was 'My Funny Valentine.'"

Len Dell'Amico remembers that once Garcia was out of the hospital and back home at Hepburn Heights, "I'd talk to Jerry on the phone and he'd always say, 'I'm fine, I'm fine.' He'd never say, 'I don't feel well.' You could never tell what his real condition was—or maybe he was being completely honest; I don't know. I'll never forget that first time I went and visited him at home. Merl was sitting at the piano—God bless Merl, because that must have taken a lot of strength, because he was there a lot—and they had sheet music out and Jerry had a guitar in his hands, but there wasn't a whole lot happening that was terribly coherent. But Merl had this very positive attitude that I'm sure was somewhat forced. And Jerry had this lost-puppy look; kind of the opposite of the leonine 'I know what I'm doing' look. But gradually what he and Merl were doing paid off."

"The first couple of times I saw Jerry try to play guitar after the coma, you could see that his mind was working faster than his hands could move," said John Kahn, who joined in the effort to get Garcia playing again after Merl and Jerry had been at it for a week or two. "But his attitude about it was always so good that I was never that worried that it wouldn't all come back. You know Jerry—he'd be playing and then he'd fuck up and he'd just laugh; like, 'Good one, Garcia!' I remember one night after he was starting to play pretty well, we played 'Like a Road,' with him on acoustic guitar and me on piano, and it was so beautiful, we both had tears in our eyes. That was when I knew it was gonna be okay."

"Gradually everything sort of came back," Garcia said, "but it wasn't without a certain amount of work. I had to do everything at least once to remind my muscles about how something worked. It was the thing of making the connection between mind and muscles, because I hadn't been away from playing for so long that my muscles had forgotten. The neural pathways were there and the reason for doing it and why it worked—the intellectual part of it—was also there, but they were all separated. I had to pick them up like, here's a hunk of how music works, over here is a hunk of why I like to play it and here's a hunk of muscles that know this stuff. It was a matter of putting my hands on the guitar and actually playing through tunes and trying to solve the structure of how each tune works—addressing the whole thing."

Garcia's illness forced the Dead to cancel their entire late-summer and fall schedule of shows, a loss of several million dollars for the Dead organization. A number of people were laid off for a few months because of the sudden cash flow shortage, and some projects that had been under way, such as the long-form video, were suspended. Ultra Sound, the company that supplied equipment for the Dead's concerts, had to scramble to find new clients to avoid taking a financial bath, and of course Deadhead vendors of T-shirts and other crafts who relied on the income they earned outside Grateful Dead shows found themselves with no outlet for their wares.

Meanwhile, the band's fans got their dose of Dead wherever they could. Bill Kreutzmann and Brent Mydland put together a group with former Santana members David Margen and Alex Ligertwood called Go Ahead, and toured clubs in the East and Midwest. In early August Bob Weir broke his shoulder in a spill from a mountain bike, but even with his arm in a sling he managed to play a gig the first week of September with a re-formed version of Kingfish at a festival called Ranch Rock '86, on the Paiute Indian Reservation near Pyramid Lake in Nevada. That show, which was billed as a healing ritual for Garcia and the Deadhead community, also included Robert Hunter's first Western appearance in two years, backed by a band featuring Mickey Hart and David Freiberg. And for the occasion, Hart assembled a group, dubbed Mickey and the Daylites, with Freiberg, Barry "The Fish" Melton, John Cipollina and Kathi McDonald, the gutsy and talented singer who had replaced Janis Joplin in Big Brother and the Holding Company.

A few nights later in San Francisco, Bill Graham Presents put on an event called "Night of the Living Deadheads" at BGP's club, Wolfgang's. The event was a benefit for the Dead's recently established philanthropic arm, the Rex Foundation (named for the late Rex Jackson), and featured a pair of Dead-inspired local bands, a Deadheads crafts bazaar and an auction that included such items as books and records autographed by the Dead and even one of Garcia's humongous T-shirts (size Big Man 4X). Phil Lesh appeared in an interview videotaped that afternoon. He talked a bit about Garcia's improving health and suggested that when the Dead eventually returned to the stage, "we're going to have a more flexible format. Some of the things that occurred in the first or second set may be switched around, and we might not take a break—I don't know. But the whole structure, the whole flow of the concert, is liable to be different when we come back."

Asked by interviewer Brian Connors (a friend of Phil's) if there was anything that Deadheads could do to help the band, Lesh replied, "Well, when we get back on the road, it would be very helpful if Deadheads wouldn't bring drugs around anymore. We'd kind of like to ask everyone to look at themselves, and look at their use of hard drugs, and kind of reconsider it, because it's not a very good trip. We've all discovered that. . . . Personally, and that's all I can really talk about, I'm down on it. I'm through with it—forever!"

No member of the Grateful Dead had ever made such a public pronouncement against drugs before, and in fact there were many Deadheads who curtailed or even eliminated their use of hard drugs around this time, at least in part to show their solidarity with Garcia, who had kicked drugs before his collapse and had told friends he intended to stay clean. It's hard to say to what degree Garcia's previous use of cocaine and heroin might have influenced some of his fans to experiment with those substances, but it can definitely be said there was a connection between his quitting drugs and many others following suit. Coke and heroin (the latter never widely popular among rank-and-file Deadheads) became branded as "bad" drugs in some circles, as opposed to pot and psychedelics, which were still regarded by their adherents as useful consciousness-expanding agents historically rooted to the social context that spawned the primal Grateful Dead experience. And quite a few Deadheads stopped using drugs altogether.

By mid-September Garcia was itching to get back to playing in front of people, so he had John Kahn call rehearsals for the JGB, and two shows were scheduled for October 4 and 5 at the Stone, an 800-seat club on Broadway in North Beach that had become a sort of home base for the band in the early '80s (as the Keystone Berkeley, which had the same owners, had been in the '70s). "When he first told me he wanted to play some shows, I nearly fell out of my chair," Kahn said, "because I wasn't sure he was strong enough to do it at that point. But we had about a week of rehearsals, and he seemed to be doing pretty good, and he was real excited to be back playing with the group. We even learned a few new songs, which we hadn't done for a while."

"I hated that he played those shows at the Stone," Mountain Girl says. "Those shows never should have been played. Jerry was still in terrible shape.

It was completely crazy. What happened was we completely ran out of money at that point. There was no money at all. Jerry owed the band a whole bunch of money and he was overdrawn. But frankly, if I wasn't around to handle the money, he was always overdrawn."

As soon as the shows were announced on the one San Francisco radio station that played Grateful Dead songs from time to time—KFOG—there was a mad scramble for tickets. All 1,600 tickets—each one trumpeting THE TRIUMPHANT RETURN OF JERRY GARCIA!—were snapped up in less than an hour, so ducats for a second set of shows about two weeks later were also put on sale. Outside the Stone the afternoon before the first show, hundreds of ticketless Deadheads clogged the area looking for some miracle ticket to appear from a kind stranger with an extra. Inside the hot, low-ceilinged club that evening, the atmosphere was giddy and electric, but tinged with apprehension. Could Garcia still play well? Was he really healthy? No one in the crowd knew for sure.

At about eight-fifteen the curtain rose slowly and there was Garcia, looking considerably thinner than he had before the coma, a big smile on his face, easing into the funky groove of Allen Toussaint's "Get Out of My Life, Woman," as the packed house exploded in cheers. And as he ripped into his first solo of the evening, the apprehension in the air turned to pure elation. Garcia's playing was surprisingly strong and confident, and his singing was markedly better, no doubt in part because he had quit smoking (for the time being). The second song of the night was a new addition to the repertoire, a gospel-flavored arrangement of Dylan's "Forever Young," which Garcia delivered with a mixture of heartfelt sincerity and a dash of irony, given his own circumstances. By the time that song had run its course, there was barely a dry eye in the house, but then Garcia took the heavy moment and transformed it to joy with a rocking version of the old Motown nugget that had been something of a theme song for Garcia's solo groups dating back to the early '70s. "How sweet it is to be loved by you!" he sang with a broad smile on his face that was returned by every person in the room.

Garcia introduced two more new cover songs at these shows, both slow ballads given strong gospel treatments—Dylan's "I Shall Be Released," and "Lucky Old Sun," popularized by Frankie Laine in the '40s and Ray Charles in the early '60s. "I got it from the Ray Charles version," John Kahn said in 1996. "He had that thing where he was able to play a song really, really slow— I understand it drove some of his musicians crazy—but they would be incredibly powerful. Jerry and I loved to play ballads more than anything. If we didn't push ourselves consciously to play fast songs, I think we would've ended up doing all ballads. Every time we'd find another song we wanted to do it was like, 'Oh, no, we have to find a fast song instead!' "

Later that fall the group did introduce an uptempo (almost frenetic) tune, Los Lobos' "Evangeline," as well as two midtempo numbers from Van Morrison's classic *Moondance* album, "And It Stoned Me" and "Crazy Love." In fact, Van's soulful early-'70s groups had certainly been a model for the JGB, deftly mixing R&B and gospel grooves.

So much of the new material Garcia and Kahn brought into the band that fall had spiritual overtones that some Deadheads wondered if Garcia had experienced some sort of religious awakening following his near-death experience. Kahn said later, "He definitely went through *something*, though I don't think it was specifically Christian or anything. We talked about it a little. I think he was mainly just happy to be alive and appreciative that he could still play and that people wanted to see him. It was a good time for the group."

"I think there's a more spiritual focus to what we're doing now," Melvin Seals commented about the mood in the band after Garcia's return. "Any time you come close to death it makes you think about things differently and it does something to you inside. I can't speak for Jerry, but I think the band has gotten deeper in feeling each other and expressing it through the music. We're all more serious about what we're doing."

By mid-October the Grateful Dead had confirmed that they were planning to return to the stage in mid-December, with three shows at the Oakland Coliseum. Even so, on October 15 there was a second "Night of the Living Deadheads" event at Wolfgang's, and this time the hundreds of Deadheads on hand were treated to a videotaped interview with Garcia—his first since the coma—done by the head of the Dead's ticketing operation, Steve Marcus. Garcia revealed that he had been working on a couple of new songs and that the group would begin recording their long-awaited album in January.

"Our plan is essentially this," he said. "We're going into the Marin Vets [Marin Veterans Auditorium] again in January with no audience and use it as a studio [as they had for the video sessions]. It turns out to be an incredibly nice room to record in. There's something about the formal atmosphere in there that makes us work. When we set up at Front Street to work, a lot of times we just sort of dissolve into hanging out."

Toward the end of the interview Garcia spoke a bit about his illness and recovery, and when asked the same question that had been put to Phil during his interview a month earlier—"Is there anything you feel Deadheads can do to help out the Grateful Dead when you start touring?"—his answer was quite different from Lesh's anti-drug plea:

"Well sure, there's all kinds of things, probably, but it's not my position to tell anybody what they should do, to modify their behavior in some direction or other to benefit anybody. That's not what I'm about, y'know—I'm the antithesis of that, hopefully. Everybody does what they want, and I'll try to stay out of the way if I get in the way.

"That's in the nature of a personal decision, and I have no business talking about that shit. I'm not a cop. I'm not into tellin' people what to do, ever—*man!*" and he burst into a throaty laugh.

The Jerry Garcia Band played the Stone a few more times in November and early December and then, on December 15, the Grateful Dead made *their* triumphant return at the Oakland Coliseum. The group's entrance onto the stage was greeted by near-pandemonium—after all, every person in the arena knew how close they had come to losing Garcia and, with him, the Grateful Dead. And when the first chords of "Touch of Grey" rose reassuringly out of the darkness on the stage, the roar from the crowd shook the building. There were tears of joy streaming down the faces of many in the crowd by the time Garcia got to the end of the first chorus and practically *shouted*, "I WILL SURVIVE!" That was all the 14,000 deliriously dancing people needed to hear. The doubts and fears dissolved. Smiles and hugs all around. Garcia was back.

CHAPTER 19
Dawn Is Breaking
Everywhere

y the end of the first of the three December '86 Grateful Dead comeback shows, it was clear that Phil Lesh's speculation that the band was going to shake up the format of their concerts wasn't going to happen immediately, if at all. The old songs were in the same slots they had occupied before Garcia's coma, but no one was complaining— the format almost felt new just because the band played with so much verve and spunk. Garcia in particular seemed like a new man onstage. He smiled often, gestured and emphasized lyrics with his picking hand, swayed and bopped the most he had since the late '70s. And he seemed to go out of his way to make eye contact with the other bandmembers, who appeared to be nearly as amazed by their comrade's demeanor as the Deadheads pressed up against the front of the stage.

Certain lyrics suddenly took on new meanings in light of Garcia's fall and resurrection. In "Althea," a huge ovation went up when Garcia came to the line "There are things you can replace, and others you cannot / The time has come to weigh those things / This space is getting hot." He delivered "Candy-man" with such gusto there was no question that when he sang the lyric "Won't you tell everybody you meet that the Candyman's in town," he was singing about himself. The bridge of "Wharf Rat," which had sometimes seemed eerily ironic during Garcia's worst junkie days, now sounded hopeful and sincere:

> *But I'll get back*
> *On my feet some day*
> *The good Lord willing*
> *If He says I may*
> *I know that this life I'm living's no good*
> *I'll get a new start*
> *Live the life I should*
>
> *I'll get up up and fly away . . .*

Garcia imbued ballads like "Stella Blue" and "Ship of Fools" with rare passion, and the life-and-death mysteries at the core of "Terrapin Station" felt richer and more personal. And "Black Peter" now seemed strikingly autobiographical:

> Fever rolled up to a hundred and five
> Roll on up, gonna roll back down
> One more day I find myself alive
> Tomorrow maybe go beneath the ground

For the rest of Garcia's career, "Black Peter," so often dirgelike in the early '80s, would be one of his most powerful tunes, no doubt because it now had a special resonance for him. This was an obvious example of a phenomenon both the bandmembers and Deadheads experienced often through the years: a lyric coming into sharp focus as it became associated with a specific personal event. In the case of lyrics that seemed to address Garcia's illness and recovery, Garcia and the audience got to experience cathartic epiphanies together, which served to further strengthen the bond between him and his fans. Raised on a steady diet of heavy songs about mortality, Deadheads had faced the metaphorical End many, many times at Dead shows; but now these songs were addressing something that was an undeniable part of their collective reality.

At the first of the three Oakland shows, too, Garcia introduced a pretty but mournful new Robert Hunter ballad of existential loneliness called "Black Muddy River":

> When the last rose of summer pricks my finger
> And the hot sun chills me to the bone
> When I can't hear the song for the singer
> And I can't tell my pillow from a stone
>
> I will walk alone by the black muddy river
> And sing me a song of my own
> I will walk alone by the black muddy river
> And sing me a song of my own

Hunter explained, "The black muddy river is a dream I've had maybe three or four times over my life, and it is one of the most chilling experiences that I've had. It's enough to turn you religious. I've burrowed under this incredible mansion, gone down into the cellars, and I find myself down at this black, lusterless, slow-flowing stygian river. There are marble columns around, and cobwebs. It's vast and it's hopeless. It's death. It's death with the absence of the soul. It's my horror vision, and when I come out of that dream I do anything I can to counter it."

Yet, typical of Hunter's writing, the composition is not all dark. By the last verse the singer not only takes solace in being able to "sing me a song of my own," but also to "dream me a dream of my own."

" 'Black Muddy River' is about the perspective of age and making a decision about the necessity of living in spite of a rough time and the ravages of anything else that's going to come at you," Hunter said. "When I wrote it, I was writing about how I felt about being forty-five years old and what I've been through. And then, when I was done with it, obviously it was for the Dead."

The other new song Garcia unveiled at the comeback shows was much lighter. Musically, "When Push Comes to Shove" was in the same loping tradition of "Ramble On Rose" and "Tennessee Jed"; musically, it was not one of Garcia's more original pieces. But lyrically, it was a hoot, a song about being afraid of everything, including and especially love. Evidently something about the song didn't ring true for Garcia after a while, because he never sang it after the summer of 1989. Two and a half years was a very short lifetime for a Garcia song.

Almost immediately after the Dead's year-end concerts at Kaiser Convention Center Garcia plunged into two projects that had been in limbo for a while—the long-form video, *So Far*, and, finally, the Dead's new studio album, *In the Dark*.

Actually, it was some of the early work on the video that suggested the approach for recording the new album: they returned to the stage of the Marin Veterans Auditorium and cut the basic tracks for the LP there live (i.e., all playing together at once), with no audience, as they had for the video shoot. Then, vocal and instrumental fixes and overdubs would be recorded at Club Front.

For the first time since *Blues for Allah* in 1975, the album's production was handled in-house—Garcia and engineer John Cutler co-produced, with plenty of input from the other bandmembers. Though Garcia said at the time that he normally didn't like being forced into "the cop role" on Grateful Dead projects, his leadership and well-known attention to sonic detail was needed to bring the album to fruition. As he noted, if others were willing to defer to him, he was not afraid to make decisions.

"It's one of the things I'm good at," he said without a hint of boastfulness, "because first of all, I have some sense of what the Grateful Dead's point of view is. The next part is that I won't let things go past unless I'm sure everyone in the band sees them or hears them. So I know enough about what the potential for political nightmares are. You want everybody to like it, and you want everybody partcipating in it fully, and that means everyone has to believe in the project.

"But you have to be able to say, 'This is it. This is the way it's going to be.' I'm flexible about what it's *going* to be, but once all the news is in—in other words, once everyone's put in an opinion—I take it into account and make changes and then I can say, 'Okay, this is it.' Nobody minds talking to me about it, and I don't mind hearing about it from anybody, so that's part of why it's fallen into my hands."

Over the course of three weeks in January, the band cut basic tracks on ten of their unrecorded songs: Hunter and Garcia's "Touch of Grey," "West L.A. Fadeaway," "When Push Comes to Shove" and "Black Muddy River"; Weir and Barlow's "Hell in a Bucket," "Throwing Stones" and "My Brother Esau" (which only made it onto the cassette versions of the LP); and Brent's rollicking train anthem, "Tons of Steel."

Meanwhile, Garcia and Len Dell'Amico had resumed work on *So Far*. By the time Garcia fell ill in the summer of '86, the duo and John Cutler had put together a seamless fifty-five-minute soundtrack that moved gracefully from "Uncle John's Band" into "Playing in the Band" into "Lady with a Fan" (from the "Terrapin" suite), followed by a segment of "drums" and "space," and closing with Weir's anti-political rant "Throwing Stones" into "Not Fade Away." The audio track consisted of material recorded at Marin Vets in 1985 with some live material from the Dead's 1985 New Year's Eve telecast. With that musical foundation in place, Garcia and Dell'Amico then began to explore various visual approaches to the soundtrack.

"We did a lot of brainstorming, just thinking, 'What kind of images do Grateful Dead songs conjure?'" Garcia said. "Well—nature, powerful forces of various sorts, volcanoes erupting, tornados, lightning, strong winds, the ocean and other archetypal things like fire and that sort of stuff. Then we got into [collecting footage of] human endeavors—everything that people do. And then we went off in a completely abstract space—okay, the music may not directly suggest these things, but these things are suggested by things that are suggested. So then we got into things like architecture, stained-glass windows, tanks, that sort of stuff. It was really a sort of free-associative thing that took place over several months, just collecting lists and lists [of images].

"Most Grateful Dead music lacks a literal quality," he continued. "Most of the lyrics don't go anywhere, exactly. Some of them have really powerful images in them, but rarely do they have specific stuff. I sort of wanted to steer away from being too literal. That got to be a byword in the studio—'Too literal! Too literal!'"

Ultimately, Garcia and Dell'Amico decided to give each song a different look. "Uncle John's Band" was mainly just the group performing at the Marin Vets, with a patchwork quilt of photos of frontier America and the Old West gliding across the screen toward the end of the tune. "Playing in the Band" was dominated by film images of dancers from the '20s, '30s and '40s, edited in time to the music and often altered by high-tech video manipulation—legs multiplied and distorted and split into intricate patterns, taking on new, unrecognizable forms—"kind of like a tantric carpet, pulsing and moving," Garcia said. "Lady with a Fan" received perhaps the most ambitious visual treatment, with elaborate (for that era) 3-D computer-generated images of tarot cards drifting through a surreal landscape dominated by a chessboard.

"If you're going to do something, it's important—for me, at any rate—to shoot high, even if you miss, or even if you're accused of being pretentious," Garcia noted. "We were after the idea of electronic mind-altering and consciousness-altering, and I think on that level it's pretty successful."

Work on the video continued up until the Grateful Dead went out on their first post-coma Eastern tour the last week of March 1987. Not surprisingly, Garcia's return was greeted as a veritable Second Coming by his fans. The ovations he and the band received every night of the tour were long and deafening, as if each Deadhead had to show his or her appreciation for the miracle of Garcia's (and the band's) survival. The Dead responded by playing a tour filled with high-energy shows that were perhaps a bit short on jamming—the big songs generally weren't as fully developed, and transitions between tunes in the second set were sometimes a bit awkward and forced—but long on joie de vivre, which was right in keeping with the celebratory mood of the crowds.

One thing the Dead hadn't counted on when they booked the tour was the thousands of people who showed up outside every venue they played, some hoping to score tickets for the sold-out concerts, but most quite content to hang out in the huge shopper's bazaar that materialized in the parking lots and surrounding streets in every city on the tour. As late as 1983–84 there had still been only a few merchants who went on tour with the Dead to peddle T-shirts, stickers, incense, handmade jewelry and food items such as premade veggie burritos and chocolate chip cookies. In that era, most of the vendors had been Deadheads who wanted to earn enough money to go on tour and see as many shows as they could. Their success, coupled with the laissez-faire environment in the parking lots, encouraged others to try their hand at selling outside Dead shows, and as the number of vendors increased, so did the number of people hanging out around the bazaar. Then, because the scene was so big and colorful, it attracted the attention of newspapers and television crews in nearly every city the Dead traveled to, and these "news" reports inspired hundreds and sometimes thousands of people, many with no particular interest in the Grateful Dead, to come down and check out what was, at least on the surface, a joyfully anarchic party. It was relatively easy to score drugs there, and you could usually find a few different kinds of bottled beer for a buck.

Even in the Bay Area, where Dead fans were considerably more blasé about their heroes simply because the band played there so often, there were signs at the mid-December '86 comeback shows, at the New Year's series and at the Mardi Gras concerts at Kaiser in early March that things were starting to get a little crazy outside the shows. But that was nothing compared with what greeted the Dead on the East Coast. Now there were hundreds of vendors outside every show, and the majority of them were people who had no intention of going inside the arenas to see the band. Whereas in the early '80s it had been common for solitary vendors to sell their wares out of their backpacks, by 1987 people were setting up large display tables, jewelry cases and even giant metal-framed booths to sell everything from tie-dyes to imported

Guatemalan clothing to every variety of drug paraphernalia. Instead of offering a couple of dozen shirts, the larger operations brought in hundreds of pieces of clothing to sell, racks to hang them on, full-length mirrors and even Visa and MasterCard processing equipment. Still, for every one of those big operators, there were probably ten subsistence-level vendors who simply liked living on the road in the Grateful Dead environment.

Almost everywhere the Grateful Dead carnival parked itself there were problems between the crowds attracted to the bazaar and people who lived near the venues, who suddenly found strange people tramping through (or even camping on) their property, using their yards and the streets as bathrooms and having loud parties into the wee hours of the morning. This, naturally, brought more police into the areas where the Dead played, and led police chiefs, mayors and angry city officials to complain to the Dead, who, it should be said, were just trying to do what they had always done: go out on the road and play music to earn a living. The band took the heat, and in what should have been their most glorious moment—sold-out houses! positive vibes rippling through the scene in the wake of Garcia's recovery!—they found themselves facing the possibility that they would be permanently banned from many cities because of the behavior a small group of people outside their concerts. In fact, some municipalities did tell the Dead to take their circus elsewhere.

And this was all before the release of what everyone fully expected would be a very successful new album. What would happen if the album was a bona fide hit, bringing in thousands of new fans? "I don't know," Garcia told me in an interview that spring. "If this translates to unheard-of record sales or something—some enormous number of records—then we'll have a serious problem. We'll have the problem of where are we going to play? We already have that problem to some extent. John Scher says he has to 'de-promote' us. We don't spend any money on advertising anymore. So where do we have to go? At this point, the Deadheads and the Grateful Dead have to get serious. We have to invent where we can go from here, because there is no place. . . . It's an interesting problem to have—the problem of being too successful. It's one of those things that completely blows my mind."

On a personal level the spring '87 tour was a supremely uplifting one for Garcia. Even though he had been the focus of intense devotion by thousands of people through the years, the spring tour was really almost like a celebration of *him*, a chance for Deadheads to express their love and appreciation. And though touring again was physically quite taxing for Garcia, his mood was very upbeat and he felt energized by the crowd's response.

Garcia was the subject of numerous magazine and newspaper profiles during this period, most of them overwhelmingly positive accounts of how he had returned from the brink, left drugs behind and been given a new lease on life. However, if the mainstream media thought that Garcia was suddenly going to become yet another recovery poster boy for Nancy Reagan's "Just Say

No" campaign, they were mistaken. Not only did he never renounce drugs, he continued to openly sing the praises of psychedelics and pot, and he advocated the legalization of all drugs in order to eliminate the criminal component of consciousness-altering.

The other angle the media just couldn't resist was Garcia's ascension to ice cream immortality. In late 1986 the Ben & Jerry's ice cream company of Vermont started producing Cherry Garcia (vanilla ice cream with chocolate-covered chunks of cherry), and it became one of the rising company's best-selling products. Unfortunately, the ice cream was named and launched without Garcia's permission. But after a minimum of legal wrangling, Ben & Jerry's agreed to pay royalties to Garcia. For a while, complimentary shipments of the confection filled the freezer in the fridge at the Dead office, until saner health practices prevailed.

Garcia handled his new megacelebrity with characteristic grace and self-deprecating humor, knowing full well that this moment in the sun would pass and that in a year or two Deadheads would probably be the only ones who cared about him again. Asked in 1987 how he dealt with his near-deification among some extremely fanatical Deadheads, who saw his survival as a mystical Sign from Above, Garcia said with a laugh, "I ignore 'em. I know better, you know? I mean, no matter who you are, you know yourself for the asshole that you are. You know yourself for the person who makes mistakes and is capable of being *really stupid.* And doing stupid things. On this earth, nobody is perfect, as far as I know. And I'm right there with everybody else. I don't know who you'd have to be to believe that kind of stuff about yourself; to believe that you're somehow special. But it wouldn't work in my house, that's all I can say. My kids would never let me get away with it. So far it hasn't been a problem. If I start believing that kind of stuff, everybody's going to just turn around and walk away from me—'Come on, Garcia!' And my friends—nobody would let me get away with it; not for a minute. That's the strength of having a group." (Asked in another interview about whether he minded being the religious focus of a segment of Deadheads who dance at Dead shows like the whirling dervishes of the Near East, Garcia quipped, "I'll put up with it until they come to me with the cross and nails.")

Sometime after his coma, Garcia joked to a member of the Dead road crew that if he wasn't going to get into trouble with drugs, he would probably get into trouble with women, in part because heroin kept his strong libido somewhat in check. It was on the spring East Coast tour, in Hartford, that Garcia hooked up romantically with a twenty-seven-year-old Deadhead from New Jersey named Manasha Matheson, with whom he had had a casual friendship for several years.

Manasha first saw the Dead at Watkins Glen in 1973, when she was just fourteen. "I went with some friends and then we separated at the show and then it was me and my clothes and nothing else," she recalls. "But I met these wonderful people from Massachusetts and they sort of took me in, which was my first exposure to that level of kindness that you hear about with Dead-heads. That was overwhelming for me. I wasn't really a fan of the Grateful Dead at that time, and I didn't really connect with the music at that show. But I do remember hearing Jerry's guitar at one point during the night and it sounded to me like it was alive, like it was a living thing. And I had this kind of primal feeling about it. It was a beautiful sound."

Five years later, when the Dead came to the Uptown Theater in Chicago in November 1978, Manasha presented a carved pumpkin (with a map showing Terrapin Ridge, Illinois, stuffed inside it) to Garcia as he arrived onstage, and after she retrieved the pumpkin following the show, someone from backstage invited her and her roommate to have lunch with Garcia the following day. So the two of them met Jerry at the White Hall Hotel in Chicago, had a pleasant chat for a couple of hours, and that night, after her roommate had departed, Manasha went to the Uptown show with Jerry.

They kept in touch a bit through the years, mainly by phone and occasional backstage visits. Jerry sometimes provided tickets for her, and they were able to communicate silently whenever she was close enough to the stage that he could see her. As she told Robert Greenfield, at one concert in San Francisco in the mid-'80s she even cut off her long hair during the show, much to Garcia's amusement. "I'd had a class back at college in living art—Fluxus, Yoko Ono, John Cage. I did it in the spirit of that kind of avant-garde weirdness."

With her hair shorn, she took to wearing shawls everywhere (she still does) and became a ubiquitous figure at West Coast Dead shows after Garcia's illness. She was still living with her parents in New Jersey and was studying art, but she spent long periods in Northern California, where she had many friends. The first time she saw Jerry after his coma was when she accompanied her onetime paramour Hamza el-Din to a Petaluma Schools benefit concert featuring Olatunji, Garcia and Carlos Santana in February 1987. "I said, 'Jerry, do you remember me?' And he said, 'Manasha, you're unforgettable,' which was so dear, and then he took my hand delicately and held it for a minute, and it was real special," she says.

It was just a month later that Jerry and Manasha got together in Hartford. She then accompanied him for most of the rest of the tour. According to Manasha, Garcia told her that his relationship with Mountain Girl was platonic; otherwise, she said, she would not have gotten involved with him.

After the Dead finished their spring 1987 tour with three concerts at Irvine Meadows Amphitheater in Orange County, California (where there was a near-riot outside the venue and a successful gate-crashing by a sizable mob during the Saturday night concert), Garcia returned to work on the album and video. He and Len Dell'Amico spent the last two weeks of April in Los Angeles overseeing the postproduction on *So Far*. While Jerry was in L.A., he flew Manasha into town and put her up at the Park Sheraton hotel, where he was staying. A few weeks later Manasha revealed that she had become pregnant—news that did not sit well with M.G.—but Manasha says she did not want Jerry to leave Annabelle and Trixie, so she elected to keep living alone in San Anselmo, seeing Jerry whenever it was convenient for him. According to Manasha, Jerry had initially suggested that she move in with him, M.G. and the girls—a bizarre notion to say the least. Beginning that summer, however, Manasha openly accompanied him on tour.

In mid-May Bob Dylan flew to Northern California to begin rehearsals with the Grateful Dead for a series of stadium concerts that summer in which the Dead would serve as Dylan's backup band—as Tom Petty and the Heartbreakers had in 1986—as well as playing their own sets. Planning for the tour, which Garcia said was a long-held dream of his, had begun around the time of the Dead's comeback shows in December 1986. Dylan secretly slipped into the Bay Area in March to finalize tour plans and attend the Dead's Mardi Gras concert at Kaiser Convention Center, where he was photographed with them backstage by Herb Greene. Dylan was spotted in the audience that night swaying to a version of his own song, "Quinn the Eskimo," which Garcia chose to open the show.

Bootleg tapes of the May '87 Dylan-Dead rehearsals have been in circulation for many years, but at the time there was a thick veil of secrecy about what was going on at Club Front. Dylan's paranoia about publicity was legendary: in March he had even threatened to cancel the summer tour after a San Francisco deejay announced some details of it. And though keeping secrets in the Grateful Dead world was always next to impossible (discreetly dispensing privileged information showed how close people were to the band, which translated to assumed power), not much information leaked out about the rehearsals other than the fact that the musicians had played a huge number of different songs, including many unusual cover tunes.

"Dylan was in ecstasy at the abuse he got from the crew," says Len Dell'Amico. "He'd come in and they'd say, 'Oh, hi, Bob,' and then turn away. And he loved that. He just blossomed because they treated him like they treated anyone else. They called him Spike because the Dead already had a Bob. But he got the crew treatment, like 'Who the fuck are you?' And he loved it. Because who's a bigger star than Bob Dylan? And he probably hated it more than anybody. And he just fit in so well with that sense of 'We're all just guys hanging around here.' "

The material Dylan and the Dead rehearsed covered an astonishing range, from old folk songs like "Stealin' " and "The Ballad of John Harding" to contemporary songs like Paul Simon's "The Boy in the Bubble" and Dylan songs from every era, many of which Dylan had either never performed live or hadn't played for years. "We'd just try 'em out," Garcia said. "[Dylan] said, 'What do you want me to do?' and we said, 'Well, we have a *small* list here of our favorite Dylan tunes.' And he said yes to just about all of them, so we just started working on them one by one."

Garcia noted shortly after the rehearsals that playing with Dylan was quite a challenge: "You really have to pay attention to him to avoid making mistakes, insofar as he's doing what he's doing and everybody else is trying to play the song. If you don't do what he's doing, you're doing something wrong," he laughed. "In that sense, he de facto becomes the leader of the band. . . . I don't know whether two weeks with us [on the tour] is going to be able to change twenty years of that kind of conditioning."

It would be a month and a half before the Dead and Dylan would get together again.

The Dead began the summer of 1987 with impressive concert stands in Ventura and at the Greek Theater in Berkeley, then traveled east to Alpine Valley Music Theater in East Troy, Wisconsin, which had become perhaps the most popular venue for the Dead in the Midwest. At each of the three concerts at Alpine Valley, more than 30,000 people packed the facility, and thousands more jammed the campgrounds outside the gates and clogged nearby roads, a pattern that repeated itself at nearly every stop on the Dead's summer tour.

Around the time the tour hit Alpine Valley, Arista Records released "Touch of Grey" to radio stations, in advance of *In the Dark*, which was to come out on July 6. "Touch of Grey" was an instant smash on rock radio all across the country, generating countless news stories about Garcia's comeback and the Dead's miraculous saga of survival and transformation into the country's most popular touring band.

Then MTV got into the act. In early May, Gary Gutierrez had shot a video for "Touch of Grey" in which life-sized puppet skeletons of the band "sang" and "played" the song in front of thousands of cheering Deadheads; then, near the tune's conclusion, the skeletons were magically transformed into the real Grateful Dead. (The video was shot at night after a Dead concert at the Laguna Seca Recreation Area near Monterey, California, using Deadheads who were camping there overnight, and anyone else who was interested, as the crowd.) MTV's execs loved the video, which was so different from the network's usual fare—in those days, most seemed to feature scantily clad women being subjugated by male rock stars, lots of fog effects and things breaking in slow motion—and the video was put in heavy rotation. Toward the end of the Dead's summer tour, MTV put together a daylong marathon called "Day of the Dead," adding to the hype that had been building since the spring tour. It was the biggest national television exposure the Dead had gotten in many years, and some believe that it mainly served to make the already overpopulated scene outside the shows even more unmanageable.

Aside from the problems of too many folks showing up without tickets to party in the parking lots, the atmosphere inside the shows changed, too. Many young people in the huge influx of 1987–88 did not understand the subtle dynamics of the Grateful Dead concert experience and hadn't gone through the natural socialization and education process that fans who saw the band repeatedly had experienced. Some of these neophytes—disparagingly labeled "Touchheads" and "In the Darkers" by veterans—came to Dead shows just to get drunk or high and to hear "Touch of Grey," which, the Dead being the Dead, the band did not play at every show (though they did at all six of their football stadium concerts on that tour). There were thousands of new fans who did not want to hear the gentle, folkish strains of "Peggy-O," who couldn't lose themselves in the sweet, sad beauty of "Stella Blue" and who were put to sleep by "drums" and "space." To be fair, there were also thousands of other newcomers who definitely "got" what was special about the Dead's music, immediately felt part of the scene and became true-blue Deadheads from that point on. So the success cut both ways.

But it wasn't just young rockers who turned out in force for the Dead's stadium shows that summer. Dylan concerts traditionally drew an older audience, and the combination of Dylan and the Dead on the same bill seemed to attract many people who might not go see either group alone, plus fans who had long since stopped going to rock shows regularly but were intrigued by the pairing or seduced by the hype. No doubt some showed up expecting to see a re-creation of a '60s concert, with the Dead and Dylan faithfully parading through their "hits." What they got was something considerably different.

Depending on the depth of their knowledge of the Grateful Dead, these fans probably heard enough songs they recognized to keep them happy. There were always several familiar early-'70s touchstones like "Truckin'," "Playing in the Band" and "Uncle John's Band" sprinkled in the Dead's sets. The Dead also made an effort to play more uptempo material than usual—ballads and slow shuffles were few and far between—and because they were also playing a full ninety-minute set with Dylan, their own sets tended to be more concise and accessible, for better or worse. At the first two Dead-Dylan shows, the Dead broke with tradition and played only one long set alone, much to the consternation of many Deadheads. By the time the tour reached Giants Stadium, however, the Dead were back to playing two sets by themselves—the New York crowd probably wouldn't have let them get away with doing only one!

The sets with the Dead backing Dylan varied tremendously in quality from song to song. The long stretch of time between the rehearsals in California and the first show had at least one negative consequence: "We rehearsed up to eighty songs, and we couldn't even remember the songs we'd rehearsed," Weir said with a laugh shortly after the tour. Garcia added, "When we went on the road we didn't have the slightest idea of what we were going to do!" In the end, the Dead and Dylan eschewed all the interesting and odd cover tunes they'd worked up in practice and instead played only Dylan songs, albeit an impressively large selection of popular and obscure ones. Besides tackling acknowledged classics like "It's All Over Now, Baby Blue," "Maggie's Farm," "Stuck Inside of Mobile with the Memphis Blues Again," "Highway 61 Revisited," "Ballad of a Thin Man," "All Along the Watchtower" and

"Knockin' on Heaven's Door," the group also played lesser-known numbers like "John Brown," "Man of Peace," "Frankie Lee and Judas Priest," "Dead Man, Dead Man," "Joey" and "The Wicked Messenger," to name just a few.

From their first moments onstage with Dylan at Schaefer Stadium in Foxboro, Massachusetts, on July Fourth, the Dead had their work cut out for them trying to keep up with Dylan's unusual phrasing and oddly atonal mumbling. Though the Dead had to work hard to keep the music together, they appeared to have a great time backing Dylan. The Dylan portion of the show always saw a slow but steady trickle toward the exits by people who were either burned out from the Dead's sets or didn't like Dylan, but those who stuck around were generally very attentive and willing to follow the musicians down every road they chose. And though Dylan was the ostensible "star" of this segment of the concert, Garcia's solos consistently drew the loudest cheers, and the biggest ovation usually came at the point in the show when Garcia sat down behind a pedal steel guitar (which he hadn't played in public since the early '70s) to pick a tune like "I'll Be Your Baby Tonight" or "Tomorrow Is a Long Time." Most Deadheads had never seen Garcia play steel onstage before.

For his part, Dylan almost never acknowledged the Dead's existence onstage with him and seemed to be off in his own world, which only occasionally intersected with the Dead's. Still, when the partnership really clicked—such as on the Dead's striking arrangements of "All Along the Watchtower," "Slow Train Coming," "Stuck Inside of Mobile" and a few others—the results were spellbinding and showed how truly magical the collaboration could have been if they'd rehearsed more, played more shows or if Dylan had made a greater effort to listen to what the Dead were playing behind him moment to moment. Even so, most fans went away satisfied. It helped that at five of the six Dylan-Dead shows the encore found Dylan joining the Dead for exuberant renditions of "Touch of Grey," which was followed at four of the concerts by either "Watchtower" or "Knockin' on Heaven's Door."

Meanwhile, in the culture at large the Dead were suddenly big news. There were innumerable articles in the press about the neo-hippie movement the Dead supposedly presided over, and much to the Dead's own surprise, most of what was being written about them was favorable. "We're sort of like the town whore who's finally become an institution," Garcia joked. "We're finally becoming respectable. I also notice there's turnover in the press. There's a whole bunch of different journalists than there were even ten years ago. There are probably a lot more of them who've grown up with the Grateful Dead as part of their—if not foreground cultural material, at least certainly something they've all heard of."

In another interview he noted, "Back in the '70s, we had the same phenomenon of all these young kids [coming to shows]. But now those are the people who are in medical school and law school; they are college people and professionals. They still come to the shows. So now there are Deadheads everywhere. They've kind of infiltrated all of American society—everybody knows one: 'I've got a cousin who loves you guys!' "

Predictably, there was also some '60s-bashing in the press, with some writers criticizing the Dead for being merchants of nostalgia, and dismissing the group's young fans as would-be hippies caught in a time warp. But Robert Hunter wondered, "Can you have nostalgia for a time you didn't live in? I think some of our music is appealing to some sort of idealism in people, and hopefully it's universal enough to make those songs continue to exist over the years."

On the same subject, John Barlow said, "I find it sort of curious that there's a pejorative attachment to the fact that there are people who refuse to let go of a certain time and place—especially when the values that that time and place represented were the best we've seen in our lifetime. These are soulless times now, and I don't see anything wrong with people who want to fix themselves on times that were a lot more enriching."

No doubt about it, the summer of 1987 was the Dead's Big Moment in America. When they had been popular in the early '70s they were still largely an underground phenomenon, supported by an unusually large counterculture. In 1987 the Dead brushed up against the mainstream in a way they never had before. They were practically inescapable that summer, between the radio and TV popularity of "Touch of Grey" and the tremendous media coverage of the Dead-Dylan tour. "Touch of Grey" became the Dead's best-selling single ever, eventually making it up to number 9 on the *Billboard* singles chart. It even hit number 15 on the Adult Contemporary chart. *In the Dark* made it as high as number 6 on the Top 200 album chart and became the first Grateful Dead album to sell more than a million copies in the year it was released. The *So Far* video, too, was hugely popular, staying on top of music video sales charts for fifteen weeks (and later winning the American Film Institute's Best Music Video award). The Dead also made the cover of *Rolling Stone* for the first time since the early '70s. Mikal Gilmore's story was the first to talk candidly about Garcia's drug problems through the years.

"Nineteen eighty-seven was like one straight peak experience," says Len Dell'Amico. "I worked every day, morning till night, in 1987, trying to help further this thing that was happening with the hit album, the tour with Dylan, the long-form video, the short videos. Obviously this was their moment to go mass. And nobody ever said, 'Well, now we'll have to do stadiums.' Nobody was really thinking of the consequences of that kind of mass success. Because nobody was planning it. It was just what had to happen. Nobody was foreseeing it or planning it, but you couldn't resist it, either. Everybody was in the same boat, just working, working, working all the time, but loving it; it was a real high. And it emanated from Jerry's rise from the ashes."

Though Deadheads were thrilled that the band had finally achieved an unprecedented level of success, many were also understandably concerned about what long-term effects mass success might have on the already over-populated Dead scene. As Robert Hunter observed, "Over the years, it seemed a blessing that we were able to work and be dynamic and stay down there out of public view. That sort of attention eats people, and it eats groups; anybody who reads *Rolling Stone* knows what happens. . . . Are we going to be eaten now? Who else ever had an underground swell as large as ours and had it meet with another wave of aboveground approval? Look out: This is critical mass.

"I'm excited about it, and I have misgivings. I would like the world to know about the Grateful Dead; it's a phenomenal band. But I don't think the Grateful Dead is going to be as free a thing as it was. That's the devil we pay."

While Garcia also acknowledged that mass success "presents itself as just a new level of problems," he admitted that the group's new popularity was "a happy surprise," and added, "it's gratifying to have an audience." In several interviews he also indicated that he was pleased that the Grateful Dead provided an alternative reality for large numbers of people disenchanted with the passionless, "lame America" of the Reagan years.

"We represent some part of the modern adventure in America—like Neal Cassady and Jack Kerouac—and just hit the road," he told the British rock magazine *Q*. "You need an excuse to be out there, and I guess the Grateful Dead is a pretty good excuse. It also provides a lot of support; there are always a lot of Deadheads traveling around, and they represent a kind of moving community. They've become more sophisticated through the years, with the older Deadheads hanging in there and younger Deadheads coming in and discovering all this stuff. I guess in the '30s, when people used to ride the rails, you'd have to learn from the old hobos how to do it, and the Deadhead traveling thing is sort of along those same lines. It's one of the last American adventures you can have—to follow the Grateful Dead on the road somewhere."

In between Dead tours, Garcia stayed extremely active. He, Weir and Brent sang backup vocals on a Robert Hunter–Bob Dylan song called "Silvio," which came out on Dylan's *Down in the Groove* CD in 1988. (A second Hunter lyric, "The Ugliest Girl in the World," was also set to music by Dylan and appeared on that record.) And Garcia contributed heavily to a Robert Hunter solo effort called *Liberty* (recorded in 1987 but released in the spring of '88), laying down bright, tuneful solos on nearly every song—it was the most Garcia had ever played on one of his partner's albums. The experience obviously had some lasting impact on Garcia, too: a few years later he re-arranged the playful title number and performed it with the Dead.

Sometime late in the summer of 1987, Jerry, Mountain Girl and the girls finally moved out of the house on Hepburn Heights and into more spacious digs on Reservoir Road in San Rafael. "It was apparently a famous house in San Rafael for parties," M.G. says. "Some big-shot developer had owned it and had major, ritzy parties in there. It was pretty big—about four thousand square feet—and it had a great pool that Jerry loved. But it was definitely kind of funky, too, so the kids couldn't ruin it. It was a wonderful house; we had a good time there. Jerry was even doing his runs on the treadmill; he was really trying to stay in shape, though it was very brief—you would have had to have been there," she chuckles. "We had an exercise bicycle, but it was very difficult to get him to commit to anything like that, so basically I boiled it down to trying to give him good food, vitamins every day, fresh juice, lots of salads."

M.G. says that for much of his adult life Garcia was afflicted by severe sleep apnea, a condition that would cause him to stop breathing for short periods while he slept. Being asthmatic as a child probably led to his later apnea, which was also exacerbated by his lifestyle. "He definitely had obstructed airways," M.G. says. "He would get into these patterns of deafening snoring that made him kind of hard to live with sometimes. As he got older it got worse. And it definitely got worse if he was smoking a lot. And it was also worse if he was really tired or fucked up. He'd be snoring away and all of a sudden he'd just stop. And a minute would go by. And then he'd almost sit up and take a huge gasp; it would be a struggle to get it in, and then he'd go back to his regular breathing pattern for several minutes and then he'd do it again.

"He used to have terrible nightmares, too, which I gather is common with sleep apnea. Your brain is trying to tell you to wake up and take a breath, so it startles you awake."

Sandy Rothman, who lived on Reservoir Road with the Garcias for a couple of months in the second half of 1987 ("basically because I was homeless living out of my car, and so Jerry said, 'Why don't you stay here?' "), clearly recalls Garcia's fitful nights, too: "I'm a night owl and he isn't, and he'd usually go to sleep long before me. My bedroom was right across the hall from theirs, and I could hear him waking up ten to fifteen times during the time I was in there reading before I fell asleep. So then sometimes his light would go on, and maybe he'd read for a bit, have a cigarette and then fall asleep again, and this could go on for hours. I felt bad for him because he wasn't getting much sleep at night."

Fortunately, Garcia never had much trouble napping on planes or backstage at gigs or just sitting in front of the TV, so he caught up on his sleep a little that way. The downside of that was that sometimes people suspected he was nodding off because of drugs rather than innocently napping.

Rothman says that when Garcia was off the road and at home, the two of them spent time listening to Jerry's huge record collection, which took up an entire wall of the house. "We'd listen to old gospel vocal groups a lot; really, all sorts of stuff. He had very broad taste." They also sat around picking acoustic instruments from time to time, which no doubt influenced Garcia's return to playing string band music that summer and fall.

Actually, Garcia first seriously expressed interest in playing acoustic music again shortly after he arrived home from the hospital in the summer of

1986, following his illness. Rothman and David Nelson, instruments in tow, visited Garcia at Hepburn Heights and the threesome ended up picking and singing one old folk and bluegrass tune after another deep into the night, Garcia plucking a banjo and singing trios with the others. Then, on Thanksgiving night in 1986, Garcia, Nelson and Rothman played informally at the annual turkey bash of the extended Dead family. That year it was held at the American Legion's Log Cabin, a wonderfully cozy, old-style redwood lodge in San Anselmo. The trio mostly played old-time country favorites, much to the delight of the gathered family. "One of our traditions," Rothman recalls, "was trying to remember all the verses to 'Little Glass of Wine,' a Stanley Brothers number. That night was no exception—David and I were impressed by how many of them Jerry could remember."

The following spring, the threesome, along with John Kahn on acoustic bass, played a few songs at a benefit concert at the Fillmore Auditorium to raise money for a coalition of '60s San Francisco poster artists who were fighting against Bill Graham and Chet Helms to gain some control of the copyrights of their posters. Garcia had always felt a kinship with the artists—particularly Rick Griffin, Kelley and Mouse, and Victor Moscoso—whom he viewed as fellow travelers on the psychedelic highway. The group's six-song miniset was very well received by the Deadheads who packed the Fillmore to see Garcia's first appearance there since the '60s, but the most enthusiastic person at the club that night just might have been Bill Graham, who came backstage after the group's set and raved about how great he thought it was. David Nelson recalled Graham saying, " 'This is such a great thing. I've got to take this somewhere. I've got to put this on somewhere. But I don't know where. I need an idea.' Jerry went, 'Uh, take it to Broadway, Bill.' And we all went, 'Yeah, right.' It was just a joke. And Bill went, 'Broadway!' He left the room and the next thing I knew we were booked to do eighteen shows at the Lunt-Fontanne theater."

Actually, the historic Broadway run took place seven months after the Fillmore gig, and during the interim the acoustic group performed only once, at a sunbaked hippie-fest on the banks of the Eel River near French's Camp, in rural Humboldt County, three hours north of San Francisco. This concert was a benefit, too—for the Hog Farm collective, which maintained a large piece of land in nearby Laytonville—and it began a tradition of Labor Day weekend Hog Farm benefits that continues to the present day. The Jerry Garcia Band was also on the bill, so the string band, sometimes a quintet with the addition of JGB drummer David Kemper, opened the show with a nine-song set; then the JGB came out and played two sets of electric music. This would provide the model for Garcia's Broadway shows, which were billed as "Jerry Garcia, Acoustic and Electric." (On Broadway the JGB played only one set per show.)

It's putting it mildly to say that Broadway and the Lunt-Fontanne had never seen anything quite like the scene that surrounded Garcia's eighteen-concert run, which stretched from October 15 through Halloween night 1987 and included five days where the groups played both a matinee and an evening show. The Lunt-Fontanne is one of the city's most historic legitimate theaters—in seventy-seven years it had hosted everything from the *Ziegfeld Follies of 1921* to *The Sound of Music* and Richard Burton in *Hamlet*. For Garcia on Broadway, Bill Graham's troops hung Grateful Dead flags on the outside of the theater and decorated the lobby. Tickets, at thirty dollars apiece (expensive by Dead standards, but cheap for Broadway), sold out in just a few hours, breaking the theater's single-day box office record. This, naturally, guaranteed that swarms of Deadheads looking for tickets would congregate outside the theater every night—quite a sight for straight theatergoers on their way to nearby productions such as *Cats, 42nd Street* and *Les Misérables*. The series had its own *Playbill* program, featuring a photograph (by Herb Greene) of a smiling Garcia dressed in a magician's cape and conjuring his electric guitar out a black top hat, cartoon lightning bolts zapping out of his outstretched fingers. Generally speaking, Deadheads were very respectful of the lovely theater, though a few people smoked pot discreetly in their seats, and there was lots of sitting around on the floor of the lobby before the show and between sets—a time-honored Deadhead tradition.

The acoustic band, which was augmented by the fine New York bluegrass fiddler Kenny Kosek, a friend of Sandy Rothman's, opened the evening with an easygoing forty-five- to fifty-minute set of old-timey, folk and bluegrass tunes. Garcia played lead guitar; Nelson, rhythm guitar; Rothman, dobro, mandolin and banjo; Kosek, the only Broadway veteran in the bunch, having played in the house band for the hit musical *Big River*, played fiddle; John Kahn played his big string bass; and David Kemper sometimes came onstage to keep time on a snare drum. Garcia sang lead on all but a couple that were handled by David Nelson, and the three-part harmonies by Garcia, Nelson and Rothman were consistently soulful and often more on-pitch than Grateful Dead harmonies. The acoustic repertoire consisted of thirty songs (ten of which were performed each night), covering a tremendous variety of folk styles, from ageless mountain tunes to bluegrass to blues. Among the American greats the band drew from were the Blue Sky Boys ("I'm Troubled," "Short Life of Trouble"), the Stanley Brothers ("If I Lose"), Flatt and Scruggs ("Gone Home"), Mississippi John Hurt ("The Ballad of Casey Jones," "Spike Driver Blues"), Big Bill Broonzy ("Trouble in Mind"), Jimmie Rodgers ("Blue Yodel #9"), Elizabeth Cotten ("Oh, Babe, It Ain't No Lie"), the Monroe Brothers ("Drifting Too Far from the Shore"), Webb Pierce ("I Ain't Never"), Leadbelly ("Goodnight Irene") and Riley Puckett ("I'm Ragged but I'm Right," which sort of became the group's unofficial theme song). The group also played "Ripple" at three shows—to no one's surprise, that tune fit in neatly with the classics from earlier eras.

Garcia appeared to relish his time onstage with the acoustic band, perhaps because it tapped so deeply into his own pre–Grateful Dead roots. He happily shared the solo spotlight with the other players—Kosek's fiddle playing and Rothman's instrumental work were especially impressive—and he seemed completely comfortable onstage in this group setting, which was not usually the case when he and John Kahn played acoustic shows together.

The electric sets by the Jerry Garcia Band on Broadway drew from completely different musical traditions than the acoustic sets. There were no new additions to the repertoire, but the selection of songs was already broad and deep, encompassing reggae ("The Harder They Come," "Stop That Train"), funky R&B ("Think," "Get Out of My Life, Woman"), Dylan tunes ("Forever Young," "Tangled Up in Blue," "The Night They Drove Old Dixie Down," "I Shall Be Released"), gospel-flavored R&B ("My Sisters and Brothers," "Lucky Old Sun"), a dash of Chuck Berry ("Let It Rock"), the Beatles ("Dear Prudence") and Los Lobos ("Evangeline"), and a healthy dose of Hunter-Garcia songs ("Run for the Roses," "Gomorrah," "Deal," "Mission in the Rain," "They Love Each Other"). By the end of each performance, Deadheads had usually heard songs from every decade of this century, all filtered through Garcia's guitar playing, singing and the strong ensemble work of his mates. It was no less a Broadway revue than *Ain't Misbehavin'* (which featured the music of Fats Waller) or *Side by Side by Sondheim*; just a little looser and less predictable from night to night, since the repertoire constantly changed.

All in all, it was quite a heady couple of weeks for Garcia and his bandmates—"definitely one of the coolest things we ever did," John Kahn enthused. "I thought it would be tiring and that maybe it would be tough switching back and forth between electric and acoustic, but everyone was so relaxed, and the crowds were so great. It was the most fun I ever had playing in New York, that's for sure, and I think Jerry had a lot of fun, too. I know he and Steve [Parish] would wander around and do stuff, and for whatever reason—maybe people were giving him his space—the New Yorkers weren't in his face as much as usual."

On December 20, 1987, Garcia became a father for the fourth time when Manasha gave birth to a girl, Keelin Noel Garcia, at her house in San Anselmo. By all accounts, Jerry was thrilled to be a dad again, and he pledged that he would be more involved with the child than he had been with his other three girls.

The year ended on another high note, with four Dead shows at the Oakland Coliseum, the last of which—New Year's Eve—was broadcast nationally on radio and televised on pay-per-view. Once again the Dead got into the spirit of the event by allowing themselves to be mocked and humiliated in a series of skits written mostly by Tom Davis. Garcia appeared as Santa Claus at one point, and wearing a chef's hat in a *Cooking with Jerry* segment in which he shared his recipe for pigs in a blanket. Not exactly Oscar-worthy, but at least he was game.

The Dead played much better this New Year's Eve than they had for their televised concert in 1985, and the difference in Garcia was like night and day. The show ended in the wee hours of the morning, January 1, 1988, when members of the Neville Brothers—one of the opening groups—joined the Dead onstage for a short third set that mixed New Orleans and Caribbean flavors ("Man Smart, Woman Smarter," "Iko Iko," "Day-O") with old-time rock 'n' roll (Bobby Freeman's "Do You Wanna Dance?") and a sobering and reflective final choice that somehow managed to bring the entire miraculous year into focus: Dylan's "Knockin' on Heaven's Door," which Garcia sang straight from the heart.

> Come wipe these tears from my eyes
> I won't shed them anymore
> The sun is setting in Western skies
> And I feel like I'm knockin' on heaven's door
>
> Knock, knock, knockin' on heaven's door
> Knock, knock, knockin' on heaven's door
> Just like so many times before . . .

CHAPTER 20

Show Me Something
Built to Last

few days after New Year's, Jerry, Mountain Girl, Trixie and Annabelle flew to Kona, Hawaii, for a couple of weeks of relaxation and fun in the sun. The Garcias had first gone to Hawaii together in November 1986, when Jerry was still recovering from the diabetic coma, and everyone had fallen in love with the Big Island's natural beauty and lazy pace. That year he took a helicopter tour of the Kilauea volcano, hung around the pool at the posh Mauna Kea resort and spent time regaining his health and reconnecting with M.G. and the kids. A few Hawaii trips later, after his strength had returned, Jerry took up scuba diving, which became one of the great passions of his later life.

"It takes up some of the space that drugs left, insofar as it's like going to a different world," he said in early 1992, when he was already a veteran diver. "You're in a different place. It's very sensual. There's lots of new information there, a lot of levels, a lot of things to think about. And physically it's good for you. But it satisfies that thing of going to space. You're in a place where there's no gravity, you're surrounded by a whole raft of interesting new life-forms, many of which are interactive. You can't go to the forest and pet raccoons, but you can go into the water and pet eels and octopuses and things. I do things I would never have believed I was capable of doing diving. I really love it; it's an amazing experience."

"What he really loved about it was the freedom of the water," daughter Annabelle says. "He and I went a couple of times together. You spend most of your life overweight and kind of low energy and doing bad things to yourself, and then you get in the water and you can pretty much do whatever you want and go wherever you want without worrying about the physical aspects. I remember him saying many times, 'It's better than taking drugs. It's better than psychedelics. It's a living theater of psychedelia; just incredibly beautiful.' "

In the late '80s and early '90s Garcia went to Hawaii whenever he had a gap of a few weeks in his insanely demanding schedule. The Hawaii vacations were his chance to really get away from the pressures of his everyday life and also, as time went on, occasions to socialize with his friends. On one trip to Kauai, Bob Weir came along. On another Big Island excursion it was Steve Parish's family. Bob and Maureen Hunter went over and at Jerry's insistence got their scuba certification, as did Laird Grant, Phil and Jill Lesh and others.

Garcia was intoxicated with Hawaii and diving and wanted to share it with the people he loved.

At the end of March the Dead went out on their first big tour of 1988, which took them to arenas on the East Coast and the Midwest. The shows sold out almost immediately in every city, and up and down the tour route, municipalities gritted their teeth and braced for the Deadhead onslaught that was certain to materialize when the band hit town. Though few ugly episodes occurred, there were still numerous complaints about unruly crowds outside the venues, and in several cities there were calls from local government officials to ban the group.

So beginning in the summer of 1988, the Dead sent a small squad into the parking lots to try to educate people about behaving responsibly—what became known as "Deadiquette." They organized groups of volunteers to pick up trash in the the parking lots after shows and filled notebooks with ideas from Deadheads about how to better control the scene. After each show, the liaison crew prepared a report outlining problems they'd seen or that had been reported to them, and in many cases they made recommendations about how things might be improved at the next stop on the tour. The bandmembers themselves took a keen interest in the reports, and they did what they could, too—they taped radio messages asking the fans to behave nicely.

Unfortunately, these preemptive maneuvers seemed mainly to reach the faithful rather than the rabble. Nearly everywhere the Dead went that summer there were problems, ranging from horrendous traffic snarls—at Alpine Valley in Wisconsin, some 20,000 people without tickets showed up—to minor gate-crashing incidents in Hampton, Virginia, and the Meadowlands in New Jersey. In Saratoga there was considerable violence when hundreds of fans stormed the fences surrounding the venue and were beaten back by panicky police.

To their credit, the bandmembers never let the intense drama that was swirling around every venue they played affect their music. Rather, they continued to improve with each tour. In general there was more jamming in 1988 than there had been in 1987, and an infusion of new material around midyear took the group into some interesting new spaces.

Garcia introduced two new songs at Alpine Valley in June. "Foolish Heart" was an immediate hit with most Deadheads, in part because it was the first Hunter-Garcia tune since "Shakedown Street" in 1978 that was clearly designed to open up to jamming. It was a clever tune, too, with a lilting melody and a flowing, slightly sensuous midtempo pace not too far removed from "Franklin's Tower." The arrangement felt relaxed and airy, yet there was also a fairly sophisticated web of interlocking lines and subrhythms being laid down by the entire band, basically for the entire song.

The lyrics were classic Hunter: in each verse Garcia instructs us to undertake some impossible, unwise or absurd task, then in the last line of each verse he sings, "But never give your love, my friend, unto a foolish heart":

Shun, shun a brother and a friend
Never look, never look around the bend
Or check a weather chart
Sign the Mona Lisa
With a spray can, call it art
But never give your love, my friend
Unto a foolish heart

"I don't even know whether 'Never give your love, my friend, to a foolish heart' is decent advice," Garcia said. "I had some trouble with Hunter about that. I said, 'Do we really want to be telling people this?' I mean, sometimes it's fun to get involved in something completely frivolous. The tone of the song is definitely ironic, but that goes over most people's heads. That doesn't surprise me anymore. A lot of songs we do are ironic in tone and people don't understand that.

"For me, though, 'Foolish Heart' is not about the text," he continued. "It's about the flow of the song. There's something about it that's charming, but as usual I don't exactly know why. I like that it's got a sort of asymmetrical melody that's very natural-sounding. That part of it is successful from my point of view."

Garcia's other new song was a slow ballad called "Believe It or Not," a love song Hunter described as "a C&W lyric reminiscent of the kind of stuff I remember hearing from tavern jukeboxes in 1948, when my father would stop in to have a few while I waited out in the car." Hunter casts Garcia in the role of a simple guy who's seen a lot of hard times ("Done time in the lockup / Done time on the street / Done time on the upswing / and time in defeat") and now longs for the simplicity of a blissful reciprocal love

Musically, the song was one of Garcia's most derivative efforts. It appropriated its main melodic motif from his own "Gomorrah," and both the glacial pace and Garcia's understated vocal phrasing were reminiscent of "Lucky Old Sun," which he performed often with the Jerry Garcia Band during this period. It even had a big, swelling R&B-style vocal ending that someone like Ray Charles could have had a field day with. Original or not, the song did have a certain quiet power. Garcia performed the song only seven times (six times in 1988 and once in 1990), so on some level it must not have worked for him. It remains a little-known curio for the most part, one of the few songs Hunter and Garcia wrote together that was never given a chance to develop much beyond its first versions.

When the Dead hit the road in September for a nearly monthlong tour, they tried something a little different, playing multiple nights in just three different venues—four each at the Capitol Centre in Maryland (outside of Washington, D.C.) and the Spectrum in Philadelphia, and then an unprecedented nine concerts at Madison Square Garden. This, naturally, cut down on the amount the band had to travel, and it also helped satisfy the incredible demand for tickets in three of the group's biggest markets.

Actually, Manhattan was one of the few places the Dead played regularly where the Deadhead presence wasn't a major nuisance—since the city is so inhospitable to begin with, and expensive to boot, the shows at the Garden didn't attract the caravans of dilapidated cars filled with would-be campers that stops on the summer tour did. Hanging out on 34th Street didn't offer much to ticketless tourheads, and the presence of so many New York policemen, some on horeseback, discouraged the usual carnival atmosphere outside the arena. Occasionally little parties would spring up in parking garages on side streets near the Garden, but it was a far cry from the scene that developed at, say, Alpine Valley.

Which is not to say that things were any less festive inside the Garden. At this series in particular, the energy surrounding the shows seemed unusually high. Part of it was the sheer length of the run, which was the Dead's longest since the 1980 Radio City stint. Producer John Scher made sure that anyone traveling past the Garden during the eleven days the Dead were in the city knew who had taken over that West Side neighborhood—over the entrance he put up a thirty-foot inflatable King Kong, decked out for the occasion in a Kong-sized tie-dyed shirt; quite a sight.

Garcia once said that playing New York under any circumstances was "a sweat," in part because the fans there were so demanding: "It's like Bill Graham used to say—they want the sword fighter, they want the juggler. In New York they really want you to sock 'em with the rock 'n' roll. I mean, they're *tough!*" Garcia laughed. The fall 1988 Garden shows were even more draining than usual because the final concert of the series was a big, high-profile, multiartist benefit that required lots of planning, preparation, promotion and rehearsal. Though the Dead had played countless benefits over the years, and in the '80s had donated money to dozens of groups through the Rex Foundation, the Garden benefit was different: It was designed to be both a money- and consciousness-raising event centered on a specific issue, namely protecting the world's rapidly vanishing rain forests.

According to Garcia, "It took us a good two years of pretty hard ferreting to find out who are the real actors in the environmental movement on a global level, especially having to do specifically with the rain forest. Once you find those, it's easier to focus on what you're going to do and what you're going to raise money for and so on." Most of the money was earmarked for three groups involved in direct action on rain forest issues—Greenpeace, Cultural Survival (which deals primarily with people indigenous to the rain forests) and the Rainforest Action Network.

On the morning of the Dead's first Madison Square Garden concert, Garcia, Weir and Hart, along with representatives from each of those organizations and the head of the United Nations Environment Program, held a news conference at the UN to articulate their concerns. Garcia tried to explain why the notoriously anti-political Grateful Dead had gotten involved:

"We've never really called on our fans, the Deadheads, to align themselves one way or another as far as any political cause is concerned because of a basic paranoia about leading someone. We don't want to be the leaders, and we don't want to serve unconscious fascism. Power is a scary thing. When you feel that you are close to it, you want to make sure that it's not misleading. So all this time we've avoided making any statements about politics, about alignments of any sort. This is even true of the notion of giving, and things like that—mercy. But this is, we feel, an issue strong enough and life-threatening enough that inside the world of human games, where people really torture each other and overthrow countries and there's a lot of murder and hate, there's the larger question of global survival. We want to see the world survive to play those games, even if they're atrocious."

Given all the extramusical activity surrounding the Garden run, it's not too surprising that a few of the shows were slightly sub-par, and that by the time the benefit concert rolled around, the band seemed a little tired and Garcia's voice was almost completely shot—the entire night he could hardly manage much beyond a scratchy croak. Fortunately, there were plenty of other musicians on hand to take up the slack, including former Rolling Stones guitarist Mick Taylor, New York singer-songwriter Suzanne Vega (a favorite of Garcia's), Bruce Hornsby and Philadelphia soulsters Hall and Oates. The concert was not the complete artistic success it might have been had Garcia not been fatigued and plagued with throat troubles, but it earned more than $600,000 for the rain forest groups and generated plenty of publicity for the cause.

On the Dead's fall 1988 Southern swing, Garcia premiered a new song, "Built to Last," which became the title song for the Dead's next album a year later. A pleasant midtempo tune, it seemed to be Hunter's meditation on the Dead's longevity, at once directed at the band and, through Garcia's voice, its fans:

There are times when you can beckon
There are times when you must call
You can take a lot of reckoning
But you can't take it all
There are times when I can help you out
And times when you must fall
There are times when you must live in doubt
And I can't help at all

Three blue stars / Rise on the hill
Say no more, now / Just be still
All these trials / Soon be past
Look for something / Built to last

Shortly after the tour, the band began working on the follow-up album to *In the Dark*, even though at that point they barely had a full album's worth of material: three Hunter-Garcia tunes ("Foolish Heart," "Believe It or Not," "Built to Last"), three Brent Mydland–John Barlow songs (the rowdy rockers "Blow Away" and "Gentlemen Start Your Engines," and a pretty ballad dedicated to Brent's little girls, called "I Will Take You Home") and just one Weir-sung effort, "Victim or the Crime." At first the band tried the same recording approach that had worked so well on *In the Dark*, cutting basic tracks live on-stage at the Marin Vets, but there was something about the new songs that didn't lend themselves to that method. So they abandoned that hall and moved out to secluded northwestern Marin County to private, rural Sky-walker Ranch, where producer-director George Lucas had built a state-of-the-art recording studio that was already becoming famous for its huge "live" room. By year's end, though, not much serious work had been done on the record and the bandmembers were already talking about trying some other approach.

At the first Dead concert of 1989, at Kaiser Convention Center in Febru-ary, Garcia introduced a song that would quickly develop into one of the great-est works of his "late" period. "Standing on the Moon" was another simple, achingly slow ballad (which immediately put off fans hoping for the next "Scarlet Begonias" to emerge), a poignant meditation on isolation, detach-ment and, ultimately, companionship. On the literal level, it depicts an astro-naut on the moon, "watching" the travails of the Earth hundreds of thousands of miles away:

> I see all of Southeast Asia
> I can see El Salvador
> I hear the cries of children
> And the other songs of war
> It's like a mighty melody
> That rings down from the sky
> Standing here upon the moon
> I watch it all roll by
> All roll by, All roll by, All roll by

By the song's conclusion, though, the homesick main character longs to be "somewhere in San Francisco / On a back porch in July / Just looking up to heaven / At this crescent in the sky." And in the emotional close of the song, Garcia sings, "Standing on the moon with nothing left to do / A lovely view of heaven / But I'd rather be with you / Be with you / I'd rather be with you. . . ." The song would build dramatically during this coda, with Garcia re-peating "be with you" over and over again, a blast of Van Morrison–style rav-ing that never failed to excite the crowd.

Hunter said, " 'Standing on the Moon' was one of those neat, sweet quick things, like 'It Must Have Been the Roses,' where the whole picture just came to me, and I grabbed a piece of paper and got it down. No changes, no nothin'. Out of the head of Zeus, full-born and clad in armor."

"Every once in a while Hunter delivers a lyric that is just absolutely clear in its intent," Garcia commented of the song. "I thought it would be really nice to do a song that you only have to hear one time and you'll get it. You don't have to listen to it hundreds of times or wonder what it's about. . . . There's something I like about it very much. It's an emotional reality; it isn't linguistics. It's something about that moment of the soul. To have those words coming out of my mouth puts me in a very specific place, and there's a certain authenticity there that I didn't want to disturb."

The Dead's spring 1989 tour was generally quite strong musically—particularly the newer material, which the band had been honing in the studio. But again there were numerous incidents outside their concerts that tainted the tour and earned the Dead even more bad press. In Pittsburgh there was a rock- and bottle-throwing melee as 3,000 people without tickets fought with police. In Cincinnati there were more than seventy arrests. There was fighting outside Irvine Meadows Amphitheater again. Even in the Bay Area, which had been spared most of the major problems associated with the overpopulation of the Dead scene, there were enough ugly incidents outside shows in 1989 that the Dead were effectively banned from the three nicest venues they played: the Greek Theater, Frost Amphitheater and Kaiser Convention Center. In the '90s, hometown shows would be played exclusively in the drab Oakland Coliseum Arena and the 20,000-seat Shoreline Amphitheater, forty minutes south of San Francisco.

That spring, too, the Dead abandoned their effort to cut their new album at Skywalker Ranch, and the action moved to Club Front and a different recording technique: building up from strong rhythm tracks, with each player recording separately and alone—the antithesis of recording together as a group.

"What we did," Garcia explained, "was we spent a lot of time trying to figure out what the right tempo for the tune was going to be, and then we took a piece of tape and a dumb-shit drum machine, and set up a basic feeling for the tune on a drum machine; like an enhanced click track. . . . So we set that up and ran it the length of the tune. So say a tune has two verses, two bridges, an instrumental bridge, another sung chorus. We set the length of the rhythm track to that idea, and then Bob and I and Phil and Brent would work together with that to get a sense of how the song would hang together. Then, once we had essentially established the length and the tempo, we started working on it individually. So Bob would go home and work on his guitar part until he felt he had one that was really successful, and so on."

This process went on for several months, as the bandmembers continually changed their parts in relation to each other's new musical ideas. This way, rather than having numerous different takes of each song, everyone essentially worked on a continually evolving single take. The main advantage to working this way was that the players could work at their own pace and to whatever degree of perfection they desired. Because they weren't ever all playing at once, each of them could really listen to the parts the others had played and put more thought into what they were trying to accomplish. As Garcia said, "The process of developing and updating, based on what you hear and what effect your part has on everybody else's playing, was speeded up tremendously by using slave reels [work copies made from the master tape]."

Garcia and John Cutler produced the record, which meant they were the ultimate arbiters of when the potentially endless process of overdubbing reactive parts was actually finished. Considering this method of working, the finished album, *Built to Last*, sounded surprisingly live; or at the very least like a band all playing at once. Garcia proclaimed himself very happy with the record, even preferring it to the mega-successful *In the Dark*.

"[*Built to Last*] is a lot more considerate of the material, and it's much more of a *record* in that each song has its own personality in a more controlled kind of way," he said shortly after the CD was released. "The fundamental sound of things is better, and also, the space in which they occur [the ambience] is better. It has better vocals and better songs, too. And the songs have an energy we haven't been able to get in the studio for quite a long time."

The final song list for the record had changed considerably as the album evolved. Garcia dropped "Believe It or Not" and added "Standing on the Moon" in addition to "Foolish Heart" and the title song. Bob Weir contributed "Victim or the Crime" and "Picasso Moon." The big surprise was that Brent had four songs, the most of anyone: "I Will Take You Home," "Blow Away" and two new songs, the ecology-minded anthem "We Can Run" and the snaky, dramatic "Just a Little Light."

"You always go with whatever your strong suit is, and in this case it was Brent that had the good songs—I mean, more of 'em," Garcia said. "Brent's getting to be more comfortable with the band. He sees it being as much his band as everybody else's. So it's just the thing of getting over the 'new guy' thing."

Still the "new guy" after ten years?

"Ten years, right," Garcia laughed. "He's been pretty conservative about getting comfortable in it, but now—I mean, [on] this record it's nice to be able to show off what he can do on a lot of different levels. And his contribution to this record is really outstanding all over. Not just his tunes and vocals, but everything else—all the keyboard parts and just ideas and general stuff."

The album also benefited from the judicious use of MIDI technology, which allowed the musicians to move away from the regular timbres of their instruments into exciting new realms. MIDI (Musical Instrument Digital

Interface) is a system that allows different electronic instruments and devices to share information, often in the form of prerecorded "samples" of sounds, which can be called up and manipulated by a controller such as a guitar, keyboard or a drum pad. So, at the flip of a switch, Garcia's guitar or Brent's keyboard could sound like a fiddle or a saxophone or church bells or wind—the possibilities were limitless. Garcia called MIDI "a whole new language." Since Bob Bralove had joined the band's technical staff in mid-1987, he'd worked with each player individually to develop his MIDI system. Brent and the drummers were the first to be up and running, but by the spring of 1989 the guitarists were experimenting with MIDI sounds onstage, too—at first they used special MIDI guitars during "space" (always the band's great testing ground) before switching back to their normal axes.

In one night's "space," Garcia might toy with the sound of a massive pipe organ; in another he became a third "drummer" for a few moments. He played MIDI panpipes and bassoon and ethereal choral washes that made his guitar sound like the breath of angels. "I've started to do some stuff on ballads that's kind of interesting," he said in the early fall of '89, "where I'll add little [MIDI] voicings against the guitar so it's not actually adding to the guitar note, but sort of adding a halo around the sound. Some of it is very subtle."

After initially using his MIDI sounds exclusively during "space," Garcia began incorporating new sounds into some regular Grateful Dead material. On "Let It Grow" and "Mexicali Blues" he would often use a trumpet sound and mimic mariachi phrasing. The jams in "Bird Song" and "Playing in the Band" lent themselves to breathy "flute" flights by Garcia. If he occasionally overdid the MIDI effects in fall '89 and spring '90, it was only because he was excited and amused by the novelty of it. And when Garcia, Lesh and Weir would go wild during "space," dialing up one bizarre sound after another, the results were often hilarious. But they could just as easily turn ominous and downright frightening, too. It was difficult for the audience to tell who was playing what when the players dove deep into the MIDI zone, and that became part of the band's special fun: to mess with the crowd's expectations by having Phil, for instance, play a flute sound while Bob was somehow causing the basslike earthquake rumble.

Garcia's MIDI "trumpet" made it onto two songs on *Built to Last*: on Brent's "I Will Take You Home," which was essentially a "trumpet"-piano duet; and the title song, where Garcia's high-pitched part sounded like a Baroque piccolo trumpet—"that Purcell 'Trumpet Voluntary' sound," he said.

In the spring of 1989 Garcia had told a writer that seeing music in a stadium is "not a pleasant experience generally. I don't see why anyone would go to more than one of those shows myself." Nevertheless, when the summer of '89 rolled around, the Dead booked a number of stadium shows in the East and Midwest to satisfy ticket demand. To their credit, the band did what they could to make these cold, impersonal venues more hospitable: They developed a bigger sound system to deliver louder, cleaner sound. They hired a Polish artist named Jan Sawka to design colorful banners and cloth panels to hang from the huge stage's proscenium and wings. Lighting director Candace Brightman devised some new lighting schemes to creatively illuminate the stage and Sawka's giant panel paintings of trees, suns, moons and odd faces. Like so many bands that make it to the stadium level, the Dead added large video screens to bring the action closer to more people. And at each stadium they booked an opening band they knew most Deadheads would like—Los Lobos, Bruce Hornsby and the Range, or 10,000 Maniacs.

The tour itself was a grand success, though two of the stadium shows (in Buffalo and Washington, D.C.) did not sell out. Actually, this was considered *good* news among Deadheads, because it was the first sign that the craziness that had been following the Dead since the summer of 1987 was finally beginning to subside. In general, there were fewer crowd problems on the tour than on the previous two summer outings, in part because it rained so much that hanging around the shows was too unpleasant for many people.

The Dead played sensationally for most of the summer, particularly once the stadium part of the tour ended. Their concerts at a brand-new rural Indiana amphitheater called Deer Creek, and at the beloved Alpine Valley, were consistently inspired. Garcia's playing was charged with electricity: with each tour following his coma in '86, he became increasingly forceful and confident, his fingering faster and more dexterous, his solos more tonally varied, imaginative and well-constructed. Some of the best playing of Garcia's career occurred between 1988 and the spring of 1990, and the rest of the band was right there with him—always getting stronger, constantly upping the intensity level of the whole.

When the Grateful Dead got on a roll like this they were an unstoppable force of nature. When they were playing their best they entered a zone that can be described only as a form of perfection—where every note felt both technically and emotionally *right,* and the musicians' individual parts and rhythmic choices meshed seamlessly to create a great, ever-changing gestalt. It wasn't something the Dead could conjure exactly, because it depended on inumerable factors—the moment-to-moment disposition of each player; whether his equipment was functioning properly so that he could hear himself and the others; the appropriateness of the song selections to the overall feeling of the show; each member's sensitivity to what everyone else was playing; the responsiveness of the crowd. But when it was happening and everything was clicking, it was apparent to just about everybody; you couldn't miss it. The Dead used to say that at those times, the music played the band, meaning that as a group they were operating beyond cognition and intention—beyond the mechanics of simply playing well—to a nearly effortless state of grace, where the music was speaking through them rather than from them. It was completely tangible to both band and audience, yet also inexplicable. It had to do with being in the moment completely and surrendering to the course that the music was taking.

Garcia struggled to explain it in a 1990 interview: "For me, the experience is one of tremendous clarity. I can see the people in the audience and everybody in the band and there's nothing between me and it; my own thoughts aren't between me and it, my own effort isn't between me and it; my ambition, all of my personal baggage. . . . That is to say, it's not like thinking, it's not cerebral, but it's not purely emotional, either. I experience it as a kind of transparency, and it's very, very easy when you get to that place. It's impossible to make a wrong decision. In fact, the music is kind of playing itself in a way because I'm not making decisions about where I'm gonna be anymore or where I'm gonna end up or how long a phrase is gonna last or any of that. I'm just goin' with it and everybody else is, too.

"You kind of have to trust it," he continued. "It's like an invisible bridge over a huge chasm and if you don't look down, you'll be okay. Trust it, just put one foot in front of another and say, 'It's there! No matter what it looks like, the bridge is there and I'm walking across it.' There's that quality to it. . . .

"It's tough to talk about. I've gone all over the place looking for metaphors, but it always ends up being gibberish. You know—'What the hell's this guy tryin' to say?' It doesn't lend itself to articulation very well. But musicians know about this stuff and [so does] anybody who's ever done something where being 'on' counts."

On the summer and fall tours in 1989 the band was clearly energized by their newer material—particularly the odd, angular "Victim or the Crime," "Foolish Heart" and "Standing on the Moon." And the overall quality of their playing was so consistently high that Garcia felt confident enough to dig into the band's songbook to pull out a few old treats for the Deadheads, the majority of whom had never seen the band before the mid-'80s. That summer, the group ended several shows with a cappella versions of "We Bid You Goodnight," which the Dead hadn't played since the '70s. The next revival was "Death Don't Have No Mercy," missing from the repertoire since 1970, in a slightly different arrangement that had Garcia, Weir and Mydland each singing a verse, instead of Garcia carrying the entire song vocally.

But the Dead saved their most cherished nuggets for their October East Coast tour, which began with two hastily arranged, completely unpublicized (to keep away the touring rabble) "guerrilla" shows at Hampton Coliseum in Virginia, where the Dead were billed as "Formerly the Warlocks." Garcia brought back several favorites: "Help on the Way" and "Slipknot" were joined again with "Franklin's Tower" for the first time since 1985. "Dark Star" had been played just twice in the early '80s before the band eased into it the second night at Hampton to the deafening, ecstatic cheers of the lucky 15,000 mainly local fans who had managed to get "Warlocks" tickets. Both "Help on the Way/Slipknot" and "Dark Star" benefited tremendously from the group's MIDI setups because the open-endedness of those tunes encouraged the band to experiment freely with different timbres and textures. Deadheads attached to the sound of the early Grateful Dead argue that the versions of "Dark Star" the band played in the '80s and '90s lacked the vision, imagination and commitment to true weirdness of the song's late-'60s and early-'70s counterparts. Better or worse, it was certainly a *different* animal in its later incarnations, but its function was unchanged—it provided a framework for sonic exploration— and the exquisite simplicity of the basic melody was no less evocative in 1989 than it had been in 1969.

The final chestnut Garcia brought back at Hampton was perhaps the most surprising—"Attics of My Life," dormant since 1972 and extremely rare even in the early '70s. Here was a tune almost none of the band's current fans had ever heard performed live, and for the first time ever, the group had a harmony blend that brought out the full passion and power of the *American Beauty* version. The song fit neatly in the late-second-set Garcia ballad slot that was usually reserved for darker, more sobering meditations; by contrast, "Attics" was an uplifting, compassionate hymn—another glimpse of the otherworldly psychic landscape shared by the band and its fans:

> *In the secret space of dreams*
> *Where I dreaming lay amazed*
> *When the secrets all are told*
> *And the petals all unfold*
> *When there was no dream of mine*
> *You dreamed of me*

On Halloween, five days after the end of the Dead's East Coast tour, *Built to Last* was released by Arista Records. Like nearly every other Grateful Dead album, it proved to be a strong out-of-the-box seller, helped no doubt by the unprecedented success of *In the Dark*. But sales tapered off quickly. Arista was never able to break a single from the record ("Foolish Heart" was the only song to get substantial airplay); reviews were mainly negative (the honeymoon between the press and the Dead in the wake of Garcia's recovery had long since ended; now the Dead were regarded as dinosaurs with boorish fans); and even many Deadheads dismissed the record because it contained more Brent tunes than Hunter-Garcia songs. MTV, which had loved the "Touch of Grey" video so much, failed to embrace Gary Gutierrez's equally imaginative treatment of "Foolish Heart," and completely ignored Gutierrez's moody performance lip-synch video for Brent's "Just a Little Light." Even so, *Built to Last* sold more than 800,000 copies in the first six months, which would have been considered phenomenal in the days before *In the Dark*. And all over the country, Deadheads let out a sigh of relief that were wasn't going to be another hit of the magnitude of "Touch of Grey" to bring in thousands of new fans from the mainstream.

The same day *Built to Last* was released, Garcia played a gig at the Concord Pavilion, an hour east of San Francisco, with the Jerry Garcia Band. This had been a great year for that group, too. The freshness and vigor that marked Garcia's playing with the Dead carried over to the JGB, elevating the entire band in the process. There were a pair of new additions to the already extensive repertoire of cover tunes: John Kahn dug up "I Hope It Won't Be This Way Always" from a late-'70s record by a Philadelphia-based group called the Angelic Gospel Singers; and JGB singer Gloria Jones suggested Garcia tackle Canadian folksinger Bruce Cockburn's moving 1986 tune "Waiting for a Miracle," which became one of Jerry's favorites for a while.

As usual, most of the JGB's gigs in 1989 were in California, but the band also made one two-week foray into the East and Midwest in September, playing many of the same venues the Dead frequented—the Spectrum, the Meadowlands in New Jersey, Hartford Civic, Alpine Valley, Poplar Creek in Illinois. This was the first time the Garcia Band had undertaken an entire tour of larger venues, and the move was viewed with some skepticism by Deadheads who thought of the JGB as a club and small theater band, not an arena act. Sweetening the pot for the fans was the addition of the duo of Bob Weir and bassist Rob Wasserman as opening act for the tour. And at four of the shows the JGB was joined by E Street Band saxophonist Clarence Clemons, who had also sat in with the Dead on a few occasions. Garcia liked having the amiable and physically imposing Clemons as a visual foil and soloist, and though he is not exactly a saxophone titan, he had great spirit and added another layer to the JGB's occasionally thin sound.

Even at this peak of Garcia's personal popularity, the JGB never attracted the same sort of fanatical devotion as the Grateful Dead. The band didn't really make records, didn't tour enough to build a following around the country and, frankly, there were many Deadheads who simply never cared much for the group. Some didn't connect with the multitude of R&B, gospel and other cover songs the way they did with Hunter-Garcia tunes. Others believed that, unlike in the Dead, none of the musicians in the JGB were up to Garcia's musical level. Certainly the JGB lacked both the dynamic ensemble interplay and the exciting, reckless edge of the Grateful Dead. And then there was always a segment of listeners who simply couldn't stand hearing so many slow ballads and midtempo tunes.

But what the JGB had to offer those fans who could get beyond the Grateful Dead comparisons was a rich and varied body of music, a relaxed and friendly atmosphere with none of the pressures and expectations endemic to Dead shows, and heaping helpings of Garcia's guitar work—he played longer solos than he did with the Dead, and there was less competing with his guitar, so he crafted his lines a little differently; more precisely, perhaps. And because

Garcia fashioned the set list at each show according to what he alone wanted to sing and play, there was an intimate quality to the performances, as if the emotions in those particular songs were what he wanted to communicate to the audience at that concert. The fact that the band's repertoire ranged from earthy, direct R&B to circuitous Dylan song-paintings and Bible-thumping gospel just showed some of Garcia's inner complexity and range of musical tastes.

"Every song he chose, every note he played was a reflection of something inside him," John Kahn commented in 1996. "A lot of times it was probably more the emotional feel rather than the literal meaning of a song that appealed to him, but it had to touch him somewhere in his soul or he just wouldn't do it. It wasn't hard to tell when a song wasn't working for him—he couldn't play it or sing it that well and he'd drop it. The ones he kept were the ones that spoke to him. And if he loved a song, it was hard not to love it, too, because he'd play it so well that it would touch your soul, too."

Asked in 1997 what the Jerry Garcia Band audience wanted to get from a show, drummer David Kemper replied, "That's easy: the audience just wanted to be in a room with Jerry. They didn't care if they were hearing fast music or slow music; they wanted to be in the same room with Jerry. That's all I could see. And it didn't matter if it was good or bad or who he had onstage with him. The crowd didn't come to see me or John or Melvin. They came to be in the same room with Jerry. It's that simple. And I don't blame them. Being in the same room with Jerry was a pretty damn wonderful place to be."

By the fall of 1989 Garcia had moved out of the Reservoir Road house he'd been sharing with M.G. and the girls and settled into a house on Palm Avenue in San Rafael, across the street from the campus of Dominican College. Actually, the property had four buildings on it—three two-bedroom houses and a one-bedroom house, plus one of the largest private swimming pools in Marin County. Annabelle lived at Palm Avenue on and off for a while, but Jerry spent much of his time during this period with Manasha and Keelin at their house on Echo Court in San Anselmo. Jerry sometimes commuted between Palm and Echo Court on a four-cylinder Honda motorcycle M.G. had given him one recent Christmas, and he became a familiar sight puttering along the tree-lined streets of San Anselmo (though when he wore a helmet he was difficult to recognize).

"Jerry loved Keelin and was trying hard to be a good father," comments Gloria DiBiase, who worked as Keelin's full-time nanny during this period. "I think he may have felt as though he had failed with his other kids, so he tried to make up for that with Keelin."

Gloria and her husband, Vince DiBiase, would play significant roles in Garcia's life from the late '80s until just a few months before his death in the summer of 1995. Vince had first entered Garcia's orbit in the early '80s, when the guitarist became fascinated by Vince's pioneering work in holography—he had been involved in the field since the early '70s and was well-known in holography circles for his complex three-dimensional artworks, called Chromagrams. Vince sent a number of examples of his holographs to Garcia, and the two carried on a phone relationship for a couple of years before finally meeting. By 1985 Vince was making trippy holographic stickers and buttons with Dead iconography on them and selling them through Grateful Dead Merchandising.

Gloria, who was an artist herself and co-owner with Vince of VinGlo Designs, came into Garcia's world by a different route. One afternoon in February 1987 she left work at the San Rafael holography gallery she managed and took a bus to Oakland to attend one of the Dead's concerts at the Oakland Coliseum. On the bus she struck up a conversation with Manasha Matheson—this is before Manasha was romantically involved with Jerry—and the two became fast friends. Later, after Keelin was born, Vince and Gloria's daughter, Mariko, occasionally baby-sat for the littlest Garcia—sometimes Manasha would send a limousine to pick her up. One time, Mariko wasn't feeling well, so Gloria baby-sat in her place, and that led to her becoming a full-time nanny for Keelin.

Gloria says, "We have four children of our own and we've been together for twenty-five years now, so it was nice to relate to Jerry on that level. He was a family man and father, and he liked having our family around.

"Jerry was, like many of us, a typical hippie parent of the '60s with very few parenting skills. He was not a disciplinarian, but he was a very gentle, kind and generous father. He took a lot of pride and delight in Keelin. She was the apple of his eye." Adds Vince, "I got the impression he really wanted to make it work. He really wanted to be Keelin's daddy. He wanted to be there for her. He loved her."

In mid-December the Dead got a bad scare when Brent Mydland was secretly hospitalized after overdosing on a mixture of heroin and cocaine. Brent's main vice had always been alcohol, the abuse of which had led to a number of DUI episodes and even a brawl or two through the years, also unpublicized. But during the second half of 1989 he started dabbling more with hard drugs, to the alarm of people in the Dead organization familiar with his extreme mood swings. Whether this turn was precipitated by his separation from his wife and daughters, or by the pounding he took in the press after *Built to Last* came out, we'll never know for sure. But he recovered quickly and fully from the OD, and the Dead went on to play their traditional New Year's series at the Oakland Coliseum Arena as planned.

When the Grateful Dead traveled to the East Coast in mid-March for their first tour of 1990, spirits were high. Brent appeared to have bounced back from his drug crisis. On March 15 Phil became the first member of the group to turn fifty, and he was in terrific shape, mentally and physically. He and John Cutler had taken on the task of assembling a live album from recent recordings to help celebrate the Dead's twenty-fifth anniversary in 1990—the first time he'd gotten so involved in a Dead album project since the ill-fated live album *Steal Your Face*. The band shook the cobwebs from a few more old tunes: Brent brought back "Easy to Love You," which he'd ignored since 1980; Weir finally bowed to public pressure and revived "Black-Throated Wind"; and Garcia dusted off and improved "Loose Lucy." These last two tunes hadn't been played since October 1974.

Several shows on the tour were broadcast locally in an effort to keep crowds away from the venues, and by and large things ran smoothly. Musically, the shows were almost uniformly strong, with the runs at Knickerbocker Arena in Albany, New York, and Nassau Coliseum on Long Island being particular standouts. Lesh drew nearly a third of his selections for the 1990 live album, *Without a Net*, from the Nassau shows, and in 1996, the Dead released a triple CD from the Knickerbocker series, *Dozin' at the Knick*. The middle night of the Dead's three-show run at Nassau quickly passed into Deadhead legend when the group was joined onstage by jazz sax giant Branford Marsalis, who met the band for the first time that night. Though he had never heard much of their music, Marsalis fearlessly tackled some of the Dead's most exciting open-ended material—"Bird Song," "Dark Star," "Eyes of the World," "Estimated Prophet"—soloing as if he had been playing this music forever and returning the challenge by pushing the Dead with his own abstract musical ideas.

The band truly smoked that night, as well as on the handful of other occasions over the next four years when Branford played with them. Of all the guest musicians who shared the Dead's stage through the years—and they were many and varied—none embodied both the Dead's adventurous, questing spirit *and* their obsession with beautiful melodies and accessible structures quite like Branford did.

With the arrival of summer came a return to mega-gigs. By 1990 the Dead had more or less settled into a comfortable pattern of playing arenas in the spring and fall, and stadiums and large amphitheaters in the summer. The Dead had opted not to push the twenty-fifth anniversary angle in advertising for their concerts because they were afraid it might attract too many people to the scene outside the shows ("Twenty-five years? Parrrrty!"), but among Deadheads there was celebration in the air anyway. The opening acts were a nice selection of simpatico groups: Little Feat; Edie Brickell and New Bohemians; Crosby, Stills and Nash; Bruce Hornsby and the Range. Crowds were large but well-behaved for the most part. Most agreed that the music was as dynamic as ever.

What Deadheads didn't know, however, was that Brent Mydland was going through a rough time. Outwardly, he seemed to be fine. He sang one or two of his songs in most shows on the tour, and his playing was unusually assertive—at points distractingly so. But offstage he was obviously depressed. According to Garcia, Brent was mortified about the pospect of having to spend a few weeks in jail following the tour for an earlier DUI conviction. He turned again to heroin for relief, but vowed to go into a treatment program once the summer road trip was over.

"The last year or so Brent was taking some risks," says Bob Bralove. "I think he was pushing himself on a lot of levels, including musically. He really played some incredible shows, but in truth, to balance his nights of brilliance, there were some nights of rough playing. Things were getting very problematic for him and I think people were very concerned about him. Everyone was very moved when he could communicate in the music. Everyone understood that it was real; that he was a soul communicating right through the music—isn't that the point? He went right to the heart of it. It was completely soulful, but it was also accompanied by all sorts of other problems in his life, and things were rough and confusing for him. He expressed some seriously sorrowful stuff sometimes. It was hard to watch on one level, but it was also completely compelling."

Two nights after Brent returned to his home in the comfortable East Bay suburb of Lafayette following the summer tour, he shot up a mixture of cocaine and morphine (what's known as a speedball) into his left arm, and the potency of the combination killed him—probably almost instantaneously. The Contra Costa County coroner reported that the levels of both drugs in his system were lethal. He was thirty-seven years old, and all indications were that it was a tragic accident, not a suicide.

Naturally, Brent's death was a tremendous shock, even to those familiar with his substance-abuse problems (and most Deadheads knew him only as a drinker). The Dead office was flooded with phone calls, letters and telegrams mourning his passing. Deadheads laid flowers on the doorstep of Brent's home. In Philadelphia, more than five hundred people showed up in Rittenhouse Square for an impromptu memorial, and there were other smaller gatherings in cities coast to coast.

"I remember the evening after Brent died Jerry and I were up at Echo Court just sitting out on the deck and gazing at the stars," says Vince DiBiase. "Jerry was deeply affected by Brent's death."

Garcia made no public statement about Brent's death at the time, but a year later he reflected on it in an interview with James Henke in *Rolling Stone*: "Brent had this thing he was never able to shake, which was that thing of being the new guy. And he wasn't the new guy; I mean, he was with us for ten years! That's longer than most bands even last. And we didn't treat him like the new guy. We never did that to him. It's something he did to himself. But it's true that the Grateful Dead is tough to . . . I mean, we've been together so long, and we've been through so much, that it's hard to be a new person around us.

"But Brent had a deeply self-destructive streak," he continued. "And he didn't have much supporting him in term of an intellectual life. I owe a lot of who I am and what I've been and what I've done to the beatniks from the '50s and to the poetry and art and music I've come in contact with. I feel like I'm part of a certain thing in American culture, of a root. But Brent was from the East Bay, which is one of those places that is like *non*culture. There's nothing there. There's no substance, no background. And Brent wasn't a reader, and he hadn't really been introduced to the world of ideas on any level. So a certain part of him was like a guy in a rat cage, running as fast as he could and not getting anywhere. He didn't have any deeper resources. . . .

"It was heartbreaking when Brent died, because it seemed like such a waste. Here's this incredibly talented guy—he had a great natural melodic sense, and he was a great singer. And he could've gotten better, but he just didn't see it. He couldn't see what was good about what he was doing and he couldn't see himself fitting in. And no amount of effort on our part could make him more comfortable."

Almost immediately after Brent's death was announced, Deadheads began to speculate about his possible successor. Many wondered if the band would carry on with their planned September and October tour of the East Coast and Europe; some suggested they would call it quits altogether. However, the day after Brent's death, the band announced they would try to keep their fall commitments. Was it a money decision? Was it a hasty move by a band in denial? Was it "what Brent would have wanted; the show must go on," or some such justification?

It was probably a little of all three. And with twenty-twenty hindsight, it was also probably a mistake.

CHAPTER 21

So Many Roads
to Ease My Soul

ithin a week of Brent's funeral the Dead got their first bit of encouraging news in a while: Bruce Hornsby agreed to play with the group, if only temporarily, while they broke in a true successor, who would be chosen from several auditioning candidates. Hornsby's solo career was so successful at that point that it was unreasonable to expect him to abandon his own music completely. But he was familiar with many of the Dead's songs already, he'd played with the band on several occasions and his dynamic musicianship and effervescent stage presence were certain to make the transition into the post-Brent age a little easier.

Hornsby had deep roots in Grateful Dead music long before he shared a stage with them. As a teenager in the early '70s the Williamsburg, Virginia, native was introduced to their music by his older brother Bobby, who lived in a Deadhead-dominated fraternity at the University of Virginia in Charlottesville. Bruce was already developing into a fine pianist with diverse musical interests—his influences included Leon Russell, Professor Longhair, Bill Evans, Otis Spann, Chick Corea, Keith Jarrett and Herbie Hancock. But for kicks, he and his brother formed a band—Bobby Hi-Test and the Octane Kids—that played a slew of Dead tunes (mostly material from "Skull and Roses" and *Europe '72*) and other cover songs by the Band and the Allman Brothers at fraternity parties and dances.

"I was way into them from '71 to '76," he says. "About '76, I got really into jazz music and ended up going to school and becoming sort of a bohemian jazz musician in college. I was more into 'Trane and Keith Jarrett, Chick Corea and McCoy Tyner. I kept track of the Dead a little bit, but not nearly as much as I had."

Hornsby's own career didn't take off until the mid-'80s, when he scored a smash single with the socially conscious "The Way It Is," followed by a succession of popular AM and FM radio hits, including "Mandolin Rain," "The Western Skyline" and "Valley Road." Hornsby was the first pop pianist since Elton John to attract a large following. But he was more than some lightweight pop confectionaire. His love of jazz came through in his playing and, like the Dead, he loved to improvise and connect songs. His singing showed more folk and country influences—it's not surprising to learn that he grew up listening to Bill Monroe and George Jones. The Dead influence in his music was subtle, more evident in his approach to soloing than in what he actually played, though he performed the Dead's arrangement of "I Know You Rider" in his own sets.

"The Dead heard that there was this band riding around the country playing Dead songs, and Garcia and Phil became fans of the record," Hornsby said. "So we got a call saying they wanted us to open a couple of shows. I was just mad for this. So in May of '87 it was Ry Cooder, us and the Dead at Laguna Seca [in Monterey, California] for two days. It was a great time for me, because I had been a fan."

The next summer, at Buckeye Lake in Ohio, Hornsby's band opened again, and this time Bruce played accordion on "Sugaree" and "Stuck Inside of Mobile," to Garcia's obvious delight—he and Bruce beamed at each other practically the entire time Hornsby was sitting in. The Range appeared on several other bills with the Dead in 1989 and '90, and Bruce and Jerry's offstage relationship also deepened during this period. In 1989 Garcia played on Hornsby's *A Night on the Town* album and appeared in a live concert video based on the record.

"My band opened for the Dead in Louisville and Raleigh a couple of weeks before before Brent passed away, and I sat in with them a bunch and had a great time," Hornsby remembers. "So when Brent passed, I was in Seattle and I got a call from my production manager, a guy named Chopper who's friends with a lot of Grateful Dead–related people. He called me at about six in the morning and told me about it. Of course I was really shocked. Three hours later I was walking down the street in Seattle and some guy comes up to me and says, 'Hey Bruce, you going to join the Dead?' It was that quick. To be honest, I was a little fazed by it, and then the rumor mill really started runnin' rampant. I was on a tour with my band and all of a sudden I was hearing that everywhere I went: 'You gonna join? You gonna join?' At that point I hadn't heard from the guys in the band yet.

"A few days later I got a call from Phil—he wanted to talk about it a little. A week later we were playing the Concord Pavilion and Phil, Garcia and Cameron [Sears, Grateful Dead road manager] came out and they basically gave me the pitch. It was pretty low-key—'Hey, you want to come play with us? We'd like to start something new here, see what happens.' I think they wanted me to actually join the band. And if they'd caught me in 1984, before I got my own career going, I probably would have lived happily ever after as a Grateful Dead piano player—I think that would have been great. But they caught me in 1990. I had three records out, I'd sold a couple of million records and I didn't feel I could give that up completely.

"So I sort of mulled it over a little while, and then I called 'em up and said, 'What the hell—let's give it a go.' So we made plans for me to start at Madison Square Garden, a few shows into the tour, because I already had shows booked all the way up through that Friday night, which was the second Garden show."

Meanwhile, the Dead were auditioning keyboardists for the permanent slot in the group. Dozens of names were kicked around at Club Front, at the Dead office and among Deadheads. These ranged from sentimental "family" favorites like Tom Constanten and Merl Saunders to hot players like Little Feat's Bill Payne and Santana's Chester Thompson. In the end, only a few serious candidates were considered: onetime Dixie Dregs ace T. Lavitz; ex–Jefferson Starship members Tim Gorman and Pete Sears; and veteran Tubes and Todd Rundgren keysman Vince Welnick. Each was sent tapes of a half-dozen recent shows and then asked to come down to Club Front to see how they fit in musically with the Dead. This process took longer than anticipated, so the band had to cancel some scheduled shows at Shoreline Amphitheater— as they explained on the group's telephone hotline, Brent's shoes were big ones to fill, "and we haven't found the right foot."

Near the end of August the band unanimously agreed that Vince Welnick was the strongest candidate. He was a fast learner with a good feel for the range of the Dead's material, and he was easily the best harmony singer of those who auditioned. About a week after his tryout, Vince says, "I got a call from Bobby and the first thing he said was, 'Is your insurance paid up?' " evidently a macabre joke about the fate of his predecessors in the keyboard chair.

The job offer couldn't have come at a better time for Vince. A journeyman rock 'n' roller who had played in every imaginable situation during his years with the ultra-theatrical Tubes (best remembered for their mid-'70s anthem "White Punks on Dope") and then with Todd Rundgren, Vince by 1990 was finding it harder and harder to make ends meet playing music, and he and his wife, Laurie, were seriously thinking of leaving the Bay Area to live more cheaply in Mexico. Then Mimi Mills, former secretary for the Tubes who was working for Bob Weir in 1990, suggested to Laurie Welnick that Vince should try for the Dead's vacant slot.

Once the band settled on Vince, the real work began for him—a serious crash course on the Grateful Dead's repertoire, in preparation for the band's Eastern tour, set to begin outside of Cleveland on September 7. "Bob Bralove made a series of ten tapes, and each tape had ten songs on it and they were from recent live gigs, '89 and '90," Vince says. "First they sent me a case of CDs, but I didn't have the heart to tell them I didn't own a CD player. Then Jerry thought it would be a better idea to send the live tapes. So I'd be at home and I'd get my list of ten songs and I'd get the tape, and I might just write the title and what key it was in; others I had to completely chart out, like 'Help on the Way,' for instance, just to learn them. For a song like 'Terrapin' I had sheets that contained the chords for the three main movements, and some of the time changes. I had to work everything out myself, playing the tapes over and over again. So I'd do that for the ten songs and then hopefully the next day we'd go over those ten songs and then Bralove would give me another tape."

Since the Dead had an active repertoire of somewhere between 120 and 150 songs, Vince had his work cut out for him—ten days to catch up on twenty-five years of history. But he was a diligent student and he loved every second of it. "Every song I'd learn was like opening a new Christmas present," he says. "I'd go home and listen to tapes and sometimes I'd be so elated that I'd have tears running down my face. I'd be raving about how great this tune or this jam was and making copious notes on it."

The bandmembers gave Vince very little specific musical direction, though "sometimes Jerry would give me a little history of the song. He'd say, 'This one is a cousin of that other song,' meaning it was closely related structurally. He was like old Granddad sitting Sonny Boy down and telling how the feel of it should go. But mainly he'd say, 'Play anything. Have fun.' "

The mood inside the Richfield Coliseum (near Cleveland) the first night of the September tour was hopeful, even jubilant. Someone in the crowd passed out little stickers that said YO VINNIE! and a big banner hanging opposite the stage proclaimed, WELCOME VINCE! Vince was understandably quite nervous before his first show, but once Garcia hit the downbeat for "Cold Rain and Snow" to open the concert, it was immediately clear that the Dead had made a good choice. For the entire first tour Vince used chord charts to help him remember some of the more complex tunes, and the Dead also took the unprecedented step of playing from predetermined set lists, "though of course we didn't stick to them exactly," Vince says. In contrast to Brent's setup, which included the Hammond B-3 organ so prominently, Vince had just a single electronic keyboard—one of Brent's synthesizers—and a library of sounds that had been developed primarily by Bob Bralove. If there was a common complaint about Vince's early tenure with the group, it was that some of the sounds he and Bralove chose were unappealing or somehow inappropriate, whether too garish a texture for a delicate song like "Stella Blue" or an organ sound on another tune that was thin and reedy.

That first show at Richfield, Vince dived headlong into jamming tunes like "Bird Song," "Truckin' " and "Playing in the Band," and most agreed that he acquitted himself quite well. The second night, the band fell into a smoldering jam after "Terrapin" that sounded as if it could have come from the Carousel Ballroom, circa 1969, and that was an encouraging sign. Vince's harmonies caught some people off guard because on a few tunes he adopted Donna Godchaux's old part rather than Brent's, but his voice blended well with Garcia's and Weir's and he wasn't shy about using it. His only real deficiency was that he was not a very effective soloist at first—not too surprising in light of the fact that he hadn't had much opportunity to solo in the Tubes or Todd Rundgren's band. But he was a sympathetic ensemble player who found his place in the group's sound fairly quickly. And just as important, he was an instantly likable presence who brought a tangible lightness to the band, especially in contrast to his sometimes dark and brooding predecessor.

After Richfield, the tour headed to the Philadelphia Spectrum for three shows, then to Madison Square Garden. Deadheads generally gave high marks to the band's first few concerts. There were some detractors and a few, mainly younger fans, who believed that Brent was irreplaceable. (This was the '90s version of the mid-'70s sentiment "There is no Grateful Dead without Pigpen.") But nearly everyone agreed that when the band—including, for the first time, Bruce Hornsby as second keyboardist—hit the stage at Madison Square Garden on September 15 and opened the concert with an ebullient "Touch of Grey," that the Grateful Dead had turned "it" up a notch.

Sitting animatedly at a concert grand piano directly to Garcia's left, Hornsby instantly became Garcia's main foil. Here was a really top-drawer pianist, with a style as distinctive as Garcia's, ready and eager to jump into the musical fray with ten fingers blazing. He says he knew about a quarter of the Dead's songs when he hooked up with the band, yet he went out onstage the first night with no rehearsal. Like Vince, he used some charts at the beginning. But it was apparent from the first minute that he understood the Dead's music and had internalized their approach to playing. He seemed to be overflowing with confidence yet not at all arrogant. He and Garcia traded grins and musical licks all night. With Bruce occupying an imposing pianistic midrange in the group's sound, Vince was forced into the upper register more often, and to synth sounds that could cut through the band's suddenly dense forest of textures. Bruce was definitely a *star* in the best sense of the word— charismatic and talented. And that took getting used to for some Deadheads who were not accustomed to having such a commanding pianist onstage, taking nearly as many solos as Garcia—at Garcia's urging. Hornsby's presence allowed Garcia to lay back a little—which he undoubtedly appreciated, but which disappointed some fans—but he also pushed Garcia and the other bandmembers musically in ways no keyboardist ever had. In so doing, he fundamentally changed the group's sound.

As the six-show series at the Garden progressed, the concerts got better each night. The jams were longer and more powerful with Bruce thickening the stew, and as the week went on the music became increasingly experimental. Before "drums" the band would split into little subgroupings—"We'd break the group down to Phil and me and Garcia," Hornsby said, "or just Bobby and me and Garcia; different little side trips they weren't doing before." And the last two nights of the run were two of the best Grateful Dead concerts of the modern era—played with breathtaking abandon and conviction, and featuring great musical surprises at every turn. The music was dense but majestic, and unarguably *new*. The last night, when the band played a transcendent "Dark Star" in the post-"drums" segment for the first time ever, and closed the show with "Touch of Grey" followed by a "Lovelight" encore, the Dead hit a musical peak that had every Deadhead in Madison Square Garden believing that the band was beginning a new golden age.

That warm, sunny feeling lasted all the way until . . . the very next Dead show, at the Ice Stadium in Stockholm, Sweden, in mid-October. This was just about as bad as a Dead show could be—low-energy, sloppy and completely lacking in inspiration. Bob Weir later joked that the Dead had been replaced that night by the famous Swedish band "Jetlag." It didn't help that right before the show Garcia had gobbled a potent pot cookie, so by midpoint of the first set he could barely stand up, let alone play well. Hornsby was lucky enough to miss the show because of a prior commitment in America, "but when I got to Europe I heard how awful it was from everybody," he says. "I guess it was almost funny."

The Dead's fall 1990 Europe trek was their first trip across the Atlantic since 1981. The band did have an album to promote—the live double CD *Without a Net*—but they seemed to view the tour more as a paid vacation than an important promotional jaunt. In a sense this trip was a reward for the band's hard work between 1987 and 1989. Spouses, lovers and children were welcome, and the accommodations were deluxe every step of the way. The band traveled mostly by bus, but there was none of the zaniness that had marked their European adventure in 1972. There were more peaceful outings and expensive meals this time around. In Paris, Garcia, Manasha and Keelin, along with helpers Vince and Gloria DiBiase and their son, Chris, went on what Jerry called "the Top 40 Tour," visiting the Louvre, Notre Dame, the carousel at the foot of the Eiffel Tower and other classic tourist destinations.

The tour provided a great excuse for thousands of American Deadheads to travel overseas and experience the shining capitals of Europe (Stockholm! Paris! London! Berlin! Essen?), and to see the band in smaller venues than they usually played in America. It's a good thing those Americans came along, too—the Dead had a minuscule fan base in Europe and couldn't possibly have filled the medium-sized halls that were booked without the traveling Americans. (Were the Dead too "American" for European audiences, or simply absent from the Continent too long?) Smaller versions of the Grateful Dead bazaar sprang up outside each venue, down to the pitiable ticketless hippies with raised index fingers hoping to score "miracle" ducats.

The concerts varied in quality, but none hit the heights the band achieved those last few nights at Madison Square Garden in September. The group worked up two of Bruce's songs—"The Valley Road" and "Stander on the Mountain"—but generally stuck to the tried and true. The last couple of days of the tour, at venerable Wembley Arena in London, Garcia was sick, and he could barely sing at the final concert on November 1. Nevertheless, it was one of the best-played shows of the tour.

Garcia was obviously run-down physically when he returned from the European tour, but just eight days later he went ahead with two weeks of already booked Garcia Band shows in L.A. and the Bay Area. The shows were spirited and well-played for the most part, with Garcia exhibiting surprisingly little wear and tear from the previous months' pressures of finding a replacement for Brent and then touring the East Coast and Europe with the Dead. Perhaps he felt momentarily energized just being away from the Grateful Dead.

That fall Garcia reconnected with David Grisman for the first time in many years. Through the latter part of the '70s and the '80s Grisman had stayed away from Garcia and the Dead, apparently holding a grudge for perceived financial transgressions related to the Old and in the Way album. Grisman had gone on to become the most important mandolinist in modern folk music, an innovator whose distinctive fusion of bluegrass, jazz, old-timey and various ethnic styles influenced an entire generation of pickers. His groups were a training ground for some of the best players in acoustic music, including Darol Anger, Rob Wasserman, Mike Marshall and Tony Rice; sort of the folk equivalent of the Miles Davis or Bill Monroe bands that spawned so many great musicians. After not seeing each other for fifteen years, in early 1990 Garcia and Grisman found themselves working together on a song for an album by Pete Sears called *Watchfire*.

Later, Grisman said, "Jerry came over to my house one day, checked out my home studio and asked me, 'How about putting out some more Old and in the Way tapes?' I said, 'Frankly, Jerry, I'd rather see us put out something new. We can put out the old tapes when we're in wheelchairs.' "

A couple of weeks later Grisman received a call from the Dead office informing him that he was to be the recipient of the Rex Foundation's 1990 Ralph J. Gleason Award, a cash grant given to someone who has made a significant contribution to music. "Later, I found out that Jerry was responsible and I called him to thank him," Grisman remembered. "We made a date to get together at my house, and he showed up with his acoustic guitar. I mean, he just walked right in and said, 'We should make a record and that would give us a reason to play.' I asked him if he was under contract to a record company. Garcia told me, 'I can do anything I want; only the Grateful Dead is under contract.' When I told him about my small record company [Acoustic Disc], he said, 'Great, so we can do it for you.' When I asked, 'When do you want to start?' he said, 'Now!' "

The first day's recordings were just a foundation for a CD that would eventually include Grisman's superb rhythm section—percussionist-fiddler Joe Craven and bassist Jim Kerwin—and cover quite a range of styles: a peppy string band workout on the B. B. King hit "The Thrill Is Gone"; Hoagy Carmichael's sleepy "Rockin' Chair"; Irving Berlin's "Russian Lullaby"; the folk blues "Walkin' Boss"; and "Friend of the Devil," which was one of the two songs from *American Beauty* Grisman had played on back in 1970. A song Garcia and Grisman wrote together called "Grateful Dawg" was a fanciful marriage of their two songwriting styles, filled with the sort of intricate melodic runs that are Grisman's specialty, and the bright, country-influenced chording that marked Garcia tunes like "Bertha" and "Touch of Grey." In an interesting twist, Garcia wrote the "Grisman" part and Grisman the "Garcia" part. But the true centerpiece of the CD—titled *Jerry Garcia–David Grisman* and released in the spring of 1991—was a sixteen-and-a-half-minute multi-part instrumental written by Grisman called "Arabia," which artfully blended Arabic and Spanish themes into a dramatic mood piece.

For Garcia, playing with Grisman became an avenue to explore some of their shared roots, and it also allowed him to venture into new territory, investigating Grisman's longstanding fascination with unison melody lines, for example. Garcia was game for any style that came up, and he always managed to inject his personality into the music through his improvisational soloing.

Garcia, Grisman, Craven and Kerwin first played together live in mid-December at a private Christmas party at Village Music, a Mill Valley (Marin County) record store that specializes in hard-to-find discs and American roots music of every kind. The group's real coming-out, though, was at the Warfield Theater in early February 1991, where in addition to tunes from their forthcoming album, they played such songs as Miles Davis's "So What," the Civil War–era tune "Sweet Sunny South," the Stanley Brothers' arrangement of "I Am a Man of Constant Sorrow," and "Ripple." The group had a warm, gentle camaraderie onstage, and Garcia seemed to be unusually relaxed, perhaps because Grisman was such a commanding instrumentalist that Garcia wasn't in the spotlight every second. In interviews, Garcia freely admitted that his acoustic guitar chops weren't nearly up to the level of Grisman's mandolin playing—not surprising given the fact that Grisman is one of the best mandolinists ever, and Garcia was mainly an electric guitarist. But Grisman inspired Garcia to play cleaner and more fluidly than he had back in 1987 in the Jerry Garcia Acoustic Band (which was Jerry's first serious acoustic outing in many years), and the pair's easy onstage manner made for a friendly and intimate concert experience. The shows took place during the peak of the military buildup for the 1991 Gulf War, when the United States was pouring armaments and soldiers into Saudi Arabia and other Middle Eastern countries. So songs like "Arabia"—which Grisman admitted had been inspired in part by the recent events there—and the sad old war ballad "Two Soldiers" seemed particularly resonant.

It was difficult not to think about the Gulf War, too, when Garcia surprised the crowd at the first Grateful Dead concert of the year, at the Oakland Coliseum Arena in late February 1991, by playing the churning, apocalyptic "New Speedway Boogie" for the first time since 1970. All the doubt and confusion inherent in the lyrics, originally penned in the wake of Altamont, seemed apt for the Persian Gulf crisis, down to the closing lines, which in this new arrangement featured Garcia, Weir and Welnick singing in harmony: "One way or another / One way or another / One way or another, this darkness got to give . . ."

Those three Oakland concerts were all played without Hornsby, who had been nominated that year for a Grammy Award and elected to attend that ceremony rather than appear with the Dead. This was the way it went during the pianist's twenty-month tenure with the group. He was there most of the time, and when he was he gave his all, but he also missed certain series because of his commitment to his solo career. So it was difficult for the band to build the kind of momentum from tour to tour that they were capable of because of the uncertainty in the keyboard slot. The Dead was two different bands—with Bruce, and without Bruce. This made things doubly hard for Vince, because his role in the music was completely different if Bruce was playing, and switching back and forth between roles was difficult. On the spring '91 tour, for example, Bruce played the four-concert series at the Capital Centre in Maryland, then missed the shows at Knickerbocker Arena in Albany and Nassau Coliseum, but returned for the Southern swing, which took the band to Greensboro, Atlanta and Orlando. However, Garcia expressed gratitude that Hornsby played with the Dead at all: "It's a wonderful gift to the band to have him in it now," he said that summer. "It's a lucky break for us."

That spring, partly at Manasha's urging, Jerry reconnected with his ex-wife Sara and his daughter Heather, whom he had seen only once—fleetingly, when he was in the hospital after his coma—during the preceding seventeen years. First, Sara saw him alone.

"Manasha was extraordinarily supportive of my making contact," Sara says. "And Jerry was so grateful that I'd come and he so looked forward to seeing and meeting Heather again.

"He had planned to go see her alone, but he chickened out and called me up saying, 'I can't do it by myself, man. You gotta come with me.' It was terribly moving to see them together after all these years. I took the roses he'd brought her off to the kitchen to put into water, to give them some time together and so I could cry with relief at this momentous occasion. There they were in the other room, finishing each other's sentences—they have this uncanny similarity in certain ways, of interests and a sense of humor and the way they think. It must be genetic. He was so proud that Heather was a musician, and they talked about music together, about how he would take her to the Smithsonian to play those Stradivarius fiddles and about composers they both loved."

Heather is a classical violinist who plays in chamber groups and in the Redwood Symphony on the Peninsula. Later that year, Jerry and the conductor of the Redwood, Eric Kujawsky, hatched a plan for Garcia to commission several short works for guitar and orchestra, which he would perform with the Redwood. With great glee he told Sara, "I let him think I was doing him a favor, but I've always wanted an orchestra!" Heather would be the musical liaison between the composers and the orchestra, and would help her father learn the music. Although Jerry did contact some composers and Davies Symphony

The view from Garcia's amplifiers, Frost Amphitheater, April 30, 1988.
(Jon Sievert)

With
Manasha
Matheson and
daughter
Keelin in
Europe, fall
1990.
(Vince DiBiase)

Pickin' with David Grisman backstage at the Summer Music Festival in Squaw Valley, California, August 25, 1991. *(John Sievert)*

Hangin' at Club Front, 1992. *Left to right:* Vince Welnick, John Cutler, Bill Kreutzmann, Steve Parish, JG. *(Herb Greene)*

ABOVE: Jerry in 1992. *(Jay Blakesberg)*

RIGHT: "This parrot is deceased!" Jerry and Barbara Meier in Lahaina, Maui, January 1993. *(Courtesy of Barbara Meier)*

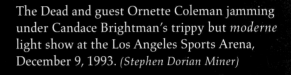

The Dead and guest Ornette Coleman jamming under Candace Brightman's trippy but *moderne* light show at the Los Angeles Sports Arena, December 9, 1993. *(Stephen Dorian Miner)*

RIGHT: Desert Sky
Pavilion in Phoenix,
March 6, 1994. *(Stephen
Dorian Miner)*

BELOW: Cal Expo
Amphitheater, June 10,
1994. *(Stephen Dorian
Miner)*

ABOVE: The JGB at Tosca's café in North Beach during a video shoot for the song "Smoke Gets in Your Eyes" from the film *Smoke*, early 1995. *Left to right:* Melvin Seals, John Kahn, Don Baldwin, *Smoke* actress Ashley Judd, Jackie LaBranch, Gloria Jones, JG. *(Jay Blakesberg)*

BELOW: At the memorial service for Garcia in Golden Gate Park, August 13, 1995. *Front row, left to right:* lyricist John Barlow, Natascha Muenter, Bob Weir, Deborah Koons Garcia. *(Stephen Dorian Miner)*

OVERLEAF: Golden Gate Park, August 13, 1995. *(Stephen Dorian Miner)*

Hall in San Francisco was tentatively booked for the performance, this was one of the great plans that Garcia never managed to complete.

Sara had been totally out of touch with the Dead scene since the early '70s, though she occasionally heard news about Jerry (much of it bad and drug-related). In the intervening years he'd become a wealthy rock star and a cultural icon, which she observed firsthand:

"I remember Leon [Day] driving us in the limo to a restaurant in Berkeley that first day we went to see Heather. Going down Telegraph Avenue we saw all the hippies and the tie-dyes and I said to him, jokingly, 'You know, you're responsible for this!' And he said, 'Yeah, man, I'm *so* sorry!' " she laughs. "And the people on the street were saying 'It's Jerry! It's Jerry!' 'cause he's got the window open for his cigarette. People were handing him gifts— 'Here, man'—and he was embarrassed by it. But he was really gracious. He never hurt people's feelings, even though it must have been incredibly annoying to be so trapped in his celebrity and have no privacy."

In the spring of 1991 a flood of CD releases kept Garcia's visibility high in the press. *Jerry Garcia–David Grisman* was an immediate success. It sold more than 100,000 copies and essentially paid for the operation of Grisman's Acoustic Disc label for the next few years. The duo granted a number of joint interviews to promote the record, mostly in guitar magazines, and in a move that was unusual for acoustic music, they also shot a conceptual video for a song, "The Thrill Is Gone," directed by Bill Kreutzmann's son, Justin. The arty black-and-white film featured the Garcia-Grisman group playing in a '30s nightclub setting, complete with couples decked out in night-on-the-town finery, cigarette girls and dancers. Garcia wore a suit and a fedora for the video, which was shot at the On Broadway club in San Francisco's North Beach. "Jerry's quote to me was, 'I'd never do this for the Grateful Dead, never in a million years,' " Justin said with a laugh. "We cut his hair, put him in a suit and tie, and had him there for twelve hours. There were Deadheads lined up outside trying to get autographs. It was a real scene."

Around the same time that album came out, the Garcia-Grisman group, augmented by keyboardist–harmonica player Howard Levy of banjoist Bela Fleck's band, went into Club Front to provide some improvised musical accompaniment for a CD by '50s "word jazz" pioneer Ken Nordine called *Devout Catalyst*. It had been many years since the deep-voiced Nordine had made an album of his hip, strange, funny and scary poems, stories and observations; for decades he had made his living primarily as a voice-over announcer. But through David Gans, Nordine did some work on the Dead's 1990 New Year's Eve broadcast, and Dan Healy was so excited about meeting this hero of his youth that he offered to record a new word jazz album with him. Garcia, too, had been a huge Nordine fan back in the '50s and offered his services.

"You've got to go back to seventeen-year-old me growing up in the Bay

Area when I first heard Ken's records—*Word Jazz* and *Son of Word Jazz*," Garcia recalled. "For me, listening to those records was like a religious experience. It was not only a completely different way of thinking, but a fantastic combination of words and music that wasn't songs. It wasn't poetry and it wasn't songs exactly and it was wonderfully peculiar. It was like the kinds of things you think that only you think about, maybe. That was from a time in my life that I was reading Kerouac and I first started smoking pot somewhere in there; a lot of things that were formative and significant and helped build my own sense of aesthetics come from right there.

"I had no idea what had happened to Ken Nordine in that intervening thirty years or so, but I was really delighted to find out he would have anything to do with us, much less come here and work with us. So for me, that was more than an honor."

In May Arista Records put out a two-CD live set called simply *Jerry Garcia Band*, culled from six performances at the Warfield Theater in 1990. The two discs, expertly recorded by John Cutler, captured the full range of the JGB's repertoire of covers—gospel songs, Dylan and Beatles tunes; a dash of Motown; one song each by the Band and Los Lobos; and the group's lone extended jamming number, "Don't Let Go," which Roy Hamilton originated in the '50s. Like a real JGB show, the CD was ballad-heavy, but the rocking tunes—"Deal," "Evangeline" and "Tangled Up in Blue"—showed the spark the band was capable of. The album was an excellent showcase for Garcia's unadulterated guitar sound at a time when so much of his Grateful Dead work was being colored by MIDI timbres. Though any number of the JGB's tunes could've benefited from a Garcia "horn" part, he chose to leave his playing essentially effect-free in that setting.

Since the introduction of compact discs in the early '80s, Deadheads had been pressing the Grateful Dead to put out CDs from the band's archive of thousands of live tapes. Everyone in the group agreed it was probably a good idea. But no one in the band was interested enough to actually go into the Dead's tape vault and wade through God knows how many shows to choose some for release. In his later days Garcia almost never listened to old tapes. He said he didn't want to look back; that he found it "embarrassing" to hear his playing from the late '60s: "I hear what I meant, as opposed to what I played." So he put no energy into the idea. After years of disinterest and inaction, Dan Healy finally sifted through some of the Dead's live multitrack tape masters and, in consultation with Phil Lesh, chose the Dead's 1975 appearance at the Great American Music Hall for a CD, entitled *One from the Vault*, that was released in the spring of '91. That show featured some of the first performances of material from *Blues for Allah*, as well as sparkling versions of jamming favorites like "Eyes of the World" and "The Other One." Released through the Dead's own merchandising company, the album sold more than 150,000 copies, making it a highly profitable venture. By the end of 1998 the band had put out more than a dozen other vintage CDs, most of them chosen by the band's vaultkeeper/archivist Dick Latvala with little input from members of the group. In 1994 Phil said, "I'm really glad there's a demand for it because that's our old-age insurance in a way." Once Garcia died, the pace of releases quickened.

Despite this flurry of exciting CDs, Garcia's upbeat pronouncements in the music press and the optimism rippling through the Dead scene because of the high quality of Dead and JGB shows, by the spring of 1991 Garcia was privately beginning to express some dissatisfaction with the Grateful Dead status quo. Since his death-defying recovery in 1986 he'd been working at a dizzying pace, with scarcely any letup, even after Brent's death. The number of gigs the band played didn't change much from year to year (about seventy-five), but the sheer size of the Grateful Dead touring machine seemed to grow each season. By the early '90s the Dead were one of the top-grossing bands in the world, bringing in tens of millions of dollars just in tour revenue, and more on top of that in merchandise and record sales. Salaries and overhead rose every year, along with employee lifestyles. The only way to support the dozens of people directly or tangentially connected to the Dead was to play more large gigs, and Garcia made no secret of his unhappiness with that state of affairs.

"We discussed that a lot and I wish everyone had heeded his warnings," Manasha says. "But he went along with the organization's agenda. People's survival was tied up in his level of output."

Did he feel burdened by that? "Yes," she says. "I don't think he expressed it to that many people, but he expressed it to me. He definitely loved the Grateful Dead, but it was very tiring for him. He was hoping to do something small with his own band for a while. He also loved that band and that collection of people and for some reason that wasn't tiring to him."

"He wanted to take a break; it was very clear," said another Dead family member who asked not to be identified. "There were some very forceful statements made in board meetings that I heard. There was one meeting where they were talking about the stadium tour of '91 and he stopped everybody and said, 'Am I the only one who thinks that stadium shows suck? I don't ever want to play in another stadium. Does anybody else feel the way I feel?' And nobody said anything. But they were trapped: big overhead, big family, dates are reserved. Who's gonna say, 'Yeah, you're right. Let's cancel the stadium tour'?"

The 1991 summer tour turned out to be one of the Dead's best in the post-Brent era, with one adventurously played show after another. Hornsby was a provocative musical prankster the entire tour, dropping musical quotes from "Dark Star" into the middle of all sorts of Dead tunes and engaging Garcia at every opportunity. There were jams at Giants Stadium, Soldier Field in Chicago and Sandstone Amphitheater in Kansas that ranked with the best moments of the first Madison Square Garden series with Bruce. And in general the band was taking chances—placing songs in unusual spots (for instance, opening a first set with "Eyes of the World," opening a second set with "Jack Straw") and steering the jams into some different directions. Later that summer, three songs from one of the Giants Stadium shows were shown on the late-night ABC-TV music series *In Concert*, so a huge national audience got to see the new Grateful Dead in full swing; quite an impressive sight.

But there was a big problem with that tour. Garcia was strung out on heroin again. There are a number of different views about the nature and degree of Garcia's drug use in the late '80s and early '90s. A few suggest that from the middle of 1987 on, Garcia dabbled with Persian on and off, mostly during tours, taking just enough to relax him a little and maybe escape some of the pressures associated with being an integral part of the accelerating Dead machine and his own manic schedule. Others, some of whom spent long stretches alone with him, swear that Garcia wasn't using at all in the late '80s. Some people observed Jerry's penchant for falling asleep at odd times and wondered if he was nodding out from drugs. But he'd had bizarre sleep habits for years, and all through 1987–90 he was usually so lucid, funny and engaging that his behavior didn't fit his mid-'80s profile as an occasionally surly, antisocial drug abuser. Whether he did or didn't take hard drugs during those years, Garcia was extremely productive and played some of the best music of his life.

Mountain Girl says, "I only learned fairly recently that during that period Jerry was taking all these pills for his teeth. After he recuperated and got back out on the road and they did 'Touch of Grey' and all that, he started to experience quite a lot of dental problems and he went in and got some implants. I think it was excruciatingly painful, so he would get these mega-prescriptions for painkillers from his dentist. So he was taking those. I couldn't figure it out. He kept falling asleep, yet I could never find his stash [of heroin] and he always denied that he was taking anything.

"Then, when he would go out on the road, someone would ring up a dentist or oral surgeon and get this pain prescription for Jerry. So I guess they had multiple dentists that they went to. So basically he went legal with his drug use, but I think ultimately it was at a pretty bad price, because he was kind of dopey some of the time. That's a word you don't hear much anymore for someone who's just a little bit off their game and not quite all there."

"When I got in the band," Vince Welnick says, "nobody in the band came out and said it, but I was under the impression that the whole band was clean, and they knew I was clean—I don't count herb as a drug—and I assumed no one was on drugs. I just thought Jerry was fragile, healthwise. He could really hold up his end when he was up onstage, and he could run through a hotel lobby faster than anybody. I'd heard stories about his health problems and the heroin thing, but I thought it was pretty much behind everybody. Particularly after the way Brent died, I'm sure the last thing they wanted was to have another drug scene."

This much seems to be clear, however: sometime after Brent's death Garcia secretly started using Persian again with increasing regularity, and by the summer '91 tour it was a matter of considerable concern within the band. His playing might still have been crisp and inventive for the most part, but he began to revert to his old junkie posture onstage—not moving as much, smiling less and not interacting with the other bandmembers to the same degree.

Offstage, various members of the band and the Dead organization approached Garcia about getting treatment after the tour, but Garcia reacted angrily to what he believed was an unfair intrusion into his personal life. He also was mortified that if he sought treatment Manasha would learn that he had been lying to her about his drug use. Nevertheless, once the tour was over, Garcia enrolled in an outpatient methadone program in San Francisco. Seven days a week for three weeks, either Jerry's regular driver, Leon Day, or Vince DiBiase, who became Garcia's personal manager around this time, picked up Garcia at his house at 8 A.M. and drove him in his BMW to the edge of the gritty Tenderloin district to get methadone. According to his doctor at that time, Randy Baker, Jerry also underwent some counseling "to explore the psychological aspects of drug addiction."

Embittered by the latest intervention attempt, Garcia reportedly lashed out at his fellow bandmembers at a meeting sometime after the summer tour, essentially saying that playing with the Dead wasn't fun for him anymore.

Asked in September 1991 about the meeting by James Henke of *Rolling Stone*, Garcia explained, "We've been running on inertia for quite a long time. I mean, insofar as we have a huge overhead, and we have a lot of people that we're responsible for, who work for us and so forth, we're reluctant to do anything to disturb that. We don't want to take people's livelihoods away. But it's *us* out there, you know. And in order to keep doing it, it has to be fun. And in order for it to be fun, it has to keep changing. And that's nothing new. But it is a setback when you've been going in a certain direction and, all of a sudden—*boom!*—a key guy disappears.

"Brent dying was a serious setback—and not just in the sense of losing a friend and all that. But now we've got a whole new band, which we haven't exploited and we haven't adjusted to yet. The music is going to have to take some turns. And we're going to have to construct new enthusiasm for ourselves because we're getting a little burned out. We're a little crisp around the edges. So we have to figure out how we are going to make this fun for ourselves. That's our challenge for the moment, and to me the answer is this: Let's write a whole bunch of new stuff, and let's thin out the stuff we've been doing. We need a little bit of time to fall back and collect ourselves and rehearse with the new band and come up with some new material that has this band in mind.

"We're actually aiming for six months off the road. I think that would be helpful. I don't know when that will happen, but the point is that we're all talking about it. So something's going to happen. We're going to get down and do some serious writing, some serious rehearsing or something. We all know that we pretty much don't want to trash the Grateful Dead. But we also know we need to make some changes."

Garcia's playing on first part of the Dead's September Northeast tour was much more erratic than it had been during the summer, an indication to those close to him that the methadone regimen didn't stick. Bruce Hornsby notes, "Truthfully, I didn't really notice Jerry having problems until the fall of '91. Or maybe I noticed it, but it didn't start pissing me off until the fall."

He continues, "I remember we played nine nights at Madison Square Garden and I thought except for a couple of really great nights, to me it was really a dogshit run. Garcia was in this place I couldn't understand. He was starting to get to that place a lot the last two or three years when I'd watch them—he'd put his head straight down and look at the floor the whole time; hunch over and not communicate with anyone. And that wasn't like him, at least as far as I was concerned. We'd always had a lot of eye contact and inter-play, really a lot of good feelings onstage. But it wasn't just that. He sort of wasn't listening and starting to run roughshod over people's solos—certainly mine—and I thought at times the music just seemed strangely lifeless. I asked Bobby about it and he explained it to me. I'd heard about it, but had never experienced it firsthand. There were nights when I wanted to push the eject button. What I would have done in my band is try to play in a different way that maybe would have jacked everybody up, tried to take a little more charge of the thing. But in this band I didn't feel it was my place. So I was caught. I felt, 'Damn, this music is not happening; the music is not going anywhere.'

"Then we got to Boston Garden and I was pretty bummed. We played this first set and it wasn't happening again, so I just said, 'Oh fuck it!' and I started playing this stuff that was very unmusical. I was playing hard and pounding and basically driving it up their ass. And sure enough, the gig got jacked up. There was a lot of energy in the set and it was a pretty good set. But I thought I was playing like crap. I was playing a way I didn't want to play.

"At the end of the set I went into Garcia's tent and he says, 'Man, I love the way you're playing tonight!' And I said, 'Garcia, I'm playing bullshit tonight. I'm playing crap, but it's all I can do because there's nothin' happening here and I really resent your coming to this gig and not putting anything into it,' or words to that effect. And he said, 'Well, man, you don't understand twenty-five years of burnout!' I said, 'Garcia, I may not understand twenty-five years of burnout, but you know what my schedule is like . . .' because in that time period I was doing stuff with my own band, playing on records all over the place—Bob Dylan, Bonnie Raitt, Bob Seger, Robbie Robertson—working on Ron Howard's movie, basically getting a lot of nice calls. The year

1990 I spent 18 days at home—I was gone 347 days of the year. The next year I spent 30 days at home, 335 days on the road. I said, 'You know, there are lots of nights I don't feel like playing because I've been playing for the last 28, but I feel it's my responsibility to get it up.' So we had it out about this. We had a good discussion, and from then on, man, the shit was happening! To me it was a great run, and I'm not trying to say that this is the reason; I'm saying that was my experience."

Indeed, the September 1991 six-show series at the Boston Garden is widely considered one of the latter-day Dead's best runs; some even consider it the group's last unarguably great run. On the sixth night, the band opened the second set with "Dark Star," segued smoothly into Weir's "Saint of Circumstance" ("This must be heaven, tonight I crossed the line . . .") and then settled into the fat groove of "Eyes of the World" before "drums." Out of "space" the group rolled into "The Other One," which went back into "Dark Star," then fell into "Attics of My Life," followed by "Good Lovin.' " The double encore paired "Brokedown Palace" with the Dead's final version of "We Bid You Goodnight." Garcia, Hornsby, *everyone* played their hearts out, and by the time the band left town the Deadhead grapevine was buzzing with excitement again.

On the night of October 25, a month after the tour was over, and just two days before the Dead were to begin a four-concert stand at the Oakland Coliseum, Bill Graham was killed in a helicopter crash, along with his girlfriend, Melissa Gold, and his pilot, Steve "Killer" Kahn. Graham was flying from a gig at the Concord Pavilion in the East Bay back to Marin County in a driving rainstorm when the helicopter struck some power lines and plummeted to earth, instantly killing all three occupants.

For a moment there was some question about whether the Dead would proceed with their scheduled shows, which were being produced by Graham's company. But carry on they did, and the next four nights became the Dead's memorial to their longtime friend. An hour before the first concert, Garcia, Weir, Hart, Wavy Gravy and Graham's grown son, David, staged a news conference for local television and newspaper reporters to fondly reminisce about the promoter.

"He's a large part of us," Garcia said. "And on a lot of different levels. We're carrying along some piece of him into the world and the future as we go along. So there's a certain part of his energy that's a part of us; it's integral. And we're pretty determined to hang in there and cover for him.

"The thing about Bill is his relationship to us is on a lot of levels like our relationship to each other. It was intimate. There's a certain kind of friendship that you have when there's somebody who understands you, and Bill was there from day one just about. We miss the personal thing—the guy who understands us. That's what hurts."

Onstage that night, the Dead opened with one of Graham's favorite songs,

"Sugar Magnolia," and during the middle of the second set the band was joined by two other members of the first generation of San Francisco rock bands, Carlos Santana and Quicksilver guitarist Gary Duncan. Garcia sang and played brilliantly all evening, and the encore, "Knockin' on Heaven's Door," couldn't have been more poignant.

At the final show of the series, Ken Kesey, dressed in a somber black suit, strode onto the stage in the middle of "Dark Star" and in a booming, urgent voice began talking about Graham, about his own son Jed, who had died in an accident in the mid-'80s, and about how the Dead's music "reaches across the distance" to talk about heavy life-and-death issues. The music behind Kesey was driving and dissonant, with Lesh thundering above Garcia's and Weir's sonic squall. Kesey closed by reciting—actually, *roaring*—poet e. e. cummings's "Buffalo Bill," which concludes with the chilling question: "how do you like your blue-eyed boy now, mr. death?" Then he left the stage as the band reached a noisy crescendo that seemed to express the *rage* so many felt about Graham's senseless death.

A few days later the Dead took part in the city's official memorial observance for Graham—a star-studded Sunday afternoon free concert in sun-kissed Golden Gate Park that drew 300,000 people; ironically, the biggest crowd ever for a BGP production in Northern California.

Two days after the Graham memorial, Garcia went back out on the road for a two-and-a-half-week East and Midwest arena tour with the Jerry Garcia Band. This did not sit well with some people in the Dead organization, given Garcia's public statements about wanting to take a break from touring. Garcia clearly felt the same sense of obligation to support the livelihoods of the people connected to that group as he did to the Dead. But at the same time he never viewed playing with the JGB as "work," exactly.

"I think our band was a refuge for him," John Kahn said. "The Grateful Dead was so big and took so much of his energy, I think he enjoyed having a place where maybe not so much was demanded of him and he could relax a little but still play music he loved. I think he was a little disillusioned with how big the Dead became, but it's hard to turn that kind of situation around. I mean, how do you become less popular?"

"The problem with the Garcia Band is that's where his [drug] connection was," Tiff Garcia says. "It wasn't with the Grateful Dead—they were pretty clean. John Kahn was the problem. Compare John Kahn and, say, John Cutler [who, in addition to recording the Dead's albums, was the JGB's live sound engineer]. It's black and white. Cutler would do everything he could to keep Jerry away from drugs. Kahn, on the other hand, made sure Jerry would be provided with, so *he* could be provided with, because he's the one who had the problem. Jerry definitely liked John a lot, no question, but Jerry was also the type who would feel sorry for somebody and take them under his wing.

Everyone needs at least one person in their life that they think needs them, and John was that person for Jerry; he fit in that."

Actually, Garcia didn't have any problem contacting drug connections on the road with the Dead, either. Dealers always managed to find their way to him, even if it meant going to the luxury hotels where the band stayed in the '90s, or sending drugs to him through overnight package couriers.

If Garcia was either tired or strung out on that fall JGB tour, he didn't show it—the band sounded as fresh and vital as they had on their last national outing in 1989. This was at least partly due to a much-needed infusion of new material during 1991: uptempo numbers like Solomon Burke's "Everybody Needs Somebody to Love," Van Morrison's "Bright Side of the Road" and Norton Buffalo's charming "Ain't No Bread in the Breadbox." Plus he added Eric Clapton's mellow "Lay Down Sally," Hoagy Carmichael's "Lazy Bones," "What a Wonderful World," a tune popularized by Louis Armstrong that Garcia sang as his encore most nights on the tour, and the consistent showstopper— the Manhattans' "Shining Star," a sappy but heartfelt ballad that let Jerry play the soul crooner to the hilt, even with his scratchy voice.

In early December the Garcia-Grisman group got together to do some recording and to play three shows at the Warfield Theater, and Garcia seemed happy and relaxed throughout the run. That group's repertoire had expanded since their last gigs, too: new songs included the traditional folk tunes "Shady Grove" (popularized by Doc Watson), "Louis Collins" (Mississippi John Hurt) and "The Wind and Rain" (from Jody Stecher, recorded and performed previously by the Jerry Garcia Acoustic Band); Jimmy Cliff's "Sitting in Limbo"; and the seasonally appropriate "God Rest Ye Merry Gentlemen," played as a jazzy instrumental with a long jam in the middle.

The Grateful Dead ended the year with four shows between Christmas and New Year's, sans Bruce Hornsby. And though the band played reasonably well, the New Year's Eve concert felt strange without Bill Graham presiding over the reverie (and making a spectacular midnight entrance dressed as Father Time as he had in years past). For several years, members of the Dead had been saying they were tired of playing New Year's Eve; that they wished they could have a normal holiday season like most people. But Graham always managed to persuade the group to play the year-end shows. It was his favorite tradition. New Year's 1991–92 showed how important Graham was to the spectacle. His death loomed large over the show, and to no one's surprise, the Dead never played on New Year's again.

It doesn't appear that the Dead ever seriously considered taking the six-month sabbatical Garcia had alluded to in *Rolling Stone.* By the time January 1992 rolled around, the band's touring schedule for the year was largely plotted and it looked an awful lot like the previous year (and the one before that), right down to the summer stadium shows in New Jersey, D.C. and Chicago.

Did something specific happen to change Garcia's mind? Or had his frustrated outbursts the previous summer just receded over time? Garcia had talked about wanting to work up some new songs as a precondition to carrying on with the Dead, and in February, when the Dead (again, without Bruce) reconvened for the first time since New Year's, he got his wish. The band learned four new songs: "Corrina," written by Hart, Hunter and Weir; Hunter and Lesh's "Wave to the Wind"; Vince's maiden songwriting effort for the Dead, "Way to Go Home," with lyrics by Hunter; and Hunter and Garcia's "So Many Roads."

"So Many Roads" sounded as if it had been penned by (or for) some weary troubadour in the autumn of his life. It was essentially an electrified folk song—an appropriate description given Hunter's lyrics, which refer to various old folk blues: "Call me a whinin' boy if you will" (as in Blind Lemon Jefferson's "Whinin' Boy Blues"); "Thought I heard that K.C. whistle moanin' sweet and low" (after "K.C. Moan" by the Memphis Jug Band). One verse works neatly as autobiography for either Hunter or Garcia:

> Thought I heard a jug band playing
> "If you don't—who else will?"
> From over on the far side of the hill
> All I know the sun don't shine,
> The rain refuse to fall
> And you don't seem to hear me when I call

Garcia ended the song with a big vocal buildup similar to ones he'd written for "Believe It or Not" and "Standing on the Moon," and it never failed to ignite the crowd. It would start with him quietly singing "So many roads to ease my soul," and then the music would swell and Garcia would play with different phrasings of the line, à la Van Morrison. For the first year after he introduced "So Many Roads," Garcia often had trouble remembering the words, mitigating some the song's power, but during the last two years of his life it was one of his most consistently powerful tunes, and obviously one that spoke to him personally.

The Dead's 1992 spring tour turned out to be Bruce Hornsby's last with the group. At the end of January his wife gave birth to twin boys and he wanted to spend as much time as he could with them. And, truth be told, he was somewhat discouraged by Garcia's ongoing drug problems and by what he saw as a disturbing complacency and stasis within the band. Bruce hadn't been in California when the band learned the new songs, and he seemed to have some difficulty finding a place for himself in the arrangements. These tunes sounded tentative for most of the spring tour, and the shows were only intermittently brilliant.

"That spring tour was not great," Bruce says, "but beyond that I got the sense that Vince was starting to feel more comfortable and I heard from the guys that there were a few shows there that I didn't make that were great nights. So I thought, 'Okay, I just had twin boys. I don't want to be an absentee father. And I do want to return the focus to my own stuff. Something needs to change here.' I think they had gotten to a point where they felt comfortable with Vince, and he was comfortable and really contributing well. So I thought it was time for me to go.

"About the last week of the tour, I said something about leaving to Cameron, maybe Mickey and a couple of guys, and it was a drag because I wanted to tell Garcia myself, but this news spread quickly through the tour ranks. And I remember sitting at my piano during a soundcheck and Garcia yelling from his tent, 'Bruce! come over here, man!' So I went in there and he was very jovial and he basically just said, 'Hey, I hear you're takin' off! It's been great. Good luck.' He was very gracious about it and so was everyone else. These people are great people.

"And I told them then that I'd still play with them from time to time when it worked out, and I did. I played with them at RFK on the very next tour and it was great—they even played 'Casey Jones' for the first time in a while [since 1984]; I loved it!"

Hornsby's high opinion of Garcia's guitar playing never wavered, and today he remembers his former bandmate as "one of the most distinctive and original players ever. To me, what he did as a soloist that was really unique in rock was his use of chromaticism. He used the five notes in the chromatic scale that aren't in the standard scale more often and more creatively, and he made more sense with them, than just about anyone. Some of it probably came from his interest in jazz, I guess, and in atonalism. Wherever it came from, he had a clearer vision of playing chromatically than any guitarist in the rock world that I know. Even on a simple song like 'Iko' he would play some shit that was like, 'Man, I wish I thought that way!'

"To me, though, one of the best parts about his playing was his sound; purely his tone," Hornsby continues. "He could play just one note and the sound moved me so much. There was a very emotional, soulful quality to his tone that to me is very important when you talk about Garcia as a musician. It was very expressive. Great phrasing and articulation. It was nothing contrived. It was a very natural-sounding electric guitar."

By the middle of 1992 Garcia was receiving almost as much attention in the mainstream press for his artwork as his guitar playing. Galleries around the country (and one in Japan) were exhibiting his paintings, drawings and lithographs, and in the cities where Garcia would show up for an opening, there was always copious press coverage. He now had two people representing his artwork to galleries and the public—Nora Sage, who handled the art

Jerry made through the middle of 1991, and Vince DiBiase, who was his rep from 1991 to 1995. Sales of Garcia's art were brisk, and a book devoted entirely to his work, entitled *J. Garcia: Paintings, Drawings and Sketches*, was a popular item among Deadheads in the fall of 1992. The book collected seventy-two different works, from intricate color airbrush paintings to graceful watercolors obviously inspired by Japanese art to simple pen-and-ink doodles, some whimsical, some serious.

Garcia seemed bemused and slightly embarrassed by all the attention his art received. As he noted, "I never saved them. It's only in the last five years that somebody said, 'People might like these things.' I thought, 'Gee, you think so?' It never occurred to me. I've never done them for any purpose. I only do them because they sort of spill out of me. I never intended for people to see them."

"He was very shy about showing the work at the beginning," says Roberta Weir (no relation to Bob), an art dealer who put on several shows of Garcia's artwork. Though Weir believes that more thought could have been put into deciding which of Jerry's pieces were good enough to exhibit, she notes, "I think he was an incredibly brilliant and talented man who, had he pursued art more deeply, would have developed a very strong personal style. My hope was that he would do that and cross over from being just a celebrity artist to being taken seriously as an artist, because he certainly had the potential for that."

Weir says she saw a connection between the way Garcia approached music and the way he executed some of his ink drawings: "Many of the drawings show that same mental state of improvisation that you find in the music. It's like, 'I'm just wandering with my pen line; I wonder where it will go.' Looking at them that way, they're not necessarily logical. Sometimes you can even turn the paper upside down and find another picture. So there's that kind of wandering, serendipitous experience of the music in the drawings."

In the summer of 1992 Garcia's artwork entered a strange new dimension when Stonehenge Ltd. introduced a line of twenty-eight-dollar silk neckties with colorful pattern designs extracted from Jerry's paintings and drawings. TIE-DYE GURU TURNS NECKTIE DESIGNER, shouted one newspaper headline reporting on this highly unlikely turn of events. After all, except in the Garcia-Grisman video, when had Garcia ever been seen wearing a tie? Garcia and the Grateful Dead represented a culture that was vehemently anti-tie. When he was first approached by Stonehenge in 1991, Garcia was adamantly opposed to the idea, but as was often the case with him, eventually he was convinced that the tie business would be handled tastefully and he relented. However, he refused to get involved in the promotion of the ties, and Nora Sage, who was his liaison with Stonehenge, said at the time, "We did ask him about wearing one for an ad, but he said, 'It's bad enough you want me to design them, now you want me to wear them?' " (Later, Garcia did reluctantly pose in his ties—

he looked good, too.) Until his dying day, however, "Jerry hated being referred to as a tie designer," Roberta Weir says. "That used to really upset him."

Incongruous or not, the tie line was an instant success—more than 150,000 were sold in the first few months after the ties appeared in Bloomingdale's and other upscale stores. The main buyers were white-collar Deadheads who, far from feeling that Garcia had sold out his hippie values, enjoyed the ties for their subversive nature: if you had to wear a tie in your job, you could at least wear one designed by someone far removed from Fortune 500 culture. Aside from appearing in corporate boardrooms, law offices and wherever cravats were required, J. Garcia ties started turning up on all sorts of prominent people, including basketball analyst Bill Walton, Chicago Bulls coach Phil Jackson, Al Franken (who wore one during his coverage of the 1992 Democratic Convention) and even Vice President Al Gore, who was photographed wearing one in a *New York Times Magazine* article. (Gore, his wife, Tipper, and one of their daughters attended the Dead's June '92 show at RFK Stadium, a mere eighteen days before he was selected to be Bill Clinton's running mate. In a newspaper story around this time, Tipper noted that she'd recently purchased *Europe '72* on CD and that she and Al were longtime fans of the group.)

The Dead's summer '92 tour was considerably stronger than their spring tour, in part because they played their new songs with more confidence, but also because Vince was able to assert himself more now that he was the sole keyboardist. He abandoned a few of his tackier synth textures in favor of more piano sounds, and he was also responsible for the season's most interesting new cover tunes: the Who's "Baba O'Riley," which he shouted with appropriate Roger Daltreyesque gusto, and the Beatles' "Tomorrow Never Knows," the trippy classic from *Revolver*. That pairing of tunes, played as the encore, was a huge hit at several of the summer stadium shows. Spicing up a few of the Dead's second sets, too, was Steve Miller, whose band opened all of the stadium shows. Miller jammed with the Dead at seven different concerts, tearing confidently through versions of "The Other One," "All Along the Watchtower," "Not Fade Away" and other rockers, and also providing silky contrapuntal lines to more delicate tunes such as "Morning Dew" and "Standing on the Moon." And at Soldier Field in Chicago, Miller invited blues harmonica great James Cotton to jam with him and the Dead on outstanding versions of "Good Morning Little Schoolgirl," "Love Light" and "Gloria."

Outwardly, Garcia seemed to enjoy himself for the most part on the summer tour, but unbeknownst to him or anyone else, his body was beginning to rebel against him again. By the time the tour was over he appeared tired and pale. But rather than taking the rest of the summer off to relax and recharge, three weeks later he went on a six-show California amphitheater tour with the Jerry Garcia Band. Fans at the first couple of shows noticed that Garcia didn't look good and that his energy seemed to come and go at random during the concerts. People who were concerned about Garcia's drug use would always be doubly worried when he would go out on the road with the JGB because of his history with John Kahn, and on this tour the rumors flew more than usual.

On Garcia's fiftieth birthday, which he celebrated with a show at Orange County's Irvine Meadows, he admitted to Manasha and others that he was feeling strange, almost as if he'd been dosed with LSD. He still managed to finish the tour with a reasonably strong performance at Southwestern College, outside of San Diego, but something was clearly wrong with him physically.

As soon as Jerry and Manasha got back to the Bay Area they moved into a spacious house in rural Nicasio, in western Marin County. This was easily the most luxurious home Garcia had ever lived in. The 7,500-square-foot pink stucco Spanish-style house was situated on a ten-and-a-half-acre plot overlooking miles of beautiful rolling hills dotted with live oaks and other trees. It was accessible only by driving up a long, twisting, single-lane private road through dense forest, yet it was still only about twenty minutes from the Dead's San Rafael headquarters. Vince DiBiase says, "It had a black-bottom pool with a circular hot tub built into it, and a fiber-optic colorwheel that changed colors around the perimeter. Jerry loved swimming in that pool. In the living room there was a ten-foot TV screen that automatically lowered down from the ceiling when the TV projection system was turned on. It was like being in your own private movie theater. Jerry also had art, music and computer studios at the Nicasio house."

Within twenty-four hours of moving into this palatial showplace, Garcia became extremely ill, exhibiting many of the same signs that he had before his diabetic coma in 1986. Garcia was later diagnosed as having an enlarged heart and chronic lung disease, and his other vital organs weren't functioning very well, either: he had little energy, in part because his system was overloaded with toxins again.

"He nearly died," Manasha says. "I had to do some quick thinking, because he didn't want to go to the hospital because his last experience there was so unpleasant for him. He was pleading for me not to call the ambulance. So I called Yen-wei Choong, the acupuncturist, and it was almost miraculous what happened—Yen-wei gave him some Chinese remedies in tea, which Jerry drank through a straw, and gave him an acupuncture treatment. And then I called the doctor, Randy Baker, down [in Santa Cruz] and he came up for a few days. He set up a vitamin drip IV and we also brought in some other doctors—Dr. McDougal for diet, Jonathan Shore for homeopathy. And I tried to keep them all coordinated. It was quite a scene!"

"He had massage therapists, personal trainers and, a little later, hypnotists to help him stop smoking," says Vince DiBiase, who, with his wife, Gloria, moved into the Nicasio house for six weeks to aid in Garcia's recovery. "During this time he was happy, looking good and feeling good, and his attitude was optimistic."

Adds Gloria DiBiase, "Manasha worked hard to coordinate this health program and to keep Jerry on it. He was taking Chinese and American herbs and vitamins and eating organically grown foods. They were buying lots of top-quality stuff from the health food stores." All in all it was quite a change for such a notoriously sedentary consumer of junk food.

This was also a particularly good time for Jerry's relationship with Keelin, who was nearly five. "I have memories of them at the Nicasio house with her on his lap at the computer and they'd be drawing something on the computer together," Vince DiBiase recalls. "Or they'd be outside watching the sunset together; or feeding the goats that roamed the property. It was just a wonderful time."

"Keelin loved dressing up in my belly-dancing scarves, veils and finger cymbals," says Gloria, who had studied belly dancing for nineteen years. "One time Keelin danced while Jerry played guitar and I sang."

The Dead canceled their late-summer and early-autumn shows, and the JGB scrapped an unannounced tour planned for November, so Garcia could take more time to get himself healthy. And he did precisely that, losing sixty pounds in five months. By the time he returned to performing, at a JGB show on Halloween 1992 at the Oakland Coliseum (with Vince Welnick's deliciously trashy but short-lived psychedelic cover band, the Affordables, opening), almost everyone agreed that Garcia looked the best he had since the late '70s. Once again, the change was plainly visible in his body language. He stood more erect, rocked on his Reeboks instead of standing stock-still, and with his new, thinner frame he could bend over easily to adjust his sea of guitar effects pedals—something he did not do when he was heavy and out of shape.

Comeback II continued in early December, when the Grateful Dead went back on the road for a short tour that took them to Colorado and Arizona for two shows each, and then returned to the Oakland Coliseum for five mid-month shows in place of the group's usual year-end stand. There were two new additions to the repertoire: the Beatles' "Rain," sung and played virtually note for note, down to the song's famous backwards vocal line, which Weir, as the designated dyslexic in the Dead, handled nicely; and "Here Comes Sunshine," which returned to the band's rotation for the first time since 1974, though in considerably different form. The impetus for the new version had come from Vince's arrangment of the tune for the Affordables, which opened nearly a cappella, eliminated the lilting singsong guitar riff and sped the song up to a chugging midtempo rhythm. "It's better than our old arrangement," Garcia enthused. "The original feel of it was a little bit dated. I prefer the stronger, rock 'n' roll feel of the new arrangement." Most veteran Deadheads disagreed, preferring the spacier, more open-ended mid-'70s arrangement, but nearly everyone was happy to hear the song in any form again. It was a bright, optimistic number that in many ways symbolized Garcia's latest re-naissance. The energetic and well-played Oakland concerts had Deadheads buzzing once more about the "new" Garcia.

Offstage, however, Garcia's personal life was in turmoil. Though he appeared to be healthier than ever, Manasha learned that he had started to dabble with hard drugs again, and she made no secret of her disappointment:

"In December we went to Colorado, and by that time I knew the symptoms of the substance problem," she says. "He'd get sleepy and perspire a lot. He'd have disappearances into the bathroom. So I noticed these things were happening again and it worried me a lot because we'd almost lost him the prior summer. So Yen-wei came to Denver and Randy came to Denver. I was concerned; it was a big issue with me. I asked Jerry about it and he didn't care to be confronted about it, and I understand that, but I was worried. And I think that sort of led to our separation. I was concerned and there was nothing I could really do. So I told him we were going to leave and he asked me not to go. But it continued and I said, 'Listen, you're going to have to make a decision about what you want to do. We have a five-year-old. . . .' "

What Manasha did not know was that Jerry had fallen in love again with Barbara Meier, his girlfriend from back when he was just nineteen and living in Menlo Park. (He had had other girlfriends during his time with Manasha, too, including one out-in-the-open relationship with a Deadhead that lasted several months.) After nearly three decades apart, Barbara and Jerry reconnected in 1989, after Robert Hunter gave Garcia a book of poetry Barbara had written entitled *The Life You Ordered Has Arrived*. According to Barbara, Jerry wrote her a letter saying how much he loved the book and that all these years later, he still loved her. By this time, she was a poet, painter and occasional program coordinator at the Naropa Institute, the Boulder, Colorado, school founded by the Buddhist teacher Chogyam Trungpa Rinpoche. When the Dead came to Denver toward the end of 1990, Barbara and Jerry nearly got together backstage, but at the last moment Garcia backed out of the meeting—she says he later told her it was because he was strung out at the time.

Then, a year later, when Barbara was in the Bay Area to do some poetry readings, the two did meet backstage at Shoreline Amphitheater for the first time in twenty-eight years, and as she said to Robert Greenfield, "My heart chakra exploded. Aside from the fact that he was in a different body with white hair and white beard, nothing had changed at all. He was sitting there and he was very nervous and smoking, but we entered a timeless space and we were right where we left off." In Denver at the end of the June 1991 tour they got together again under the pretense of Barbara interviewing Jerry for the Buddhist magazine *Tricycle*, and then, "I started creating every opportunity I could to go to the Bay Area, where we'd go out to lunch or just hang," she said.

When the Dead came to Denver in December 1992, Garcia promised Barbara that he would figure out a way to extricate himself from his situation with Manasha, so he and Barbara could have a relationship again. He said he didn't want to drop this bombshell on an unsuspecting Manasha before Christmas, so he waited until a couple of days before New Year's—and then had someone else give Manasha the news. In what even the most charitable Garcia apologists would have to admit was an act of extreme cruelty and cowardice, he left his Nicasio home one afternoon and simply never went back. Instead, he hooked up with Barbara at Hunter's house and the two lovebirds flew to Hawaii for nearly a month, leaving poor Vince DiBiase to deliver a breakup note to Manasha. Garcia never saw Manasha or Keelin again.

If guilt was eating away at Garcia in Hawaii he didn't show it. He and Barbara had a blissful time on Maui and the Big Island, taking long beach walks, diving and spending endless carefree hours reconnecting with each other, trying to understand the twists and turns their lives had taken in the intervening decades. They shopped at a health food store to find the proper nonfat foods for Jerry's strict diet (fortunately, Barbara was already a vegetarian), and after a few days they met some hippies who regularly brought them meals. For the last two weeks the couple was joined by Robert and Maureen Hunter. It was a happy and creative time for Garcia and Hunter, who worked on several new songs while they were in the Islands.

"That whole month we were in Hawaii was so unbelievable," Barbara says. "It really did feel like we had created a time warp and we were right back where we left off. He called it 'psychic fascia' that we had that between us. And that really was true, and continued to be true. We were able to have this great month together, and he even asked me to marry him."

A day before Jerry and Barbara returned to the Bay Area, Gloria DiBiase found the couple a furnished condominium rental on Red Hill Circle in Tiburon, with a spectacular view of the harbor there, and for a couple of months things went along smoothly. Garcia spoke effusively to anyone who would listen about how he'd finally found true love and how his life was heading in the right direction.

People throughout the Dead family remarked that they hadn't seen Garcia this happy in years, and because of this Barbara was welcomed warmly wherever she traveled in Grateful Dead circles. This had not been the case with Manasha, who was never really embraced by some members of the inner circle and largely stayed apart from the Dead family by choice. Barbara even befriended Mountain Girl, Sara, and Jerry's daughters.

Annabelle Garcia remembers, "He introduced me to Barbara and told me they were engaged to be married and he was happier than I'd ever seen him. *Ever.* It made me so happy. It seemed like perfection. I'd never seen him glow like that. He was jumping around introducing her to everybody. I was all for it."

"Everyone around Jerry at that time kept saying that it felt so good," Barbara says. "It really felt like a rebirth of those early Menlo Park days, that same energy. It was there. It was happening. I thought, 'M.G. loves me, Sara loves me, the girls love me; we can all work together. There's all this love around, and Jerry's writing songs again with Hunter and it's all coming together.' Everyone was saying it. Even he was saying it: This is going to be the golden age of the Grateful Dead. We're really going to sail off to the sunset now, and everything's going to be healed and resolved, and we're going to do all these great things—we're all going to rent a live-aboard dive boat. It really felt like the community was coming together in a way that it had not for many, many years."

"Every once in a while, if you're lucky, you get to have the feeling that you've been given another chance and it's like you get a clean slate," Garcia said in early 1993. "That's the way it feels to me now with Barbara."

CHAPTER 22
A Broken Angel
Sings from a Guitar

he hopeful mood in the Dead scene spilled over to the band's first two concert series of 1993 at the Oakland Coliseum. At the Chinese New Year shows at the end of January, Carlos Santana sat in with the band one night. And during the final night of the February Mardi Gras series, Ornette Coleman, whose band opened the Fat Tuesday concert, played screeching, mind-bending sax on "space" and "The Other One," then added tasteful lines to "Stella Blue," "Lovelight" and "Brokedown Palace." Earlier, Garcia had played on the final number of Ornette's set. The real news from the February shows, though, was the introduction of several new songs, including three by Hunter and Garcia.

"Lazy River Road" was one of the warmest love songs the pair ever wrote, a nifty fingerpicking tune that sounded like a cross between an Elizabeth Cotten or Mississippi John Hurt folk blues and an early pop-jazz tune such as "Russian Lullaby." No doubt it was influenced musically by Garcia's acoustic guitar outings with David Grisman during this period; it was certainly of that genre. It was the only song from the Hunter-Garcia Hawaii writing sessions to be completed, and anyone who was aware of the relationship between Garcia and Barbara Meier couldn't help but be struck by the sentiment of the lyric:

> *Thread the needle right through the eye*
> *The thread that runs so true*
> *All the others I let pass by*
> *I only wanted you*
> *Never cared much for careless love*
> *But how your bright eyes glowed*
> *Way down, down along*
> *Lazy River Road*

The second new Hunter-Garcia song was a musical rewrite of an existing Hunter lyric—"Liberty" had been the title track of Hunter's 1988 solo album, which Garcia played on. Garcia junked Hunter's "Scarlet Begonias"–like melody and reset the words in an arrangement reminiscent of the Dead's version of "Samson and Delilah." The lyrics were like an anthem for libertine misfits; perfect for Garcia, who loved to think of himself as an incorrigible and untamable noncomformist rebel, which he certainly was to a degree.

> *Say what I mean and I don't give a damn*
> *I do believe and I am who I am*
> *Hey now, mama, come and take my hand*
> *Whole lot of shakin' all over this land*
> *If I was an eagle, I'd dress like duck*
> *Crawl like a lizard and honk like a truck*
> *If I get a notion I'll climb this tree*
> *Or chop it down and you can't stop me*

Then Vince and Bob would join in for the sing-along chorus:

> *Ooo freedom, Ooo liberty*
> *Oh, leave me alone*
> *To find my own way home*
> *To find my own way home*

Whereas the mood of both of those songs was light and uplifting, the haunting ballad "Days Between" had a reflective, almost melancholy tone. This turned out to be the last song Hunter and Garcia wrote together, and it was one of their most powerful efforts. "I wrote a verse while Jerry was working out something on piano," Hunter recalled of the song's genesis. "I gave it to him, he said he liked the rhyme scheme and idea, and began working out the melody. As he was doing that I wrote the rest of the verses. An hour's work."

Enigmatic and highly evocative, "Days Between" is painted in an emotional chiaroscuro, at once fond and foreboding, filled with promise and dread. In one verse, "Summer flies and August dies / The world grows dark and mean." But in another "a hopeful candle flickers / in the land of lullabies." One part of the final verse has "Hearts of summer held in trust / still tender young and green," then immediately offsets that with "left on shelves collecting dust / not knowing what they mean."

" 'Days Between' joined the Grateful Dead oeuvre right at the time—1993—when old-time Deadheads were asking themselves if Garcia and Hunter were still capable of creating art that had a primordial, frightening intensity: the beauty at the edge of terror that Rilke described," comments Steve Silberman. "As the other songs written roughly in the same period seemed to mine well-worn images and attitudes—almost reveling in their seasoned facility to create an archetypal mood, like 'Lazy River Road'—'Days Between' slipped between your clothes and your skin like a chill wind out of a grave. I think it's the most uncompromisingly adult lyric Hunter ever wrote.

"The verses present a panorama or mandala of existence in which each thing is in its place, but no place is completely safe. It's a world where both the sighs of young passion in springtime and the lonely horseman, leaving only his torn song in the world as he vanishes—as the singer himself was about to vanish—coexist and inform each other, together creating a universe of joy and horror side by side. 'Days Between' was the final battlefield where the Dead dared to face the elementary questions of existence, and refused to flinch. It has the same fated, tragic majesty that bears witness to the life force in all truly great art."

Hunter offered this tantalizing glimpse of what inspired the song in a "letter" to Garcia, written on the first anniversary of the guitarist's death and posted on the Internet:

"Obviously, faith in the underlying vision which spawned the Grateful Dead might be hard to muster for those who weren't part of the all-night rap sessions circa 1960–61—sessions that picked up the next morning at Kepler's Bookstore, then headed over to the Stanford Cellar or St. Mike's to continue over coffee and guitars. There were no hippies in those days and the Beats had bellied up. There was only us versus '50s consciousness. There were no jobs to be had if we wanted them. Just folk music and tremendous dreams. Yeah, we dreamed our way here. I trust it. So did you. Not so long ago we wrote a song about all that, and you sang it like a prayer. 'The Days Between.' Last song we ever wrote."

There were days
There were days
And there were days I know
When all we ever wanted
Was to learn and love and grow
Once we grew into our shoes
We told them where to go
Walked halfway 'round the world
On promise of the glow
Stood upon the mountaintop
Walked barefoot in the snow
Gave the best we had to give
How much we'll never know
Never know

The song did not have a conventional pop structure. There was no chorus, no bridge; just four long verses that started with spare and simple accompaniment and then built in intensity as the instruments played increasingly grand ornamental fills. Vince Welnick described it nicely: "It would go from this poignant but intense space to this big, majestic thing that would just *pour out.*

That song and 'So Many Roads' really meant a lot to Jerry; you could tell." In its early versions, the song had no solo break between the verses, but it had a moody and unusual open-ended instrumental coda that wasn't tied to the melody of the song, but rather spilled off in other more musically abstract directions.

Garcia's relationship with Barbara Meier, so filled with hope and promise in early 1993, fell apart during the beginning of the Dead's spring tour that year. Barbara had observed that Jerry had periodically gone through moods when he seemed dark and distant, and at the Dead's first tour stop in Chicago he seemed "cold and withdrawn," she said. According to her account of the breakup, Barbara learned that Jerry was using heroin again and confronted him about it, stressing that she would stick with him through thick and thin. But Garcia reacted angrily, and out of the blue asked her to leave. Before the tour, at the urging of a hypnotherapist who was trying to help him quit smoking, Jerry had admitted to Barbara that he was having "thoughts" about his old flame from the '70s, Deborah Koons, whom he had encountered outside a health food store in Mill Valley a few weeks earlier and secretly contacted afterward. At that time he had insisted he wanted to be with Barbara, but now, out on the road, he acknowledged that he was in love with Deborah. "I cannot tell you how weird, brutal and shocking it was to hear all this," Barbara says. Nevertheless, she and Jerry spent the next day and night together, and they parted sadly but without rancor. After that, Barbara never saw him again.

She left hurt, confused and disappointed that heroin exerted such a strong pull on him and transformed him from an open, loving person to a brooding, emotionally closed loner. Did Barbara understand what Garcia got out of heroin? "Absolutely—oblivion," she says. "He had let things slide so terribly for so long that to do the kind of fine-tooth combing one needs to do to set things straight—make amends, tie up loose ends, complete things, have closure, just tidy up your psychic emotional life—was too daunting for him."

She was disillusioned to learn that the Dead's touring retinue seemed to accept Garcia's addiction as a fact of life. "I can remember raving to Steve Parish that I couldn't believe how enabling and co-dependent the whole scene was with Jerry," she says. "And Steve said, 'Listen, man, you know we're just going, and we gotta go forward. This is moving down the road and we've gotta move it down the road, okay? And we're gonna just do it the way we gotta do it.' It just felt like there was this machine—the gears were in gear—and there was no way to stop it."

In fairness to Parish, it should be noted that Barbara was probably unaware of how many times over the years he and everyone else on the road crew had tried to help Garcia take steps to conquer his addiction. There was no lack of compassion there; more a resignation born of futility. As Bob Bralove put it, "I think the reality is, there is only so much you can do. If you respect all these freedoms, you can state your concern. But you can't lock somebody up because they're doing something bad to themselves. You can't make somebody stop those bad behaviors. You can take them aside and tell them you're concerned, but beyond that, what can you do? I know some of that went on with Jerry. Should it have gone on more? I don't know. How many interventions are you doing to do? If you've put yourself out several times over thirty years and you get slapped down each time, and it doesn't seem to do anything, and then you stop doing it, is that noninterventionist?"

By the end of the spring tour Jerry had brought Deborah out on the road to be with him, and their relationship continued to deepen back in Marin County after the tour was over. The news that Garcia had broken up with Barbara and was back with Deborah spread quickly through the Dead organization and was, frankly, greeted with disapproval and disappointment in some quarters. There were a number of people in the organization who simply never liked Deborah—some even referred to her as Black Deborah because of her penchant for wearing black and what they perceived as a malevolent streak in her. Others who did not know her at all in the '70s had heard negative stories—some perhaps true, some undoubtedly groundless—that had become part of the Grateful Dead oral mythology. This was always an extremely gossipy scene in which people who fell out of favor for whatever reason were branded as pariahs and privately scorned. Deborah, who had spent much of her time since the late '70s establishing her own documentary film company, Signs of Life Films, reentered the Dead world with two strikes against her in many people's minds: She was viewed as the woman who had broken up Jerry and M.G.'s supposedly idyllic (but actually very complex and troubled) relationship in the early '70s—a gross oversimplification at best—and now Deborah had come between Garcia and the widely liked Barbara Meier, the golden girl who was going to once and for all bring Jerry the personal happiness he'd been seeking his whole life. But the fact is that heroin was starting to come between the two of them before Deborah did, and on some level Jerry resented the idea that he would have to "change" for anyone.

Deborah had her share of supporters, too, mostly among people who had known her in the '70s. "I think it was as much destiny as anything else that brought them back together," says Richard Loren, "and you know what—I don't think the circle was complete with them when they broke up. Sometimes in your life something gets interrupted and it's left a semicircle, and I think with them it was a case where it wasn't finished."

Emily Craig, who maintained a close relationship with Deborah through the years, says, "I think that in the '70s and again in the '90s Deborah had a lot to do with with Jerry getting in touch with his authentic self. I know she was a good influence on him. Because he was so happy with her he didn't need everybody else as much, and that made her a threat in some people's eyes."

"Deborah is a really special person," comments Thayer Craw, who had been in or on the periphery of the Dead family since 1969. "I've never seen Jerry happier than he was with Deborah, either go-around. I'm not really clear what happened the first time when she was no longer around. It was too bad because they seemed to have something really special then. In my opinion she couldn't have been a better match for him; they really set each other off well. You could tell he was head over heels in love with her."

Despite the turmoil in his personal life, Garcia played well on the spring tour. His new songs garnered mainly favorable reviews from Deadheads, particularly "Days Between," which had such a different feel from Garcia's other heavy second-set ballads; it truly felt new. On that tour Garcia introduced two new cover songs, which he slotted as encores. The Beatles' 1967 psychedelic classic "Lucy in the Sky with Diamonds" immediately became a sing-along favorite among Deadheads. But the Bobby Fuller Four's oft-covered "I Fought the Law" was derided by some fans for its brevity. It contained no solo and usually clocked in at under three minutes, making it the shortest song in the Dead's live repertoire.

An offstage highlight of the spring tour for Garcia was his visit to the White House during the Dead's series at the Capitol Centre. Garcia, M.G., Phil and Jill Lesh, Mickey and his wife, Caryl, and a few others were even escorted into the Oval Office (alas, the president was elsewhere). Then they had a private meeting with Vice President Gore, followed by more than an hour chatting with the veep's wife, Tipper. "They were both really, really nice," M.G. reports. That members of the Grateful Dead—*the* acid band, fathers of the counterculture—would be invited to the White House with nary a ripple of protest after the fact showed how much respect the band commanded by the mid-'90s. Jack Ford, the son of President Gerald Ford, had been a Dead fan, but it was unimaginable in the late '70s that the group would be allowed anywhere near the White House. Garcia liked Gore because the vice president was a strong environmentalist, but in keeping with Jerry's lifelong distrust of government and those who seek power, he didn't vote in the 1992 election. The Dead were approached about playing at one of the Clinton-Gore inaugural balls in January '93, but the band politely declined. Bob Weir and Rob Wasserman did play at an event called the Reunion on the Mall, and Garcia noted with a laugh, "If Clinton doesn't fuck up too bad in the next four years, maybe we can go back and play his second inauguration!"

Two weeks after the end of spring tour, Garcia took part in another uniquely American ritual. He, Weir and Welnick sang an a cappella version of "The Star-Spangled Banner" at Candlestick Park in San Francisco to celebrate the opening of the San Francisco Giants' 1993 baseball season. It's difficult to estimate how many Deadheads attended the game mostly to see Jerry, Bob and Vince, but the singers received a loud and long ovation for their efforts. Though Garcia was understandably a little nervous before he went out to sing, he seemed to thoroughly enjoy the Opening Day spectacle, and he was thrilled to meet the man who served as their "opening act" at the stadium— Tony Bennett, who crooned "I Left My Heart in San Francisco" to the adoring throng. The sight of members of the Grateful Dead singing the national anthem was incongruous enough that the event received coverage from media all over the country.

In July 1993 Jerry, Deborah and a couple of friends vacationed in Ireland, which Jerry had been keen on visiting for many years, as he had strong roots there on his mother's side. By all accounts he fell in love with the land and its people, and it was refreshing for him to be able to travel unmolested—very few people recognized him, and the few who did didn't bother him. Garcia relished these moments when he could be like everyone else; they brought home just how weird his day-to-day life was under the microscope in America. To her credit, Deborah always tried to get Jerry away from the pressures and celebrity of his Grateful Dead life. Whenever he did make the time for real rest and relaxation, whether it was in Hawaii or on other travels, he thrived, but finding those windows of opportunity for vacations was difficult because he allowed himself to be pulled in so many different directions by his myriad musical loyalties.

By the summer of 1993 the Dead had more than enough unrecorded original songs to fill a CD, but the group didn't seem to be in any rush to make an album, even though it had been nearly four years since *Built to Last* had come out. Garcia's excuse was that he wanted to have even more material for the group to choose from. "I'd like to spit out another five or six tunes this year, and hopefully it'll happen," he said in the summer of '93. "Really, it's pretty easy: all Hunter and I have to do is get together. I find it hard to write without being in his presence, but when we're together, it starts snapping. But it's also the hardest thing to do, because writing music is probably my least favorite thing in the world. I mean, I'd rather throw cards in a hat. Anything is more interesting than the idea of writing." (This was a theme Garcia returned to often in his later interviews: "Writing is one of those things . . . I'd rather fill in all the 'O's in the phone book," he said with a laugh to one writer. He told another he'd rather feed the cat than work on a new song; quite a change from the Garcia who could barely keep up with the new songs that spilled out of him in the early and mid-'70s.)

With the Dead album still on the back burner, Garcia continued to record sporadically with David Grisman at the mandolinist's casual home studio. Initially it appeared that the follow-up to their successful first album might be another eclectic mélange, but then Grisman zeroed in on a completely different approach: "Me and David are working on a children's album right now," Garcia said that summer. "It's something I never would have thought to do."

The material they ultimately chose for the CD *Not for Kids Only* was a far cry from what was on most of the kid-oriented albums coming out at that time. Many of the tunes were old folk songs that had been rediscovered and recorded by the New Lost City Ramblers in the late '50s and early '60s; others, such as Elizabeth Cotten's "Freight Train" and the folk standard "Shenandoah," were well-worn numbers plucked from the folk music ether. There was a splendid version of "Teddy Bears' Picnic" and the infinitely weird "A Horse Named Bill." On the duo's first album, Garcia had handled nearly all the vocals, but on *Not for Kids Only* Grisman harmonized with Garcia on most tracks. And on a few—such as "Jenny Jenkins," "There Ain't No Bugs on Me," "Hot Corn, Cold Corn"—the two dexterously engaged in some nifty wordplay that practically begged to be sung along to.

In interviews promoting the album, Garcia said he thought it was important to make a children's album with some edge to it. He believed too many kids' records and videos had been "made to be as inoffensive as they could possibly be. . . . Kids like weird shit in there. They like crazy stuff lurking around, things with teeth, crazy people. They're realistic. They know the world is full of weird stuff and kids sort of prefer weird stuff; they rejoice in it. It's no big thing, but it's nice to be able to throw some music back in there that's originally from that world; bring some of the weirdness back, take a chance a little. I mean, it's sort of trusting the kids, that they can handle something more than terminal niceness," he added, laughing.

After Garcia and Grisman had recorded enough tunes for the album, Jerry went on the road with the Dead for a couple of tours, so Grisman finished up the record without him, bringing in all sorts of other players to complete the arrangements. Their version of "Teddy Bears' Picnic," for instance, was fleshed out with another guitar, bass and a Dixieland-style trumpet-trombone-clarinet trio. A few songs featured sawing fiddles; others had twanging jew's harps. The lovely, intentionally soporific "Shenandoah Lullaby" (got to get those kiddies to sleep) was augmented by piano, oboe and a small string section that included Garcia's daughter Heather. And Grisman added all sorts of sound effects that perked up this music for wee ones—buzzing flies and mosquitoes, birds, even the chugging locomotive for "Freight Train" (courtesy of Joe Craven's percussion and mouth).

It was all a very low-key affair that was meant mainly for a young audience and their parents; it certainly wasn't designed to show off Garcia's and Grisman's instrumental prowess. When it was released in September 1993, it received overwhelmingly favorable reviews—including ones in such unlikely sources as *Parenting* and *Family Life* magazines—and it sold very well. It's also worth noting that the cover illustration by Garcia, which depicts him and Grisman picking and singing for an audience of eight distracted rug rats, is Jerry's only published self-portrait. A limited edition of five hundred lithographs of the cover illustration was sold through the album to raise money for the Carousel Fund and the Nordhoff Robbins Music Therapy Clinic.

It was an up-and-down summer and fall for the Grateful Dead. On the plus side, crowds on the summer tour were large but well-behaved. At first, many Deadheads wondered if having Sting, the jazzy popster with new wave roots, as the opener for the stadium shows would be an odd match, but it proved to be a good fit. As always, Sting had a great, tight band that could also jam, and he mixed up his set lists from show to show so the touring Deadheads wouldn't be bored with the same set all the time. Garcia, who dubbed Sting "an A-list guy," jammed with Sting's group at a few stops on the tour, and sounded surprisingly at home on Sting tunes like "Tea in the Sahara," "Walking on the Moon" and "Consider Me Gone."

Bruce Hornsby brought his accordion down to the Dead's two dates at RFK Stadium in Washington, D.C., and Garcia obviously enjoyed having his old mate beside him again. At Autzen Stadium in Eugene, Oregon, Huey Lewis blew harp on a few tunes one day, raising the energy level of the set a couple of notches. On the September East Coast tour, Edie Brickell turned up onstage at Madison Square Garden one night during "space" for some some vocal improv noodling. And at the last Garden show, the progressive young jazz sax player David Murray added some wonderfully inventive squeaks, squalls and bleats to "Bird Song," "Estimated Prophet," "Dark Star," "Wharf Rat" and a few other tunes. (Later that autumn Murray also played an entire show at the Garden with the Garcia Band.)

But there were also stretches of Grateful Dead music in the fall that sounded listless and uninspired, and in the crowd there was considerable antipathy for some of the band's new material, particularly Phil's "Wave to the Wind," Vince's "Way to Go Home" (which was the most-played Dead song that year) and Weir's cumbersome "Easy Answers." Garcia's singing and playing was fitfully uneven. He had been historically guilty of lyric lapses, but these increased on the fall tour to the point where he rarely made it through a song without a flub. Instrumental errors by him became more common as well, leading many in the crowd to suspect that he had fallen back into some of his bad habits. Reports of Garcia's sloppy performances also followed him on the JGB's three-week tour of East Coast arenas that November.

Nevertheless, friends said he seemed to be happy at year's end. The Dead's shows in Los Angeles and San Diego in early December had many good moments, with Deadheads especially buzzing about appearances by Ornette Coleman and Branford Marsalis on consecutive nights at the L.A. Sports Arena.

The end of 1993 might have been an ideal time for the Dead to take the break from performing they'd talked about a year earlier, but it was impossible to slow down the momentum of the organization. Arenas and stadiums had to be reserved nearly a year in advance, and anyway there didn't seem to be much support within the Dead to take a break. Garcia was notorious for being out of touch with his own health needs, and he also now had a new set of financial realities that no doubt played into his own desire to keep working. He was paying nearly $21,000 a month to M.G. as part of their divorce settlement; he'd agreed to give $3,000 a month to Barbara Meier for three years; plus he was responsible for child support for Keelin and a huge mortgage for Manasha and Keelin's new house in northern San Rafael.

In January 1994 the Grateful Dead were inducted into the Rock 'n' Roll Hall of Fame. This was actually their second year of eligibility for the honor, which is bestowed annually by a panel of rock critics and music biz veterans, but incredibly enough, they were beaten out the first time by the likes of the short-lived (but highly influential) band Cream, Frankie Lyman and the Teenagers and Creedence Clearwater Revival. The Dead had long been ignored by the country's hip critics, who believed the group was a quaint and irrelevant anachronism playing for an army of drugged-out zombies, so the slight was not surprising; just myopic. All of the bandmembers except Garcia attended the black-tie induction ceremony at New York's Waldorf-Astoria Hotel ballroom. At an accompanying press conference, Garcia was represented by a life-sized cardboard-cutout photograph. The media were told that Garcia didn't attend because he had a cold. He may well have been under the weather, but it was also common knowledge in the Dead scene weeks before the awards that Garcia was planning to skip the event. Generally speaking, Garcia disliked awards and was embarrassed by such public recognition.

Healthy or not, this was a good period for Garcia's relationship with Deborah Koons. They went diving in Hawaii and Deborah occasionally accompanied Jerry on tour (though he always insisted on having his own room to retreat to). Sometimes when she would be on the side of the stage during Dead shows, Jerry would play to her and smile, and more than a few Deadheads observed them cuddling and smooching behind the band's equipment between sets. They undoubtedly had chemistry.

Even so, many people in the Dead family were surprised when Jerry and Deborah decided to get married on Valentine's Day in 1994. The twice-married Garcia had told each of his two previous girlfriends—Manasha and Barbara—that he wanted to marry them, so he was definitely the marrying kind, so to speak. But Jerry and Deborah had only been a couple for a year at that point, and he wasn't in very good health in early 1994. Some members of the crew and in the Dead office expressed considerable concern about him, and the Deadhead rumor mill was filled with supposedly reliable reports that Garcia's opiate use was on the rise. (For her part, Deborah claimed to have no knowledge of Garcia's drug use until much later.)

The site of the wedding was kept secret until the morning of the event. Then, the invited elite—about seventy family, bandmates, crew and office folks, and a few of Deborah's friends from Ohio and the East Coast—called a number and were instructed to convene at Christ Episcopal Church in Sausalito, a cozy, beautiful, brown-shingle redwood church high in the hills above San Francisco Bay. The Reverend Matthew Fox, a former Catholic priest who had become well-known in New Age circles, presided over the ceremony. David Grisman and his guitarist bandmate Enrique Coria played "Ave Maria," and JGB singer Gloria Jones sang Stevie Wonder's "You and I" for the couple.

Garcia wore a dark suit but no tie; Deborah was dressed in a traditional, flowing wedding gown. A friend of Deborah's named Jamie O'Meara told the *Cincinnati Post* that Jerry "took one look at [Deborah] walking down the aisle and he couldn't keep his hands off her all during the ceremony. It was cute."

For the reception at the casually tony Corinthian Yacht Club in upscale Tiburon, "We popped in our limos they had rented for everyone, and had a dinner of ten vegetarian dishes," O'Meara said. "I'd never seen so much champagne in my life. There was no wild partying. Deborah rarely touches alcohol and I didn't see [Jerry] drinking." Jerry, Deborah and the other happy revelers danced the night away to an Irish band, and the festivities went on until about 11 P.M.

"It was a thrill to see them so happy and dancing at the wedding," Thayer Craw says. "They were doing all the traditional stuff; it could have been any couple in the world. Jerry was way into it—you could tell it wasn't just Deborah putting on the kind of wedding she wanted. He was a full participant. It couldn't have been sweeter."

There was no time for an extended honeymoon—Grateful Dead shows at the Oakland Coliseum the last week of February had been booked for some time; then, as always, the Dead's schedule was paramount. After the wedding, Jerry and Deborah continued to maintain separate residences, she in Mill Valley, he on Red Hill Circle in Tiburon. A few months later Garcia moved to more spacious digs just up the hill from Red Hill Circle, on Audrey Court. This rented contemporary house had an even more spectacular view of Richardson Bay, San Francisco Bay, San Francisco, the Golden Gate Bridge and Mount Tamalpais. The mother of actor Paul Newman was one of his neighbors in the decidedly upscale but unpretentious neighborhood.

When he was home alone, Jerry's house was like a multisensory playground for him. "The TVs were on in his house almost all the time," says Vince DiBiase, his personal assistant and art liaison during this period. "At Audrey Court he had a TV in his living room, his bedroom, his exercise room, in the den and in the little bedroom—five televisions, and a lot of times all five of them would be going and on different channels. He had two satellite dishes. I think he had every English-speaking channel in the world." Vince says that Jerry was particularly fond of watching movies from the '30s, '40s and '50s.

"He was more in 'the now' than anyone I've ever met in my life," Vince notes. "He was always creating. He couldn't turn it off. He always had half a dozen sketch pads around, a number of books he was reading—a couple of mystery thrillers, the *Oxford English Dictionary*, health books, esoteric books, music books—as well as magazines and newspapers. He'd have his main computer on in one room and he'd be working on something in there. He'd have his laptop on his bed and he'd be working on something else in there. He had a couple of guitars and a banjo lying next to the bed he might pick up. He had a synthesizer in another room with other guitars, plus another dozen guitars lying around."

"He would take catnaps throughout the day and night," adds Gloria DiBiase, who took care of the household. "He snored like a bear, and if he stopped breathing [from the sleep apnea] I would wake him up."

"In my opinion he was overworked," Vince says. "Too much traveling, too many tours. And the art business was picking up, with more demands for Jerry to show up for openings and do art interviews. Then, when he was home, everybody wanted him for something—play on their album, do this, do that. People were always groping at him to work on their projects and he couldn't say no. Some of them were musicians he'd known for twenty or thirty years, and how do you say no to those guys, especially when he *wanted* to play with them?"

On the Dead's tour of the Midwest and East in March and early April 1994, Garcia was once again highly erratic—muffing lyrics, missing cues and, most disturbing, seemingly unable to execute certain musical passages that required a high degree of fingering dexterity. On fast runs he sometimes resorted to a sort of guitar shorthand in which he'd simply play fewer notes than he usually did in that situation, or else he'd play chords instead of clusters of individual notes. Even when he could get his fingers to play complicated parts—such as on "Slipknot" or the speedy instrumental interludes in "Samson and Delilah"—he occasionally lagged a split second behind the rest of the band, so everything would either be slightly out of sync, or the other players would have to slow down to play at his pace. But Garcia's malaise was completely unpredictable. He might play brilliantly on one song and then seem inept and even disoriented on the next. By and large, he was best on his ballads—there were versions of "Stella Blue" and "Days Between" on the spring tour that were overflowing with emotional singing and sensitive playing. And at many shows the rest of the group played well enough that Garcia's deficiencies were not apparent to the casual observer.

Most of the grousing among Deadheads came from hard-core fans who followed part or all of the tour and could see the disturbing pattern in Garcia's performances. Not surprisingly, most of the critical Deadheads were concerned that Garcia's lapses were a result of his drug use. It appears more likely, however, that there were physical reasons for his slide. For several years he had been afflicted with carpal tunnel syndrome in his left hand and forearm which had caused him to periodically lose feeling in the tips of his fingers. This is actually fairly common among musicians, and Vince, Bob and Mickey also complained of the problem. Garcia's condition was exacerbated by the heaviness of his guitar, which pulled down on his left shoulder, and by the hand position he had developed for his left-hand fingering through the years.

While Garcia said in a 1993 interview that he felt his problem was in check, by the following year it had started to bother him again, and the numbness had even traveled up the underside of his arm to just below the elbow.

"Having something like the carpal tunnel is not something one is pleased to announce," says Bob Bralove, "so I would think it was probably even worse than he indicated. It must have been scary for him. It would scare me." According to Steve Parish, by the middle of 1994 the problem was serious enough that he and Garcia were looking into getting Jerry a more ergonomic guitar. Garcia also saw a hand specialist, who recommended certain exercises.

"Jerry told me he was losing the feeling in his hands," Vince Welnick says. "I think some of it was carpal tunnel, but he also had diabetes on top of that, and it's a very common side effect of diabetes to lose the feeling in your extremities."

Garcia did nothing to curtail his busy schedule after the spring of 1994. In the second half of April he played a series of shows with the Jerry Garcia Band at the Warfield Theater, and in mid-May the Garcia Band went out on another Western tour, playing five shows in large amphitheaters in Southern California, and one in Phoenix. Actually, he only played half a show in Phoenix. Garcia was so sick when he went onstage at the Desert Sky Pavilion there that he only made it through five songs in the first set before he took a break and collapsed backstage. The rest of the show was canceled, and though some of those close to Jerry urged him to go the hospital because he looked so bad, he refused and instead flew back to the Bay Area that night.

"It was pretty awful," John Kahn remembered. "He was sick and weird and he was playing bad, and if there's anything he hated it was that. He knew he was in terrible shape, but he would never ditch a gig in a million years. I finally went and asked him if he wanted me to set it up so he could split, and he said, 'Yeah.' And it was to save him from having to play bad; that was part of it. I was worried about him. I knew there was something wrong with him. I don't know exactly what it was, but it wasn't a drug thing.

"I caught crap from everyone. The band hated me for losing the money. The Grateful Dead hated me; I should think they would have liked that we canceled the show for his health. But I can see why they wouldn't like it, because they should have done that a lot of times in the past. He played [Dead] gigs where he had to piss in a garbage can on the side of the stage, he was so sick. But they'd never cancel a gig for him."

There was considerable antipathy between some people in the Dead organization and John Kahn because they believed Garcia's drug intake increased whenever he gigged with the JGB. Vince Welnick is unusually blunt on the subject: "I swear to God, if it would've been up to me, John Kahn would've been out of the picture a long time ago. I don't know if that would've saved Jerry. A lot of people say that Jerry would've done what he did with anybody he could've done it with, but there was something about Kahn I felt was bad news. More than a couple of times I thought of dealing with John on my own; I'm going to leave it at that."

A more sympathetic view is expressed by Annabelle Garcia: "Yeah, Dad did drugs with John and Linda [Kahn], but that was just the way it was. They offered my dad a safe haven—a place he could come to get some drugs if he wanted it, and a place to sleep if he needed it, and the company that he needed. Dad was one of those classic lonely folks who had a lot to talk about and talked a lot, but he didn't have that many super-close friends when it came to really talking about his feelings. And I think that John and Linda offered him a place to really let out his feelings. And even though drugs were involved, I can't really condemn that, because drugs were *always* involved. In my mind, I can't separate the old man from that, 'cause it's one and the same. It's just the way he was, for almost as long as I can remember. John and Linda were very sweet people and I know at least they made my dad feel comfortable."

Once Garcia was back home from Phoenix, his doctor, Randy Baker, determined that Jerry was was suffering from a recurrence of the diabetes that had nearly killed him eight years earlier. Garcia bowed out of a scheduled trip to Ireland with Deborah (who went anyway), and Vince and Gloria DiBiase moved into Garcia's house for about a month in an attempt to help restore the guitarist's health. Dr. Baker devised a health regimen that included certain medications and herbs, and he suggested various diet and lifestyle changes, which Jerry paid lip service to but largely ignored.

The Dead's summer touring schedule began in early June, when Garcia was clearly in no condition to be onstage. Before the first concert at Cal Expo in Sacramento, one member of the sound crew wondered aloud whether the summer tour would finally be the one on which Garcia would keel over onstage. Another complained that the band was running on inertia and that the only reason they were out on the road was to make money. Many Deadheads were alarmed at Garcia's ghostly pallor and slumping posture at Cal Expo. His playing rarely rose above the ordinary, and at times it was simply awful. True, there were some hot musical moments in Sacramento and at most of the dates on the summer tour, which took them to amphitheaters and stadiums in the East and Midwest. But Garcia was obviously struggling to keep up with the other members of the band, and at points he seemed either bored or spaced out (or both), unable to muster enough will or energy to bring many of his songs fully to life. Again, he seemed most comfortable and engaged on his ballads— perhaps because they were his most personal songs, with their intimations of mortality and existential longing.

"I think except for Jerry the band was playing great," Bob Bralove says. "I think they also knew they had to play great to get a performance across. If they didn't deliver it, there was no guarantee. I think everyone was worried about Jerry and that they all rallied on some level. I also think that what you do as a friend to somebody who's having trouble with a dependency problem sometimes is say, in effect, 'Look, we've got *this* to offer. We've got a cooking band here. Why don't you come play with us, man?' Give him some place to be inspired to clean up for. Not that I think they were just playing well for him—they were playing well for themselves and the fans, too."

Among Deadheads, the summer '94 tour was probably the most negatively criticized tour the Grateful Dead ever played. Many of the fan reviews on the various Internet computer bulletin boards devoted to the Dead were quite harsh—but at the same time nearly everyone expressed great concern about Garcia.

There were several shows on the summer tour that were fairly solid, with flashes of real brilliance. Even so, the word of mouth about the summer tour was so bad that when the Dead went on the road again in late September, for the first time since anyone could remember the group's shows at Boston Garden and Madison Square Garden did not sell out in advance. The band's spokesperson chalked this up to playing too many shows in the Northeast in too short a time span, but privately bandmembers admitted that they needed to play better if they were going to keep the fans coming back. And on that fall tour they rose to the occasion more often than not. The biggest difference was in Garcia, who seemed more alert than he had been at any time since the spring of '93. There were several excellent shows on this tour—with colossal versions of "Scarlet Begonias" > "Fire on the Mountain" in Boston and New York, for example—prompting more than a few Deadheads to believe that Garcia's troubles were behind him. But closer inspection of Garcia's playing revealed that there were still periods in which he had difficulty getting his fingers to do what his mind wanted them to, and other times when he seemed to be playing on autopilot—noodling aimlessly with no clear intent of where he wanted to go in a jam.

In November the Dead finally began work on their new album at a secluded studio in the wilds of West Marin called the Site. The Dead worked on basic tracks for nearly all of their unrecorded songs, but after about twelve days of sessions they didn't have much on tape to build upon. Garcia seemed distracted and out of sorts much of the time. He arrived late for some sessions, left others shortly after arriving and skipped a few altogether. But the problem wasn't just with Jerry. In Vince's opinion, "We weren't getting a good sound in the studio. Here we were in this great studio, great view, great equipment and it just didn't sound good.

"It was frustrating that we couldn't get a decent take," he continues. "We'd do the song and somebody would inevitably ruin it, which was kind of like how the way we played live came back to haunt us. You can get away with that onstage, but when it's supposed to be for keeps, that can be tough. I mean, I have a rehearsal tape of us doing 'Days Between' that sounds much better than any of the thirteen takes or whatever we did of it at the Site."

Despite the largely positive word of mouth the Dead's fall East Coast tour had received, Bay Area Deadheads were apparently still wary about the state of the band: only one of the group's four shows at the Oakland Coliseum in early December sold out, and at the last two there were thousands of empty seats. Even news that the band soundchecked "Saint Stephen"—which they hadn't played in eleven years—before the penultimate show in the run wasn't enough to fill the coliseum the next night. (Some cynics suggested that the sound check was actually a ploy to sell tickets for the last show. At the sound check the band didn't perform the entire song, and they didn't play it at the show, either.)

Besides the poor ticket sales, the other major topic of Deadhead conversation at these shows was the band's use of video monitors to help the singers remember the words to their newer songs. This wasn't unprecedented in the rock world—the Rolling Stones used lyric monitors on their 1994 tour. And Garcia had employed a discreet music stand with sheets of lyrics for his appearances with David Grisman (nothing easy about remembering all the verses of those old sea chanteys and murder ballads) and for a couple of songs at '94 Dead shows, such as "Days Between" and "Lucy in the Sky with Diamonds." But the move still raised a few eyebrows, and most people assumed it was primarily a face-saving measure for Garcia. The monitors did make an immediate difference in the group's performances of their '90s songs, but they did nothing to stop the musical miscues, and Garcia still suffered from lyric amnesia on his older songs, which were not programmed into the monitors.

In strictly financial terms 1994 was the Grateful Dead's most successful year ever. The band played eighty-four shows and grossed $52.4 million dollars from touring alone, making them the fifth most popular road act that year, behind the Rolling Stones, Pink Floyd, the Eagles and Barbra Streisand. (The previous year the Dead was the number one touring attraction in the United States, grossing $45.6 million dollars on the road with weaker competition.) Add to that the income from merchandising and CDs and you have an improbable corporate giant—a millionaire band that still had a hippie image in the straight world. And Garcia's income was augmented further by his work with the JGB, recording royalties and money he pulled in from his artwork and line of ties.

Despite the overflowing coffers, which, as usual, translated to generous bonuses throughout the Dead organization, there wasn't much jubilation in San Rafael as 1994 turned to 1995. True, by December most of the next year's touring schedule had been preliminarily sketched out, and it promised to bring in even more cash than the group had earned in '94. But there was a deep-seated concern about Garcia's health and well-being that gnawed at everyone, from the bandmembers to the good folks who staffed the Dead's ticket operation. A sense of fatalism gripped some people—a few even began quietly investigating job possibilities in preparation for that dark day they believed might be a tour or two away if Garcia didn't get into shape. Others hoped for the best and took comfort in the knowledge that there had always been a return from the brink before. But even the optimists admitted that something had to give.

CHAPTER 23
There's Nothing You Can Hold for Very Long

f the Grateful Dead had been a typical American show-business phenomenon, they would have turned 1995 into a yearlong celebration of their thirtieth anniversary, and earned tens of millions of dollars on top of what they would ordinarily make on the road. They would have finished their new album and released it in June in time for a big thirtieth-anniversary stadium tour, sponsored by a giant corporation. The group, at the urging of some high-powered New York publicity firm, would make strategic television appearances to support the album and tour— *The Tonight Show*, the *Late Show with David Letterman*, maybe an *MTV Unplugged* appearance that could later be spun off into a CD and commercial video. Or they could have gone the classier cable TV route—half a million people in Manhattan's Central Park for a free concert broadcast live on HBO; a Woodstock of the '90s. They probably could have played the White House for the ultimate ironic photo op. A world tour would have taken them across Europe, Asia and Australia, culminating on New Year's Eve with a meticulously planned pay-per-view event from some exotic locale—the Great Wall in China; Ayers Rock in Australia; Easter Island!

Instead, the Dead basically chose to ignore the anniversary, as if they knew that with Garcia's tenuous health a threat to their future, there was no reason to be popping champagne corks or attracting global attention when they weren't playing their best. To the outside world, which understood the Dead only as a successful sociocultural phenomenon and couldn't be expected to have tracked Garcia's subtle musical decline, the Dead appeared to be sitting pretty. They were more than just survivors of the rock 'n' roll wars; they were living icons whose very existence in 1995 was symbolic of the durability of some of the ideals of the '60s. Garcia generally disavowed the '60s mantle, but Phil Lesh noted in 1994 that the Grateful Dead were "the last holdout—the last piece of that culture that really exists in this era. It's history, and for some, I suppose, it's nostalgia. But it's very much alive—that's the key. . . . If it is the only remnant of the '60s, thank goodness there's something left. Because there really isn't much else that survived the '60s intact."

Garcia's first three gigs in 1995 were Jerry Garcia Band shows at the Warfield Theater in mid-January. He seemed to be in fine spirits at these concerts, which broke no new musical ground but were fairly well played. By this time Garcia could do JGB shows at the Warfield in his sleep—and there are those who will tell you he did nod off at a few gigs there. The atmosphere around those smaller shows was always more relaxed than at any Dead concert. People's expectations were perhaps lower, too, so they were rarely disappointed.

On January 19, four days after the last JGB show in that series, Garcia was involved in a frightening single-car accident on busy Highway 101 in Marin County. Driving a $32,000 loaner BMW 525i while his own larger BMW was in the shop, Garcia lost control of the car, smashed several times into the center divider on the highway and spun around before coming to a stop facing the opposite direction. He was shaken up but not hurt, and he told police he wasn't sure how he'd lost control. Vince DiBiase says that Garcia was not high at the time, and though the police at first believed some hand-rolled cigarettes Garcia had in his briefcase might contain marijuana, they turned out to be an especially pungent type of tobacco. (Had Garcia been busted following the accident, who knows how events would have unfolded in 1995?)

Two days later the JGB went into Fantasy Studios in Berkeley to record two songs for the soundtrack of Wayne Wang's film *Smoke*, a fine, character-driven art film centered on a Brooklyn smoke shop. Wang, the acclaimed director of *Chan Is Missing*, had a personal connection to Garcia—he had worked as a roadie for the Garcia Band in the mid-'70s. He had long wanted to use Garcia on one of his soundtracks and *Smoke* finally seemed like the right vehicle. Wang chose the '30s Jerome Kern song "Smoke Gets in Your Eyes," which Kahn and Garcia rearranged with a reggae lilt. It is possible that this was the only time Garcia played a song by the man he was named after. Kahn suggested the JGB's other tune on the soundtrack, the hazy ballad "Cigarettes and Coffee." Even though this was the JGB's first appearance in a recording studio, "The sessions went amazingly fast," Kahn said. "We did it in a couple of days and had a great time. I kind of wish we'd had the time to do a whole album with that band."

In some ways, the hectic pace of Garcia's life in 1995 wasn't much different than it was in 1971, when he was playing with both the Dead and the New Riders, jamming regularly with Howard Wales at the Matrix and showing up at his friends' recording sessions around town. Then, as in 1995, he was obsessed with playing music in as many different contexts as possible. He never lost that desire, but the particulars of his life had changed completely over twenty-five years.

The enormity of the Grateful Dead juggernaut had become burdensome for him—it was almost as if he were the de facto CEO of some multimillion-dollar corporation, at once responsible for both the company and the product. The demands on his time were overwhelming. He did only a fraction of the things asked of him, and who knows how many hundreds of other projects and ideas he would have been bombarded with if he hadn't had a protective wall around him? Some have been intensely critical of the Grateful Dead road crew's role in supposedly isolating Garcia through the years, but it's abundantly clear that he was at times desperate to stay away from the frenetic hordes who wanted him to do something with them or for them. The isolation—and heroin—provided him with some measure of peace and relaxation, but took their toll in other ways. By 1995 he had been a junkie for much of the past seventeen years, an experience that had periodically weakened his body and soul. Once the proud possessor of an iron constitution, he was now racked with physical ailments, including chronic bronchitis, carpal tunnel syndrome, recurrent diabetes and, as we later learned, advanced heart disease.

But health be damned, he seemed constitutionally unable to slow down. So he toured with the Dead and JGB, did sessions with Grisman and others, went to Grateful Dead business meetings, sat on the Rex Foundation board and consulted about his art and the J. Garcia clothing line (which was expanded from ties to include scarves, blouses and more). He had a personal financial burden to match his workload, too. Now, in addition to paying $20,800 a month to Mountain Girl, $3,000 a month to Barbara Meier, child support and mortgage payments for Manasha's and Keelin's upkeep, he was also spending about $22,000 a month to pay for Deborah Garcia's rather extravagant lifestyle; this despite her mid-six-figure income from her family trusts.

According to John and Linda Kahn, Garcia was unhappy about Deborah's apparent obsession with his finances, and he disliked her attempts to regiment his life. "She had him backed into this rigorous schedule of meetings and all these various things, which he ditched all the time—he had a trainer and he'd show up there like eight hours late and be there for fifteen minutes," John said. "She had him boxed in where he had to be places at certain times. So it ended up the only time I'd see him would be like four in the morning or something; that was the only time he could get away."

"The last couple of years he was at our house every night he was in town," Linda says. "He'd come over to our house after he'd leave [Deborah's] house. . . . He was just real lonely. He thought he was getting married to have a partner to hang out with and it didn't turn out that way. He came over to our house a lot of times almost in tears. It was real sad. He didn't understand the way he was being treated.

"He said she didn't have any faith in him. She wanted money in the bank because she didn't think he could go out and make it. She didn't have faith in his ability, and that really hurt him. He'd say, 'Linda, haven't my girlfriends always had everything they wanted?' Which was true. He gave all his money away to his girlfriends, always."

Annabelle Garcia comments, "Here was another situation where he was looking for that true love that everyone's looking for and it turned out again that here was someone who wanted to manipulate his life more for their own purposes than he was comfortable with. I think he really wanted someone who would roll over and let him live however he wanted. But he was a tough match. I'm not sure he ever quite got matched properly.

"I think he had a long history of letting the ladies in his life say, 'C'mon,

Jerry, let's clean you up and get you off drugs, let's get your life together.' And he'd say, 'Sure, sure, sure, you betcha,' and then he wouldn't help them, and he'd go off in the middle of the night, get what he needed, not come back for a couple of days. Then he'd kind of make the effort again and drop it when they weren't looking. He really didn't want someone making him do something [to clean up], even though that's what he needed. And he would never do anything on his own. That's the common thread with all these ladies: 'Well, he said he wasn't taking drugs, but he was and then I didn't know what to do.' He was extremely stubborn."

In early February 1995 Jerry and Deborah took a belated honeymoon trip to Bonaire, a Dutch island off the northern coast of Venezuela famous for its many diving spots. When he returned he had planned to play a series of JGB shows at the Warfield to warm up for Dead shows in Salt Lake City and Oakland. The night of the first show, the Warfield was packed as usual with expectant Heads. But as showtime rolled around, Garcia informed Steve Parish and BGP production chief Bob Barsotti that he didn't think he could play. He said he'd been stung in the hand by a jellyfish while he was scuba diving and later slept on his arm while it was in an awkward position. Now he was having difficulty moving his hand and fingers. Parish also noted that Garcia was experiencing carpal tunnel–related problems that made playing problematic, so it's hard to say how much of his acute condition was the jellyfish sting and how much was a result of a general health decline. Whatever the cause, Garcia was in no shape to play, so Barsotti told the crowd that Garcia was having trouble with his hand but that he expected to be able to play tomorrow's concert, and that tickets for the canceled show would be honored two nights later. However, in the end Garcia didn't recover enough to play any of the shows, so all the tickets had to be refunded.

Between the auto accident and the cancellation of the JGB gigs, Deadheads had a lot of bad Garcia news to deal with in the first weeks of 1995. But with Jerry again able to play, the Dead pressed on with their Salt Lake City concerts in the third week of February, and received generally favorable notices from most Deadheads. Garcia revived two songs he hadn't played in many years— the perennial crowd-pleaser "Alabama Getaway," absent from the repertoire since 1989; and Dylan's haunting and cynical "Visions of Johanna," which Garcia had sung only twice in 1986. The latter song became a real powerhouse in this later incarnation. Thanks to the new lyric monitors, Garcia delivered the song's long, complicated verses and dense swirl of images and shadowy characters with unbridled passion. There was obviously something about the song's bleak settings and the sense of confusion and foreboding mixed with ennui that Garcia related to personally.

In late February Annabelle came to the Bay Area from Eugene, Oregon, to have a heart-to-heart talk with "the old man," as she often refers to him, about her future. "I had called him and told him that I'd gotten engaged and I was getting married and he was extremely excited about that. He was really looking forward to the ol' walking-the-daughter-down-the-aisle. So I took Scott [McLean, her fiancé] down there to meet him, and we met with him over a couple of days and he gave us these big, drawn-out lectures about how to make a marriage work. And it basically boiled down to 'Don't live together, don't see each other. Have separate houses and have somebody to take care of all your stuff.' I'm like, 'That's very realistic, Dad, thanks! You want to lend us twenty million dollars so we can do that?' But he was totally serious. It was funny but it was also sad that that was what he had learned.

"He was very energetic, but I think he was very nervous as well, because here's his daughter bringing in some guy who wants to marry her. That's a big deal. And he was expected to do some fatherly thing, and he was always terrified of that kind of stuff—having to lecture or give opinions or advice. He was very hands-off and this was putting him on the spot a bit. I gave him a big hug and a kiss and I noticed he was really, really skinny—his arms and legs seemed tiny. He was still kind of round around the middle. But he seemed short to me; kind of small. He seemed frailer than I'd ever seen him before, yet his inside stuff was really lit. He was very excited about stuff in general. He was excited about me getting married and he talked about playing with Grisman—that was the one thing that I know made him supremely happy. Whenever I talked to him about that, he'd talk ten times faster, which was a sure sign that he was excited.

"Then the day after we saw him I had a weird dream about this old horse of mine that had passed away, and in the dream I was riding the horse around the field. It seemed like the next day Dad was dead." Actually, Garcia died months later, but this was the last time Annabelle saw her father alive.

The Grateful Dead's three-week spring tour took them mainly to Southern destinations, including Charlotte, Atlanta, Memphis (where they hadn't played since 1970), Birmingham and Tampa. The big news on this tour was that after twenty-three years of fan requests, Phil Lesh finally played "Unbroken Chain" onstage with the Dead. (In the end it wasn't because of the fans' pleadings; rather, Phil's son Graham asked him to and he obliged.) Phil made a point of playing the song once in each city on the tour (except Birmingham), and it was ecstatically greeted each time, particularly by older Deadheads who'd worn out copies of the *Mars Hotel* album in the era before Dead bootleg tapes became widely available, when records were still the main medium for listening to the Dead. A convoluted composition with numerous dynamics and tempo shifts, "Unbroken Chain" proved quite a challenge for the band. Garcia in particular appeared to have some difficulty negotiating the tune's many twists and turns, sometimes lagging a little behind the others. It's one of those songs that probably would have evolved into something quite magnificent after a couple of years of tinkering onstage, but as it was it never developed much beyond the album version. Even so, hearing it was a highlight of the year for many Deadheads.

The band's fortunes on spring tour went up and down with Garcia's condition, which remained unpredictable. In Philadelphia he seemed full of energy most of the time, and in Charlotte he was clearly buoyed by the presence of Bruce Hornsby, who played grand piano the whole night. Hornsby, rather than Garcia, was the dominant melodic player at that show, pushing the other bandmembers the way Garcia used to but now seemed nearly incapable of.

Garcia played what turned out to be his final shows with the Garcia Band near the end of April at the Warfield. Once again, his playing seemed painfully uneven—inspired one moment, inept the next—and even John Kahn could see the writing on the wall.

"Our band was all but finished by the end," he said. "We were working very little; he basically wasn't allowed to work with us. That's the impression I got. We were going to do a tour in the fall but it got canceled before it even got booked because Steve [Parish] and all the Dead people didn't think he should go out with us. Our band was stretched to the limit where we were on the verge of not being a band, and it was starting to sound like it. We had been doing pretty well before that year; I think we'd reached a sort of a peak and were now maybe on the other side of that. I didn't know what the reason was—if he was sick or what—but I could tell Jerry was sort of falling apart, and our band was falling apart as well. The rest of the people weren't playing as well, either, which is something that happens.

"It was like he lost interest," Kahn continued. "That's what I was talking about with our band—it was headed nowhere. We weren't rehearsing at all. We weren't learning any new songs. He stopped caring, or something." Why? "I think he wanted out. He wanted to change his life around. I don't exactly know how. But the last conversations I had with him, I don't think there was going to be a Jerry Garcia Band. We would still find stuff to do, him and me. He had talked about doing Old and in the Way again, which would have been a pretty all-encompassing thing. That's more than just a little side thing—it involves a lot of work, and it also involves a degree of health. He was saying he wanted to do it after he was healthy again, which never happened. But he was talking seriously about that a couple of weeks before he died."

On and off the road, Garcia did have one project that seemed to bring him a great deal of pleasure. The book *Harrington Street* was to be his memoir of growing up in San Francisco in the '40s and '50s—a pastiche of recollections accompanied by sketches and paintings illustrating events from his early life and his childhood fantasies. In early 1994 he had signed a six-figure deal with Delacorte Press to produce the book, and he and Deborah spent many hours probing his memory and trying to shape the book. As with many of his later artworks, he scanned his ink drawings into a computer and then manipulated and colored them using a computer "paint" program. This occupied him hour after hour, and it was something he could work on in hotel rooms on tour, whether he was writing in his distinctive, messy calligraphic scrawl, or using a laptop computer. As Deborah wrote in the preface to the book, which was completed by her and published posthumously, "He was a big kid, with a beard. Of all the ways someone might go back and explore childhood, the one Jerry chose suited him ideally: create a marvelous picture book."

In May the Grateful Dead went back to the Site to work more on their new album, but once again the sessions, which lasted ten days, were disappointing. Garcia seemed unfocused and uninterested much of the time. Vince Welnick recalls, "Jerry was there, but nobody in the band would press upon him to complete his guitar track or to put down a definitive vocal track. Occasionally Jerry would say, 'I'll get back to it later,' or, 'I'm going to sit it out because I've gotta hear what you guys are doing; I haven't decided what I'm going to play.' We didn't get a whole lot done." Indeed, when Phil Lesh listened to the session tapes after Garcia's death to see if there was anything salvageable he came up empty-handed.

The band's Western tour stretched over the second half of May and the beginning of June, and included stops in Las Vegas (where the group's annual three-show run at the Silver Bowl on the outskirts of town had become a pilgrimage point for Deadheads all over the West), Seattle, Portland and Shoreline Amphitheater. As had been the case on most of their tours in the mid-'90s, the quality of the shows varied widely from night to night, set to set, even song to song. Though almost everyone agreed that Garcia didn't look very good—his skin had taken on a slightly unreal yellow pallor and his complexion appeared waxy—he seemed fairly energetic most of the time; or at least until "drums" in the second set, after which he usually flagged a bit.

June 2, 3 and 4 at Shoreline Amphitheater turned out to be the last three Dead shows I ever attended, twenty-five years and more than 350 concerts after my first, at the Capitol Theater in Port Chester, New York, when I was sixteen. There were plenty of sixteen-year-olds at Shoreline in 1995, as well as babes in arms, ten-year-olds, twenty-five-year-olds, fifty-year-olds (the Dead's contemporaries), sixty-year-olds and beyond. Like many others, I had gone into the shows feeling some measure of trepidation because Garcia had been so inconsistent at other concerts I'd attended in '95, and the rumors of his ongoing drug dependency preceded him.

So it was heartening to find Garcia in such a positive mood and playing so well at the first two Shoreline concerts. His song choices on the opening night of the run hit all sorts of stylistic realms. There was a rousing "Alabama Getaway," with its Chuck Berry riffing (this just a few days after Berry opened for the Dead in Portland); the loping "Candyman," like something off the stage of the Dodge City Music Hall; "Ramble On Rose," puttering and backfiring like a Model T Ford; a jazzy, at times dissonant musical flight into the unknown via "Bird Song." And that was just in the first set. In the second set Garcia served up sparkling, imaginatively played renditions of "New

Speedway Boogie"; Paul McCartney's little half-song "That Would Be Something," which became a launching pad for a lengthy group jam; a stately but not somber "He's Gone"; "Standing on the Moon," sure and emotional; and the feel-good encore of "Lucy in the Sky with Diamonds," complete with the 20,000-voice Shoreline chorale on the choruses.

But the concert's most magical moments didn't come from the band. During "drums," ten maroon-robed members of the Tibetan Buddhist Gyuto Monks, who had a long association with the Dead, mostly through Mickey Hart and Danny Rifkin, came onstage and electrified the crowd with their hypnotic, guttural chanting. What does it say about a Grateful Dead concert that the band could surrender the stage to a group of Tibetan holy men for fifteen minutes and nobody in the crowd thought it was the least bit out of place? To the contrary, the audience was transfixed, and the appreciative roar when the monks slowly filed off the stage had the Tibetans beaming and waving. Whether it was Olatunji or Ornette Coleman, Carlos Santana or Edie Brickell joining the Dead onstage, Deadheads were always open to new infusions of interesting energy from whomever or whatever. It was all in the noble service of blowing minds.

At the second Shoreline show, on Saturday night, Garcia was in fine fettle again. In the first set he was the earnest but convivial storyteller, regaling the throng with atmospheric pieces about three very different women: "Althea," Delilah Jones from "Brown-Eyed Women" and Delia DeLyon, the heroine of "Stagger Lee." The second set opened with a perky, neatly executed "China Cat Sunflower" segueing (as usual) into the always uplifting "I Know You Rider." Through all his ups and downs, Garcia almost never played a bad version of "I Know You Rider." Musically and lyrically, the old folk blues tune was one of the simplest songs in the Dead's repertoire and that's precisely why it was always so effective. Every person in the arena, amphitheater or stadium—from the bandmembers to the Heads spinning in the farthest reaches of the venue—could relate to the song's determined optimism, as Weir sang the second verse, straight out of American mountain music:

> Well, the sun's gonna shine in my back door someday
> You know the sun's gonna shine in my back door someday
> March winds gonna blow all my troubles away.

Then Garcia would step up to the microphone, and his verse, which he always delivered with as much passion as he could muster, tapped into everyone's natural wanderlust:

> I wish I was a headlight on a northbound train
> I wish I was a headlight on a northbound train
> I'd shine my light through the cool Colorado rain

Later in the set Garcia led a triumphal sing-along on "Uncle John's Band," and in his post-"drums" ballad slot he offered a spellbinding version of "Stella Blue" that was filled with heart. Garcia seemed completely inside Hunter's lyric that night—the giant video screens showed his face in extreme close-up and he couldn't have looked more clear-eyed and present. When Garcia was truly in the moment on his ballads, he was able to communicate the most complex feelings and emotions with a directness and simplicity that could touch almost any soul. He was singing about life and death, "broken dreams and vanished years." It was sad and beautiful, especially when he came to the last verse. The music dropped to a whisper—the silence between each note palpable—and the crowd hung on every word as he sang

> *It all rolls into one*
> *And nothin' comes for free*
> *There's nothing you can hold for very long*
> *But when you hear that song*
> *Come crying like the wind*
> *It seems like all this life*
> *Was just a dream*
> *Stella Blue*

And he smiled ever so slightly, recognizing that the crowd and band had experienced a moment of the soul together—had walked in the same shoes and seen from the same eyes, if only briefly. It was that kind of enlightened moment, a shared reality full of spiritual nourishment and humanity, that kept Deadheads coming back for more. I'll always carry with me the vision of Garcia, his eyes scanning the crowd, desperately trying to connect with every person at Shoreline, and in the process drawing them into the depths of his own soul.

The show ended on a bright note with "Liberty," Garcia charging through it with delight and gusto, rocking back and forth on his heels to the beat and seemingly as full of energy as he'd been during the evening's first song. I was ready to believe that bright days were ahead.

But Sunday afternoon's show was another story altogether. Garcia was distracted by equipment problems for much of the first set, and spent an inordinate amount of time conferring with Steve Parish about the vexing sound gremlins. His attention appeared to wander at times while he was singing, and his playing lacked the crispness of the first two nights. During "Victim or the Crime" in the second set, he sounded completely lost, hitting "clams" and wrong chords left and right, and even during "Unbroken Chain"—which was the first version ever played in California—he wasn't in sync with the rest of the band and his melodic fills sounded perfunctory. He rallied enough energy to deliver "Eyes of the World" at a robust clip, but basically he'd run out of gas by "drums," and the late-second-set "Days Between" was mostly a shambles. Still, "Brokedown Palace" was a sweet and nicely played encore, more in spirit of the first two concerts than the disjointed and occasionally disturbing third. And as fate would have it, the last words I ever heard Jerry Garcia sing were a moving good-bye:

> *Fare you well, fare you well*
> *I love you more than words can tell*
> *Listen to the river sing sweet songs*
> *To rock my soul*

June was the last time Mountain Girl saw Jerry, too—they sat across from each other at a Rex Foundation meeting. "We had a really nice chat," she reports. "He was kind of pale; his color wasn't good. I noticed that his shoulders were a lot thinner. When he was swimming a lot he'd develop these big swimmer's shoulders; he just loved our pool [on Reservoir Road] and of course he liked swimming in Hawaii. But his spirits were good."

It was around this time, too, the Deborah Garcia came to grips with the fact that Jerry was strung out on heroin again. As she recounted to *Rolling Stone* after his death, "I said to him, 'I know you're doing drugs. I want to tell you that if you want to keep doing drugs for the rest of your life, I will love you anyway. We will deal with it, and at least it won't be something you have to hide or be afraid of. But do you want to stay on them?'

"And he said, 'No, I don't. It's a pain in the butt.' That's exactly what he said. 'I don't want to do this for the rest of my life.' It was right before the summer tour. We decided it would be better for him to go to a treatment place."

But first Garcia had to make it through one more tour—a monthlong trek that took the Dead to stadiums, amphitheaters and arenas in the East and Midwest, and paired them with Bob Dylan's band on five of the first seven concerts. (Dylan opened the shows and never played with the Dead.) It would be the Dead's final tour.

In the summer of 1994 the Dead had played a very successful concert in a giant field surrounded by beautiful pine-covered hills in Highgate, Vermont. The show had drawn about 60,000 people from all over the Northeast, and though there were some logistical problems with the site—the traffic jams coming and going were horrendous—it proved to be a mellow setting for such a big event. The Dead began their summer '95 tour at Highgate, with Dylan opening, and this time there was trouble. More than 100,000 turned up and there was an ugly gate-crashing episode in which some fences were knocked down, injuring a number of people in the process, and thousands of rowdy fans swarmed into the concert site.

The Dead later determined that there was a large element of party animals who were not necessarily Deadheads who had decided on a lark to be part of the madness at a big outdoor Dead show and didn't think twice about the consequences of their disruptive behavior. It was widely reported by fans that Garcia was in poor shape at this show, blowing lyrics and not doing much on the guitar.

By the next concert, three nights later at Giants Stadium, Garcia was playing a little better, but he still went through periods during the show when he seemed zombielike and out of it. Bob Bralove remembers, "There was a moment where he got caught in the beginning of 'Wharf Rat' and he didn't seem to be able to get out. He got lost; he couldn't find his way out. And that's when I started getting scared: 'Is this drugs? Is this physical? What's goin' on?' "

The sound at the show was terrible, in part because Garcia kept the volume of his guitar turned so low he could barely be heard at times, so the group sounded unbalanced. This was a problem at numerous Dead shows in 1994 and 1995—on nights when he lacked confidence, Garcia would turn himself down in the mix, and as a result the sound seemed to have a hole in it. Mixer John Cutler was powerless to control it from the soundboard; it was Garcia's choice, and it frustrated his fans to no end.

From Giants Stadium the caravan moved on to Albany, New York, where there was another (much smaller) gate-crashing incident outside Knickerbocker Arena that culminated in numerous arrests and a few injuries to fans and police. The scene outside hot, humid and occasionally rainy RFK Stadium in Washington, D.C., was less chaotic, but there was weirdness there, too: three fans were struck by lightning before one of the concerts (all survived). Bruce Hornsby played piano with the Dead a final time at the first of the two RFK shows, but he seemed unusually restrained. Garcia, on the other hand, was surprisingly lively, and he even joined Bob Dylan at the end of his set for a bluesy reading of "It Takes a Lot to Laugh, It Takes a Train to Cry" and a festive romp through "Rainy Day Women #12 and 35" that had nearly every person in the stadium shouting out the famous refrain: "I would not feel so alone / Everybody must get stoned!"

Things went well during the next three shows on the tour. Like Knickerbocker Arena, the Palace in Auburn Hills, Michigan—home to professional basketball's Detroit Pistons—felt like a relatively intimate venue for the Dead in the midst of their stadium tours, and they usually played well there. This summer was no exception: though Garcia had trouble with lyrics on both nights, the level of his playing was generally high. Even with Jerry playing respectably (but not consistently) at most of the tour stops, backstage there was great concern about his health. His breathing was often labored, he looked uncomfortable much of the time and it appeared to be a struggle for him to get from place to place.

"During the summer tour we were all aware he was pretty sick," Vince Welnick says. "I was actually worried that he was putting himself in a position where he would become incapacitated or unable to play. He was unhappy, he was tired, he was asleep a lot. When he wasn't asleep he was kind of grouchy. He seemed a little bit disoriented and he wasn't the happy-go-lucky Jerry. He was obviously suffering. And you know the guy had enough money to buy whatever drug he wanted to make him feel right, but that wasn't working. I think he knew he was dying, and I guess the truth of it is he was. But I think everybody in the band thought, 'Well, let's just get through this tour and it'll all be better.' "

Was there ever any thought of not doing the tour? "No, because when we went out, it wasn't that apparent. In the spring tour prior to that it wasn't that noticeable."

After a stadium show in Pittsburgh, the tour went to Deer Creek amphitheater in Indiana, which was probably the most popular Midwestern venue for the Dead since the band had stopped playing Alpine Valley after 1989. The band had a history of playing good shows there, also, and because it was a lovely, midsized venue, holding 20,000 people in seats and on a sprawling lawn in the back, the demand for tickets was always extremely high. The previous couple of years when the band played Deer Creek there had been the usual hordes of ticketless fans outside, but there hadn't been any real problems. That changed on July 2, 1995.

Unbeknownst to the thousands of people attending the show, Garcia had received what everyone in the Dead camp regarded as a very serious death threat from someone who claimed he was going to gun down the guitarist. On a tour plagued with disturbing violent episodes, this was the last straw.

"That was scary," Vince Welnick says. "I remember Phil wanted to pack up and leave right then and there, and then we decided, well, if it's Jerry's life, let him call it. And Jerry said, 'There's no way I'm going to let that stop me; hell no.' He said, 'I've been getting crackpots all my life.' But if he hadn't said that, we absolutely would have gone home, because Phil was already packed."

Both the local police and the FBI were put on alert, and metal detectors were quickly set up at the gates to the venue. "We didn't know about the death threat at the time," says Peter Toluzzi, who attended the show. "And the scene outside was fairly mellow before the show. There were an awful lot of people with no tickets, but that wasn't particularly unusual. It's interesting in retrospect that during the band's sound check that afternoon, which we could hear outside, Garcia played the first verse of 'Death Don't Have No Mercy,' which they hadn't played since Brent died. Then he stopped it and went into 'Visions of Johanna' and then 'Here Comes Sunshine,' which they opened the show with.

"The metal detectors made it so it took a long time for most people to get inside," Toluzzi says. "Then, once the show started, I thought it was strange that there were so many security people up in the catwalks and in the front rows. We didn't know what that was all about."

If Garcia was nervous, he didn't show it. In fact, he provided his own ironic commentary on the situation when he chose to play "Dire Wolf," with its chipper "Don't murder me" refrain. (This closely mirrored a night in 1979 at Madison Square Garden when he received a death threat and played "Dire Wolf.")

But two-thirds of the way through the set, while Phil was leading the band through his arrangement of Robbie Robertson's moving "Broken Arrow," something very disturbing happened. Thousands of ticketless kids broke down the rear fence of the venue, pushed aside security guards and swarmed onto the back lawn, as many fans inside cheered them on. At the perimeter of the amphitheater, police used tear gas, pepper spray and German shepherd attack dogs in an attempt to keep order, but the fighting continued for some time. Within a couple of hours of the incident, CNN broadcast video footage of the Deer Creek riot, and those pictures then popped up on news programs all over the country.

The inundation of ticketless rowdies made the amphitheater crowded and uncomfortable for many people, and the security forces inside realized that the breach of security could have let in a potential assassin, so tensions were high backstage and in the area in front of the stage. "The whole thing was really very weird," Bob Bralove says. "You look out [from backstage] and the lights are on and you're watching everybody and you can see the guys with the bulletproof vests on and all the security people are looking so serious. It was very creepy. It was a shock to look out at this sea of faces that had been a source of nothing but positive energy—you know, the dark, warm, fuzzy area out there—but it was brightly lit and you were looking for people *with guns*. Then you look up at the fence and people are pouring over it, so there goes your security."

In the face of this frightening anarchy, it's amazing Garcia was able to play at all, much less play quite well in spots. The house lights were left on during the entire second set for security reasons, adding to the strangeness of the event. Obviously distracted, Garcia sang only one of the three verses of "Fire on the Mountain" during the second set, but his guitar work on the song was quite intense; darkly inspired. In this setting, his struggle through "New Speedway Boogie" seemed like a plaintive entreaty, and the celestial harmonies of "Attics of My Life" washed over the chaotic scene like a soothing balm.

The next morning, after consulting with police and the management of Deer Creek, the Dead decided to cancel the second scheduled show there. The next stop on the tour was Riverport Amphitheater near St. Louis three days later, and when Deadheads arrived they found a massive police presence awaiting them, complete with dogs and extra barbed-wire fencing.

Things were peaceful, even subdued, the first night at Riverport. There was obviously some residual weirdness from the Deer Creek debacle; it was in the air. The house lights were left on during the show again, which added to the constrictive vibe of the event. Even though the show went on without incident, there was bad news this first night. A couple of hours after the concert, about 150 Deadheads were injured—some seriously—when a porch at a campground collapsed under the weight of too many people. This incident, on top of the Highgate and Deer Creek disasters, also became a national news story. The band dedicated the next night's show to the injured Heads, and put in a solid performance. By the second set that night the house lights were turned out, and most believed that things were returning to what passes for normal at a Grateful Dead show.

The Tour from Hell, as it was dubbed by many Deadheads, limped into its final port of call, Chicago's venerable Soldier Field, on July 8. Even though the Dead had played the stadium without incident the previous four years, the negative press from the tour got some city officials in such a lather that Mayor Richard Daley had to reassure them that extra security precautions would be taken. Outside the show, a number of Deadheads took it upon themselves to spread the word about responsible behavior at Dead shows. One group sold black-and-yellow GATECRASHERS SUCK! bumper stickers.

Inside, the mood was considerably more festive than it had been in St. Louis. The Band opened the two Chicago dates, and their hit-heavy sets were very well-received. This wasn't exactly a reunion of two of the titans of Watkins Glen—both groups were ragged and on the other side of their best years—but their shared history added to the warmth of the event.

The Dead's sets at Soldier Field weren't much better or worse than most of the ones that preceded them on the tour. Garcia flubbed lyrics left and right but occasionally turned in a great performance of a song; the rest of the band sounded comparatively strong and confident. The first night, Jerry's standout was the one song where he was aided by the lyric monitor, "Visions of Johanna." He dug into Dylan's words with tremendous feeling, even pumping his fist into the air to punctuate the line "Mona Lisa must've had the highway *blues* / You can tell by the way she smiles."

Although no one knew it at the time, the July 9 concert at Soldier Field would be the Grateful Dead's last. For that reason it has taken on a perhaps unjustified historicity, with some scouring the tapes for clues to prove that Jerry knew he was dying and was playing his final show. This much is clear: by that last night, Garcia was spent. He looked pale and drawn, he had trouble even getting up the stairs to the stage and some backstagers observed that he appeared fidgety and uncomfortable. Did he know that exactly one month later he'd be dead? Certainly not. Otherwise, why would he reaffirm his commitment to clean up after the tour? Why open his final concert with "Touch of Grey"? Not for irony's sake.

His most vital and revealing number that night was "So Many Roads," with its compelling mixture of weariness, resignation and, ultimately perhaps, acceptance. "So Many Roads" is a song aimed at someone in the late autumn of life—not at a typical fifty-year-old—and it seemed more meaningful to Garcia each time he sang it. That final set at Soldier Field, he sang the repeated ending refrain, "So many roads to ease my soul," with as much verve and passion as he could physically muster in his obviously weakened state. He changed the phrasing each time through, and built to a crescendo in which he was nearly shouting the words, like some testifyin' preacher. This was Garcia's soul laid bare, and the audience responded by cheering him on, empathizing with him, struggling with him. Many people were in tears by the end of the song, and the deafening ovation it received showed that Jerry and most of the crowd had truly connected and experienced the song together. This mystical union of artist and audience was at the core of the Grateful Dead's appeal. There was always a sense that the band was using these songs—this immeasurably rich body of tunes that encompassed cautionary tales, swirling seas of metaphors and allegories, little bursts of wisdom at every turn, black comedy, fantasies, surrealism and the down-home "I know you rider, gonna miss me when I'm gone" blues—in the same way the crowd was: as constantly shifting touchstones for their own lives.

Garcia's final musical statement at Soldier Field couldn't have been more appropriate for the ultimate outcome of the Garcia saga—the darkly existential "Black Muddy River," played as the encore. The moment that song ended, Phil launched into a powerful, hope-filled version of "Box of Rain" that lifted everyone's spirits. But the poignant last words of that song work as a closing quotation mark on Garcia's life journey: "Such a long, long time to be gone / And a short time to be there." Fireworks exploded over the stadium as the crowd filed out, and no doubt there were thousands of animated conversations about catching some or all of the *next* Dead tour.

The mood of the band was considerably more serious. "I was just glad we got through it," Vince says. "I thought, 'Thank God that's the last date!' There was always something cool about playing Soldier Field, especially with the fireworks show and everything. But when you play for that many people, you always want it be spectacular and all you could really say about that was, 'Thank God it's over.' "

Once he returned home to the Bay Area from the summer tour, Garcia had a week of leisure before he went down to the Betty Ford Clinic in Rancho Mirage, California, near Palm Springs, to go through their famous detox program. In his many years of battling heroin addiction, this was the first time Jerry had ever agreed to try a multiweek residential facility. It was at Deborah's urging, and his acquiescence showed that he knew he was seriously ill and strung out. The move caught many in the Dead scene off guard because it was such a radical departure for him.

"I was pretty surprised when he went into Betty Ford," said John Kahn, who also offered this unorthodox minority view: "I don't think he was hooked on drugs at the time, to tell you the truth. I really doubt that he was. He didn't have a very hard time down [at Betty Ford] on that level. The drugs were the least of his problems."

On July 16, exactly a week after tour's end, Garcia played on his final recording session—a version of the Jimmie Rodgers song "Blue Yodel #9 (Standing on the Corner)" cut at David Grisman's studio for a Rodgers tribute album spearheaded by Bob Dylan. The band that day consisted of Garcia on acoustic guitar and lead vocals, Grisman on mandolin and banjo-mandolin, Kahn on stand-up bass, jazz drummer George Marsh on percussion and Bay Area string band veteran Sally Van Meter on dobro.

"Jerry said he was getting over a bronchitis cold," Van Meter says, "but his spirit was totally there. He was completely professional and in a good mood and really very friendly. Very talkative. Obviously very intelligent. Actually, when John Kahn arrived, I thought he looked worse than Jerry did."

Shortly after the session, Garcia flew to Southern California accompanied by Deborah and Steve Parish and checked in to the Betty Ford Clinic for what was to be a monthlong detox program.

"The first week he was there," Deborah told *Rolling Stone*, "he called and said he really liked all the people there and that he was really sick—he had a pretty serious jones going. But he was very committed to getting off [heroin], and he did—the hard way. He suffered physically.

"Then, after two weeks he called me and said it was really hot, he hated the food, he wanted to come home. So Parish and I went down. Jerry came out, and he looked just great. He'd lost weight and he was smiling. He was doing really well, and he was strong. He was clean. You're supposed to stay a whole month, but he wanted to come home. So I said, 'You can come home if you continue in the recovery stuff.' "

Parish suggests that once Garcia was clearheaded and apparently on the road to physical recovery, he was turned off by the Ford clinic's rehab rhetoric and generally stifling milieu. And though Parish acknowledges that Garcia's decision to leave before his program was completed was potentially dangerous, he supported the guitarist's urge to continue his rehabilitation in a more pleasant and laid-back environment. So Garcia got his wish, and he was able to spend his fifty-third birthday back in the Bay Area.

Over the days that followed his release, Garcia lay low, attending a few AA-style meetings and talking with a couple of recovery psychiatrists "who he felt understood him," Deborah said. A number of people in the Dead scene had their last encounters with Jerry during the first week of August, and to a person they reported that he was extremely warm and optimistic about the future. At the same time, they recognized his physical frailty.

Steve Parish says that Jerry went to the Dead's brand-new recording studio in Novato and talked excitedly about building a special guitar room there. Vince Welnick was there that day and he heard Garcia's upbeat rap about the guitar room, too. Vince adds, "He was in a great mood. He was telling these old 'war stories' about being in the clinic. He had a Kentucky Fried Chicken sack with him; yup, he'd been to the Colonel! Anyway, he was one of the main proponents for building Club Front 2. He was very enthusiastic.

"But I could tell right away his guts were fucking with him, which could be expected. He looked like he was in pain. You could sort of hear the fluid on his lungs when he talked. But if he knew he was dying he was fooling everybody, because he was making plans like he was going to live. I don't think he knew he was dying; I think he just felt particularly cruddy, which could be expected from just getting out of rehab."

On August 4 Jerry called his old friend Bob Hunter out of the blue. A couple of weeks after Garcia's death, Hunter attempted to reconstruct this last conversation in his journal (and later shared it with the world on his personal Web site). Parts of it went like this:

RH: Hey, Bozo!
JG: Hey, Hunter, it's Garcia. I just got out of the Betty Ford Center!
RH: How was Betty?
JG: She was a great fuck, man!
RH: Did they wean you off or what?
JG: Naw, it's strictly cold turkey. They give you some pills to help the sleep and convulsions, but basically it's the shits. And the food—*aargh*— it makes airplane food seem like gourmet dining. It's a good thing I wasn't hungry! I think the plan is to make you so miserable you don't ever want to go back. The only good thing was this old guy who watched the ward at night—he used to play with Django, man! You shoulda heard his stories. I sat up all night talking to him a couple of times; I couldn't sleep anyway, and it was incredible. I'll tell you about it later.

Garcia mentioned his excitement about working on the *Harrington Street* book, even recounting an episode from his childhood that was part of the book. Then he told Hunter:

JG: . . . What I called about was I'm feeling real creative and I'm hot to get writing. I got to thinking about all the stuff we've done while I was at Betty Ford. I don't seem to be able to get to it without you—somehow when we get together the ideas start coming. You know, I've been singing some of those songs for over twenty-five years, and they never once stuck in my throat, I always felt like they were saying what I wanted to be saying . . . It's like they're . . . It's like they're . . .
RH: Real songs?
JG: Yeah, that's it! Real songs! And besides, I miss you, man.
RH: Hey, don't get sentimental on me . . . Get your ass over here and let's start crankin'.
JG: All right! I'd come over now but I think the wifey has some plans for the weekend.
RH: What's a couple more days? We got forever.

There's Nothing You Can Hold for Very Long   **453**

Hunter and Garcia never did get together for that songwriting session. Racked with pain, Garcia turned to heroin for relief again. Then he unilaterally decided that he needed to go into another rehab program to get the medical help he knew he needed.

"Jerry said that when he was in Betty Ford, they were giving him medication for his heart, for his cholesterol, for everything the whole time he was there," Linda Kahn says. "And when he left they told him he should go to a doctor and have those medications continue; that if he didn't take them he'd die. But I guess instead he went to some holistic doctors or something.

"That's why he went to Serenity Knolls [a drug rehab facility in Forest Knolls, in northwest Marin County]. He was originally planning on going up to [a program in] Napa for three months. He hadn't picked out a place, but he was so scared because of what they'd said at Betty Ford about the medication that he hadn't been getting, that he went to Serenity Knolls thinking that he would get it there. But it wasn't that kind of a place."

John Kahn recalled, "I saw him at my house a couple of days before and he didn't seem very well at all. He told me he was an old man. He was trying to explain to me how bad he felt. I was saying, 'Naw, c'mon. It's not that bad. You'll be okay.' And he was saying, 'No, really.' He put it in terms of being a seventy-year-old man in a fifty-year-old body. I know he'd lived a lot of life. But there was something really wrong with him. He wasn't getting enough oxygen. He told me the hardest thing was just getting out of bed in the morning.

"He told me he was going to go somewhere where nobody could find him, and then he'd let me know. I know he had a big argument with his old lady the night before he went in—a big fallout. She really hurt him in a lot of ways—things about money. I felt for him. It was kind of sad to be hassling about that.

"I really got the feeling that he was going to cut a lot of things loose," Kahn continued. "He didn't exactly say what; my feeling was everything—the Grateful Dead, Jerry Garcia Band, his wife, drugs. He really wanted to get away from everybody. That was the last thing he told me. That was the way he thought he could do it. I guess he got away."

Garcia told John and Linda Kahn that one reason he chose Serenity Knolls is that it used to be a Boy Scout camp where he and the band had crashed occasionally in the mid-'60s. Garcia planned to stay at the facility for twenty-one days. He told very few people of his plan; most people in the Dead organization believed he was going to Hawaii. He even kept the news from Deborah, who found out shortly after he'd checked in on the afternoon of August 8, and, according to Linda Kahn, was very angry about having been kept in the dark. She received permission from Serenity Knolls to take Jerry out to dinner, and the two dined together at a Mill Valley Italian restaurant called Piatti. Then she drove him back to Serenity Knolls, a twenty-minute drive.

A Serenity Knolls counselor passed by Garcia's room at around 4 A.M. and heard him snoring loudly. Twenty minutes later the counselor passed Garcia's room again, and this time he didn't hear any sound. When he went into the room to check on Garcia, he found him dressed in a blue polo shirt, gray sweatpants and white socks, lying on top of his bed, his eyes open slightly, apparently lifeless. The orderly called in a staff nurse and Marin County paramedics and they tried to resuscitate Garcia, to no avail. Jerry Garcia was pronounced dead at 4:23 A.M. on August 9, and the county coroner was called in. Pending the results of an autopsy, the cause of death was listed as a massive heart attack.

Deborah Koons Garcia later wondered if Jerry's chronic apnea had contributed to his death: "It's when you're sleeping and you can't breathe. You stop breathing and then you snap out of it. He'd had it for thirty years. And I think he was too weakened to breathe through it. He just stopped breathing. They tried to revive him, and they couldn't."

Garcia's body was moved to a Marin funeral home, and Deborah went over right away. "It's strange to say, but he looked so peaceful," she said. "And Jerry had this smile on his face. I said to the guy at the funeral home, 'Look, he's smiling. Did you do that to him?' And he said, 'No, that's exactly the way I found him.' His face was so at peace. At the funeral we decided to have an open casket because he looked so good."

Word of Garcia's death spread quickly through the media, and the many Grateful Dead conferences on the Internet were inundated with stunned fans looking for comfort and sharing their feelings and memories. By the time Garcia died, most hard-core Deadheads had already heard through the Grateful Dead grapevine about his stay at the Betty Ford Clinic, and there was a widespread feeling of optimism that Jerry was beating his demons and raring to get healthy again. The last year of his life there was no concealing how sick he was—he wore it on his face—yet when the end actually came, nearly everyone professed shock and disbelief. Garcia seemed like one of those guys who, despite his reckless and abusive lifestyle, would probably outlive us all. He might have believed that, too.

In San Francisco a couple of thousand grieving fans crowded onto Haight Street, some banging on drums and playing flutes, while others kept a silent and respectful vigil outside 710 Ashbury. A large group of mourners headed over to the Polo Fields in Golden Gate Park for an impromptu get-together at the site of the Human Be-In twenty-eight years earlier. In New York City, about a thousand people gathered in Central Park at Strawberry Fields—a shrine to another fallen rock star, John Lennon. In cities all over the country, from Philadelphia to Chicago to Portland to Los Angeles, Deadheads gathered to console each other, to mourn and to celebrate Garcia's legacy.

Garcia's death received prominent coverage on the national news broadcasts that evening, and the next morning the story was front-page news in many of the country's largest newspapers, including the *New York Times*, which ran a fond but sober headline: JERRY GARCIA OF GRATEFUL DEAD, ICON OF '60S SPIRIT, DIES AT 53. Within hours of Garcia's passing, television, radio and the news wires were cluttered with fond remembrances from Garcia's musical peers, from friends, admirers and even President Clinton, who said that he and his daughter, Chelsea, represented two generations of Dead fans, and that he wore J. Garcia ties and gave them away as gifts. "He was a great talent; he was a genius," he told MTV. "He also had a terrible problem that was a legacy of the life he lived and the demons he dealt with. And I would hope that all of us who loved his music would also reflect on the consequences of self-destructive behavior."

The most heartfelt tributes came from musician friends past and present, and Jerry's counterculture peers.

Carlos Santana: "He was a profound talent both as a musician and as an artist, and he cannot be replaced. I take solace in the thought that his spirit has gone to join the likes of Bill Graham, Jimi Hendrix, Marvin Gaye, Miles Davis and other greats who have left us too soon."

David Crosby: "Musicians and people who love music have lost one of the brightest, most articulate minds of this generation. He was a great man, a friend and the creator of an incredible amount of wonderful music."

Ornette Coleman: "Jerry Garcia was one of the original American icons. He played naturally and beautifully."

Branford Marsalis: "There is not a sentence in the world that could respectfully do justice to the life and music of Jerry Garcia."

Paul Kantner: "The universe is a cold, indifferent place if you don't believe in Jesus. As Jerry Garcia said, '[Rock 'n' roll] provides what church provided for in other generations.' The Grateful Dead went a long way toward providing something appropriate to this current universe that worked. Jerry was the master of that particular paradigm. He was an exquisite man despite all his faults, many of which we all have. Let us all remember exquisite men."

Maria Muldaur: "He had a flock. He didn't choose it. He didn't say, 'I want to be a big icon and guru' to what is now several generations. But I think it was because in his own unassuming way he made himself completely an instrument of higher good energy, which is the real reason people need music so much. They don't get their money's worth most of the time, but with Jerry Garcia, they sure did."

Ken Kesey: "Jerry was a great warrior. If he was a good leader, then we don't need him anymore; it should be time for people to become active and follow instructions, and his instructions were fairly simple. He's just a straight-out Christian acidhead, speaking of love and mercy and mischief, all those wonderful things from the '60s.

"Jerry knocked a chink out of the wall and let the light shine through, and it's up to us to keep that light shining through, or someday we are going to have to answer to him."

But perhaps the most moving and eloquent tribute of all came from a man unaccustomed to public pronouncements—Bob Dylan: "There's no way to measure his greatness as a person or as a player. I don't think eulogizing will do him justice. He was that great—much more than a superb musician with an uncanny ear and dexterity. He is the very spirit personified of whatever is muddy river country at its core and screams up into the spheres. He really had no equal.

"To me he wasn't only a musician and friend, he was more like a big brother who taught and showed me more than he'll ever know. There are a lot of spaces between the Carter Family, Buddy Holly and, say, Ornette Coleman, a lot of universes, but he filled them all without being a member of any school. His playing was moody, awesome, hypnotic and subtle. There's no way to convey the loss. It just digs down really deep."

The surviving members of the Grateful Dead made no official comment at first. The three who were in the Bay Area at the time—Mickey, Phil and Vince—got together briefly and shared their grief with others in the Dead organization. Bill Kreutzmann was out of town on vacation when he got the news, and Bob Weir was in New Hampshire with his side band, Ratdog. Weir went on with his scheduled performance that night at the Casino Ballroom in Hampton Beach, telling the shell-shocked crowd, "If our dear, departed friend proved anything to us, he proved that great music can make sad times better."

The funeral service for Garcia took place at St. Stephen's (no irony intended) Episcopal Church in Belvedere, in Marin County, on August 11. The location of the ceremony was a closely guarded secret to keep away curious fans, but members of the press found out and showed up in force to gape at the mourners as they entered and left the church. About two hours before the funeral, a retinue of Hell's Angels roared up on their Harleys, went inside for a few minutes, then came out dressed in black suits to help with security. The guest list of about 250 was controlled by Deborah Garcia and included all the current and former bandmates, Grateful Dead staff, Jerry's three grown daughters, his ex-wife Sara, Barbara Meier and assorted friends and colleagues ranging from Kesey to Dylan to Bill Walton. Among those pointedly left off the list were Mountain Girl, Manasha and John Kahn, mean-spirited exclusions that were roundly criticized later by many in the Dead community. M.G. had the opportunity to see Garcia in repose, dressed in a black T-shirt and sweatpants, at a wake the night before. In *Living with the Dead* Rock Scully recounts a conversation in which Garcia supposedly said he didn't want his body to be on display after he died, and art dealer Roberta Weir recalls a remark Jerry made to her in early 1994:

"I told him that I'd always been sort of death-obsessed, that it was in my own [art] work a lot. And he said he thought it was too bad that death had been mystified for people, because dead bodies were taken away and people didn't get a chance to see them. He said, 'If society wasn't hiding the bodies all the time people would realize that the body is just a hunk of meat.' I said,

'Well, what do think about practices that delay burial so that people can talk to the body?' Like in Buddhism there's the idea that the confused soul lingers around the body. And he looked down at himself, he pulled his shirt out from his belly and he said, 'Hang around for *this*? You've got to be kidding. When I'm dead. I'm *outta* here!' "

"It was weird seeing him like that at the funeral," said John Kahn, who showed up with his wife, Linda, anyway and stood in the back. "I crashed the funeral, because I wasn't invited. I just said, 'Fuck it,' and went anyway. It was so ridiculous. I went late after everybody was in and just walked in the back door. They could have stopped me, probably. I went there with the attitude, 'This is the last I'm going to see any of these people, because I'd just as soon not see them anymore.' I was kind of pissed off at them about Jerry. The Grateful Dead was really hassling Jerry at the end—all those people, his wife, the Grateful Dead. He wasn't very happy there at the end and it pissed me off."

The Reverend Matthew Fox (who had presided over Jerry and Deborah's wedding) conducted the service, which lasted about an hour and a half and featured a number of speeches, many of them laced with humor, from friends and family. It was an open-casket funeral and several attendees later noted—with affection and not a trace of disrespect—that they'd seen Jerry look much worse. Reverend Fox called Jerry "a wounded healer" and sprinkled quotes from Heidegger, Jung and St. Thomas Aquinas in his remarks. "Jerry is in a place where the ancestors gather, his musical ancestors," he said, "and one can only imagine the jamming going on there."

Kesey praised Garcia as a warrior, and Steve Parish spoke movingly about his friend who had treated him and others so well through the years. David Grisman and Enrique Coria played "Amazing Grace" and the ancient Hebrew melody "Shalom Aleichem." Gloria Jones and Jackie LaBranch of the JGB sang a spiritual called "My Living Shall Not Be in Vain" backed by Melvin Seals on piano. Annabelle Garcia, beaming a pranksterish grin, noted that Jerry "may have been a genius, but he was a shitty father." This widely reported remark was viewed by people who don't know her mischievous sense of humor—so much like both her father's and mother's—to be out of place at the funeral, but everyone in attendance knew what she meant and took it in the spirit she intended.

Toward the end of the service Robert Hunter stood in front of the mourners and with shaking hands but a strong voice read a poem he'd written for the occasion. As usual, his eloquence struck the perfect chord for the event. It read, in part:

> *Jerry, my friend,*
> *you've done it again,*
> *even in your silence*
> *the familiar pressure*

comes to bear, demanding
I pull words from the air
with only this morning
and part of the afternoon
to compose an ode worthy
of one so particular
about every turn of phrase,
demanding it hit home
in a thousand ways
before making it his own,
and this I can't do alone.
Now that the singer has gone,
where shall I go for the song? . . .

. . . May she bear thee to thy rest,
the ancient bower of flowers
beyond the solitude of days,
the tyranny of hours—
the wreath of shining laurel lie
upon your shaggy head,
bestowing power to play the lyre
to legions of the dead.

If some part of that music
is heard in deepest dream,
or on some breeze of Summer
a snatch of golden theme,
we'll know you live inside us
with love that never parts
our good old Jack of Diamonds
become the King of Hearts.

I feel your silent laughter
at sentiments so bold
that dare to step across the line
to tell what must be told,
so I'll just say I love you
which I never said before
and let it go at that my friend,
the rest you may ignore.

At the end of the service Reverend Fox asked the mourners to give Garcia one last standing ovation, and they obliged, tears flowing from most eyes. As they left the church, many filed by the open casket, pausing for a moment to say good-bye one more time.

After the funeral some of the crowd repaired to a gathering at Bill Graham's former hilltop mansion in Mill Valley, known as Masada, while others, including M.G., went to Robert and Maureen Hunter's house. Sara Ruppenthal says, "We had a wonderful time at Hunter's. And for that whole week there was this extensive sort of house party going on, with Hunter taking care of people who needed to come and connect with each other. It was extraordinarily nurturing."

Two days after the funeral, at the Polo Fields in Golden Gate Park, there was an official public celebration of Garcia's life. The day broke sunny and warm, and by 8 A.M. thousands of Deadheads from all over the Bay Area, and scores more who had flown in or driven long distances to be part of the event, had congregated on the field in the bright morning sunshine. Bill Graham Presents had set up loudspeakers and erected a small platform with a rostrum and a single microphone surrounded by enormous sprays of flowers. Multicolored triangular banners flanked the stage, and an arch of purple and green balloons blew silently above the stage in the early morning breeze. From outward appearances, it could almost have been a stage set from a latter-day Dead show except for the main element in the scene: a striking thirty-foot painted cloth portrait of a smiling Garcia, guitar in hands. In front of the stage there was a makeshift shrine which over the course of the day became filled with thousands of personal mementos from Deadheads—photos, old Dead T-shirts, poems, flowers, stuffed animals, ticket stubs, messages to Jerry—all sorts of big and little items.

At 10 A.M. a Mardi Gras–style funeral parade passed slowly around the edge of the field, led by a Dixieland band playing from the back of a flatbed truck. Among those in the procession were a dozen or so people carrying Grateful Dead and Tibetan prayer flags, and the Hog Farm's Chinese New Year dragon, Flash, who'd been part of so many Grateful Dead shows. By late morning there were about 25,000 people on the field—about the same number that attended the Human Be-In there. Clusters of Deadheads who'd been to untold numbers of shows together assembled on blankets and bedspreads as if they were at a show. Children chased each other and blew bubbles. There were hugs, more than a few tears, but mostly smiling faces.

The great Nigerian drummer Babatunde Olatunji, dressed in a flowing white African robe, was the first to speak before the crowd. He offered words of consolation, urged those gathered to celebrate Garcia's spirit and led everyone in call-and-response chanting that echoed across the giant field.

Then Olatunji introduced Deborah Garcia, who lifted the crowd's mood when she came to the microphone and said, "What a great guy Jerry was! He would have loved this; he *is* loving it! He was a big-hearted, generous, wonderful, hardworking man. I want everyone to know that he died in his sleep with a smile on his face. He was working hard to purify himself, and we thought it was going to be for a good long life, but it was for another journey.

And he loved his life. He loved all of you. And what I learned from Jerry was to open my heart and live fully in the moment. And for that, and for everything else, and for all the beauty in his life, I want to say thank you, Jerry, I love you."

Annabelle Garcia lauded her father as "one of the greatest Americans ever born" and urged Deadheads "to respect each other and love each other. And think to yourself when something's wrong: What would Jerry do? And keep it up, you know? You gotta keep together, and be grateful."

Fighting back tears, his voice breaking with emotion, Bob Weir thanked Jerry for "showing me how to live with joy and mischief. And so, what I want is to give some of that back to him now, make him complete, make him whole." With his arms outstretched, his hands open toward the sun, he asked the crowd to "Take your heart, take your faith, and reflect back some of that joy he gave you. He filled this world full of clouds of joy. Just take a little bit of that and reflect it back up to him, or wherever he is, just shine it back to him."

Steve Parish, a private man with a tough exterior, said simply, "You've seen us up here scurrying around all these years. I wanna just tell you we did it because we love you, too; all of you, you were great! You're the best people there are!"

Then the other members of the band spoke.

Mickey Hart told the crowd that the Grateful Dead had empowered them and that now, "You have the groove, you have the feeling. We've been working on it for thirty years now. So what are you going to do with it? That's the question. . . . This means a lot to all of us, and you kept us going; you were the fuel. You were a part of it; a big part of it. . . . We all love you for that!"

Phil Lesh called Jerry "my brother. He was a wounded warrior. And now he's done with becoming. Now he is being Jerry, God bless you. Go with God. I love you."

Bill Kreutzmann noted that "the highest moment of my life was when the band was playing and cooking . . . with Jerry and these guys behind me. That's the best."

And Vince Welnick said, "The first time I ever laid eyes on Jerry I believed in Santa Claus. He could be ornery at times, but that was his body talking, not his soul. Because I never met a kinder man in the whole world. Everybody's asking the big question, and love is the answer. And I'll always believe in Santa Claus."

The last speaker was John Barlow: "They asked me to come up here and speak a word, and rarely in my life have I had so few of them. And so I'll just speak one: Love."

For the entire afternoon, David Gans and Dick Latvala played Grateful Dead tapes over the huge sound system, and thousands of Deadheads danced, swayed, sang along and cheered as if it were "the boys" themselves up there, beneath the smiling Jerry portrait, cranking out rock 'n' roll and space music and heartrending ballads. The crowd whooped during "Scarlet Begonias" and "Sugar Magnolia," seemed scattered and confused during a long, painfully loud psychedelic jam from a '68 tape, and looked appropriately somber during "Death Don't Have No Mercy."

As the shadows from the towering cypress trees that ring the Polo Fields grew long in the late afternoon, an unmistakable air of sadness floated over the field. The last few songs brought back tears once more: the gentle strains of "Box of Rain" from *American Beauty*; the band, circa 1968, struggling to keep their harmonies together on "We Bid You Goodnight," the lovely a cappella spiritual the band closed so many shows with in the late '60s; and finally, the soothing orchestral version of "Greensleeves" that Bill Graham loved to use to gently usher people back out into the real world after shows at the Fillmores and Winterland. The day had been a celebration *and* a wake; a perfect day with only one thing missing: Jerry Garcia.

EPILOGUE
Sleep in the Stars

he mainstream press reaction to Garcia's death in the weeks following August 9 was remarkable. He was on the cover of *Newsweek, People* and *Rolling Stone. People* and *Entertainment Weekly* each put out special commemorative issues devoted entirely to him. Most of what was written about Garcia after his death was filled with genuine respect and affection. Jerry's iconic persona was that of a laidback, good-natured hippie—*People* dubbed him "rock's happy warrior" on their August 21 cover. To the non–Deadhead world, he was the grizzled, grinning embodiment of the acid-soaked Summer of Love, a pied piper to young and old hippies; "Thirty years and still truckin'!" He was free concerts in the park and "Touch of Grey." He was even forgiven his love of drugs: LSD was far in the past; stoned Deadheads were practically cultural icons themselves, funny to people the same way beatniks were in the '50s; and because Garcia died in a drug treatment facility, the public perception was that he was finally trying to beat his addiction. If he had died of a drug overdose backstage at a show, the spin of most of the stories would have been quite different. But America loves recovery, because nearly everyone can relate to some form of excess.

As a media story, Garcia's death faded from view within a month. Many newspapers and magazines didn't even bother to report the autopsy findings, which confirmed what everyone had suspected: Garcia had died of a heart attack. The coroner's investigator, Gary Erickson, observed that Garcia had advanced heart disease and that two of the three arteries leading into Jerry's heart had been reduced to "a pinpoint," with 85 percent blockage. "He was a fifty-three-year-old man with hardening of the arteries," he said. "This was a mechanical process." A coronary bypass operation at the end of summer tour might have saved Garcia, but he went into drug rehab, not a hospital, so the facility he checked in to was looking primarily at his addiction, not his overall health. After Jerry's death several of his friends remarked that the strain of going through detox, then taking more drugs, and subsequently trying to clean up again was probably more than his weakened body could take.

"Everyone should note that the worst thing he ever did for his health was the cigarettes—the two and three packs a day for years and years and years," Len Dell'Amico says. "That over the long haul, obesity and smoking cigarettes are two of the main indicators for a heart attack. That's why the doctors said [after Garcia's 1992 collapse], 'If you don't quit this you've probably got two years.' And he never really quit smoking."

This may be true, but it must also be said that heroin had the extremely deleterious effect of making him not care about what he ate, whether he slept or if he got any exercise. And though heroin is widely considered the great dark force of this saga, because it turned him inward and away from people, the prodigious amounts of cocaine Garcia took through the years also must have taken a toll on his body—prolonged use of the drug has been shown to cause heart damage.

If the media mourning of Garcia was largely finished a month after his death, in the Grateful Dead community—the Dead family and all the Deadheads—the enormity of the loss was just beginning to sink in. The shock was wearing off, denial was no longer an option and hundreds of thousands of people—from bandmembers to roadies to that twenty-year-old hippie girl from Santa Cruz selling veggie burritos outside Dead shows to earn enough scratch to make it to the next concert—were now confronted with the frightening and incomprehensible prospect of a world without the Grateful Dead. This was the Big One, a reckoning if there ever was one. Can You Pass *This* Acid Test?

One can only imagine what the band—with their unfathomably rich shared history and their psychic (and psychedelic) bonds as strong as any blood ties—must have experienced in the first months after Jerry's death. Steeled though they may have been from years of secretly expecting Garcia's imminent demise, no one could foresee the emotional ramifications of the event when it finally happened. There was sadness, rage, confusion, emptiness—many of the same feelings Deadheads went through.

Bob Weir was the first to make a public statement about Garcia's death, when he appeared in a brief interview with MTV's Kurt Loder on September 9. Asked if grieving Deadheads had been approaching him on the streets, Weir remarked, "All the time. They're pouring out a little bit of their hearts. They're assuming that I'm taking this a lot harder than I am. Death is so final that I can't really react to it that much. Because it's a change you absolutely have to accept, right now. I can't take Jerry's death personally; he didn't do that to me. When they come up to me on the street, I think they're trying to give me a little strength that I don't really need; they could keep it for themselves. But if they feel like they have to share something with me, well, here I am."

Mickey Hart says that after Garcia died, "I couldn't play Grateful Dead music around the house for a long time. It was just too painful to hear his guitar. Three years later it's still painful for me; it's still a little close. And I really thought I would never play Grateful Dead music again. But you have to put the past behind. I dug in here at my studio for months and didn't come out." Hart was already working on a solo album—called *Mystery Box*—that featured songs with lyrics by Robert Hunter. But Garcia's death gave the project a new urgency and also a new direction: some of Hunter's lyrics seemed to address the uncertainty Deadheads and the musicians were facing in the post-Jerry age, while at the same time optimistically positing the notion that love and music were the keys that could unlock life's mystery box: "Depend on the wind of distant drums / We'll know the next step when it comes." Another song, "Down the Road," included a touching verse about Garcia, written just days after August 9:

> From the corner of my eye I saw the sun explode
> I didn't look directly 'cause it would have burned my soul
> When the smoke and thunder cleared enough to look around
> I heard a sweet guitar lick, an old familiar sound
> Heard a laugh I recognized come rolling from the earth
> Saw it rise into the skies like lightning giving birth
> It sounded like Garcia but I couldn't see the face
> Just the beard and glasses and a smile on empty space

Interestingly, the bandmember who was perhaps the most severely affected by Garcia's death was the most recent addition, Vince Welnick. "When Jerry died my whole world came apart," he says. "I don't think I'll ever be the same again. That was the happiest time of my life, playing with those guys. Jerry's death completely changed my life from the happiest time in my life to the unhappiest. I'm only now [a year and a half later] even able to talk about it. If you had tried to interview me a year ago, I would've had nothing to say; there was nothing I *could* say. I was like a vegetable. I could barely stand to go to the wake and the funeral. I remember when I was seeing Jerry in the coffin I was thinking, 'He moved!' And the thing in Golden Gate Park was like the worst acid trip of my life, because you're out there seeing all these people and it's a beautiful day and Jerry's fucking dead and you can't believe it, not even for a minute, and you can't change it.

"I was just not ready, not in the slightest, for that to go down. It took every bit of life out of me; I've never been in a darker time. I was like a walking zombie. I was very depressed and wound up in a depression clinic around Christmas of '95."

Not coincidentally, it was in early December that it became clear that the Grateful Dead would not continue without Garcia. Throughout the fall there had been rampant speculation that the band might try to carry on with a new guitarist—popular choices of the rumor mill included Carlos Santana, Eric Clapton, Los Lobos' David Hidalgo and Jorma Kaukonen. One scenario had Branford Marsalis and Bruce Hornsby filling the vacant slot; another suggested that the Dead would use a number of different players over the course of a tour. But all this was little more than wishful thinking. In truth, no one was ever approached about taking Garcia's place. December 7 was to be the first full band meeting since Jerry's death, but Bill Kreutzmann elected not to attend, effectively scuttling any serious talk about the future. Kreutzmann made it clear that he had no intention of going on without Garcia; still, a couple of his bandmates were miffed that he didn't even show up to discuss the situation. Nevertheless, the others talked for nearly five hours. The following day, December 8, the Dead formally broke the suspense by announcing that they had officially disbanded.

"Everybody sort of knew inside," Mickey Hart told the *San Francisco Chronicle*. "Of course it was hard. But everybody had a feeling. It just wasn't there. We put it to pasture, righteously, as it should be. We went out looking good.

"I think we've done it about as good as it can be done," Hart reflected. "This thing was a conversation, a very intimate conversation between us; the band and the audience. It's something you can't really manufacture. It's not something you sign up for or sign out of. Think about it: We went through presidencies, Vietnam. Thirty years. It was never planned. It was spontaneous, with a giant helping of magic. It was a great ride."

Garcia's passing had an immediate and calamitous economic impact on the Dead organization and various businesses that depended on the band for a sizable percentage of their income, such as Ultra Sound (which supplied the Dead's sound system), Bill Graham Presents and John Scher's Metropolitan Entertainment. At Dead headquarters in San Rafael, there were a number of layoffs, and several people from the office staff were reassigned to work at Grateful Dead Merchandising (GDM), which was inundated with orders after Jerry died. Ironically, the person in charge of handling the huge volume of orders at GDM in Novato was Tiff Garcia. Salaries were slashed across the board, and those who had been connected primarily with the Dead's touring operation found themselves struggling to justify a position on the payroll. Despite Garcia's collapses in 1986 and 1992, the organization had no real plan for what would happen if the Grateful Dead ceased to exist.

Deadheads coped with the loss however they could. There isn't a Deadhead alive who doesn't remember where he or she was when the bad news came in—that paralyzing phone call; the dispassionate radio report; the newspaper headline seen in a sidelong glance; the sobbing friend at the door. The myriad Grateful Dead on-line conferences provided an important outlet for thousands of Heads to express their feelings and stay connected with each other in the absence of Dead concerts, as did Robert Hunter's Web site. David Gans, whose syndicated *Grateful Dead Hour* radio program continued to bring music and interviews to more than eighty different radio markets, compiled a moving book called *Not Fade Away: The On-line World Remembers Jerry Garcia*, filled with eloquent reflections and memories plucked from cyberspace in the month following August 9.

Many Deadheads found that they were unable to listen to Dead tapes for months after Jerry's death because it made them too sad. Others listened obsessively in hopes of absorbing some joy from the music. Bands that played mainly Grateful Dead music—from unassuming little combos with acoustic guitars to highly evolved and ambitious electric groups that could truly summon the fire of the '68 (or '77, or '89) Dead—took up some of the slack. Bars and clubs that played Dead tapes one night a week (or sporadically) for dancing Deadheads also proliferated. *Of course* it wasn't the same as going to a Dead show; no one expected that. But many found familiar flashes of that Grateful Dead high here and there—"in the strangest of places if you look at it right." And, above all, there was the warm camaraderie that had always suffused Deadhead events. That did not die with Garcia.

Where did the tourheads go? By the time Garcia died, some were already following the popular band Phish, a tremendously skilled, vibrant, fun-loving and eclectic quartet with a penchant for jamming, big grooves and playing long sets of highly improvisational music. Phish is more like the Grateful Dead in approach and in sound, and though there was an overlap of fans for years, Phish has always attracted its own, mainly younger, crowd of non-Deadheads, too. A similarly obsessive subculture has grown around Phish, too, with tapers and statisticians and merchants and hard-cores who hit entire tours.

Other commercially popular bands that attracted large followings of young Deadheads in the mid-'90s were the Dave Matthews Band and Blues Traveler. The next tier of less mainstream groups admired by many Deadheads for their jamming prowess included Rusted Root, moe., Widespread Panic, God Street Wine, String Cheese Incident, Zero, Max Creek, Leftover Salmon and Medeski, Martin and Wood. None of those bands sound like each other; mostly they share a sense of adventure and musical daring that is attractive to Deadheads.

On the fringes of the Dead family, there were a number of groups that provided a sense of musical continuity for Deadheads: Merl Saunders's Rainforest Band played a number of the tunes that the old Garcia-Saunders group used to perform in the early '70s, as well as jazzy versions of "Sugaree," "Fire on the Mountain," "Franklin's Tower" and occasionally "Dark Star." David Nelson's band also played a few Dead covers, as well as songs from his New Riders days and a scattering of impressive original songs, including a few with lyrics by Robert Hunter. The Nelson Band's Barry Sless was the most overtly Garcia-like lead guitarist of all the Dead family bands, though he was much more than a clone.

Without question the most controversial Dead family group to tour in the long shadow of Garcia's death was Bob Weir's band, Ratdog. Here was a group consisting entirely of rhythm players and no lead instrumentalist. The contrast between the Grateful Dead, where Garcia's guitar lines spun graceful melodies that danced in the air, and this group, with its thin and monotonous sound, could not have been more striking. Weir made a point to *not* play his best-loved Grateful Dead material—"Let It Grow" "Sugar Magnolia," "Estimated Prophet," etc.—yet he did play some of his least popular Dead tunes in Ratdog—"Victim or the Crime," "Throwing Stones" and "Eternity." The band was able to fill small theaters and clubs, but the word of mouth from their first tour was not good. Maybe in some other time they would have been embraced more, but in the wake of Jerry's death they seemed pale and surprisingly joyless.

Nevertheless, Ratdog was chosen to headline the first Furthur Festival in the summer of 1996. Sensing that Deadheads might still be interested in turning out to see a lineup of bands that were capable of rekindling some of the Dead's spirit, Weir, John Scher, Dead tour manager Cameron Sears and Mickey Hart conceived a roving festival along the lines of already popular summer touring rock cavalcades such as Lollapalooza and HORDE, and named it after Kesey's bus, that eternal icon of '60s fearlessness. They assembled a strong bill for their first tour: Hot Tuna, Los Lobos, Bruce Hornsby's band, Ratdog and Mickey Hart's Mystery Box (which included several world-class percussionists and a black British female vocal sextet called the Mint Juleps). Each Furthur show offered seven hours of music, culminating in a mini jam session that found Weir, Hart, Hornsby, Jorma Kaukonen and members of Los Lobos trading licks on a wide variety of classic rock tunes, from "Not Fade Away" to "White Rabbit." Hippie vendors paid for the right to sell their wares inside the amphitheaters and parks where the tour traveled, and the Dead's ticket operation, GDTS, handled some of the ticketing. The tour was a moderate success commercially, selling an average 65 percent of capacity— not terrific by the Dead's lofty standards, but, as John Scher notes, "better than either Lollapalooza or HORDE did in their first years."

Though the tour was not specifically designed to be a tribute to Jerry Garcia, there was no escaping his ghost—his absence was like a great unseen presence. At the Shoreline Amphitheater Furthur concert I attended, Los Lobos dedicated a spellbinding rendition of Marvin Gaye's "What's Goin' On?" to Jerry before slamming into "Bertha." Bruce Hornsby played a piano fantasia based around "Terrapin" during his set, and later brought out both Hart and Weir for a "Jack Straw" that featured the same sort of deftly executed dynamic shifts that made the tune soar with the Dead. At many shows Hornsby also played "Wharf Rat," which had long been one of his favorite Hunter-Garcia songs. Mickey closed each of his sets on the tour with with his spoken-rapped version of "Fire on the Mountain," one of the first songs he and Hunter wrote together.

At Shoreline, Phil Lesh joined the group for "Fire on the Mountain," playing a thundering bass solo over the song's fat, loping rhythm—something he never did with the Dead. After the song, he and Mickey embraced warmly in a touching show of deep kinship. And Phil, Mickey, Bobby and Bruce were reunited for the show-closing jam session, which included "Truckin' " and

"The Other One," with David Hidalgo, Jorma Kaukonen and hard rocker Sammy Hagar (a friend of Mickey's) blazing away on guitars, each in his own style. It offered a glimpse of how exciting a tour by the surviving Dead members could be if they ever decided to make the leap.

While the former members of the Grateful Dead pondered their next moves in the year after August 1995, a very different kind of drama connected to Garcia's will was unfolding in the Marin County court system. The will, which was written in May 1994, was quite straightforward and simple; so much so that it was praised by *Money* magazine for the clarity of its intent. Jerry left one-third of his estate and the bulk of his material possessions to Deborah Koons Garcia. Of the remaining two-thirds, he left a fifth to each of his four daughters—Heather, Annabelle, Theresa and Keelin; and the remaining fifth split between Sunshine Kesey (whom he helped raise for several years) and his brother, Tiff. Additionally, Jerry willed the custom guitars that had been built for him by Doug Irwin back to the luthier. At the time of Jerry's death there was no detailed accounting of either his assets or the potential value of the estate, so it wasn't immediately clear how much money there was to divide.

And then things started to get complicated. Within a few months, more than $38 million in claims had been filed against the estate, ranging from a $980 claim from Jerry's personal trainer, Sherwood Cummins, to a $15.6 million claim from Vince DiBiase, whose ownership of a number of Garcia's original artworks and his right to sell reproductions of those works was challenged by the estate—represented by Deborah. In between those two figures there was a wide array of other claims, among them:

Carolyn Garcia (Mountain Girl) asked for $4.6 million still owed her under a $5 million divorce agreement she and Jerry signed in 1993 guaranteeing her more than $20,000 a month for the next twenty years. Jerry had been making the payments up until his death, when Deborah abruptly stopped them and then decided to challenge the fairness and legal authority of the thirteen-line document Jerry and M.G. had signed. Theresa Garcia asked for $22,000 she said was owed her after the estate stopped making payments on a Toyota 4-Runner car. Jerry's daughter Heather Katz filed a claim for $30,000 she said Jerry had promised toward a down payment on a home she was buying in Oakland. Barbara Meier sued to receive the remaining $21,000 due her under her 1993 agreement with Jerry to pay her a total of $108,000; the monthly $3,000 payments had been cut off by Deborah in May 1995. Manasha Matheson filed a claim for $3 million, saying that was the figure owed her under an agreement Jerry had made in return for her dropping her option of suing him for palimony and child support. John Kahn claimed he was owed an undetermined amount of JGB royalties and money for a recording console he'd purchased. Perhaps the most bizarre claim was filed by Eric Storace, who asked for $10,000, saying that back in 1970 Garcia had agreed to buy the rights for a never-completed concert film that included the Dead called *Pot Luck Sock Hop Dog Fuck.*

In late May 1996 John Kahn died in his sleep in the Mill Valley house he shared with his wife, Linda. As fate would have it, I had interviewed him for this book just a week earlier. That night he looked pale and drawn, but he was in good spirits and he spoke optimistically about the prospects for his new band—featuring Melvin, Jackie and Gloria from the JGB and a new guitarist and singer—which had played a couple of gigs in Santa Cruz. As had happened with Garcia, Kahn's heart simply gave out. Though there were drugs in his system at the time of his death, it was not ruled an overdose. In a particularly cruel twist, the police who came to the Kahns' house to investigate the death busted Linda for possession of a small amount of cocaine found in a search of the premises. A celebration of John's life at the Log Cabin in San Anselmo a few days later drew dozens of friends and former musical partners who swapped stories about this kind and gentle man, as a CD player blasted music by the JGB, the Jerry Garcia Acoustic Band and Old and in the Way. Stanley Mouse dropped by with a whimsical cartoon he'd drawn of Garcia and Kahn happy together in heaven; a nice thought, everyone agreed.

At the end of 1996 the court battle between Carolyn Garcia and Deborah Koons Garcia came to trial in the futuristic Frank Lloyd Wright–designed Marin County courthouse. This legal contest probably would not have drawn much interest outside Deadhead circles had it not been for the decision by the Court TV cable network to televise the trial nearly in its entirety, assuring that the "War of the Wives" (as *People* magazine dubbed it) would be a spectacle.

The estate's strategy in the case was to prove that Jerry's marriage to M.G. was a sham carried out for business reasons, and that Jerry had been coerced into signing the $5 million divorce settlement without obtaining anything tangible in return. Though Judge Michael Dufficy ruled early in the trial that he viewed the 1981–93 marriage between Jerry and M.G. as legal and binding, the estate's blustering and aggressive lawyer, Paul Camera, produced a series of reluctant witnesses, including Phil Lesh and Steve Parish, to testify that M.G. rarely traveled with the Dead and didn't live with Jerry during the time of their marriage, except for a few years after Jerry's coma. (Later in the trial it came out that Jerry and Deborah had not lived together during their marriage, either.)

"The reason that Jerry and I made an agreement outside of the legal system was because we were afraid of just this kind of stuff," M.G. said after the trial. "Neither of us wanted to go to court; we didn't want to submit ourselves to the scrutiny."

Court TV had a slew of legal analysts covering the proceedings, dissecting the minutiae of the testimony the way they had for the O. J. Simpson murder trial a year earlier, and day after day the "experts" came up with the same conclusion: that the one-paragraph divorce agreement, drawn up by Carolyn Garcia at Jerry's request and signed in the presence of a lawyer, was valid. In the end, Judge Dufficy came to the same conclusion and let the divorce settlement stand.

Deborah appealed the judgment and the ruling seemed to be heading for years of expensive appeals when, in the summer of 1998, M.G. decided to end the court battles by settling with the estate for $1.25 million. Since that bruising trial, Deborah has settled several of the other claims against the estate as well.

Ultimately the trial and all the mudslinging in the press had little effect on most Deadheads, who—like Jerry himself—have always been more interested in music and celebration than digging through the dirty laundry of their heroes. And to the fans' delight, in 1997 all of the former members of the group were active musically, making their way through uncertain times by finding new creative ventures.

Bill Kreutzmann, now living on the Hawaiian island of Kauai, joined a local trio called Backbone, which played bars there and a few gigs in Northern California to mixed reviews.

Vince Welnick came out of his funk with a strong, eclectic group called Missing Man Formation, which played a mixture of Grateful Dead tunes (including "Saint Stephen," "Cosmic Charlie," "The Wheel" and others), unusual cover songs from the '60s and '70s (Led Zeppelin, the Stones, et al.) and a handful of originals, including three that addressed Jerry's death and its aftermath. "I plan to carry on in the tradition of the Dead as much as I can," Vince says, "but respectfully and without trying to steal the thunder. I want to be with those people [Deadheads] and to serve the music, just like Jerry did. That's my goal."

Bob Weir, Mickey Hart and Bruce Hornsby took their groups out on the second Furthur Festival in the summer of 1997. Ratdog added a young sax player named Dave Ellis, who brought the band a powerful melodic voice, and a new keyboardist, Jeff Chimenti. The group's songbook also underwent a much-needed transformation: this time out, Ratdog's Furthur sets consisted mostly of Grateful Dead material, including crowd-pleasers such as "Saint of Circumstance," "Truckin'," "Sugar Magnolia" and "Cassidy," and even a few Garcia tunes—"Touch of Grey," "West L.A. Fadeaway," "Loose Lucy." Mickey's band, Planet Drum, featured the same top-notch percussionists as Mystery Box, but not the Mint Juleps, so most of their material was new and not so vocally oriented. Instead, Planet Drum fell into a sort of organic techno-ambient groove space—modern dance music with a tribal feeling. Hornsby's sound and repertoire changed little between the 1996 and 1997 tours. Robert Hunter, who that spring returned to the stage after a seven-year absence, also performed at a number of Furthur dates, to a rapturous reception.

Financially, Furthur '97 was a bust, particularly on the East Coast, before the tour's uniformly strong word of mouth had a chance to work. The tour undoubtedly suffered from the bad rap that Ratdog received in 1996, but also, many Deadheads were turned off by the '97 headliner, the hard-rocking Georgia band the Black Crowes.

Phil Lesh strapped on his bass in public only a few times in 1997. He jammed with Weir, Hart and Hornsby at the Furthur show at Shoreline Amphitheater; he joined David Crosby for a few songs at a pair of Bay Area gigs; and he sat in twice with David Gans's occasional band, the Broken Angels, gleefully playing on a wide selection of Dead tunes, from "Scarlet Begonias" to "The Other One," and singing a few himself—"Broken Arrow," "Just Like Tom Thumb's Blues" and "Box of Rain."

During the first few months of 1998 Phil stepped out even more, playing monthly gigs at the Fillmore and Warfield with a variety of different musicians, billed as Phil and Friends. (All the shows were benefits for a philanthropic group Phil and his wife, Jill, started called the Unbroken Chain Foundation.) The first couple of shows featured the Broken Angels as the core band, augmented by players ranging from Vince Welnick to pedal steel player Joe Goldmark. Bob Weir showed up at the late February Fillmore show, rocking and jamming through two generous sets of mostly classic Dead material. The format was loose as could be, and Phil was clearly up for anything, whether it was long-neglected songs from the Dead's past, such as "Saint Stephen" and "Alligator," or numbers like Coltrane's "A Love Supreme" and the Stones' "Wild Horses." Anything was fair game; Phil even took a stab at singing "Days Between."

By spring, rumors that had been swirling through the Dead scene since December 1997 were confirmed: Lesh, Weir, Bruce Hornsby and Mickey Hart had agreed to put together a band for the summer 1998 Furthur tour. John Molo, from Hornsby's band, was brought in as a second drummer. Ratdog sax man Dave Ellis was also invited to be part of the group. They even had a clever and fitting new name: the Other Ones.

Not surprisingly, the toughest position to fill was the lead guitarist slot. For a while, a young player from David Murray's jazz group named Stan Franks appeared to have the inside track—he played at several Phil and Friends shows, and Weir in particular seemed to favor him. But when rehearsals for the Other Ones' tour began in earnest in May it was decided that Franks was not such a good fit after all. With time running short, the group settled on a versatile journeyman guitarist named Mark Karan. Originally from Marin County, but more recently living in L.A., Karan was already familiar with the Dead's music and, unlike Franks, was comfortable anchoring Dead-style melodic jams.

Just a few days before the tour began, however, the Other Ones added a second guitarist—Steve Kimock, who played in Zero and had been a member of Missing Man Formation through most of 1997. Months earlier, Kimock had been passed over by the Other Ones, in part because Weir felt his style was too close to Garcia's. But he also had his advocates in the Dead camp, and when he went back to the Dead's Novato studio to see how he would mesh with Karan and the rest of the group, the chemistry was clearly there.

"I happened to swing by the studio the day they were auditioning Steve Kimock," M.G. relates. "I swung by and it was lunch hour and they weren't really rehearsing yet; they were just warming up. But I'll tell you—when I heard the sound of Phil's bass and those guitars and the drums all coming together it was so exciting I nearly passed out! It sounded like the real thing. When I hear that sound my whole being goes into some fugue state of anticipation and ecstasy. I'm just wired up that way, and think of how many thousands of other people are, too. There's nothing else like that sound. And *this* was that sound."

It was *that sound*, only different, of course. The Other Ones had a bigger, fuller, denser sound than the Dead ever did—not surprising given that Garcia was "replaced" by two guitarists and a saxophonist, and that Weir, Lesh, Hornsby and Hart all viewed themselves as leaders of the octet to a degree. Although the repertoire was dominated by Grateful Dead songs, the musicians took great pains to get away from some of the Dead's ingrained habits. Instead of playing two sets, they played one two-and-a-half- to three-hour set each night. They abandoned the Dead's tired formula of playing short songs at the beginning and extended pieces toward the end, making sets very unpredictable. They also changed the arrangements of many Dead tunes. "Friend of the Devil," sung by Weir, went back to its original fast clip; "Uncle John's Band" was transformed into a brisk, lilting tune with African and West Indian shading. Hunter-Garcia tunes dominated, with Weir singing songs such as "China Cat," "Touch of Grey," "Loose Lucy" and "Bird Song"; Lesh trying "U.S. Blues," "China Doll" and "Mississippi Half-Step," among others; and Hornsby leading the band through "Scarlet Begonias," "Wharf Rat," "Tennessee Jed" and "Ramble On Rose." The group also fearlessly tackled a few songs that Garcia either rarely played in his later days, or hadn't attempted for years, including "Saint Stephen," "The Eleven," "Dark Star" and "Mountains of the Moon."

"It was illuminating and refreshing going back to some of those musical places," Mickey says. "Things were organic in a way they were for years and years in the Grateful Dead, with different guys suggesting approaches. Somewhere along the line the Dead stopped doing that; we lost that fire. So we reclaimed some of that spirit, and like the Dead, the Other Ones were able to turn spirit into form.

"Backstage one day on the tour someone asked me, 'What would you say to Jerry if he walked into this room right now?' I'd say, 'Hey man, we could really use you. You wanna join the band?' And you know what? I bet he'd join this band. Because in some ways it's better than the Grateful Dead was when we stopped. It's more enthusiastic, more poised. And I know Jerry would want to be part of something this good. He'd get off on it," he adds, a trace of sadness behind his smile.

Sometimes there were clashing soloists, way too much going on in the music, and it was hard not to yearn for the delicacy, simplicity and directness Garcia brought to his playing (and singing). But the flip side of that is that the Other Ones were capable of building sonic tidal waves. They were serious about jamming and serious about taking the Grateful Dead songbook to some new spaces. This wasn't meant to be nostalgia; it was a new thing. And the fact that both the musicians and the large, jubilant crowds that turned up at every tour stop seemed to enjoy themselves so much is proof that *it worked*.

"When we got out there onstage the first night of the tour it felt like we'd only been gone for three days, not three years," Mickey says. "The heat coming from the audience was tremendous. They were hungry and we were hungry and we all sat down together for a big feast. We were all desperate for that Grateful Dead feeling. It was mutual, and it all seemed quite soulful and real."

"I think it's great that Deadheads are still getting together and the musicians are still out there making music and trying new things," says Dick Latvala, who has stayed busy turning out a steady stream of live shows from the vault—the *Dick's Picks* CD releases—as well as spinning tapes at occasional dance parties. "But let's face it: There ain't ever gonna be another Grateful Dead. They belonged to that time and they can't be replaced, because Jerry's role was central to the essence of everything. People might say I'm crazy, but I really believe that the Grateful Dead was one of the most awesome things to ever happen in the universe, because they succeeded at getting people together in ways that they never had before, and they were about peace and love and all that corny stuff, which is obviously what we need to survive into the future.

"It was totally magical at the same time it was real," he continues. "Talk to Deadheads, man. Every one has a great story—or a million of 'em! But I've always felt that at the core there was a commonly shared perception and all people were the same when we were in there at the shows. We were all spirits and it didn't matter what age you were; we were all receiving the same information and sharing in the joy of celebrating it together and that's what was so compelling about being at a show. The band and the audience produced this effect together and it was something that existed uniquely in that space at that time. That's why Deadheads wanted to go to every show. That's what they'll be trying to explain in the future—why did these people go to every show? Why did this guy have six hundred tapes of this band? They'll be forever answering that question. And one answer is that it was as high as you can get in a group, and people like to be together. But beyond that it's like trying to explain sex to someone who's never had it."

"One of the things I think the Dead teaches us about spirituality is that commonality of experience—that we're more alike than we realize," notes Peter Toluzzi. "There are so many commonly recognizable truths, if I may use that scary term, embodied in the experiences described in the lyrics, and there is whatever is the musical equivalent of truth—the perfect segue, the perfect chord, the perfect arpeggio. And some of the magic lies in our simultaneous appreciation of these truths—one of art's most powerful aspects is the ability to allow us to experience powerful emotions together and feel a sense of unity. I think the Dead were very, very good at what they did, and we were ready to have those buttons pushed because that's a basic part of the human spirit."

"People need celebration in their life," Garcia said. "It's part of what it means to be human. We need magic and bliss and power, myth and celebration in our lives. And music is a good way to encapsulate a lot of it."

If the Grateful Dead and the Deadheads constituted a modern mobile tribe, then Garcia would have to be considered the principal shaman of the tribe—magician, conjurer, healer and holy man. Of course he would say he was just a guy who played the guitar and sang, but everyone who loved his music and every musician who played with him knows better.

"In the tribal culture, the shaman isn't in society—he lives in the tent outside," comments Len Dell'Amico. "He's usually considered crazy, and he lives in poverty and he's happy. But a shaman in America today becomes a multimillionaire, because what he is doing is in such incredible demand.

"Jerry was a shaman who was put in a certain position to perform a certain task, and I think he carried a heavy burden as well as he could for as long as he could, and that was it. And it was a long time, and it was a heavy fucking burden for somebody who was the most happy-go-lucky person I've ever known—who would be happy living in a car; who would've been happy as long as he had a guitar and someone to play with."

He never aspired to guruhood; in fact, he ran away from it at every opportunity—"I don't want to be a leader," he once said, "because I don't want to be a misleader." But everyone viewed him as a leader anyway, because he was smart and articulate and had lots of great ideas.

When Barbara Meier interviewed Jerry for the Buddhist journal *Tricycle* in 1991, the first question she asked was whether he considered himself a bodhisattva. Naturally, Garcia demurred, but when I asked Barbara if *she* considered Jerry one, she was emphatic: "Yes. He was phenomenally generous on many, many levels. And then, something would snap and he'd become phenomenally closed. But when he was in the generous mode, you felt listened to, embraced, acknowledged, included, *grokked*. He was generous with his attention. He was generous with his energy, his money, everything. He created a lot of light."

"He had an enormous compassionate streak that was a huge part of him," M.G. says. "He deeply believed in the sameness of souls. He didn't believe in people's egos. And for better or worse he was drawn to people who were fucked up, pathetic, sad, downtrodden. He thought homeless drunks were sort of saints of the streets. I don't know whether it was from his early experiences in San Francisco or just some inner thing, but he always had this link with people who were down and out. He would radiate this compassionate heart for those kinds of people.

"He brought that attitude to the Grateful Dead's business, too. Whenever there was a discussion about ticket prices, he was always the one who wanted to keep prices down. From the beginning to the end he always wanted the music to be available to people. He didn't want the funky people shut out. He hated people being shut out because of money, status or class."

"One thing I loved about him is he found nearly everything funny," Barbara Meier notes. "He found the slightest thing hilarious. He could bring tremendous levity to almost any situation. But of course you know the other side of it—where the blackest, darkest cloud would come over him. It was very hard to make plans for what kind of mood he was going to be in."

Steve Brown concurs: "My relationship with Jerry was mostly just laughing and having fun, and you'll probably find a lot of people who will say the same thing. I've only known a couple of people in my life who were always ready for a joke, always ready to be 'Oh wowed,' always ready to be turned on to something cool, always ready to be just giggling or catching something that was weird. He was that guy. He really liked to be able to enjoy something that way, discover new trips. You could even pull him out of a crotchety thing with something funny oftentimes. And if you didn't, you better leave the room, 'cause he'd really be in a bad way!" he adds with a chuckle.

"As far as I can tell, the battle cry 'Louder and funnier!' summed up Jerry's attitude better than anything else ever solemnly pondered and enunciated," says Willy Legate, who knew him for thirty-five years. "To a question about how he could stand in front of a loudspeaker like that, he said, 'It's like a dog riding in a car—he likes to stick his head out the window.' "

Someone could probably fill an entire book about Garcia with fuzzy anecdotes about his humor and great spirit. And they could just as easily fill a volume with stories that detailed his foibles. He had extremely complex relationships with most of the people he was close to, and in his later years he kept many of his older friends at arm's length and chose isolation over deep friendships.

"He knew he was a fire," says Len Dell'Amico, "and he knew he would burn people near him; he knew he had a history of that and I think after a while he developed a protective mechanism: 'I don't want to let people get too close because I'll disappoint them. They'll get hurt when I do X or Y or Z.' He had experiences of people getting close to him and then he didn't want to see them anymore for whatever reason, and they seemed overly broken. Well, that's disturbing. If you're a raging ego, you just say, 'Fuck 'em, I don't care.'

But he was more of a regular, amiable, warm guy and he didn't like seeing people hurt that way."

With any luck, the bad times will recede into the distance as the years pass, and Garcia's friends and family will be left with mostly fond thoughts and golden memories. And of course there are some who carry a part of him with them wherever they go. It's somehow heartening to know that daughter Heather is a violinist, Theresa a budding artist, and that, in July 1997, nine-year-old Keelin had her first piano recital, performing "Swing Low, Sweet Chariot," a tune her dad sang in coffeehouses when he was twenty and on Broadway when he was forty-five.

And then there's Annabelle—spittin' image of Jerry, with the plucky spirit to match. Always an artist, in the summer of 1997 she discovered something else inside of her:

"I busted up my leg this summer and I had a lot of time sittin' on my butt, so I picked up the five-string banjo and I've been playing that. And that's my own personal connection with the old man. I taught myself out of a book and it's going pretty well. I'm playing one of my dad's banjos that he gave me years ago—the one he didn't like. But I've never played music in my life, and my mom always tried to keep us away from the guitars because she didn't want us to knock 'em over. And I always figured, 'Well, Dad kind of covered the whole music scene. I don't want to get involved with that.' Plus, I wasn't attracted to the guitar.

"But right after I broke my leg I had a dream about him handing me a banjo, so I picked up a book and three months later I've got a pretty good repertoire, and my neighbors are starting to applaud instead of sneer. I haven't quite started singing yet; I think I'll learn how to play and then maybe I'll croak out a few tunes. But either way, it's just fun, and I can feel sometimes that I'm connecting with my grandfather and my great-grandfather and my dad and the whole thing. I'm actually happier now that I've picked up the banjo. It's actually made me more mellow. It's the funnest thing that's happened to me in a long time, and it makes me feel like my dad is always nearby."

No doubt there will be endless dissections of Garcia in the years to come, as other biographers try to explain this charismatic and enigmatic figure, and his friends and colleagues write their memoirs, each offering different glimpses into Garcia's character. As David Grisman noted, "It's just hard to describe the enormity of his personality and the depth of the guy. Because basically his shtick was trying to be invisible in a way, trying to be nothing special."

"Even though Jerry was quite obviously a great virtuoso player," Mickey Hart says, "he would be the first to tell you that his greatest strength was playing in the ensemble, weaving in and out. He wasn't a guy who asked for the spotlight, musically speaking, but he wasn't uncomfortable if the spotlight fell on him, either. When he was 'on' he could really take command. But he was happy just being one of the guys in the band; we all were and that's one reason it lasted for thirty years."

What will survive every deconstruction of the Garcia myth is his music— that sublimely soulful guitar wordlessly speaking volumes, saying different things to each person who listens to it; and his ragged voice, creaky as a back-porch rocking chair, spinning old tales and modern parables, wisdom from and for the ages.

"Jerry got a lot of flack for that voice," Robert Hunter said after Garcia's death. "People kept putting it down because it wasn't a trained voice; it was thin, it was reedy. I never knew what they were talking about. I thought that was one of the most glorious voices in popular music or folk. Maybe I had to believe that to write [for] it; but I still do."

"My heartfelt prayer is that Jerry's music will retain its freshness and excitement forever," M.G. says. "When it's all said and done, the music is what's left—that music, that sound and the memories of the wonderful thing that Grateful Dead music could do and the way it all felt. And so much of that was Jerry. That sweetness he had is something that just emanated from him, and it's so much in the music. It was such a unique thing. God, he could be amazing! He could play these musical tricks that would absolutely dumbfound you. You weren't even quite sure what he'd just done half the time. He would pluck these melodies from the air and you'd wonder, 'Where did *that* come from?' They had a life of their own, he'd play them once and then they were gone. That's pretty high art. Thank God for the tapes!"

In the thousands of hours of tapes and CDs that survive Garcia's corporeal departure there is an infinite and inexhaustible bounty of emotions to be experienced, from frightening hells to transcendent realms of ecstasy, from deep blues to the most buoyant and uplifting rock 'n' roll imaginable. His guitar could cry tears born of existential longing one moment and roar like a fire-breathing dragon the next. Sometimes one crystalline, perfectly formed note was all it took to draw a tear or a smile or even ask a question. Often the search was as interesting as the final destination. Whether it was a Dead concert, a JGB show or a quiet night with Garcia and Grisman, at the end of the night you always felt as if you'd been somewhere special and learned something about yourself and what it means to be a thinking and feeling person. The tapes and CDs have that power as well, though they lack the immediate, real-time experience of being in a room with the musicians and thousands of people twirling, swirling, bopping and sometimes singing together—the ancient ritual reenacted anew each time.

"In the music there is room for space, there's room for quietness, room for sorrow, room for passion, anger, hate, violence," Garcia said in 1981 when a particularly hostile British interviewer told him that he found the Dead's music "dead dull." "It's not my desire to say there is only this or that. For me it's a full range of experiences, and within that it includes things like boredom.

Sometimes boredom is what is happening in life; that's what it's about sometimes. Sometimes the tension between boredom and discovery is an interesting thing. The idea of noodling around aimlessly for fifteen minutes—and we are notorious for that—and then hitting on some rich vein of something that we might never have got to any other way—that's the reward. I want there to be a complete vertical experience. I want it to be the full range."

"There was a quality to his playing that made you want to trust it," comments Steve Silberman. "You wanted to go where it was going. Part of that was that Garcia was an incredibly subtle musician, so you would be rewarded for expecting novelty at every moment. Also, even though he certainly had a lot of blues sensibility, I heard an essential optimism or buoyancy in his note choices. I remember when I heard 'Eyes of the World' for the first time, it contained a kind of brightness that seemed slightly tropical, but I'd never heard anything quite like it before. 'Uncle John's Band,' too. It was a kind of optimism that didn't seem to surrender any intelligence to get to its positive place. It owned all of the quizzical nature of being human and yet it still said 'yes' on some level.

"Also, he always had a way of making you feel included—that there was a cosmic joke that you were both getting, and that you were included in a wry understanding of the goofy quality of fate or existence, and that you and he were both enjoying it. William Blake had this phrase: 'Energy is eternal delight.' I felt that Garcia's personal presence communicated that feeling—a sort of delight in the varieties of experience. He radiated engagement and delight in the next thing."

He was both guide and participant on a personal and collective journey of exploration, as vulnerable as the rest of us, maybe a little more fearless, but always goin' down the road with the hope and belief that there might be sunshine around the next bend and better days ahead. To believe otherwise would be to give in to despair, and that was not an option—not as long as there was love and friendship to experience, not as long as there were "songs to fill the air," as he sang in "Ripple." And though now he's gone—and "nothin's gonna bring him back"—there is still solace to be found in what he left behind; in a note, a chord, a turn of phrase. As he sang so beautifully in the heartbreaking but reassuring ballad "Like a Road":

> When the dark clouds start to blow
> And you need somewhere to go
> And you want some company
> That really cares
> Turn around, turn around
> Turn around and I'll be there
> Like a road, like a road
> Leading home.

ACKNOWLEDGMENTS

Writing this book was a tremendously challenging and cleansing experience for me. Begun in the sad aftermath of Garcia's death, this project stretched over two and a half years and occupied a part of my brain every second of those years, even in my dreams. Although writing is a solitary, soul-searching craft, there are many people to thank for their generous help and support.

First of all, this book would not have been written if it hadn't been for my friend (and agent) Dan Levy. It was his idea; blame him!

Many thanks to my good friends and fellow chroniclers of the Dead scene, David Gans and Steve Silberman, who offered so much valuable advice and information along the way. I have learned much from David during the twenty-plus years we've known each other. He has long been one of the Dead scene's brightest lights, and it has been my great fortune to have worked on a parallel track with him. And the passion and poetry that spill so naturally out of Steve is a never-ending source of inspiration to me.

My sincere gratitude to the good people I interviewed specifically for the book (whose names appear in the Bibliography). These interviews ranged from a few minutes on the phone to many hours in person, deep into the night. Thank you for sharing your memories and your hearts at a difficult time. Special thanks to a handful of interviewees who put up with an unending stream of follow-up queries: Carolyn Garcia (aka Mountain Girl), Sara Ruppenthal, Barbara Meier, David Nelson, Owsley Stanley, Alan Trist, Steve Brown and Vince and Gloria DiBiase. John Kahn gave me a wonderfully soulful interview just a week before his untimely passing; may he rest in peace.

Thanks also to those good souls who, while not sitting down for formal interviews, were very helpful resources: Robert Hunter, Steve Parish, Willy Legate and Nora Sage.

Several writers were nice enough to provide me with tapes or unpublished transcripts of interviews they had done with Garcia—*merci beaucoup* to Joel Selvin, Alice Kahn, Oliver Trager, Jeffrey Pepper Rodgers and Paul Grushkin. And a special tip o' the hat to Dick Latvala for sending some rare interview tapes my way.

I'd also like to sing the praises of the following folks for their encouragement and/or assistance: Eileen Law, Robert Greenfield, Tiff Garcia, Daniel Grayson, Kris Clifford Crow, Jack Ortman, Michael Zipkin, David Housden, Len Dell'Amico, Rick Sullivan, Robert Wagner, Michael Getz, Lou Tambakos, David

Dodd, Jeremy Marre, Peter Albin, Ron Rakow, Jay Blakesberg, John Dwork, Michael Bailey, Herb Greene, Rae Lyn Winblad, Harvey Kubernik, Eric Levine, Nick Meriwether, Rick and Jerry Melrose, Jon Sievert, Peter Toluzzi and all my co-workers at *Mix* magazine.

Salutations to my old show buddies, with whom I've shared a million profound, funny, scary, transcendent, embarrassing, tearful and joyous moments: MZ, Jon and Deb Hoffman, John Larmer, Alyssa DiFilippo, Carol Gould, John Leopold, T'res Buika, Steve Schmid, Jim Buika, Barb Treadwell, Ken Schwartz, Chris Fuller, Chuck Culbertson, Andrew Wernick, Bill and Kristy Buckley, Paul and Melanie Nichols, Hale and Ann Milgrim, Bobby Lawrence, Bennett Falk, Mary Eisenhart, Barbara Lewit, the Sundance Books gang, Dave Leopold, Mark Leviton and Aloha Steve Lipschultz.

I am indebted to my original editor at Viking, David Stanford, and to the many fine people there who nudged this book toward publication.

My heartfelt appreciation to Sandy Rothman—one of Garcia's old pickin' pals in the mid-'60s and late '80s—who served as a first editor on my manuscript. Sandy, your insights were invaluable, your instincts always correct, and thanks for all the jokes and insults in the margins. In the immortal words of JG, "We appreciates it!"

Finally, thanks to my family for cheering me on: Mom, Pop, Kathleen, Roger, Pam, Ian and Uncle Ted. My loving wife, Regan, was with me every step of the way—hashing out ideas, helping me gather research materials, making countless great suggestions about every aspect of the book, editing each chapter, lifting my spirits when I was down and, most difficult of all, giving me the time and space I needed to complete this mammoth undertaking. Regan, I'm sure you know what I was singing all those late nights and weekends: "I'd rather be with you . . ."

BIBLIOGRAPHY

INTERVIEWS BY THE AUTHOR

Ozzie Ahlers (1996); Peter Albin (1992); Brooks Arthur (1995); Ken Babbs (1990, 1996); Todd Barkan (1996); Steve Barncard (1996); Bill Belmont (1996); Bernie Bildman (1985); Elvin Bishop (1995); Jay Blakesberg (1995); Bob Bralove (1996); Steve Brown (1996); Betty Cantor-Jackson (1997); Vassar Clements (1996); Dennis Clifford (1996); Tom Constanten (1984); Emily Craig (1995); Thayer Craw (1995); Susan Crutcher (1995); John Dawson (1985, 1996); Len Dell'Amico (1987, 1996); Dave Dennison (1995); Gloria DiBiase (1997); Vince DiBiase (1997); Rodney Dillard (1996); Spencer Dryden (1985); Martin Fierro (1996); Annette Flowers (1993); Paul Foster (1996); David Freiberg (1996); David Gans (1996); Annabelle Garcia (1992, 1996); Carolyn "Mountain Girl" Garcia (1985, 1996, 1998); Daniel Garcia (1996); Jerry Garcia (1981 [twice with David Gans], 1985, 1987 [twice, once with Paul Grushkin], 1988, 1989, 1991, 1993), Tiff Garcia (1996); Leon Gast (1996); David Getz (1996); Donna Godchaux MacKay (1985, 1996); Bill Graham (1985); Laird Grant (1993, 1996); Phoebe Graubard, (1996); Richard Greene (1996); Paul Grushkin (1996), Gary Gutierrez (1985); Don Hall (1997); Mickey Hart (1979, 1991, 1998); Dave Hassinger (1985); Dan Healy (1985); Tom Heckley (1997); Wally Hedrick (1996); Levon Helm (1996); Bruce Hornsby (1996); George Hunter (1985); Robert Hunter (1988, 1991, 1992); Gloria Jones (1992); John Kahn (1986, 1992, 1996); Linda Kahn (1997); Henry Kaiser (1996); Paul Kantner (1996); Bill Keith (1996); Alton Kelley (1984); Ken Kesey (1986, 1991); Kenny Kosek (1996); Bill Kreutzmann (1989); Nikki Lastretto (1995); Dick Latvala (1996); Eileen Law (1993, 1996); Marshall Leicester (1996); Phil Lesh (1990, 1994); Charles Lloyd (1996); Richard Loren (1996); Gary Lyons (1995); Alan Mande (1996); Greg Mann (1995); Steve Marcus (1992); Manasha Matheson (1997); Bob Matthews (1993, 1996); Rosie McGee (1996); Jon McIntire (1987, 1993); Barbara Meier (1996); Sanjay Mishra (1995, 1996); Victor Moscoso (1997); Brent Mydland (1987); David Nelson (1993, 1996); Art Neville (1986); Keith Olsen (1996); Brooks Adams Otis (1996); Dave Parker (1996); Ron Rakow (1996); Jonathan Reister (1996); Danny Rifkin (1993); Neil Rosenberg (1996); Leonor Garcia Ross (1996); Sandy Rothman (1988, 1996); Sara Ruppenthal (1996); Ralph Sall (1991); Ira Sandperl (1996); Merl Saunders (1996); John Scher (1996); Rock Scully (1990, 1993); Melvin Seals (1985); Bob Seideman (1995); Steve Silberman (1996); Owsley Stanley (1996); Sue Swanson (1992); Peter Thea (1995); Eric Thompson (1996); Peter Toluzzi (1996); Alan Trist (1996, 1997); Sally Van Meter (1997); Danya Veltfort (1996); Bill Vitt (1996); Howard Wales (1996); Bill Walker (1987); Butch Waller (1996); Rob Wasserman (1992); Bob Weir (1985, 1989, 1992, 1993); Roberta Weir (1997); Wendy Weir

(1996); Vince Welnick (1997); Roland White (1996); Suzy Wood (1996); William Wynans (1995).

BOOKS

Anthony, Gene. *The Summer of Love: Haight-Ashbury at Its Highest.* Celestial Arts, 1980.

Brandelius, Jerilyn Lee. *Grateful Dead Family Album.* Warner Books, 1989.

Brown, David Jay, and Rebecca Novick. *Voices from the Edge.* Crossing Press, 1995.

Dodd, David, and Robert Weiner. *The Grateful Dead and the Deadheads: An Annotated Bibliography.* Greenwood Press, 1997.

Gans, David. *Conversations with the Dead: The Grateful Dead Interview Book.* Citadel Press, 1991.

———, ed. *Not Fade Away: The On-line World Remembers Jerry Garcia.* Thunder's Mouth Press, 1995.

Gans, David, and Peter Simon (photo editor). *Playing in the Band: An Oral and Visual Portrait of the Grateful Dead.* St. Martin's Press, 1985. Revised edition, 1996.

Garcia, Jerry. *Harrington Street.* Delacorte Press, 1995.

Gleason, Ralph. *The Jefferson Airplane and the San Francisco Sound.* Ballantine, 1969.

Greenfield, Robert. *Dark Star: An Oral Biography of Jerry Garcia.* William Morrow & Co., 1996.

Greenfield, Robert, and Bill Graham. *Bill Graham Presents: My Life Inside Rock and Out.* Doubleday, 1992.

Grinspoon, Lester, and James B. Bakalar. *Psychedelic Drugs Reconsidered.* Basic Books, 1979.

Grushkin, Paul. *The Art of Rock: Rock Posters from Presley to Punk.* Abbeville Press, 1987.

Grushkin, Paul, with Jonas Grushkin and Cynthia Bassett. *The Official Book of the Deadheads.* Quill Books, 1983.

Harrison, Hank. *The Dead, Vol. 1.* The Archives Press, 1973. (Originally published as *The Dead Book.*)

———. *The Dead, Vol. II.* The Archives Press, 1980.

Hart, Mickey, with Jay Stevens. *Drumming at the Edge of Magic: A Journey into the Spirit of Percussion.* HarperCollins, 1990.

Hunter, Robert. *Box of Rain.* Penguin, 1993.

Jackson, Blair. *Grateful Dead: The Music Never Stopped.* Delilah, 1983. (Out of print.)

Lee, Martin, and Bruce Shlain. *Acid Dreams.* Grove Weidenfeld, 1985.

Perry, Paul, and Ken Babbs. *On the Bus.* Thunder's Mouth Press, 1990.

Reich, Charles, and Jann Wenner. *Garcia: Signpost to New Space.* Straight Arrow, 1972. (Out of print.)

Scott, John W., Mike Dolgushkin, and Stu Nixon. *DeadBase IX: The Complete Guide to Grateful Dead Songlists.* DeadBase, 1995. (Also, *DeadBase VI*, 1992.)

Sculatti, Gene, and Davin Seay. *San Francisco Nights: The Pychedelic Music Trip, 1965–1968.* St. Martin's Press, 1985.

Scully, Rock, with David Dalton. *Living with the Dead: Twenty Years on the Bus with Garcia and the Grateful Dead.* Little, Brown, 1995.

Selvin, Joel. *Summer of Love.* Dutton Books, 1994.

Shenk, David, and Steve Silberman. *Skeleton Key: A Dictionary for Deadheads.* Doubleday, 1994.

Stevens, Jay. *Storming Heaven: LSD and the American Dream.* Perennial Library, 1991.

Troy, Sandy. *One More Saturday Night.* St. Martin's Press, 1991.

———. *Captain Trips: A Biography of Jerry Garcia.* Thunder's Mouth Press, 1994.

Watson, Steven. *The Birth of the Beat Generation: Visionaries, Rebels and Hipsters, 1944–1960.* Pantheon Books, 1995.

Wolfe, Tom. *The Electric Kool-Aid Acid Test.* Bantam, 1968.

NEWSPAPER AND MAGAZINE ARTICLES

Abbott, Lee. "Dead Reckoning and Hamburger Metaphysics." *Feature* (March 1979).

Adamson, Dale. "Jerry Garcia Says Grateful Dead Aren't Dead—They Are Just De-Controlled." *Houston Chronicle* (March 28, 1976).

———. Title not available; interview with Garcia. *Houston Chronicle* (January 7, 1979).

Aronowitz, Alfred. "Closed Circuit Concerts." *New York Post* (December 21, 1971).

Barich, Bill. "Still Truckin'." *New Yorker* (October 11, 1993).

Barlow, John Perry. "Cassidy's Tale." *Literary Kicks* (date unknown).

Bashe, Philip. "What a Long, Strange Trip It's Been: A Conversation With Jerry Garcia." *Good Times* (April 22, 1980).

Bell, Max. "The Grateful Dead's First Annual Pyramid Prank." *New Musical Express* (September 30, 1978).

Block, Adam. "Garcia on Garcia, 1977." *BAM* (December 1977 and January 1978).

Bowman, Rob. *Grayfolded* liner notes (1996).

Bromberg, David N. "Interview: Jerry Garcia of the Grateful Dead." *Jazz & Pop* (February 1971).

Carlin, Peter, and Ken Baker. "War of the Wives." *People* (January 27, 1997).

Carlini, John. "Jerry Garcia and David Grisman: The Continuing Process." *Guitar Extra!* (fall 1991).

Cincinnati Inquirer. "New Mrs. Garcia from Cincinnati" (February 16, 1994).

Crowe, Cameron. "Grateful Dead Show Off New Bodies." *Creem* (January 1974).

Dead Heads newsletter, 1972–75.

Drabanski, Emily. "Dead Heads Rejoice! The Dead to Play Santa Fe." *The New Mexican* (October 15, 1982).

Duncan, Harry. "Grateful Dead Rides Again." *Madison Kaleidoscope* (March 31, 1971).

Dwork, John. "DDN Interviews Owsley." *Dupree's Diamond News* (issue 25, August 1993).

Eisenhart, Mary. "Aging Gratefully: The Dead's Flattering Touch of Grey." *BAM* (December 18, 1987).

Epand, Len. "State of the Artful Dead." *Zoo World* (August 15, 1974).

Fedele, Frank. " 'Fuck No, We're Just Musicians': An Interview with Jerry Garcia." *Long Beach Sunset Press* (December 1971).

Fields, Rick. "A High History of Buddhism." *Tricycle* (fall 1996).

Forte, Robert. "Domains of Consciousness: An Interview with Jack Kornfield." *Tricycle* (fall 1996).

Gans, David, and Marty Martinez. "Grateful Dead's Bob Weir and Phil Lesh on the 1972 European Tour." *Goldmine* (February 2, 1996).

Garbarini, Vic. "In Search of the Grateful Dead." *Musician* (September 1981).

Gates, David. "Dylan Revisited." *Newsweek* (October 6, 1997).

Golden, Tim. "Why a Star Is Spinning in His Grave." *New York Times* (December 31, 1996).

The Golden Road. Material was drawn from most of the twenty-seven issues published by Blair Jackson and Regan McMahon from winter 1984 through the 1993 annual. Articles *not* written by Blair quoted in the book:

Brown, Steve. "If I Told You All That Went Down: A Fond Look Back at Grateful Dead Records" (issue 11, summer 1986).

Eisenhart, Mary. "Robert Hunter: Songs of Innocence, Songs of Experience" (issue 4, fall 1984).

Groenke, Randy, and Mike Cramer. "One Afternoon Long Ago . . . : A Previously Unpublished 1967 Interview with Jerry Garcia" (issue 7, spring 1985).

Levy, Dan. "Branford Blows with the Dead" (issue 23, summer 1990).

Marcus, Steve. "Garcia: 'The Point Is I Survived It. Here I Am' " (issue 12, fall 1986).

Gorman, Peter. "Albert Hoffman: An Interview." *High Times* (May 1993).

Greuber, Mike, et al. "The Dead Just Keep On Truckin'." *Harvard Independent* (March 4, 1971; part 2: March 11, 1971).

Guitar Player magazine (in chronological order):

Stuckey, Fred. "Jerry Garcia: It's All Music" (April 1971).

Sievert, Jon. "Jerry Garcia: Founder of the Grateful Dead" (October 1978).

———. "Jerry Garcia: New Life with the Dead" (July 1988).

———. "Garcia and Weir: Further." Special Grateful Dead issue (fall 1993).

Obrecht, Jas. "Turn On, Turn Up, Trip Out: The Rise and Fall of San Francisco Psychedelia" (February 1997).

Hard Road. "Jerry Garcia" (July 20, 1970).

Henderson, Randi. "Jerry Garcia: 'Dead' Head Is Keeping the Sixties Alive." *Baltimore Sun* (April 8, 1982).

Herbst, Peter. "A Message from Garcia: Nothing Exceeds Like Success." *Boston Phoenix* (November 19, 1974).

Hinckle, Warren. "May the Baby Jesus Open Your Mind and Shut Your Mouth: The Hippies." *Ramparts* (March 1967).

Horowitz, Donna. "Garcia vs. Garcia: Two of Jerry's Three Wives Fighting Tooth and Nail." *San Francisco Examiner* (January 5, 1997).

Hunt, Ken. "Jerry Garcia: Folk, Bluegrass and Beyond." *Swing 51* (issue 7).

———. " 'Sometimes the Cards Ain't Worth a Dime, If You Don't Lay 'Em Down': The Robert Hunter Interview." *Dark Star Magazine* (November 1979 interview, publication date unknown).

Hunter, Robert. "Robert Hunter, Dark Star." *Crawdaddy* (January 1975).

Itkowitz, Jay. "Rapping with the Dead's Jerry Garcia." *Good Times* (November 1970).

James, Viola. "Garcia Takes Legion on Funk Crusade." *Circus* (July 1975).

Johnson, Greg. "A Dead Head for Business." *Los Angeles Times* (August 18, 1996).

Kates, Marcy. "The Image Is Hippie, but 'Grateful Dead' Also Know Business." *Wall Street Journal* (November 22, 1974).

Kent, Bill. "The Grateful Dead Is Just Circling." *Camden (N.J.) Courier-Post* (August 29, 1980).

Kokot, John. "A Summer Day of Music: Allman Bros., the Band, the Dead." *New Times* (July 28, 1973).

Lake, Steve. "Rock 'n' Roll Misfit." *Melody Maker* (September 14, 1974).

———. "Weir: 'Rock Has Ceased to Progress.' " *Melody Maker* (September 21, 1974).

Levy, Arthur. "Jerry Garcia: Up from the Dead." *Creem* (August 1975).

Lindenmuth, Gary. "Rock Star Flies In, Gets One-Year Suspension." Unknown origin (March 1973).

McClanahan, Ed. "A Brief Exegesis of Certain Socio-Philosophical Themes in Robert Hunter's Lyrics to 'New Speedway Boogie.' " *Realist* (March–April, 1971).

McEnroe, Colin. "The Grateful Dead's Weir Ponders Group Character." *Hartford Courant* (May 9, 1980).

McKaie, Andy. "Bob 'Ace' Weir: Inside Straight on the Dead's Full House." *Crawdaddy* (August 1972).

Meyer, Bruce. "The Grateful Dead Still Alive and Vibrating." *Latrobe (Pa.) Bulletin* (July 1, 1976).

Morley, Paul. "What a Long, Predictable Trip It's Become." *New Musical Express* (March 28, 1981).

Morse, Steve. "Hunter Finds Life Beyond the Dead." *Boston Globe* (March 7, 1997).

Oliver, Christopher. "Onions and Orchids at the Rockfest." *New York Daily News* (July 29, 1973).

Peterzell, Paul. "Heated Fight Over Garcia's Estate." *Marin Independent Journal* (August 4, 1996).

Platt, John. "Rhythm Devil: An Interview with Mickey Hart." *Comstock Lode* (Autumn 1981).

Relix magazine (in chronological order):

Moore, Jerry. "Six Hours Before the Mast" (November 1976).

Hall, John. "Jerry Garcia: True Confessions in Hartford, Parts 1 and 2" (November 1977, January 1978).

Dym, Monte, and Bob Alson. "The Man Behind the Words: An Interview with Robert Hunter" (January and June 1978).

Brown, Toni. "So Far: A Transcript of a Grateful Dead Press Conference" (February 1988).

Peters, Steve. "Built to Last: An Exclusive Interview with Jerry Garcia" (December 1989).

Ruhlmann, William. "Mickey Hart Interview" (October 1991).

Jones, Greg, and Andrew Pickard. "Crazy Fingers: Jerry Garcia and the Banjo" (April 1992).

Juanis, J. C. "Dawgwood Revisited: David Grisman Remains at the Forefront of the Acoustic Music Movement" (April 1993).

Robinson, Lisa. "Creem Interview w/Grateful Dead." *Creem* (December 1970).

Rodgers, Jeffrey Pepper. "In the Dawg House: Jerry Garcia and David Grisman's Acoustic Reunion." *Acoustic Guitar* (January 1994).

Rolling Stone magazine (in chronological order):

"Dead Head for Paradise and Points East" (March 9, 1968).

"Fillmore Scene Moves to New Carousel Hall" (August 10, 1968).

"Grateful Dead Ungrateful; Sued" (July 26, 1969).

"New Orleans Cops and the Dead Bust" (March 7, 1970).

" 'The Stones Have Not Acted Honorably' " (April 30, 1970).

Fong-Torres, Ben. "New Riders in the Circus Circus" (September 2, 1971).

"Grateful Dead Bust Their Dad" (September 2, 1971).

Hopkins, Jerry. "The Beautiful Dead Hit Europe" (June 22, 1972).

Gleason, Ralph. "Perspectives: Full Circle with the Dead" (September 29, 1972).

"Garcia Arrested: Watch Your Speed" (April 26, 1973).

Grissim, John. "Garcia Returns to Banjo: Splendor in the Bluegrass" (April 26, 1973).

Siegel, Joel. "Watkins Glen Jam Tops Woodstock; 600,000 Fans" (August 30, 1973).

Perry, Charles. "Alembic: Sound Wizards to the Grateful Dead" (September 27, 1973).

———. "A New Life for the Dead: Jerry Garcia Is Checking Cash-Flow Charts" (November 22, 1973).

Epand, Len. "Garcia and Saunders: A Most Informal Group" (June 20, 1974).

Grissim, John. "The Dead After a Decade: 'Allah' Means Business" (November 6, 1975).

Young, Charles M. "The Awakening of The Dead" (June 16, 1977).

Fong-Torres, Ben. "15 Years Dead" (August 7, 1980).

Gilmore, Mikal. "The New Dawn of the Grateful Dead" (June 16, 1987).

Goldman, Fred. "On a Roll: The Rolling Stone Interview with Jerry Garcia" (November 30, 1989).

Henke, James. "Alive and Well: The Rolling Stone Interview with Jerry Garcia" (October 31, 1991).

DeCurtis, Anthony. "The Music Never Stops: The Rolling Stone Interview with Jerry Garcia" (September 2, 1993).

Fricke, David. "He Had Faced His Demons: Deborah Koons Garcia on Jerry" (September 21, 1995; expanded interview in the *Rolling Stone* book *Garcia*).

Wilkinson, Alec. "Bob Weir: Friend of the Devil" (July 9, 1998).

Rothman, Sandy. "Reflections on Jerry Garcia's Banjo Playing." Unpublished manuscript (1995).

Rowland, Mark. "Bring Me the Head of Jerry Garcia." *St. Louis Post-Dispatch* (August 14, 1980).

———. "Jerry Garcia and Elvis Costello: Strange Bedfellows." *Musician* (March 1991).

———. "Days of the Living Dead." *Musician* (October 1996).

San Francisco Chronicle (in chronological order):

Bess, Donovan. "Far-Out Voices in the Debris" (January 1, 1966).

Robertson, Bob. "Kesey Wears a Tie—For a Few Hours" (January 21, 1966).

Gleason, Ralph. "Censure, Praise for 'Trips' Festival" (January 30, 1966).

———. "The Tribes Gather for a Yea-Saying" (January 16, 1967).

"Cops Raid Pad of Grateful Dead" (October 3, 1967).

Gleason, Ralph. "Stones' Plan for Free S.F. Concert" (November 24, 1969).

———. "A Few Guesses on Rolling Stones" (November 28, 1969).

———. "Bad Vibes for Rolling Stones" (December 5, 1969).

———. "The Rolling Stones Are Right On" (December 5, 1969).

———. "Who's Responsible for the Murder?" (December 8, 1969).

———. "More Questions for Rolling Stones" (December 12, 1969).

"An Arrest in Grateful Dead Embezzling" (August 11, 1971).

"Minister Gets Six Months" (March 3, 1972).

Hunt, Dennis. "Playing the Small Rock Clubs Is a 'Release from the Dead' " (April 1, 1972).

Selvin, Joel. "Garcia Returns to a First Love" (March 14, 1973).

"Garcia Arrested—With Drugs" (March 30, 1973).

Selvin, Joel. "The Grateful Dead Decides to Try a Guiding Hand" (July 28, 1977).

———. "End of the Road for Grateful Dead" (December 9, 1995).

———. "Garcia's Final Trip Takes Him to India" (April 9, 1996).

Saporita, Jay. "Keith and Donna on the Road." *The Aquarian* (December 3, 1975).

Sekuler, Eliot. "Grateful Dead and Round: Innovative Independence." *Record World* (April 12, 1975).

Selvin, Joel. "Hello/Goodbye: Mickey Hart and the Grateful Dead." *Mojo* (November 1996).

Silberman, Steve. "Standing in the Soul: Robert Hunter Interview." *Poetry Flash* (December 1992).

Silver, Sam. "Merl Saunders' Musical Fire." *Night Times* (May 2, 1972).

Simon, Peter. "Making Musical Miracles: An Interview with Jerry Garcia." *New Age Journal* (May 1975).

Smolin, Barry. "Drumming at the Edge of Jerry: An Interview with David Kemper." *Dupree's Diamond News* (issue 36, summer 1997).

Snyder-Scumpy, Patrick. "The Allman Brothers: Boogie or Bust." *Crawdaddy* (October 1973).

Stafford, Peter. "Bill Graham on Acid." *Crawdaddy* (May 1969).

Staska, Kathie, and George Mangrum. "Jerry Garcia Discusses Grateful Dead, Albums." *Hayward Daily Review* (October 12, 1972).

Sutherland, Steve. "Tripping in the Timeless Zone." *Melody Maker* (March 28, 1981).

Swenson, John. "The Sound and the Fury." *College* (October 1973).

———. "Back from the Dead." *Guitar World* (December 1987).

Territo, Joe. "A Talk with Jerry Garcia" (three parts). *Marin Independent Journal* (June 3, June 10 and June 17, 1982).

Thompson, Hunter. "The 'Hashbury' Is the Capital of the Hippies." *New York Times Magazine* (May 14, 1967).

Tolces, Todd. "Deadlines." *Melody Maker* (January 24, 1976).

Watrous, Peter. "Touch of Grey Matter: The Grateful Dead Are Different from You and Me." *Musician* (December 1989).

Watts, Michael. "Honour the Dead." *Melody Maker* (April 15, 1972).

———. "Curse of the Pharaohs Nixes Dead's London Gigs." *Melody Maker* (September 23, 1978).

———. "Dead on the Nile." *Melody Maker* (September 23, 1978).

White, Steven. "We Got L.A. by the Balls." *Staff* (December 10, 1971).

White, Timothy. "From the Beatles to Bartok: Jerry Garcia and Bob Weir Trace the Roots of the Dead." *Goldmine* (November 2, 1990).

Miscellaneous Sources

Transcripts of Joel Selvin's interviews with Jerry Garcia (April 30, 1992) and Robert Hunter (January 7, 1992), undertaken for his book *Summer of Love*.

Transcript of Oliver Trager's interview with Jerry Garcia (January 25, 1993), undertaken for a story in *Entertainment Weekly*.

Transcript of Alice Kahn's interview with Jerry Garcia (October 1984), undertaken for an article in the *San Jose Mercury News*.

Source unknown: Interview with Jerry Garcia in Room 1503 of the Radisson Hotel in St. Paul, Minnesota (July 19, 1981).

WBRU (Providence, Rhode Island) interview with Jerry Garcia and John Kahn (March 11, 1978).

Gary Lambert's interview of Jerry Garcia and Phil Lesh for KPFA (Berkeley, California; February 11, 1993).

Paul Krassner's interview of Jerry Garcia (May 1984), broadcast nationally during the set break of the June 21, 1984, Grateful Dead concert at Kingswood Music Theatre in Ontario.

David Gans's July 1993 interview with Ken Nordine for KPFA.

July 1993 interview with Garcia on WBEZ in Chicago.

Obey Benz's interview with Jerry Garcia for the Time-Life History of Rock 'n' Roll series, conducted in 1994.

1976 interview with Jerry Garcia for the Bay Area television program *Miracles*, hosted by Father Miles.

The on-line journal of Robert Hunter, posted on www.dead.net.

A lengthy correspondence from Willy Legate.

Jeremy Marre's 1997 documentary *Anthem to Beauty*.

Testimony from the Carolyn Garcia vs. Deborah Koons Garcia trial, 1997.

Want to Read More?

In the course of editing this book for space considerations, a number of colorful anecdotes and entire topic areas had to be excised. These are available for your perusal on my Web site, www.blairjackson.com. The site also includes an extensive critical discography of Garcia's work, detailed bibliographical information (the source of each quote in the book), an essay on the process of researching and writing *Garcia: An American Life*, and much more.

INDEX